Same-Sex Couples before National, Supranational and International Jurisdictions

Daniele Gallo • Luca Paladini • Pietro Pustorino
Editors

Same-Sex Couples before National, Supranational and International Jurisdictions

Foreword by Prof. Gráinne de Búrca

Springer

Editors
Daniele Gallo
Department of Law
Luiss University
Rome
Italy

Luca Paladini
University Institute SSML Carlo Bo
Rome
Italy

Pietro Pustorino
Department of Political and
International Sciences
University of Siena
Siena
Italy

ISBN 978-3-642-35433-5 ISBN 978-3-642-35434-2 (eBook)
DOI 10.1007/978-3-642-35434-2
Springer Heidelberg New York Dordrecht London

Library of Congress Control Number: 2013955027

Printed on acid-free paper

Springer is part of Springer Science+Business Media (www.springer.com)

Foreword

Recent years have seen exciting developments across many jurisdictions as far as the legal recognition of the rights of same-sex couples is concerned. It seems as though—at least in certain parts of the world—a tipping point has been reached in relation to legal recognition and protection for the rights of same-sex couples. These include the right to workplace benefits, the right to have relationships legally recognized and formalized, and the right to marry. Needless to say, there are a great many parts of the world where harsh forms of discrimination against same-sex couples are still enshrined in law and where few or no legal rights are accorded to same-sex couples. On the other hand, there has also been a cascade of reforms in recent years in Europe, in North and South America, and in many parts of the Commonwealth and elsewhere. Many of these reforms have been triggered or developed through litigation and adjudication before national, regional, and international courts and tribunals, and sometimes before several of these.

This book is a wonderfully timely and an impressively wide-ranging survey of these judicial developments in the law relating to same-sex couples.

Part I of this book contains a series of analyses of these developments in a range of national jurisdictions across the globe. There are chapters dealing with the US and the evolution of American Supreme Court jurisprudence on same-sex relationships, chapters on Canada and a range of Central and South American jurisdictions as well as Mexico, and chapters covering South Africa, Australia, and New Zealand. Some of the chapters are explicitly comparative, such as that which contrasts the legal background to developments within South Africa and Canada, while other chapters point to some of the similarities in context and culture within certain groups of states—such as Mexico and parts of Central and South America—which have traditionally adhered to a more conventional conception of the 'family'. The chapter covering Australia and New Zealand, by comparison with many of the aforementioned jurisdictions, points to the leading role of the legislature rather than the courts.

The chapters dealing with European states similarly cover what might be called clusters or 'varieties' of European jurisdiction insofar as their approach towards judicial recognition of the rights of same-sex couples is concerned. The UK enjoys a chapter to itself, which outlines the 40-year revolutionary road taken by the UK, by means of its equality law and human rights law, towards significant recognition of the rights of same-sex couples. The Nordic chapter looks at five Nordic states and identifies a lack of radical judicial activism in this field (as in others) and a more significant role for the democratic process—including civil society and governmental entities—in the gradual expansion of same-sex relationship rights. A more sobering chapter covering a range of Eastern European countries, including Croatia, Hungary, Slovenia, and Poland, challenges any conception of unidirectional progress towards greater legal recognition for same-sex couples, outlining the continuing social prejudice and discriminatory attitudes evident even in domestic parliamentary debates. The chapter on France and Belgium similarly points to the primary role played by the political process, and notes that while courts are not the main actors in the same-sex debate in these countries, they have nevertheless played a certain incremental role in framing the debate and advancing elements of legal protection for same-sex relationships. The coverage of Germany, Austria, and Switzerland indicates once again a leading role played by legislatures, but with the constitutional framework of the state setting the contexts for occasional judicial intervention, and ultimately a 'separate but equal' regime of registered partnerships rather than marriage for same-sex couples. Perhaps unsurprisingly, the case law from the Catholic-dominated jurisdictions of Italy, Spain, and Portugal demonstrates that the courts are not what the authors call 'avant-garde' actors, but instead mainly defer to the legislature against the backdrop both of domestic constitutional law and also, to some extent, the developments of the European Court of Human Rights. Finally, the chapter on Greece and Cyprus similarly refers to the likely future influence of both ECHR law and in this instance also EU law on the question of the legal protection of same-sex couples, even though at the time of writing it seems that same-sex couples can neither marry nor enter civil unions in either jurisdiction.

These national law analyses are followed by a section of the book devoted to private international law issues, with three chapters—one on the law governing *formation* of same-sex marriages, one on the law governing *recognition* of foreign same-sex partnerships and marriages, and one on the treatment of same-sex families (procreation, surrogacy, parenthood, etc.) across borders. These chapters address many of the thorny conflicts-of-law issues raised by the existence of differences in the national legal treatment of same-sex couples when there is a transnational dimension to the relationship.

Part II of this book is then devoted to the treatment by regional (or supranational, as the book calls them) and international courts of issues relating to same-sex couples. There are two chapters on the case law of the European Court of Human Rights—one dealing with the right to marry (not yet recognized by the ECtHR) and the other with other rights of same-sex couples—and a chapter on the jurisprudence of the Inter-American Commission and Court of Human Rights. Two chapters on EU law follow, the first looking at the uneven free movement rights of same-sex couples and the other at employment benefits (where same-sex couples working as EU staff have been accorded greater rights by the CJEU than employees in Member

States), while the last two chapters deal with labor law rulings of international organizations (such as the UN and the ILO administrative tribunals), and finally with the jurisprudence of the UN Human Rights Committee which monitors the International Covenant on Civil and Political Rights.

Overall, this book is a rich compendium of important national and international legal developments in the arena of the legal recognition of the rights of same-sex couples. It contains thorough and up-to-date analyses of these trends across most of the relevant parts of the world in which change has been occurring. The inclusion of chapters on private international law, regional human rights law, EU law, and international human rights law nicely supplements the analysis of domestic jurisdictions in the first half of the book, and makes this work an essential reference point for all of those interested in global legal developments in this important field.

New York, USA

Gráinne de Búrca
Florence Ellinwood Allen Professor of Law
New York University School of Law

Contents

Detail Contents

List of Contributors

Giacomo Biagioni is Assistant Professor of International Law at University of Cagliari, where he teaches international law and global governance law. He holds a degree in law (*magna cum laude*) from University of Florence and a Ph.D. in EU Law from University of Trieste. He taught at several institutions in Europe. He is regular speaker at various meetings and author of a monograph and about 30 articles, especially on private international law and international civil procedure, as well as the co-editor of two books.

Adam Bodnar is Assistant Professor of Human Rights at Warsaw University, Faculty of Law and Administration. He is a graduate of the Warsaw University (M.A., 2000) and the Central European University in Budapest, Department of Legal Studies (LL.M. in Comparative Constitutional Law, 2001). He holds a Ph.D. from Warsaw University. Previously, he worked as an associate for Weil Gotshal & Manges, Warsaw office. Vice-President of the Management Board and Head of the legal division of the Helsinki Foundation for Human Rights in Warsaw, he is also the senior legal expert within the FRALEX network of the EU Agency for Fundamental Rights. He taught on homosexuality and the law and on anti-discrimination law at several institutions, including the Academy of European Law in Trier. He is author of several publications on, *inter alia*, the protection of fundamental rights, anti-discrimination law and EU citizenship. In 2011 Dr. Bodnar was awarded the Tolerance Award by the Campaign against Homophobia and Warsaw Lambda Association for his activities aimed to enhance the protection of LGBT rights. He is also Marshall Memorial Fellow 2013.

José Miguel Cabrales Lucio graduated with honors at University Autonomous of Tamaulipas (México), where he teaches human rights, constitutional law, and comparative law. He is coordinator of postgraduate research studies at the Faculty of Law and president of Board of Advisors of *Humanistica Review*. He holds a Ph.D. in Fundamental Rights and Public Liberties from Castilla-La Mancha University and Pisa University. He also coordinated the annual colloquium of Social Rights, Theory of Argumentation and Rule of Law at University Carlos III of Madrid. He holds a Master in Public Law at the latter university and a specialization in international human rights from the International Institute of Human Rights in Strasbourg. Previously, he was a researcher at University of Pisa. Former case law analyst in the Spanish Constitutional Court for a year. Correspondent for Latin American Countries for the International Survey in *Public Law Review*. Dr. Lucio is author or co-author of several publications on human rights, constitutional law, such as, amongst others, the textbook *Derecho Constitucional Europeo* (Tirant lo Blanc, 2011). Member of several national and international academic associations including the International Association of Constitutional Law.

Aristoteles Constantinides is Assistant Professor of International Law and Human Rights at the Law Department of the University of Cyprus. He holds a law degree and a Ph.D. in International Law from Aristotle University of Thessaloniki. He has been academic responsible of the project week of the European Master's Degree in Human Rights and Democratisation organized by the EIUC in Venice and Visiting Scholar at the Amsterdam Center for International Law and the University of Grenoble. He reports on Cyprus for the Oxford Reports on International Law in Domestic Courts and is a member of the Cyprus National Bioethics Committee and various academic networks, including the ILA Committee on non-State actors and the ILA Committee on Recognition/Non-Recognition in International Law. Dr. Constantinides is author of several articles on international law and human rights.

Francesco Crisafulli is judge at the Rome Court (civil cases) and Vice-Chair of the Steering Committee on Legal Cooperation of the Council of Europe. He holds a law degree from Sapienza University (Rome). Previously he was the Italian co-agent at the European Court of Human Rights for about 10 years and legal counselor at the Presidency of the Republic for about 5 years. Member of various boards of editors, Dr. Crisafulli is the author of several essays on ECHR Law as well as the editor of a textbook on Constitutional Law.

Antonio D'Aloia is Full Professor of Constitutional Law at University of Parma, where he was also Director of the Law Department. At the same University he teaches also Biolaw. He delivered conferences and lectures at many universities in Italy and abroad (Barcelona, Nancy, Mexico City, Lima, Prague, Baltimore, etc.). Member of numerous boards of editors, he was responsible of many research projects financed by Italian as well as by European institutions. He has been consultant to the Ministry for European Affairs and to the Ministry for Territorial and social cohesion. Prof. D'Aloia is author or editor of ten books, as well as of more than 100 articles and essays on Public and Constitutional Law.

Spyridon Drosos is a Ph.D. Researcher at the European University Institute (Florence). He has been Visiting Researcher at UC Berkeley School of Law. Prior to obtaining an LL.M. in Law from University College London, he read law at the National and Kapodistrian University in Athens. A member of the Athens Bar Association, Mr. Drosos has authored numerous articles in the field of EU law.

Tiago Fidalgo de Freitas is a Ph.D. Researcher at the European University Institute (Florence, Italy) and Guest Lecturer at the University of Lisbon School of Law (Lisbon, Portugal). On the former capacity, he has been a Visiting Doctoral Researcher at the Getúlio Vargas Foundation School of Law (Rio de Janeiro, Brazil). Beforehand, he completed an LL.M. at New York University School of Law as a Hauser Global Scholar and has taught as a Guest Lecturer at the Portuguese Catholic University School of Law (Lisbon, Portugal). He also holds the Diploma of the Academy of European Public Law (Legraina, Greece) and a law degree, *magna cum laude*, from the University of Lisbon School of Law. Admitted to the Portuguese Bar Association, Tiago has authored published and forthcoming articles in the fields of constitutional law, fundamental rights, EU law, and national and global administrative law.

Hrefna Fridriksdóttir is Associate Professor at the Law Faculty of the University of Iceland, where she graduated in 1989 (Cand.jur). Prof. Friðriksdóttir has an LL.M. degree in law from Harvard Law School (1996) and the title of her master thesis was "The Nordic gay and lesbian 'marriage': No children allowed". She passed the bar exam and worked at Iceland's biggest law firm for 6 years, and she also worked for 13 years as Head of the Legal Department for The Government Agency for Child Protection. Her research interests focus on family law, children's rights, child protection, inheritance law, social law and policy and sexual orientation law. Prof. Fridriksdóttir has written several articles on same-sex partnership and, in 2010, she also wrote the bill for the Icelandic gender-neutral marriage laws.

Daniele Gallo is Assistant Professor of EU Law at Luiss Guido Carli University (Rome) where he teaches also advanced EU law and international environmental law and where he previously taught international economic law. He holds an advanced degree in law (*magna cum laude* and special mention) and a Ph.D. in International Law and EU Law both from Sapienza University (Rome). He has been European Union Fulbright Schuman Scholar at Fordham Law School (New York), DAAD Fellow at Max Planck Institute for Public International Law and Comparative Law (Heidelberg), and Jean Monnet Fellow at the European University Institute (Florence). He taught at several institutions in Europe and the USA. Co-Director of Luiss Working Papers Series, editor of *Diritto del commercio internazionale* and of the Italian Society of International Law's blog, Dr. Gallo is author of a book (reviewed in journals such as CMLRev, LIEI, RDUE) as well as of about 40 contributions on international law and EU law (in journals such as *International Organizations Law Review*, *Revue du Droit de l'Union européenne*, *Revue des affaires européennes*). Attorney-at-Law, he has pleaded before the ECtHR, the UNIDROIT Administrative Tribunal and the ILO Administrative Tribunal.

Nelleke Koffeman is a Ph.D. candidate at the Europa Institute of Leiden University, where she graduated in 2006. Her research focuses on the question how cross border movement within the EU affects national choices in morally sensitive issues, such as reproductive rights and the legal recognition of same-sex relationships. In the course of her research Ms. Koffeman has been Visiting Researcher at the Humboldt University in Berlin and at Fordham Law School in New York. She has published on human rights in various Dutch legal journals and volumes and contributed to the Fundamental Rights Agency Group of Legal Experts (FRALEX). At Leiden Law School, Ms. Koffeman teaches several courses in European (human rights) law.

Laura Magi is Assistant Professor of International Law at the University of Florence, where she also taught international economic law and EU law. She earned her law degree at the University of Florence and her Ph.D. in International Law at University of Padua. Previously she was Max Weber Fellow at the European University Institute (Florence). Dr. Magi is the author of a book and of various articles, one of which was awarded, by the Italian Society of International Law, the price as the best article written by a young scholar in 2010. Laura has recently been interested in the topic of gay couples, as it is shown by a recent essay published in *Rivista di diritto internazionale*.

Edmondo Mostacci obtained the qualification as Associate Professor of Comparative Public Law in 2010. He currently teaches constitutional law at Bocconi University (Milan) from which he obtained the degree in law. He holds a Ph.D. in Public Law from the University of Genoa. Dr. Mostacci is author of a book on Soft Law in Comparative Public Law published by Cedam (Kluwer Publisher) in 2008 as well as of more than thirty publications on constitutional and comparative public law.

Aidan O'Neill is a Queen's Counsel, Edinburgh and London, Chairman of the Edinburgh Centre for Constitutional Law and Honorary Fellow in the School of Law of Edinburgh University. He holds two law degrees, one from University of Edinburgh [LL.B. (Hons.) (First Class)] and one from Sydney University [LL.M. (Hons.) (First Class)] and he also obtained an LL.M. in European and International Law from the European University Institute (Florence). In the academic year 2007–2008 he was the inaugural University Center for Human Values/Law and Public Affairs Fellow in Law and Normative Inquiry at Princeton University and subsequently Visiting Professor at Princeton University. He has written three legal textbooks on EU law—amongst others *EU for UK lawyers*, second edition, Hart, 2011—and several chapters in a number of legal books, as well as several articles in various academic journals, particularly in the field of human rights, constitutional law and EU law. Aidan O'Neill is qualified to appear as counsel in Scotland, as well as in the courts of England and Wales. He has appeared as senior counsel before the ECJ, the UK Supreme Court, the Judicial Committee of the Privy Council, the House of Lords, the Court of Session (Inner and Outer House), the ECtHR, and the High Court of England & Wales (Administrative Division), as well as before the sheriff courts in Scotland and the county court in England and Wales.

Massimo Francesco Orzan is Legal Secretary (*référendaire*) of the President of the EU General Court. He graduated in political science at Luiss Guido Carli University (Rome) and in law at University of Cassino. He holds a Ph.D. in International Law and EU Law from Sapienza University (Rome). He has been Post-Doc Fellow in EU Law, Assistant Professor of EU Law and Adjunct Professor of International Economic Law at Luiss University as well as of International Law at Italian Navy Academy (Leghorn). He has been speaker at various conferences and workshops. Admitted to the Bar of Rome, Dr. Orzan is also author of numerous articles published in Italian and foreign journals.

Luca Paladini is Adjunct Professor of International Organizations at the University Institute SSML Carlo Bo (Rome) and Visiting Scholar at the University of Siena. He has also been Adjunct Professor of EU Law at Italian Navy Academy (Leghorn). He graduated in political sciences and specialized in EU law at the University of Milan. He holds a Ph.D. in EU Law from the University of Bologna. He was Jean Monnet Fellow and then Visiting Fellow at the European University Institute (Florence). Dr. Paladini is author of about 20 contributions on EU law and international law. He is Member of the University of Florence Equal Opportunities and Anti-Discrimination Committee for the period 2013–2016.

Pietro Pustorino is Tenured Associate Professor of International Organizations at Siena University, where he teaches also EU law, and Professor of Human Rights Law at Luiss Guido Carli University (Rome). He graduated in law at Sapienza University (Rome) and was a researcher in International Law at National Research Council (CNR) and after at Luiss Guido Carli University as well as legal adviser to the Ministry for Foreign Affairs. He taught at several institutions in Europe and the USA and was Visiting Scholar at Fordham Law School (New York). He is regular speaker at various meetings and was scientific coordinator of various workshops. Prof. Pustorino is member of various boards of editors, author of two monographs and about 50 articles as well as the co-editor of three books.

Giorgio Repetto is Assistant Professor of Constitutional Law at the Faculty of Law of University of Perugia and Adjunct Professor of Public Law at the University of Tuscia. He has a degree in law earned at Luiss "Guido Carli" (*magna cum laude* and special mention) and holds a Ph.D. in Public and Constitutional Law from Sapienza University (Rome). His doctoral thesis has received the Edoardo Ruffini Award granted by *Accademia dei Lincei*. Dr. Repetto is author of a book on the role played by comparative arguments in the case-law of the European Courts of Strasburg and Luxemburg and editor of a volume on the constitutional relevance of the ECHR in domestic and European law (Intersentia 2013) as well as of more than 30 publications concerning Italian and comparative constitutional law.

Philippe Reyniers is a Ph.D. Researcher at the European University Institute (Florence) where he focuses on the paradigm of difference in the theory of discrimination law. He obtained a *Licence en Droit* (*Grande Distinction*) and a Master of laws in EU Law both from the *Université Catholique de Louvain* where he has been researcher for several years. He also took part in several projects financed by the European Commission. As Member of the Brussels Bar, he practised employment and EU Law and appeared several times before the ECJ, both in appeals and preliminary ruling procedures. Mr. Reyniers has mainly published on the interaction between fundamental rights and labour law.

Jorrit Rijpma is Assistant Professor at the Europa Institute of the Leiden Law School (The Netherlands). He is a graduate from the European Law School in Maastricht and the College of Europe in Bruges. In 2009 he defended his Ph.D. thesis at the European University Institute on the regulatory framework for the management of the external borders of the European Union. His research focuses on EU migration law and policy and institutional developments in the EU's Area of Freedom, Security and Justice. Jorrit Rijpma is a frequent speaker on EU migration and asylum policy. He has been involved in various research projects on topics related to the EU's migration and asylum policy for the Italian and Dutch government, the ILO, and the European Commission. As part of his doctoral research he spent 3 months working for the European Union's border agency Frontex in Warsaw. Recently he was seconded to the European Law Department of the Dutch Ministry of Foreign Affairs. He is a member of the Standing Committee of Experts on International Immigration, Refugee and Criminal Law (Meijers Committee) and a guest lecturer at Koç University in Istanbul.

Graziella Romeo is Assistant Professor of Constitutional Law at Bocconi University (Milan) where she also teaches civil liberties and human rights. She holds an advanced degree in law from that university and a Ph.D. in Constitutional Law from University of Milan. She has been Visiting Scholar at Fordham Law School (New York) where she gave several lectures on citizenship and equality. She is the author of a book on citizenship and immigration in European constitutionalism as well as of several essays on comparative constitutional law issues, including equality and sexual orientation.

Olivia Rundle is Lecturer in Law at the University of Tasmania, Australia. She teaches, researches and participates in community engagement activities in the areas of family law, dispute resolution and civil procedure. In the family law field Dr Rundle's particular area of interest is in diverse family forms, including same-sex couples and same-sex parented families. Her current projects include: co-authoring a book regarding legal and social issues experienced by same-sex couples and same-sex parented families; developing a decision-making framework around ethical and legal issues arising from commercial surrogacy; and co-authoring a booklet to disseminate information about the Tasmanian deed of relationship scheme of non-married relationship recognition. Dr Rundle is also a registered family dispute resolution practitioner and a mediator accredited under the Australian National Mediator Accreditation Standards.

Anna Śledzińska-Simon is Assistant Professor of Constitutional Law at the Department of Law, Administration and Economics of the University of Wrocław. She holds the MA in law (2002) and international relations (2003) (University of Wrocław), the LL.M. (2002) and the S.J.D. (2007) in comparative constitutional law (Central European University). She was a Fellow Researcher at Columbia University (New York), Max Planck Institute (Heidelberg) and the European University Institute (Florence). Currently, she is a national legal expert in the FRALEX network and the Israel Democracy Institute as well as a member in the Legal Research Panel at INTERIGHTS. Since 2007 she cooperates with the Polish Helsinki Human Rights Foundation in various projects. She teaches constitutional law, human rights, equality and non-discrimination law and gender in law courses.

Diletta Tega is Legal clerk (*referendario*) at the Italian Constitutional Court, Assistant Professor of Constitutional Law at Milan Bicocca where she teaches advanced constitutional law and constitutional law, and Adjunct Professor of Fundamental Rights at the University of Bologna. She holds a law degree from University of Bologna and a Ph.D. in Constitutional Law from University of Bologna and University of Paris X. She has been Emile Noël Research Fellow at the Jean Monnet Center at NYU School of Law (New York). Previously, she was the Italian legal junior expert for the EU Fundamental Rights Agency. Dr. Tega has published widely in the field of European constitutionalism and constitutional law. Her book focuses on the relationship between national legal order and the ECHR.

Roberto Virzo is Assistant Professor of International Law at University of Sannio (Benevento), where he teaches also International Organizations, Adjunct Professor of International Law of the Sea at University of Florida, Levin College of Law, and Adjunct Professor of International Organizations at Luiss Guido Carli University. He holds a degree in political science (*magna cum laude*) from Luiss Guido Carli University and a Ph.D. in International Law and EU Law from University of Bari. He has been Visiting Professor at University of Rennes I and University of Picardie Jules Verne as well as Post-Doc Fellow in International Law at Luiss-Guido Carli University. He served as Italian Delegate at the XVI Session of the Procurement Group of UNCITRAL at UN. Dr. Virzo is author of a book, reviewed, *ex multis*, in *American Journal of International Law*, as well as of about 40 articles on international and EU law published in journals such as *The Law and Practice of International Courts and Tribunals*, in the *Max Planck Encyclopedia for Public International Law* and in a number of edited volumes.

Matteo M. Winkler is Adjunct Professor of International Law at Bocconi University (Milan). He holds a degree in law from Catholic University of Milan, an LL.M. from Yale Law School (New Haven) and a Ph.D. in International Economic Law from Bocconi University (Milan). He has been Visiting Scholar at Yale Law

School. He is Associate Attorney-at-Law in a law firm in Milan where he practices, *inter alia*, international law. He is author of a book on international law, co-author of a book on sexual orientation and the law, as well as author of about 50 contributions in English, French and Italian.

Chapter 1
Same-Sex Couples, Legislators and Judges. An Introduction to the Book

Daniele Gallo, Luca Paladini, and Pietro Pustorino

Abstract The volume focuses on the jurisprudence of national, supranational and international jurisdictions (and quasi jurisdictions) as regards the legal status of same-sex couples. The book tries to convey the complexities and controversies that derive from the judicial recognition of same-sex couples across the world, considering the relationship of the judiciary with the executive and the legislature.

The legal discourse on the status of same-sex couples before the courts raises problems in terms of legitimacy, democracy and separation of powers. What is at stake is the balance between the prerogatives of the judiciary and (especially) those of the legislature. The courts of some jurisdictions have been progressive, dynamic, activist and even creative in their interpretation of the law, while others have been conservative, static, literal and *originalist*.

In any case, regardless of the final outcome, it is undisputable that the continuous flow of new decisions has produced a considerable body of jurisprudence that deserves close attention. This is precisely the main objective of the present book.

> We know that people of the same sex often love one another with the same passion as people of different sexes do and that they want as much as heterosexuals to have the benefits and experience of the married state. If we allow a heterosexual couple access to that wonderful resource but deny it to a homosexual couple, we make it possible for one pair but not the other to realize what they both believe to be an important value in their lives [...]. The cultural argument against gay marriage is therefore inconsistent with the instincts and insight captured in the shared idea of human dignity. The argument supposes that the culture that shapes our values is the property only of some of us – those who happen to

D. Gallo (✉)
Law Department, Luiss Guido Carli University, Rome, Italy
e-mail: dgallo@luiss.it

L. Paladini
University Institute SSML Carlo Bo, Rome, Italy
e-mail: l.paladini@ssmlcarlobo.it

P. Pustorino
Department of Political and International Sciences, University of Siena, Siena, Italy
e-mail: pietro.pustorino@unisi.it

D. Gallo et al. (eds.), *Same-Sex Couples before National, Supranational and International Jurisdictions*, DOI 10.1007/978-3-642-35434-2_1,

> enjoy political power for the moment – to sculpt and protect in the shape they admire. That is a deep mistake: in a genuinely free society the world of ideas and values belongs to no one and to everyone. Who will argue – not just declare – that I am wrong?
>
> R. Dworkin, The New York Review of Books, 21 September 2006

> The Constitution does not forbid the government to enforce traditional moral and sexual norms [. . .]. It is enough to say that the Constitution neither requires nor forbids our society to approve of same-sex marriage, much as it neither requires nor forbids us to approve of no-fault divorce, polygamy, or the consumption of alcohol.
>
> A. Scalia, Dissenting Opinion, 26 June 2013, *United States v. Windsor*

1.1 A Brief Prologue: Harry, Sally and the Present Time

The reasons for this book may be better understood by recalling Rob Reiner's *When Harry Met Sally*. . . (1989). This widely acclaimed movie is about a man and a woman who, after completing their undergraduate studies, share a car trip to New York. When they arrive, they go their separate ways with no particular feelings for each other (except, maybe, some sort of mutual dislike). They meet again 5 years later and, from that moment on, the plot follows the development of their relationship from friendship to love and, finally, marriage. The narrative is brilliantly interspersed with short documentary-style clips of married couples telling the stories of how they met.

In most parts of the world, the type of development described above—which may sound familiar to many—is impossible for same-sex couples. At the time of this writing,[1] most countries in the world do not grant any form of legal recognition to LGBTI (lesbian, gay, bisexual, transgender and intersex) couples; and of the 18 States providing some form of legal recognition other than marriage, only 13 have passed legislation on same-sex marriage.[2]

These asymmetries—in terms of rights protection—between straight and gay couples, on the one hand, and, on the other, among same-sex couples, prompted us to investigate the challenging issue of the legal situation of same-sex couples' relationships in the world. As a consequence, we decided to limit this study to the rights of LGBTI people as couples, leaving aside other important legal issues

[1] Developments in this field are fast, as shown by those occurred in 2013 in Brazil, France, New Zealand, United Kingdom, United States, and Uruguay (all covered in this book).

[2] Countries that have legalized same-sex unions at the national (but not sub-national) level, or where these unions are recognized *de facto*, include: Andorra, Australia, Austria, Colombia, Costa Rica, Croatia, Czech Republic, Ecuador, Finland, Germany, Hungary, Ireland, Israel, Liechtenstein, Luxembourg, Slovenia, Switzerland, and the UK. The following countries have recognized same-sex marriage: Argentina, Belgium, Brazil, Canada, Denmark, France, Iceland, The Netherlands, Norway, Portugal, Spain, South-Africa, Sweden. For a comprehensive list of countries, including some sub-national jurisdictions—such as parts of Mexico and the US—where legal partnerships and/or same-sex marriages have been legalized, see www.iglhrc.org/.

arising all over the world from discrimination based on sexual orientation, such as the criminalization of LGBTIs as individuals.[3]

1.2 Aim and Scope

The present volume focuses on the jurisprudence of national, supranational and international jurisdictions (and quasi-jurisdictions, as is the case of the UN Human Rights Committee) as regards the legal *status* of same-sex couples.

This collection of essays is by no means intended to provide an exhaustive treatment of the statement of the law. Our aim is rather to explore the content, functioning and opportunities of the different jurisdictions' reasonings and their contribution to the strengthening of LGBTI rights (and duties). As a consequence, the book tries to convey the complexities and controversies that derive from the judicial recognition of same-sex couples across the world, considering the relationship of the judiciary with the executive and the legislature.

Nowadays, more and more same-sex couples are going to court to claim that their rights are not protected. In response to these issues, the courts of some jurisdictions have been progressive, dynamic, *activist* and even creative in their interpretation of the law, while others have been conservative, static, literal and *originalist*. In any case, regardless of the final outcome, it is undisputable that the continuous flow of new decisions has produced a considerable body of jurisprudence that deserves close attention.

The nature of the claims brought before the courts (or *quasi*-courts) varies depending on the legal system in question.

At the national level, in States where there is a gap in the ordinary law as regards the *status* of same-sex couples, homosexual partners mainly ask that their rights as a 'couple' be recognised, while in countries where same-sex couples can marry, register as partners, or obtain at least the most basic forms of legal protection, judges are asked to recognize more specific (and thus more advanced) rights, such as survivor's pension or adoption rights.

At the supranational and international levels there are more variables. With the exception of international administrative tribunals, which have competence in labour law matters concerning international organizations' staff members, individuals are normally entitled to seek protection once they have exhausted all available domestic remedies. That being said, the legal effect of the decision of a supranational and international judicial (or *quasi*-judicial) body depends on two conditions (a) the extent and limits of the competence of the court (or *quasi*-judicial body),

[3] According to the EU Foreign Affairs Council's "Guidelines to promote and protect the enjoyment of all human rights by Lesbian, Gay, Bisexual, Transgender and Intersex (LGBTI) persons" (Brussels, 24th June 2013, para. 15), around 80 States still consider homosexuality as a crime. See www.consilium.europa.eu/uedocs/cms_Data/docs/pressdata/EN/foraff/137584.pdf.

which are generally established in its Statute; and (b) both the efficacy and the role accorded to international norms and judgments by national legal systems.

Given the above, a further preliminary remark is necessary. Focusing on jurisprudential developments does not mean in any way downplaying the importance of the legislature. On the contrary, the essential role of legislative bodies[4] in understanding and providing a legal framework for the changes occurred in society must be acknowledged and taken into account. This holds true especially when what is at stake is the interpretation and application of the principle of non-discrimination, that is, a general principle of law which is evolving and whose content seems to be historically and geographically determined.

Furthermore, the extent to which judges acknowledge the existence of an inviolable core of rights implied in such principle and the way in which they interpret it are two factors that have a strong impact on the powers and functions of the legislature. The interpretation of the courts can, indeed, have the effect of urging or even requiring lawmakers to take action, i.e., to pass new legislation or amend existing laws. In this regard, the dialogue between the judiciary and the legislature shows that the two form an 'inseparable *couple*': in this volume, the first will play the lead, while the second will be the co-star.

1.3 Structure

The book consists of two parts: Part I is on (selected) national jurisdictions; Part II is on supranational and international jurisdictions (and *quasi*-jurisdictions).

1.3.1 Part I: National Jurisdictions

Part I deals with same-sex couples before national jurisdictions. We have tried to cover as many countries as possible,[5] without ever purporting to include all relevant national legal systems. Many Asian countries (such as Nepal)[6] as well as some EU

[4] Not only national but also international and supranational bodies, such as the institutions of the European Union.

[5] As already noted, national legal systems where homosexuality is criminalized—that is, countries where there can be, *a priori*, no case law on same-sex couples' rights—are not discussed in this book.

[6] In 2007 the High Court ruled on LGBTI rights, asking the Government of Nepal to form a committee in order to produce a study on the issues raised by same-sex marriage. The judgment is available at www.bds.org.np/publications/pdf_supreme_eng.pdf.

Member States, such as The Netherlands[7] or Ireland,[8] are not discussed in the book. Of course, this does not diminish the importance of their legal systems or their courts' positive action in recognizing, and giving 'tangible' meaning to, the rights of same-sex couples.

Part I is divided in two sections. Section 1, entitled "Domestic Law Issues", contains 12 chapters written by scholars and practitioners with considerable expertise in constitutional and public comparative law. While the US[9] and the UK[10] are the subject of separate chapters, other countries are discussed together in chapters concerning different States that share similar legal institutions and concepts[11] or, more frequently, a common historical and geographical background.[12]

Besides purely national legal orders, the three chapters of Section 2 focus on crucial issues of private international law regarding same-sex couples: the law applicable to the formation of same-sex partnerships and marriages[13]; the recognition of foreign same-sex partnerships and marriages[14]; and, finally, the impact of the transnational movement of same-sex families on private international law mechanisms at the national level.[15]

1.3.2 Part II: Supranational and International (and Quasi-*) Jurisdictions*

Part II contains three sections and deals with same-sex couples before supranational and international jurisdictions.

Section 1 concerns supranational courts with human rights jurisdiction. Section 2 is devoted to the Court of Justice of the European Union (CJEU). Section 3, entitled "International Labour Law Issues and *Quasi*-Jurisdictional Bodies", covers both the jurisprudence of international administrative tribunals and the decisions rendered by the UN Human Rights Committee (UNHRC).

---

[7] In 2000, the Netherlands were the first country in the world to legalize same-sex marriage. An English version of the Dutch civil code is available at www.dutchcivillaw.com/civilcodebook01.htm.

[8] In Ireland, civil same-sex partnerships became legal in 2011 and the recognition of the right to marry is currently under discussion. For the text of the Civil Partnership and Certain Rights and Obligations of Cohabitants Act, see www.irishstatutebook.ie/2010/en/act/pub/0024/.

[9] Chapter 2 by Romeo and Chap. 3 by D'Aloia.

[10] Chapter 8 by O'Neill.

[11] Chapter 4 by Mostacci.

[12] Chapter 5 by Cabrales Lucio; Chap. 6 by Rundle; Chap. 7 by Friðriksdóttir; Chap. 9 by Bodnar and Śledzińska-Simon; Chap. 10 by Reyniers; Chap. 11 by Repetto; Chap. 12 by Fidalgo de Freitas and Tega; Chap. 13 by Drosos and Constantinides.

[13] Chapter 14 by Virzo.

[14] Chapter 15 by Biagioni.

[15] Chapter 16 by Winkler.

Section 1 is divided in three chapters. In Chap. 17, Pustorino conducts an in-depth analysis of the well-known decision of the European Court of Human Rights (ECtHR) in *Schalk and Kopf v. Austria*, examining also the most recent cases before the Court, some of which are still pending. Chapter 18, by Crisafulli, focuses on rights other than the right to marry, which lie at the heart of cases such as *Christine Goodwin v. the United Kingdom* (ECtHR): the right to private and family life, patrimonial rights, parental rights, and the expulsion of aliens. Chapter 19, by Magi, discusses the case-law of the Inter-American Commission of Human Rights (IACHR), as well as that of the Inter-American Court of Human Rights (IACtHR), with particular attention to the decision in *Atala Riffo and daughters v. Chile*. The importance of the jurisprudence of the ECtHR, the IACtHR and the IACHR lies in an innovative interpretation of the notion of 'family' and its impact on the legal orders of Member States.

Section II is devoted to EU law. Chapter 20, by Rijpma and Koffeman, deals with same-sex couples from the point of view of the free movement rights in the EU, in connection with the notions of European citizenship and family reunification. Chapter 21, by Orzan, addresses the issue of employment benefits for same-sex couples, with regard to both EU staff cases and references for preliminary rulings.

Part II ends with Section 3 on International Labour Law Issues and *Quasi*-Jurisdictional Bodies. In Chap. 22, Gallo focuses on the UN Administrative Tribunal (UNAT) and the ILO Administrative Tribunal (ILOAT) as a privileged instrument of analysis, examining their evolutive interpretation of concepts such as 'spouse', 'couple', and 'marriage' with regard to the internal law governing employment relations in international organizations as well as to the application of the *lex patriae* of the staff members concerned. Chapter 23, by Paladini, investigates the case-law of a *quasi*-jurisdictional body—the UN Human Rights Committee—reporting on several cases concerning the rights of same-sex couples, especially the right to marry and the right to a 'widow's pension'.

1.4 The *Vis Expansiva* of Same-Sex Couples's Rights Across the World and the Role of the Judiciary

Already in 1994 Kees Waldijk, writing about the recognition of same-sex couples' rights across the world, pointed out that:

> [t]here seem to be a general trend of progress: where there is legal change it is change for the better. Countries are not all moving at the same time and certainly not at the same speed, but they are moving in the same direction: forward.[16]

Some years later, Robert Wintemute observed that:

[16] Waldijk (1994), p. 51.

civil marriage will gradually be opened up to same-sex couples in more and more countries.[17]

This book confirms the *vis expansiva* implied in the above quotations, showing how the promotion and protection of same-sex couples' rights have progressed as a result, depending on the jurisdictions and in varying degrees, of the activities performed by both the judiciary and legislature,[18] or mainly by the judiciary,[19] or mainly by the legislature.[20] Said tendency applies equally to the rights of same-sex (registered) partners and those of same-sex (married) spouses.[21] Therefore, we can say, first of all, that there is a general trend towards the recognition of same-sex couples' rights[22] and, second, that this trend has often been due to the courts' interpretation and application of the law.[23] However, the way in which judges have enforced the rights of same-sex couples, and thus, pioneered legal changes and reforms in this area of law, varies from one legal system to another. In fact, when, based on a case-by-case approach, (more or less *activist*) judges recognize certain rights in contexts where there are no laws recognizing LGBTI's rights, that does not resolve the issue of discrimination due to the absence of specific legislation, since it is the task of the legislature to *actively* provide citizens with guarantees and rights.[24] This is even clearer when the executive violates the rights and independence of the judiciary and, by doing so, chooses to deny LGBTI people the legal protections granted to straight couples.[25]

1.5 Interactions, Dialogues and the Rights of Same-Sex Couples

The present volume book shows that the recent progress in the recognition and protection of same-sex couples is characterized, in varying degrees and with different consequences, by horizontal and vertical dialogues between national

---

[17] Wintemute (2004), p. 594.

[18] See Chap. 2 by Romeo; Chap. 3 by D'Aloia; Chap. 4 by Mostacci; Chap. 5 by Cabrales Lucio, as to Argentina and Brazil for example; Chap. 8 by O'Neill; Chap. 10 by Reyniers; Chap. 11 by Repetto; Chap. 20 by Rijpma and Koffeman; Chap. 21 by Orzan.

[19] See Chap. 5 by Cabrales Lucio, as to Colombia for example, and chapter by Fidalgo de Freitas and Tega, as to Italy.

[20] See Chap. 6 by Rundle; Chap. 7 by Friðriksdóttir; Chap. 9, as to the Czech Republic for example; Chap. 12 by Fidalgo de Freitas and Tega, as to Spain and Portugal.

[21] Depending on the legal system, the term 'spouse' does not necessarily imply marriage. On this point see, for instance, Chap. 22 by Gallo with regard to the Staff Regulations and Rules of international organizations.

[22] But see Chap. 13 by Drosos and Constatinides.

[23] But see Chap. 5 by Cabrales Lucio, as to Chile for example.

[24] See, for instance, the case of Italy discussed in Chap. 12 by Fidalgo de Freitas and Tega.

[25] See Chap. 9 by Bodnar and Śledzińska-Simon, with regard to Hungary.

legislatures and domestic/supranational courts. Although less evident, a dialogue exists also in the case of international tribunals and *quasi*-jurisdictional bodies, i.e. international administrative tribunals[26] and the UNHRC.[27]

In the case of a national legislature, the recognition of same-sex couples' rights may cross-fertilize other national legislatures, with the result that those rights and their legitimacy penetrate from a purely national dimension in different cultural, social and, ultimately, legal traditions. At the same time, however, it must be noted that this transnational legislative transplant can work only if there is some degree of homogeneity between the countries concerned.[28]

As regards the horizontal and vertical dimensions of the judicial dialogue, in some national jurisdictions' reasonings are grounded on comparative law as well as on the case-law of supranational courts, such as the ECtHR[29] and the IACtHR.[30] This shows the "maieutic" force[31] of legal pluralism as well as a desire on the part of national judges to find an external legitimization for their rulings. As to supranational courts, the decisions of the ECtHR,[32] the CJEU's[33] and the IACtHR's[34] have been crucial in paving the way for national legislation recognizing same-sex couples' rights,[35] including, in some countries, marriage equality.[36] Indeed, those courts have elevated 'new' values and principles of equality from a national level to a supranational level. However, they do not require Member States to recognize same-sex partnerships or marriage; instead, they have chosen to opt for the highest possible degree of rights protection, adopting a flexible interpretation, respectively, of the ECHR, EU law and the American Convention on Human Rights. This means, for example, that the Strasbourg Court recognizes the rights of a same-sex couple if the law of the applicant's State of nationality has legalized same-sex marriages and/or registered partnerships. Moreover, another factor contributes to the promotion of LGBTI rights: a teleological, systemic and inclusive interpretation of both Art. 8 and Art. 12 of the ECHR which has enabled the Court to abandon a literal interpretation of the law. When confronted with the protection of same-sex couples, the Court, even though it does not require Member States to adopt specific

[26] See Chap. 22 by Gallo on the cross-references made by the UNAT and ILOAT.

[27] See Chap. 23 by Paladini, on the references made by national and international judges to the case-law of the UNHRC.

[28] Chapter 7 by Friðriksdóttir.

[29] See, for instance, Chap. 8 by O'Neill and Chap. 12 by Fidalgo de Freitas and Tega.

[30] See, for instance, Chap. 5 by Lucio Cabrales.

[31] Von Bogdandy and Schill (2011). See also Von Bogdandy (2008); Walker (2008); Delmas-Marty (2009); Poiares Maduro (2009); Focarelli (2012), pp. 316–321.

[32] Chapter 17 by Pustorino and Chap. 18 by Crisafulli.

[33] Chapter 19 by Magi.

[34] Chapter 20 by Rijpma and Koffeman and Chap. 21 by Orzan.

[35] See, for instance, Chap. 8 by O'Neill and Chap. 11 by Repetto.

[36] See, for instance, Chap. 12 by Fidalgo de Freitas and Tega.

legislation, clearly supports the full recognition of same-sex couples' rights.[37] And yet, one thing is to use a broad interpretation of applicable laws, so as to ensure that applicants' rights will be protected if the State of nationality recognizes same-sex marriage or registered partnership; another thing is to require Member States to adopt such laws. One thing is to encourage national legislatures to step in, or hope that they will do so; another is to impose legislative changes through the "denationalization"[38] of crucial national family-law regimes. Nevertheless, it must be emphasized that the rulings rendered by supranational judicial bodies, as well as the norms adopted by international and supranational institutions, generally lead to large debates, at both legal and social levels, that greatly contribute to a positive and fruitful interaction between international, supranational and national legal—and especially judicial—systems.

Finally, it must be recalled that there is a horizontal dialogue also between supranational jurisdictions, when they act both in the same and different regional context, as shown by the numerous references made both by the CJEU[39] and the IACtHR[40] to the case-law of the ECtHR.

1.6 'Couple', 'Family', 'Marriage', 'Sex' in Context and Related Problems Concerning Legitimacy, Democracy and the Separation of Powers

The legal discourse on the *status* of same-sex couples before the courts raises problems in terms of legitimacy, democracy and separation of powers. What is at stake is the balance between the prerogatives of the judiciary and those of the legislature. The issue becomes even more complicated when, as in the present book, the courts in question are not only national but also supranational, and when their jurisprudence has an impact on both national legislators and judges. In this case, legitimacy, democracy and the separation of powers tend to be naturally seen as a matter of State sovereignty in family law—that is, in an area no longer solely within the scope of national jurisdiction.

In this context, the authors of the following chapters try to answer a number of questions. To mention a few: what is the boundary between judicial activism and the judicial recognition of human rights as a remedy to the inertia of the legislature? When can legislative action, insofar as resulting from the democratic process, no longer be regarded as the best way to ensure that the rights of citizens are protected? To what extent can judges urge/require the legislature to take the rights of 'same

[37] Chapter 17 by Pustorino and Chap. 18 by Crisafulli.

[38] De Búrca and Gerstenberg (2006). See also Nollkamper (2010).

[39] Chapter 20 by Rijpma and Koffeman and Chap. 21 by Orzan.

[40] Chapter 19 by Magi.

sex-couples' seriously'? Judges do not create the law,[41] but they interpret and even shape it—in addition to protecting it—and thus represent an indispensable antidote against populism, as well as a fundamental barrier to the tyranny of the majority, no matter whether that majority exists among the people or the members of Parliament. It is our conviction that, when rights resulting from social and cultural changes are at stake, the courts, without being necessarily 'creative'[42] agents of change, should be active in acknowledging the socio-cultural transformations occurred in modern society and providing a legal framework for them.

The problem with a static, *originalist*, formal constructivist interpretation of the law is that it leads us to establish an *ex-ante*[43] connection between the law and the specific period in time when it was enacted, whereas concepts such as equality and discrimination change over time. It is also in this process of change that lies the universal—but not immutable—nature of human rights, as well as that of the fundamental international, supranational and national norms aimed at their protection.

Therefore, the issue of same-sex couples and their *status* before the courts serves as a privileged touchstone for assessing the rationale, scope, potential and limits of judicial activity, especially with regard to the role of judges when facing issues that are replete with cultural, religious, social and, in a broad sense, political implications.[44] In this respect, the jurisprudence examined in the next 22 chapters of this book clearly shows the existence of different kinds of judicial behaviour: from a deferent and/or self-restrained interpretation of the law, to a resilient/flexible or even activist approach.

Considering the position adopted by national, supranational and international jurisdictions vis-à-vis same-sex couples, we can conclude that the legal protection of LGBTI people is, ultimately, a matter of equality. In particular, as observed by Nussbaum, the right to marry:

> is a fundamental liberty right of individuals, and because it is that, it also involves an equality dimension: groups of people cannot be fenced out of that fundamental right without some overwhelming reason. It's like voting: there isn't a constitutional right to vote, as such: some jobs can be filled by appointment. But the minute voting is offered, it is unconstitutional to fence out a group of people from the exercise of the right. At this point, then, the questions become, Who has this liberty/equality right to marry? And what reasons are strong enough to override it?[45]

---

[41] In these terms Klabbers et al. (2009), p. 127.

[42] On the risks deriving from such 'creativity' see Cappelletti (1984) and Waldron (2006).

[43] See Rubenfeld (2001), p. 188.

[44] See, in this perspective, the relationship between constitutional/supreme/high courts and legislatures as discussed in Zagrebelsky (2005).

[45] Nussbaum (2009). See also Nussbaum (2010).

1.7 A Working Tool

This book is addressed to academics, legal practitioners (mostly lawyers and judges) and policy makers who work in the fields of international law, constitutional law, private law, comparative law, EU law and human rights, and who must face the issue of the protection of LGBTI rights. Throughout its chapters, it tries to combine an informative account and a critical analysis of the jurisprudence of international, supranational and national courts.

This volume, however, is not for legal 'experts' only, but also for readers who wish to know more about this complex, fascinating and evolving issue, which represents a crucial test for modern democracies and contemporary societies.

Acknowledgements The editors wish to thank: Dr. Elena Miraglia for revising the English of this and other chapters; the team at *Springer*, especially Anke Seyfried, for their help, support and efforts, which have led to a timely publication of the present volume.

References

Cappelletti M (1984) Giudici legislatori? Giuffrè, Milano

De Búrca G, Gerstenberg O (2006) The denationalization of constitutional law. Harv Int Law J 47:243–262

Delmas-Marty M (2009) Ordering pluralism. A conceptual framework for understanding the transnational legal world. Oxford University Press, Oxford

Focarelli C (2012) International law as social construct. The struggle for global justice. Oxford University Press, Oxford

Klabbers J, Peters A, Ulfstein G (2009) The constitutionalization of international law. Oxford University Press, Oxford

Nollkamper A (2010) National courts and the international rule of law. Oxford University Press, Oxford

Nussbaum M (2009) A right to marry? Same-sex marriage and constitutional law. Dissent – a quarterly of politics and culture 2009. http://www.dissentmagazine.org

Nussbaum M (2010) From disgust to humanity: sexual orientation and constitutional law. Oxford University Press, Oxford

Poiares Maduro M (2009) Courts and pluralism: essay on a theory of judicial adjudication in the context of legal and constitutional pluralism. In: Dunoff JL, Trachtman JP (eds) Ruling the world: constitutionalism, international law, and global governance. Cambridge University Press, Cambridge, pp 356–379

Rubenfeld J (2001) Freedom and time – a theory of constitutional self-government. Yale University Press, New Heaven

Von Bogdandy A (2008) Pluralism, direct effect, and the ultimate say: on the relationship between international and domestic constitutional law. Int J Const Law 6:397–413

Von Bogdandy A, Schill S (2011) Overcoming absolute primacy: respect for national identity under the Lisbon treaty. Common Market Law Rev 48:1417–1453

Waldijk K (1994) Standard sequences in the legal recognition of homosexuality—Europe's past, present and future. Australas Gay Lesbian Law J 50:50–72

Waldron J (2006) The core of the case against judicial review. Yale Law J 115:1346–1406

Walker N (2008) Beyond boundary disputes and basic grids: mapping the global disorder of normative orders. Int J Const Law 6:373–396
Wintemute R (2004) International trends in legal recognition of same-sex partnerships. Quinnipiac Law Rev 23:577–595
Zagrebelsky G (2005) Principî e voti. La corte costituzionale e la politica. Einaudi, Torino

Part I
Selected National Jurisdictions

Section 1 Domestic Law Issues

Section 2 Private International Law Issues

Chapter 2
The Recognition of Same-Sex Couples' Rights in the US Between Counter-Majoritarian Principle and Ideological Approaches: A State Level Perspective

Graziella Romeo

Abstract The chapter analyzes the issue of same sex couples' right to marry from a State level perspective. Before describing different models of recognizing same sex couples' rights, the essay deals with the argumentative structure of State Courts decisions in an attempt to demonstrate that the continued interaction among legal formants fosters the recognition of rights. The State Supreme Courts indeed seem to develop a counter-majoritarian attitude that encourages a theory of constitutional interpretation that conceives constitutions as evolving documents.

2.1 The Recognition of Rights Between Counter-Majoritarian Dilemma and Ideological Approaches

Studies on same-sex couples in the United States usually take for granted the distinction between Red and Blue States, emphasizing two opposing models of society behind the recognition or the denial of homosexual relationships, which in turn express conflicting views of basic values and deep ideological beliefs that define political inclinations.[1]

There are at least two reasons why this approach is arguable. Firstly, this methodology, although generally capable of explaining some data, tends to underestimate the process through which a claim, originally supported by a specific faction or group,[2] achieves an ideologically enfranchised position in public (and

[1] See McClain (2008–2009), p. 415.

[2] Earlier analyses of homosexuals' rights had a primarily militant motive: see T. Stoddard and P. Ettelbrick's debate in *Out/Look Magazine* during the 1980s, now retraced in Hull (2006), p. 77. Stoddard believed that allowing same-sex marriage was the best way to end discrimination for political reasons and a part from practical reasons such as tax regulation. By contrast, Ettelbrick

G. Romeo (✉)
Department of Law, Bocconi University, Milan, Italy
e-mail: graziella.romeo@unibocconi.it

D. Gallo et al. (eds.), *Same-Sex Couples before National, Supranational and International Jurisdictions*, DOI 10.1007/978-3-642-35434-2_2,

political) debate. The State of Washington could serve as an illustration of this: it recently moved from being cited as an example of a State with quite a conservative attitude towards same-sex couples' rights[3] to a State that advocated the complete recognition of same-sex marriages[4] without significant changes in political scenario. Virtually every State seems to adopt an incremental approach to gay rights that usually develops from a statutory ban on homosexual intimate relationships to a statutory guarantee of (at least) some spousal rights. These developments do not appear to depend directly upon changing political attitudes. In almost every case the evolving vicissitudes of rights recognition involve struggles among courts, legislatures and civil society—as the preferred terrain of the liberty/authority dialectic—rather than the mere transformation of political preferences.[5]

Secondly, the ideological dichotomy between Red and Blue States represents a structural division that is for instance insensitive to specific or temporary changes in voters' attitudes. Progresses in the affirmation of civil rights reflect cultural shifts in people's beliefs[6] towards specific issues without necessarily encompassing a broader change in political inclination.

In other words, the recognition of a previously denied right owes more to the dynamic interaction among judges, legislatures and civil society initiatives than to the predominance of a political party. There will undoubtedly be instances in which the full recognition of rights is combined with the State's progressive political attitude, but this does not mean that the division between Red and Blue States can be interpreted as self-explanatory. Therefore, the analysis of same-sex couple's rights needs to be placed within the democratic process understood in wider terms, as a communicative process in which multiple actors, even the non-political ones, play significant roles.[7]

---

maintained that marriage would not have had the effect of liberating gays and lesbians, rather it would have forced them into the mainstream, undermining "some of the most cherished goals of gay liberation, including the recognition of and the respect for a diversity of family forms and intimate relationships" (Hull 2006, p. 80). Along the same lines, the modern feminist critique of the marriage model extends to same-sex marriages as they tend to 'map-on' the traditional prototype of marriage. See Barker (2012), p. 198: "there have been some strong arguments made for same-sex marriage, from the necessity of accessing legal protections and the symbolism of legal recognition to feminist claims that same-sex marriage would transform the institution and suggestions that marriage could be queered". In other words, the struggle for homosexuals' rights missed the chance to move beyond marriage and conjugality.

[3] See the decision of *Andersen v. King County*, 138 P.3d 963 (Wash. 2006).

[4] Same sex marriages came into effect on December 6th, 2012 (see note 62).

[5] On the contrary, J. Toobin seems to support the view according to which there is an immediate correlation between the outcome of Presidential elections and the outcome of cases before the Supreme Court: "[...] So in time of great polarization between the parties, Democratic and Republican judicial appointees see the world, and the law, in very different ways". See Toobin (2013), p. 20.

[6] See Tribe and Matz (2011–2012), p. 471.

[7] This idea, of course, owes a debt to the theory of communicative democracy, better known as discourse ethics, formulated by Habermas (1990).

Neither the exclusive reference to the history of legislative proposals (or popular initiatives) nor the sole mentioning of Courts' decisions are capable of explaining the *status* of same-sex couples' rights protection in the United States. It is the continued interaction among legal formants[8] on the one hand and public debate on the other that marks progress or regression in this field. Courts cannot ignore commonly held opinions as always happens when the recognition of controversial rights is concerned. Judges indeed face the counter-majoritarian difficulty[9] each time they are required to deliver decisions that affect society's fundamental choices. Nevertheless, the issue of the rights of same-sex couples appears to be a typical area of the law in which the counter-majoritarian approach encourages theories of constitutional interpretation that conceive constitutions as evolving documents,[10] capable of leading to results that are not entirely predictable.

In order to be consistent with the general premise, this chapter disregards the ideological division between conservative and progressive States and addresses same-sex couples' rights from a dual perspective: the competing arguments within the public debate and the Courts, and the models of same-sex couples' relationships, shaped as result of the competition among possible solutions.

Before considering the issue of same-sex couples' rights from an argumentative standpoint, Sect. 2.2 focuses on the implications of the federalist system for the regulation of marriage, while Sect. 2.3 deals with the competing solutions to the same-sex couples' issue supported by courts, legislators and public opinion. In an attempt to summarize the contents of public discourse, in which each legal formant plays its role, Sect. 2.4 describes and analyzes the contending views with a particular focus on judicial argumentation. Section 2.5 explores four models of recognition of homosexual couples' rights in order to systematize legislative and judicial instruments that influence the current scenario. Eventually, Sect. 2.6 offers some concluding remarks on counter-majoritarian approach and its role in fostering evolving standards of protection of rights.

---

[8] "Legal formant" is here used to denote legislators, Courts' decisions and scholars' opinions "who are never in complete harmony" as has been taught by Sacco (1991), p. 343.

[9] See the well-known analysis of Bickel (1986).

[10] Consider the Connecticut Supreme Court decision of *Kerrigan v. Commissioner of Public Health*, 957 A.2d 407 (CT 2008) which holds that the State ban on same-sex marriage violates the Constitution. The ruling clearly states: "we are mindful that State "[c]onstitutional provisions must be interpreted within the context of the times ... The Connecticut Constitution is an instrument of progress, it is intended to stand for a great length of time and should not be interpreted too narrowly or too literally so that it fails to have contemporary effectiveness for all of our citizens". See also Conkle (2006), p. 121 discussing *Lawrence v. Texas*, 539 U.S. 601(2003) as an example of a decision based on interpretative flexibility and dynamic theory of those national values that guide constitutional interpretation (see note 44).

2.2 Marriage Federalism and Its Implications

Marriage as a legally recognized social relation involves both the State's power to regulate internal affairs (and the internal order)[11] and the guarantee of a personal right. This dual nature of marriage, a subject matter of police power and an individual right,[12] implies that it is incorrect from a methodological perspective, when discussing the rights of same-sex couples, to disregard issues like State interest in pursuing public goals connected with marriage (such as procreation, childrearing, preservation of traditional family) or federal interactions with State level regulation.

As far as State interests in marriage are concerned, the case law offers a variegated map of reasons that governments supported to justify the regulation of marital (and non-marital) relationships. Although the promotion of procreation is the most cited interest in State's litigation, it does not represent the only concern of courts and legislatures. Childrearing and protection of the traditional model of family[13] are often alleged to be the justifications of public regulation. Those interests, of course, are interconnected: procreation and childrearing need a stable and committed relationship that usually takes the form of marriage. States that refuse to recognize same-sex relationships maintain that their interests in marriage justify the prohibition. Sometimes even other reasons peer out from the case law and are claimed to be supportive of the banning of same-sex relationships. The preservation of State finances, threatened by the extension of social or tax benefits recipients, can be cited as an example of asserted interest.[14]

The issue of same-sex couples, however, is not a purely State's problem. It necessarily involves also federal law because, as always happens in American constitutionalism, recognition of rights has consequences for federalism.[15] Indeed when a right is guaranteed by both State and federal law, minimal interferences or overlaps occur between the two levels of government.[16] When the dynamics of federalism allow or imply differentiation in matter of rights, however, tensions may appear insofar as State law or judicial interpretation attempt to find a constitutional foothold at federal level.[17] Indeed within American constitutionalism there is in any case no general need to pursue homogeneous grounds of protection across the

[11] The reference is to state police power as described by Dubber (2005), *passim*. The Author underlines the prevailing purpose of the exercise of police power, essentially aimed at guaranteeing the ordered and safe existence of civil society.

[12] See *ex multis Loving v. Virginia* 388 U.S. 3 (1967).

[13] *Baker v. Vermont*, 744 A.2d 864, 884 (Vt. 1999).

[14] *Baehr v. Miike*, No. 20371, 1999 HI LEXIS 391 (HI December 9, 1999). See Sects. 2.4 and 2.4.1.

[15] See Abraham and Perry (2003), p. 38. See also Powell (1996–1997), pp. 81–82 and Collins (1992), p. 78. who argues that American federalism has seldom been interpreted "in the sense in which [Justice] Black had newly christened it – as a way of referring to our concerns for harmonious state-federal relations, and with more than a hint of special solicitude for states' rights".

[16] See Marks Jr and Cooper (2003), pp. 35–38.

[17] The issue is clearly addressed by Sandalow (1965), p. 187. The Supreme Court of the United States seems to be jealous of its mandate to interpret the provisions of the Constitution and the Bill of Rights.

whole federation.[18] Nevertheless, a State guarantee that does not have a federal counterpart may raise issues such as a specific supra-state interest to regulate the matter or inconsistent interpretations of the Bill of Rights between federal and State Courts; in the same way there may be instances in which the recognition of a right relies upon State provisions (with or without constitutional standing) and, at the same time, no federal interest can be identified. Consequently only State constitution and statutory law occupy the scene.

This seemed to be the case for same-sex couples rights up to the 1990s. In *Baker v. Vermont*,[19] Vermont Supreme Court held that the banning of homosexual marriage amounted to a violation of rights secured by the state Constitution. The Massachusetts Supreme Court ruled that the right to marry the person of one's choice is granted under the state Constitution in the celebrated decision of *Goodridge v. Department of Public Health.*[20] Conversely, in *Baehr v. Miike*,[21] Hawaii Supreme Court found that the interpretation of statutory provisions in a way that allows same-sex marriage to be performed was inconsistent with the State Constitution. In all cases, judicial interpretation rested upon State constitutional grounds, excluding federal law from the issue.

In the second half of the 1990s, federal law came to the fore in the field of same-sex couples' rights. In 1996, Congress passed the Defense of Marriage Act (DOMA),[22] defining marriage as the union between a man and a woman and denying the recognition of same-sex marriages, performed in State jurisdictions, for federal law purposes such as social security benefits or tax benefits. This piece of legislation was specifically designed to preserve "marriage federalism"[23] without forcing the Nation to share choices made by a few States.

DOMA served somehow as an example for State jurisdictions. Seven States passed similar statutes,[24] and the vast majority of them approved constitutional amendments to define marriage as a relationship between a man and a woman.[25]

---

[18] Federal constitutional and statutory laws establish a minimum national standard for the exercise of individual rights but do not prevent State governments from affording higher levels of protection for the same rights: see *State v. Morales*, 232 Conn. 707, 716, 657 A.2d 585 (1995), quoting *State v. Barton*, 219 Conn. 529, 546, 594 A.2d 917 (1991).

[19] See note 13.

[20] 798 N.E.2d 941, 948 (MA 2003).

[21] See note 14.

[22] Pub.L. 104–199, 110 Stat. 2419, enacted Sept. 21, 1996, 1 U.S.C. § 7 and 28 U.S.C. § 1738C.

[23] See Knauer (2008), p. 421.

[24] Delaware (DE Code, Title 13, Ch. 1, §101); Hawaii (HI Code, Title 31, Ch. 572, § 1); Indiana (IN Code, Title 31, Ch. 1, sect. 1); Illinois (750 IL Code 5/212); Minnesota (MN Code, Ch. 517, sect. 03); Pennsylvania (PA Code, Title 23, Ch. 11, § 1102), West Virginia (WV Code, Ch. 48); Wyoming (WY Code, Title 20, Ch. 1, Art. 1).

[25] See para 5. Scholars refer to Super-DOMAs to describe those laws that prohibit any kind of recognition of same-sex relationships, including civil union and domestic partnership. Nebraska, Ohio and Virginia passed statutes expressly not permitting even those forms of domestic relationships. See Cahill (2004), p. 9.

As a result, the recognition of marriages performed in jurisdictions issuing licenses for homosexual couples is left to the discretion of each State. In a limited number of cases, States refusing such a right recognize marriages from other jurisdictions such as civil unions or domestic partnerships so as not to contradict their own position on same-sex relationships.[26]

This composite framework did not come to an end after the Supreme Court reached the decisions in *United States v. Windsor*[27] and *Hollingsworth v. Perry*.[28] The former involved Sect. 3 of DOMA, which expressly circumscribes marriage to the union of a man and a woman. The latter concerned the State of California Proposition 8, which bans same sex marriages. The judgments called into question not only homosexuals' rights, but also State prerogatives and even, in broader terms, the way in which federalism is supposed to be framed.[29] An essential point behind these cases was the extent to which State interests in regulating marriage prevent the 'constitutionalization' of same-sex couples' rights and in parallel the extent to which the federal government is allowed to ignore States' decision to dignify homosexual relationships. The Supreme Court seems to have chosen to preserve marriage federalism by declaring on the one hand that Sect. 3 of DOMA is unconstitutional under the Fifth Amendment due process clause and, on the other hand, by deciding not to address the constitutionality of Proposition 8, hiding itself behind a procedural issue.[30] The concrete outcome of the two cases is that States may regulate same-sex couples' right to marry without incurring in denial of homosexuals' marriage under federal law. At the same time, States are not compelled to recognize marriage equality.

Against this background, exploring the issue of homosexuals' rights at State level should imply focusing on the competing arguments that have influenced scholarly as well as public debate around this topic. They are indeed the most powerful forces that can challenge (and even survive) the constitutional decisions.

Before reaching the core of competing opinions, the analysis should address the mutual influences among legal formants that continuously reshape models of recognition of homosexuals' rights.

---

[26] See Illinois Religious Freedom Protection and Civil Union Act of 2011 (codified as 750 IL Code 75/60). By contrast, the West Virginia Code expressly refuses recognition of same-sex marriages performed in another State (WV Code, Ch. 48, sect. 2–603).

[27] 570 U.S. ___ 2013 (Docket No. 12-307).

[28] 570 U.S. ___ 2013 (Docket No. 12-144).

[29] From this standpoint, it is worthwhile mentioning those studies that analyze the coefficient of successful gay rights litigations in federal and state courts. See Cross (2004–2005), p. 1196 who underlines: "states courts decided in favor of gay rights more than twice as often as did federal courts, at both intermediate and supreme courts level". Similarly, claims brought under state constitutions were resolved more favorably than federal constitutional cases.

[30] In *Hollingsworth v. Perry* the Court failed to reach the merit because it affirmed that the petitioners, who were the sponsors of ballot initiative, lacked standing to sue under federal law.

2.3 Courts, Legislature and Public Debate

In recent American legal thought it is not unusual to find authors supporting the thesis of the limited impact of judicial decision in advancing gay rights protection.[31] There are even arguments clearly asserting that judicial activism resulted in severe backlashes for the cause of same-sex couples' equality.[32]

Undoubtedly homosexuals' rights litigation was not always capable of achieving enduring results. There are at least three cases in which the outcome of judicial decisions provoked legislative or popular retorts. In 1993, Hawaii Supreme Court held that the denial to recognize same-sex marriage violates the State equal protection clause. On April 29, 1997, both Houses of the legislative branch passed a bill proposing an amendment to the Hawaii Constitution defining marriage as being limited to the union of a man and a woman. Similarly, the California Supreme Court ruling declaring the ban on same-sex marriage to be unconstitutional was overruled in a referendum. Indeed, in 2008 voters approved an amendment designed to define marriage as the relationship between two persons of the opposite sex (the so-called Proposition 8). After the above-mentioned decision *Goodridge v. Department of State*, a wave of legislative and popular initiatives sought to insulate marriage laws from the judicial process.[33]

According to some scholars, had the Courts decided to leave the choice to legislators and their constituencies, there would not have been such sweeping backlashes.[34] In other words, instead of establishing a fruitful dialogue with the judiciary, lawmakers tried to put the issue of same-sex couples beyond the reach of judges resulting in a substantial impairment of homosexuals' rights at least in the long term.

The recognition of rights is not something that develops at an even pace. It is rather a history of struggles in which Courts act as watchdogs of the legislative branch and sometimes succeed in developing a 'civilization' of fundamental rights. One cannot trace a perfect harmony among legal formants: it is indeed the communication among them that marks the upholding of (formerly denied) rights.

Thus it is not surprising that same-sex marriages are legalized following fluctuating vicissitudes. The Maine Legislature approved "An Act To End Discrimination in Civil Marriage and Affirm Religious Freedom".[35] The voters firstly invalidated the law by referendum, and then changed their opinion supporting same-sex marriage in a ballot held in 2012.

In some instances, Courts have engaged in a virtuous dialogue with legislators. Though urging lawmakers to adopt statutes on marriage equality, judges left them free to choose any form of legally recognized relationship that was capable of guaranteeing spousal rights on an egalitarian basis. The Vermont Supreme Court

---

[31] See Toobin, in note 5.

[32] See Klarman (2013).

[33] At least 25 States had enacted constitutional amendments that define marriage as the union between a man and a woman after the Supreme Court of Massachusetts decision: see Cole (2013).

[34] See Klarman (2013), p. 35.

[35] ME Rev. Stat. Ann. tit. 19-A, § 650.

for instance left the legislature with the ultimate decision on how to secure gay couples' rights without compelling the State to provide them with the institution of marriage.[36]

In virtually every case one can trace a strong connection between political process and litigation in the field of gay rights. It does not necessarily require that there should also be a complete syncretism. Arguments discussed in the courtroom become the subject of public debate and public debate, in turn, influences lawmakers and, indirectly, judges. The Hawaii Supreme Court declared the ban on same-sex marriage to be in violation of the State equal protection clause but was then compelled to recognize that a constitutional amendment and a statutory provision had been approved. Consequently, the ruling could not withstand a change that was of a political nature.[37]

These kinds of changes are, however, not irreversible; indeed they are constantly subjected to challenges as the cases of Maine and Washington show. In both circumstances, political shifts are incapable of *per se* explaining why public opinion moved from anti-gay to pro-gay positions.

In modern democracies *consensus* around shared values is built in a process where opinions compete in a public arena. However, even in an open and democratic debate constitutional arguments are compelling. It is therefore unavoidable to turn to strictly legal argumentation in order to understand the way in which same-sex couples' rights receive protection.

2.4 The Choice Over the Scheme of Argumentation in State Litigation

Arguments used to oppose same-sex marriages in States' litigations seem to be of a circular kind: that is they often assume what they are attempting to prove. The circular logic has been shown both by State governments' lawyers that have tried to resist the right to same-sex marriage in court and by legal scholars, to such an extent that the debate has been virtually built around one single issue: the biological basis

[36] See *Baker v. Vermont*, in note 13. Chief Justice Amestoy wrote: "in the faith that a case beyond the imagining of the framers of our Constitution may, nevertheless, be safely anchored in the values that infused it, we find a constitutional obligation to extend to plaintiffs the common benefit, protection, and security that Vermont law provides opposite-sex married couples. It remains only to determine the appropriate means and scope of relief compelled by this constitutional mandate". It must be mentioned that civil unions or domestic partnerships are not a "consolation prize" (Tribe and Matz 2011–2012, p. 481): there are views, even within the gay community, that do not share the need to have homosexual relationships recognized in the form of marriage as part of a broader critique to the marriage institution itself: see note 2.

[37] See note 24.

(i.e. the *natural* foundation) of the human bond that generates a family and requires a legal/formal structure called marriage.[38]

Even leaving out the most radical rhetoric based on the laws of nature[39] and taking a closer look at recent academic debate and judicial rationale, the 'basic biology' (or 'basic understanding' of biology), i.e. the need for a man and a woman to give birth to a child, is at the same time the starting point of the theory that justifies the different treatment of straight and homosexual couples and the reason why same-sex marriage could not be conceived in a ordered society.[40] In other words, marriage is an institution that is designed to protect the essential nucleus of our society (the family), possibly completed by children. The argument could be essentially synthesized as follows: biological differences create the family *because* the family derives from biological differences. From this perspective, only heterosexual couples are able to establish a family and thus need the institution of marriage. It has been far too simple to respond that same-sex partners have and raise children and that they need a secure and committed relationship as much as heterosexual couples do.[41]

Considering the argument from the point of view of the interests of the State[42] in regulating marriage leads to the same conclusion. If state regulation of conjugal relationships is essentially designed to secure a stable and healthy environment for childrearing, it is unreasonable to deny protection to those who happen to have parents with homosexual orientation. To some authors[43] the doctrine of State interest seems to afford another reason to support same-sex couples' rights and at the same times reveals that the real interest served by State legislations is basically the protection of the heterosexual conception of marriage (and thus a traditional way of conceiving family).[44]

Hence, the first difficulty encountered by States' Supreme Courts is the choice of the scheme of argumentation. Judges' opinions always need to be perceived as acceptable from the perspective of the common starting points in legal contexts.[45] This means, *inter alia*, that judicial reasoning should put to one side extra-legal/traditional/cultural arguments so as not to transform the rationale into a sort of political argumentation.

---

[38] It is worthwhile recalling that in a number of U.S. Supreme Court decisions marriage is expressly defined as heterosexual and as "the foundation of the family and society without which there would be neither civilization nor progress": *Reynolds v. United States*, 98 U.S. 145, 165 (1879); *Murphy v. Ramsey*, 114 U.S. 15, 45 (1988). See also Gallagher (2003), p. 17.

[39] For a comprehensive explanation of a natural law approach see George (1993).

[40] See for example arguments presented in decisions such as *Anderson v. King County*, 138 P. 3d 963, 982–983 (WA 2006); *Conaway v. Deane*, 932 A.2d 571 (MD 2007); *Morrison v. Sadler*, 821 N.E. 2d 15 (IN Ct. App. 2005).

[41] See Sect. 2.4.1. See also Strasser (2003), p. 36.

[42] See Wardle (2001), p. 771.

[43] See Strasser (2003), p. 36.

[44] "Traditional family" is used to denote the idea of family that has its origins in a specific socio-cultural context. See for instance George (2003), p. 116. See also the classical study on marriage and family written by Witte Jr. (1997).

[45] See Feteris (2009), pp. 91–92.

Even Justice Scalia, who cannot be described as an advocate of homosexuals' rights, appears to believe that some traditional conceptual tools are weak or completely inadequate to face the challenging arguments supporting gay equality.[46] Procreation is maybe the clearest example: it is constantly brought up in State litigation[47]; nonetheless it can be held as a general opinion that marriage has assumed "profound expressive, personal, and financial significance in modern society".[48] This new understanding of marital relationships, whether or not embracing an alternative model of family, overlooks the procreation-oriented prototype of marriage.[49]

Therefore, the competition between opposing views should be dealt with on a strictly legal basis where the quality of conflicting opinions can be measured with positive law and theories of constitutional interpretation.

2.4.1 Equal Protection v. Due Process

Within the cultural debate among gay rights supporters, some authors recall the rhetoric of the civil rights movement[50] and favor a political and cultural crusade based on the inspiring principle of equality. In terms of judicial litigation though, equality can be less effective than it is frequently perceived to be, at least in those fields in which the law is persistently influenced by cultural heritage and traditional understandings of human relationships. Even the litigation on civil rights has shown the limited meaning that judicial interpretation can give to equality when it comes to deciding "hard cases".[51]

Nevertheless claims supporting gay rights tend to be based on grounds of equal protection both at the Federal and State level. From a legal standpoint, this trend could easily be justified because the scheme of equal protection reasoning is perfectly suitable for arguments affirming same-sex couples' rights. Both the technique of

---

[46] See *Lawrence v. Texas*, in note 10, Scalia J. dissenting: "preserving the traditional institution of marriage is just a kinder way of describing the state's moral disapproval of same-sex couples". The point is also well illustrated by Walfson (2004), pp. 79–80.

[47] *Ibidem*, at 75.

[48] See Tribe and Matz (2011–2012), p. 481.

[49] Witte Jr. (1997), p. 75.

[50] Walfson (2004), p. 23 and Cole (2013). Novak (2010), p. 711 criticizes this approach stressing that there is a difference between pre-political institution like marriage and political (and strictly legal) institutions like the ones involved in civil rights litigation, citing as an example public education.

[51] See Ball (2011–2012), p. 1. Examples can also be derived from the controversial "separate but equal doctrine", elaborated within the equal protection clause jurisprudence before the upheaval of *Brown v. Board of Education*, 47 U.S. 483 (1954). An interesting case is *Pace v. Alabama*, 106 U.S. 583 (1883), cited by the Supreme Court in *Loving v. Virginia*, 388 U.S. 1 (1967). In that case, the Court upheld an Alabama statute forbidding adultery or fornication between a white person and a Negro and imposing a greater penalty than that of a statute proscribing similar conduct by members of the same race. The Court maintained that the statute could not be conceived as a discriminative measure against Negroes because the punishment was the same for each participant in the offense.

suspect or quasi-suspect classifications and the corresponding model of scrutiny fit the structure of the argumentation presented to support marriage equality.

Although the equality principle does not ensure a successful litigation, there are at least four cases in which constitutional or statutory bans on same-sex marriages have been struck down on equal protection grounds[52]; by contrast, a different legal basis seems to have been successfully invoked only in two cases.

In *Kerrigan v. Commissioner of Public Health*,[53] the Connecticut Supreme Court ruled the ban on homosexual marriages to be unconstitutional and rejected the government argument according to which same-sex and straight couples are not similarly placed as far as the desire to develop a conjugal relationship is concerned. In other words, the Court refused to adopt a sort of socio-cultural approach that characterizes homosexual couples as being basically indifferent to the aspiration of forming a family and adopted the equal protection analysis on a rigorous basis.

Comparably, the equality principle was influential in judges going against traditional beliefs and opinions in *Varnum v. Brien*.[54] The Supreme Court of Iowa cited the *Kerrigan* case and justified the application of the heightened level of scrutiny over classifications based on sexual orientation such as the one contained in a statute that excludes same-sex marriages. Neither the State interest in preserving traditional marriage, nor the interest connected to the promotion of the optimal environment for childrearing can withstand the intermediate scrutiny because the Court found that neither interest was supported by clear evidences justifying the classification operated by the statute. Even the promotion of procreation is conceived as a 'too tenuous' argument to overcome the heightened test of constitutionality.

The equal protection clause can be a powerful weapon in litigation concerning the rights of same-sex couples, but it can be used to justify discrimination as well. In a number of cases the principle of equality is invoked to reach opposing conclusions, essentially based upon the fact that gay and heterosexual couples are not similarly situated as far as the right to marry is concerned.[55] In *Standhardt v. Superior Court*,[56] the Arizona Appeals Court applied the same rationale to conclude that there is a reasonable link between opposite-sex marriage, procreation and childrearing.

The due process clause, on the contrary, has hardly been used at all to decide gay rights cases even if it generally demands a more intrusive standard of review. Massachusetts Supreme Court resorted to both due process and equal protection in the famous decision of *Goodridge v. Department of Public Health*.[57] Due process has been applied according to the rational basis test. It has been construed as requiring that the statute "bear[s] ... a real and substantial relation to the public health, safety, morals, or some other phase of the general welfare".

---

[52] For a complete list of examples see Ball (2011–2012), p. 41.

[53] See note 10.

[54] 763 NW 2d 862 (IA 2009).

[55] See *Morrison v. Sadler*, in note 38, or *Hernandez v. Robles*, 855 N.E. 2d 1, 21 (N.Y. 2006).

[56] 77 P. 3d 451 (AZ Ct. App. 2003).

[57] See note 20.

The equal protection standard required that:

> an impartial lawmaker could logically believe that the classification would serve a legitimate public purpose that transcends the harm to the members of the disadvantaged class.

The Court systematically rejected the justifications of the ban on same-sex marriages offered by the Government, including procreation, childrearing and preserving the institution of traditional marriage, and found that the statutory ban could not withstand even the rationale basis test.

The majority opinion is heavily influenced by Supreme Court decision in *Lawrence v. Texas*[58] and develops a rationale that is a sort of matching of the classical due process and equal protection analysis.

The approach adopted by the California Supreme Court is somehow bolder. In *Re Marriage Cases*[59] is indeed entirely construed as a due process claim. The State judges appear to believe that the issue cannot be confined to the equal protection clause. Accordingly they perform a liberty analysis that recognizes the fundamental right to marry as being applicable to same-sex couples because marriage is not to be grounded in procreation and childrearing, but more broadly viewed as a stable commitment that gives formal recognition to an intimate relationship.

Some scholars argue that it is not by chance that due process has been applied to reach such a strong position on same-sex marriage as a fundamental right.[60] In other words, the liberty review should be held as the most effective standard in gay rights litigation.

This position supports the rediscovery of the due process clause[61] and ultimately transfers the key point of the debate around same-sex couples from equal treatment, that could mean fairly comparable treatment, to complete recognition of rights enjoyed by straight couples.[62]

---

[58] Crane (2003–2004), p. 465. *Lawrence v. Texas*, in note 10, dealt with sodomy law, an area of legislation where it may be generally difficult to apply equal protection because law criminalizing sodomy may be facially neutral. The Texas statute however was not facially neutral, but expressly targeting homosexual intimate relationships. See Ball (2011–2012), p. 40.

[59] 183 P. 3d 384 (CA 2008).

[60] See Ball (2011–2012), p. 38.

[61] Supreme Court Justices developed an interesting debate around the rediscovery of the due process clause and its substantive dimension. The discussion arose from Justice Kennedy concurring opinion and Scalia response in *Stop the Beach Renourishment, Inc. v. Florida Department of Environmental Protection*, 130 S.Ct. 2592, 2613 (2010). The debate is retraced by Stone et al. (2010), pp. 98–99. I have discussed this issue elsewhere: Romeo (2011), pp. 4063–4064. In general see Musgrove (2008), p. 137.

[62] Nussbaum (2010), pp. 669ff. seems to stress that the debate around same-sex couples must address primarily this issue when she argues that: "The public debate ... is ... about marriage's expressive aspects. It is here that the difference between civil unions and marriage resides, and it is this aspect that is at issue when same-sex couples reject the compromise offer of civil unions, demanding nothing less than marriage. It is because marriage is taken to confer some kind of dignity or public approval on the parties and their union that the exclusion of gays and lesbians from marriage is seen ... as stigmatizing and degrading".

In most cases, the outcomes of the litigation that was centered on equality review were indeed partial solutions (or victories) such as the recognition of non-marital relationships, labeled as domestic partnership or civil unions, or of a particular package of rights.

2.5 Models of Recognizing Same-Sex Couples' Rights: A Kaleidoscopic Framework

From a purely theoretical standpoint, possible approaches to same-sex couples' rights are essentially limited to the dialectic between traditional and modern conceptions of marriage and family relations. By contrast, positive law offers nuanced solutions, sometimes even combined with each other and not entirely congruent from a strictly legal perspective. In this regard, it happens that civil unions, with the recognition of the whole set of spousal rights, characterize States in which legislatures have simultaneously passed a statutory ban on same-sex marriages.[63] In other words, homosexual couples enjoy the same rights and almost the same status as married couples but without being allowed to marry.

The overview of State level solutions should distinguish among different ways of recognizing couples' rights. Following an ideal rights-declining approach but without claiming to be complete, it is possible to classify at least four prototypes: the first covers those States where same-sex marriages are allowed.[64] The second designates States which recognize only civil unions (and possibly domestic partnerships).[65] The third labels States which expressly do not allow homosexuals marriage and introduce domestic partnerships.[66] Finally, the fourth covers States which prohibit same-sex marriages by means of constitutional[67] or

---

[63] This is the case for Hawaii, Delaware and Illinois (see Sect. 2.2 and note 24).

[64] Connecticut (An Act Implementing the Guarantee of Equal Protection Under the Constitution of the State for Same Sex Couples, Public Act No. 09-13); Iowa (by judicial decision); Maine (Title 19, Domestic Relations, Ch. 1, § 34); Maryland (Civil Marriage Protection Act 2012); Massachusetts (by judicial decision); New Hampshire (Title XLIII, Domestic Relations, Ch. 457, § 457:1-a); New York (The Marriage Equality Act, 2011); Vermont (An Act to Protect Religious Freedom and Recognize Equality in Civil Marriage, 2009); Washington (Civil Marriage and Domestic Partnership law, 2012); District of Columbia (Jury and Marriage Amendment Act of 2009).

[65] Delaware; Hawaii; Illinois (see note 24); New Jersey (NJ Code, Ch. 103, P.L. 2006); Rhode Island (RI General Laws, Title, 15, Ch. 3.1-1).

[66] California (CA Family Code, sections 297–297.5); Nevada (NV Code, Ch. 122A); Oregon (OR Code, Title 11, Ch. 106).

[67] Alabama (Am. 774(d)); Alaska (Art. 1, sect. 25); Arizona (Art. XXX); Colorado (Art. II, sect. 31); Florida (Art. I, sect. 27); Georgia (Art. I, sect. IV); Idaho (Art. III, sect. 28); South Carolina (Art. XVII, sect. 15); South Dakota (Art. XXI, sect. 9); Kansas (Art. XV, sect. 16); Kentucky (sect. 233 A); Louisiana (Art. XII, sect. 15); Michigan (Art. I, sect. 25); Mississippi (Art. XIV, sect. 263A); Missouri (Art. I, sect. 33); Montana (Art. XIII, sect. 7); Nebraska (Art. 1, sect. 29); North Carolina (Art. XIV, sect. 6); North Dakota (Art. XI, sect. 28); Ohio (Art. XV, sect. 11); Oklahoma

statutory provisions,[68] without providing homosexual couples with alternative forms of union.

Within the first two models, same-sex marriages and civil unions are often presented as an alternative. That is to say, recognizing the former implies denying the latter. The solution could be perceived to be surprising, but it is probably coherent with the incremental approach followed by those States in which civil unions were the first step towards the full recognition of marriage equality between homosexual and straight partners.[69] Therefore, marriage licences for homosexual couples tend to replace previously enacted civil unions.[70] On the other hand, civil unions are sometimes introduced as a compromise solution specifically designed to avoid the recognition of same-sex marriage. Massachusetts's Legislature engaged in a form of struggle with the judiciary after the Supreme Court delivered a decision in the case of *Goodridge v. Department of Public Health*. The State Senate played its part and introduced a bill on civil unions in order to provide same-sex couples with an institution that is *de facto* equivalent to marriage,[71] without being compelled to allow homosexuals to marry.

Allowing same-sex marriages does not, however, rule out domestic partnerships that survive as alternative form of recognized union,[72] clearly distinguishable from marriage due to the explicit purpose they are designed to serve and thus the specific nature of the rights they grant to individuals. Domestic partnerships are aimed at protecting property rights, usually granted to married couples, within a stable relationship in which it is undeniable that one partner contributes to the other partner's property and economic situation.[73] The recognition of such a union does not imply that the law supports same-sex relationships, since domestic partnerships are available for straight as well as for homosexual couples.

Some States, in which a constitutional or statutory provision defines marriage as being between a man and a woman, often choose to recognize domestic partnerships as a substitute option for expressing a stable and legally recognizable commitment. As a result, States afford some spousal rights but tend to exclude most of

(Art. II, sect. 35); Tennessee (Art. XI, sect. 18); Texas (Art. I, sect. 32); Utah (Art. I, sect. 29); Virginia (Art. I, sect. 5-A). It must be mentioned that the State of Ohio instead of simply amending the Constitution, passed a far-reaching statute on defence of marriage that does not recognize civil unions and State employee domestic partner benefits.

[68] Indiana; Minnesota; Pennsylvania; West Virginia; Wyoming (see note 24).

[69] This was certainly the case at least for New Hampshire, Vermont and Connecticut: see Sect. 2.3.

[70] The State of Vermont passed the Marriage Equality Act in May 2009. As of September 1, 2009, civil unions are no longer available; however civil unions entered into prior to September 1, 2009 remain valid.

[71] See Crane (2003–2004), pp. 477ff.

[72] See Maine (ME P.L. 2003, c. 672); District of Columbia (Jury and Marriage Amendment Act of 2009; Health Care Benefits Expansion Act of 1992 and Domestic Partnership Registration Rule); Washington (WA Rev. Code Title 26, Ch. 26.60).

[73] Anyway, the right to enter a domestic partnership never implies that unmarried couples also enjoy those federal guarantees that married couples are normally provided with, one example being the social security survivors' benefits, financed by federal programs.

social security rights.[74] Within States which refuse same-sex marriage licenses this model is of a 'recessive' kind: out of 28 States in which legislatures have passed constitutional provisions to prohibit same-sex marriages, only three[75] have extended the right to homosexual couples to enter into a domestic partnership. Reasons can be found in the intensely ideological debate that led to the approval of constitutional amendments, often cited as examples of backlashes of judicial hyper-activism in affirming marriage equality.[76] As has been mentioned before, constitutional amendment proposals are often designed to prevent judicial decisions, which recognize the fundamental right of every couple to marry. The hesitancy of legislatures to guarantee spousal rights to unmarried homosexual couples seems to derive from a defensive attitude towards those controversial claims catching judicial attention.

Besides their strong legal foundation, these models do not describe a static layout, they rather express a dynamic situation in which the recognition of same-sex couples' rights seems to undergo phases of progress and of backlash, sometimes even in rapid succession. Virtually every State in America has experienced two or three of the models. This statement does not imply that there is such a thing as an inescapable and progressive path towards the full recognition of marriage equality. The general framework rather suggests that the recognition of rights depends on unpredictable interactions between legal formants and the public debate. Indeed each model results from (that is, it is shaped by) a string of 'dialogues' among judges, legislatures, scholarship and public opinion.

2.6 Final Remarks

This chapter focuses upon the recognition of same-sex couples' rights in the United States of America from a rigorous State level perspective. However, same-sex couples' rights are not only a State concern. As was mentioned above,[77] the Supreme Court will rule on this issue during the present term. The future of 'marriage federalism' is thus directly related to the outcomes of the pending cases.[78]

Within US scholarships, opposing views of what the Justices will decide coexist.[79] Without becoming involved in prophetic hypothesis, it is important to stress that the brief history traced here reveals that the recognition of rights proceeds with

---

[74] See for example the case of Oregon (OR Family Fairness Act, P.L. 2007-99) and Wisconsin (WI P.L. 2009-28, Assembly Bill 75, sect. 774).

[75] Nevada and Oregon (see note 64); Wisconsin (WI Code, Ch. 770).

[76] See Sect. 2.3.

[77] See Sect. 2.2.

[78] See the chapter by D'Aloia in this volume.

[79] Tribe and Matz (2011–2012), p. 478. See also Eskridge (2012), p. 97.

phases of progress and phases of inaction, both having the effect of stimulating debate and sometimes even bringing about cultural shifts in public opinion.

Courts, however, seem to be aware of their mandate: that is to act as the watchdog of legislative power when the choices of legislatures conflict with constitutional principles. This counter-majoritarian vocation is upheld even where a legislative action coincides with a viewpoint which is broadly accepted in terms of public debate. The Iowa Supreme Court made clear this approach in *Varnum v. Brien*,[80] stating that:

> Our responsibility ... is to protect constitutional rights of individuals from legislative enactments that have denied those rights, even when the rights have not yet been broadly accepted, were at one time unimagined, or challenge a deeply ingrained practice or law viewed to be impervious to the passage of time.

The same can be held for the other State Supreme Courts facing same-sex couples' rights issue.

Judges, scholars and legislatures normally deal with the counter-majoritarian difficulty, recognizing its role in a mature democracy.[81] When it comes to issues that involve basic social values though the risk of a backlash in the protection of rights can hardly be ignored. However, the mere fact that there is a strong link between the democratic process and recognition of rights should not restraint Courts from addressing controversial issues and coming to a decision in a way that is inconsistent with the majoritarian choice as long as the judgment can be founded upon constitutional principles.

Principles, though, are subject to interpretation more than norms. The above-mentioned approach represents an emerging trend that reveals how, especially in times of values polarization, the counter-majoritarian attitude encourages a theory of constitutional interpretation that conceives constitutions as evolving documents. The rulings based on the application of State equal protection clause can confirm this assumption.[82]

Such an emerging trend is far from being completely persuasive to the federal Supreme Court. In American constitutionalism, the recognition of new rights or of 'new' areas of protection of existing rights seems to be founded upon an evaluation of the existing needs of the society. At the same time, the character of 'fundamentality' of the right pertains to the legal position as it is rooted in the history and culture of the United States of America. In other words, the expectation

---

[80] See note 52. The Iowa Supreme Court proceeds citing *Lawrence v. Texas* and *Callender v. Skiles*, 591 N.W.2d 182, 190 (Iowa 1999): "Our Constitution is not merely tied to tradition, but recognizes the changing nature of society."

[81] See Redish (1989–1990), p. 1346.

[82] *Kerrigan v. Commissioner of Public Health*, part II, stating: "The Connecticut Constitution is an instrument of progress, it is intended to stand for a great length of time and should not be interpreted too narrowly or too literally so that it fails to have contemporary effectiveness for all of our citizens". *Goodridge v. Department of Public Health*, part B, citing Loving. Virginia: "As it did in Perez and Loving, history must yield to a more fully developed understanding of the invidious quality of the discrimination". *Varnum v. Brien* in notes 52 and 77.

of a constitutional protection is necessarily related to the appreciation of a change already (neither *in fieri*, nor merely possible) occurred in the society. This is the way in which Justices appear to find a link between "past values" and "future demands".[83]

State Courts that developed an activist approach on same-sex couples' rights may exert a modest influence towards the Supreme Court or, with the help of *Lawrence v. Texas* and its due process basis, may force Justices to take a sharp position on one of the most delicate issue in contemporary political agenda.[84]

In any case, judicial rationale becomes part of the public debate and shapes the discussion of such a divisive problem. Solutions or equilibrium reached in 'hard cases' are rarely long lasting[85]; they are rather a moment in the complex history of individuals' rights. For all these reasons, it is only within the dialectical confrontation among arguments that rights can, in the end, be affirmed.

References

Abraham HJ, Perry B (2003) Freedom and the courts: civil rights and liberties in United States. Kansas University Press, Lawrence

Ball CA (2011–2012) Why liberty judicial review is as legitimate as equality review: the case of gay rights jurisprudence. Univ Pa J Const Law 41:1–76

Barker N (2012) Not the marrying kind. Palgrave, MacMillan, London

Bickel A (1986) The least dangerous branch. The Supreme Court at the bar of politics. Yale University Press, New Haven

Cahill S (2004) Same-sex marriage in the United States. Focus on the facts. Lexington Books, Lanham

Cole D (2013) Getting nearer and nearer. The New York Review of Books, New York, January 10th, 2013. http://www.nybooks.com/articles/archives/2013/jan/10/getting-nearer-and-nearer

Collins MJ (1992) Whose federalism? Const Commentaries 9:75–86

Conkle D (2006) Three theories of substantive due process. N C Law Rev 85:63–148

Crane JMA (2003–2004) Legislative and constitutional responses to *Goodridge v. Department of Public Health*. N Y Univ J Legis Public Policy 7:465–485

Cross FB (2004–2005) Gay politics and precedents. Mich Law Rev 103:1186–1212

Dubber MD (2005) The police power. Patriarchy and the Foundation of American government. Columbia University Press, New York

Eskridge WN Jr (2012) The Ninth circuit's Perry decision and the constitutional politics of marriage equality. Stanford Law Rev Online 64:93–100, http://www.stanfordlawreview.org/online/perry-marriage-equality

Feteris ET (2009) Strategic manoeuvring in the justification of judicial decision. In: van Eemeren FH (ed) Examining argumentation in context. John Benjamins Publishing Company, Amsterdam/Philadelphia, pp 91–114

[83] In general see Thomson (1981–1982), p. 601 discussing theories of constitutional interpretation.

[84] See Toobin (2013), p. 19.

[85] Considering for instance the New Hampshire Republicans initiatives to revoke same-sex marriages briefly mentioned by Tribe and Matz (2011–2012), pp. 471–472, note 4.

Gallagher M (2003) Normal marriage: two views. In: Wardle LD, Strasser M, Duncan WC, Orgon Coolidge D (eds) Marriage and same sex unions. A debate. Praeger, Westport, pp 13–24
George RP (1993) Making men moral: civil liberties and public morality. Clarendon, Oxford
George RP (2003) Neutrality, equality and "Same Sex Marriage". In: Wardle LD, Strasser M, Duncan WC, Orgon Coolidge D (eds) Marriage and same sex unions. A debate. Praeger, Westport, pp 119–132
Habermas J (1990) Moral consciousness and communicative action. Massachusetts Institute of Technologies, Cambridge
Hull KE (2006) Same sex marriage. The cultural politics of love and law. Cambridge University Press, Cambridge
Klarman MJ (2013) From the closet to the altar: courts, backlash, and the struggle for same-sex marriage. Oxford University Press, Oxford
Knauer NJ (2008) Same-sex marriage and federalism. Temple J Polit Civ Rights 17:421–442
Marks Jr C, Cooper JF (2003) State constitutional law. West, St. Paul, Thomson West
McClain LC (2008–2009) Red versus blue (and purple) states and the same sex marriage debate: from values polarization to common ground? UMKC Law Rev 77:415–455
Musgrove W (2008) Substantive due process: a history of liberty in the due process clause. Univ St Thomas J Legis Public Policy 2:125–140
Novak D (2010) Response to Martha Nussbaum's a right to marry. Calif Law Rev 98:706–720
Nussbaum M (2010) A right to marry? Calif Law Rev 98:667–696
Powell KJ (1996–1997) The other double standard: communitarism, federalism, and American constitutional law. Seton Hall Const Law J 7:69–102
Redish MH (1989–1990) Political consensus, constitutional formulae, and the rationale for judicial review. Mich Law Rev 88:1340–1365
Romeo G (2011) La giurisprudenza della corte suprema degli stati uniti nei *terms* 2009/2010 e 2010/2011. Giurisprudenza Costituzionale 5:4039–4072
Sacco R (1991) Legal formants: a dynamic approach to comparative law. Am J Comp Law 39:343–401
Sandalow T (1965) Henry v. Mississippi and adequate state ground: proposals for a revised doctrine. Supreme Court Rev 1965:187–240
Stone GR, Seidman LM, Sunstein CR, Tushnet MV, Karlan PS (2010) Constitutional law, 4th edn. Wolters Kluwer, New York
Strasser M (2003) The state interest in recognizing same sex marriage. In: Wardle LD, Strasser M, Duncan WC, Orgon Coolidge D (eds) Marriage and same sex unions. A debate. Praeger, Westport, pp 33–42
Thomson JA (1981–1982) Principles and theories of constitutional interpretation and adjudication: some preliminary notes. Melb Univ Law Rev 13:597–616
Toobin J (2013) The people's choice. The New Yorker, New York, pp 19–20
Tribe LH, Matz J (2011–2012) The constitutional inevitability of same sex marriage. Md Law Rev 71:471–489
Walfson E (2004) Why marriage matters. America, equality, and gay people's right to marry. Simon and Schuster, New York
Wardle LD (2001) "Multiply and Replenish": considering same sex marriage in light of state interest in marital procreation. Harv J Legis Public Policy 24:771–814
Witte J Jr (1997) From sacrament to contract. Marriage, religion and law in the western tradition. Westminster John Knox Press, Louisville

Chapter 3
From Gay Rights to Same-Sex Marriage: A Brief History Through the Jurisprudence of US Federal Courts

Antonio D'Aloia

Abstract In their jurisprudence on same-sex marriage, the U.S. Federal Courts have touched on almost all aspects of constitutionalism, combining issues of federalism (e.g., the Full Faith and Credit Clause, the Tenth Amendment, and State or Federal jurisdiction in marriage and family cases) and substantial variations of concepts such as equality, dignity, and the anti-discrimination principle. In this sense, same-sex marriage is a unique lens through which to examine the development of constitutional commitments. The struggle for same-sex marriage has now reached a new crucial stage, after the decisions of the U.S. Supreme Court in *Hollingsworth v. Perry* and, above all, *United States v. Windsor*. The U.S. Supreme Court ruled that Section 3 of DOMA—which, for the purposes of 1,000 federal laws and multitudes of official regulations, defines marriage as the union of one man and one woman only—violates the Fifth Amendment and is, therefore, unconstitutional. Even after the decisions of the Supreme Court, however, the issue will continue to be controversial and to animate the political and legal debate, especially with respect to the question of parenting and child rearing.

3.1 Introductory Remarks. Same-Sex Marriage at the Crossroads: Between State and Federal Legislative and Judicial Powers

Two preliminary observations are necessary before discussing the topic of this chapter.

In the first place, it is not easy to write about American Federal jurisprudence on same-sex marriage in the wake of the recent decision (26 June 2013) by which the U.S. Supreme Court has rewritten the legal history of the subject. The cases *United*

A. D'Aloia (✉)
Department of Law, University of Parma, Parma, Italy
e-mail: antonio.daloia@unipr.it

D. Gallo et al. (eds.), *Same-Sex Couples before National, Supranational and International Jurisdictions*, DOI 10.1007/978-3-642-35434-2_3,

States v. Windsor and *Hollingsworth v. Perry* can be considered as the final chapter of a long and difficult path that has seen State and Federal powers, both judicial and legislative, intersect in such a way as to make it very hard to analyse them separately. In other words, this last stage seems to reflect precisely the intersection between the two levels of institutional power.

For sure, the decision in *Windsor* will have a strong impact on future developments in this field, as regards both legislation and the case-law.

A closed subject? I do not think so, for a number of reasons.

In the first place, the judgment in *Windsor* dealt with the issue of same-sex marriage from a particular point of view, namely that of the relationship between State and Federal jurisdiction, adopting a perspective which combined the doctrine of equal protection and that of federalizing process.

As I will point out in the final parts of the chapter, several questions are still to be resolved (not only with regard to Section 3 of DOMA, which has been declared unconstitutional, but also to the ways in which the Supreme Court's ruling will be enforced) and will probably lead to new decisions in both State and Federal courts. Moreover, we should not forget that the *Windsor* judgment was approved by a scanty majority (5/4) and that dissenting opinions were very clear-cut and emphatic.

The debate is thus still open, at least in part. This is also why it seems useful to illustrate the arguments that have so far been put forward in the case-law. Furthermore, we must take into account the interpretive approaches and tools underlying the two cases, that is the way constitutional principles and language are interpreted.

In the second place, it should be emphasized that, of course, Federal case-law is not limited to the decisions of the US Supreme Court. The particular characteristics of the Supreme Court's constitutionality review, especially the writ of certiorari and other instruments allowing the Supreme Court "to decide not to decide",[1] make the study of other segments of the American judicial system necessary and appropriate: the State segment on the one hand, and, on the other, the 'smaller', 'Federal' segment in the District and Appeals Courts of the various Circuits. This chapter will focus on the latter, and the discussion will not be limited to the jurisprudence of the Federal Supreme Court.

Given this premise, we may identify three turning points in the history of the American jurisprudence (and legislation) on same-sex marriage and, previously, on gay rights: the *Bowers v. Hardwick* case (1986), the *Lawrence v. Texas* case (2003), and the Supreme Court judgments of these last weeks. Following the development from one to the other, we will try to understand the evolution of legal thought on this very thorny topic, which in recent years has been one of the most important constitutional issues in the United States.

[1] Bickel (1986), p. 133.

3.2 The *Bowers* Case: A Wall with Many Cracks on the Road Towards Gay Rights Recognition

For many years, *Bowers* has been considered as a symbol of the typical American attitude to gay rights and same-sex marriage, or rather, as an obstacle that has strongly weighed against their recognition. Indeed, there is no room even to start discussing same-sex marriage if homosexual conduct is regarded, in itself, as a behavior that can be legitimately criminalized.

Seventeen years later, *Lawrence* overruled *Bowers*, bridging the gulf between the American attitude and the legal culture that had developed in Europe.

But let me not jump ahead. Before *Bowers*, there were two other cases concerning sodomy laws. The first was in Virginia, where a Federal Court refused to extend to homosexual behaviors the right to privacy, which had been affirmed by the US Supreme Court in *Griswold v. Connecticut* (1965), on the grounds that *Griswold* addressed the issue of privacy in a "marital situation". The Federal Court of Virginia was also clearer and more direct with regard to homosexual relations, establishing, in the majority opinion, that "homosexual conduct is likely to end in a contributing to moral delinquency".

The matter came to the Supreme Court, which, without an opinion, confirmed the judgment of the lower court. The decision in *Doe v. Commonwealth's Attorney for the City of Richmond* (1976) is basically an approval lacking in motivation: it is impossible to understand whether the Supreme Court (or, at least, the six judges who gave the majority judgment) agreed on the merits with the conclusions of the District Court of Eastern Virginia, whether it simply wanted to give deference to the State's punitive power, or whether it considered the issue to be culturally and socially premature.

It remains a fact that some years later—paradoxically the same year as *Bowers*—the Supreme Court denied certiorari in another sodomy case, this time a case from Texas (*Baker v. Wade*).[2]

The facts of *Bowers* are well known, therefore I will not comment on them at length. In short: the constitutional review concerned the Georgia sodomy law under which Michael Hardwick had been arrested at his home, while engaging in sexual acts with his male partner.

It should be emphasized that the Court had many uncertainties about the possibility to accept the judgment. The certiorari was granted only by four Justices, which was the minimum number required. Moreover, the motivations of the Justices who 'decided to decide' were deeply divergent: White (who wrote the Court's opinion) and Rehnquist aimed to restrict the right to privacy; Brennan, on the contrary, was convinced that it was possible to reach a majority of five votes to invalidate the Georgia law.

[2] Barsotti (2002).

The decision was short and, perhaps, unclear. Its background, however, is way more straightforward, in that it reveals the actual cultural approach of the defenders of the sodomy law. The concurring opinion of Justice Burger, for example, is a moral, as opposed to legal, condemnation of homosexuality:

> Decisions of individuals relating to homosexual conduct have been subject to State intervention throughout the history of Western civilization. Condemnation of those practices is firmly rooted in Judaeo-Christian moral and ethical standards. Homosexual sodomy was a capital crime under Roman Law [. . .]. [Eighteenth-century English legal scholar Sir William] Blackstone described the infamous crime against nature as an offense of deeper malignity than rape, a heinous act the very mention of which is a disgrace to human nature, and a crime not fit to be named [. . .]. To hold that the act of homosexual sodomy is somehow protected as a fundamental right would be to cast aside millennia of moral teaching.[3]

The underlying debate concerned, therefore, the following issues: the interpretation of fundamental rights; the weight of history; the evolution of social and cultural dynamics as regards the identification of a society's fundamental values; and the meaning acquired over time by general constitutional provisions, such as those on privacy, due process, and equal protection. Laurence Tribe and Kathleen Sullivan supported Hardwick's reasons, trying to demonstrate that, if there was a public interest in "protecting public sensibilities", purposes like "protecting vulnerable persons such as minors from possible coercion" and "restricting commercial trade in activities offensive to public decency" could not apply to the facts of the case at issue.[4]

Bowers was a sodomy case and did not concern same-sex marriage. However, a connection between the two issues emerged at various levels. Chief Justice Burger, for example, identified the protection of traditional marriage as one of the possible purposes of the Georgia law. In the brief of the case, openness to gay marriage—which, quite significantly, was associated with polygamy, fornication, adultery, and incest—was indicated as the risk of a decision against the Georgian law. Finally, in contrast with Burger's position—who, in the summary of the case, stated that there was "no fundamental right to engage in sodomy, an activity that had been criminalized for centuries" and that "a privacy decision in favor of Hardwick would undermine laws against incest and prostitution"—Justice Blackmun noted that the decision in *Loving v. Virginia* (1967), a leading case on interracial marriage, could be an important precedent.[5]

---

[3] Similar considerations can be found in the brief of the petitioner. In order to emphasize the difference from the previous case of *Stanley v. Georgia*, which concerned the right to use obscene materials in the privacy of one's home, the petitioner stated that: "homosexual sodomy as an act of sexual deviancy expresses no ideas. It is purely an unnatural means of satisfying an unnatural lust, which has been declared by Georgia to be morally wrong". Richards (2009), p. 79, recalls that "the brief also argued (and is a very harsh and unpleasant argument) 'the relationship of homosexual sodomy in the transmission of Acquired Immune Deficiency Syndrome (AIDS) and other diseases'".

[4] *Ibidem*, pp. 88–89.

[5] *Ibidem*.

As mentioned above, the judgment in *Bowers* was not straightforward with regard to its purpose. The question of privacy (and of gay–lesbian identity) was almost hidden, thus denying any relationship between homosexual activity and personal liberty, family, marriage and procreation, which were the reference points of cases such as *Carey*, *Griswold* and *Roe*. In White's opinion, nothing in the decisions in those previous cases made it possible to legitimize "any kind of private sexual conduct among consenting adults" or to support the notion that "any State limitation is constitutionally invalid".[6]

As a matter of fact, in addition to this initial definition of the scope of the issue, the majority opinion focused on the existence of a fundamental right to practice homosexual sodomy, and the possibility to identify that right in the Constitution and in the wording of the due process clauses (5th and 14th Amendment).

The Court did not deny, also in the light of its precedents, that the Due Process Clauses aimed to guarantee substantial rights. The problem was whether a Judge could identify such rights, or better, to what extent he or she could do so.

According to Justice White, who wrote the opinion of the Court, the category of rights qualifying for "heightened judicial protection" included "those fundamental liberties that are implicit in the concept of ordered liberty". Moreover, he added that:

> the Court is most vulnerable and comes nearest to illegitimacy when it deals with judge-made constitutional law having little or no cognizable roots in the language or design of the Constitution.

And he concluded his premise stating that:

> neither of these formulations would extend a fundamental right to homosexuals to engage in acts of consensual sodomy. Proscriptions against that conduct have ancient roots. [...] [T]o claim that a right to engage in such conduct is "deeply rooted in this Nation's history and tradition" or "implicit in the concept of ordered liberty", is, at best, facetious.[7]

The fact that homosexual behavior occurred in domestic settings was mentioned only briefly and nonchalantly. The right in question was not considered in connection with the First Amendment and the freedom of expression. Therefore, the case of *Stanley v. Georgia*—which concerned the possession of pornographic material—could not be cited as a precedent. On the other hand, according to White:

> otherwise illicit conduct is not always immunized whenever it occurs in the home. Victimless crimes, such as the possession and use of illegal drugs, do not escape the law where they are committed at home. [...] And if respondent's submission is limited to the voluntary sexual conduct between consenting adults, it would be difficult, except by fiat, to limit the claimed right to homosexual conduct while leaving exposed to prosecution adultery, incest, and other sexual crimes even though are committed in the home.

[6] *Ibidem.*

[7] See Tushnet (2005), p. 157: "Gays rightly heard overtones of homophobia in White's opinion; the word facetious was particularly insensitive", even though "Burger's separate opinion was even worse".

The decision was adopted by a 5-4 majority, with Powell as a 'swing Justice'—just like in *Bakke*, the famous 1979 affirmative action case. By the term 'swing Justice' I refer not only to the judge who decides, breaking the balance of the Court, but also to the fact that his or her involvement in the opinion of the Court is asymmetric and his or her consent is based on fragile, unstable elements, in the sense that, had the judgment had a different line of reasoning, the position of that judge could have been different.

In this specific case, Powell considered that "imprisonment for homosexual sodomy would be cruel and unusual punishment"[8] and firmly supported the decision in *Roe*. However, he also doubted that the practice of homosexual relations could be a constitutional right deriving from the Due Process Clause. Unfortunately, the issue came before the Court in those terms. As recalled by Richards, Powell, who had already left the Court 3 years earlier, admitted to his mistake in a public debate at the NYU in 1990. In this sense, *Bowers* was a heavy precedent, whose relevance has been compared to the *Dredd Scott* case of 1837 on slavery and the rights of the black minority. At the same time, it was based on shaky grounds and, thus, destined to be challenged.

It is no coincidence that the Georgia sodomy law was declared unconstitutional by the Georgia Supreme Court and repealed in 1998, before *Lawrence* overruled *Bowers*. However, this somehow reflects an American dualism between State and Federal levels as regards the protection of fundamental rights.

In fact, the arguments in *Bowers* immediately seemed "highly questionable". The uncritical use of the historical argument and the dismissal of the constitutional principle of privacy—a dismissal which was barely justified and contradicted a number of opinions delivered by the same majority Justices in other cases (e.g., the 1992 Planned Parenthood case on abortion)—were 'weak' points destined to be modified by later case-law.[9]

As often happens in American jurisprudence, dissent paved the way for a possible overruling. The positions of Blackmun and Stevens were very clear. The first Justice maintained that:

> sexual intimacy is "a sensitive, key relationship of human existence, central to family life, community welfare, and the development of personality" [...]. The fact that individuals define themselves in a significant way through their intimate sexual relationships with others suggests, in a Nation as diverse as ours, that there may be many "right" ways of conducting those relationships, and that much of the richness of a relationship will come from the freedom an individual has to choose the form and nature of these intensely personal bonds.

Both of them, moreover, emphasized that arguments based on dominant or conventional moral opinion, majoritarian offense, or long-standing religious tradition are insufficient to justify serious restrictions on a constitutionally protected right (like that claimed by Hardwick). In particular, while the opinion of the Court

[8] Richards (2009), p. 113.

[9] Richards (2009), pp. 113–114.

stated that the law "is constantly based on notions of morality", Stevens asserted that the fact that the governing majority in Georgia viewed sodomy as immoral was "not a sufficient reason for upholding a law prohibiting the practice" and that "neither history nor tradition could save a law prohibiting miscegenation from constitutional attack".

While the Supreme Court was going to address the *Bowers* case, 26 American States had already removed sodomy from their penal codes. Illinois was the first to do so in 1971, 2 years after the Stonewall riot, which had drawn media attention to discrimination against homosexuals and to the fight for gay rights.

At the same time, the situation in Europe was well advanced—gay/lesbian sex acts had already been decriminalized, in many countries since as early as the nineteenth century. In 1978, the decision of the European Court of Human Rights (further referred to as ECtHR) in *Dudgeon v. United Kingdom* established that legislation criminalizing homosexual acts violated Art. 8 of the European Convention of Human Rights (further referred to as ECHR), which provides for the right to respect for one's private and family life.[10]

3.3 After *Bowers*: *Romer v. Evans* and Justice Kennedy's Doctrine

Both the 'weak arrogance' of the Court in *Bowers* and the 'competition' on fundamental rights between Federal and State Courts (and, in general, between political institutions at the two levels)—a competition which is typical of US dual federalism—can explain a series of reactions and consequences.

First of all, those who feared that the Court's judgment would force States to keep sodomy laws, or even to re-criminalize homosexual conduct, have been contradicted. No State has reintroduced laws that punish homosexual relations, while many States have removed the crime of homosexual sodomy from their codes, starting with Kentucky, which was the first to do so in 1992.

As it has been already mentioned, *Bowers* was overruled 17 years later in *Lawrence*, but, in fact, homosexuality had already been largely liberalized. Thirteen States, however, kept sodomy laws in force, and four of them also imposed heavier penalties.

More interestingly, *Bowers* triggered a strong cultural mobilization on the part of the gay movement. As emphasized by B. Friedman, *Bowers* was a second Stonewall, "a display of antihomosexual spleen that fueled public responses from gay people and their growing number of allies".[11]

The Court called to hear the *Lawrence* case was deeply renewed. A remarkable six Justices of the Court had retired at the time of *Bowers*; however, the

[10] See the chapters by Crisafulli and Pustorino in this volume.

[11] Friedman (2009), p. 573.

appointment of Chief Justice Rehnquist and the entrance of Scalia and Thomas—who would, in fact, fiercely dissent from the opinion of the Court in *Lawrence*—seemed to preserve the conservative majority.

A key role in the overruling decision was played by Justice Kennedy, who had already agreed with the decision made by the majority of the Court in *Romer v. Evans* (1996), where the Supreme Court had declared that the amendment to the Constitution of Colorado that forbade all laws protecting gays and lesbians from discrimination was unconstitutional.

Romer v. Evans was the major step in the process that led to the overruling of *Bowers*, a process which took place mainly at the level of State case-law.

The first step in this process was *Commonwealth v. Watson*, where the Kentucky Supreme Court[12] struck down a state sodomy law, thus promoting the constitutional right to privacy denied in *Bowers*. The Court took an interesting position on the issues discussed here, relating them to the American system of dual sovereignty:

> it is our responsibility to interpret and apply our state constitution independently. We are not bound by decisions of the United States Supreme Court when deciding whether a state statute impermissibly infringes upon individual rights guaranteed in the State Constitution [. . ..]. [T]he Bill of Rights in the United States Constitution represents neither the primary source nor the maximum guarantee of State constitutional liberty.

Other cases of invalidation of sodomy laws concerned Minnesota, Tennessee, and—as mentioned earlier—Georgia itself, where the Supreme Court, 12 years after *Bowers*, invalidated the law it had previously saved.[13]

At the same time, the US Supreme Court was active in two other cases of discrimination based on sexual orientation. In both cases, the issue was the balance between the principle of non-discrimination (in this case related to sexual orientation) and the freedom of speech of groups and associations. The outcome was substantially the same, but the composition of the majority seems to reflect the evolution begun in *Romer* and completed in *Lawrence*.

In *Hurley v. Irish-American Gay, Lesbian, and Bisexual Group of Boston* (1995), the Court unanimously found that it is the private citizens organizing a public demonstration who choose the groups to be included in their demonstration.[14] On the other hand, in *Boy Scouts of America v. Dale* (2000) only a 5-4 majority approved the opinion of Chief Justice Rehnquist that a private organization, such as the Boy Scouts, can exclude a gay person from membership, in accordance with the principle of 'freedom of expressive association', if the presence of that person affects in a significant way the group's ability to advocate public or private viewpoints.

Let me now turn to *Romer v. Evans*. The case concerned an amendment to the Constitution of Colorado, approved by a referendum that was immediately 'blocked' on the initiative of the District Court of the State. The amendment was

---

[12] *Commonwealth v. Wasson*, 842 S. W 2d 487 (Ky. 1992).

[13] For an in-depth analysis of these cases, see Montalti (2007), pp. 115–117.

[14] Richards (2009), p. 120.

clearly 'anti-gay': a "non-protected status based on homosexual or bisexual orientation"[15] was obviously a way to perpetuate a form of denial and "segregation" of homosexuality, although on a slightly less punitive level than sodomy laws. Basically, the shift was from criminalization to discouraging the public acceptance of homosexuality[16] and, at the same time, identifying homosexuals as a distinct class, according to criteria unrelated to any legitimate State interest.

In fact, in the majority opinion (approved 6-3), Kennedy referred to the dissent of Justice Harlan in *Plessy v. Ferguson* (1896)—the famous case on racial segregation that was overruled by *Brown v. Board of Education* in 1954—stating that: "[T]he Constitution neither knows nor tolerates classes among citizens".

The judgment was apparently neutral on the issue of sexual orientation and homosexuals as a discriminated minority and, above all, did not refer to the *Bowers* case. Paradoxically, only Justice Scalia mentioned the connection with that case in his dissenting opinion: "In holding that homosexuality cannot be singled out for disfavorable treatment, the Court contradicts a decision, unchallenged here, pronounced only 10 years ago, see *Bowers v. Hardwick*". In other words, the authority of *Bowers* was hanging by a thread: it is hard to believe that a decision considering the constitutional legislative choice to punish homosexual sodomy could maintain its value, while a law (or rather, a State constitutional amendment) that "merely" prohibited rules in favor of homosexuals was declared unconstitutional.

3.4 A Parallel Story: The First Same-Sex Marriage Cases in Federal Courts

While the battle over gay rights was still formally at a standstill, and homosexual conduct still criminalized (in accordance with the position expressed in *Bowers*), the issue of same-sex marriage and/or legislation on same-sex couples began to be discussed at various levels of jurisdiction.

The first Federal cases on same-sex marriage occurred at the same time as the first sodomy cases. When compared to the European experience, this is yet another anomaly: the theme of homosexual partnership appeared only after sodomy or similar laws had been repealed or invalidated. However, it is clear that the issue was not yet fully developed. The judgments delivered by the courts seem 'overhasty' due to the surprise caused by the novelty of the problem: they just dismiss the claims at issue, often without any detailed discussion of their implications.

In *Baker v. Nelson*,[17] a same-sex couple who had applied for a marriage license in Minneapolis challenged the refusal of a clerk of the Hennepin County District

[15] Montalti (2007), p. 230.

[16] Richards (2009), p. 116.

[17] *Baker v. Nelson*, 191 N.W. 2d 185 (Minn. 1971).

Court to issue the license, alleging that said refusal was contrary to various provisions of the Federal Constitution (1st, 8th, 9th and 14th Amendments). The trial court dismissed the couple's claims without discussion, but distinguished the case from *Grinswold*, a leading case in the field of privacy, and especially *Loving v. Virginia*, a landmark civil rights decision that invalidated laws prohibiting interracial marriage (also known as "anti-miscegenation laws"), on the grounds that "there is a clear distinction between a marital restriction based merely upon race and one based upon the fundamental difference in sex".

The following year, the case came before the US Supreme Court through mandatory appellate jurisdiction, thus giving the judges the opportunity to rule on the constitutional rights at issue and deliver a decision on the merits. However, the US Supreme Court summarily dismissed the appeal for "want of a substantial federal question".[18]

Another dismissal—this time on the merits—was made by the Washington Court of Appeals in *Singer v. Hara* (1974).[19] The judgment includes a short but meaningful passage on the Marriage Statute of the State of Washington, which is considered valid and constitutional insofar as it does not grant same-sex couples access to marriage. According to the Court, the state marriage law promoted "the public interest in affording a favorable environment for the growth of children".

Numerous other court decisions excluded same-sex partners from the institution of marriage and from the legal definition of "spouses". The judgment in *Adams v. Howerton* (1980)[20] is especially noteworthy. In this case, the Ninth Circuit Court of Appeals decided that there were rational bases for excluding homosexual partners from the legal definition of 'spouses', since "same-sex couples do not procreate, most or all States do not recognize marriages between persons of the same-sex, and same-sex marriages violate traditional mores".

Substantially restrictive positions of this kind led gay activists to move the battle for same-sex marriage from federal to state courts, whose jurisdiction is more suitable for dealing with cases concerning marriage and family. The strategy of gay rights groups aimed to avoid a face-off with the Federal judicial power, whose negative reaction could have much more devastating effects on the outcome of their struggle. As Evan Wolfson wrote in 1994, "the wrong case, wrong judge, or wrong forum could literally set us all back years, if not decades".[21] On the other hand, 'local' victories could gradually contribute to change public attitudes and promote a progressive acceptance of a sexually open model of marriage.

However, besides raising problems with respect to the theory of federalism and the separation of powers, this strategy does not prevent multiple connections between federal and state levels. These connections do not simply relate to

[18] *Baker v. Nelson*, 409 U.S. 810 (1972). On this point, see Duncan (2006), pp. 30–31.

[19] *Singer v. Hara*, 522 P. 2d 1187 (Wash. Ct. App. 1974).

[20] *Adams v. Howerton*, 673 F. 2d 1036, 1038 (9th. Cir. 1980). See also *Bowers*, *Dean v. District of Columbia*, 653 A. 2d 307 (D.C. App. 1995): "we cannot overlook the fact that the Supreme Court has deemed marriage a fundamental right substantially because of its relationship to procreation".

[21] See Wolfson (1994), p. 611.

corresponding functions (i.e., federal congress/state legislatures, and federal courts/ state courts), but are way more complex. This is clearly shown by two facts: first, the decisions taken at the state level with regard to legislative and constitutional review, and which defended a traditional definition of marriage, have been attacked on federal constitutional grounds even before being challenged in state courts; and second, the best response to the activism of state courts came from the Federal legislature with the famous Defense of Marriage Act of 1996 (DOMA).

3.5 The Federal Congress' 'Studs Up Tackle': DOMA and the Power to Reserve Marriage to Opposite-Sex Couples

The DOMA is a symbol of the double conflict between Federal/State and legal/ judicial levels. It encompasses both perspectives; and, in the end, it is mainly a means to protect Member States against (legislative or judicial) decisions made by other States. It was followed by a series of reactions: to begin with, Hawaiian voters approved a referendum for a constitutional amendment adding the following provision to the Hawaii Constitution: "Marriage. The legislature shall have the power to reserve marriage to opposite-sex couples".

The fundamental reason for the intervention of the Federal Congress was certainly the decision of the Supreme Court in the Hawaii case of *Baher v. Lewin* (1993). The Supreme Court found that Hawaii's prohibition of same-sex marriage violated the Equal Protection Clause of the State Constitution—or better, it could violate that constitutional provision—and asked the trial court to demonstrate that the same-sex marriage ban furthered "compelling state interests".

In response to the court's ruling, in 1998 Hawaiian voters approved the aforementioned amendment to the state constitution, allowing the state to reserve marriage to opposite-sex couples. This enabled the Supreme Court, to which the trial court had once again asked to dismiss the case, to rule that the marriage amendment was decisive.

Apart from the outcome of the case (the State of Hawaii recognized some 'reciprocal' rights, or benefits, to same-sex couples, similar to those granted by the French *PACS*), the judgment in *Baher* marked the beginning of a path on which several other states followed.[22] The decision of the Massachusetts Supreme Court in *Goodridge v. Department of Public Health* (18 November 2003), for example, is especially noteworthy, also because it produced stable effects with regard to the recognition of same-sex marriage in Massachusetts.[23]

---

[22] Montalti (2007).

[23] After *Goodridge*, another important ruling was that of the New Jersey Supreme Court in *Lewis v. Harris* (2006), where the Court held that limiting the access of opposite-sex couples to civil marriage violated the state constitution, but did not rule that the State should allow same-sex couples to marry. Moreover, in 2008 the California Supreme Court ruled in favor of same-sex marriage in case *In re Marriage Cases*. See Knauer (2008), p. 101.

This judgment radically challenged the reservation of marriage to people of the opposite sex. The fundamental nature of the right to marry led the Court to emphasize that a marriage ban was contrary to the respect of individual autonomy, protected by the Due Process Clause and the Equal Protection Clause of the 14th Amendment, because it worked "a deep and scarring hardship on a very real segment of the community for no rational reason".[24] In the same way, it found that the attempt to distinguish between marriage, reserved to opposite-sex couples, and civil unions, open to same-sex couples, was unacceptable because it maintained "an unconstitutional, inferior, and discriminatory status" for homosexuals.

As already noted, *Baher* was the first case to challenge the idea of marriage as the union between a man and a woman; in particular, it was the sign that the battle had to be fought at the federal level, which shows that the relationship between central and local authorities was not as rosy as suggested by Justice Brandeis in his famous 1932 dissent in *New State Ice Co. v. Liebmann*:

> It is one of the happy incidents of the federal system that a single courageous State may, if its citizens choose, serve as a laboratory; and try novel social and economic experiments without risk to the rest of the country.

Indeed, the decision was followed by an immediate reaction at Federal level, namely the DOMA,[25] which served as a model for a whole series of similar and sometimes more radical initiatives in many States,[26] such as the amendments to State constitutions known as "Mini-DOMAs".[27] Moreover, in some of the States that have amended their constitutions to include Mini-DOMAs, State courts have refused to establish the right to same-sex marriage as a matter of state constitutional law.[28]

That is not an obvious choice, since defining marriage and family has traditionally been a State matter. In *Sosna v. Iowa* (1975),[29] for example, the US Supreme Court found that the regulation of domestic relations was an area that had long been regarded "as a virtually exclusive province of the States".

There was a strong divide between the legal culture and society's perception of same-sex marriage, which has been partially solved only in recent times. State legislatures and voters basically opposed the attempts of the courts to invalidate same-sex marriage bans, or to extend the concept of marriage (or at least some marriage rights) beyond the traditional idea of the union between a man and a woman.

---

[24] Montalti (2007), pp. 434–435.

[25] It is useful to remember that the Congress approved the DOMA by a large majority: 342-67 in the House of Representatives, and 85-14 in the Senate.

[26] On DOMA and the *Baehr* case, see Strasser (2011). It should be emphasized that DOMA was approved by a large majority: 342-67 votes in the House of Representatives and 85-14 in the Senate.

[27] See again Strasser (2011), *passim*.

[28] Solimine (2010), pp. 105–107.

[29] 419 U.S. 393, 404 (1975).

At present, 41 States still have statutory and/or constitutional provisions under which same-sex marriage is invalid or which simply state that it is not marriage at all.[30]

The situation is indeed very complex and multifaceted. Apart from Massachusetts and California, after the 2008 Supreme Court's decision *In re Marriage Cases* and before the introduction of Proposition 8, which recognized same-sex marriage, some States (New Jersey, Connecticut, New Hampshire, Oregon, Vermont) granted same-sex couples the same benefits or rights as married heterosexual couples, while others (Maine, Washington, District of Columbia) extended at least partial benefits.[31] In other words, the DOMA has in its turn unleashed a series of reactions: this confirms the essential pluralism of the American system, which encompasses both a federalist approach and the ancient conflict between legislative and judicial powers (especially in the field of fundamental rights).

This interplay of reactions and setbacks has been possible because the circle is not closed yet. The attempt to directly transfer into the US Constitution only heterosexual marriage has failed, and the Federal Marriage Amendment—according to which "Marriage in the United States shall consist only of the union of a man and a woman. Neither this Constitution or the constitution of any State, nor State or Federal Law, shall be construed to require that marital status or the legal incidents thereof be conferred upon unmarried couples or groups"[32]—has not been adopted.

3.6 Constitutional Problems Raised by DOMA. The Full Faith and Credit Clause in the Conflict Between the Judicial and Legislative Branches, and the 'Incidents' of Federalism

Let me now go back to the Defence of Marriage Act and examine the related constitutional issues. DOMA does not expressly prohibit same-sex marriage, even though it certainly "comes out strongly against same-sex marriage".[33] Moreover, it

[30] Among these, 17 states have particularly aggressive provisions that not only prohibit same-sex marriage, but also purport to prohibit all other forms of relationship recognition (Knauer 2008, p. 103). The only states without marriage restrictions are Massachusetts, New Jersey, New Mexico, New York, Rhode Island.

[31] In any case, there is no doubt that anti-marriage measures—some of which extremely hostile to same-sex relationships—were predominant: see Knauer (2008), p. 109.

[32] On this point, *ibidem*, p. 112, and Montalti (2007), p. 409.

[33] Simson (2010), p. 43.

does not exclude the possibility that some States will legalize same-sex marriage or enforce the laws or decisions adopted in the States that have already recognized this institution—namely, those States that have legalized it or passed legislation granting rights and benefits to same-sex couples, while still maintaining a distinct *status* (i.e., civil unions) for these couples.

At the same time, the DOMA allows States opposing same-sex marriage not to feel obliged to follow the decisions and regulations of other States in favor of giving homosexual couples access to marriage.[34] In essence, a couple legally married in Massachusetts has no guarantee that their status will be recognized also in other States and their marriage will have the same legal effects as those required under the Federal legislation.

The DOMA is divided into two parts: the first has a 'horizontal scope', since it concerns the interstate effects of a same-sex marriage contracted in a given State[35]; the second concerns the relationship between State and Federal powers. It seems appropriate to analyze them separately.

The first provision (Section 2) states that:

> No State, territory, or possession of the United States, or Indian Tribe, shall be required to give effect to any public act, record, or judicial proceeding of any other State, territory, possession, or tribe respecting a relationship between persons of the same sex that is treated as a marriage under the laws of such other State, territory, possession, or tribe, or a right or claim arising from such relationship.

Quite clearly, the purpose is here to avoid the risk of a 'progressive' use of legislative or judicial decisions that recognize same-sex marriage in individual states. In particular, this provision aims to prevent other states from being forced into adopting laws that may recognize same-sex couples by virtue of the Full Faith and Credit Clause doctrine.

As is well known, the Full Faith and Credit Clause is contained in Art. IV(1) of the US Constitution. It provides that:

> Full Faith and Credit shall be given in each State to the public Acts, Records, and judicial Proceedings of every other State. And the Congress may by general Laws prescribe the manner in which such Acts, Records and Proceedings shall be proved, and the effect thereof.

This Clause is essential in order to make the complicated system of federalism work.[36] As noted by the US Supreme Court in *Milwaukee County v. M.E. White Company*,[37] the clause produced a change in the status of the States, transforming them into "integral parts of a single nation throughout which a remedy upon a just obligation might be demanded as of right, irrespective of the State of its origin".

---

[34] See Kramer (1997).

[35] "(I)t is horizontal because it primarily concerns the relations among the co-equal sovereign States of the Union" (Wardle 2010, p. 149).

[36] Jackson and Tushnet (1999), p. 193.

[37] 296 U.S. 268, 277 (1935). See Strasser (2011), p. 89.

It is basically a source of federal unity and loyalty, expressing a sense of convergence towards uniformity even in those areas where the weight of and the claim for state competences are stronger. The Clause itself contains elements of flexibility; in other words, it contains its exceptions, namely the possibility for the Congress to introduce provisions derogating from the Full Faith and Credit mechanism.

The point here is to understand the limits of this right to derogate from the Full Faith and Credit Clause. The connection of the Clause with important constitutional interests means that the individual states are not "free to ignore obligations created under the laws or by the judicial proceedings of the others".[38]

First of all, according to the most authoritative interpretation, it is only possible to disregard the Full Faith and Credit Clause when there are important or overriding public policy reasons, which, of course, must not be contrary to the Federal Constitution.

Moreover, judgments and statutes are not on the same level. Many decisions of the US Supreme Court agree that a distinction is necessary between "the credit owed to laws (legislative measures and common law) and to judgments".[39] As regards laws, the US Supreme Court recognized, in *Pacific Employers Company* (1998), that:

> The very nature of the Federal union of States, to which are reserved some of the attributes of sovereignty, precludes resort to the full faith and credit clause as the means for compelling a State to substitute the statutes of other states for its own statutes dealing with a subject matter concerning which it is competent to legislate.[40]

However, in other cases it has maintained that the Constitution does not support a "roving public policy exception to the full faith and credit due judgments".[41]

Section 2 of DOMA seems indeed to reflect the quest for a constitutional balance among the different States, protecting state sovereignty on certain issues reserved to the individual States, such as marriage and domestic relations, and preserving the right of each State to decide for itself whether to recognize same-sex marriage.[42]

It is difficult to assess with certainty whether the DOMA has exceeded the exception to the Full Faith and Credit Clause. Of course, we cannot but take into account the fact that, as noted above, at present the majority of States prohibit or do

---

[38] See, again, *Milwaukee County v. M.E. White Company*.

[39] See *Baker v. General Motors Corp.*, 522 U-S. 222, 232 (1998).

[40] See *Pacific Employers Insurance Company v. Industrial Accident Commission*, 306 U.S. 493, 591 (1939).

[41] See *Baker v. General Motors Corp.* and *Sherrer v. Sherrer*, 334 U.S. 343, 356 (1948), on divorce and marital status. See also Strasser (2011), pp. 89–90.

[42] Wardle (2010, pp. 1345 and 1353) emphasizes that the DOMA "is an architectural provision protecting the architecture of federalism" and "the constitutional allocation of authority to set public policy regarding recognition of same-sex marriage", and that "it protects each State from aggressive Federal judges, and other governmental officials, who would use the supremacy of Federal law to force States to recognize same-sex marriage in their internal domestic relations laws".

not recognize same-sex marriage. However, this is a 'quantitative' argument, which may not be decisive per se, even though several years ago (*McKeiver v. Pennsylvania*, 1971) the US Supreme Court stated that:

> the fact that a practice is followed by a large number of States [. . .] is plainly worth considering in determining whether the practice offends some principle of justice so rooted in the traditions and conscience of our people as to be ranked as fundamental.

The issue is far more complex. A Federal State is based on a series of interests of the Union, which in their turn affect the fundamental rights of US citizens. The freedom of movement and the right to work in all the States of the Union seem to imply that all citizens can move from one state to another, taking their rights and fundamental freedoms with them, including the right to marry as recognized in any one of the States of the Union.[43] If connected to these fundamental 'interests', the Full Faith and Credit Clause seems to acquire greater strength: the procedural dimension is enriched with elements that recall the due process, equal protection, and individual autonomy doctrines and, ultimately, the exception to the recognition of other States' laws and judgments appears to need more rigorous justifications, which perhaps are now difficult to find.

Moreover, this provision combines horizontal and vertical effects, the latter concerning the relationship between the States and the Federation. The Full Faith and Credit Clause, as already noted, provides the Congress with the authority to regulate interstate recognition processes and their effects, which also includes the power to "tell the States when they must, and when they may not, recognize the domestic relations laws, records, judgments of other states".[44]

To conclude on this point, the critical issue is "[w]ho decides whether, when, and to what extent same-sex marriages created in one American state will be recognized by other state governments, and by the Federal government".[45] DOMA resolves it as follows: Congress cannot prevent a given state and its courts to legalize same-sex marriage, but it protects the discretionary power of other American states to do the same, or to recognize 'external' laws and judgments, or to maintain their own system, above all the legislative one.

Section 3 of DOMA, also known as the 'vertical section', is not less important, nor does it pose fewer problems. It provides that:

> In determining the meaning of any Act of Congress, or of any ruling, regulation, or interpretation of the various administrative bureaus and agencies of the United States, the word 'marriage' means only a legal union between one man and one woman as husband and

---

[43] In this regard, Strasser (2011, p. 197) notes that: "Marriage is a fundamental interest for right-to-travel purposes, and states have a heavy burden of justification when making citizens sacrifice their marriages as a price of migrating to the State. That right-to-travel guarantees are triggered when states force citizens seeking to immigrate to leave their marriages at the border does not somehow create National marriage law".

[44] Wardle (2010), p. 149.

[45] *Ibidem*.

wife, and the word 'spouse' refers only to a person of the opposite sex who is a husband or wife.

The aim seems here stated more directly, and the provision is less ambiguous than Section 2.[46] For all purposes, regulations, and programs that may be provided for by Federal laws, the definition of 'marriage' only includes opposite-sex unions. We are thus facing a legislative issue, which can be overcome only through constitutional judicial review.

Once again, we are confronted with the question of the complicated relationship between the legislative and judicial branches.[47] In other words, the legislature 'raises the stakes'; it explains itself and tries to impose the scope of application/ interpretation of the law. However, that is an impossible task, especially in the field of fundamental rights, which, as noted by Finnis,[48] is a complex terrain on which nobody can really have the last word. Of course, this applies also to mini-DOMA statutes, which can be overturned by a judicial interpretation of the State Constitution: the Iowa Supreme Court, for example, declared unconstitutional a State statute defining marriage as the union of a man and a woman.[49]

3.7 Development of the Federal Case-Law on DOMA

In *United States v. Windsor*, the Supreme Court struck down the DOMA, in particular its Section 3, a decision that was to be expected since, as noted above, the signs were never very encouraging. All the same, it seems important to examine the development of the case-law on this Act.

It cannot be denied that, at least in a first stage, the DOMA proved effective in developing substantive objectives. In the individual States, legislative and jurisprudential 'progress' (as regards the recognition of same-sex marriage or of equal rights and benefits for same-sex couples) stopped at a 'middle' stage, and was thus "inadequate to secure broad based minority rights".[50] As we have seen, this Federal law has addressed and influenced the evolution of legislation in most American States, which have taken a strong position against the option of same-sex marriage.

Moreover, the DOMA was not declared unconstitutional in many Federal cases where there was an attempt to prove that making law by creating a classification

[46] Strasser (2011), p. 74.

[47] Wardle (2010, p. 177) notes that Section 3 has both federalism and separation of powers dimensions, which protect Congress "from aggressive federal judges and executive branch officials who may use their power to force the recognition of state-created same-sex marriages into federal programs, policies, laws, without congressional approval".

[48] See Finnis (1980), p. 220.

[49] See *Varnum v. Brien*, 763 N.W. 2d 862, 907 (Iowa 2009).

[50] See Knauer (2008, p. 118): "this confusing and conflicting status of relationship recognition weighs heavily on same-sex couples, [. . .] creates a level of uncertainty that complicates daily life in ways that opposite-sex couples need never consider".

based on sexual orientation—which has a disparate impact on homosexuals—is unreasonable and contrary to the Equal Protection Clause.

For example, in *Smelt v. Orange County* (2005),[51] the Central District of California rejected the claim that the DOMA constituted discrimination based on sex, since the law had no disparate impact on either men or women, and found that a classification based on sexual orientation was rationally justified, since it encouraged "the stability and legitimacy of what may reasonably be viewed as the optimal union for procreating and rearing children, by both biological parents". Moreover, the Federal judge maintained that the often-cited precedent set in the case *Loving v. Virginia*, which concerned interracial marriages and anti-miscegenation laws, was not relevant to same-sex marriage cases, for the simple (and, to some extent, unfounded) reason that the "fundamental right to marry was not a fundamental right to same-sex marriage".[52]

Similarly, other Federal Courts have ruled that the DOMA is not unconstitutional. In particular, in *Wilson v. Ake* (2005),[53] the Florida District Court concluded that DOMA did not violate the Full Faith and Credit,[54] Equal Protection, or Due Process Clauses; and in *In re Kandu* (2004)[55] the US Bankruptcy Court rejected the claim that DOMA violated the Fifth Amendment's guarantees of due process and equal protection, and the Tenth Amendment's reservation on the power of States to regulate marriage. In the latter case, the Court found that there was no conflict between State and Federal policy, noting that "Washington State has adopted its own definition of marriage identical to DOMA, defining marriage for State purposes as the legal union of one man and one woman".[56]

More recently, however, very different positions have emerged,[57] showing the vulnerability of DOMA[58] under different concurring aspects. This seems to point to a path leading close to what many consider as the final chapter on the issue (namely, the *Windsor* case).

The turning point in this case-law, which seemed consistent in rejecting the claim of unconstitutionality of DOMA, can be found in two 2010 decisions of the

[51] 374 F. Supp. 2d 861 (C.D. Cal. 2005).

[52] Duncan (2006), pp. 40–43.

[53] *Wilson v. Ake*, 354 F. Supp. 2d 1298 (M.D. Fla. 2005).

[54] See *Wilson v. Ake*, 354 F. Supp. 2d, 1302, where it is stated that DOMA was an appropriate exercise of Congress' power to regulate conflicts between the laws of different States, and that holding otherwise would create "a license for a single State to create National policy". The Federal District Court also rejected the argument that "Congress may only regulate what effect a law may have, it may not dictate that the law has no effect at all" (1303).

[55] *In re Kandu*, 315 B.R. 123 (Bankr. WD. Wash. 2004).

[56] *Ibidem*, p. 132.

[57] According to Strasser (2011, p. 147), "this lack of uniformity is unsurprising, both because the language in one State Constitution might differ from that of another and because, even where the language is the same, the jurisprudence in the respective states fleshing out the depth and breadth of the guarantees might differ".

[58] *Ibidem*, p. 85.

Massachusetts Federal Court,[59] where Judge Tauro declared the law of 1996 unconstitutional—in particular its Section 3—on the grounds that it violated the Fifth Amendment's Equal Protection Clause, the Spending Clause (which prevents Congress from exercising its spending power in such a way that may induce any of the States to violate its citizens' constitutional rights), the Tenth Amendment and constitutional principles of federalism, because only the States—and not the Federal government—have valid constitutional interests in regulating marriage. The District Court, moreover, enjoined federal officials and agencies from enforcing Section 3.

These judgments have been heavily criticized as contradictory and even 'ideologically' biased. More specifically, putting together the arguments concerning the competence of individual states on marriage and the Equal Protection Clause has been regarded as a 'startling' move in that the "two opinions are at war with themselves".[60]

In any case, the US Court of Appeals for the First Circuit confirmed Judge Tauro's opinion, even though for different reasons. In fact, some arguments put forward at first instance were overturned and struck down by the higher court on appeal.

In particular, the Court of Appeals accepted that the DOMA violated the Tenth Amendment and the Spending Clause, but declined to apply intermediate scrutiny in its equal protection analysis of the Act ("extending intermediate scrutiny to sexual preference classifications is not a step open to us"), since that would have meant overruling a US Supreme Court precedent (which a lower court is never allowed to do), namely the precedent set in *Baker King*, which had not been affected by *Lawrence* and *Romer* (the latter case did not specifically concern same-sex marriage).

The DOMA failed to pass even the 'rational basis' test (i.e., the lowest standard of review), which in this case, however, was somehow 'reinforced' by the connection with the issue of federalism[61] and that of the protection of the States' power to regulate marriage.

---

[59] *Gill v. Office of Pers. Mgmt.*, 699 F. Supp. 2d 374, 397 (D. Mass. 2010), and *Massachusetts v. U. S. Dep't of Health and Human Servs.*, 698 F. Supp. 2d 234, 249 (D. Mass. 2010). The year before, two Federal courts of appeals had expressed strong doubts about the constitutionality of the DOMA. Chief Judge Kozinski, of the 9th. Circ., *In re Golinsky* (587 F. 3d 901, 903, 2009), expressed doubts about the possibility of identifying "legitimate governmental end" for the exclusion of same-sex spouses from the coverage of the Federal Employees Health Benefit Act (FEHBA); Judge Reinhardt, also from the 9th Circ., *In re Levenson* (560 F. 3d 1145, 1149, 2009), stated even more firmly that "the denial of benefits here cannot survive even rational basis review, the least searching form of constitutionality scrutiny".

[60] According to Jack M. Balkin (quoted in Wardle 2010, p. 1347): "the credibility of the judgments was undermined for several reasons: the District Court, in an 'Alice-in-wonderland' judicial moment, brushed aside all differences between conjugal marriages and same-sex relationships; Judge Tauro was painfully unpersuasive in his attempt to ignore the long history of Federal preemption of State marriage law for purposes of Federal programs; and he desperately focused on 'straw man' equality arguments."

[61] The Court of Appeals stated that: "In our view, neither the Tenth Amendment nor the Spending Clause invalidates DOMA; Supreme Court precedent relating to federalism-based challenges to federal laws reinforce the need for closer than usual scrutiny of DOMA's justifications and diminish somewhat the deference ordinarily accorded".

The Court of Appeals considered the reasons given by the House Committee Report for supporting the DOMA, namely (1) defending and nurturing the institution of traditional heterosexual marriage; (2) defending traditional notions of morality; and (3) preserving scarce government resources. It concluded that these reasons were not sufficient to justify the exclusion of same-sex married couples.[62]

The Court reached the same conclusions with regard to the argument that the law supports child-rearing in the context of stable marriage, for the simple (and maybe elusive) reason that:

> The evidence as to child rearing by same-sex couples is the subject of controversy, but we need not enter the debate. Whether or not children raised by opposite-sex marriages are on average better served, DOMA cannot preclude same-sex couples in Massachusetts from adopting children or prevent a woman partner from giving birth to a child to be raised by both partners.[63]

As for the moral disapproval of homosexuality, the Court regarded the argument as completely unfounded, since *Lawrence* (and *Romer*) had ruled that moral disapproval alone could not justify legislation discriminating on that basis.

Finally, the Court also found that the argument that DOMA would save money for the federal government was not decisive:

> This may well be true, or at least might have been taught true; more detailed recent analysis indicates that DOMA is more likely on a net basis to cost the government money.
>
> But, where the distinction is drawn against a historically disadvantaged group and has no other basis, Supreme Court precedent marks this as a reason undermining rather than bolstering the distinction.[64]

In other words, the weakness of a group or class (in this case, homosexuals), which alters the normal balance of the financial costs connected with the choice to invalidate or legitimize a law, has a greater weight than the type of legal review (intermediate scrutiny or rational basis standard).

Moreover, before confirming the judgment of the District Court, the Court of Appeals stated that:

> [M]any Americans believe that marriage is the union of a man and a woman, and most Americans live in states where that is the law today. One virtue of federalism is that it permits this diversity of governance based on local choice, but this applies as well to the states that have chosen to legalize same-sex marriage.[65]

---

[62] In particular, Judge Boudin's ruling concluded that: "Under current Supreme Court authority, Congress' denial of federal benefits to same-sex couples lawfully married in Massachusetts has not been adequately supported by any permissible federal interest."

[63] See the decision written by Judge Boudin, p. 26, which also states that: "Although the House Report is filled with encomia to heterosexual marriage, DOMA does not increase benefits to opposite-sex couples [...] or explain how denying benefit to same-sex couples will reinforce heterosexual marriage."

[64] *Ibidem*, p. 25.

[65] *Ibidem*, p. 30.

This is a perfect description of the virtues of federalism and of the 'anti-majoritarian' (or 'non-majoritarian') role of the judiciary, which, as noted by Dogliani,[66] gives greater consideration to constitutional judicial review.

These decisions visibly extended the debate,[67] which eventually came to involve the Federal Administration.

As a matter of fact, it was the US Supreme Court that, with its decision in the *Lawrence* case, set in motion the questioning of DOMA's constitutionality and the erosion of its legitimacy, whether intentionally or not. Once again, gay rights and same-sex marriage cases intersect and show their intimate connection. For this reason, it seems appropriate to make some observations on this important 'precedent'.

3.8 *Lawrence*, or the Case That Put a Positive End to the Quest for Individual Gay Rights and Opened Up the Possibility of Homosexual Partnership and Same-Sex Marriage

The *Lawrence* case is considered one of the leading cases in the American jurisprudence on civil rights and, in particular, gay rights. The judgment did not directly concern the issue of same-sex marriage, but somehow paved the way and legitimated the case-law which, especially at the State level, had begun to establish gay rights in all their dimensions, extending their protection beyond the principle of non-discrimination to include not only individual rights, but also relational rights.

If sexual orientation is part of the individual's liberty and personal identity, this identity must have the possibility to be fully realized also in terms of relationships, (sexual) intimacy, companionship, mutual responsibility, and love.[68] As noted by L. Tribe:

> *Lawrence* laid the groundwork for striking down bans on same-sex marriage in much starker terms than did Brown for invalidation of anti-miscegenation laws (in the case *Loving v. Virginia*).[69]

I will not comment on this comparison, but the quotation is meant to emphasize the importance of *Lawrence* for the topic here discussed.[70]

According to the Court's ruling (adopted 6-3), the Texas sodomy statute at issue was unconstitutional. Significantly, *Bowers* was totally overruled, and considered

[66] Dogliani (1982), p. 40.

[67] See also *Diaz v. Brewer*, 656 F. 3d 1008, 1014–1015 (Court of Appeals of the 9th Cir. 2011).

[68] Nussbaum (2010), p. 1.

[69] Tribe (2011), p. 1.

[70] In this sense, see also Montalti (2007), pp. 447–448 and Sunstein (2003), 30 ss.

as a wrong decision at the very moment it was adopted. As emphasized by Justice Kennedy,

> our laws and traditions [...] show an emerging awareness that liberty gives substantial protection to adult persons in deciding how to conduct their private lives in matters pertaining to sex

and these developments "should have been apparent when Bowers was decided".[71]

His conclusion is even clearer: "*Hardwick* was not correct when it was decided, and it is not correct today".[72]

The Supreme Court held that the sodomy ban violated the constitutional principle of privacy and was not only a matter of equal protection, since the law prohibited homosexual sodomy but allowed heterosexual sodomy.

In Justice Kennedy' view, liberty is a shifting concept,[73] whose meaning and components can reveal themselves in "manifold possible ways" which reflect the evolution of times and social issues,[74] so that "as the Constitution endures, persons in every generation can invoke its principles in their own search for greater freedom".

This is a demonstration of the dynamism of American jurisprudence thanks to the different types of Justices' opinions (majority, dissenting and concurring). Stevens's dissent in *Bowers* became the crucial point of the Court's reasoning in *Lawrence*: the protection of the Due Process Clause of the 14th Amendment "extends to intimate choices by unmarried, as well as married, persons".[75]

Paradoxically, the link between sodomy cases and the problem of same-sex marriage (or same-sex relationships), which seems unrelated to the issue in *Lawrence* (which "does not involve whether the government must give formal recognition to any relationship that homosexual persons seek to enter"),[76] becomes

---

[71] Justice O'Connor concurred with the majority opinion in *Lawrence* that the Texas criminal statute, which banned only gay/lesbian sexual acts, was unconstitutional, but she did not agree that a statute such as the Georgia ban in *Bowers*, equally applicable to heterosexual and homosexual forms of non-procreational sex, should be regarded as unconstitutional. For O'Connor, therefore, it was not necessary to reverse *Bowers*. On this point, see Friedman (2009), p. 339.

[72] Tribe (2008, p. 135) considers this conclusion "unusual (indeed, I think, unprecedented)".

[73] D'Aloia (2003).

[74] Sunstein (2009), p. 55.

[75] Tushnet (2005), p. 157.

[76] And maybe only implicitly hinted at, as noted by Nejaime (2012, p. 1216), according to whom Kennedy's rhetoric moved beyond "(private) same-sex sex and instead gestured toward the (potentially public) same-sex relationships that enact lesbian and gay identity [...] thereby suggesting the way in which relationships are linked to the actualization of identity". Nejaime also notes that: "Lawrence constitutes a crucial moment in the developing shift toward recognizing that unequal treatment of same-sex relationships is unconstitutional sexual orientation discrimination" (p. 1218). A connection between same-sex relationships and lesbian and gay equality is supported also by Strasser (2004) and Glazer (2011). The latter notes that: "it seems reasonable to argue that Lawrence paved the way for successful same-sex marriage decisions".

apparent especially in the dissenting opinion of Justice Scalia,[77] which is the most direct and radical criticism[78] of the Court's opinion.[79] Here, the Justice's usual skepticism with regard to the constitutional principle of privacy is expressed in very aggressive terms. According to Scalia, the overruling of *Bowers* would entail a "massive disruption of social order", because:

> State laws against bigamy, same-sex marriage, adult incest, prostitution, masturbation, adultery, fornication, bestiality and obscenity are [...] sustainable in light of Bowers' validation of laws based on moral choices.

This is clearly a stronger position against same-sex couples, whereas Kennedy's opinion simply stated that the question involved "two adults who, with full and mutual consent from each other, engaged in sexual practices common to a homosexual lifestyle".

According to Scalia, Kennedy's opinion was a "bald unreasoning disclaimer". He concludes: "what justification could there possibly be for denying the benefits of marriage" to homosexuals?

Same-sex marriage had already made its appearance on the stage, becoming the new goal of gay rights activists, once the obstacle of sodomy laws had been removed. It is no coincidence that many cases which in the last years have attacked the DOMA as unconstitutional (starting from the recent decisions of the Federal Courts of Massachusetts, examined above) have identified precisely in *Lawrence* the starting point of that new approach to liberty and equality, which, on the one hand, made it possible to secure the protection of individual rights for homosexuals and, on the other hand, opened the debate on same-sex relationships.

The constitutional impact of *Lawrence* goes beyond the gay rights issue. The two fronts, symbolically represented by Kennedy and Scalia, fought also on the issue of whether the case-law and legislation of other countries was relevant to American constitutional law. Kennedy referred to a major decision of the Strasbourg Court in *Dudgeon* (1981), holding that bans on consensual homosexual conduct violated the fundamental human rights enshrined in the ECHR.[80]

Justice Scalia's dissent was clear-cut and original also on this point—according to Tribe, its tenor was 'anti-globalist'. Indeed, Scalia saw the Constitution as embodying "American conceptions of decency", not international ones; therefore,

---

[77] As observed by Richards (2009, p. 168), although "*Lawrence* held that gay/lesbian sex may not be criminalized, not that gay/lesbian relationships must be accorded marriage rights. Justice Scalia may nonetheless be right that grounding the holding of *Lawrence* in the right of constitutional privacy [...] must have normative implications for the recognition of same-sex marriage".

[78] Or "ferocious criticism", according to Tribe (2008), p. 183. See also Friedman (2009), p. 338, who underlines that in his dissent, Scalia wrote that the decision was "the product of a Court, which is the product of a law-profession culture, that has largely signed on to the so-called homosexual agenda".

[79] In fact, rather than being in favor of sodomy ban, Justice Thomas was persuaded that the legislator was entitled to decide whether to maintain it. On this point, see Tushnet (2005), p. 96.

[80] On this topic, see Bychkov Green (2011).

he regarded as a danger the fact that the Supreme Court thought of imposing foreign styles, trends, and opinions on Americans.

As is well known, this issue had emerged also at other times in the history of the case-law of the US Supreme Court, in both of the Court's opposing sides (i.e., conservative and liberal). Indeed, in his minority opinion in *Lawrence* Chief Justice Rehnquist had previously claimed that:

> constitutional law is [now] firmly grounded in so many countries, it is time that the United States courts begin looking to the decisions of other constitutional courts to aid in their own deliberative process.

For example, in *Roper v. Simmons* (2005), which concerned the application of death penalty to people under 18 years of age, the Supreme Court referred to values (especially human dignity) adopted in other countries in order to conclude that:

> the execution of individuals who were under 18 when they committed their capital crimes is prohibited by a combination of Eighth Amendment's ban on cruel and unusual punishment and the Fourteenth Amendment's ban on deprivation of life without due process of law.[81]

Again with regard to the application of death penalty, but this time to mentally retarded criminals, we should mention the decision in *Atkins v. Virginia* (2002), where the Court noted that executing "mentally retarded offenders is overwhelmingly disapproved [. . .] within the world community", an argument that Scalia considered "rhetorical". Finally, another reference to precedents set by the Constitutional Courts of other democracies can be found in *Washington v. Glucksberg* (1997), a case concerning physician-assisted suicide. In particular, the concurring opinion of Justice Souter referred to the fact that "in almost every western democracy [. . .] it is a crime to assist a suicide", and emphasized the risk of abuse under Dutch law.

The divide in the American constitutional debate seems irreversible also in this regard. The two extremes are reflected, respectively, in the position of L. Tribe and that of R. Bork. According to Tribe:

> it is hard to imagine that the attempt to isolate the American Constitutional thought from events elsewhere in the word will last very long or get very far. [. . .] the global mode of construction deserves a continuing place in the panoply of tools for making more concrete the norms that define the invisible Constitution.[82]

On the other hand, according to Bork (who was substituted by Anthony Kennedy after his appointment to the Supreme Court by President Reagan was not approved by the Senate)[83] there is a "New Class of militantly secular, eclectically socialist, faux intellectuals, [. . .] whose international agenda contains a toxic measure of anti-Americanism".[84]

---

[81] Tribe (2008), p. 183.

[82] *Ibidem*, p. 189.

[83] On this case see Fisher (1988), pp. 139–140.

[84] Bork (2003), pp. 2–16.

As noted by Justice Breyer in his opinion in *Prinz v. United States*, despite the reference to foreign precedents, the Supreme Court interprets the Constitution of its own country, not that of other nations: it simply makes use of solutions and approaches belonging to a wider juridical context in order to examine problems that may have universal importance.

3.9 Beyond the Question of Powers and Federalism. Same-Sex Marriage and the Embarrassing (and, Perhaps, Not Entirely Correct) Comparison with the Precedent of the Interracial Marriage Ban (the *Loving* Case)

From the overview so far provided, which has included both gay rights and same-sex marriage cases, there emerges an irregular development in which different positions have encompassed all fields of constitutionalism.

More generally, the issue of same-sex marriage is extraordinarily multifaceted, almost a kaleidoscope of all the main conceptual categories of constitutional law (and of their conflicts) with regard to both rights and powers. This issue shows how these two sides affect each other, in the sense that the potential conflicts arising out of the great dilemmas concerning the application of the great constitutional values and the general clauses reflecting fundamental individual rights (dignity, equality, privacy, personal autonomy and liberty) have an impact on the issue of the division of powers, and, in their turn, the various decisions of the state and federal apparatus (i.e., legislative, judicial, and administrative institutions) fuel debate on the purposes of these clauses.

Whatever the issues related to federalism (such as the Full Faith and Credit Clause, the Tenth Amendment and the Spending Clause), the crucial arguments in favor or against same-sex marriage include: the principles of dignity, equal protection and anti-discrimination; the possibility to extend the right to marry beyond the traditional, subjective concept of marriage; and the consequences of a possible recognition of the rights of procreation and child-rearing for same-sex married couples.

The strongest and most widespread position is to treat same-sex marriage cases in the same way as previous cases on the prohibition of interracial marriage, which was declared unconstitutional by the Supreme Court in the famous case of *Loving v. Virginia* (1967).

This is an important and tragic analogy, especially for the history of American law. Anti-miscegenation laws, such as those on the segregation from public services, were the "poisoned fruit" of the tragedy of slavery. *Brown v. Board of Education and Loving* removed the last two formal "gears" of racial discrimination, thereby starting the long and complicated process that, through various desegregation cases, led to the Civil Rights Act, and the controversial strategy of affirmative action—and we may say that Obama's presidency symbolically summarizes and concludes this process.

Considering gays and lesbians in the same was as black people and, similarly, regarding them as a suspect class means using an argument that admits almost no opposition, and that actually ends up condemning the defense of heterosexual marriage, putting it through an almost insuperable test of strict scrutiny.

However, is this argument really so obvious? I am not entirely convinced of this, for a very simple reason: the prohibition of marriage between whites and blacks was the mirror of a frightening ideology of racial superiority. Those who fought against interracial marriage and defended the anti-miscegenation laws wished to protect the superiority of the white race over the black minority. On the contrary, those who have opposed same-sex marriage do not necessarily think that gays and lesbians are inferior or immoral, but may simply be persuaded that marriage is traditionally linked to the two roles of man and woman, also with regard to its effects on procreation and child rearing.

In other words, the defense of heterosexual marriage might have no links with discriminatory ideas, but only reflect a particular vision of the institution of marriage.

Even leaving aside the comparison with *Loving*, and with the highest levels of discrimination, I believe that before claiming a fundamental right and alleging discrimination if that right is not recognized, it is essential to identify the content of such right.

In this case, is marriage an empty 'container', open to various uses? What is the relationship between marriage and procreation? Can gay/lesbian rights be suitably protected only by granting homosexuals access to marriage? There is no 'conclusive' answer to these questions. Or, at least, I do not have such an answer. I will expand on this in my final remarks.

3.10 *United States v. Windsor* and *Hollingsworth v. Perry*: The Final Turning Point. The US Supreme Court Declared Section 3 of DOMA Unconstitutional

In any case, the US Supreme Court has now written what is perhaps the final chapter of this intriguing history.

After all, the two cases heard on 26 and 27 March 2013 concerned the very essence of the issues discussed here: on the one hand, the relationship between State constitutions and the Federal Constitution and, on the other, the doubts concerning DOMA's constitutionality.[85] This last aspect was dealt with in the more significant of the two decisions.

[85] The question of whether Section 3 of DOMA violates the Fifth Amendment's guarantee of equal protection as applied to same-sex couples legally married under state law is also presented in the government's petition for a writ of certiorari in *United States Department of Health and Human*

A brief description of each case seems appropriate here—not only to follow the historical perspective of this chapter (which aims to outline the path that gradually led to the judgment in *Windsor*), but also to better understand the importance and consequences of the recent decision of the Supreme Court.

Hollingsworth v. Perry concerned a complex Californian story I will briefly summarize. In May 2008, the Supreme Court of California[86] ruled that the State Constitution guaranteed the fundamental right to marry to same-sex couples and invalidated a State Statute restricting civil marriage to opposite-sex couples. In response to this decision, a constitutional referendum was announced and approved, which introduced a provision (the famous Proposition 8) providing that "only marriage between a man and a woman is valid or recognized in California".

At the same time, gay and lesbian couples had full access to the legal incidents of marriage through domestic partnerships. The judicial response against the initiative for a constitutional amendment was immediate and direct and led a District Judge (Justice Vaughn R. Walker, from San Francisco) to hold Proposition 8 unconstitutional under the Equal Protection and Due Process Clauses of the 14th Amendment.[87] The case was tried in the Court of Appeals of the Ninth Circuit and then referred to the US Supreme Court.[88]

The second case on which the Federal Supreme Court was called to rule, and which led to the landmark decision of a few days ago, is *United States v. Windsor*. It focused on Section 3 of DOMA and, therefore, marriage as defined within the heterosexual paradigm. The plaintiff and his partner were legally married in Canada (State of Ontario) but domiciled in the State of New York, which, for tax purposes, does not recognize the marriage celebrated in Canada. Without entering into the facts of the case, which was referred to the US Supreme Court, it should be noted, in order to better identify the issues involved, that the position of the district court was as follows: even though the DOMA is sufficiently related to an interest of the government in ensuring the uniform distribution of federal benefits nationwide, this interest is illegitimate because under the Constitution it is the States and not the Congress that have the power to define 'marriage', including for Federal law purposes.

The new element in both cases was the Federal administration's position that any law or provision limiting or preventing same-sex marriage is unconstitutional. Indeed, according to the brief filed by Solicitor General Donald B. Verrilli Jr. (on 28 February 2013), the President and the Attorney General determined that

Services v. Massachusetts (filed 3 July 2012), and in the government's petition for a writ of certiorari before judgment in *Office of Personnel management v. Golinski* (filed same day).

[86] See *In re Marriage* cases, 183 P. 3d 384 (Cal. 2008).

[87] See *Strauss v. Horton*, 207 P. 3d 48 (Cal. 2009). It is interesting to note that the Court first found that gays and lesbians were the type of minority strict scrutiny was designed to protect and that strict scrutiny was the appropriate standard of review to apply to legislative classifications based on sexual orientation, but then ultimately held that Proposition 8 was unconstitutional under any standard of review, because proponents had failed to identify any rational basis for Proposition 8 in denying the right to marry to same-sex couples.

[88] On this case, see Conte (2012).

"classifications based on sexual orientation should be subject to heightened scrutiny for equal protection purposes". Their reasons were as follows:

(1) Gays and lesbians have "suffered a significant history of discrimination in this country", not only because, before *Lawrence*, criminal laws in many States prohibited their private sexual intimacy, but also as regards discrimination in a variety of contexts, including but not limited to employment, immigration, criminal violence and voter referenda[89];
(2) Sexual orientation "generally bears no relation to ability to perform or contribute to society"[90];
(3) Discrimination against gay and lesbian people is "based on an immutable or distinguishing characteristic" that defines them as a group; and
(4) Despite the fact that the situation has begun to change, it is undisputed that gay and lesbian people, as Proposition 8 itself underscores, are a minority group with limited power to protect themselves from adverse outcomes in the political process. In other words, the advancement of gay rights has resulted mainly from "judicial enforcement of constitutional guarantees", not political action, and:

> The recent history of marriage initiatives confirms that gay and lesbian people continue to lack any consistent or widespread 'ability to attract the favorable attention of the lawmakers.'[91]

The "heightened scrutiny" mentioned by the Administration is neither the strict scrutiny still reserved for laws that classify based on race or ethnicity (see the well-known *Korematsu* case), nor the rational basis review that in certain areas of federal law had already been considered sufficient to strike down the DOMA, but, rather, the so-called intermediate scrutiny. According to such scrutiny, the classification must be justified by a significant and appropriate purpose, whereas, in the case of a rational basis review, a rational connection to a legitimate governmental purpose is sufficient, and the burden of proving that a statute is unconstitutional falls on the parting challenging that statute.[92] In addition, an enhanced measure of protection

---

[89] U.S. Merits Brief (*Windsor*), p. 23. Concerning employment, the brief states that: "By the 1950s, based on Presidential and other directives, the federal government investigated its civilian employees for 'sexual perversion,' i.e., homosexuality. Until 1975, '[t]he regulations of the Civil Service Commission for many years ha[d] provided that [...] immoral or notoriously disgraceful conduct, which includes homosexuality or other types of sex perversion, are sufficient grounds for denying appointment to a Government position or for the removal of a person from the Federal service" (p. 23). With regard to immigration, the brief noted that: "For decades, gay and lesbian noncitizens were categorically subject to exclusion from the United States on the ground that they were 'persons of constitutional psychopathic inferiority,' 'mentally ... defective,' or sexually deviant" (p. 24). As for voter referenda: "Efforts to combat discrimination have engendered significant political backlash, as evidenced by a series of successful state and local ballot initiatives [...] repealing anti-discrimination protections for gay and lesbian people" (p. 26). See also Wintermute (1995).

[90] U.S. Merits Brief (*Windsor*), pp. 27ff.

[91] U.S. Merits Brief, cit., p. 33.

[92] See *Baker v. Carr*, 369 U.S. 186, 266 (1962).

must be provided where there is a higher risk that the classification may be the result of impermissible prejudice or stereotypes.[93]

It is important to briefly examine the observations of the Administration in the two cases: on the one hand, they represent a 'new mood' that is the outcome of a long, complex process of cultural and political development in the fields of gay rights and same-sex partnerships; on the other, they have certainly helped the US Supreme Court to become quickly aware of this 'new mood'.

To begin with, we should note that the precedent in *Lawrence* underlies this new position (not only on the part of the Administration, but also of 'lower' courts), at least for three main reasons: first, the premise that "sexual orientation is a core aspect of human identity, and its expression is an integral part of human freedom" (Brief); second, as mentioned above, the opportunity to rely on a "more searching form of rational basis review" (*Lawrence*); and third, the argument that "the fact that the governing majority in a State has traditionally viewed a particular practice as immoral is not a sufficient reason for upholding a law prohibiting the practice"(Justice Stevens in *Bowers*, quoted also in *Lawrence*).

At the same time, the similar precedent of *Baker v. Nelson* is set aside, since summary dispositions are "not of the same precedential value as would be an opinion of this Court treating the question on the merits" (*Hollingsworth v. Perry*).

Moreover, the Administration believed that none of the arguments supporting the DOMA or Proposition 8 would pass the test of heightened scrutiny, and some of them not even the 'more searching' rational basis standard, according to O'Connor's 'doctrine' in *Lawrence*.

The "proceeding with caution" argument was rejected, for the simple reason that: with regard to the DOMA, "there is nothing temporary or provisional about Section 3", which "contains no sunset provision" (US Merits Brief Windsor); with regard to Proposition 8, it "permanently amends the California Constitution to bar any legislative change to the definition of marriage" (US Government Amicus Brief (*Hollingsworth v. Perry*)); and this permanent amendment really contradicts the "step by step" approach.

The aim of protecting the traditional form of marriage can be 'catching' as well. In fact, the DOMA does not prevent States from recognizing same-sex marriages or partnerships. Moreover, according to the US briefs, the 'historical' argument can be dangerous, since it relies on notions found in *Bowers* that have now become useless and basically reflect the moral disapproval of homosexuality.

The point here is that constitutional language changes over time. It evolves and acquires new meanings according to the evolution of society.

Indeed, the US Amicus Brief states that: "reference to tradition, no matter how long established, cannot by itself justify a discriminatory law under equal protection principles".

In *Windsor* and *Hollingsworth*, another argument opposing same-sex marriage is that decisions regarding the recognition of same-sex marriage must be left to the

[93] See *City of Richmond v. J.A. Croson*, 488 U.S. 469, 493 (1989).

democratic process. In other words, we should take into account the fact that Proposition 8 was the result of a voter initiative and that the US Congress passed DOMA by a large majority.

Yet, this is the classic dilemma of constitutional democracy. A quick answer is that constitutional principles are also a challenge to political and social majorities.

For sure, that is true and incontrovertible, but the issue is more complex, especially considering that the Constitution is made of visible and invisible parts, of formal elements and interpretations, which are the resources through which constitutional language can keep up with the flow of time and maintain relevance and the ability to have an impact on current issues. Therefore, it is not easy to determine what issues are constitutionally relevant, and who has the power to establish that.

The conflict between political process and judicial power, and between different levels of these two "institutional giants", is confined in this space; the Constitution is a fixed and unchangeable reference (according to constitutional originalism, or at least its most radical version), but there are also other factors that must be taken into account: constitutional ideas; the expansive force of principles; the fact that cases may be enlightening; and the pressure of cultural and social movements. This is especially true with regard to rights, or to the contents or implications of clauses such as equality and dignity, which are the outcome of a social as well as an individual struggle.

In any case, the Administration has come to the following conclusion concerning Section 3 of DOMA:

> Section 3 of DOMA violates the fundamental constitutional guarantee of equal protection. The law denies to tens of thousands of same-sex couples who are legally married under state law an array of important federal benefits that are available to legally married opposite-sex couples. Because this discrimination cannot be justified as substantially furthering any important governmental interest, Section 3 is unconstitutional (US Merits Brief in *Windsor*).

The Court eventually decided the cases, reaching different conclusions in each: in one case it refused to examine the merits, whereas in the other it accepted the claim of inconstitutionality of Section 3 of DOMA. The majorities in the two cases, moreover, were clearly asymmetric: in *Hollingsworth v. Perry* the opinion of the Court was delivered by Chief Justice Roberts, joined by Scalia, Ginsburg, Breyer and Kagan; in *Windsor*, however, Roberts and Scalia (together with Alito and Thomas, even though for different reasons) dissented from the opinion of the Court, which was delivered by Kennedy and supported by Ginsburg, Breyer, Sotomayor and Kagan.

This is a strange situation, and the foreseeable effects of the judgment also on Proposition 8 do not seem to justify the reversal between majority and dissenting positions within the Supreme Court.

But let me follow the order of events.

The outcome of the *Hollingsworth* (*Perry*) case was a 'procedural' decision. The US Supreme Court denied that the petitioners (who opposed same-sex marriage, asking the US Supreme Court "to decide whether the Equal Protection Clause prohibits the State of California from defining marriage as the union of a man and a woman") had standing to appeal the District Court's order. As a consequence, the Supreme Court concluded that it did not have authority to decide the case on the merits and "neither did the Ninth Circuit".

The decision was far from obvious as regards the new constitutional principle. The Chief Justice himself wrote in the Court's opinion that: "We have never before upheld the standing of a private party to defend the constitutionality of a state statute when state officials have chosen not to. We decline to do so for the first time here".[94]

According the Supreme Court, when a state's voters have approved new legislation or a new state constitutional amendment, and the State's own officials refuse to defend it in court, the sponsors of the ballot measure "have no personal stake in defending its enforcement that is distinguishable from the general interest of every citizen of California".[95]

The Supreme Court's majority decision focuses on Article III of the US Constitution, which establishes special requirements for justifying the intervention of Federal courts, in particular: the need to decide an actual case or controversy—as noted in the opinion of the Court, "those words do not include every sort of dispute, but only those historically viewed as capable of resolution through the judicial process"—and that the parties have suffered a concrete and particularized injury. Also this latter requirement was not met in this case.

It is not easy to foresee the practical consequences of this decision.

On the one hand, Proposition 8 is unaffected; therefore, under the Constitution of California access to marriage is still limited to people of the opposite sex. This seems in line with that part of the *Windsor* decision where the Supreme Court emphasized that the competence on marriage and family matters has traditionally lied with the individual states. In other words, also Proposition 8 is a result of a political process, and it must be complied with, just like state legislation allowing same-sex marriage is complied with.

This is also consistent with another passage of the opinion of the Court, where Chief Justice Roberts underlines the connection between a strict (and thus 'negative') interpretation of standing requirements and the need "to ensure that we act as judges, and not engage in policymaking properly left to elected representatives".[96]

For sure, the opinion of the Court does not mention the question of how Judge Walker's injunction should be applied. This means that such injunction remains in effect the law of the case,[97] also because the US Supreme Court concluded that the

---

[94] 570 U.S., 26 June 2013, p. 17.

[95] *Ibidem*, p. 8. Contra, see the dissent of Justice Kennedy (570 U.S., 2013, dissenting, p. 14), which sustain that "In California and the 26 other States that permit initiatives and popular referendums, the people have exercised their own inherent sovereign right to govern themselves. The Court today frustrates that choice by nullifying...".

[96] *Ibidem*, p. 2.

[97] See Lederman (2013).

Ninth Circuit was without jurisdiction to consider the appeal: its judgment "is vacated, and the case is remanded with instructions to dismiss the appeal for lack of jurisdiction".[98] As noted by Justice Kennedy in his dissenting opinion, "the Court's opinion today means that a single district court can make a decision with far-reaching effects that cannot be reviewed".

There is no doubt, then, that the two same-sex couples who sued in the case were entitled to the marriage licenses they requested. But what about all the other same-sex couples in California?

In my opinion, there cannot be automatic effects. Other officials (i.e., county clerks) may keep on refusing to grant these benefits pursuant to Proposition 8, which remains the constitutional provision in force in California.[99]

Nevertheless, three factors seem to undermine California's status as a non-marriage-equality state[100]: the now explicit claim that Proposition 8 of the State jurisdiction is unconstitutional, the US Supreme Court's denial of standing in *Perry* and, at the same time, its observations on DOMA's unconstitutionality in *Windsor*. It is very unlikely that state officials (including the Governor and the Attorney General) will decide to take a position that can be successfully challenged before state courts, as well as district courts and circuit courts.

In *Windsor*, the US Supreme Court accepted to bear the burden of a decision on the merits; it declared Section 3 of DOMA unconstitutional; and, despite basing its reasoning on the protection of the competence of individual states as regards family and marriage matters, it strongly asserted the connection between same-sex marriage, personal dignity and equality, and the conclusions reached in previous cases (e.g., *Lawrence*) with regard to individual gay rights.

Also in this case, however, the judgment does not seem decisive. As we will see, it does not create a constitutional obligation to fully recognize homosexual marriage, and each state is free to choose whether to define marriage only as the union of a man and a woman.

Let me examine in detail the arguments of the Court.

The basic premise of the majority opinion is linked to the issue of the division of powers between the Federation and the States. Since the competence on marriage, family, and their implications (including the minimum age for marriage, consanguinity, and other requirements) has traditionally been reserved to the States, DOMA "disrupts the federal balance", and "departs from this history and tradition of reliance on state law to define marriage".

---

[98] *Ibidem*, p. 17.

[99] Also the Supreme Court, in a sentence of the majority opinion (*ibidem*, p. 3), seems to highlight that the officials in charge of applying the Judge Walker's injunction should be those "named as defendants" in the case.

[100] At present, the "marriage equality States" are: Connecticut, Delaware (where a new law took effect on 1 July 2013), Iowa, Maine, Maryland, Massachusetts, Minnesota (where a new law will take effect on 1 August 2013), New Hampshire, New York, Rhode Island (where a new law will take effect on 1 August 2013), Vermont, Washington, and District of Columbia. See Lederman (2013).

Moreover, the main problem lies in the general, absolute nature of Section 3 of DOMA. On the one hand, the Court acknowledges that the Federal Congress has the power to make determinations that have a bearing on marital rights and privileges, but only through specific, limited measures. On the other, it maintains that the DOMA "has a far greater reach", since it enacts a directive concerning social security, housing, taxes, criminal sanctions, and veterans benefits that is "applicable to over 1,000 federal statutes and the whole realm of federal regulations". In other words, the Act does not only amend or harmonize state family law with a number of important federal laws (e.g., immigration law), but, in many ways, it ends up in blocking legislative measures that the individual states are free to introduce (e.g. the recognition of same-sex marriage).

Besides, the issue of the division of powers is intertwined with and strengthened by the rights discourse. For this reason, the review concerns whether Section 3 of DOMA violates the Fifth Amendment.

When State competence is violated, "a class of persons that the laws of New York, and of 11 other States, have sought to protect"[101] is unreasonably affected. The Supreme Court expressly attacks the decision of the legislature, even though, in order to do so, it provides an interpretation of the purposes of the DOMA that seems far-fetched. In its eyes, these purposes cannot consist only in the expression of "a moral disapproval of homosexuality, and a moral conviction that heterosexuality better comports with traditional (especially Judeo-Christian) morality".[102]

However, the two perspectives remain closely connected, which may be a way to make the decision more acceptable in a social and cultural context that is still sharply divided on this issue. The Fifth Amendment thus represents a framework allowing the states that oppose same-sex marriage some scope for action and, as already noted by Scalia in his dissenting opinion, this issue must be addressed by the democratic process. According to the Court, the DOMA (1) "is unconstitutional as a deprivation of the liberty of the person"; (2) "*demeans the couple, whose moral and sexual choices the Constitution protects*" (it's important, here, the reference to Lawrence); and (3) "*humiliates tens of thousands of children now being raised by same-sex couples*". The couples to which *Windsor* refers are, however, those "*whose relationship the State has sought to dignify*", and the persons suffering a 'deprivation of liberty' are "*those persons who are joined in same-sex marriages made lawful by the State*".[103]

To sum up, once a State has recognized same-sex marriage, no Federal law can annul that legislative decision, refusing to grant a certain class a status that the State finds to be dignified and proper and, thus, "creating two contradictory marriage regimes within the same State".[104]

---

[101] *Ibidem*, p. 16.

[102] *Ibidem*, p. 21.

[103] *Ibidem*, p. 25.

[104] *Ibidem*, p. 22.

This means that the ruling on the unconstitutionality of Section 3 of DOMA will have an impact on the States that have already allowed same-sex marriage, since access to federal benefits will no longer depend on the status of 'spouse'. By contrast, the decision will have no direct, immediate impact on the states that do not recognize homosexual marriage (still the majority of states) and that use a legislative parameter which duplicates the DOMA at the State level.

The fact that the doctrine of equality is combined with that of 'family/marriage federalism' probably means that the so-called 'traditionalist' states are not obliged to allow and recognize same-sex marriage.

However, what happens if a same-sex couple, legally married in a State that allows it, wants to transfer their domicile, for work or other reasons, in a State that prohibits same-sex marriage?

In this case, there is a conflict between two fundamental principles of the Federal system: on the one hand, the power of individual states to decide issues that are so delicate from an ethical and social point of view; on the other hand, the freedom of movement, which seems to imply that all citizens can move from one state to another, taking their rights and fundamental freedoms with them.

Quite clearly, the question has not been fully resolved, and it will probably be dealt with at other levels, starting with lower courts. As noted by Roberts in his dissenting opinion:

> While the state's power in defining the marital relation is of central relevance to the majority's decision to strike down DOMA here, that power will come into play on the other side of the board in future cases about the constitutionality of state marriage definitions [. . .]

Moreover, the US Supreme Court did not made any explicit observation on Section 2 of DOMA, which gives the States the right to refuse to recognize same-sex marriages performed in other States.

3.11 Final Remarks: Some Doubts Concerning Same-Sex Marriage, the Anti-Discrimination Principle, and Homosexual Parenting

To sum up, after the recent decisions of the US Supreme Court, same-sex marriage is a constitutionally legitimate option, and individual States are free to legalize and regulate it. Moreover, it is an option that, once adopted, cannot be limited by Federal law.

This is now the prevailing position in the legal and political culture of the United States, and we feel that it will gradually become widespread also in the states that have not yet fully acknowledged it in their laws.

Furthermore, it should be noted that this is a global trend, as shown by the case of France and by the recent decisions of the ECtHR on same-sex parenting.

In this regard, I would like to make some final observations concerning the 'irresistible' rise of the issue of same-sex marriage. I will try to proceed in order. First of all, I believe that same-sex couples deserve, or rather, are entitled to have their relationships legally recognized. Certain rights, benefits, and consequences are always part of the decision of two people, whether of the same or the opposite sex, to live together, to create a loving environment, to be mutually responsible for each other, and to share an intimate and sexual relationship.[105]

This position has been expressed also by the Italian Constitutional Court, even though the constitutional validity of the heterosexual paradigm of marriage has been, in my view, confirmed. To my mind, regulating same-sex unions through an institution other than marriage, as is often the case in many countries, does not constitute discrimination. According to Nussbaum, as well as to some Federal Courts, that is a second-class status,[106] but I think that it is just a different *status*, not necessarily second-class or less important.

There is an obvious objection to this point of view: why not marriage? If marriage is a fundamental right, why should it be denied to homosexuals? That marriage is a fundamental right is an absolutely uncontested truth, and even a commonplace assertion. With regard to American law, let it suffice to recall that in a number of famous cases (such as *Turner v. Safley*, *Loving v. Virginia*, *Skinner v. Oklahoma*, and *Zablocky v. Redhail*) the marriage was considered "a fundamental right" or "a basic right", crucial to our very existence and survival. What I do not believe—or, at least, what I do not see as an automatic, mandatory next step—is that everyone is entitled to the right to marry, that it belongs to the individual as such, and that everybody can marry everybody, whether a person of the same or the opposite sex.

I do not think that this matter can be addressed in terms of opposite constitutional options. The statements on the right to marry refer (at least in the American case-law) to a particular form of marriage. In fact, marriage is not only an individual right, but also an institution based on a series of principles, structural elements, and requirements that, so far, have been typical of the traditional model of marriage.

I concede that some people might consider this point of view as a "circular"[107] or tautological argument. Yet, on the other hand, also the argument that denying marriage to homosexuals constitutes discrimination based on personal circumstances (i.e., sexual orientation) appears to be self-referential in that, as far as legal reasoning is concerned, its premise should actually be a conclusion: marriage is an institution that can be modified on the basis of the development of social customs and cultural forces; it is an "empty shell", undefined and therefore open to any 'reconstruction'[108] or 'deconstruction'.[109]

---

[105] Nussbaum (2010), pp. 1–2.

[106] *Ibidem*, p. 10.

[107] See Eskridge (1993), pp. 1419 and 1495.

[108] See also Novak (2010), p. 713.

[109] For an in-depth analysis, see Lee (2010), pp. 126–127.

I also think that there is another aspect that should be carefully considered in connection with the possible recognition of same-sex marriage: the relationship between marriage, procreation and child rearing.

Of course, family and marriage do not necessarily imply procreation and parenthood (couples may choose not to have children, or they may be prevented from doing so because of a physical condition or because they do not satisfy certain legal requirements, as in the case of adoption); otherwise, it would be easy to maintain that "marriage never has been limited [. . .] to the fertile, or even those of an age to be fertile".[110]

Nevertheless, this is an important connection; family, marriage, and parenting represent a 'preferred' progression, or at least an important one also in terms of mutual interaction.

If this is true, once we recognize that marriage is an institution constitutionally open to same-sex relationships, we have to draw some consequences with regard to these couples' child-rearing. Saying that no parental relationship is required in order to protect marriage as a fundamental right is one thing; saying that there should not be a parental relationship, that it should be prohibited, that the main elements of a legal institution (i.e. marriage) can (or rather, must) take different and not necessarily related forms is another thing.

Accepting same-sex marriage raises the issue of accepting same-sex parenting (of course, in its legal forms, such as adoption and medically assisted procreation), or that of finding a rational justification for denying parenting rights only in the case of this specific kind of marriage.

Do we want this? Do we think that the prohibition of homosexual parenting (along with the same-sex marriage ban) is no longer reasonable or rationally justifiable? Do we think that the presence or the absence of different (in terms of gender) parental figures is essentially irrelevant for the purpose of parenting?

In this case, marriage and parenting are not and cannot be the same thing, especially because on this second level of the debate there is a new question to be taken into consideration: the child, and his or her best interests, is crucial to the legal definition of parenting relationships. Therefore, we cannot address this problem only with regard to the rights 'of existing and future parents'.

The link between procreation and heterosexuality is truly and objectively 'natural', and I don't know whether the law can completely do without its natural reference points (what we often call "the nature of things") and thus become a purely technical activity, capable of modelling any institution or relationship.[111] On the other hand, there is no proof that removing the 'legal' requirement of the two traditional parental figures is not relevant to the need of a harmonious development of the child's personality in all its aspects.

[110] Nussbaum (2010), p. 679.

[111] For similar observations, see Novak (2010), p. 715.

It is true that the ECtHR, since its 1999 decision in *Salgueiro*, has maintained that (homo)sexual orientation is not sufficient to reject a fostering application, and that same-sex couples can be considered fully capable of child-rearing.[112]

So far, however, the Court has always dealt with cases where the child was the son of one of the same-sex partners, which is different from granting a same-sex couple the right to adopt or to access assisted reproduction.[113]

Obviously, I do not dispute the sensitivity and the affective ability to educate that same-sex couples may have or not in comparison with heterosexual couples. The problem is more general and concerns the suitability of a parental structure of this type (in this social and cultural context) in relation to the development of the child's personality; on this point, doubts and uncertainties are still strong, as shown by the psycho-pedagogical literature.

This is the last in a series of arguments that can no longer justify the uniqueness of heterosexual marriage and that oppose the last step in the gay rights strategy: same-sex marriage.

However, this seems to apply more in Europe, where there is a certain way of connecting marriage, the family, and child protection—which is reflected also in the Italian Constitution, in particular Art. 29 (on the family as the natural society based on marriage), 30 (responsible procreation and the rights and duties of parents and children) and 31 (promotion and protection of families, especially large ones).

As for the American debate, a fact is undeniable. In recent cases, the argument based on marriage as a stable institution for responsible procreation and child rearing has been easily overturned, by noting that in many States same-sex couples have the same parental rights as married heterosexual couples (they can adopt and can access assisted procreation). For this reason, Proposition 8 and the DOMA neither promote child rearing by married opposite-sex couples, nor prevent same-sex parenting.

In addition to the argument of the inconsistency of the law or that of its inability to achieve the aim pursued, it has been more and more recognized that "no sound basis exists for concluding that same-sex couples who have committed to marriage are anything other than fully capable of responsible parenting and child-rearing", and that "children raised by gay and lesbian parents are as well adjusted as children raised by heterosexual parents".[114]

If also this distinction is dropped, the question of State competence will no longer be center stage, since there will be no reasonable legal obstacles to same-sex marriage, which could thus become, as noted by others, constitutionally unavoidable.[115]

---

[112] See, recently, *X* et al. *V. Austria*, n. 19010/07, 19th February 2013 on which see the chapters by Crisafulli and Pustorino in this volume.

[113] This distinction can be found also in Novak (2010), p. 718.

[114] Brief Administration, case *Windsor*, 42-43.

[115] Tribe (2011) states "in the end the Court must do its duty and recognize a right to same-sex marriage. There is no other way".

References

Barsotti V (2002) Il sodomita messo al bando dalla Corte Suprema degli Stati Uniti trova protezione presso le Corti statali – Il federalismo americano e la tutela dei diritti. Rivista critica del diritto privato 20:637–658

Bickel AM (1986) The least dangerous branch. The Supreme Court at the bar of politics, 2nd edn. Yale University Press, New Haven

Bork RH (2003) Coercing virtue: the worldwide rule of judges. Aei Press, Washington

Bychkov Green S (2011) Currency of love: customary International law and the battle for same-sex marriage in the United States. Univ Pa J Law Soc Change 14:53–133

Conte L (2012) Lezioni americane: la Corte d'Appello federale californiana sulla Proposition 8 in materia di matrimoni omosessuali. Quaderni Costituzionali 2:420–422

D'Aloia A (2003) I diritti come "immagini in movimento": tra norma e cultura costituzionale. In: D'Aloia A (ed) Diritti e costituzione. Profili evolutivi e dimensioni inedite. Giuffrè, Milano, pp 7–93

Dogliani M (1982) Interpretazioni della Costituzione. Franco Angeli Editore, Milano

Duncan WC (2006) Avoidance strategy: same-sex marriage litigation and the federal courts. Campbell Law Rev 29:29–46

Eskridge WN (1993) A history of same-sex marriage. Virginia Law Rev 79:1419–1495

Finnis J (1980) Natural law and natural rights. Oxford University Press, Oxford

Fisher L (1988) Constitutional dialogues. Princeton University Press, Princeton

Friedman B (2009) The will of the people. Farrar, Straus and Giroux, New York

Glazer EM (2011) Sodomy and poligamy. Columbia Law Rev 111:66–78

Jackson VC, Tushnet MV (1999) Comparative constitutional law. Foundation Press, New York

Knauer NJ (2008) Same-sex marriage and federalism. Temple Polit Civ Rights Law Rev 17:421–442

Kramer L (1997) Same-sex marriage, conflict of laws, and the unconstitutional public policy exception. Yale Law J 106:1965–1979

Lederman M (2013) The fate of same-sex marriage in California after Perry. SCOTUSblog (26 June 2013, 11.32 p.m.). http://www.scotusblog.com/2013/06/the-fate-of-same-sex-marriage-in-california-after-perry/

Lee K (2010) Equality, dignity, and same-sex marriage. Brill, Leiden

Montalti M (2007) Orientamento sessuale e costituzione decostruita. Storia comparata di un diritto fondamentale. Bononia University Press, Bologna

Nejaime D (2012) Marriage inequality: same-sex relationships, religious exemptions, and the production of sexual orientation discrimination. Calif Law Rev 100:1169–1238

Novak D (2010) Response to martha nussbaum's a right to marry. Calif Law Rev 98:709–720

Nussbaum M (2010) A right to marry? Same-sex marriage and constitutional law. http://www.dissentmagazine.org/article/symposium-martha-nussbaum

Richards DAJ (2009) The sodomy cases. University Press of Kansas, Lawrence

Simson GJ (2010) Religion, same-sex marriage, and the Defense of Marriage Act. Calif West Int Law J 41:35–46

Solimine ME (2010) Interstate recognition of same-sex marriage, the public policy exception, and clear statements of extraterritorial effect. Calif West Int Law J 41:105–141

Strasser M (2004) Lawrence and same-sex marriage bans: on constitutional interpretation and sophistical rhetoric. Brooklyn Law Rev 38:1003–1036

Strasser M (2011) Same-sex unions across the United States. Carolina Academic Press, Durham

Sunstein CR (2003) What did Lawrence hold? Of autonomy, desuetude, sexuality, and marriage. Supreme Court Rev 27:30–74

Sunstein CR (2009) A constitution of many minds. Princeton University Press, Princeton

Tribe L (2008) The invisible constitution. Oxford University Press, Oxford

Tribe L (2011) The constitutional inevitability of same-sex marriage. SCOTUSblog (26 August 2011, 2:41 p.m.). http://www.scotusblog.com/2011/08/the-constitutional-inevitability-of-same-sex-marriage/

Tushnet MV (2005) The court divided. The Rehnquist Court and the future of constitutional law. W W Norton and Company Incorporated, New York/London

Wardle LD (2010) Who decides? The federal architecture of DOMA and comparative marriage recognition. Calif West Int Law J 41:1–5

Wintemute R (1995) Sexual orientation and human rights. Clarendon, New York

Wolfson E (1994) Crossing the threshold: equal marriage rights for lesbians and gay men and the intra-community critique. N Y Univ Rev Law Soc Change 21:568–615

Chapter 4
Different Approaches, Similar Outcomes: Same-Sex Marriage in Canada and South Africa

Edmondo Mostacci

Abstract The chapter analyses the path followed within the Canadian and South African case-law to recognize same-sex marriage on an equal footing with heterosexual couples. It highlights the similarity of their points of arrival as well as the differences between the Canadian and the South African approaches. Within the Canadian legal system, Courts decisions played a leading role in legitimating same-sex family from a social point of view, granting them legal significance and recognizing same-sex unions and same-sex marriages. On the contrary, the case-law of the South African Constitutional Court was facilitated by a legal formant which was very favourable to legal recognition of same-sex marriage.

4.1 Canada and South Africa: Different Approaches with Similar Outcomes

When compared with each other, experiences in Canada and South Africa regarding the recognition of same-sex marriage show considerable similarities. Moreover, recognition occurred during the same period—2003–2006—and in both legal orders was the consequence of specific judicial rulings and came in the wake of an evolution within case-law which started from questions of a secondary nature and ended up ruling unconstitutional the rule excluding same-sex couples from the institution of marriage.

Furthermore, the similarities are not limited to the above. The two countries are rooted in the common law tradition, in which a debate of primary interest had been established between the traditional rules on marriage—under the law of the land—and the provisions of constitutional law; it should also be pointed out that the constitutional law of these two countries is remarkably similar as regards the

E. Mostacci (✉)
Department of Law, Bocconi University, Milan, Italy
e-mail: edmondo.mostacci@unibocconi.it

D. Gallo et al. (eds.), *Same-Sex Couples before National, Supranational and International Jurisdictions*, DOI 10.1007/978-3-642-35434-2_4,

prohibition on discrimination, i.e. the legal basis which led to the ruling that the prohibition on same-sex marriages was unconstitutional. These points of contact then operate within a more general framework in which Canadian law has exerted an influence—from a cultural and legal policy perspective—on the formant of case-law and, at least in part, that of the literature from the South African legal system.[1]

Essentially, an initial analysis appears to reveal two experiences which are absolutely similar, one of which could have played a decisive role in providing inspiration for the other.

However, this initial impression is misleading. There are numerous differences between the situation in Canada and that in South Africa. In Canada the principle developed gradually, having established its roots in the first half of the 1970s. Although it of course did experience periods of rapid acceleration, the last of which occurred at the start of the new millennium, this does not alter the fact that these decisive moments resulted form a long and important period of incubation in which the development of the super-primary normative source of law—the adoption of the 1981 Charter—and the social context laid the basis for the most significant judgments, and subsequently for the enactment of ordinary legislation.

On the contrary, in the South African legal system the evolution was much more rapid, and resulted from specific provisions of the Constitution which did not leave scope for uncertainty within case-law. The Constitution of the "Rainbow Nation"[2] is rooted in the fight by the native population against the segregationist apartheid regime, and is inspired by the broadest recognition of diversity and the multiplicity of social reality. Consequently, the prohibition on discrimination is not only formed in terms which are much more in keeping with contemporary society, but is less amenable to differences in treatment, the essential justification for which may be found in the common sentiment of the majority of the population.[3]

These preliminary observations explain why, leaving aside the (albeit important) point of contact, the two national experiences are in reality profoundly different and need to be considered separately. This is above all because the purpose of this study is not only to indicate the point of arrival of the evolution which has occurred in the two countries, but above all to demonstrate the paths which have been followed, including from the perspective of their possible imitation in other countries. For that purpose, this contribution is divided into six sections, in addition to this introduction. The first section will analyse the more long-standing experience in Canada, along with the case-law on issues relating to the legal recognition of same-sex relationships (in relation to work, pensions, inheritance etc.), which will lead into an analysis of the period which led to the adoption of the Civil Marriage Act 2005. At

[1] *Ex multis*, see Grant (1996), p. 568, Robinson and Swanepoel (2004), pp. 2–8.

[2] As Nelson Mandela, the first President of the post Apartheid South Africa, said during his *Inaugural Speech* (Pretoria, 5/10/94): "We enter into a covenant that we shall build the society in which all South Africans, both black and white, will be able to walk tall, without any fear in their hearts, assured of their inalienable right to human dignity - a *rainbow nation* at peace with itself and the world" (www.africa.upenn.edu/Articles_Gen/Inaugural_Speech_17984.html).

[3] See De Vos (2007), pp. 435–443.

this stage, attention will be shifted to the African continent in order to analyse the particular constitutional framework in South Africa, and subsequently applying to that country the second and third points from the analytical framework applied to Canada. Finally, several observations of a comparative nature will be offered regarding the two countries and the role which the formant of case-law has played within them.

4.2 Same-Sex Marriage in the Courts: The Initial Experience in Canada

The first case in which a Canadian court was called upon to discuss the question of marriage involving same-sex couples dates back to 1974, shortly after the adoption of the weighty Criminal Law Amendment Act 1968–69 in which—in the wake of the legislation enacted 2 years before by the Westminster Parliament in the Sexual Offences Act 1967—the Canadian Parliament had repealed the sodomy laws in force in the country at the time. The case involved a possible interpretation of the Marriage Act for the Province of Manitoba,[4] the provisions of which regulating the institution of marriage were in fact apparently neutral—with regard to the sex of the married couple—and thus appeared to open up the door to the recognition of same-sex unions,[5] especially given that sexual relations between persons of the same sex had been legalised throughout Canada.

However, the Court rejected the claimant's action, inferring from the law of the land the heterosexual foundation to marriage, which had been disregarded—or perhaps implied—by Parliament. To that effect, the district court did not content itself with references to Canadian precedents, but preferred to engage in a much broader analysis of the institution of marriage under the Common Law. For that purpose, it even referred to a renowned US precedent from 1866 in *Hide v. Hide and Woodmansee* which, in line with the sentiment of its times, inferred the necessarily heterosexual and monogamous nature of marriage—understood as an institution rather than a contract[6]—from arguments of a traditionalist nature and *latu sensu* religious,[7] alongside the more recent English precedent of *Corbett v. Corbett.*

[4] *North v. Matheson* (1975) W.W.D. 55, 52 D.L.R. 280.

[5] See Casswell (2001), p. 222.

[6] This approach has many consequences: see Bailey (2003–2004), pp. 1030–1032.

[7] Judge Penzance wrote: "Marriage has been well said to be something more than a contract, either religious or civil – to be an Institution. It creates mutual rights and obligations, as all contracts do, but beyond that it confers a status. The position or status of "husband" and "wife" is a recognised one throughout Christendom ... What, then, is the nature of this institution as understood in Christendom? Its incidents vary in different countries, but what are its essential elements and invariable features? If it be of common acceptance and existence, it must needs (however varied in different countries in its minor incidents) have some pervading identity and universal basis. I conceive that marriage, as understood in Christendom, may for this purpose be defined as the

Leading aside the analysis conducted into the heterosexual basis for marriage under the Common Law, the case of *North v. Matheson* is also of interest for another reason. In fact, the court refused to update the traditional concept of marriage, as provided for under the Common Law, by virtue of the fact that it coincided with the meaning of marriage according to the common sentiments of the body of society. This assertion highlights how, already at that time, the courts were aware that the need for a potentially modernising reinterpretation of a certain legal institution arose within the context of a minimum level of shared values throughout society and that any guiding role played by case-law in the evolution of the law would need to be allied with favourable views which were sufficiently widespread amongst the general public.

A second case of interest arose 20 years later within a changed constitutional context. Indeed, the Charter of Rights and Freedoms, some of the provisions of which would be destined over time to have a profound impact in this area, had been in force for a decade. In particular, section 15 of the Charter is dedicated to equal protection under law and imposes a prohibition on discrimination on the grounds, inter alia, of religion and sex.[8]

In the case of *Layland v. Ontario*, the claim no longer related to the legal concept of marriage, but focused on its necessary heterosexual nature, arguing that this ran contrary to the prohibition on discrimination which was clearly enshrined in the Charter of Rights and Freedoms. However, arguing on strictly formalist grounds, which curiously were circular in nature, the majority opinion refused to endorse the claimant's view. On the contrary, according to the Court, nobody prevents gays and lesbians from contracting marriage with a partner of the opposite sex, in the same manner as any other person; if this does not occur, it is the result of a mere individual preference which has nothing to do with the rights and obligations enshrined under law.[9]

Despite the majority opinion, the entry into force of the Charter of Rights and Freedoms and the changed political and social framework have not been entirely without effect for the matters of interest in this paper. First, the Court's decision was not unanimous. On the contrary, Justice Greer wrote a dissenting opinion which was characterised by a marked openness towards the claimant's demands and towards same-sex marriages. In the first place, Greer endorsed the position of the

voluntary union for life of one man and one woman, to the exclusion of all others" ([L.R.] 1 P. and D. 133).

[8] Sec. 15, first clause, of the Charter sets out: "Every individual is equal before and under the law and has the right to the equal protection and equal benefit of the law without discrimination and, in particular, without discrimination based on race, national or ethnic origin, colour, religion, sex, age or mental or physical disability".

[9] "The fact that many homosexuals do not choose to marry, because they do not want unions with persons of the opposite sex, is the result of their own preferences, not a requirement of the law. Unions of persons of the same sex are not "marriages", because of the definition of marriage. The applicants are, in effect, seeking to use s.15 of the Charter to bring about a change in the definition of marriage. I do not think the Charter has that effect" (Ontario Divisional Court, *Layland v. Ontario*, para. 14–104 DLR (4th) 214).

Metropolitan Community Church of Ottawa, an intervener in the proceedings, according to which within a changed social context, the common law rules on marriage could no longer be considered to exclude same-sex unions. Moreover, the judge highlighted that the reasoning underlying the majority opinion was exclusively formal in nature and failed to engage with the factual context within which the legislation applied. The provision that marriage was to be exclusively heterosexual contrasted openly with the prohibition on discrimination; in fact, the State must respect the individual lifestyle choices made by private individuals, and may not differentiate between them on the basis of pre-constituted ideological opinions.

4.2.1 Continued: Its Consequences for the Approach to the Issue of Rights for Same-Sex Couples

The *North* and *Layland* cases did not obtain practical results. However, they were decisive in the subsequent development of Canadian society and its view of same-sex marriage for two parallel reasons. In the first place, they stimulated debate within the LGBT community as to which strategies should be pursued in order to obtain recognition for certain types of right, whereas debate had initially focused on which types of rights should be pursued. On this point, it is important to note the gradual shift from principles inspired by a philosophical outlook rooted in Communitarian values to decidedly more liberal visions. The first positions stated at the start of the 1990s by LGBT associations were focused on the claim to special status by same-sex couples and the fact that they could not be brought within the relationship frameworks which had traditionally been applied to heterosexual couples. Indeed, it was only in the second half of the decade that arguments gained ground which were more open to the plurality of individual relations within the social reality and which were more sensitive to the needs and requirements of couples who wanted to give legal stability to their relationship.

As regards the contents of the claims and the overall strategy for achieving legal equality between same-sex unions and heterosexual unions, the path which was eventually pursued was to adopt an intentionally gradualist approach. It was no longer seen as appropriate to apply to the courts seeking immediate recognition of a concept of marriage which was indifferent to the sex of the two partners, and above all to the fact that they had the same sex. On the other hand, it was considered important to focus on intermediate objectives, in order to establish the prerequisites—in both social and legal terms—for the recognition of same-sex marriage, as will be noted below.

On the other hand, the second consequence of the initial rulings concerns procedural strategies. In other words, these initial experiences provided counsel representing the requests of same-sex couples with the minimum amount of material which was necessary in order to ascertain the claims that needed to be brought before the courts, along with the legal and factual bases for the claims, which thereby increased the likelihood that they would be accepted. In this second regard, it is interesting to note the attention dedicated to the facts of individual cases, in increasingly articulate and detailed terms, along with the assessment of the contribution of scientific disciplines other than the law.[10] This fact will come as no surprise. The developments—which were at times ground-breaking—in the case-law on equality, above all in common law countries which give particular importance to the principle of *stare decisis*, were almost always supported by and derived argumentative force from references to the principal social sciences, which performed the delicate task of linking up the fundamental principles under the Constitution with the calls emerging from society, and of giving a new depth to their meaning and effect.

4.3 The Rights of Same-Sex Couples and Discrimination on the Grounds of Sexual Orientation in the 1990s

The cases which followed throughout the 1990s in a certain sense paved the way for the change which occurred within the case-law on same-sex marriage after the turn of the millennium.

These developments occurred along two principle lines, which to some extent complemented each other. On the one hand, there was a significant increase in the cases brought seeking recognition for same-sex couples of the benefits which Canadian law granted to unmarried couples. Here, the courts almost completely equalized the position of the former with that of the latter. This point is of major importance for one essential reason: in granting or refusing these benefits to same-sex couples on the basis of the rules in place for unmarried heterosexual couples, the courts appeared to presume that the two types of union were entirely similar, and disregarded the substantial difference that, at the time, only heterosexual couples were able to marry. In some sense, this appeared to set out the logical prerequisites for the recognition of same-sex marriage.

On the other hand, a specific interpretation of the prohibition on discrimination emerged.[11] In other words, the courts—and in particular the Supreme Court of Canada—asserted that discrimination on the grounds of sexual orientation was entirely equivalent to discrimination on the grounds of criteria expressly indicated as suspect under section 15 of the Charter of Rights and Freedoms. Whilst it is certain that, for the time being, the particular restrictive rules on same-sex unions are justified under the terms of section one, it is nonetheless clear that the recognition of the discriminatory nature of these rules represented an important turning point.

[10] See Manderson and Yachnin (2003–2004), pp. 484–485.

[11] See MacDougall (2000–2001), p. 252.

As regards the first issue, it is important to mention certain significant judgments of the Canadian courts in which the position of same-sex couples was deemed to be equivalent to that of unmarried heterosexual couples.

In reality, Canadian case-law moved along a twin-track approach. On the one hand the courts displayed an openness to claims seeking the 'social' recognition of same-sex unions,[12] whilst on the other hand expressed much greater deference to the choices made by Parliament where the claimants' requests were aimed at obtaining benefits directly from the public authorities.

As regards the first prong of the approach, at the start of the 1990s the courts began to display a general openness to unmarried couples and to interpret the concept of spouse—which is often provided for under Canadian law[13]—as also including individuals who are united by a bond of affection.[14] This occurred for example in *Miron v. Trudel*, in which the Supreme Court of Canada held that it was not permitted to discriminate between married couples and unmarried couples in relation to the payment of damages for personal injury resulting from a road traffic accident, provided that the couple is co-habiting and that the bond of affection uniting them also includes a promise of mutual assistance, including of a material nature.[15]

A similar ruling was made in relation to employment benefits. Here, the reference legislation already covered unmarried heterosexual couples. The exclusion of homosexual couples was ruled unlawful by the British Columbia Supreme Court on the grounds that it breached the prohibition on discrimination in the judgment *Knodel v. British Columbia*,[16] which also had an impact outwith the province in providing guidance to the Ontario Human Rights Board of Inquiry, starting from the case of *Leshner v. Ontario*.[17]

However, the position which emerged from the decisions in *Rosenberg v. Canada* and above all *Egan v. Canada*[18] appears to contradict with the cases cited above. The latter case related to a claim, made by a same-sex couple, seeking a supplementary pension provided for under the Old Age Security Act for heterosexual couples only, where their income fell below a particular threshold. Similarly, the *Rosenberg* case involved a claim brought by a woman seeking recognition of a survivor's pension following the death of her same-sex partner. The claims were rejected in both cases. However, a certain deference towards the choice by Parliament to define the range of beneficiaries of public benefits may be noted in the

[12] See Lahey (2001), pp. 243–247.

[13] For a broad analysis on case-law, see Chaplick (1997).

[14] Rusk (1993–1994), pp. 174–203, who explores the discriminations faced by same-sex couples claiming spousal rights at the beginning of 1990s.

[15] *Miron v. Trudel* (1995) 2 S.C.R. 418.

[16] *Knodel v. British Columbia* (1991) W.W.R. 728.

[17] *Leshner v. Ontario* (1992) 16 C.H.R.R. 184. Its consequences are analysed by Berg and Nunnelley (2002), pp. 218–221.

[18] (1995) 2 S.C.R. 513.

judgments, which manifested itself in the choice to justify the difference in treatment on the basis of section one of the Charter of Rights and Freedoms.

The natural evolution of the case-law under examination occurred in the case of *M. v. H.*, involving a dispute between two women who had been united for a long time as a same-sex couple. At the end of the relationship, one of the women sought financial support from the other pursuant to section 29 of the Ontario Family Law Act. In contrast to the two previous cases, this case involved relations between private individuals[19] and, in particular, the obligation for a former partner to support the other partner who is in financial difficulty where the situation of economic weakness of the former is a result of the relationship. Consequently, there were no grounds to exercise deference towards Parliament,[20] and the Supreme Court of Canada held that this case could be distinguished from *Egan*. This means that the limitation of the obligation to provide maintenance to heterosexual couples alone not only ran contrary to the prohibition on discrimination, but also had no justification within a 'free and democratic society'.

One last issue which is of certain interest relates to the issue of adoptions. Here, the Canadian system displays features of absolute originality since the courts of Ontario have allowed minors to be adopted by same-sex couples[21] since 1995. In the case of *K. and B. Re*[22] in fact, the Provincial District Court held that the prerequisite of heterosexuality provided for under applicable legislation was incompatible with the principle of non-discrimination and that such discrimination could not in any way be justified given the legislation's purpose of favouring the minor's interest in having a nuclear family of his or her own.[23]

This line of case-law is significant in that it opened up the path towards the legal recognition of same-sex unions, and above all resulted in a profound cultural change in relation to homosexuality and the consideration of homosexual relations. However, from a strictly legal point of view, the second issue to be analyzed is absolutely decisive since it provided the basis for establishing the material from case-law which, over the following decade, would enable the courts to rule unconstitutional the requirement that marriage must involve heterosexual couples.

In essence, the situation saw an evolution in the interpretation of section 15 of the Charter of Rights and Freedom. In fact, the wording of the Charter expressly prohibits only discrimination based on "race, national or ethnic origin, colour, religion, sex, age or mental or physical disability" and gives no consideration to sexual orientation. However, case-law ended up holding that this feature had equivalent *status* to those which were expressly listed, according to an approach adopted following a claim by a lesbian woman to (to continue to) serve in the

---

[19] See Radbord (2003), pp. 20–22.

[20] "The possibility of increase demands on public founds is not an issue".

[21] For a broad analysis about adoption law of the nine Canadian Provinces regarding same-sex couples, see Dort (2010).

[22] (1995) 31 C.R.R. (2D) 151. See also *Fraess v. Alberta*, 2005 A.B..Q.B. 889.

[23] Dort (2010), p. 297.

Canadian army. In the case of *Douglas v. R.*,[24] the Federal District Court held that the army's policy of excluding homosexuals was to be deemed to breach the prohibition on discrimination enshrined in the Charter. Whilst the case in itself amounted to a judgment on a policy of a State administration, as a matter of principle the Court recognised that discrimination on the grounds of sexual orientation was unconstitutional.

The next stage came with the judgment in *Haig v. Canada*[25] by the Ontario Court of Appeal which supplemented by content of the Canadian Human Rights Act insofar as it did not include sexual orientation under the suspect classifications which cannot be used as a basis for different treatment. In other words, the Court held that sexual orientation is to be deemed to be entirely equivalent to the grounds for discrimination expressly specified in section 15 of the Charter of Rights and Freedoms. This position was then reasserted 3 years later by Canada's highest court in *Egan v. Canada*,[26] and was also applied to relations between private individuals, again by the Supreme Court of Canada, in 1998 in *Vriend v. Alberta*.[27]

The Egan case concerned, *inter alia*, the recognition of the rights of same-sex couples in relation to social security benefits. As noted above, the Court rejected the claim, but only in a highly circumscribed majority opinion, which was accompanied by a rather lively dissenting opinion, which was drawn up by Justice Iacobucci. In summary, the majority opinion openly recognised that, in the light of section 15 of the Charter, discrimination on the grounds of sexual orientation is prohibited in the same way as discrimination on the grounds of race, sex, religion, etc.[28] The legislation limiting the rights of homosexual couples was however upheld on the basis of section 1, in the light also of the fact that Parliament is vested with a certain margin of appreciation and flexibility when recognising situations which require social protection by the State.

The judgment gave considerable *impetus* in the drive towards the recognition of same-sex marriage. On the one hand, it enshrined the principle that regulations based on sexual orientation are inherently suspect. This significantly reduces the range of arguments which may be used in order to justify the requirement that marriage must be heterosexual in nature.[29] In particular, it is no longer acceptable to argue that gays and lesbians may marry a partner of the opposite sex, and that if they do not marry due to their sexual orientation, this is merely the result of their free choice. On the contrary, the traditional rule that marriage must be heterosexual in nature must, according to the Supreme Court, be deemed to constitute

[24] 16 C.H.R.R. D-226.

[25] 94 D.L.R. (4th) 1.

[26] *Egan v. Canada*, see note 18.

[27] (1998) 1 S.C.R. 493.

[28] "Sexual orientation is a deeply personal characteristic that is either unchangeable or changeable only at unacceptable personal costs, and so falls within the ambit of s[ect]. Fifteen protection as being analogous to the enumerated grounds". *Egan*, see note 18, at 514.

[29] See, for example, Schnurr (1996–1997), pp. 34–38.

discrimination. The issue with reference to which it is now necessary to argue whether same-sex marriages should be recognised or by contrast whether their prohibition is legitimate now turns upon whether or not it is justified to enact specifically discriminatory legislation[30] within a free and democratic society. This is an area which is evidently more amenable to the demands of LGBT movements than to conservative views, and provided fertile ground for a turning point within the case-law which, on the facts, was not late in arriving.

4.4 The Courts, the Federal Parliament and the Recognition of Same-sex Marriage

At the start of the new millennium, the battle seeking legal recognition within the courts of same-sex unions was engaged with as a matter of priority by the LGBT[31] community, and led first to the adoption of two foundational judgments—*EAGLE* and *Halpern*—and later, on the basis of these judgments, the approval of the Civil Marriage Act 2005 which completed the journey towards full recognition of same-sex marriage.

In reality, both the *Halpern* judgment and the appeal judgment in the *EAGLE* case did nothing other than infer the consequences of the case-law analysed in the previous paragraph.

However, in spite of the fact that all legal and constitutional prerequisites had been met, the shift was nonetheless of considerable importance and was difficult to implement in practice. And it was not by chance that, as late as 2000, in the proceedings at first instance in the *EAGLE* case,[32] the District Court of British Columbia refused to endorse the claimant's view, and even reached diametrically opposed conclusions: it not only held that there was an express prohibition under the common law on same-sex marriages, but also that the Canadian Constitution had chosen to endorse by reference the concept of marriage contained in the law of the land at the time it was adopted, and therefore that ordinary legislation could not provide for any form of recognition beyond the simple civil partnership. As regards equal protection under law on the other hand, the Court held that the provision requiring that marriage must be heterosexual in nature was discriminatory, but that such discrimination is to be deemed to be lawful in the light of section one of the Charter of Rights, given the (alleged) reproductive goals of the institution of marriage.[33]

It was only thanks to the federal form of the Canadian State that the decisive rejection by the British Columbia court did not constitute a serious obstacle to the

---

[30] See Kuffner (2000), p. 262.

[31] Among Canadian LGBT associations, EAGLE played the most active and significant role.

[32] 2001 BCSC 1365 (CanLII).

[33] Loosemore (2002), p. 53.

process under analysis. In fact, whilst the legal concept of marriage is exclusively a federal matter, powers over the celebration of marriage are vested in the provinces. Consequently, disputes relating to the law on marriage are brought in the first instance before the circuit courts of the individual provinces, which also rule on the concept of marriage and its constitutionality, according to the normal arrangements applicable to questions of constitutionality brought before the lower courts. In any case however, every citizen of the Federation is fully at liberty to contract marriage in the province of his or her choosing.

This explained why the decision by the District Court of British Columbia could be contradicted within such a short space of time by that given by the circuit courts of a different province, Ontario, and why as such the latter decision generated a domino effect within such a short space of time which was capable of spreading throughout the Federation. First, the principle of *stare decisis* does not apply within horizontal relations, or between the courts of different provinces. Secondly, the recognition of the admissibility of same-sex marriage within one province renders that institution available to any Canadian couple—provided that they contract marriage in the province in which the court which decided to that effect is based—and thus has a trail-blazing effect which cannot fail to have an impact on judgments by the courts of other provinces.

Following the judgment at first instance in *EAGLE*, the general schema set out above was applied in practice by the judgment of *Halpern v. Canada*,[34] given by the District Court of Ontario.

In the *Halpern* case, the process of refinement of the procedural strategy highlighted above reached its culmination. On the one hand, the writ of summons sought to contextualise the facts of the case and to enrich them with contributions from the social sciences regarding the most salient points.[35] The claimant couples and their requirements are described in entirely normal terms; sociology and psychology are used in order to demonstrate the harm suffered due to the limitation imposed by the strictly heterosexual nature of marriage, as regulated at that time in the Country[36]; it was demonstrated that the law plays an irreplaceable role in processes of self-identification and social recognition and acceptance.

On the other hand, as regards the legal basis on which the claimant's claim was based, the utmost prominence was given to the case-law on the prohibition on discrimination.[37] The argument, which was already experimented in *EAGLE*, that the common law needs to evolve in order to keep pace with the emerging needs of society, was not placed at the forefront. On the contrary, the emphasis was placed on section 15 of the Charter of Rights and Freedoms, and on the specific prohibition—already recognised by the Supreme Court in *Egan*—on discrimination

[34] 225 DLR (4th) 529.

[35] Van Kralingen (2004), pp. 159–160.

[36] See Davies (2008), p. 123.

[37] Davies, see note 36, p. 112.

on the grounds of sexual orientation.[38] In particular, the risk that differences in treatment may be justified on the basis of section 1 of the Charter was pre-empted. To that effect, the claim asserted that the inability of the claimant couples to marry was at odds with the model of a free and democratic society, as expressly enshrined in the Charter of Rights and Freedoms,[39] and ultimately with the value of human dignity which asserted on various occasions within constitutional case-law.

The trial court accepted the claimants' action. However, given the delicate nature of the issue and the fact that the ruling struck down as unconstitutional federal legislation in this area, notwithstanding that it had been adopted by reference to the provisions of common law, it also ruled that the effect of the judgment was to be deferred, and allowed Parliament 2 years in order to regulate the situation in a manner compatible with the prohibition on discrimination laid down by the Charter of Rights.[40]

The *Halpern* judgment led to a rapid change in the courts' perspective of the issue of same-sex marriage.[41] Less than 10 months later, in the appeal proceedings in the *EAGLE* case,[42] the British Columbia court endorsed the position adopted by the Ontario court, and went so far as to declare that only equal access to the institution of marriage—and not the mere recognition of 'civil partnership'—could satisfy the prohibition on discrimination,[43] whilst agreeing that Parliament should be granted a 2-year period in order to take action. For its part, the Ontario Court of Appeal upheld the trial court's judgment and ruled that it should take effect forthwith.

The judgments examined immediately gave rise to a round of rulings by the provincial courts which, over the following 2 years, acknowledged that same-sex marriage should be recognised within the majority of Canadian provinces,[44] and above all called for urgent action by the political authorities. In the first place, a few weeks after the judgment in the appeal in Ontario, Canadian Prime Minister Chrétien announced that the government did not intend to pursue an appeal and that it would table draft legislation in Parliament on the regulation of same-sex marriages. Amongst other things, the procedure which led to the adoption of the

[38] "If the Halpern and Rogers application for a marriage licence said Colin Rogers instead of Colleen Rogers, Hedy Halpern would today be legally married. ... The State therefore denies Hedy Halpern the mate of her choice. In doing so, the law draws a distinction between the applicant and others, based on the personal characteristics of sex and sexual orientation".

[39] "Similarly being restricted from affirming relationships and domestic life in the public sphere through the virtually universal currency of marriage constitutes a curb on public recognition as a valid actor in civil society".

[40] Van Kralingen (2004), pp. 153–156.

[41] See Casswell (2004), pp. 710–716.

[42] *Barbeau v. British Columbia*, 2003 BCCA 251 (CanLII).

[43] See Romano (2003), pp. 6–10.

[44] See: *Hendricks and Leboeuf v. Quebec*, 2002 CanLII 23808 (QC CS)—Quebec; *Dunbar and Edge v. Yukon and Canada*, 2004 YKSC 54—Yukon; *Vogel v. Canada* (2004) M.J. No. 418 (QL)—Manitoba; *Boutilier v. Canada and Nova Scotia*; (2004) N.S.J. No. 357 (QL)—Nova Scotia.

Marriage Act 2005, which definitively enshrined the neutral *status* of marriage throughout the Federation, involved a further court ruling. In fact, the federal government seised the Supreme Court of Canada on a consultative basis seeking answers to four questions, namely (1) whether the Federal Parliament has exclusive powers to enact legislation stating the prerequisites for individuals who wish to contract marriage; (2) whether freedom of religion provides religious ministers with a guarantee that they may refuse to celebrate same-sex marriages; (3) whether the recognition of the right to marry also to homosexual couples was constitutional; and (4) whether the necessarily heterosexual nature of marriage is contrary to section 15 of the Charter of Rights and Freedoms.

In its ruling in Reference *Re Same-Sex Marriage*, the Supreme Court refused to consider the merits of the third and fourth questions, considering that the government had decided not to appeal against the judgments in *Halpern* and *EAGLE*, thereby implicitly endorsing the rulings of the two lower courts[45]; as regards the other questions, the Court stated that the area of law fell within the exclusive jurisdiction of Parliament, and that the principle freedom of religion dictated that religious ministers could not be required to celebrate unions which were contrary to their belief.[46]

The Supreme Court's judgment represented the last and definitive move prior to the enactment of the Marriage Act 2005, which to all intents and purposes provided for equality between same-sex and heterosexual marriage. It should be pointed out however that there were certain minor differences, in addition to the right for celebrants—and religious confessions—to state a general refusal to celebrate same-sex marriages. The federal nature of Canada also had an implication on the legislation applicable to marriages, with the result that certain forms of different treatment provided for under provincial legislation are still in force, and will remain so until a court rules that they breach the principle of non-discrimination. In any way, these are now residual elements which only the passage of time will sweep away, and bring the law into line with the new path inaugurated by *Halpern* and *EAGLE*.

4.5 The Constitution of the Rainbow Nation and Sexual Orientation

The process which led to the recognition of same-sex marriages under South African law was certainly less complex than that followed under Canadian law. There are two reasons for this. First, the historical background is certainly of significance: the watershed provided by the move from the apartheid regime to the constitutional democracy represented a historic change to the very form of the

[45] Murphy (2005), p. 25.

[46] See MacDougall (2006), pp. 360–363.

State, which means that experiences in the two countries are incommensurable. Moreover, the South African Constitution, which was adopted in 1996, is a highly modern document which implements the experiences accrued in matters relating to equality and the protection of rights from the principal countries of the Western Legal Tradition.

The 1993 provisional Constitution already laid down a principle of equality imposing a prohibition on unfair discrimination on the grounds, *inter alia*, of sexual orientation[47]; the 1996 Constitution reasserted and expanded the provision from the provisional Constitution,[48] provided for its effect also in horizontal relations and expressly established a rebuttable presumption that any difference in treatment grounded on the characteristics listed would be unlawful.[49] On the other hand, the 1996 Constitution also contains a clause on the limitation of fundamental rights which enables the legislature to limit such rights only by general legislation and provided that the limits are reasonable and justifiable within an "open and democratic society based on human dignity, equality and freedom".[50]

The wording of section 9 and section 36 appears in part to have been inspired by the analogous provisions of the Canadian Charter of Rights and Freedoms. However, there are two differences which are not negligible. On the one hand, the South African experience imposes a prohibition on discrimination on the grounds of sexual orientation, whereas this principle was only adopted into Canadian law a decade after the entry into force of the Charter and as a result of judicial interpretation. On the other hand, any justification of discriminatory treatment must be deemed to be justified not only within an open and democratic society, but also in one based *inter alia* on the principle of equality laid down under section 9. This means that different treatment may only be deemed to be justified in specific limited situations, and provided that the differences are directly and strictly aimed at implementing other principles of constitutional standing.

In this regard, section 15, which authorises Parliament to grant legislative recognition to the plurality of unions present within society, thus seems to be particularly significant in relation to same-sex marriages.[51] This provision, which is aimed at granting equal consideration to all traditions and religious confessions present in South Africa, as part of the Rainbow Nation principle, is particularly suited to providing specific cover to laws recognising homosexual marriage,[52] and

[47] Sec. 8.2, Const. 1993.

[48] See sec. 9.3, Const. 1996: "The state may not unfairly discriminate directly or indirectly against anyone on one or more grounds, including race, gender, sex, pregnancy, marital status, ethnic or social origin, colour, sexual orientation, age, disability, religion, conscience, belief, culture, language and birth".

[49] See Lind (2001), p. 285.

[50] See sec. 36.1, Const. 1996.

[51] Wolhuter (1997), p. 395.

[52] See Williams (2004), pp. 47–51.

above all precludes constitutional interpretations aimed at limiting access to marriage on the basis of traditional interpretations of the institution.

4.6 Recognition of Same-Sex Unions, from *Langemaat* to *Fourie*

Within the constitutional framework described above, the first case of significance for same-sex couples concerned the *status* of the partner of a woman employed by the State Police and her entitlement to be eligible for medical scheme aid, under the same conditions as the spouses of other police officers. In the *Langemaat* case,[53] the High Court of Pretoria did not rule directly on the principle of non-discrimination, but approached the question from a different perspective, ruling that the legal *status* of the union was not relevant since "the relationship between the two parties create a duty to maintain" and the duty to maintain was based on principles such as equality, affection and the sense of decency. On the other hand, the Court went on, both marriages and *de facto* unions deserve equal respect and protection; consequently,

> parties to a same sex union which has existed for years in a common home, must surely owe a duty of support, in all senses to each other.[54]

The Court did not consider the problem of discrimination on the grounds of sexual orientation, which would inevitably have led the Pretoria court to reach conclusions which would either have been inconclusive or incompatible with the principle that the court order must rule on the remedy sought. However, on the facts it held that the social significance and need for consideration and protection of any couple was fully equivalent, irrespective of sexual orientation.[55] On the contrary, it may without doubt be asserted that the Court would regard as unacceptable any difference in treatment which depended upon whether or not the couple was heterosexual. Similarly, it endorsed a kind of legal fiction by on the one hand disregarding the impossibility for same-sex couples to contract marriage, whilst on the other hand deciding whether the law and the Police Regulations provided for different treatment solely on the basis of the free choice by the partners over whether to contract marriage.

Similar findings[56] were reached in the *Satchwell* case,[57] which was considered by the Constitutional Court with more reference to the principle of equality and

[53] *Langemaat v. Minister of Safety and Security and Others* (1998) 4 B.C.L.R. 444.

[54] *Langemat*, see *supra* note 53.

[55] Dupper and Garbers (1999), pp. 766–769.

[56] On the case-law about discrimination in the employment benefits, see Wood-Bodley (2008), pp. 484–488.

[57] *Satchwell v. President of the Republic of South Africa and Another*, 2002 (9) BCLR 986 (CC).

human dignity underlying the right to marry, and the *Du Toit* case[58] on adoptions by same-sex couples, which was resolved in their favour on the basis of the intimate connection between human dignity and full recognition of the fundamental right to family life.[59]

The question left unaddressed by the Pretoria Court soon arose again in a decisive case which enabled the Constitutional Court to rule on the issue: *Minister of Home Affairs and Another v. Fourie and Another.*[60]

The heart of the decision by the Constitutional Court did not concern the violation of the principle of non-discrimination by the strictly heterosexual nature of marriage, as enshrined under the common law and enacted in the Marriage Act.[61] In this regard it is sufficient to note, in the wake of the *Satchwell* and *Du Toit* cases, that the group excluded from marriage has been historically vulnerable, disadvantaged and the victim of prejudice.[62] Consequently, the different treatment causes immediate harm to human dignity[63] and is unfair—the prerequisite for ruling unconstitutional any situation which *in re ipsa* appears to constitute discrimination.[64]

The issue on which the Court focused was rather the lack of any justification for the different treatment. The most controversial aspects were two intimately related issues: in the first case, whether the extension of capacity to marry is liable to undermine the fundamental nature of the institution, thereby compromising its legal and social significance; and secondly, whether this would also run contrary to the religious sentiment of (heterosexual) couples who decide to marry. The Court considered the alleged grounds provided as justification to be entirely inconsistent. With regard to the former, it held that the principle that the degree of social dissemination of a prejudice can never justify the retention of discriminatory legal institutions was all-embracing. In fact, the task of the law, given the *drittwirkung* of the principle of equality, is to avoid detriment also through the removal of all forms of unfair discrimination. On the other hand, the South African Constitutional Court argued, the legal recognition of same-sex marriage does not have any impact on the ability of each couple to contract marriage in accordance with the requirements of their own religious belief.

Essentially, the Court concluded, marriage has both a practical and a symbolic impact. Consequently, there is no plausible justification which can salvage a regulation of the institution which discriminates on the grounds of sexual orientation. On the other hand, any provision for same-sex unions which fell short of full

---

[58] *Du Toit and Another v Minister of Welfare and Population Development and Others (Lesbian and Gay Equality Project as amicus curiae)*, 2002 (10) B.C.L.R. 1006 (CC).

[59] Himonga (2004), p. 731.

[60] 2006 (13) BCLR 355 (CC).

[61] See Marriage Act, Sec. 30.

[62] Barnard (2007), p. 510.

[63] See Romeo and Winkler (2010), pp. 391–392.

[64] De vos and Barnard (2007), pp. 802–806.

recognition for their capacity to contract marriage would be at odds with history and with the fundamental characteristics of the Rainbow Nation; it would amount to a reassertion of the principle of "separate but equal", in opposition to which the Republic of South African reconstructed its essential features from the foundations upwards. Essentially,

> in a context of patterns of deep past discrimination and continuing homophobia, appropriate sensitivity must be shown to providing a remedy that is truly and manifestly respectful of the dignity of same-sex couples.[65]

Whilst ruling that the requirement that marriage be heterosexual was unconstitutional, the Constitutional Court deferred the efficacy of the judgment for 1 year, in order to enable Parliament to regulate the question, in accordance with the findings of the *Fourie* judgment.

Parliament responded to the Court's judgment within the required time-scale, although on the facts the judgment encountered considerable political and social resistance, which resulted in an initial draft of the Civil Union Bill that betrayed the essence of the Constitutional Court's decision and merely created a regime providing for the legal recognition of homosexual couples. However, the incontrovertible clarity of the judgment's findings, which was stressed by the State Law Advisor, and the desire of the parliamentary majority to avoid conflicts with the Constitutional Court,[66] led to the bill being redrafted. This bill, which was then approved, involved the institutionalisation of a dual level of recognition for couples—civil unions and marriage—both of which are available under fully equal conditions for any couple, irrespective of the sexual orientation and sex of the couple.[67]

4.7 The Recognition of Same-Sex Couples Between the Courts and the Legislature: Some Comparative Comments

As the previous pages have attempted to demonstrate, the path followed within the Canadian case-law was not particularly similar to that followed in South Africa. Only the point of arrival is similar: the recognition of same-sex marriage on an equal footing with heterosexual couples. Whilst officials may only raise objections on the grounds of conscience[68] against same-sex couples, it may easy be understand that this option was provided in order to ensure that the move from a traditional legal framework to a decidedly more liberal arrangement was less divisive and traumatic.

---

[65] *Fourie*, see note 29, at 153.

[66] *De Vos and Barnard*, see note 64, pp. 806–807.

[67] See the Civil Union Act 2006.

[68] On this issue, see MacDougall et al. (2012), p. 148, and Bonthuys (2008), pp. 477–482.

The differences between the two approaches do not relate solely to the length of time taken in Canada, compared to the relatively short time required by South African case-law. On the contrary in fact, the case-law of the South African Constitutional Court was facilitated above all by a legal formant which was very favourable to full legal recognition of same-sex unions, thus enabling it to force through a change which caused social strains, going by the heavy pressure exerted on Parliament during the discussion of the Civil Union Bill seeking to limit the impact of the *Fourie* judgment on the recognition of civil partnerships and civil unions, and thus excluding same-sex marriages.

Conversely, the Canadian experience was in part different. The case-law was able to use a legal formant which was suited to this purpose, especially following the *Egan* judgment of the Supreme Court according to which sexual orientation had become a suspect discrimination for all intents and purposes. However, the social rooting of the battle for same-sex marriage, within a country which is rooted in the liberal culture,[69] had a predominant influence. It is not by chance that the political initiatives adopted to combat the recognition of same-sex marriages did not take root even in Alberta, the most conservative Canadian province, in spite of the fact that they would nonetheless have been practicable—at least on a symbolic level. In fact, it must not be forgotten that, from a formal point of view, the *Halpern* and *Eagle* judgments were not binding on the other Canadian provinces and that the courts of Alberta never accepted that the strictly heterosexual conception of marriage was discriminatory in nature.

Within the Canadian experience, the gradual evolution of the formant of case-law was itself of fundamental import. The decisions of the courts which started granting legal significance to same-sex unions also legitimized that kind of family from a social point of view and led to a diffuse culture which was finally free from stereotypes and open to re-assessing in positive terms first and foremost same-sex relationships, and thereafter same-sex unions.

In other words, the Canadian example shows how much open public debate may bear fruit within a free and democratic society and how important the contribution of law, and above all of the courts, is to its orderly development.

On the other hand, the South African example started from a much more explicit legal formant compared to the Canadian experience, and specifically benefited from the experience gained in other countries both in relation to equality and equal protection before the law as well as the protection of rights and their connection with the schema of values underlying the Constitution, along with the over-arching value of human dignity, with all of the consequences for the prerequisites for and purposes of any limitation, as elaborated within late twentieth century constitutional theory.

Within this framework, the insights provided by comparative law are particularly prominent, as they are useful not only in the process of constitutional amendment and the elaboration of the principal categories within the literature, but also

[69] See Montalti (2008), pp. 73–77.

where a legal operator—here, the Constitutional Court—is confronted with complex and stimulating issues and problems.

This is the situation for same-sex marriage; in fact, the evolution of case-law in South Africa was facilitated by the reference—which is moreover typical of a newcomer—to judgments from foreign legal systems which, given the partial similarity within the legal formant, often originated precisely from Canadian law. These references were undoubtedly useful in rooting the domestic case-law approach in tendencies common to the countries of the Western Legal Tradition. However, they also appear to have left the social dimension to law excessively exposed, resulting in a divide between the legal country and the real country, which risks partially thwarting the modernizing effort made by case-law and legislation.

References

Bailey M (2003–2004) Same-sex relationship across borders. McGill Law J 49:1005–1033

Barnard J (2007) Totalitarianism, (same-sex) marriage and democratic politics in post-apartheid South Africa. S Afr J Hum Rights 23:500–525

Berg BE, Nunnelley S (2002) Working out there: same-sex employment benefits in Ontario. Can Labour Employ Law J 9:213–241

Bonthuys E (2008) Irrational accommodation: conscience, religion and same-sex marriages in South Africa. S Afr Law J 125:473–483

Casswell DG (2001) Any two persons in Canada's Lotusland, British Columbia. In: Andenas MT, Wintemute R (eds) Legal recognition of same-sex partnerships, A study of national, European and international law. Hart Publishing, Oxford/Portland, pp 215–236

Casswell DG (2004) Same-sex marriage: equality for lesbian and gay people. Advocate (Vancouver) 62:709–722

Chaplick ND (1997) An update on employment benefits for same-sex spouses. Can Labour Employ Law J 5:321–340

Davies C (2008) Canadian same-sex marriage litigation: individual rights, community strategy. Univ Tor Fac Law Rev 66:101–134

De Vos P (2007) The 'Inevitability' of same-sex marriage in South Africa's post-apartheid state. S Afr J Hum Rights 23:432–465

De Vos P, Barnard J (2007) Same-sex marriage, civil unions and domestic partnerships in South Africa: critical reflections on an ongoing saga. S Afr Law J 124:795–826

Dort M (2010) Unheard voices: adoption narratives of same-sex male couples. Can J Fam Law 26:289–338

Dupper O, Garbers C (1999) The provision of benefits to and discrimination against same-sex couples. Ind Law J Juta 20:772–807

Grant B (1996) Homosexual marriage and the constitution. S Afr J Hum Rights 12:568–574

Himonga C (2004) Same-sex unions and guardianship of children. S Afr Law J 121:730–735

van Kralingen A (2004) The dialogic saga of same-sex marriage: EAGLE, Halpern, and the relationship between suspended declarations and productive political discourse about rights. Univ Tor Fac Law Rev 62:149–192

Kuffner KL (2000) Common law and same-sex relationships under the matrimonial property act. Sask Law Rev 63:237–273

Lahey KA (2001) Becoming "Persons" in Canadian law: genuine equality or "Separate But Equal?". In: Andenas MT, Wintemute R (eds) Legal recognition of same-sex partnerships, A study of national, European and international law. Hart Publishing, Oxford/Portland, pp 237–277

Lind C (2001) Politics, partnership rights and the constitution in South Africa (and the problem of sexual identity). In: Andenas MT, Wintemute R (eds) Legal recognition of same-sex partnerships, A study of national, European and international law. Hart Publishing, Oxford/Portland, pp 279–294

Loosemore S (2002) EAGLE v. Canada: the case for same-sex marriage. Univ Tor Fac Law Rev 60:43–63

MacDougall B (2000–2001) The celebration of same-sex marriage. Ottawa Law Rev 32:235–267

MacDougall B (2006) Refusing to officiate at same-sex civil marriage. Sask Law Rev 69:351–373

MacDugall B, Bonthuys E, McK Norrie K, van den Brink M (2012) Conscientious objection to creating same-sex unions: an international analysis. Can J Hum Rights 1:127–164

Manderson D, Yachnin P (2003–2004) Love on trial: nature, law, and same-sex marriage in the court of Shakespeare. McGill Law J 49:475–511

Montalti M (2008) La separazione dei poteri e il riconoscimento del matrimonio tra persone dello stesso sesso. In: Billotta F (ed) Le unioni civili tra persone dello stesso sesso. Profili di diritto civile, comunitario e comparato. Mimesis, Milano, pp 69–103

Murphy R (2005) Same-sex marriage and the same old constitution. Const Forum 14(3):21–32

Radbord JL (2003) A wedding story. Windsor Rev Leg Soc Issues 15:15–29

Robinson JA, Swanepoel J (2004) Same-sex marriage in South Africa: the road ahead. Potchefstroom Electron Law J 7:1–21

Romano M (2003) "Do You Take This Man to Be Your Lawfully Wedded Husband?" – a case of form following substance. Windsor Rev Leg Soc Issues 15:3–14

Romeo G, Winkler MM (2010) «Yet footnotes matter»: osservazioni a margine di una tradizione. In: Bin R, Brunelli G, Guazzarotti A, Pugiotto A, Veronesi P (eds) La "società naturale" e i suoi "nemici". Sul paradigma eterosessuale del matrimonio. Giappichelli, Torino, pp 389–393

Rusk P (1993–1994) Same-sex spousal benefits and the evolving conception of family. Univ Tor Fac Law Rev 52:170–205

Schnurr BA (1996–1997) Claims by common law spouses and same-sex partners against estates. Estates, Trusts Pensions J 16:22–46

Williams K (2004) 'I Do' or 'We Won't': legalising same-sex marriage in South Africa. S Afr J Hum Rights 20:32–63

Wolhuter L (1997) Equality and the concept of difference: same-sex marriage in the light of the final constitution. S Afr Law J 114:389–411

Wood-Bodley M (2008) Same-sex couples discrimination in employment benefits: where to now? S Afr Law J 125:483–488

Chapter 5
Same-Sex Couples Before Courts in Mexico, Central and South America

José Miguel Cabrales Lucio

Abstract Latin American Countries have been historically influenced by Catholic European Countries, such as Spain and Portugal. This influence has resulted in a deeply-rooted traditional culture that has shaped most civil institutions, including marriage and civil unions, and the way they are perceived. As a result, relationships between people of the same sex have usually been prohibited and, at times, criminalized. A process of change, however, has been at work in some parts of Latin America since 2001, and national courts (especially supreme or constitutional courts) have played a major role in the legal, social and constitutional recognition of the rights of same-sex couples. This chapter aims to examine how the main jurisdictions in México, Central and South America have been influenced by this unprecedented trend, which has been accompanied by the legal recognition of other important social rights, such as pension, social security, health care, inheritance and property rights. In Latin America, homosexuals are gradually being granted rights equal to those enjoyed by heterosexuals, and this change is in line with the universal recognition of human rights for all, regardless of sexual orientation or any other social and personal circumstances.

5.1 Introduction

Marriage and civil unions have always been regulated by social and religious principles, which, in their turn, have influenced the law in most Countries in the Americas, especially in Central and South America. The close connection between the Church and the law has had an impact on civil institutions, especially in conservative Catholic Countries such as the former Spanish colonies.

J.M.C. Lucio (✉)
Department of Legal and Social Sciences, Autonomous University of Tamaulipas, Tampico, Mexico
e-mail: jmcabrales@uat.edu.mx

D. Gallo et al. (eds.), *Same-Sex Couples before National, Supranational and International Jurisdictions*, DOI 10.1007/978-3-642-35434-2_5,

As a consequence, same-sex civil unions have been the subject of a legal, constitutional, political, social, and moral debate in Central and South America, as they were in European Countries in the second half of the twentieth century and the beginning of the twenty-first century. Constitutional judges have played a major role in the recognition of most of the rights now enjoyed by gay people in Mexico, Central and South America, such as the right of a couple to unite their lives, regardless of gender.

This chapter will try to provide an overview of the situation in each country, focusing on the legislation of Mexico, Central and South America and the case law developed by their respective courts. More specifically, it will examine the legal and constitutional grounds for gay marriage, civil unions and related rights, as well as the role of the courts in consolidating the social rights of sexual minorities, including civil unions, marriage and adoption rights. The direct consequences of the major legal and constitutional decisions on gay marriage in the most representative Countries will also be discussed.

The geographic scope of this study will not include Latin American Caribbean Countries due to the early development of their legislation in this field, which however does not exclude the possibility that they may, in the future, be influenced by the significant changes that are now taking place in neighbouring Countries.

This chapter does not intend to explain or illustrate the political aspects of the regulation of same-sex couples. Nor does it aim to be a detailed study on the legal *status* of civil unions and their history, even though those factors will be taken into account to pursue the specific purpose of our discussion. In accordance with that purpose, special attention will be paid to key judgments that are closely related to the progressive recognition of same-sex couples at the national level, as well as to the developments towards the establishment of same-sex marriage. Some of these judgments are real landmarks, and we will examine the legal arguments put forward by the courts. Most of the grounds for legitimizing the rights of same-sex couples have been discussed by important authors and the media in order to inform society of these rulings and create awareness on the issue. We will try to examine the different Countries based on their constitutional relevance.

5.2 The Situation of Same-Sex Couples in Latin America

Needless to say, same-sex couples have always existed. Until the end of the twentieth century, however, there was no intention to recognise them legally. The region of Latin America includes a large number of Countries that have a strong conservative Catholic tradition, which is easily explained by their historical background. For this reason, many social and political forces are opposed to the recognition of homosexuals and their right to free sexual orientation, which leads to a slower development of the legislation on same-sex couples. Judges are sometimes strongly influenced by this conservative trend, which hinders the progress of human rights in general, with the result that the rights of homosexuals as a traditionally vulnerable group are notoriously violated.

If Mexico and Argentina have somewhat led the way in regulating same-sex marriage, the approach to the status and rights of same-sex couples is extremely varied in Central and South America, reflecting different degrees of openness or conservatism on the part of the courts. At present, the constitutional judges of the Countries in question are extremely protective as regards the interpretation of legal and constitutional provisions.

Parliamentary debate has been underway in Latin American nations since 2001, leading to the legalization and regulation of same-sex couples, either in terms of marriage or civil partnership. Parliamentary initiatives are often in response to very controversial judgments delivered by the highest national courts (i.e., supreme and constitutional courts), which shows that judges usually have a continuing dialogue with the legislators to ensure that democratic States protect human rights of all. This is a worldwide trend[1] that has been particularly felt in Latin American Countries after Argentina legalized same-sex marriage in 2010.[2] Following a legal and constitutional struggle before national courts,[3] some governments have already passed legislation allowing same-sex couples to marry and adopt children. This is the case not only of Argentina, but also Mexico, even though the law applies only in Mexico City. In 2010 Argentina became the first Latin American country to legalize same-sex marriage all over its territory. On 13 April 2013, Uruguay became the second nation in the region to recognize same sex marriage. Other Countries—including Chile, Costa Rica, Peru and Colombia—have drafted specific legislation on this matter. These draft laws provide for same-sex couples in different ways, from the recognition of civil unions to the granting of certain rights, but do not define such unions as marriage. Some Countries have introduced special legislation, while others have simply amended the Civil Code so as to extend access to marriage to same-sex couples.

Some Countries, such as Brazil, legally recognize informal cohabitation or unions between people of the same sex. Others, however, have a more conservative approach and tend to avoid gay marriage at all costs: Art. 63 of the 2009 Bolivian Constitution, for instance, strongly confirms the traditional understanding of marriage as heterosexual. The cultural and economic development of Central American Countries is directly proportional to the tolerance of society towards same-sex couples, as is the case in Peru and Nicaragua. Homosexuality was a crime under the former text of Art. 204 of the Penal Code of Nicaragua, but it is no longer illegal under the new Criminal Code (March 2008). At the time of this writing, the

[1] Waaldijk (2011).

[2] Rodríguez et al. (2010).

[3] Bustillos (2011), pp. 1033–1034.

Constitution of Peru defines marriage as the exclusive relationship between a man and a woman, and does not permit unions or marriages between same-sex partners.[4]

Allowing the registration of same-sex unions with the civil authorities was the first step in the long road to equality for homosexuals, a step taken first in Buenos Aires, Argentina, in 2003, and later in Rio Grande do Sul, Brazil, in 2004. These registered unions, however, did not provide sufficient rights and maintained a clear distinction between same-sex couples and people eligible for marriage. This distinction perpetuated the unequal treatment of homosexuals.

In other Countries, not only same-sex civil unions and marriage, but also other important social rights—including pension, social security and other rights—have been recognized through judicial decisions. This recognition has been achieved indirectly, that is, through the extensive and broad interpretation of anti-discrimination clauses. From this point of view, Colombia has the one of the most advanced constitutional courts. Other Countries, such as Mexico[5] and Ecuador,[6] have amended their constitutions so as to literally expand the scope of anti-discrimination clauses.

The understanding of discrimination has changed nowadays and some Countries have passed legislation to avoid it, not only as regards single individuals but also the community. In Venezuela, for example, a draft law on gender equity and equality is under discussion, whereas in Chile two bills on same-sex civil unions are now at the House of Representatives. The first of these bills concerns the creation of the *Acuerdo de Vida en Pareja* (Life Partnership Agreement), aimed at protecting the property rights of same-sex couples; the second concerns the Civil Union Pact, which has the same purpose. On the other hand, Paraguay's 1992 Constitution[7] is very strict on the formation of marriage and *de facto* unions, which are not allowed for same-sex partners; accordingly, unions or marriage between people of the same sex are not permitted under general law.

Latin American Countries share the same cultural and political ideology and identity with regard to the concept of the family as the foundation of society. Recent years, however, have seen a significant development in the region with respect to conservative notions of the family, the couple, marriage and other relationships. This trend is reflected in the fact that the State has been moving in a more progressive direction, trying to protect different family structures based on affective relationships, freedom and personality development. This transformation has been certainly strengthened by the courts. With their extensive interpretation of notions such as family, equality, and prohibition of discrimination, they have often torn down barriers and promoted equal rights for same-sex couples.

[4] A first draft law on same-sex civil unions was submitted in 1993. In 2011, due to the presidential election campaign, another draft law on equal civil marriage for same-sex couples was proposed.

[5] Art. 1 (2011), on the prohibition of discrimination based on sexual orientation.

[6] Art. 37 (1998 and 2008), on the definition and protection of the family.

[7] Art. 51 and 52.

5.3 Mexico

5.3.1 General Overview

Nothing in the Mexican Constitution expressly prohibits same-sex marriage or civil unions. Art. 4, for example, does not define the family as composed of a man and a woman, but only states that the law (in a broad sense) regulates and protects the organization and development of the family, affirming the principle of equality of men and women before the law. In addition, Art. 1 as amended on 10 June 2011 explicitly prohibits all forms of discrimination, including discrimination based on sexual orientation.[8] These two provisions would be enough to protect the rights of same-sex couples, such as the right to marry and form a family, at the constitutional level.

In Mexico, constitutional reforms have been strengthened by other social, economic and political circumstances. The concept of 'family', for example, has changed dramatically, due to the openness to diversity on the part of society and the law. This openness has made it possible to recognize different categories of family types beyond the traditional family composed of a man and a woman, whose main purpose is procreation. Several studies have emphasized the existence of different family structures, as noted in the 2012 Annual Report of the CONAPRED.[9] No longer "an idealized institution (father, mother and children)" defined by social norms and state laws, the family has thus become "a network of relationships defined by what the person or people decide".[10]

5.3.2 Mexico City

5.3.2.1 Civil Unions: The 'Law for Coexistence Partnerships'

The first law legalizing same-sex civil unions was called *Ley de Sociedades de Convivencia* (Law for Coexistence Partnerships). Initially presented as a bill in 2000, it was repeatedly opposed and intensely debated. However, it was finally passed by the Mexico City Legislative Assembly on 9 December 2006 and entered into force in March 2007.

[8] Bustillos (2011), p. 1035.

[9] The CONAPRED, or *Consejo Nacional para Prevenir la Discriminación National* (Anti-Discrimination Council), is a State Agency created in Mexico in 2003 to prevent discrimination. It receives and resolves complaints of discrimination, including racial, ethnic, religious, and sexual orientation discrimination. For more information, visit www.conapred.org.mx. The report is available at http://www.conapred.org.mx/index.php?contenido=noticias&id=3021&id_opcion=108&op=214.

[10] Rafael De La Madrid (2012), p. 39.

The Law for Coexistence Partnerships allowed certain rights similar to those arising from marriage, such as social, property and inheritance rights. Art. 1 states that the law is of public order and social interest, and that its provisions govern relationships based on coexistence partnerships. These are defined as bilateral legal acts between two adults of opposite or same sex with full legal capacity, whereby they establish a common home, commit to a permanent relationship and undertake to look after each other.

5.3.2.2 Same-Sex Marriage: The 2009 Reform

The definition of marriage adopted in Mexico City until 2009—namely, the free union of a man and a woman[11]—expressly excluded same-sex couples.

On 29 December 2009, however, the Legislative Assembly approved a reform of the Civil Code of Mexico City allowing same-sex couples to marry,[12] a reform promoted by the Party of the Democratic Revolution (PRD). The amended legislation, which entered into force in March 2010, grants homosexual couples also the same adoption rights as heterosexual couples. More specifically, the amendment to Art. 146 of the Civil Code states that:

> Marriage is the free union of two persons in the community of life, in which both owe each other respect, equality and mutual support. Marriage must be celebrated before the Civil Registry and according to the formalities set out in this Code.

The reform has made it necessary for the Supreme Court to develop new criteria to address the subject. With regard to the question of adoption rights, which has been especially problematic, the Supreme Court has made no distinction between homosexual and heterosexual couples and has argued that adoption—whether by same-sex or opposite-sex couples—is not automatic, since the interests of the child must always prevail.[13]

5.3.2.3 Same-Sex Marriage: Court Decisions

Before the approval of the Law for Coexistence Partnerships (2007), there were no jurisdictional issues that may allow us to speak of a judicial intervention in the battle for the rights of same-sex couples. Indeed, the legal debate started after the law allowing same-sex couples to marry and adopt children took effect. In 2010, five states with conservative governments—namely, Morelos, Guanajuato, Tlaxcala, Sonora, Baja California and Jalisco—brought constitutional proceedings in which they challenged the amendments to Art. 146 of the Civil Code and Art.

[11] See the previous text of Art. 146 of the Civil Code.

[12] The draft was passed with 39 votes in favour, 20 against, and 5 abstentions.

[13] Suprema Corte de Justicia de la Nación, *Acción de Inconstitucionalidad 2/2010*, 16 August 2010.

391 of the Code of Civil Procedure (which grant same-sex couples access to marriage and adoption rights), invoking the principle of the child's best and that of equality. The Supreme Court rejected their claims as manifestly inadmissible and lacking legitimate interest.[14]

On 27 January 2010, another constitutional action was brought against the Mexican legislative reform allowing same-sex marriage,[15] this time by the *Procuraduría General de la República* (Attorney General's Office) on behalf of the Government. The Court ruled by a 8-2 vote that the amendments in question were not unconstitutional.[16]

The *Procuraduría General* claimed that the new articles of the Civil Code were contrary to Art. 4 (on the family) and 16 (motivation and principle of legality) of the national Constitution.

First of all, the Attorney General's Office maintained that the local legislator had no reason for introducing the bill and amending the current legislation, since the rights of same-sex couples were already protected under the *Ley de sociedades de convivencia*: hence, the Congress had failed to comply with the principles of reasonability and proportionality. The *Procuraduría General* also submitted that the amendments were not consistent with Art. 16(1) of the Universal Declaration of Human Rights, since that provision only prohibits limitations to the right to marry that are due to race, nationality or religion—and not to sexual orientation.

Secondly, the Attorney General's Office emphasized that the founding fathers of the Constitution had had an "ideal model of family" in mind, i.e., a family composed of a father, mother, and their children, with procreation as its main goal (Art. 4). Hence, the amended Art. violated the Constitution because in that they permitted changes to this family model. In sum, according to the Attorney General, the different treatment of gay and heterosexual marriage was just a question of 'appropriateness' of the law to the specific case.

The Court held that the protection of the family is a duty of the State, and that the concept of 'family' must include the variety of family structures existing in society; therefore, same-sex marriage is not contrary to Art. 4 of the Constitution.[17] According to the Court, natural procreation is no longer essential to the idea of marriage, since nowadays families are based first and foremost on affection, mutual care and commitment. This argument was supported by numerous sociological studies carried out by prestigious research institutions in Mexico.

In addition, the Court found same-sex marriage constitutional on grounds of the right to human dignity and the right to the free development of personality enshrined in Art. 1 of the Constitution (prohibition of discrimination). In the eyes of the Court, the State must protect not only the individual rights of homosexuals,

[14] Suprema Corte de justicia de la Nación, Controversia constitucional 13/2010, 23rd January 2010.

[15] Bustillos (2011) p. 1041.

[16] *Supra*, note 14.

[17] *Ibidem*.

but also their right to marry a same-sex partner. Pursuant to Art. 121. IV of the Constitution, the Court also ruled that all of the Mexican states must recognize the validity of same-sex marriages entered into in Mexico City, regardless of whether the formation of gay marriages is allowed only in that district. Finally, the Court concluded that there was no reason to preclude homosexual couples from enjoying the right to adopt, since heterosexual couples who cannot or do not wish to procreate have the right to do so and, according to professionals, children do not suffer any psychological or social disadvantage as the result of being raised by same-sex parents.

Since Mexico has federalist government system, there is a great variety of local laws, which could lead to inconsistencies in the regulation of marriage and civil unions. Nevertheless, the Court has ruled that all Mexican states are obliged to recognize marriages contracted in Mexico City, regardless of their internal legislation.[18] This means that, even though the formation of same-sex marriage or other forms of civil unions is not allowed in individual states, gay marriages celebrated in Mexico City will be fully valid in the states that have not passed legislation on the subject. As a consequence, problems may arise when there is a contradiction between laws, for example if same-sex marriage is prohibited by a state law or local constitution but permitted in Mexico City. In that event, the issue will be resolved by the Supreme Court, which will have to reaffirm its earlier conclusions and the prohibition against discrimination.

5.3.2.4 Social Security and Social Rights for Same-Sex Couples

Same-sex couples have faced many difficulties with regards to social security. From a legal point of view, the first marriage contracted in Mexico under the new Mexico City law (4 March 2010) is particularly worthy of notice. In this case, one of the partners requested to nominate her spouse as the beneficiary of certain social security benefits. The Mexican Social Security Institute (IMSS), however, refused said benefits to the couple on 2 August 2010, based on a strict and reductive interpretation of the applicable law (the IMSS Act), which provides that an applicant can only nominate as a beneficiary a person of the opposite sex. Given this sexual orientation discrimination, the couple filed an *amparo* (action for protection of fundamental rights), which was eventually ruled on by the Supreme Court on 9 November 2010. The competent court for the case—the IV Federal District Court for Labour Matters (Mexico City)—was then asked to obtain the registry of beneficiaries from the Social Security Institute.

Following the decision of the Supreme Court in case No. 590/2011-3, also the Institute for Social Security and Services for State Workers (*Instituto de Seguridad y Servicios Sociales de los Trabajadores del Estado*, or ISSSTE) had to recognize

[18] *Ibidem.*

the rights of a same-sex couple.[19] In this case, registration with the Institute, and thus the granting of health care and social security benefits, occurred after the CONAPRED issued its Resolution No. 2/2011, according to which discrimination based on sexual preference is contrary also to Art. 1 of the Constitution. This Resolution is aimed at recognizing and guaranteeing the right to social security benefits for same-sex couples, based on the duty to protect the family in its broadest sense. It was issued in response to a number of complaints brought against the IMSS and ISSSTE for discrimination against homosexual couples married or registered in Mexico City (where same-sex unions are legal) and for the refusal to register a member's same-sex partner as a beneficiary. The first-instance administrative courts had denied benefits to same-sex partners based on a strict interpretation of the law, thereby violating the right of civil partners to receive social security benefits and have their union recognized.[20] These are all examples of the problems same-sex couples may face even when their relationship is recognized as equivalent to marriage for all legal purposes.

The decisions and actions of the institutions that protect equality have triggered legislative safeguards. In particular, on 30 April 2012 the House of Representatives approved a bill to amend the ISSSTE and IMSS rules and regulations,[21] so as to grant all same-sex couples in a civil partnership, marriage or domestic partnership the same access to social security as heterosexual couples.

5.3.3 Mexican Federal States

Mexican states have had an ambivalent approach to same-sex civil unions. In this regard, the first observation to be made is that the Capital and each of the 31 states have the legislative power to regulate marriage as they think fit and, if necessary, to alter their domestic laws, including their local Constitution.

Until 31 December 2012, 19 states defined marriage in their civil codes as a relationship between one man and one woman,[22] while 11 states did not define marriage or civil partnership in those terms.[23] This second group of states, however, seem to take it for granted that a marriage or civil partnership is the union between a man and a woman, since 'husband' and 'wife' are recurring terms in their civil codes. Quintana Roo is the only state where ordinary civil law uses gender-neutral

[19] IV District Labour Court, *amparo* No. 590/2011-3.

[20] CONAPRED Resolution No. 2/2011 of 6 July 2011.

[21] The draft was approved with 252 votes in favour, 80 against and 15 abstentions.

[22] States of Aguascalientes, Baja California, Baja California Sur, Chihuahua, Estado de México, Hidalgo, Jalisco, Michoacán, Morelos, Nuevo León, Nayarit, Oaxaca, Puebla, Querétaro, San Luis Potosí, Sonora, Veracruz, Zacatecas and Yucatán.

[23] States of Campeche, Chiapas, Coahuila, Colima, Durango, Guanajuato, Guerrero, Sinaloa, Tabasco, Tamaulipas and Tlaxcala.

terms when defining or regulating marriage. Art. 602*bis* of the Civil Code, for instance, provides that the "family is a permanent, social institution composed of a group of people joined together by the legal bond of marriage".

Following the introduction of the Mexico City law and the increasing public demand for the recognition of the rights of sexual minorities, gays, lesbians and transsexuals, several State Congresses have considered draft legislation allowing same-sex unions. These bills are at different stages of the legislative process.

In Yucatán, for instance, a bill called "Marriage for All" was presented in November 2012 on the initiative of the parliamentary group of the PRD (the same party that had submitted the bill on same-sex marriage passed in Mexico City). It aims to afford same-sex couples the same right to marry as heterosexual couples. Some local Congresses have been considering for several years the possibility of introducing legislation on same-sex civil unions. In the State of Puebla, the issue has been under discussion since 7 December 2006, while in the State of Sonora a draft law to allow same-sex marriage was presented in January 2010. In other States, such as Tabasco (Southern Mexico), the main political parties (including the Institutional Revolutionary Party, also known as PRI or PRD) support the introduction of legislation on the subject, even though no bill has been discussed. In Tamaulipas, a draft Law for Coexistence Partnerships has been submitted to protect the rights of same-sex civil partners. In Quintana Roo, same-sex marriage became legal in January 2012 without any legislative reform, since the law of that state does not define marriage as the union of one man and one woman.[24] Other states are following in the footsteps of Mexico City: in 2007, for example, Coahuila allowed 'civil solidarity', that is, the registration of both opposite and same-sex partnerships.

In this perspective, the state of Oaxaca is an exception. Art. 143 of the local Civil Code expressly defines marriage as the union between one man and one woman whose purpose is procreation: "Marriage is a civil contract between one man and one woman, whereby they are united in order to perpetuate the species and support each other for life."

On 5 December 2012, however, the Supreme Court of Justice, after long judicial proceedings started in August 2011,[25] declared Art. 143 unconstitutional on grounds of discrimination and, therefore, authorized same-sex marriage directly, that is, without any legislative reform being needed.[26] This judgment is the first of its kind in the country. It sets a precedent for the other states and, therefore, encourages them to file applications for *amparo* before the Supreme Court against any legislation excluding same-sex couples from marriage.

---

[24] See Anderson-Minshall (2012).

[25] Second District Court of Oaxaca, Section II, *Mesa* III-A, Writ of Amparo No. 1143/2011.

[26] Supreme Court Decision of 5 December 2012, cases 457/2012, 567/2012 and 581/2012. The Court exercised its 'power of attraction' (i.e., legal authority to bring important cases under its jurisdiction).

Same-sex marriages are still prohibited in Oaxaca, and the Supreme Court is currently examining another case of sexual orientation discrimination. On 27 February 2013, the First Chamber of the Court decided unanimously to bring under its jurisdiction an *amparo* case concerning Art. 143 of Oaxaca's Civil Code and potential discrimination based on sexual orientation.[27] This time, the Court will have to decide whether Art. 143, which defines marriage as the union between a man and a woman, is in itself discriminatory—and not whether a law implementing Art. 143 is contrary to constitutionally protected equality rights. In this sense, the Court may eventually decide on a new legal concept in Mexican law: that of 'legitimate interest', introduced in the 2011 constitutional reforms to the *amparo* system.

With regard to the recognition of same-sex civil unions, the adoption of legislative and jurisprudential measures has not been unambiguous in Mexican states. Not all measures are aimed at recognizing these unions, and some states have used their legislative power to prevent the introduction of gay marriage. Baja California (Northern Mexico), for instance, has amended its Constitution to reaffirm a conservative position on family and marriage. Moreover, its Civil Code excludes same-sex couples from marriage, since it defines that institution as the union between one man and one woman.

Finally, it should be emphasized that, even if individual states (except the Federal District) do not allow same-sex couples to register their unions, marriage or adoption rights granted by the laws of Mexico City or another State will be valid, by order of the Supreme Court, also in the other Mexican States. This follows from Art. 121 of the Federal Constitution of Mexico, which states that: "Complete faith and credence shall be given in each State of the Federation to the public acts, registries, and judicial proceedings of all the others."

This does not mean that if same-sex unions, marriages or adoption rights are legal in Mexico City or another State they will be automatically legal in other States, but that they must be recognized in accordance with Art. 121 [28] Therefore, same-sex couples cannot ask state or federal courts to be allowed to marry based on a law of another State, since para. 1 of Art. 121 provides that "[t]he laws of a State shall have effect only within its own territory and consequently are not binding outside of that State".

In any case, the legislative sovereignty of each State must be considered within the context of the Federal Constitution as amended in 2011, whose Art. 1 and 4 establish the duty of the State to protect the family, and to do so without discrimination. In conclusion, due to the differences between Mexican states as regards the (judicial or legal) situation of same-sex couples and their adoption rights, each case is determined individually. We must wait and see if Mexico will introduce a federal law to address the issue, and how that law will protect the rights of sexual minorities.

[27] Case 387/2012, Appellate Court for Civil and Administrative Matters, 13th Circuit.

[28] See Art. 121(4) of the Federal Constitution.

5.4 Central America

5.4.1 Guatemala

Due to the historical influence of Spain, Guatemala is a conservative Catholic country. For this reason, marriage, civil partnerships and any other form of union between people of the same sex have not been taken into consideration in ordinary laws or in the Constitution. In Guatemala, as in most Central and South American Countries, marriage is defined as the union of a man and a woman.

Art. 47 of the 1993 Constitution, which concerns social rights, specifically protects the institution of the family, but it does not define marriage as the relationship between a man and a woman. Art. 48 protects *de facto* unions without defining them, while Art. 54 guarantees adoption rights without specifically excluding same-sex couples. This does not imply that gay marriage, civil unions and/or adoption by same-sex couples are permitted; at the same time, however, it means that they are not explicitly prohibited. As a consequence, the recognition of civil unions, marriage, and adoption rights depends on the legislators.

In this regard, Art. 78 of the Civil Code states that: "Marriage is a social institution whereby a man and a woman are legally united, with the intention of permanence and with the purpose of living together, procreating, nourishing and educating their children, and helping each other."

At least three distinctive features emerge from this definition: the union is between a man and woman only; it is intended to be permanent; and it has the purpose of procreating. In Guatemala, as also in other Countries of the region, marriages between people of the same sex may be (or seem to be) authorized by the case law, and this possibility is based on the constitutional principle of equality enshrined in the Constitution (Art. 4).

5.4.2 Costa Rica

Same-sex civil unions or marriages are not legal in Costa Rica.

As in most Latin American Countries, the legislation on marriage and civil unions covers heterosexual relationships only. According to Art. 11 of the Family Code, the objectives of marriage include cohabitation, cooperation and mutual assistance. Moreover, Art. 14(6) of the same Code expressly states that marriage between people of the same sex is legally impossible. Finally, Art. 242 provides that only *de facto* unions between a man and a woman who have legal capacity to marry are comparable to marriage. This definition of marriage and its purposes, as well as the explicit exclusion of same-sex couples from *de facto* unions, have led to a number of interesting court decisions.

5.4.2.1 Court Decisions

In Costa Rica, the battle for the right of gay people to register their civil unions or marriages has been fought in the courts.

A first action for judicial review was brought before the Constitutional Chamber of the Supreme Court on 29 July 2003. The main pleas put forward in the application concerned: sexual orientation discrimination, arising from the fact that Art. 14(6) of the Family Code expressly prohibits same-sex marriage; and a breach of the principle of autonomy enshrined in Art. 28 of the Constitution. The case was referred to the Supreme Court by a Family Court, according to which it raised constitutional issues.

The Supreme Court thus had the opportunity to rule for the first time on same-sex marriage. It delivered its judgment in 2006, ruling by a 3-2 vote that Art. 14 (6) of the Family Code was not unconstitutional, on the grounds that it did not infringe the principle of equality (Art. 33 of the Constitution) or that of autonomy.[29] The Court held that homosexual relationships could not be treated as equal to heterosexual relationships, and that there was no breach of the principle of freedom enshrined in Art. 28 of the Constitution. In order to support its position, the Court provided an interpretation of Art. 17 of the American Convention on Human Rights, which recognizes the right of men and women to marry and raise a family.[30] The judges maintained that if the Convention had wanted to include gay marriage, it would have used the term 'person', as it did in other provisions,[31] and that the same held true for Art. 23 of the International Covenant on Civil and Political Rights.[32] Without denying a certain inequality of treatment with regard to access to marriage, the Court ruled that it was up to the ordinary legislator to solve the problem of possible discrimination. Rather than declaring the challenged provision unconstitutional, the Court recognized that there is a difference in the treatment of heterosexuals and homosexuals, which must be resolved exclusively by the Legislature. The Court did not recognize that same-sex marriages or civil unions should be legally regulated, but simply maintained that the Legislature should remedy any inappropriate regulation, or lack of regulation (i.e., a legislative gap). This statement of the Court is a plea to the Legislature to regulate unions or, at least, establish legal measures to reduce or eliminate differences and discrimination between heterosexual and homosexual couples. As of April 2013, in Costa Rica there is no legislation addressing this issue.

On the other hand, the existing legislation on civil unions has been the subject of judicial discussion. A constitutional complaint against Art. 242 of the Family Code, which only recognises heterosexual relationships, was filed in 2003.[33] The main

[29] Constitutional Chamber of the Supreme Court, Judgment No. 7262-06, Action for Judicial Review (*Acción de inconstitucionalidad*) No. 8127-03.

[30] See also the Chapter by Magi in this volume.

[31] Art. 2, 3, 5, 8 and 10 of the Declaration.

[32] See the Chapter by Paladini in this volume.

[33] Avalos (2012).

ground of the complaint was the indirect exclusion of same-sex couples from the right to form a family and to receive health, pension and other social benefits derived from civil unions. The Constitutional Court rejected the complaint[34] and did not address the merits because of a procedural default, since there was no case pending before a lower court that required a judgment on the merits.

On 16 May 2011, two marriage applications were filed with the civil courts, one of which by a gay couple. This application was rejected by the Second Family Court of San Jose based on Art. 14 of the Family Code, which expressly precludes same-sex couples from marrying.

Another landmark case concerning the rights of same-sex couples is the constitutional objection filed on February 2008 against Decree No. 33876-J on Technical Regulations of the National Penitentiary System, whose Art. 66 defines 'conjugal visit' as "the right of the detainee to private contact with another person of their choice that is of the opposite sex". In other words, conjugal visits are permitted only in the case of an opposite-sex relationship, which constitutes discrimination against same-sex relationships.

The case went to the Constitutional Chamber of the Supreme Court through an action for judicial review that had been preceded by an injunction. On 13 October 2011, the Court ruled by a 4-3 vote that the expression 'that is of the opposite sex' was unconstitutional, insofar as it violated the principle of equality, the prohibition of discrimination and the principle of human dignity.[35] The Court also added that the contested legislation violated the right to privacy and sexuality, since it made an arbitrary and unreasonable distinction between homosexuals and heterosexuals. The decision of the Supreme Court retroactively overturned the previous judgment on the case, protecting the rights acquired in good faith. This is the first and only ruling in Costa Rica that has been in favour of same-sex couples.

5.4.2.2 Electoral and Constitutional Battle Over the Bill on Same-Sex Civil Unions

Two important bills presented on 27 September 2006 are currently under discussion: the draft law on "civil unions for same-sex couples"[36] and that on same-sex "coexistence partnerships". Even though the bills have polarized public opinion, there is consistent support for the introduction of same-sex civil unions.[37]

Since their submission, these draft laws have met some opposition in the courts. More specifically, on 26 June 2008 a group opposed to same-sex unions requested the *Tribunal Supremo de Elecciones* (or TSE, the Costa Rican electoral authority)

---

[34] Constitutional Chamber of the Supreme Court, Judgment No. 2009-8909.

[35] Constitutional Chamber of the Supreme Court, Case No. 13800-11.

[36] Bill No. 16390 (Official Gazette No. 214, 8 November 2006), examined by the Special Commission for Human Rights.

[37] González Suarez (2009).

permission to collect the signatures required by law to authorize a referendum on the bill on civil unions for same-sex couples. On 1 July of the same year another group made the same request, and the two applications were considered jointly. The TSE eventually authorized the collection of signatures and asked the public whether they agreed or disagreed with the bill.[38] By doing so, it was essentially fulfilling procedural requirements.[39] In the meantime, numerous individuals and organizations with a legitimate interest initiated an *amparo* proceeding, requesting the Supreme Court to review the legality of the proposed referendum. On 10 August 2010, the Supreme Court ruled that said referendum was unconstitutional, on the grounds that allowing a non-gay majority to decide on the rights of a minority group, such as homosexuals, would expose the latter to the risk of discrimination and violate the principle of human dignity.[40] Therefore, the Supreme Court not only annulled the decision of the TSE authorizing the collection of signatures, but also made it clear that the organization of a referendum on this subject, including the collection of signatures, was to be avoided by all means. Indeed, the Court ruled that any entity engaging in such activities would be liable to imprisonment from 3 months to 2 years. Despite this legal battle, the bill on civil unions for same-sex couples has not been stopped. On the other hand, the draft law on coexistence partnership was criticised by the Special Committee for Human Rights in its opinion of 6 June 2012.

Finally, we should mention another action for judicial review. Submitted in 2010, it challenged the refusal to grant social security benefits to same-sex couples. In particular, the claimants alleged that Art. 10 of the Regulation of the *Caja Costarricense de Seguro Social* (CCSS, Costa Rican Social Security Fund) was unconstitutional, on the ground that it breached the principle of equality (under Art. 10 CCSS, only opposite-sex couples can register with the Fund). The Supreme Court rendered its judgment on 2 May 2012, concluding that the refusal to grant same-sex couples the same social security benefits as those enjoyed by heterosexual couples did not breach the principle of equality. This decision continues the trend started with judgment No. 7262-06 of 2006, which excluded same-sex couples from marriage.

5.4.3 El Salvador

The Constitution of El Salvador does not expressly prohibit marriage between people of the same sex. However, its Art. 32 states that:

---

[38] *Supremo Tribunal de Elecciones*, application No. 195-E-2008, decision No. 3401-E9-2008.

[39] Art. 6 of the Costa Rican law on referendums.

[40] Constitutional Chamber of the Supreme Court, application No. 10-008331-0007-CO, decision No. 2010013313.

> The family is the fundamental basis of society and shall be protected by the State, which shall dictate the necessary legislation and create the appropriate organizations and services for its integration and wellbeing, as well as its social, cultural, and economic development. The legal foundation of the family is marriage and rests on the juridical equality of the spouses. The State shall encourage marriage; but the lack thereof shall not affect the enjoyment of the rights established in favour of the family.

And Art. 33 provides that:

> The law shall regulate the personal and patrimonial relations of spouses amongst themselves, and between themselves and their children, establishing the rights and reciprocal duties on an equitable basis; and shall create the necessary institutions to guarantee its applicability. Likewise it shall regulate the family relations resulting from the stable union of a man and a woman.

It should be noted, moreover, that a draft to amend Art. 33 of the Constitution, submitted to the Congress in 2005, proposes to add the expression *así nacidos* (born as such) after "a man and a woman". Besides, according to Art. 11 of the Family Code, marriage is:

> the legal union of a man and a woman, in order to establish a full and permanent life together.

Quite clearly, the above legal provisions categorically exclude the possibility of same-sex marriage. Any discussion of openness to same-sex marriage or civil unions in El Salvador must take this fact into account.

In 2012, the legal *status* of marriage and civil unions between people of the same sex was the subject of a constitutional debate, especially as regards the possibility of treating these unions as being, in certain circumstances, equal to heterosexual marriage and unions. As mentioned above, a proposal to amend the Constitution so as to protect the institution of marriage as understood by the conservative Catholic tradition—that is, as the union of 'a man and a woman born as such'—was presented in 2005. The surrounding debate was, and still is, intensely political.

The conservative proponents of the amendment, which is meant to expressly prohibit same-sex marriage, have already managed to have it discussed and voted once, even though unsuccessfully (based on the number of members of the Congress, at least 56 votes are required). It was first discussed in the legislature for the years 2007–2009. In order to take effect, it required adoption by a majority vote of the next legislature (2009–2012), but eventually it was not approved. However, it can still be considered in 2012–2015 and, if approved, ratified in 2015–2018.

The proposed amendment is also intended to prevent same-sex couples from adopting children and marriages contracted in other states from being recognized in El Salvador. From a constitutional perspective, it goes much further than a ban on same-sex marriage or a restriction on the rights of discriminated minorities. In fact, it is aimed at strengthening the traditional concept of the family as the cornerstone of the state and society.

5.5 South America

5.5.1 Colombia

5.5.1.1 Constitutional Framework and Court Decisions

Colombia has legalised civil unions only for heterosexual couples. According to Art. 113 of the Civil Code, marriage is "a solemn contract whereby a man and a woman unite in order to live together, procreate and help each other". The current legislation is thus quite clear about marriage. In recent years, however, a number of judicial decisions, especially by the Constitutional Court,—have changed the actual situation.

With respect to domestic partnerships, Law No. 54 of 1990 states that:

> for legal purposes, a domestic partnership is a stable union between an unmarried man and an unmarried woman who form a permanent household together. Likewise, for legal purposes, the man and woman who form part of a domestic partnership are defined as permanent companions.[41]

The Constitutional Court reviewed this law in Case No. 098/96, concluding that giving special protection to heterosexual couples did not constitute discrimination against same-sex couples.[42] According the Court, a distinction between heterosexual and homosexual couples was indeed justified, for the following reason:

> Insofar as they represent a form of family, heterosexual domestic partnerships are recognized by the law in order to ensure the "full protection" of the family and, in particular, that "men and women" have equal rights and duties (P.C. arts. 42 and 43), which clearly cannot apply to homosexual couples.[43]

Moreover, the judgment states that, even though the family structure (also in the form of a domestic partnership) does not necessarily include children, it can be reasonably assumed that procreation is one of the traditional purposes of marriage. As a consequence, special protection is further justified by the need to protect the patrimonial rights of children born within heterosexuals unions.

While acknowledging a difference in how same-sex couples were treated, the Court maintained, however, that such difference was not due to the law at issue, which was aimed at preventing the unequal treatment of unmarried opposite-sex

---

[41] The original text reads as follows: "para todos los efectos civiles, se denomina unión marital de hecho, la formada entre un hombre y una mujer, que sin estar casados, hacen una comunidad de vida permanente y singular. Igualmente, y para todos los efectos civiles, se denominan compañero y compañera permanente, al hombre y la mujer que forman parte de la unión marital de hecho."

[42] Constitutional Court, C-098/96, 7 March 1996 (No.14).

[43] The original text reads as follows: "Las uniones maritales de hecho de carácter heterosexual, en cuanto conforman familia son tomadas en cuenta por la ley con el objeto de garantizar su "protección integral" y, en especial, que "la mujer y el hombre" tengan iguales derechos y deberes (C.P. arts. 42 y 43), lo que como objeto necesario de protección no se da en las parejas homosexuales."

couples. In short, according to the Court there was a gap in the law with regard to same-sex couples, which did not per se constitute discrimination. The Court observed, however, that this legislative omission must be remedied in the future in order to ensure that homosexuals are protected.

In 2007, the Court adopted a different position when reviewing the constitutionality of Law No. 54 of 1990 as amended by Law No. 979 of 2005.[44] In its judgment, it declared the unconstitutionality of the law in question, concluding that the protection provided by law to heterosexual couples must apply also to homosexual couples.[45]

As regards the protection of patrimonial rights, same-sex partners can decide to legally share their lives and property, so that if one of the partners dies, the surviving partner is entitled to its part of the shared property. In its judgment No. 811/07, the Constitutional Court ruled that same-sex partners, just like heterosexual couples, are entitled to benefit from social security schemes, including survivor's pensions, provided they have lived together in a stable relationship for at least 2 years.[46] Proof of this permanent relationship must be given in the form of a declaration authenticated by a notary.

In its judgment No. 029/2009, the Constitutional Court reaffirmed the jurisprudential line that the Constitution prohibits all forms of discrimination based on sexual orientation.[47] It also held that there are substantial differences between heterosexual and homosexual couples, which justify a different treatment by the legislature. Therefore, any legislative provision reflecting this distinction is not, in itself, unconstitutional. Even though it did not specify what differences in treatment are non-discriminatory, the Court maintained that the Congress has the responsibility to define the necessary measures to give special protection to minority or marginalized groups, such as same-sex couples.

In sum, according to the Court there are differences in the way the law treats same and opposite sex couples amounts to discrimination, but these differences in treatment are constitutionally permissible if, and only if, they obey the principle of sufficient reason. Therefore, one must examine the specific circumstances of each case in order to determine whether the different treatment provided for by a specific provision is discriminatory (and thus contrary to the Constitution), or whether it complies with the democratic principle of equality.

This approach was a very important step towards the recognition of the civil and political rights of same-sex couples, including nationality, residence permits, property protection, and social security benefits.

---

[44] Constitutional Court, C-075/07, 7 February 2007 (application No. D-6362).

[45] The original text reads as follows: "es contrario a la Constitución que se prevea un régimen legal de protección exclusivamente para las parejas heterosexuales [. . .] en el entendido que el régimen de protección allí previsto también se aplica a las parejas homosexuales."

[46] Constitutional Court, C-811/07, 3 October 2007 (application No. D-6749).

[47] Constitutional Court, C-029/2009, 29 January 2009 (application No. D-7290).

All the legal provisions reviewed by the Court in this decision must henceforth be considered as applying also to same-sex couples, due to the broad interpretation adopted by the Court in order to give these couples equal rights. This change in interpretation means that same-sex couples are granted equal rights as regards the following (1) the real property where a same-sex couple reside can be declared to be the principal "dwelling of the family" and cannot be seized; (2) civil obligation to pay maintenance; (3) legal guardianship; (4) migration rights to acquire Colombian nationality; (5) right to not incriminate the same-sex partner; (6) aggravating circumstances when the victim is the same-sex partner; (7) being included as possible perpetrators of the crimes of embezzlement and squandering of family property, domestic violence and threats to witnesses, when the victim is the same-sex partner; (8) right to justice and reparation for victims of heinous crimes (the definition of 'victim' now includes same-sex couples); (9) right to claim and receive the dead body; (10) right to know the measures taken to search for the missing person; (11) right to family reunification of displaced persons; (12) civil protection measures for victims of heinous crimes; (13) benefits in the retirement and health plans for members of the Armed Forces and National Police; (14) eligibility for government benefits in health and educational programs; (15) eligibility for government benefits for family housing; (16) access to land ownership, also on behalf of both partners; (17) death compensation in case of a traffic accident; (18) being included in conflict-of-interests restrictions for the exercise of public functions and the award of state contracts.[48]

Not only have same-sex couples been granted equal rights as heterosexuals, but several decisions of the Constitutional Court have also established that, like heterosexual spouses, same-sex partners have obligations towards each other, including nourishment, maintenance and other family duties, although these are not fully comparable to the obligations arising from marriage.

In a 2010 judgment concerning economic and survivor's pension rights, the Court specified the extent to which the State grants these rights to same-sex couples.[49] This judgment is particularly important in that it established that, in order to be eligible for survivor's pensions, same-sex partners are not expressly required to produce a notarized statement as proof of the fact that they have lived together for at least 2 years. Moreover, a series of rules of a generally binding nature (*grupo de órdenes con efectos intercomunis*) were applied for the first time in the context of same-sex couples' social rights, thus becoming applicable to all people in the same situation as the claimants in the case. In this way, the Court extended legal protection to same-sex couples and recognised their right to a due process in administrative proceedings. In short, it used the principle of favourable interpretation to ensure the greatest protection for all human beings.

---

[48] *Ibidem.*

[49] Constitutional Court, T-051/10, 2 February 2010 (file No. T-2.292.035, T-2.299.859, T-2.386.935). On this judgement, see also the Chapter by Paladini in this volume, with specific regard to the case *X. v. Colombia,* decided by the UN Human Rights Committee.

In 2011, the Constitutional Court took three important steps forward in the struggle for the rights of same-sex couples.[50] First of all, it ruled that all civil code provisions relating to inheritance laws applicable to heterosexual domestic partners must apply to same-sex unmarried couples.[51] This was based on a wider interpretation of (rather than on any amendments to) those provisions, which means that the Court did not interfere with the work of lawmakers, who enjoy democratic legitimacy. For the first time, however, the Court urged lawmakers to take action and regulate the *status* of same-sex couples.[52] A few days after this judgment, it issued a special statement asking the Congress to pass legislation on the effects of same-sex unions. In another decision, the Court examined Art. 113 of the Civil Code, which restricts marriage to the union of a man and a woman for the purpose of procreation and forming a family.[53] The Court declared that it could not change the definition of marriage used in the Civil Code, but it did not rule on the merits with regard to procreation as a purpose of marriage, or on the expression 'a man and a woman' in special laws.[54] In addition, once again the Court urged the Congress of the Republic to pass legislation on the rights at issue in the decision, so as to make up for the 'lack of protection' for same-sex couples.[55] This time, the Court also established a deadline (20 June 2013) and ruled that if Congress failed to regulate same-sex unions within that deadline, Colombian homosexual couples would be free to have their partnerships formalized by Colombia's courts or notaries, with full legal effects.

According to another important judgment delivered by the Constitutional Court in 2011, denying a surviving same-sex partner social security benefits because of his or her sexual orientation violates many fundamental rights, including the right to equality, the right to the free development of personality and the rights to social security.[56] This judgment paved the way for the decision in case C-336/2008,[57] which established the right of the surviving same-sex partner to receive pension benefits. As for the issue of adoption, case law on this matter dates back to 2001, when the Constitutional Court categorically stated that same-sex couples did not have the right to adopt children.[58] The Court justified its position on the basis that, since there are differences between heterosexual and homosexual couples, the

[50] Constitutional Court, C-577/11, 26 July 2011 (file nos. D-8367 and D-8376); C-283/11, 13 April 2011 (file No. D-8112); T-716/11, 22 September 2011 (file nos. T-3.086.845 and T-3.093.950).

[51] *Ibidem*, C-283/11.

[52] *Ibidem*, C-577/11.

[53] *Ibidem*.

[54] See Art. 2 of Law No. 294 of 1996 (domestic violence) and Art. 2 of Law No. 1361 of 2009 (protection of the family). Both laws implement Art. 42 of the Constitution (protection of the family), which also defines marriage as the union between a man and a woman.

[55] *Supra*, footnote 48, C-577/11.

[56] Constitutional Court, T-860/2011, 15 November 2011(file No. T-3.130.633).

[57] Constitutional Court, C-336/2008, 16 April 2008 (file No. D-6947).

[58] Constitutional Court, C-814/2001, 2 August 2001 (file No. D-3378).

provisions on adoption contained in the Juvenile Code cannot apply to same-sex couples.[59] The Court noted that there was a gap in the law that could be indirectly discriminatory. However, it held that the legislative omission was not unconstitutional on the ground that the law reflects the demands of society, which in 2001 still conceived of the family as monogamous and heterosexual, in accordance with Art. 42 of the Constitution.

5.5.1.2 Legislative Reactions to the Decisions of the Constitutional Court

Recent years have seen the Legislature trying to meet the demands of the Constitutional Court to regulate same-sex marriage and civil unions.

A bill on same-sex civil unions was presented on 3 August 2011 (No. 47/2011). In its Art. 1, it defines 'Civil Union' as "a legal act, made before a notary, whereby two same-sex partners publicly express their free and informed consent to live together as a couple and support each other permanently."[60]

The following bills on same-sex marriage are currently under discussion in Congress: Bill No. 047 of 2012 ("Law on equal marriage"), together with Bill No. 67 of 2012, and laws nos. 101 and 113 of 2012 instituting same-sex marriage and amending the Civil Code and other provisions.

Bill No. 47 ("Law on equal marriage"), which amends Art. 113 of the Civil Code, must be voted four times in order to take effect. In its Art. 1, it states that the purpose of the proposed law is to legalize same-sex marriage and establish its legal effects in accordance with the principles of human dignity, equality and plurality enshrined in the Political Constitution of Colombia.[61]

Initially approved by a Committee of 15 members by a 10-5 vote, it was rejected by the Colombian Senate in April 2013.

5.5.2 *Venezuela*

Same-sex marriage and civil unions are not legal in Venezuela. Art. 77 of the 1999 Constitution only allows marriage and civil unions between a man and a woman, and no alternative interpretation of the law is currently being considered.

[59] See Art. 89 and 90 of Decree No. 2737 of 1989 on the Juvenile Code.

[60] República de Colombia Camara de Representantes (2011).

[61] The original text reads as follows: "La presente ley tiene por objeto reconocer legalmente el matrimonio de las parejas del mismo sexo y determinar sus efectos legales de conformidad con el principio de dignidad humana, igualdad y pluralismo que establece la Constitución Política de Colombia". Congreso de la República de Colombia Senado (2012), available at http://es.scribd.com/doc/111038927/PONENCIA-PRIMER-DEBATE-P-L-47-12.

5.5.3 Ecuador

Like most Latin American Countries, Ecuador has a strong, conservative Catholic tradition. The Third Section of the 2008 Constitution, which concerns the family, is especially noteworthy with regard to same-sex civil unions and marriage. In particular, Art. 37 guarantees the protection of the family, but—unlike the constitutions of other Countries—it does not define 'family' or specify the purpose(s) of its protection or mention the union of a man and a woman. Furthermore, it uses the gender-neutral term 'spouses' when establishing the equality of the members of a couple, thus making it possible to interpret it as referring also to homosexual couples. A reference to gender and procreation, however, is implied in the fact that Art. 37 expressly mentions motherhood. As for civil unions comparable to marriage and allowed by the Constitution, Art. 38 expressly refers only to heterosexual partners.

A number of court cases deserve attention with regard to the recognition of same-sex couples. In June 2010, two women who had formalized their civil union before a notary were refused recognition of their union by a Civil Registry official. After filing a petition for injunction before the competent court, which rejected it, they lodged an appeal before the Provincial Court of Pichincha. The Court authorized registration of their union on the grounds that the State must guarantee the free development of personality, in accordance with its constitutional duty to ensure that all people have equal access to legal protection. This duty also implies that the State must guarantee the right to equality and non-discrimination, including non-discrimination based on sexual orientation.

Unlike civil unions, same-sex marriage is constitutionally banned in Ecuador. However, there is an increasing recognition of the rights of same-sex couples, especially in court decisions. This recognition includes the protection of the economic rights of unmarried couples, regardless of sexual orientation and on the sole condition that the partners have lived together for at least 2 years. Unlike heterosexual couples, however, same-sex partners are not granted adoption rights.

5.5.4 Brazil

Like other Latin American Countries, such as Mexico and Argentina, Brazil has a federal government system that gives individual states considerable legislative autonomy. The issue of same-sex unions and marriages has thus been addressed first at the local level and then at the federal level, mainly through same-sex union litigation and adjudication. The path towards the recognition of homosexual couples' rights has not been an easy one, and legalization has been the result of same-sex couples seeking access to the institutions that regulate domestic cohabitation, such as the *União Estável* (Stable Union). These unions have gradually unleashed an intense debate on the concept of family, especially because there have been cases of polygamous relationships. The idea of family is now broader and includes gay and lesbian couples, who have contributed to the creation of this type of unions and, thus, to the protection of the economic rights of the family.

Brazilian legislation has always has tried to prevent discrimination based on sexual orientation, and this has paved the way for same-sex partnerships and adoption by gay and lesbian couples. In particular, Art. 226 of the 1988 Constitution establishes that the State must give special protection to the family, which is "the foundation of society". Moreover, para. 3 specifies that the "stable union between a man and a woman" is recognized as a family entity, and that "the law shall facilitate the conversion of such entity into marriage". Even though this early characterization of the family has not made it easy to allow same-sex couples to enter into civil unions or marriages, it has not been a significant obstacle to the recognition of their economic rights. Indeed, there are some grounds for considering the concept of family protected by the Brazilian Constitution as broad enough to include same-sex unions.[62]

The rights of homosexuals have been gradually recognized mainly with the support of the courts, which have interpreted existing legislation so as to achieve full equality for same-sex couples. An important step was taken in 1989, when the *Superior Tribunal de Justiça* (STJ, Superior Court of Justice) recognized same-sex unions as *de facto* partnerships (*sociedade de fato*).[63] The Court ruled that the union between two people of the same-sex constituted a *de facto* partnership, which guaranteed equitable division of property only upon evidence of common economic efforts towards the acquisition of that property. From a legal and constitutional point of view, this notion of same-sex civil partnership has remained virtually unchanged over the years.

The legislative debate on gay rights and homosexual unions started in 1995, when a same-sex civil union bill was presented to the Brazilian Congress.[64] Since then, it has focused especially on the protection of property and inheritance rights. An important step was taken in this regard on 10 February 1998, when the STJ ruled that the legislation did not prevent the judiciary from granting access to property rights to same-sex couples. In this way, the STJ set a precedent for lower courts.

In 2008, the Attorney's Office of the state of Rio de Janeiro brought an action before the Brazilian Supreme Court, claiming that same-sex couples in a stable relationship had the right to register their unions with *cartorios* (public notary offices). A similar action was brought in 2009 by the Attorney General's Office. These lawsuits gave the Court the opportunity to rule that same-sex couples who could prove that they were living in a stable union had the same rights as heterosexual couples.

In 2006, two women living together in a long-term relationship were denied registration of their union, first by a notary office in Rio Grande do Sul and then by a

[62] De Oliveira Nusdeo and De Salles (2009), p. 5.

[63] STJ, Special Appeal No. 648.763—RS (2004/0042337-7), 7 December 2006.

[64] Vianna and Carrara (2013), p. 45.

state court of first instance. The case was then referred to the Superior Court of Justice, which delivered its decision on 25 October 2011. The judges found that homosexuals lacked legal protection[65] and that the Civil Code[66] did not expressly ban same-sex marriage. They also noted that, by virtue of the democratic principle, lawmakers had a duty to remedy the lack of protection for homosexuals. Therefore, the Court ruled that all same-sex couples have the right to marry and adopt children. Although it did not legalize same-sex marriage, the ruling recognized that homosexual couples have the same rights as heterosexual married couples. In this way, the Court confirmed its previous case law, according to which the State must protect all families, whether formed by different- or same-sex couples, in accordance with the constitutional principle of pluralism.

In its ruling of 21 June 2011, the Brazilian Superior Court of Justice declared that nothing in the Constitution expressly prohibited the extension of stable unions to same-sex couples,[67] and that a restrictive interpretation of Art. 226(3) would, therefore, violate the principle of equality and non-discrimination. Confirming its position that homosexuals have the same human dignity as heterosexuals, the Court thus ruled that same-sex couples were legally entitled to civil unions.

As for legislation, many Brazilian states recognized same-sex marriage before it was finally legalised at the federal level in May 2013. Alagoas was the first state to pass legislation on the subject in 2011; Bahia, Piauí, Holy Spirit, Sau Paulo, Brasilia, Sergipe, Federal District, Mato Grosso do Sul and other states followed in 2012. In March 2013, the Department for the Administration of Justice of Ceará issued an administrative order requiring notaries to formalize same-sex unions and/or convert them into marriage,[68] while the state of Paranà ruled that homosexual couples could register their unions with the civil authorities without seeking the approval of a court.[69]

With regard to same-sex adoption, it must be noted that, even though several judges have given favourable rulings in this respect, Brazilian laws do not specifically allow homosexuals to adopt children. Art. 39 of Law No. 8069/90, also known as the Statute on Children and Adolescents, provides that two people who are married or in a stable relationship shall have adoption rights.[70] In both cases, under federal laws these rights are still limited to heterosexual couples. As noted in the literature, this means that same-sex adoption depends on whether the marriage or civil union of the couple who wish to adopt has been recognized by the State. Moreover, since there is no official information on the issue, it is very difficult to provide a comprehensive view of all the cases that have been examined by the

[65] STJ, Special Appeal No. 1.183.378—RS (2010/0036663-8), 25 October 2011.

[66] Art. 1514, 1521, 1523, 1535 and 1565 of the 2002 Civil Code.

[67] STJ, Special Appeal No. 827.962—RS (2006/0057725-5), 21 June 2011.

[68] *Corregedoria Geral de Justiça, Provimento* No. 02/2013, 7 March 2013.

[69] *Corregedoria Geral de Justiça, Instrução Normativa* (Normative Instruction) No. 2/2013, 26 March 2013.

[70] De Oliveira Nusdeo and De Salles (2009), p. 8.

courts since 2006. In 2008, for example, a woman who was in a stable same-sex relationship lodged an application for adoption with the Youth Court of Porto Alegre, unaware that in Brazil it was possible to apply for joint adoption. This example shows two things: first, homosexuals wish to be granted adoption rights; second, they are unaware that the existing legislation can be interpreted in such a way as to extend those rights to same-sex couples. Another case dates back to 2010, when the Superior Court of Justice, by unanimous vote, allowed two women in a civil partnership to adopt a child. It is important to note that the First Instance Court of Rio Grande Do Sul had already ruled in favour of homosexual couples, but the Attorney General's Office decided to appeal the decision in order to protect the child's best interests. According to the Superior Court, however, it was necessary to take into account also what the child actually wanted.

On 18 December 2012, the Supreme Court decided on another case concerning a same-sex couple wishing to adopt.[71] The Court authorized the adoption on the following grounds: the recognition of full citizenship to homosexuals; the absence of prejudice against them; the clear need to extend adoption rights; the child's best interests; and the irrelevance of sexual orientation for determining the quality of parenting.

Although courts all over the country already permitted same-sex marriage, some still refused to recognize it. For this reason, in May 2013 the *Conselho Nacional de Justiça* (CNJ, National Justice Council), according to its competences and based on previous case law, issued a ruling ordering all civil authorities to perform same-sex marriages and, if so requested by a couple, to convert civil union into marriages.[72] In addition, if a judge or other authority refuses to recognize same-sex marriage, the refusal must be immediately reported to a special judge, who will take all appropriate measures. With this ruling, Brazil became the third country in Latin America to legalize same-sex marriage at the federal level.

A number of bills against discrimination based on sexual orientation are still under discussion in the Brazilian Congress,[73] namely: Bill No. 1151 of 1995, which aims to introduce special contracts for same-sex marriages; Bill No. 2.285/07, on the status of the family; and, finally, Bill No. 67 of 1999, which is intended to amend the constitutional provisions on non-discrimination[74] by adding an explicit reference to sexual orientation.

[71] STJ, Special appela No. 1.281.093—SP (2011/0201685-2), 18 December 2012.

[72] CNJ, Decision No. 174, 14 May 2013.

[73] De Oliveira Nusdeo and De Salles (2009), p. 7.

[74] Art. 3(IV) and art. 7(XXX).

5.5.5 *Chile*

Art. 102 of the Chilean Civil Code defines marriage as a contract between a man and a woman, thus implicitly excluding same-sex marriage. Several bills on gay marriage and *de facto* unions were introduced on the initiative of activists fighting for the rights of discriminated minorities and for the protection of sexual and reproductive rights. The bills failed to pass due to the opposition of conservatives, who are a majority group in Chile. Moreover, the proposed laws were criticised in a number of studies as potentially violating children's rights and other legal and constitutional principles.[75] The hostility of Chilean society is reflected also in the conservative, reactionary approach of the courts to this issue.

5.5.5.1 The Constitutional Court Rejects Same-Sex Marriage

In 2010, three same-sex couples applied to the Constitutional Court for judicial review, following the decision of the Civil Registry of Santiago de Chile, which had refused to recognize the marriage of two of the couples and to grant the other couple permission to marry.[76] The first two couples had contracted marriage abroad, respectively in Argentina, which legalized same-sex marriage in 2009, and Canada, which legalized it in 2005. The Civil Registry rejected their applications on the grounds that Art. 102 of the Civil Code clearly states that marriage is a solemn contract between a man and a woman. In addition, officials are required to verify that marriages performed abroad are not contrary to Chilean legislation: in order to be valid on the national territory, they must be contracted by a man and a woman (Art. 80 of the Civil Marriage Act).

The main issue to be decided by the Constitutional Court was whether the civil regulation of marriage was contrary to Art. 19(2) of the Constitution, which guarantees the right to equality. However, without addressing the issue, the Court decided (by a 9-1 vote) that Art. 102 of the Civil Code (which defines marriage as a solemn contract between a man and a woman) was not unconstitutional. The ruling of the Court has thus left unresolved a question that will certainly be raised again in the near future. All the same, it made very important points on gay marriage. For example, the only judge who voted against the decision, Vodanovic, maintained that refusing homosexuals access to marriage means denying them human dignity and, therefore, violating a principle enshrined in the Constitution.

Even though the Court did not rule on whether the civil regulation of marriage violated the right to equality enshrined in the Constitution, some observations made by the judges touched on the merits of the case: the argument that it is up to the legislator (rather than the constituent legislator or the Constitutional Court) to

[75] Cf. Universidad Austral (2010), available at http://www.thefamilywatch.org/doc/doc-0142-es.pdf.

[76] Constitutional Court, No. 1881/2010, Judgment of 3 November 2011.

regulate same-sex marriage, and that allowing gay marriage would be contrary to the Constitution. Quite clearly, this position leaves the debate open as to the constitutionality of same-sex marriage.

5.5.5.2 Bills on Same-Sex Couples

A significant step could be taken towards the recognition of same-sex relationships if the bills already submitted to the Congress were approved.

A bill on non-discrimination and same-sex unions was presented to the House of Representatives on 10 July 2003 and filed on 4 August 2009. Another draft law on civil partnership agreements and their patrimonial consequences (*Contrato de Unión civil y sus consecuencias patrimoniales*) has been pending since 19 December 2007, going through several stages. In 2008, yet another bill was introduced to regulate the rights of same-sex couples and the patrimonial consequences of civil unions, while a draft law on 'civil union pacts' presented in 2009 is currently under discussion. A bill on 'Life Partnership Agreements', which would regulate and protect the relationships between unmarried same-sex partners, was introduced in 2010. The proposed law confirms the duty of the State to protect the family, recognizing the variety of family structures in present-day Chilean society, including same-sex couples in a *de facto* relationship (more than 15 % of people over 18 years of age).[77]

5.5.5.3 Lack of Protection at the National Level: The *Atala Riffo* Case

In this important case the claimant was a Chilean judge, Ms. Karen Atala Riffo. In 2002, she and her husband decided to end their marriage through a de facto separation, and established by mutual consent that Ms Atala would maintain the care and custody of their three daughters. However, when Ms Atala's new partner, a woman, began living with her and the three girls, her ex-husband claimed custody alleging that her sexual orientation and her co-habitation with a partner of the same sex would cause harm to their daughters.

On 14 January 2003, the father of the three girls filed a custody suit with the Juvenile Court of Villarrica, which granted him provisional custody of the girls on 2 May 2003, regulating also the mother's visits. The decision was based on Ms Atala's sexual orientation and its possible consequences on her daughters. Maintaining that cohabitation with the mother and her partner was contrary to the best interests of the girls, the Juvenile Court then granted permanent custody to the father. In the final decision on the merits of 29 October 2003, however, the Judge concluded that the respondent's sexual orientation was not an impediment to carrying out responsible motherhood, that homosexuality is not a manifestation of

---

[77] Lecaros (2012).

a pathological conduct, and that no concrete evidence had shown that the presence of the mother's partner in the home was harmful to the physical and psychological wellbeing of the girls. Custody was thus granted to the mother, and the Juvenile Court ordered that the girls be handed over to their mother. However, the girls' father had already appealed to a higher court, requesting that the case be reviewed on the merits. After granting temporary custody to the father on 24 November 2003, the Court of Appeals of Temuco confirmed the conclusions of the Juvenile Court and granted permanent custody to the mother.

On 5 April 2004, the girls' father filed a remedy of complaint (*recurso de queja*) with the Supreme Court against the Court of Appeals of Temuco. He also requested that the girls remain in his care on a provisional basis, and the Supreme Court granted his request. On 31 May 2004, the Supreme Court rendered its final judgment, deciding on whether denying Ms Atala custody of her daughters because of her stable relationship with another woman amounted to sexual orientation discrimination. In a split 3-2 decision, the Court granted permanent custody to the father.[78]

In 2012 the Inter-American Court of Human Rights, based in Costa Rica, ruled that the State of Chile had violated the American Convention on Human Rights.[79]

5.5.6 Uruguay

Same-sex marriage is not legal in Uruguay, but homosexual couples can enter into civil unions that grant similar property rights. Uruguay is thus the first Latin American country to have legalised same-sex civil unions at the national level.

Due to the lack of specific legislation, a fierce legal battle has been fought in the courts for the recognition of same-sex marriages. On 5 June 2012, the Family Court of Montevideo delivered the first important judgment on the matter (No. 1940/2012). A Uruguayan and a Spanish national who had contracted marriage in Spain in 2010[80] sought a declaratory relief concerning the recognition of their marriage in Uruguay. Due to the lack of legislation at the national level, the Court granted the declaratory judgment pursuant to Art. 11(3) of the General Code of Procedure.[81]

From the point of view of private international law, the Court agreed to the preliminary recognition of a juridical relationship validly established in a foreign State. In that sense, the Court declared that the marriage was valid in Uruguay for all purposes of law, in accordance with Arts. 2 and 7 of the Inter-American Convention on General Rules of Private International Law.[82] This reasoning was

[78] *Supra*, footnote 69.

[79] See the Chapter by Magi in this volume.

[80] Spain legalised same-sex marriage in 2005.

[81] XXVIII Family Court, Montevideo, Decision No. 1940/2012, 5 June 2012.

[82] Held in Montevideo, 8 May 1979.

based also on the right to a due process—in its broadest sense, i.e. including access to justice and effective judicial protection—guaranteed by the American Convention on Human Rights (Art. 8), to which Uruguay has been a party since 1985.

In assessing the validity of the marriage legally contracted abroad, the Court of Montevideo applied national civil laws (there is no *ad hoc* international treaty between Uruguay and Spain). In particular, the Court referred to Art. 2395 of the Civil Code of Uruguay, which provides that the law of the State of celebration governs the legal capacity to marry as well as the formal validity of the marriage. Therefore, it applied both international human rights law and domestic law.

The Court also rejected the argument of the Prosecution that the public policy exception in private international law applied. Indeed, it maintained that the recognition of the marriage contracted in Spain was not in breach of constitutional principles, noting also that the principle of heterosexuality in marriage could no longer be considered a principle of Uruguayan international public policy after the entry into force of Law No. 18.246 (2008) on civil unions and Law No. 18.620 (2009) on gender identity. In the eyes of the Court, and according to legal theory, the concept of international public policy should be restrictive to ensure implementation of and compliance with international law. More specifically, the Court stated same-sex marriage is possible, even though not explicitly allowed, under Uruguayan law, in particular Law No. 18.620 on gender identity (which allows the biological sex of a person to be different from the gender identity as recorded on official documents).

For the above reasons, the Court of Montevideo declared the same-sex marriage contracted in Spain to be valid in Uruguay for all purposes of law. Thus, for the first time in history, a Uruguayan court recognized marriage between two people of the same sex. This judgment extended the possibility for same-sex couples to have their marriages recognized under existing national laws and, at the same time, emphasized the need for specific legislation on the subject.

Court decisions have indeed spurred legislative action. For example, a bill on "equal marriage" has been introduced on the initiative of the Ministry of Education and Culture, in addition to a similar project already in Congress. This bill, which would allow same-sex couples to register their unions as marriages, has been intensely debated. On 26 December 2012, it was passed by the Chamber of Deputies with 81 votes. On 20 March 2013, it was approved by a special Committee of the Senate (Constitution and laws) and then, on 2 April 2013, fully approved by a 23-8 vote. After Argentina, Uruguay is the second country in Latin America to pass a national law on same-sex marriage.

5.5.7 *Argentina*

5.5.7.1 General Overview

In Argentina, as in most Latin American Countries, the Constitution provides special protection to the family. Art. 14*bis* of the 1994 Constitution mentions the "full protection of the family" and the "protection of the homestead". However, it does not provide a definition of 'family' or expressly exclude same-sex couples. As a result, the issue of whether the rights arising from same-sex civil unions are comparable to those arising from marriage has been debated at the level of laws and judicial decisions.

The first step towards the legal recognition of the rights of same-sex couples dates back to 12 December 2002, when the law on civil unions (Law No. 1004) was passed in Buenos Aires. Under this law, couples of any sexual orientation who have lived together for 2 or more years in Buenos Aires have rights and duties comparable to those of husbands and wives. However, civil partners are not granted adoption rights and certain inheritance rights. Buenos Aires was the first city in Latin America to legalize same-sex civil unions. Other regions or cities that have followed its example include the Provincia de Rio Negro, Carlos Paz and Rio Cuarto.

5.5.7.2 Court Decisions

As in many other Countries, in Argentina the battle for same-sex marriage has been fought in the courts. In this respect, the most interesting decisions have been taken by lower courts, due to the type of judicial review available in those courts. The process leading to the recognition of the right to marry for same-sex couples is reflected in the many cases brought before the national and provincial courts. On 14 February 2007, for instance, two women tried to register their marriage before the Civil Registry. Their application was rejected on the grounds that Art. 172 and 188 of the Civil Code did not allow same-sex marriage, since marriage is permitted only between a man and a woman. The applicants thus initiated *amparo* proceedings (claim for protection of fundamental rights) claiming that their fundamental rights under the 1994 Constitution, in particular the right to equality, had been violated.

5.5.7.3 Court Decisions in Buenos Aires: Constitutional Principles Supporting Same-Sex Marriage

On 10 November 2009, the Administrative Court of the City of Buenos Aires accepted the *amparo* brought by a same-sex couple wishing to marry. They challenged the constitutionality of Art. 172 and 188 of the Civil Code of Buenos

Aires, according to which marriage is the union between a man and a woman.[83] The judge found that the articles in question were unconstitutional in that they violated the right to equality. In a comparative law perspective, the constitutional grounds for this decision are very interesting.

The Court's reasoning was based on the principle of non-discrimination, and the judge also referred to Art. 11 of the Constitution of the City of Buenos Aires, which includes the prohibition of discrimination based on sexual orientation:

> All persons have equal dignity and are equal before the law. The right to be different is recognized and guaranteed, without any sort of discrimination leading to marginalization based on race, ethnicity, gender, sexual orientation, age, religion, ideology, opinion, nationality, physical characteristics, psychophysical, social, or economic condition, or any other circumstances involving difference, exclusion, restriction or impairment. The City of Buenos Aires promotes the removal of any obstacles to freedom, equality, or the full development of the person and encourages the effective participation in the political, economic and social life of the City.

The Court held that, in this case, there was a change in the burden of proof required to defend the constitutionality of a law that creates differences in treatment according to a suspect category such as sexual orientation. The State must prove that there is sufficient reason for such differences; the evidence must be strong enough to rebut any presumption of unconstitutionality with regard to the law creating said differences in treatment. The judge made some interesting points on the applicable standard of review and its impact on the final decision:

> the standard of review that applies to classifications based on sexual orientation means that these categories should not be directed at creating or perpetuating stigma, scorn or legal inferiority for persons belonging to sexual minorities.[84]

The judge also added that any other classifications based on sexual orientation should be directed only at identifying the negative discrimination historically suffered by homosexuals. On these grounds, the Court authorized the same-sex marriage and declared that Art. 172 and 188 of the Civil Code were unconstitutional. Moreover, it ruled that the marriage could be registered with the Civil Registry.

In response to this ruling, an action for the annulment of the permission to celebrate the marriage was filed with the Civil Court of First Instance.[85] On 30 November 2009, the Civil Court issued its decision, granting a special injunctive relief called *medida cautelar innovativa*, i.e., a temporary suspension. The suspension was based on a strict interpretation of the requirements for marriage, including sexual orientation, which was considered essential by the Court to ensure the validity of the marriage. In the decision, it was also observed that the claimants

---

[83] *Freyre Alejandro v. GCBA* (Art. 14 CCABA), No. 34292, 10 November 2009. See also Cabrales Lucio (2010), pp. 413–414.

[84] *Ibidem*, pp. 413–414.

[85] First Instance Civil Court, Buenos Aires, No. 85, Judgment of 30 November 2009.

intended to use the Court to reform the Civil Code, which is a power resting only with the Congress and political decision-makers.

Finally, although the couple had been granted permission to marry in Buenos Aires, they could not register their marriage there. They had to move to the city of Tierra del Fuego, where it was possible for them to register their marriage. This city thus became the first city in Latin America to register a same-sex marriage of two people of the same-sex. The constitutional and legal grounds used in this case are easily transferable to other cases, as demonstrated by other important rulings concerning on the registration of same-sex marriages with the Civil Registry of Buenos Aires.

5.5.7.4 Legislative Reaction to Judicial Decisions

The court decisions in favour of same-sex marriage led to the introduction of a number of bills to regulate this institution. The first was presented on 30 April 2007, on the initiative of the Argentinian LGBT Federation and two Deputies. In October 2007, the Law on equal marriage went to the Senate, and another bill was submitted on the initiative of the President of the National Institute against Discrimination, Xenophobia and Racism.

In 2010, Argentina became the first country in Latin America to allow same-sex marriage nationwide: the bill on equal marriage was finally approved on 15 July 2010, and Law No. 26618 entered into force on 21 July 2010.

The new law grants same-sex couples the same rights as heterosexual married couples, including adoption rights. Its Art. 2 represents a radical change from the past, as it amends Art. 172 of the Civil Code: that is, the definition of marriage as the union of a man and a woman, which was repeatedly criticised in court decisions. A very problematic issue has thus been resolved, and same-sex couples are no longer excluded from marriage.

References

Anderson-Minshall D (2012) Same-sex marriages legal in Cancun. http://www.advocate.com/news/daily-news/2012/01/01/same-sex-marriages-legal-cancun

Ávalos A (2012) Sala IV estudia acción para legalizar unión de hecho entre personas del mismo sexo. Diario Nación. http://wvw.nacion.com/ln_ee/2009/marzo/24/pais1916544.html

Bustillos J (2011) Derechos humanos y protección constitucional. Breve estudio sobre el matrimonio entre personas del mismo sexo en México en perspectiva comparada. Boletín Mexicano de Derecho Comparado 132:1017–1045

Cabrales Lucio JM (2010) Argentina – Judges contest same sex marriage, Freyre Alejandro contra GCBA sobre amparo (art.14 CCABA), Administrative Court, Buenos Aires, exp 34292/0. Public Law (April):413–414

De Oliveira Nusdeo AM, De Salles CA (2009) Adopción por Homosexuales: El Discurso Jurídico. http://www.law.yale.edu/documents/pdf/Student_Organizations/SELA09_NusdeoSalles_Sp_PV.pdf

República de Colombia Camara de Representantes (2011) Proyecto de Ley Por medio de la cual se regula la Unión Civil entre parejas del mismo sexo y se dictan otras disposiciones

González Suarez M (2009) Proyecto de Ley de Unión Civil entre personas del mismo sexo. Posiciones a favor y en contra. Rev Electrón Estud Escuela Psicología Univ Costa Rica 4(1):11–30, http://dialnet.unirioja.es/servlet/articulo?codigo=3921916

Lecaros M (2012) Efectos de las uniones civiles: un análisis comparado. http://diarioconstitucional.cl/mostrararticulo.php?id=65

Rafael De La Madrid R (2012) Reporte sobre la discriminación en México 2012 proceso civil. http://www.conapred.org.mx/userfiles/files/Reporte_2012_ProcesoCivil.pdf

Rodríguez M, Mariano B, Rea Tizcareño C, Gil Hernández F, Pezoa P, Cisneros R (2010) América Latina. Ecos del matrimonio igualitario. http://www.pidhdd.org/v3/index.php?option=com_content&view=Article&id=1955:amica-latina-ecos-del-matrimonio-igualitario-&catid=1:noticias&Itemid=62

Universidad Austral (2010) Informe de estudios científicos y jurídicos Matrimonio homosexual y adopción por parejas del mismo sexo. http://www.thefamilywatch.org/doc/doc-0142-es.pdf

Vianna A, Carrara S (2013) Sexual politics and sexual rights in Brazil: a case study. In: Parker R, Petchesky R, Sember R (eds) Sexpolitics – reports from the front lines. http://www.sxpolitics.org/frontlines/book/pdf/capitulo1_brazil.pdf

Waaldijk K (2011) Same-sex partnership, international protection. In: Max Planck Encyclopedia of Public International Law. www.mpepil.com

Chapter 6
Following the Legislative Leaders: Judicial Recognition of Same Sex Couples in Australia and New Zealand

Olivia Rundle

Abstract The rights of same-sex couples in Australia and New Zealand have been progressed significantly, primarily through legislative action. The New Zealand Parliament recently legislated for same-sex marriage. Despite attempts, same-sex marriage has not been achieved in Australia, although at the time of writing there were bills before Parliaments that, if passed, would enable same-sex marriage at either the State/Territory or Federal level. This chapter describes the legal order and legislative regimes in each country. It explains the contributions of the judiciary to law reform, judicial reflection of societal attitudes and the way that judges have applied laws to same-sex couples. The judiciary have generally embraced the legislature's lead towards equality enthusiastically, although some examples of homophobia and homo-ignorance are evident. Judges have been less able or prepared to promote same-sex couples' rights where the legislature has not taken the lead.

6.1 Introduction

Australia and New Zealand have some of the most progressive and egalitarian laws regarding the recognition of non-married same-sex couple relationships. The judiciary have, for the most part, embraced legislative reforms enthusiastically through their application and interpretation of laws to same-sex couples.

The willingness of the legislature and judiciary to recognise same-sex *de facto* relationships and to treat them equally to heterosexual *de facto* relationships can be

On 22nd October 2013, as this book went to print, the Australian Capital Territory passed the *Marriage Equality Amendment Bill*. The Commonwealth Attorney-General immediately announced an intention to challenge the ACT law on constitutional grounds in the High Court of Australia. This highlights the difficulties arising from Australia's federal system and uncertainty about where power lies to legislate for same sex marriage. A High Court determination will resolve the uncertainty.

O. Rundle (✉)
Faculty of Law, University of Tasmania, Hobart, TAS, Australia
e-mail: Olivia.Rundle@utas.edu.au

D. Gallo et al. (eds.), *Same-Sex Couples before National, Supranational and International Jurisdictions*, DOI 10.1007/978-3-642-35434-2_6,

contrasted with their unwillingness to grant same-sex couples the opportunity to legally marry (to date).

The legal framework and culture in both countries means that the legislature rather than the judiciary must be the initial driver of law reform towards marriage equality. The New Zealand Parliament enacted legislation on 17th April 2013 that enables same-sex couples to marry. The Australian Parliament has yet to legislate for same-sex marriage. This remains a significant and symbolic barrier to equality for same-sex couples in Australia. Judicial consideration may follow legislative action, particularly in Australia, where the constitutional issues raised by same-sex marriage have yet to be tested in the High Court.

6.2 Australia

In Australia the legal rights of married and non-married couples as well as heterosexual and same-sex couples are largely equal. The residual differences are: first, non-married couples may need to prove the existence of their relationship in order to access rights and secondly, same-sex couples are excluded from the opportunity to be married. Therefore, same-sex couples may experience more difficulty accessing their legal rights than heterosexual married couples.

The role played by the judiciary in regard to same-sex couples in Australia has been partly shaped by the absence of a constitutional or legislative Bill of Rights at the National level. Reform in Australia has been led primarily by political lobbying and legislative action rather than judicial decisions.[1] Some legislative action has been a response to litigation and has had the effect of taking questions away from the judiciary. Nonetheless, the judiciary has played an important role in its interaction with same-sex couples through applying the law and comments made by judges about same-sex family relationships. Sometimes judicial officers have highlighted problems in the law explicitly, other times their decision making has generated publicity about inadequacies in the law. This has provided material for those advocating for reform. Judges have also reflected or highlighted societal prejudices. Of particular significance are decisions about the legal recognition of same-sex *de facto* relationships. Another important site of interaction between judges and same-sex couples is the interpretation and application of laws relating to legal parentage of children born into same-sex parented families through assisted reproductive technologies.

6.2.1 Background: The Australian Legal Order

Australia is a Federation of States (known as the Commonwealth of Australia). Eight legislative systems operate simultaneously. There are five Australian States

---

[1] Sifris (2010).

(New South Wales, South Australia, Tasmania, Victoria and Western Australia) and two mainland Territories (Australian Capital Territory and the Northern Territory). The Australian Constitution is the "supreme law" governing the Commonwealth and can only be changed by an absolute majority in both Houses of the Bicameral Federal Parliament and a *referendum* of a majority of Australian voters, with a majority in a majority of States.[2] The Commonwealth's powers are sourced from either the Australian Constitution or by referral of power from the States. The Constitution gives the Commonwealth power to make laws concerning "marriage"[3] and "matrimonial causes" including divorce, property adjustments, parental rights and custody of children of married couples.[4] These powers are held concurrently by the States.[5] A State or Territory law that is inconsistent with a Commonwealth law is invalid to the extent of the inconsistency.[6] The States (except Western Australia) have referred power to the Commonwealth over children's family matters for children born outside marriage[7] and in respect of *de facto* property and financial matters.[8] Some residual children's matters remain exclusively in the State and Territory jurisdictions, including adoption,[9] assisted reproduction (including surrogacy)[10] and registration of births, deaths and marriages.[11]

Australia is a common law jurisdiction. The most superior court is the High Court, which hears constitutional matters and appeals from the lower tier. Below the High Court there are the Federal Courts and State and Territory Courts. The Federal Courts include the Federal Court and Family Court, which have appeal divisions, and below them sits the Federal Circuit Court.[12] The Supreme Courts are the superior State and Territory courts, with some States having a middle tier of District Courts and all having Local or Magistrates Courts at the lower level. The State of Western Australia has its own Family Court, which exercises the

[2] The Constitution 1901, Chapter VIII.

[3] *Ibidem*, sect. 51(xxi).

[4] *Ibidem*, sect. 51 (xxii).

[5] *Ibidem*, sections 51 and 107.

[6] *Ibidem*, s. 109.

[7] Commonwealth Powers (Family Law) Acts 1986 (SA); 1987 (Tas); Commonwealth Powers (Family Law—Children) Acts 1986 (NSW); 1986 (Vic); 1990 (Qld).

[8] Commonwealth Powers (De facto Relationships) Acts 2003 (NSW); 2003 (Qld); 2004 (Vic); 2006 (Tas); 2009 (SA).

[9] Adoption Acts 1984 (Vic); 1988 (Tas); 1988 (SA); 1993 (ACT); 1994 (WA); 2000 (NSW); 2009 (Qld); Adoption of Children Act (NT).

[10] Status of Children Acts 1974 (Tas); 1974 (Vic); 1978 (Qld); 1996 (NSW); (NT); Family Relationships Act 1975 (SA); Artificial Conception Act 1985 (WA); Parentage Act 2004 (ACT). The Family Law Act 1975 clarifies the legal recognition of parentage of children born through assisted reproduction for the purposes of Commonwealth law.

[11] Registration of Births, Deaths and Marriages Act 1997 (ACT); Births, Deaths and Marriages Registration Acts 1995 (NSW); (NT); 1996 (SA); 1996 (Vic); 1998 (WA); 1999 (Tas); 2003 (Qld).

[12] Formerly the Federal Magistrates Court, name changed by Federal Circuit Court of Australia Legislation Amendment Act 2012.

jurisdiction of the Family Law Act as well as State jurisdiction. It is for this reason that Western Australia has not referred powers over children's and *de facto* property matters to the Commonwealth, as it already hears those matters in its own Family Court. Various tribunals exist at the State, Territory and Federal level.

There is no constitutional or legislative Bill of Rights at the Commonwealth level in Australia.[13] Consequently, a law that breaches human rights in Australia may nonetheless be valid law. It is not possible to challenge Australia's discriminatory marriage laws through the courts, as has occurred elsewhere, because the courts lack power to strike down legislation solely on the ground that it is discriminatory.[14] Nonetheless, in Australia there is a

> strong political tradition of support for principles of equality and non-discrimination, and these values have been articulated through numerous State, Territorial and some Federal statutes.[15]

Although there is no prohibition against discrimination on the basis of sexual orientation at the Federal level,[16] it is a recognised ground of discrimination in the States and Territories.[17]

There has been successful challenge to laws that breach Commonwealth laws prohibiting discrimination on the basis of marital *status*. *McBain*[18] involved a challenge to Victorian legislation preventing single women or women in a *de facto* relationship from accessing Assisted Reproductive Technology (ART) services. The High Court found this to be discriminatory under Commonwealth anti-discrimination law, thereby rendering the Victorian law invalid to the extent of its inconsistency with Commonwealth law.[19] The Commonwealth's response was to introduce a bill to enable discrimination on grounds of marital *status* in the context of access to ART.[20] The bill was abandoned after the Senate Legal and Constitutional Legislation Committee "highlighted how such an enactment would breach Australia's obligations under international treaties."[21] States that regulate ART in legislation have enabled women in lesbian relationships to access ART services.[22]

The Australian Capital Territory (ACT) and Victoria have both enacted a legislative Charter of Rights to guide the work of Parliament and the courts in those jurisdictions.[23] There is at least one example of a lost opportunity to highlight

---

[13] Walker (2007) noted that this is unusual for a Western democratic country.

[14] *Ibidem*, p. 122.

[15] McNamara (2007), p. 143.

[16] Discussed in Human Rights and Equal Opportunity Commission (2011). See the Exposure Draft Human Rights and Anti-Discrimination Bill 2012, in the consultation stage at the time of writing.

[17] McNamara (2007), p. 143.

[18] *Re McBain; Ex Parte Australian Bishops Conference* (2002) 209 CLR 372 ("*McBain*").

[19] *McBain*; Sifris (2010), p. 17.

[20] Sex Discrimination Amendment Bill (No 1) 2000 (Cth).

[21] Young et al. (2013), para. 7.24.

[22] *Ibidem*, para. 7.25.

[23] Human Rights Act 2004 (ACT); Charter of Human Rights and Responsibilities Act 2006 (Vic).

discrimination against same-sex couples through the use of a Charter of Rights in judicial decision-making. Sifris and Gerber have commented on the *AB* case,[24] a County Court of Victoria decision interpreting sect. 11(3) of the Adoption Act 1984, which empowers a court to make an adoption order in favour of "one person" but not in favour of a non-married couple.[25] The applicant was a man in a long term relationship with another man (the couple were married in Canada, a marriage not recognised in Australia) who wanted to adopt their 11 year old foster child.[26] One of the men applied to adopt the child as an individual, as they were not eligible to adopt as a couple because under Australian law they were not legally married. The question before the court was whether a person in a couple relationship was eligible to adopt as an individual. Pullen J concluded that Parliament had not expressly excluded people in same-sex relationships from adopting as individuals, therefore there was no basis for a narrow interpretation of the relevant provision and the adoption application was granted.[27] Sifris and Gerber have criticised Pullen J for failing to use the Victorian Charter of Human Rights and Responsibilities[28] or to take the opportunity to "comment on whether precluding same-sex couples from adopting purely on the basis of their sexual orientation amounted to discrimination."[29] The Charter could be have been used to challenge discriminatory legislation.[30]

McBain and the *AB* cases demonstrate that anti-discrimination laws have been able to be used in the courts to progress the rights of same-sex couples, notwithstanding the absence and then under-utilisation of the Victorian Charter of Rights.

6.2.2 Same-Sex Marriage

Marriage remains a site for differential treatment of opposite and same-sex couples. Marriages entered into by people of the same-sex in other countries are not recognised as marriages in Australia.[31] Prior to 2004, these marriages could potentially have been legally valid in Australia[32]; however, in 2004 the Commonwealth

[24] As the judgment was not reported, Sifris and Gerber's report and analysis has been relied upon.

[25] Sifris and Gerber (2011b) regarding *AB and Victorian Equal Opportunity & Human Rights Commission and Department of Human Services and Separate Representatives of J* Unreported, County Court of Victoria, Case No AD-10-003, Pullen J, 6 August 2010 ("the *AB* case").

[26] Sifris and Gerber (2011b), pp. 275–276.

[27] *Ibidem*, pp. 278–280, referring to the *AB* case, paras 59–60.

[28] Charter of Human Rights and Responsibilities Act 2006 (Vic).

[29] Sifris and Gerber (2011b), pp. 281–282.

[30] *Ibidem*, p. 115.

[31] Same-sex marriages entered into in some overseas jurisdictions are recognised as significant relationships under the Relationships Act 2003 (Tas).

[32] Although some commentators argue that this was unlikely. See for example McNamara (2007), p. 151.

enacted amendments to the Marriage Act that clarified the definition of marriage to be between a man and a woman, thus explicitly preventing same-sex marriages from being recognised in Australia.[33] This legislative action was partly in response to an application to the Family Court of Australia by two same-sex couples who had married in Canada and who wanted their marriage to be legally recognised in Australia.[34] As a consequence of the legislative amendment, the case was discontinued and the Family Court did not make a determination on this point. McNamara has wondered whether the absence of a "suprapolitical human rights standard for guiding and scrutinising the policy formulation process and reform agenda" created the environment in which the 2004 amendments could be made and the prohibition of same-sex marriage continued.[35] He also suggested that the Government's legislative action characterised the judicial role as one carrying dangers and unknown qualities that needed to be controlled.[36] This reflects Australian legal culture that privileges the law making role of the legislature over that of the courts.

If a law for same-sex marriage was enacted by the Federal, a State or Territory Parliament, the validity of that law could possibly be challenged in the High Court on constitutional grounds. There is no certainty that such a challenge would be made or would be successful. It is widely acknowledged that any laws, State or Commonwealth, that propose to legalise same-sex marriages create multiple challenging and unresolved constitutional questions.[37] Essentially, these constitutional questions emerge because of the Australian Federation of States. Because no Australian legislature has exercised the marriage power in respect of same-sex couples in Australia, and the Australian High Court has not been asked to interpret the power in that context, these legal questions remain unresolved.[38] Consequently, there is little judicial commentary about the issue of same-sex marriage and same-sex relationship recognition, particularly from the High Court.

There have been multiple bills attempting to legalise same-sex marriage presented to the Federal Parliament, but none have been passed.[39] The 2012 Marriage Equality Amendment Bill went to a vote and was defeated, and another bill was presented to Parliament in February 2013. Same-sex marriage bills have been presented to Parliaments but have not been passed into law in Tasmania, New

---

[33] Marriage Amendment Act 2004 (Cth), inserting the definition in sect. 5(1) of the Marriage Act 1961 (Cth).

[34] Walker (2007), p. 110. McNamara (2007) has suggested that the government's move was an over-reaction, as in the absence of a superior human rights framework the applicants had little chance of success (p. 151).

[35] McNamara (2007), p. 145.

[36] *Ibidem*, p. 152.

[37] See the overviews of these issues in Griffith (2011), pp. 25–31; Walker (2007), pp. 112–119; and Tasmanian Law Reform Institute (2013).

[38] Walker (2007), p. 113.

[39] Marriage Amendment Bill 2012; Marriage Equality Amendment Bills 2013; 2012; 2010; 2009; Marriage (Relationship Equality) Amendment Bills 2008; 2007; Same-Sex Marriages Bill 2006.

South Wales, Victoria, South Australia and Western Australia.[40] The 2012 bills presented in some of these jurisdictions were responses to the defeat of the Commonwealth bills in September 2012. The Tasmanian Same-sex Marriage Bill 2012 was defeated and none of the others had gone to a vote at the time of writing. The ACT government has committed to legislating for marriage equality but so far no bill to this effect has been introduced.[41]

There have been some comments made by Australian High Court judges about the power of the Commonwealth to legislate to recognise same-sex marriage.[42] Most notably, McHugh J in *Re Wakim* speculated

> The level of abstraction for some terms of the Constitution is, however, much harder to identify than that of those set out above. Thus, in 1901 "marriage" was seen as meaning a voluntary union for life between one man and one woman to the exclusion of all others. If that level of abstraction were now accepted, it would deny the parliament of the Commonwealth the power to legislate for same sex marriages, although arguably "marriage" now means, or in the near future may mean, a voluntary union for life between two people to the exclusion of others.[43]

Notwithstanding this comment and its citation by other judges,[44] the Commonwealth Parliament has not adopted a broad interpretation of the marriage power. Rather, it has specifically legislated to clarify that marriage under Federal law must only be between a man and a woman.[45]

6.2.3 Same-Sex Relationship Recognition

6.2.3.1 Non-Married Relationship Registration

Non-married relationship registration options include civil unions, civil partnerships, deed of relationships or registration of personal relationships. Such schemes

---

[40] Same-sex Marriage Bills 2010 (Tas); 2008 (Tas); 2005 (Tas); State Marriage Equality Bill 2012 (NSW); same-sex Marriage Bills 2006 (NSW); 2005 (NSW); Marriage Equality Bills 2012 (Vic); 2012 (WA); 2012 (SA); 2011 (SA); Griffith (2011), pp. 23–25.

[41] Parliamentary agreement for the 8th Legislative Assembly for the Australian Capital Territory 2012, available at act.greens.org.au/sites/greens.org.au/files/2012%20parliamentary%20Agreement.pdf (accessed 8 February 2013), Schedule 1 clause 8.3.

[42] Walker (2007), p. 113 identified comments about the meaning of marriage by Brennan J in *The Queen v. L* (1991) 174 CLR 379, p. 392 and Higgins J in *Attorney-General for New South Wales v. Brewery Employees Union of New South Wales* (1908) 6 CLR 469, 610. The Full Court of the Family Court in *Kevin and Jennifer* (2003) 30 Fam LR 1, p. 22-4 discussed High Court judicial comments on the meaning of marriage. See discussion in Nicholson (2005).

[43] *Re Wakim* (1999) 198 CLR 511, para. 45.

[44] Kirby J in *Grain Pool of WA v. Commonwealth* (2000) 202 CLR 479, para. 127, noting that the House of Lords cited McHugh J in *Fitzpatrick v. Sterling Housing Association Ltd* [1999] 3 WLR 1113.

[45] Marriage Amendment Act 2004 (Cth).

are separate and distinct from marriage.[46] These options provide couples who are excluded from marriage or who choose not to marry with a way of attracting certain legal recognition of the existence of their relationship as well as symbolic state recognition that their relationship is valued by the community.[47] There is no non-married relationship registration option at the Commonwealth level in Australia. There are schemes in Tasmania, Victoria, the Australian Capital Territory, New South Wales and Queensland.[48] All of these schemes are open to both opposite sex and same-sex couples.

6.2.3.2 *De Facto* Recognition of Same-Sex Couples

Australia has a long tradition of recognising "marriage like" relationships[49] and there has been progressive change to equalise the legal position of married and non-married couples.[50] Recognition was first extended to heterosexual non-married couples.[51] Same-sex couples now have recognition of their relationship *status* equivalent to non-married heterosexual couples in most contexts, including at Commonwealth and State/Territory level.[52] The most recent changes at the Commonwealth level in 2008 extended the jurisdiction of the Family Law Act to financial matters after the separation of *de facto* couples (defined to include both heterosexual and same-sex couples). These reforms "built upon 20 years of State based case law interpreting *de facto* relationships."[53] It was through these reforms that same-sex couples obtained access to redress in the Federal family courts upon the breakdown of their relationship (previously restricted to couples who had been married). Additionally, the 2008 Federal reforms provided for recognition of same-sex couple relationships for purposes such as pensions, superannuation, taxation

---

[46] Rundle (2011).

[47] *Ibidem.*

[48] Relationships Acts 2003 (Tas); 2008 (Vic); Civil Unions Act 2012 (ACT) (superseded the Civil Partnerships Act 2009 (ACT)); Relationships Register Act 2010 (NSW); Relationships Act 2011 (Qld) (renamed by the Civil Partnerships and Other Legislation Amendment Bill 2012).

[49] Walker (2007), p. 110.

[50] Graycar and Millbank (2007).

[51] See for example: Property (Relationships) Act 1984 (NSW); Property Law Act 1974 (Qld); Family Relationships Act 1975 (SA) (limited recognition); De facto Relationships Act 1996 (SA); Family Court Act 1997 (WA); De facto Relationships Act 1999 (Tas) (no longer in force); Relationships Act 2003 (Tas); Domestic Relationships Act 1994 (ACT); De facto Relationships Act 1991 (NT) (cited by Walker (2007), at note 12).

[52] Examples of amending legislation include: Property (Relationships) Legislation Amendment Act 1999 (NSW); Statute Law Amendment (Relationships) Act 2001 (Vic); Discrimination Law Amendment Act 2002 (Qld); Statutes Amendment (Domestic Partners) Act 2006 (SA); Relationships Act 2003 (Tas); Acts Amendment (Lesbian and Gay Law Reform) Act 2002 (WA) (cited by Sifris and Gerber 2011a, p. 96).

[53] Family Law Amendment (*De facto* Financial Matters and Other Measures) Act 2008 (Cth), which came into effect on 1 March 2009; Millbank (2009), p. 193.

and social security.[54] The reforms responded in part to the Australian Human Rights and Equal Opportunity Commission's 2007 Report, which followed the UN Human Rights Committee's view in *Young v Australia* and identified 58 Commonwealth laws that discriminated against same-sex couples.[55]

There are some residual distinctions in State and Territory laws between married and non-married couples (which also means that there are distinctions between heterosexual and same-sex couples), but the general move has been towards parity rather than differential treatment.[56] In Australia, once a relationship is found to fall within the legally recognised category, the rights and responsibilities of married couples are automatically applied to that relationship. For some purposes it may be necessary to establish that the relationship was of a particular duration as well as the fact that the relationship satisfies the relevant definition.[57] There is therefore a policy presumption that people in intimate personal relationships require legal protection and ought to enjoy the same benefits as married couples. This approach has been preferred over granting same-sex couples an option to marry.

In all jurisdictions in Australia, the existence of a legally recognised non-married (but "marriage like") relationship is dependent upon whether the parties have a relationship "as a couple".[58] The various pieces of legislation contain similar non-exclusive lists of indicators which may be taken into account in determining this question of fact,[59] none of which are necessary to find that a recognised relationship exists.[60] The legislative indicators evolved from State case-law that considered the existence of *de facto* relationships,[61] which essentially reversed the

[54] Same-Sex Relationships (Equal Treatment in Commonwealth Laws—General Law Reform) Act 2008; Same-Sex Relationships (Equal Treatment in Commonwealth Laws—Superannuation) Act 2008.

[55] See the discussion of *Young v Australia* HRC Communication No 941/2000 and the Australian response in the Chapter by Paladini in this volume.

[56] A notable exception to the trend towards equality is the Queensland government's current proposal to deny access to surrogacy by same-sex couples. See Australian Broadcasting Commission (2012), available at http://www.abc.net.au/news/2012-06-22/no-more-surrogacy-for-same-sex-couples-in-qld/4086064.

[57] See for example some provisions relating to intestacy. Administration and Probate Acts 1929 (ACT) s 45A(1)(a); 1969 (NT) Pt III cl 1(a). The Family Law Act 1975 (Cth) s. 90SB requires that *de facto* relationships be of 2 years duration before a property adjustment can be made, unless the relationship has been registered in a recognised State or Territory scheme or there is a child of the relationship.

[58] See discussion in Young et al. (2013), para. 5.95.

[59] Per Murphy J in *Jonah v. White* (2011) 45 FamLR 460, p. 467; approved by the Full Court in *Ricci & Jones* [2011] FamCAFC 222 and *Jonah & White* [2012] FamCAFC 200.

[60] Family Law Act 1975 (Cth) s. 4AA(2); Property (Relationships) Act 1984 (NSW) s. 4(2); De facto Relationships Act 1991 (NT) s . 3A(2); Acts Interpretation Act 1954 (Qld) s. 32DA(2); Relationships Act 2003 (Tas) s. 4(3); Relationships Act 2008 (Vic) s. 35(2); Interpretation Act 1984 (WA) s. 17(2).

[61] *D v. McA* (1986) 11 Fam LR 214.

criteria for assessing whether a married couple had separated.[62] The criteria include: the length of the relationship, the nature and extent of common residence, whether or not the parties have a sexual relationship, the degree of financial interdependence, arrangements for financial support, ownership, use and acquisition of property, degree of mutual commitment to a shared life, care and support of children, performance of household duties and reputation and public aspects of the relationship.[63]

6.2.3.3 Judicial Recognition of Same-Sex Couples

The judiciary's treatment of same-sex relationships in Australia occurs in a context where same-sex marriage is not recognised and the judiciary lacks the tools to address this area of discrimination. Legislative provisions treat non-married heterosexual couples and same-sex couples equally. This raises the question of whether applying the same law is equitable when the "norms" of same-sex couple relationships may differ from those of heterosexual couples. To truly achieve equality, it is necessary; first, that judges perceive same-sex relationships as being of equal worth as heterosexual relationships and secondly, that the judiciary takes account of inherent differences between same-sex and heterosexual relationships when applying the law. If true equality is to be achieved, the judiciary should not apply inappropriate hetero-normative assumptions to same-sex relationships when determining whether those relationships are "worthy" of legal recognition.

One of the first cases applying the 2008 Federal *de facto* provisions involved a female couple and stands out as a case where hetero-normative assumptions may have been applied unfairly to that relationship. *Keaton v. Aldridge*[64] concerned parentage and the question before Chief Federal Magistrate Pascoe was whether or not two women were in a *de facto* relationship at the time of the assisted conception procedure.[65]

Pascoe CFM noted that at the time of conception there was no avenue for the legal recognition of the co-mother as the child's legal parent.[66] His Honour found that the parties were not in a *de facto* relationship at that time, relying in part on their maintenance of separate dwellings (including independent responsibility for household cleaning), lack of sexual intimacy at the time of conception, financial independence and absence of shared property.[67] This was despite the fact that most

[62] As established by Watson J in *Marriage of Todd (No 2)* (1976) 1 FamLR 11,186 at p. 11,188 and approved and added to by the Full Court in *Marriage of Pavey* (1976) 1 FamLR 11,358.

[63] Millbank (2008), p. 9.

[64] *Keaton v Aldridge* (2009) 223 FLR 158.

[65] As required by sect. 60H(1)(a) of the Family Law Act 1975.

[66] *Keaton v Aldridge* (2009) 223 FLR 158, para. 111.

[67] *Ibidem*, para. 115; Behrens (2010), p. 355.

of their nights were spent together at one of their residences.[68] Evidence that could have supported a finding that the parties were in a relationship at the relevant time included that they had a shared social life, were mutually committed to their relationship throughout the relevant times, socialised and attended outings together and referred to one another as "my partner."[69] The parties' joint commitment to planning for and parenting the child together was also relevant. The applicant attended the ART clinic with the respondent and engaged in intake and counselling sessions, signed the consent forms for the treatment as the partner of the respondent, was present when the ART procedure took place and at the birth.[70] However, Pascoe CFM concluded that the couple had not made a decision about the role that the applicant would play in the child's life, and this was critical to his conclusion that they were not in a *de facto* relationship at the time of conception.[71] Millbank has criticised this interpretation of the evidence of "a shifting and negotiated understanding of shared parenthood between the women"[72] because it failed to take account of the context of legal non-recognition of and absence of established norms around lesbian co-parenting.[73]

Pascoe CFM appears to have applied an expectation of equal co-parenting roles on the female couple, when the traditional division of contributions in heterosexual relationships often involves one parent taking primary responsibility for parenting of the children of that relationship, sometimes also dictating the extent of involvement of the other parent.[74] Pascoe CFM also characterised the applicant's contributions of: attending pre-natal activities, being involved in the birth, sharing care of the child, and the child being given her last name as a middle name, as being "supportive" of the respondent rather than indicative of a *de facto* relationship.[75] These kinds of contributions indicated the applicant's intention to parent the child, but her legal parentage *status* depended upon whether or not she was in a *de facto* relationship with the respondent at the time of conception. Millbank has criticised the circularity of the decision, where parentage depended upon relationship *status* which was judged partly by evidence of parenting.[76]

Keaton v. Aldridge does appear to sit as an anomaly in post 2009 judicial decisions regarding same-sex couple recognition.

Despite some fears about the absence of some of the *de facto* criteria in many relationships, the application of the legislative provisions demonstrates that "judges have generally been alive to the idea of difference and been flexible and adaptive in

[68] *Ibidem*, para. 115.

[69] *Ibidem*, para. 116; Behrens (2010), pp. 355–356.

[70] Millbank (2009), pp. 185–186.

[71] *Keaton v. Aldridge* (2009) 223 FLR 158, para. 113; Behrens (2010), p. 356.

[72] Millbank (2009), p. 188.

[73] *Ibidem*, p. 188.

[74] *Ibidem*, p. 188.

[75] *Ibidem*, pp. 188–189.

[76] *Ibidem*.

their interpretation."[77] The inherent diversity in intimate human relationships has therefore generally been recognised by the judiciary. Justice Coleman in *Barry & Dalrymple*[78] explicitly commented on the application of the definition of *de facto* relationship (sect. 4AA) in the Family Law Act to same-sex couples:

> Section 4AA(5) of the Act leaves no scope for doubt that the same criteria apply to "working out if persons have a relationship as a couple" for the purposes of s 4AA, whether those persons are of the "same" or "different" sexes. Thus, no gendered assumptions or stereotyping can impact upon the determination… There is a substantial degree of consensus as to what is, and is not consistent with the existence of heterosexual de facto relationships within the meaning of s 4AA of the Act. Some of the "traditional" indicators of a heterosexual de facto relationship cannot, or usually will not apply to same sex relationships.[79]

Coleman J recognised that although the same legislative criteria were to be applied in determining whether a *de facto* relationship existed, it would be wrong to apply hetero-normative assumptions to same-sex relationships.[80]

In *Estrella v McDonald and Ors,*[81] Associate Justice Lansdowne considered whether it was significant that the alleged relationship between the applicant and the deceased was homosexual. Her Honour concluded that although the same law applied to heterosexual and homosexual relationships, the fact that the relationship was a same-sex relationship was relevant and significant for two main reasons. First, because the couple did not have the option of publicly confirming their relationship by marriage, there was no need to apply the same degree of caution as when finding whether a heterosexual *de facto* relationship existed.[82] Secondly, the legal changes regarding same-sex relationships were recent developments, which meant that community acceptance of those relationships may not have kept pace with the law:

> In particular, if indeed the relationship was a sexual and romantic one, embarrassment on the part of the deceased and the plaintiff as to its homosexual nature or consciousness that the relationship may not be accepted by their families or the community may provide explanation for their failure to openly acknowledge the relationship, the actions they took to conceal its true nature, and, in the case of the deceased, his denials that it was a sexual relationship.[83]

There is some judicial understanding of the social issues that same-sex couples face, such as the varying degrees and variable contexts in which lesbian, gay and bisexual people might publicise their relationships.

---

[77] *Ibidem*, p. 10.

[78] *Barry & Dalrymple* [2010] FamCA 1271.

[79] *Ibidem*, para. 236.

[80] *Ibidem*, para. 237.

[81] *Estrella v. McDonald and Ors* [2012] VSC 62.

[82] *Ibidem*, para. 35 citing *Re the Estate of Sigg (deceased)* [2009] VSC 47.

[83] *Ibidem*, para. 36. This approach was also adopted by Justice McCready in *Morwood v. Dalgleish* [2007] NSWSC 32.

6.2.4 Same-Sex Parenting

In addition to the legal recognition of couple relationships, same-sex parented families are also affected by laws around parentage and care of children. There have been significant law reforms affecting the legal recognition of parentage of children born through artificial reproduction.[84] This means that where a lesbian *de facto* couple plan a child together through assisted conception, the child is regarded as a child of the non-birth mother.[85] However, it remains the case that many parents who have children in same-sex relationships are not regarded as the legal parents of children.

Laws about parenting in Australia focus upon the best interests of the child rather than a concept of parental rights. A person without legal parentage *status* may acquire parenting orders either when the same-sex relationship is ongoing or after separation. Non-parents with an interest in the care, welfare and development of a child can approach the family courts[86] for parenting orders.[87] Therefore, step-parents and other non-legal parents may seek orders for sole or shared parental responsibility, orders that a child lives with, spends time with and/or communicates with that person.[88] There are some distinctions between parents and non-parents: presumptions of equal shared parental responsibility and the child's "right" to know and be cared for by a parent do not apply to non-legal parents and the relevant factors in determining parenting order applications also distinguish between parents and non-parents.[89] However, there is a "catch all" provision in parenting matters of "any other fact or circumstance that the court thinks is relevant", and the family courts have used this provision to consider the factors that apply exclusively to parents as they apply to non-legal parents such as co-mothers, biological fathers and partners of legal or biological parents.[90]

There are two main issues affecting same-sex parented families. First, whether or not a non-biological co-parent will be recognised as a legal parent.

---

[84] Sect. 60H Family Law Act 1975, as amended in 2008; Status of Children Acts 1974 (Tas) sect. 10C; 1974 (Qld) sections 19B–19E; 1974 (Vic) sections 13–14; 1978 (NT) sect. 5DA; 1996 (NSW) sect. 14(1A); Family Relationships Act 1975 (SA) sect. 10C(3) and Artificial Conception Act 1985 (WA) sect. 6A.

[85] One recent example of the application of the Federal provision to a lesbian couple is *Connors & Taylor* [2012] FamCA 207.

[86] Family Court of Australia, Federal Circuit Court (formerly Federal Magistrates Court) and Family Court of Western Australia.

[87] Family Law Act 1975 (Cth), sect. 65C.

[88] *Ibidem*, sections 64B, 64C.

[89] *Donnell & Dovey* (2010) 237 FLR 53; *Aldridge & Keaton* (2009) 235 FLR 450. See Rundle and Hardy (2012), part 3.3.

[90] See for example *Aldridge & Keaton*; *Wilson and Anor & Roberts and Anor (No 2)* [2010] FamCA 734.

Secondly, how the courts will view homosexuality when making decisions about parenting.[91]

6.2.4.1 Judicial Recognition of Legal Parentage

Judges made comments about the inadequacy of the law to deal appropriately with same-sex parented families in *B v. J*[92] and *Re Patrick*.[93] Both of these cases involved known donors of sperm to a lesbian couple. *B v J* concerned the question of whether the donor was a parent of the child for the purposes of child support. It was concluded that he was not a parent for this purpose, and therefore was not required to support the child financially. *Re Patrick* concerned the degree to which a known sperm donor to a lesbian couple would be involved in the child's life. At the time of *Re Patrick* there was no legal recognition of the parentage of a co-mother. Both cases contributed to the political movement toward 2008 reforms to the Family Law Act, which, as well as bringing *de facto* financial matters into the jurisdiction of the Family Court, introduced some recognition of co-mothers as parents of children born through artificial conception and specified that donors should not be treated as parents.[94]

Justice Guest in *Re Patrick* took the opportunity to make a judicial plea for legislative action to improve the state of parenting laws and recognise the reality of the diverse forms of family into which children were being born.[95] In *Re Patrick*, Guest J was quite clear that he considered Patrick's family to be comprised of his mother and co-mother and that the male donor was not part of the primary family unit.[96] This was despite choosing to use the term "father" when referring to the donor in the judgment.[97] In asserting the family *status* of Patrick and his two mothers, His Honour commented:

> In my view it would stultify the necessary progress of family law in this country if society were not to recognise the applicants as a 'family' when they offer that which is consistent and parallel with heterosexual families, save for the obviousness of being a same-sex couple. The issue of their homosexuality is, in my view, irrelevant.[98]

---

[91] In the Australian family law system the overall term for care of children is "parenting" (distinct from "parentage", which relates to legal *status* as a parent). Equivalent terms in international law are guardianship ("parental responsibility"), custody ("living with") and access ("spending time and/or communicating with").

[92] *B v. J* (1996) 135 FLR 472 per Fogarty J, at 483. Sifris (2010), p. 20.

[93] *Re Patrick: An application concerning contact* (2002) 168 FLR 6 ("*Re Patrick*") per Guest J, at 78. Sifris (2010), p. 20.

[94] Family Law Amendment (De facto Financial Matters and Other Measures) Act 2008 (Cth). See discussion in Sifris (2010), pp. 21–22.

[95] *Re Patrick*, Part 9 headed "Possible Recommendations".

[96] *Ibidem*, paras 323–326.

[97] *Ibidem*, para. 2.

[98] *Ibidem*, para. 325.

There is no doubt that judicial commentary has contributed to the legal reforms in relation to same-sex parentage in Australia. Judges have raised awareness and stimulated discussion about the issues faced by same-sex parented families.

The Full Court of the Family Court commented about the new 2008 provisions in *Aldridge v Keaton*[99]

> ...the Act in its present form enables a court dealing with a parenting application the flexibility to recognise and accommodate "new" forms of family, including families with same-sex parents, when making orders which are in the best interests of a child who is part of such a family.[100]

Judicial commentary since the reforms has reinforced the intention of the legislature and the state of the law in Australia, whereby the family law framework is able to respond to the needs of diverse family forms.

6.2.4.2 Judicial Views on Parenting by Same-Sex Couples

While family court judges tend to make statements about equality and an intention to focus on parenting ability, there has been evidence of discrimination and prejudice in some judges' decisions. Family Court judges have historically and consistently stated that parenting ability rather than sexuality is relevant for decisions affecting children of gay, lesbian and bisexual parents.[101] However, past parenting decisions demonstrate that homosexuality has been raised as an issue in some cases. Parents in same-sex relationships have been subjected to scrutiny that would not be applied to parents in heterosexual relationships.[102] Some have had discriminatory conditions imposed upon them, such as not displaying affection to their partner in the presence of their children.[103] Such treatment reflected judicial prejudice against same-sex couples.

In recent years there has been a notable shift away from judicial comment about or differential treatment of homosexual parents.[104] This shift is evident not from judicial comment, but rather its absence. For example, in *Craven & Crawford-Craven*[105] a father formed a same-sex relationship after his separation from the mother. This fact was stated by the Full Court, but no further comment was made about him being in a homosexual relationship and no concerns were raised about this being of concern for the children.

---

[99] *Aldridge v. Keaton* (2009) 235 FLR 450.

[100] *Ibidem*, para. 77.

[101] See discussion in Young et al. (2013), para. 9.68.

[102] *L and L* (1983) FLC 91–353; *Marriage of Doyle* (1992) 15 FamLR 274; discussed in Young et al. (2013), para. 9.68.

[103] *Marriage of Spry* (1977) 3 FamLR 11,330.

[104] Young et al. (2013), para. 9.68 citing *D v. N* [2002] FMCAfam 66 and *Craven v. Crawford-Craven*.

[105] *Craven & Crawford-Craven* [2008] FamCAFC 93.

Although concerns have been raised in the past about potential detrimental impact of prejudice against homosexuals on children of gay, lesbian or bisexual parents, in keeping with advances in law that have addressed legal discrimination, there are fewer concerns raised about this issue in more recent cases. Perhaps the judiciary have treated legislative actions as a guide to public standards and expectations. Justice Dessau emphasised in *Wilson & Roberts* (*No 2*) the diversity of family forms and the irrelevance of socio-politics about families to parenting decisions in the Family Law Act:

> This Court deals with a full spectrum of families: parents who have lived together as a unit with children for many years, parents who have met only briefly but through happenstance have parented a child together, heterosexual parents, homosexual parents, parents who have changed gender, parents from a wide range of cultures, and for example, in some medical procedure and other cases, parents who are firmly united in what they seek from the Court. It is always the particular child and his or her particular needs that must be at the centre of a decision.[106]

The family involved in the case before Dessau J was a family formed by a female couple and a male couple, whose preferences had changed when the realities and stresses of first time parenthood were experienced. Although the female couple were treated as the child's parents, the circumstances leading to the child's birth were taken into account and the male couple were accepted as being persons of significance in the child's life. They were therefore able to apply for orders regarding parental responsibility, spending of time and communicating with the child.

6.3 New Zealand

Despite the existence of a human rights framework at the national level, the role of the judiciary in respect of same-sex couples in New Zealand has been limited by the primacy of the legislature and a judicial culture of reinforcing this *status quo*. Despite the fact that there is a legal framework and culture in New Zealand that means judges have rarely directly changed laws affecting same-sex couples, there are a number of different ways in which judges have contributed to same-sex law reform. Sometimes judges have demonstrated societal (or at least, judicial) prejudices through the language that they have chosen when determining cases involving people in same-sex relationships.[107] On other occasions judges have taken the opportunity to comment about inequalities in the law, notwithstanding their inability to actually change those inequalities. The judiciary also interact with same-sex couples through identifying and applying the law to their family relationships.

---

[106] *Wilson and Anor & Roberts and Anor* (*No 2*), para. 330.

[107] Clark (2006).

6.3.1 Background: The New Zealand Legal Order

New Zealand has a common law tradition. Decisions of superior courts are binding on lower courts. The final appellate court in New Zealand is the Supreme Court, which hears appeals from the Court of Appeal.[108] The Court of Appeal hears appeals from the High Court as well as some specialist courts. The High Court has a broad general jurisdiction.[109] It hears serious criminal and civil matters as well as appeals from the District Court and some other courts, tribunals and authorities. The District Court divisions include the Family, Civil, Criminal and Youth Divisions.

Parliamentary sovereignty is prioritised in New Zealand and Acts of Parliament are the highest law.[110] The Acts of Parliament that are relevant to the discussion here include the New Zealand Bill of Rights Act 1990 (BORA) and the Human Rights Act 1993 (HRA). Because they are not entrenched in a higher law, these Acts can be amended or repealed by a simple majority in the unicameral New Zealand Parliament.[111]

BORA outlines the rights that citizens can expect from the State.[112] Because it lacks higher law *status*, BORA has been said to provide mere guidance to judges.[113] Judges are guided by section 6 to interpret legislation in a way that is consistent with BORA wherever possible.[114] However, there are limits to the extent to which judges can act upon inconsistencies between an enacted law and BORA. Section 4 of BORA provides that no court shall

> (a) Hold any provision of the enactment to be impliedly repealed or revoked, or to be in any way invalid or ineffective or
> (b) Decline to apply any provision of the enactment -
> by reason only that the provision is inconsistent with any provision of this Bill of Rights.

The HRA contains anti-discrimination provisions and "significantly expanded the range of grounds upon which a non-discrimination claim could be founded."[115] The HRA introduced the ground of sexual orientation, defined as "a heterosexual,

[108] The New Zealand Ministry of Justice (2013), available at http://www.justice.govt.nz/services/access-to-justice/civics-education-1/nz-court-system/the-role-of-courts-and-judges.

[109] Courts of New Zealand (2013), available at http://www.courtsofnz.govt.nz/about/system/structure/overview.

[110] McK Norrie (2011), p. 265.

[111] *Ibidem*, p. 265.

[112] *Ibidem*, p. 265.

[113] *Ibidem*, p. 266.

[114] BORA, sect. 6.

[115] Erdos (2009), p. 99.

homosexual, lesbian, or bisexual orientation."[116] Erdos has claimed that when the HRA was enacted in 1993, New Zealand became the first country to offer explicit protection in its Bill of Rights against discrimination on grounds of sexual orientation.[117] However, the way that the majority considered the non-discrimination issue in *Quilter v Attorney-General* ("*Quilter*")[118] effectively rendered the provision "legally nugatory."[119]

In 2001, legislative amendments to HRA empowered appeal courts and the Human Rights Review Tribunal to issue formal "declarations of inconsistency" where they determined that primary legislation was inconsistent with the standards of non-discrimination in BORA.[120] This provided courts with a clear mandate to make judicial comment about inconsistency with BORA, notwithstanding that it is beyond the courts' powers to invalidate legislation on the basis of inconsistency with BORA.[121] This option has not been exercised in respect of the human rights of same-sex couples.

Culturally, New Zealand judges are reluctant to interfere with Parliament's legislative function.[122] McK Norrie has observed that

> New Zealand courts do not stretch the meaning of legislative provisions to achieve consistency with the Bill of Rights Act, in the way that UK courts do in order to achieve consistency with the European Convention on Human Rights.[123]

Unlike in the UK, New Zealand Parliaments and courts have not had to respond to a body such as the European Court of Human Rights in developing and implementing human rights law.[124]

6.3.2 Same-Sex Marriage

Until August 2013, marriage was restricted to heterosexual couples in New Zealand.[125] Legislative action was necessary, because attempts to recognise same

---

[116] HRA, sect. 21(1)(m); Erdos (2009), p. 99; McK Norrie (2011), p. 265.

[117] Erdos (2009), p. 105.

[118] *Quilter v Attorney-General* [1998] 1 NZLR 523.

[119] Erdos (2009), p. 108, discussed further below.

[120] Human Rights Amendment Act 2001, inserting (*inter* alia) sections 92J and 92K; Erdos (2009), p. 99.

[121] Rishworth (1998) noted some uncertainty about the appropriate approach of courts, the court of appeal noted in *Moonen v Film and Literature Board of Review* [2000] 2 NZLR 9 (CA) that there was an implied ability to make a declaration, but the legislative action in 2001 provided a clear mandate and process for a response from the legislature (see Erdos 2009, p. 99).

[122] McNamara (2007), p. 133.

[123] McK Norrie (2011), p. 265; on UK see the Chapter by O'Neill in this volume.

[124] McNamara (2007), p. 139.

[125] Marriage Act 1955 as interpreted by *Quilter*. At the time of writing the Marriage (Definition of Marriage) Amendment Bill 2012 had passed its third reading in the New Zealand Parliament on

sex marriage through judicial action were unsuccessful. *Quilter* was an appeal from the registrar of Births, Deaths and Marriages' refusal to issue marriage licences to three lesbian couples. The applicants argued that the right to freedom from discrimination on the grounds set out in HRA,[126] which included sexual orientation,[127] meant that the traditional heterosexual definition of marriage was unjustifiably discriminatory against homosexual people. The judges of the Court of Appeal held by a majority that there was no discrimination and unanimously declined to reshape the definition of marriage to include same-sex unions, because to do so would repeal the Marriage Act and this would contravene sect. 4 of BORA.[128]

Quilter is the highest New Zealand Court decision dealing with same-sex relationships.[129] The judges in that case responded in mixed ways to the opportunity to declare the heterosexual definition of marriage to be discriminatory. Two judges (Gault and Keith JJ) concluded that there was no such discrimination in the Marriage Act. Richardson P recorded his agreement with Gault and Keith JJ's views on the issue of discrimination, but did not think that it was necessary to determine that question in the case.[130] Two judges (Thomas and Tipping JJ) concluded that

> on an impact analysis restricting marriage to opposite-sex couples was prima facie discriminatory.[131]

Tipping J did not express an opinion as to whether this *prima facie* discrimination was justifiable, because the Marriage Act legitimised the *prima facie* discrimination.[132] Thomas J alone concluded that the Marriage Act was discriminatory against same-sex couples.[133] Gault J presented the applicants' same-sex relationships as being a "choice" as opposed to a consequence of their core identities[134]

> They contend, however, that because of the choice of partner they have made the effect of the law preventing their marriages bears upon them and persons in like situations and not upon others and so is discriminatory. But denial of choice always affects only those who wish to make that choice. It is not for that reason discriminatory.[135]

17th April 2013 (New Zealand Parliament (2013), available at http://www.parliament.nz/en-NZ/PB/Legislation/Bills/2/c/4/00DBHOH_BILL11528_1-Marriage-Definition-of-Marriage-Amendment-Bill.htm). The commencement period means that the first same-sex marriages in New Zealand could occur from August 2013.

[126] BORA, sect. 19.

[127] HRA, sect. 21(1)(m).

[128] See Butler (1998); McNamara (2007), pp. 130–133; Erdos (2009), pp. 106–115 for critiques of this decision.

[129] *Quilter* was heard in the Court of Appeal. The Supreme Court has not heard any matters regarding same-sex couples.

[130] *Quilter*, p. 526.

[131] Butler (1998), p. 400.

[132] *Quilter*, pp. 575–576.

[133] *Ibidem*, p. 528.

[134] *Ibidem*, p. 527.

[135] *Ibidem*, p. 527.

Butler has highlighted that Gault J's argument about choice is unconvincing, because the choice that the law denied related directly to the prohibited ground of discrimination based on sexual orientation: "homosexuals' desire to marry a person of the same-sex is a core aspect of their sexual orientation."[136] This point was made by Thomas J in his judgment:

> Just as the sexual orientation of heterosexual men and women leads to the formation of heterosexual relationships, so too it is the sexual orientation of gays and lesbians which leads to the formation of homosexual relationships. Sexual orientation dictates their choice of partner in both cases. To a heterosexual person that sexual orientation can lead to a valid marriage relationship; to a gay or lesbian person it cannot.[137]

Another aspect of Gault J's discussion about choice was his drawing of parallels between a choice to form a same-sex relationships and a choice to form a prohibited relationship between a (homosexual) man and a child:

> Denial of the choice of marrying a child or someone already married could not be said to be discriminatory on the grounds of sex or sexual orientation just because a homosexual male wants to make such a choice.[138]

Clark has noted that judicial statements such as this reinforce societal stereotypes linking homosexuality and paedophilia.[139] He also pointed out that the *Quilter* case was brought by three lesbian couples, making the analogy even less relevant to the case.[140] Thomas J responded to these kinds of analogies in his judgment when he said:

> Any person who wishes to marry anyone within these prohibited categories, it is argued, is denied the partner of his or her choice as much as a gay or lesbian person seeking to marry a same sex partner. Apart from the fact the analogy with persons who are under age, mentally incapable, or bigamists is demeaning to gays and lesbians, I believe the proposition only has to be stated to be seen to be self-evidently untenable.[141]

Another criticism of Gault J's judgment was that he concluded that discrimination in the Marriage Act was permissible because marriage had been defined as a heterosexual union for such a long time and only the legislature should rule this discrimination to be unjustifiable.[142] As Butler has argued, longevity is not a reasonable justification for discrimination.[143]

By declining to find discrimination in the exclusion of same-sex couples from an institution that is available to heterosexual couples, Richardson P, Gault and Keith JJ sent a message that it is not discriminatory to exclude same-sex couples from

---

[136] Butler (1998), p. 398.

[137] *Quilter*, p. 537.

[138] *Ibidem*, p. 527.

[139] Clark (2006), p. 209.

[140] *Ibidem*, p. 209.

[141] *Quilter*, p. 538.

[142] *Ibidem*, p. 527 critiqued in Butler (1998), pp. 397–398.

[143] Butler (1998), p. 398.

opportunities that have traditionally been reserved for heterosexual couples. This message runs *contra* to the message sent by the New Zealand Parliament in recognising same-sex couples as *de facto* couples, and equalising the treatment of married and non-married couples. At the time that *Quilter* was decided, there had been a substantial degree of incremental reform towards this equalisation.[144] Further reforms have continued this process towards equality, ultimately resulting in the passing of the amendment to the Marriage Act that enables same-sex couples to marry. It should also be noted that post-*Quilter* there have been judicial findings elsewhere that heterosexual marriage is discriminatory (for example, in Canada).[145]

Furthermore, McNamara has observed that a "deference to parliamentary supremacy" was behind the majority's conclusions that the heterosexual definition of marriage was not discriminatory.[146] Therefore, the two separate questions of (a) whether or not the Marriage Act was discriminatory and (b) whether or not the Court could overturn parliamentary intention, were conflated.[147] This highlights the missed opportunity of the majority in the *Quilter* judgments, whereby some of the reasoning was circular and avoided the central question.

Following *Quilter*, despite the judgments having gone against the applicants, recognition of same-sex couples became prioritised on the New Zealand government's agenda.[148] Numerous reforms were made between 1999 and 2004, culminating in the Civil Unions Act 2004.[149] A parallel relationship category was created rather than pursuing marriage equality. Marriage equality became particularly unlikely to succeed politically after the decision of the UN Human Rights Committee in *Joslin v New Zealand,* where the Committee determined that New Zealand's refusal to enable same-sex couples to marry did not breach the International Covenant on Civil and Political Rights.[150] Consequently, international law obliges signatories to recognise heterosexual marriage, but not same-sex marriage.

McNamara has noted that the difference in outcomes on this issue in New Zealand and Canada can be explained by the different legal forms of the respective human rights frameworks

> the Canadian judiciary enjoys an interpretive supremacy over the terms and demands of the Charter, including the equality guarantee in s 15, which is simply not extended to New Zealand courts under the BORA.[151]

Erdos has argued that additional factors, including judicial culture, have also played a part.[152] *Quilter* has been said to demonstrate the New Zealand judiciary's

---

[144] For an overview of the state of the law in 1998 see Keith J in *Quilter*, pp. 565–570.

[145] McNamara (2007), p. 132; on Canada see the Chapter by Mostacci in this volume.

[146] *Ibidem*, p. 131.

[147] *Ibidem*, p. 131.

[148] *Ibidem*, pp. 134–135.

[149] McNamara (2007), p. 129.

[150] *Joslin v. New Zealand*, Communication No 902/1999, 30 July 2002; see discussion in Walker (2007), pp. 116–117 and the chapter by Paladini in this volume.

[151] McNamara (2007), p. 132.

[152] Erdos (2009), pp. 106–127.

cautious approach to shaping social policy in the non-discrimination area.[153] This contrasts with New Zealand courts' willingness to stretch the requirements of BORA and interpretation of primary legislation in the criminal justice sphere.[154]

There was an attempt, through a private member's bill presented in 2005, to reinforce the heterosexual definition of marriage.[155] The bill contained amendments to the Marriage Act that would have reinforced the heterosexual definition of marriage and expressly prevented the recognition of foreign same-sex marriages in New Zealand. It was based upon the 2004 amendment to the Australian Marriage Act. It was unsuccessful, despite being presented to Parliament twice.[156] In 2012, a private member's bill to enable same-sex couples to legally marry was introduced into the New Zealand Parliament.[157] The bill passed its second reading by a vote of 77 to 44.[158] It then passed through a Committee of the whole house on 27th March 2013 and the third reading stage on 17th April 2013. New Zealand thereby became the first nation in the Asia-Pacific to extend the definition of marriage to all couples, regardless of their sex.

6.3.3 Same-Sex Relationship Recognition

6.3.3.1 Non-Married Relationships Registration

A civil union attracts essentially the same rights and entitlements as marriage.[159] Civil unions are open to both same-sex and heterosexual couples (for whom it is an alternative to marriage). The requirements for entering into a civil union are based upon the requirements for entering into a marriage.[160] Partners to a civil union cannot access adoption either as a couple or of a partner's child in the way that married persons can.[161]

---

[153] *Ibidem*, p. 110, citing Bigwood (2006).

[154] Erdos (2009), p. 111, contrasting *Quilter* with *Attorney-General v. Zaoui* [2005] NZSC 38.

[155] Marriage (Gender Clarification) Amendment Bill 2005.

[156] The New Zealand Parliament did not pass the Marriage (Gender Clarification) Amendment Bill 2005; see McK Norrie (2011), p. 266; McNamara (2007), p. 142.

[157] Marriage (Definition of Marriage) Amendment Bill 2012.

[158] AAP (2013), available at http://www.theage.com.au/world/nz-gay-marriage-bill-passes-second-reading-20130313-2g14k.html.

[159] Civil Union Act 2004. See discussion of some differences between marriage and civil unions in McK Norrie (2011), pp. 267–268.

[160] McK Norrie (2011), p. 266.

[161] *Ibidem*, pp. 267–268.

6.3.3.2 *De Facto* Recognition of Same-Sex Couples

The rights and responsibilities of formalised (by marriage or civil union) and non-formalised (*de facto*) couples are largely equivalent in New Zealand.[162] In 2001 the property division regime was extended from married couples to those living in *de facto* relationships (inclusive of heterosexual and same-sex partnerships).[163] In 2005 the New Zealand Parliament passed the Relationships (Statutory References) Act, which amended at least 103 existing statutes to update the references to relationships contained within them, specifying whether laws applied to married, civil union partners, *de facto* heterosexual couples and same-sex couples.[164] The policy statement that accompanied the bill made it clear that the intention was to have neutral laws on relationships that applied equally to all relationship categories.[165]

6.3.3.3 Judicial Recognition of Same-Sex Couples

Despite the failed attempts to achieve same-sex marriage equality in *Quilter*, the New Zealand judiciary have been willing in other cases to legally recognise same-sex relationships.

In 1998, Fisher J of the High Court determined in *P v. M*[166] that although *Quilter* had confirmed that same-sex partners could not marry, there was clear legislative intent to define family in a broader sense for the purposes of the Domestic Violence Act.[167] His Honour commented that:

> It would scarcely be radical for the legislature to have recognised that for present purposes live-in same sex partnerships exhibit most of the functional indicia of heterosexual marriage. Exclusive emotional commitment, a shared household, pooled financial and property resources, cooperative division of labour, sexual exclusivity, shared social and recreational activities, joint presentation as a couple and substantial duration are some of the main examples. As with heterosexual relationships, all or some may be present in any given relationship.
>
> If those features can be found in either type of relationship it is difficult to see any policy reasons for distinguishing between homosexual and heterosexual relationships for the purpose of protecting against domestic violence. Within the relationship itself one assumes that heterosexual relationships do not have a monopoly on violence.[168]

---

[162] *Ibidem*, p. 278.

[163] The Property (Relationships) Amendment Act 2001 renamed the Matrimonial Property Act 1976 the Property (Relationships) Act 1976. *De facto* relationship is defined in s 2D of the Property (Relationships) Act 1976.

[164] Discussed in *In the matter of AMM and KJO* [2010] CIV 2010-485-328, paras 59–60.

[165] *Ibidem*.

[166] *P v. M* [1998] 3 NZLR 246.

[167] *Ibidem*, p. 251.

[168] *Ibidem*, p. 252.

Accordingly, the brother of a woman in a same-sex relationship was recognised as a family member of the woman's partner for the purposes of the Domestic Violence Act. It is interesting to note that it was the same-sex couple who challenged the final protection order on the basis that no family relationship should be recognised between the complainant and his sister's female partner.

Mixed judgments have been made about the interpretation of "spouse" in legislation. In a family court case, Justice Walsh interpreted the word "spouse" in the Adoption Act to mean "2 persons in a relationship in the nature of a marriage," thereby determining that *de facto* couples could apply for adoption.[169] In his judgment, reference was made to the impact that a stricter interpretation would have on same-sex couples, who are unable to legally marry. However, a subsequent High Court case which involved the question of access to adoption for heterosexual *de facto* couples was used as an opportunity to cast doubt on this interpretation of the legislation.[170] Justices Wild and Simon France explicitly restricted the question before them to whether

> "the word "spouses", which is normally used to refer to a married couple, be read to apply also to a de facto couple of the opposite sex."[171]

However, several *obiter* comments were made that reflected Their Honours' view that different issues were raised to the question of enabling adoption by same-sex couples than the issues that were raised for *de facto* heterosexual couples. For example, when considering the purposes of the Adoption Act, Their Honours said:

> ...it must be thought that the purpose of limiting joint applications to married couples was to ensure that the applicants were a man and a woman, and that they were in a committed relationship. The traditional concept of the family unit would seem central to the limitation.
>
> Obviously extending the word "spouses" to a de facto couple is consistent with the first of these purposes. The necessary profile of the applicants, namely that they offer a mother and a father, is achieved.[172]

The family unit comprised of a mother and father was apparently seen by the court to be superior to the family unit comprised of two mothers or two fathers.

KL L-A v. EA[173] involved similar issues to the Australian case of *Keaton v. Aldridge*, namely, whether a lesbian couple were in a *de facto* relationship at the time of an artificial conception procedure. The co-mother was seeking a declaration of parentage. Justice Maude was satisfied that the parties were living in a *de facto* relationship at the time of conception. His Honour took into account: the joint planning of the insemination and birth, joint signing of consent and

---

[169] *In the matter of C* [*Adoption*] [2008] NZFLR 141, [77]. There were inconsistent previous judgments on the issue: Boshier J in *Re Adoption by Paul and Hauraki* [1993] NZFLR 266; von Dadelszen J in *Re TW* [*adoption*] (1998) 17 FRNZ 349; *In the matter of R* (*adoption*) [1999] NZFLR 145.

[170] *In the matter of AMM and KJO* [2010] CIV 2010-485-328.

[171] *Ibidem*, para. 4.

[172] *Ibidem*, paras 35–36.

[173] *KL L-A v. EA* [*Care of Children*] [2008] NZFLR 536.

parentage documentation, the birth mother's change of name to a hyphenated last name (which was also given to the child), joint financial decisions (including purchase of a motor vehicle and an insurance policy in joint names), sharing of a common residence (apart from times when the birth mother stayed in a women's shelter, when they worked in different locations and when they slept separately when visiting relatives in South Africa), and sharing of a sexual relationship. The relationship appeared to be a difficult one, but Maude J put the issue of allegations of family violence to one side when determining the preliminary question of whether the parties were in a *de facto* relationship at the time of conception, which was the issue that determined legal parentage.

The 2002 Court of Appeal Case of *King v. Church*[174] involved appeal from the High Court's determination of a claim in equity, for division of property between former partners. It was argued by counsel for one of the men that the court should distinguish between the societal norms that apply to opposite and same-sex couples.[175]

The Court of Appeal preferred an approach that treated same-sex and heterosexual couples equally. Anderson, Baragwanath and Potter JJ noted that the rules of equity were to be applied:

> ...against a background of current social norms. They can now include the perception of a particular same sex relationship as closely analogous to what has in the past been seen as a stereotypical opposite sex partnership.[176]

The circumstances of the relationship in *King v. Church* were such that Mr Church could be treated in a way analogous to that of the wife whose contributions to the matrimonial home largely comprised of household duties.[177] His gender was an irrelevant difference.

The difficulty in determining whether or not a *de facto* relationship exists between two people of the same-sex is demonstrated by *TJD v. TLB*.[178] Justice von Dadelszen was faced with very conflicting accounts of whether two women, who had lived together for 12 years, were sharing a house as best friends or were in a *de facto* relationship. His Honour was reluctant to jump to conclusions:

> Before discussing the evidence itself I want to say that I am not prepared to make any assumptions at all about the way that people choose to live their lives, be they gay or heterosexual.[179]
>
> ...I am not going to assume (as perhaps I was invited to do) that just because neither of the parties here had a relationship with another person during those 12 years, they must have been together as a gay couple.[180]

---

[174] *King v. Church* [2002] NZFLR 555.

[175] *Ibidem*, at 7, counsel for King's submissions considered at 26 and 29.

[176] *Ibidem*, at 18.

[177] *Ibidem*, at 31.

[178] *TJD v. TLB* (Family Court, Napier, FAM-2005-041-591, von Dadelszen J, 17 May 2007).

[179] *Ibidem*, para. 20.

[180] *Ibidem*, para. 38.

Ultimately, von Dadelszen J was not satisfied that the applicant had discharged her onus of proof that a *de facto* relationship existed. Relevant evidence included: attendance at family and special occasions together, joint signing of greeting cards, the lack of evidence of shared finances or property ownership, lack of planned future together. There was conflicting evidence of other relevant factors including sexual and public aspects of the relationship. The applicant had not provided adequate detail to the court about the sexual relationship that she alleged she had with the respondent. Because many couples may not share finances, publicise the nature of their relationship or gather proof of their sexual encounters, this case demonstrates that same-sex couples can experience great difficulty if they are called to prove the existence of their relationship to a court.

6.3.4 Same-Sex Parented Families

6.3.4.1 Legal Parentage

Co-mothers of children born into lesbian relationships through artificial conception have been recognised as the parents of the child in New Zealand since 2004. The litigation in the case of *T*[181] illustrated some conflicted outcomes for co-mothers prior to these reforms. The co-mother could not apply for second parent adoption because she was not married to the mother. Therefore, she applied to adopt their third born child, the legal effect of which would be to extinguish the legal parentage of the biological mother.

On appeal, the High Court determined that although adoption would attract many benefits for the child, the artificial legal relationship that would be created was not in his best interests, and a guardianship order would have the same effect.[182] The parties subsequently separated, after which the co-mother had little contact with the children. The biological mother obtained orders terminating the co-mother's guardianship of the children and also applied for an order declaring the co-mother to be the step parent of the children and therefore liable to pay child support.[183] On the basis of her attempt to adopt the third child, the Family Court (Brown J) determined that the co-mother had accepted responsibility for the children through her adoption application and she was declared to be a step-parent for the purposes of the Child Support Act.[184] On appeal the High Court (Penlington and Hammond JJ) affirmed the Family Court's decision.[185] It was clear that for the

[181] *Re an Application by T* [1998] NZFLR 769 (HC); *T v. T* [1998] NZFLR 776; *A v. R* [1999] NZFLR 249.

[182] *Re an Application by T.*

[183] *T v. T*, p. 7.

[184] *Ibidem.*

[185] *A v. R.*

purposes of child support, a same-sex partnership could be treated as a relationship in the nature of a marriage, and that child support was a separate issue to time spent with a child. Clearly, there were inconsistencies in parentage *status* applied to the co-mother. She was left without the benefits of legal recognition and carrying the financial burden of parenthood.

The litigation about parentage in the decisions of *P v. K*[186] also provided an opportunity for judicial comment about same-sex parenting. In *P v. K* the child's conception was planned and negotiated between a female couple and a male couple. The disputes essentially resulted from a breakdown in the relationship between the two couples, which led to disagreement about the involvement of the men in the child's life. At the time of the 2003 High Court decision, there was a distinction in the legislative provisions applying to parentage of children born from artificial insemination of married and unmarried women.[187] This prompted Priestley J to note that the distinction between the provisions was significant, because where the woman was not married, only the rights and obligations between child and donor were extinguished, rather than the donor not being the father of the child for any purpose.[188] In analysing the distinction, Priestley J said:

> One can thus start to see an explanation for the distinction, for in the case of a marriage or a relationship between a woman and a man in the nature of a marriage there are plausible policy reasons for treating the child resulting from a medically contrived donor pregnancy as being exclusively the child of the marriage or the relationship and for totally excluding the donor. Speaking in 1987 terms, there are however in terms of s 5(2) no such policy reasons for protecting the security of the traditional nuclear family in that way where there is either no traditional nuclear family to protect (as in the present case, though I accept that there may here be a 'psychological' nuclear family) ...[189]

This commentary reflects a view that there is no policy reason to protect and secure a primary two parent family headed by two women in the way that a heterosexual two parent family ought to be "protected and secured." It was common ground that the agreement between the couples was that the women would be the primary parents of the child, with a not insignificant parenting role also played by the male couple. Priestley J commented later in his judgment that the legislative provision ensured that "a child born of an artificially inseminated unmarried woman is not fatherless"[190] and later "parliament's clear intention by enacting sect. 5(2) of the SCAA was to preserve a father for this child."[191] This view was echoed by Harrison J in the later High Court decision where he responded to an argument that

---

[186] *P v. K* [2003] 2 NZLR 787; *P v. K and* M [2004] NZFLR 752; *P v. K* [2004] 2 NZLR 421; *P v. K* [2006] NZFLR 22.

[187] Status of Children Amendment Act 1987, sect. 5(1) and (2). Note: these provisions were repealed and replaced by the Status of Children Amendment Act 2004, sect. 14. See Status of Children Act 1969 as amended, Part 2.

[188] *P v K* [2003] 2 NZLR 787, p. 795.

[189] *Ibidem*, p. 795.

[190] *Ibidem*, p. 807.

[191] *Ibidem*, p. 819.

the child's need for a male role model could be satisfied by interaction with the friends of the mother and her partner:

> This informal and likely transitory arrangement could never be a substitute for a boy's right to a special and formalised relationship with his biological father or, in the reverse situation, a girl's right to a special and formalised relationship with her biological mother.[192]

It could be suggested that had the functional primary family been a heterosexual couple and the child, these policy reasons behind the legislative provision may not have been emphasised by the courts. The judges' views may have been different if the birth mother's partner (in the position of non-biological parent) would be a father figure for the child. It seems that despite the emphasis on biological connection, it was actually access to a father that was the concern behind the comments. Priestley J treated the donor as a father on a number of bases, including that he was the biological father, was named on the child's birth certificate as such and it had been agreed that he would have a parental relationship with the child.[193] His Honour referred to the UN Convention on the Rights of the Child as supportive of recognition of the child's right to have a relationship with his "parent."[194] Notwithstanding these factors, the effect of the applicable provision in the Status of Children Act was that the father could not exercise the statutory rights of a parent under that Act.[195] Priestley J closed his judgment with the observation that:

> It is undesirable that fathers and children in the situation of this father and this child should be left legally marooned. The current review of the Act should address the situation as a matter of urgency.[196]

Heath J agreed with Priestley J's reasons and added his own comments about the policy issues raised by the case.[197] His Honour raised a number of issues for consideration by Parliament, including the question as to whether a distinction should be drawn between known and unknown donors.[198] In relation to agreements between same-sex couples and donors of sperm (or eggs and gestation in the case of surrogacy), Heath J suggested that:

> In either case the law needs to recognise the need for involvement of a person of the opposite sex and to specify what will happen in the event of a dispute arising between the surrogate mother and the gay couple (on the one hand) or the donor of semen and the lesbian couple (on the other).[199]

---

[192] *P v K* [2004] 2 NZLR 421, 430.

[193] *P v K* [2003] 2 NZLR 787, p. 804.

[194] *Ibidem*, p. 804. See also Harrison J in *P v. K* [2004] 2 NZLR 421.

[195] *Ibidem*, p. 808.

[196] *Ibidem*, p. 820.

[197] *Ibidem*, Heath J's decision commences at p. 820.

[198] *Ibidem*, p. 822; Although subsequent law reforms have not addressed this question, the reasoning in *P v. K* was applied to an anonymous donor when Robinson J ordered that the anonymous sperm donor be served with the co-mother's application to be appointed as a guardian in *M v. C* [2004] NZFLR 695.

[199] *Ibidem*, p. 823.

The legislature responded to concerns about the current laws of parentage. The Status of Children Amendment Act 2004 inserted a Part 2 in the Act with the stated purposes to remove uncertainty and facilitate recognition of co-mothers.[200]

The Amended Act extinguishes the parental *status* of a donor "for all purposes" regardless of whether the birth mother is partnered (married, in a civil union or a *de facto* relationship with a man or a woman) or a single woman acting alone.[201] A male or female partner of the birth mother (married, civil union or a *de facto* of either sex) who consents to the AHR procedure is, "for all purposes" the parent of the child.[202] Clearly, the exploration of the policy issues by the judges in *P v. K* contributed to the subsequent legislative reforms. The legislative response was to treat lesbian couples as the parents of children born into their relationships and to extinguish the legal parental *status* of donors, whether known or unknown, a somewhat different outcome than the stated judicial preference.

6.3.4.2 Parenting by Same-Sex Couples

Like in Australia, parenting is not tied to parentage in New Zealand. The Care of Children Act 2004 provides that any person may apply for a guardianship order, which includes a person in the position of the known donor father in *P v. K*. Judges in New Zealand appear to have, over the past 20 years, declined to view lesbian relationships as being a concern in parenting matters.[203] Sometimes this has been stated explicitly:

> There is no evidence before me to suggest that his mother is hampered in her ability to parent W by reason of her sexual orientation.[204]

Male same-sex relationships appear to have attracted more prejudicial statements. Clark examined New Zealand judicial writing to identify the way that homosexuality was constructed in judicial language.[205] He concluded that there were tendencies to: frame male homosexual sex as "indecent," view same-sex relationships as lacking longevity, prefer heterosexual rather than same-sex parented households, and reward parents in same-sex relationships for hiding

[200] Status of Children Act 1969, sect. 13, inserted by Status of Children Amendment Act 2004, sect. 14.

[201] Status of Children Act 1969, sections 19–22. The only exception is where a donor later becomes the birth mother's partner (sections 23–25).

[202] Status of Children Act 1969, sect. 18. For application see *HU v. SP* [*Parenting Order*] [2008] NZFLR 751.

[203] *Neate v. Hullen* [1992] NZFLR 314 (the mother's lesbian relationship was problematic for other reasons); *B v. P* [1992] NZFLR 545 (prejudice of the other applicants towards same-sex relationships was seen to be potentially damaging to the child, whose mother was in a lesbian relationship).

[204] *B v. P*, p. 6.

[205] Clark (2006).

their sexual orientation and/or relationship from their children.[206] However, Clark's analysis did not focus on judgments that did not portray such stereotypes and therefore cannot be relied upon as evidence of overall judicial tendency (although expressions of prejudice by the judiciary are significant).[207]

6.4 Comparison of Australia and New Zealand

There are many similarities in the treatment of same-sex couples in Australian and New Zealand law. Some differences in the human rights frameworks have affected the way that the judiciary have been able to play a role in legal developments.

6.4.1 *Legal Orders and Human Rights Frameworks*

Both Australia and New Zealand have a legal framework and culture of parliamentary supremacy. New Zealand has a national statutory Bill of Rights, whereas Australia has none at the Federal level.

McNamara concluded in 2007 that the absence of a Charter of Human Rights in Australia was a significant barrier to same-sex marriage and other recognition of same-sex relationships.[208]

In the absence of an overarching Bill of Rights, the judiciary have not been able to draw guidance from a human rights framework to determine whether or not the denial of marriage equality is discriminatory or breaches human rights. However, the New Zealand case of *Quilter*, which was determined within a human rights framework, does not bode well for the benefits of that legal form in any event. In Australia, an additional inhibiting factor is the complex constitutional issues raised by the Federal system, which has discouraged legislatures from exercising the marriage power to legalise same-sex marriage.

McNamara's conclusion about the impact of the absence of a Charter of Rights is less convincing when the sweeping law reforms that have occurred in relation to same-sex relationship recognition in Australia are observed. These fundamental changes occurred in the absence of an overarching human rights framework. They also occurred despite the need for legislative action by States and Territories as well as at the Federal level.

The Australian experience suggests that where there is political will, human rights can be promoted in the absence of an overarching human rights framework.

[206] *Ibidem*, referring to cases such as: *Quilter*; *VP v. PM* (1998) 16 FRNZ 621 (FC); *K & M* (2002) FRNZ 360 (FC); *P v. K* [2003] 2 NZLR 787 (HC); *R v. Ali* HC AK CRI-2003-292-1224.

[207] *Ibidem*, p. 200.

[208] McNamara (2007), p. 148.

The New Zealand experience, where there is a human rights framework, but it is not framed in higher law, demonstrates that such a framework has limited effect where political will is lacking.[209] However, there is questionable longevity and security where human rights depend upon the whims of Parliament.

Together, the New Zealand and Australian experiences demonstrate the limitations created by the absence of a Human Rights Charter that has higher law *status*. Otherwise there is a need for political will by the legislature to promote the human rights of same-sex couples and this is susceptible to changes in government. The legislature can advance human rights for same-sex couples in dramatic and widespread ways, arguably effecting change more fundamentally and rapidly than the judiciary could. However, without a Human Rights Charter with higher law *status*, there is a limited degree to which the judiciary can or will hold the legislature to account for discrimination.

6.4.2 Marriage Inequality

In Australia, marriage is defined as a heterosexual union. The Parliaments have not acted to legalize same-sex marriage. The situation was the same until very recently in New Zealand, where the Parliament has now passed a bill for marriage equality. In both jurisdictions, lesbian couples have applied to register their same-sex marriage. In Australia the legislature intervened to reinforce marriage as a heterosexual union and thereby silenced the judiciary. In New Zealand the application went to the judiciary in *Quilter*, who said that the applicants could not enter a legal marriage. A bill replicating the Australian amendment that reinforced marriage as between a man and a woman failed to pass in New Zealand. More recently, same-sex marriage bills have been presented to various Parliaments in Australia. None have passed into law.

In both countries, the consequence of the legislative and judicial actions refusing to legalize same sex marriage were that political campaigning for same-sex marriage increased. In Australia it is a prominent topic in the public debate and there are several bills currently before Australian Parliaments. However, unresolved constitutional questions remain about the appropriate way to implement same-sex marriage law reform. Australia's Federal system itself has been a barrier to same-sex marriage. No court has been asked to determine the constitutional questions directly. In New Zealand an application was made to the UN Human Rights Committee (*Joslin* case) and this failed. The result in *Joslin* possibly reassured both governments that failing to enact same-sex marriage laws is not a breach of international human rights. In New Zealand this led to the enactment of the Civil Unions bill, a way of imparting the rights of marriage without enabling same-sex marriage. There is no national relationships registration scheme in Australia,

[209] *Ibidem*, p. 157.

although the possibility has been mooted. The Federal system may also prove to be a barrier to this proposal, as the Constitution does not grant the Commonwealth power over "family" or "relationships" but "marriage" and "marital causes". A Federal civil union scheme may require a referral of powers from the States, many of whom have already implemented their own relationship registration schemes (which are all recognized by the Commonwealth for the purposes of Commonwealth law). There are clearly limits to what the Australian and New Zealand legislatures have been prepared to do to promote equality for same-sex couples (until very recently). New Zealand has led the way by becoming the first nation in the Asia-Pacific region to legalise same-sex marriage. It is possible that Australia will legalize same-sex marriage in the foreseeable future.

6.4.3 Treatment of Same-Sex Couples

The judiciary has played a mixed part in respect of the legal treatment of same-sex couples. Historically, there are examples of judicial prejudice against same-sex couples in both jurisdictions. Judges have made statements that same-sex couples should be treated equally as compared to heterosexual *de facto* couples. In Australia, post *Keaton v. Aldridge*, there is evidence of judicial appreciation for some of the factors that make the application of hetero-normative assumptions to same-sex couples inappropriate. The Australian and New Zealand judiciary have embraced the widespread and fundamental changes to the legal treatment of same-sex couples that were introduced by the legislature.

Where the legislature has reformed the law to equalise the treatment of opposite and same-sex couples, the Australian and New Zealand judiciaries have, in most cases, embraced that reform enthusiastically. Judicial application of the law to same-sex couples has at times evidenced an appreciation that a hetero-normative lens of coupledom and family life is inappropriate for many same-sex couples. The judiciary has also appreciated that prejudice does exist against same-sex couples and that can affect the way that same-sex couples conduct and/or publicise their relationships.

6.4.4 Recognition of Same-Sex Parents

A remaining site of contention is parentage of children of same-sex parents. Both Australia and New Zealand recognize co-mothers as legal parents of children born into their relationship, provided that certain pre-conditions are met at the time of conception. This is a positive reform that provides certainty and security for lesbian parents and their children. However, judicial comments in New Zealand have reflected a preference for heterosexual parenting. Relatively recent decisions regarding adoption[210] and parenting by known donors[211] have been taken as an opportunity by some judges to raise concerns about children's need to be parented by a mother and a father. This approach is consistent with conservative commentators who claim that the heterosexual parenting relationship is a reason to treat same-sex couples differently to heterosexual couples, particularly where it comes to the right to marry.[212]

Both jurisdictions also exclude donors from recognition as legal parents, regardless of the parenting arrangements and preferences of the adults involved. This essentially reflects an expectation of a two parent family model, which is appropriate in most circumstances. However, in some circumstances it may be more appropriate to recognize the parentage of more than two individuals, particularly where all involved intend that a biological father will co-parent the child.[213] This may be the case for a known donor to a female couple (or single woman) or a commissioning male couple (or single man) in a surrogacy arrangement, where it is anticipated that the donor or gestational mother will play a parenting role in the child's life. Judges in both Australia and New Zealand have recognized the reality of parenting arrangements in such families, despite legal parentage being limited to two parents.[214]

6.5 Conclusion

Same-sex couples in Australia and New Zealand enjoy most of the same rights as non-married heterosexual couples. The current situation has been achieved with the benefit of judicial commentary contributing to law reform. Judges have, for the most part, embraced the spirit of legislative moves toward equality. Their role has been less pro-active than in jurisdictions where there is a Bill of Rights contained in higher law.

Acknowledgements Acknowledgements and thanks to Charlotte Hunn, University of Tasmania, for her research assistance, and Associate Professor Samantha Hardy, James Cook University, for her valuable feedback.

References

AAP (2013) NZ gay marriage bill passes second reading. The Age
Australian Broadcasting Commission (2012) No more surrogacy for same sex couples in Qld

---

[210] *In the matter of AMM and KJO*.

[211] *P v. K*.

[212] See for example Scott (2010).

[213] Surtees (2011); Rundle and Hardy (2012).

[214] *Wilson & Roberts (No 2); P v. K*.

Behrens J (2010) 'De facto relationship'?: some early case law under the FLA. Aust J Fam Law 24:350–360
Bigwood R (ed) (2006) Public interest litigation: New Zealand experience in international perspective. Wellington Lexis Nexis, NZ
Butler A (1998) Same-sex marriage and freedom from discrimination in New Zealand. Public Law (Autumn) 396–406
Clark E (2006) The construction of homosexuality in New Zealand judicial writing. Vic Univ Wellington Law Rev 37:199–221
Courts of New Zealand (2013) The structure of the court system
Erdos D (2009) Judicial culture and the politicolegal opportunity structure: explaining bill of rights legal impact in New Zealand. Law Soc Inq 34:95–127
Graycar R, Millbank J (2007) From functional family to spinster sisters: Australia's distinctive path to relationship recognition. Wash Univ J Law Policy 24:121–164
Griffith G (2011) Same sex marriage. NSW parliamentary Library Research Service. Briefing Paper 3 (July 2011)
Human Rights and Equal Opportunity Commission (2007) Same-sex: same entitlements. Final Report
Human Rights and Equal Opportunity Commission (2011) Addressing sexual orientation and sex and/or gender identity discrimination. Consultation Report
McK Norrie K (2011) National report: New Zealand. Am Univ J Gend Soc Policy Law 19:265–271
McNamara L (2007) Human rights controversies: the impact of legal form. Routledge, New York
Millbank J (2008) The role of "functional family" in same-sex family recognition trends. Child Fam Law Q 20:1–28
Millbank J (2009) De facto relationships, same sex and surrogate parents: exploring the scope and effects of the 2008 federal relationship reforms. Aust J Fam Law 23:160–193
New Zealand Parliament (2013) Legislation: bills: marriage (definition of marriage) bill 2012
New Zealand Ministry of Justice (2013) Civics education: the role of courts and judges
Nicholson A (2005) The legal recognition of marriage. Melb Univ Law Rev 29:556–572
Rishworth P (1998) Reflections on the bill of rights after *Quilter v Attorney-General*. N Z Law Rev 4:683–699
Rundle O (2011) An examination of relationship registration schemes in Australia. Aust J Fam Law 25:121–152
Rundle O, Hardy S (2012) Australian birth certificates: the best interests of no-one at all. Aust J Fam Law 26:116–141
Scott A (ed) (2010) The jurisprudence of marriage and other intimate relationships. William S. Hein and Co Inc., Buffalo
Sifris A (2010) Lesbian parenting in Australia: demosprudence and legal change. Law Context 28:8–27
Sifris A, Gerber P (2011a) Same-sex marriage in Australia: a battleground for equality. Aust J Fam Law 25:96–120
Sifris A, Gerber P (2011b) Victorian Court circumvents prohibition on adoption by same-sex couple. Aust J Fam Law 25:275–283
Surtees N (2011) Family law in New Zealand: the benefits and costs for gay men, lesbians, and their children. J GLBT Fam Stud 7:245–263
Tasmanian Law Reform Institute (2013) The legal issues relating to same sex marriage. Research paper number 3
Walker K (2007) The same-sex marriage debate in Australia. Int J Hum Rights 11:109–130
Young L, Monahan G, Sifris A, Carroll R (2013) Family law in Australia, 8th edn. Lexis Nexis Butterworths, Chatswood, NSW

Chapter 7
The Nordic Model: Same-Sex Families in Love and Law

Hrefna Friðriksdóttir

Abstract The Nordic Countries share a common history and have a long tradition of legal cooperation. Their systems of government are often referred to as *the Nordic model* modelled on principles of equality and social security. The Nordic Countries were the first in the world to incorporate same-sex relationships into the sphere of traditional family law. One of the most outstanding features of the legal development in this area is the trust in the democratic processes and lack of challenges through the judiciary. This chapter discusses some key elements of the Nordic model and Nordic constitutional theory and follows the development of the legal regulations of same-sex relationships within family law in each of the Nordic Countries: Denmark, Norway, Sweden, Iceland and Finland.

7.1 Introduction

The Nordic Countries[1] share a common history, culture and social values and have a long tradition of legal cooperation. They are democracies with parliamentary governments. They are also strong welfare States with unique characteristics which are often embodied using the terms the Nordic welfare state model, or the Nordic model. Historically the Nordic model is molded on principles of social security, equality and opportunities for every individual.

These principles have greatly affected the development of the Nordic legal systems in different areas. The Nordic Countries were the first in the world to incorporate same-sex relationships into the sphere of traditional family law. This

[1] The Nordic Countries consist of five sovereign states: Denmark, Finland, Iceland, Norway and Sweden. The Faroe Islands and Greenland enjoy a high degree of self-goverance under the sovereignty of Denmark and the same applies to the Åland Island under Finland.

H. Friðriksdóttir (✉)
University of Iceland, Reykjavík, Iceland
e-mail: hrefnafr@hi.is

D. Gallo et al. (eds.), *Same-Sex Couples before National, Supranational and International Jurisdictions*, DOI 10.1007/978-3-642-35434-2_7,

recognition is generally accepted as having made a genuine and striking impact on the development in many other Countries.[2] One of the special features regarding the development of favorable same-sex legislation within family law in the Nordic Countries is the fact that changes have come about exclusively through the democratic process.

The aim of this chapter is to give an overview of how regulations of same-sex relationships have developed step by step in the area of family law in the Nordic Countries. Family law regulates formal relations between individuals in close emotional relationships. Legal reforms within the field of family law thus deal with the framing and reframing of concepts such as marriage, cohabitation, partnership, parentage and parental responsibilities. The chapter will begin with some notes on Nordic cooperation and characteristics of the Nordic Model that have been instrumental in the development of laws regulating same-sex relationships in the Nordic Countries. The chapter will then briefly outline the developments and major milestones in each of the five Nordic Countries. The conclusionary remarks will at last attempt to identify further similarities and divergences between the legal orders.

7.2 Nordic Family Law and Same-Sex Relationships

7.2.1 The Nordic Model

The Nordic Countries are thought to comprise one of the most stable regions in the world of parliamentary democracy, albeit each one with distinctive parliamentary models. They are characterised as consensual democracies where governments engage in dialogue with opposition parties. It has been argued that a distinctive model of political decision making has evolved in the Nordic Countries with a particular emphasis on compromise and pragmatic solutions.[3] The Nordic Countries are relatively small in population size and some have argued that the smallness has contributed significantly to a consultative and consensus based Nordic style politics.[4]

The Nordic Countries are well known as strong welfare states. Friedman argues that maximization of freedom is at the very core of welfare States and that they pursue individual freedoms through a quest for security and social guarantees.[5] This resonates with the general goal of the Nordic model to actively encourage strong

[2] Scherpe (2007), p. 266.

[3] Persson and Wiberg (2011), p. 17.

[4] Arter (2006), p. 5.

[5] Friedman (1990), p. 74.

social cohesion based on core values of equality, social solidarity, security and opportunities for all.

One of the central aspects of the Nordic Countries is their high social capital which reflects their general reliance on a consensual approach on how to develop legal norms and social policy.[6] The State has been understood as virtually identical with society as a promoter of the interests of its citizens[7] and in that sense Nordic legislation is both normatively and ideologically powerful. The pursuit of individual freedoms is thus broadly accepted as an organized, institutionalized activity rooted in the rule of law.[8]

7.2.2 *The Nordic Legal Family*

The legal systems in the Nordic Countries are generally considered a legal family of its own. As Bernitz points out the Nordic Countries are

> remarkably similar to each other as regards the fundamental perception of the legal system, its design, methodology and basic principles.[9]

These similarities are based on their common heritage, culture and social values. The Nordic Countries are all characterized as civil law Countries and judicial review in some form is an integral part of Nordic constitutional law.

The Nordic Countries have a long history of cooperation in the area of law. An underlying aim has to some extent been to achieve as much conformity as possible but also to actively exchange information and experiences.[10] The first step to the current formal, legal and political cooperation was taken in 1952 when the Nordic Council was formed.[11] The Nordic Council of Ministers, which is an equivalent cooperation between the Nordic governments, was established in 1971. Contemporary cooperation is based on the 1962 Nordic cooperation agreement known as the Helsinki Treaty. The preamble to the treaty states that the Nordic Countries will strive towards uniform rules in the Nordic Region in as many respects as possible.[12]

[6] Greve (2007), pp. 44–45.

[7] Svenson and Pylkkänen (2004), p. 18.

[8] According to comparative research elements of social capital are among the highest in the Nordic Countries, with the highest levels of generalized trust and confidence in political actors, see Giczi and Sik (2009), p. 79.

[9] Bernitz (2007), p. 18.

[10] The Nordic states are in many ways influenced by global developments and increased Europeanization, though to different degrees. All the Nordic Countries are Council of Europe Member States. Denmark (not the Faroe Islands and Greenland), Finland (along with the Åland Islands) and Sweden are members of the EU, but Norway and Iceland are EFTA Countries within the EEA (European Economic Area).

[11] The Nordic Council, www.norden.org.

[12] *Ibidem*. Accessed 15 December 2012.

7.2.3 Nordic Milestones

As stated above the Nordic Countries were forerunners in accepting and legitimizing same-sex relationships within the sphere of family law.

There are some common trends discernible in Nordic family law reform in the twentieth century that undoubtedly paved the way.[13] The Nordic Countries cooperated closely in reforming their marriage laws in the first decades of the twentieth century, placing great emphasis on gender equality and joint, equal responsibility of both spouses. This was a modern concept of marriage—as a contractual union of two equal individuals creating common financial and emotional needs and obligations.

Another step was the ensuing abolishment of the distinction between legitimate and illegitimate children emphasizing equality for children regardless of parental *status*. The most important aspect of this was to distinguish between on one hand the material consequences of marriage for the adults involved and on the other hand procreation and the needs of children; thus effectively challenging the links between marriage and procreation.

The Nordic Countries have also in general operated a dynamic approach to the definitions of families with the broad acceptance of non-marital cohabitation in society. All the Nordic Countries emphasize marriage as the preferred model for legal recognition of couples and unmarried cohabitation as a distinctly different choice of family formation. On one hand family law deals with some of the core marital rights and obligations that do not apply to non-marital cohabitation, such as dissolution and division of property and inheritance rights. Cohabitants on the other hand enjoy certain comparable rights and obligation in many other areas of law, most notably within social welfare legislation.[14]

The Nordic Council took important steps in 1984 that in many ways laid the foundation for the development of legal regulations with regards to same-sex relationships in the Nordic Countries. The Nordic Council issued two recommendations on 1st March 1984. In recommendation 17/1984 the Council urged the Nordic Countries respectively to study and collect information about the situation of homosexuals in each Country, examine the possibilities of abolishing laws discriminating against homosexuals and the possibility of adopting laws to secure the equality of homosexuals and their protection against discrimination. In recommendation 18/1984 the Council urged the governments of the Nordic Countries to cooperate within the UN and other international organizations on issues involving the human rights of homosexuals, with the objective to abolish discrimination.[15]

[13] Important necessary changes have also taken place outside the realm of family law, such as the decriminalization of same-sex sexual acts and the acceptance of different forms of anti-discrimination legislation.

[14] Friðriksdóttir (2012), pp. 151–152.

[15] Friðriksdóttir (1996), p. 9.

Table 7.1 Same-sex relationships in the Nordic Countries—some important milestones

Milestones	Denmark	Norway	Sweden	Iceland	Finland
Registered partnerships acts in force	1989	1993	1995	1996	2002
Step-parent adoption	1999	2001	2003	2000	2009
Joint custody	2010	2009	2003	1996	2002
Formal access to reproductive technologies	2006	2009	2005	2006	2006
Full adoption	2010	2009	2003	2006	n.a.
Gender neutral marriage	2012	2009	2009	2010	n.a.[a]

[a]A motion to introduce a bill proposing same-sex marriage and full adoption was rejected by the Finnish Parliament in 2012

The Nordic Council's actions were in part inspired by activity within the Council of Europe but the Nordic recommendations were much wider in scope.[16]

Before looking more closely at the developments in each of the Nordic Countries it is worthwhile to give an overview of the important milestones in legislative reform within family law.[17]

As evident from Table 7.1, the Nordic Countries have step by step taken action to reduce/abolish exclusion of same-sex couples in family law, starting with the adoption of laws on registered partnership leading up to the acceptance of a gender neutral marriage in all of the Countries except Finland.

7.2.4 Same-Sex Relationships in the Nordic Countries

This section takes a closer look at family law reform in each of the Nordic Countries. A special attention will be given to the reasoning for passing the groundbreaking laws on registered partnership and the reasoning for subsequent amendments.

7.2.4.1 Denmark

The first proposals to equate marriage with other forms of cohabitation, including same-sex relationships, was introduced in the Danish Parliament as early as in 1968, albeit unsuccessfully. The Ministry of Justice did appoint a committee to

[16] In 1981 the parliamentary Assembly of the Council of Europe adopted recommendation no. 1981 urging member states to apply the same minimun age of consent for same-sex and opposite sexual activity and to ensure equal treatment in employment and child custody decisions. The Council of Europe also adopted resolution no. 756/1981 urging the World Health Organization to remove homosexuality from its International Classification of Diseases. It may also be noted that the Parliament of the European Community adopted a resolution in 1984 requestiong member states, among other things, to legalize homosexual relationships.

[17] Countries are put in the order in which they introduced Acts on Registered Partnerships.

consider issues such as whether some provisions giving legal effects to marriage should also apply to certain marriage-like family forms but the idea of same-sex marriage was rejected by the committee in 1973 as in breach with traditional views.[18] An active debate followed, both within the LGBT community and between the community and ministerial experts in family law. In 1984 the Danish Parliament adopted a resolution to appoint a special commission to elucidate the social circumstances of homosexuals. The commission's mandate was as follows:

> Recognizing that homosexuals ought to have the possibility of living in accordance with their identity and of arranging their lives in society thereafter, and recognizing that adequate possibilities of doing this are not present, the commission shall collect and present available scientific documentation on homosexuality and the homosexual way of life as well as institute investigations to elucidate the legal, social, and cultural circumstances of homosexuals.
>
> In this connection, the commission shall propose measures aimed at removing the existing discrimination within all sectors of society and at improving the situation of homosexuals, including proposals making provisions for permanent forms of cohabitation.[19]

The Commission published an extensive report in 1988. The report deals with homosexual identity and discrimination in general, criminal law, labor law, immigration law, social law, tax law and specifically family law. The Commission states:

> [I]t must be emphasized, that the freedom of homosexuals to come forward with their own special, divergent identities, free from all types of differentiated treatment, is dependent upon society's acceptance of their existence as different, but just as worthy as other members of society. This depends on enlightenment with the objective of enhancing understanding and tolerance, and here both the school system as a whole and the media can play a part. This also depends on the legislature allowing for homosexuals by abolishing all existing differentiated treatment and taking care not to create laws that may have discriminatory effects [...] the exists a permanent obligation to ensure that homosexuals can freely seek fulfillment of their wishes in life in the same degree as others.[20]

Despite these broad statements the Commission could not reach a *consensus* on a proposal for laws allowing marriage or formal cohabitation for same-sex partners. The Commission stated that laws regulating marriage reflected society's view of the ideal family and could not as such apply unconditionally for same-sex relationships.[21] The majority of the Commission also rejected the idea of any kind of registration of same-sex relationships. The reasoning was that there was no real need for such laws as the number of homosexuals living together in family type relationships was unknown in Denmark, and that regulations protecting individuals or informal cohabitation would offer sufficient protection for any such couples. The

[18] In *Betækning* No. 1127/1988 *Homoseksuelles vilkår* [Official Governmental Report: The situation of homosexuals].

[19] *Ibidem*, p. 7.

[20] *Ibidem*, at note 19, p. 21.

[21] *Ibibem*, pp. 109–110.

majority also pointed out that Sweden had recently rejected the idea of extending further protection to homosexuals in family law context, other Countries might strongly object to such legislation and that there was no need for Denmark to be the only Country in the world to legalize homosexual partnerships.[22]

The minority of the Commission stressed the overriding importance of equality which could not be achieved without the adoption of formal registered partnership legislation. Real equality could thus not be achieved without formal equality, which required having the same rules for homosexuals and heterosexuals. The minority argued:

> In trying to achieve cultural and social equality for homosexuals, it is of absolute importance that society underlines its acceptance of homosexuals, by securing legal equality in forms of cohabitation [...] Law on partnership for two persons of the same sex can better than any other legal regulation of partnerships create a framework for families, secure each members emotional and economic loyalty and underline the mutual obligations in the same manner as marriage for heterosexuals [...] It is hard to see how discrimination against homosexuals can be avoided without offering them the same type of legal regulation as heterosexuals. Also, only be doing this can one give homosexuals the opportunity of choosing what legal regime they wish to have governing their partnership.[23]

A bill was presented by members of the Danish Parliament in 1988 relying heavily on the reasoning of the minority of the Commission.[24] The bill was passed without much debate and in May 1989 the Danish Parliament adopted law No. 372/1989 on registered partnership.[25] The law was simple in design. It allowed two persons of the same sex, to register their partnership in Denmark, following the same procedures as applied to civil marriages.[26] According to Art. 3 the registration had all the same (material) consequences as heterosexual marriage, with the explicit exception of certain (parental) consequences further enumerated in Art. 4, such as regarding adoption, joint parental responsibility and rights specifically conditioned on a person's sex (such as rules on paternity of children).

In 1997 Denmark passed laws on reproductive technologies for the first time.[27] Before that lesbian women in Denmark had access to private clinics for inseminations but the new law formally restricted access to reproductive technologies to different-sex couples.[28]

In 1998 the Government introduced a proposal widening the categories of those able to register their partnership in Denmark. In Parliament it was further proposed

[22] *Ibidem*, pp. 126–128.

[23] *Ibidem*, p. 123.

[24] Bill no. 117 and 118/1998 on registered partnership.

[25] Greenland adopted the Danish law on registered partnership in 1996 (Resolution no. 320/1996) but the partnership law is not valid in the Faroe Islands.

[26] With the exception that at least one of the partners had to be a Danish national residing in Denmark. This condition changed gradually over the years, allowing persons from other Countries with similar legislation to register their partnership in Denmark.

[27] Law No. 460/1997 on reproductive technologies.

[28] Bill No. 5/1996–1997 for law on reproductive technologies; Lund-Andersen (2003), pp. 19–20.

to open up step-parent adoption for same sex couples. This was a very important step as the discussion in Denmark for the first time moved away from rhetorical speculations surrounding the best interests of children focusing instead on the needs of children actually living with same-sex parents, thus acknowledging functional same-sex family relationships. It was argued that the legal *status* of these children was not equal to that of children in different-sex families and that their situation was even more vulnerable as they often only had one biological parent.[29] The proposals were accepted by the Danish Parliament in 1999.

After legitimizing step-parent adoptions the Danish Parliament routinely turned down proposals to diminish further the difference between registered partnership and heterosexual marriage until the year 2006. In that year the Danish Parliament changed the law on reproductive technologies allowing access for single women and lesbian couples. At this point in time the reasoning was to avoid discrimination based on sexual orientation and to underline equality, i.e. same-sex parents as equality qualified to parent a child. Reference was made to the fact that many children were growing up in same-sex families with no known adverse effects.[30]

In 2009 the Danish Parliament ordered the government to prepare a bill allowing for full adoption rights for same-sex couples. The bill was introduced in Parliament soon after along with the proposal to change the law on parental responsibility equating different-sex and same-sex couples with respect to joint custody. The goal was to secure full equality for same-sex couples with regards to adoption and custody of children. A special reference was made to the fact that single persons could adopt children in Denmark and that any regards to sexual orientation in that respect would be considered discriminatory.[31] These changes came into force in 2010.

Finally in 2012 the Danish Parliament legalized same-sex marriage and abolished the law on registered partnership.[32] This was based on the government policy document from 2011, stating that: "Freedom of the individual, equal opportunities for all, community, respect and tolerance are our values." The main goal was to secure the rights of same-sex couples to have a church wedding equal to different-sex couples.[33] The reasoning was as follows:

> Since [1989] our laws have gradually changed equating registered partnership and marriage more and more and today registered partnership has almost identical legal consequences as

[29] Parliamentary Law Committee Report 6 May 1999. With respect for Countries of origin step-parent adoptions were not available if the child had been adopted from another Country.

[30] Bill No. 151/2005–2006 for changes to the law on reproductive technologies.

[31] Bill No. 146/2009–2010 for changes to the law on registered partnership.

[32] Law No. 532/2012 on changes to the law on marriage, law on marital consequences, law on procedure and the abolishment of the law on registered partnership. This was not the first proposal of its kind that was introduced in Parliament, see for example Bill No. 123/2009–2010 for changes to the law on marriage etc.

[33] *Et Danmark – der står sammen* (2011) [A Denmark that stands together]. An English summary available at http://www.stm.dk/multimedia/Regeringsgrundlag_uk_2011.pdf. Accessed 17 December 2012.

> marriage. The difference is that registered partnership can only take place before a civil official but cannot be solemnized in a church as a marriage. Even though marriages and registered partnerships have almost identical consequences, these are still considered two distinct legal institutions in Danish law. [...] The proposal is considered as having positive effects on basic equality.

7.2.4.2 Norway

In the wake of the Nordic Council's resolution of 1984 some members of the Norwegian Parliament urged the government to appoint a committee to analyze the situation of homosexuals. The Norwegian government opted for appointing a Commission in 1985 to consider the circumstances where two people choose to live together outside of marriage and to propose changes providing for better legal protection if necessary. In 1991 the Norwegian Parliament adopted a law on joint households, providing some economic security for any two persons sharing a household for a certain period.[34]

A few members of the Norwegian Parliament proposed a bill in 1991 on registered partnership which was referred to the government for further analysis. The government then introduced an almost identical bill in 1992, based on an analysis favoring the Danish solution. The explanatory remarks accompanying the bill emphasized marriage as a fundamental institution in society but stated that:

> [T]he majority of rules surrounding marriage are based on the need for a regulation of the legal end economic aspects on a partnership and the relationship between the marriage and society. [...] Homosexual partners have the same need for legal regulation and are in this respect more like a married couple that other persons, such as kinfolk or friends that live together, because their emotional closeness will have an equivalent effect on their economic and practical relationship.[35]

In April 1993 the Norwegian Parliament adopted law No. 40/1993 on registered partnership, in all respects similar to the Danish legislation.

The government introduced a bill allowing for step-parent adoption in 2001 with the aim of securing the rights of children living with a biological parent and its same-sex partner.[36] It was argued that these families had the same need for a secure legal regulation in the event of divorce or death as other families for whom step-parent adoption was an option. Children living with a biological parent together with a social same-sex parent in a stable family relationship should therefore be able to enjoy the rights and protection that step-parent adoptions could offer.[37] The law was passed and came into force soon after.

---

[34] Law No. 45/1991 on joint households.

[35] Ot.prp. No. 32 (1992–1993) [Bill for law on registered partnership].

[36] Following the Danish example in excluding children adopted from another Country.

[37] Ot.prp. No. 71 (2000–2001) [Bill for changes to the law on adoption and law on registered partnership].

In 2005 a newly reformed coalition government in Norway issued its major policy document promising to recommend changes opening up marriage to same-sex partners. In 2007 the government introduced a bill for the repealing of the law on registered partnership along with changes to the law on marriage, law on children, law on adoption and law on reproductive technologies. The overarching aim was to secure the rights of same-sex persons, to support same-sex partners allowing them to live openly and to actively fight against discrimination.[38] The bill was accepted as law in the Norwegian Parliament in 2008 and came into force on 1st January 2009.[39] Norway thus became the first of the Nordic Countries to allow persons to enter into marriage regardless of gender. At the same time all the former restrictions on parental consequences of registered partnerships were abolished, effectively allowing same-sex partners to adopt children and lesbian partners the use of reproductive technologies. In debating the best interests of children the bill stated:

> In reviewing the current knowledge on children growing up in same-sex families the government refers to changes recently made in Sweden allowing same-sex partners to adopt children, which were founded on a thorough analysis of all relevant research. The result in Sweden was as follows: "Research strongly indicates that same-sex partners are generally qualified to provide stable homes for adopted children and to meet the special needs such children may have."[40]

Importantly the government also noted that in general restrictions on parenting for same-sex couples were likely to have negative stigmatizing effects on children already living in same-sex families.[41]

According to the law on gender neutral marriage those already in a registered partnership in Norway were offered the possibility of changing this to a marriage by a simple declaration. They could also choose to remain in their registered partnership which would then have all the same legal consequences as a marriage.

7.2.4.3 Sweden

In 1973 the Swedish Parliament passed a statement to the effect that cohabitation by two persons of the same sex was a perfectly acceptable form of family life. This statement marked a path towards acceptance and legitimacy in Sweden.[42]

---

[38] Ot.prp. No. 33 (2007–2008) [Bill for changes to the law on marriage, law on children, law on adoption, law on reproductive technologies (one marriage law for heterosexual and homosexual partners)]. The Norwegieans took due note of the Swedish report SOU 2007:17 *Äktenskap för par med samme kön: Vigselfrågor* [Swedish Government Official Reports: Marriage for person of the same sex, Formalities for entering into marriage] and subsequent proposals in Sweden, see further below in the section on Sweden.

[39] Law No. 53/2008.

[40] Ot.prp. No. 33 (2007–2008), p. 50.

[41] Ot.prp. No. 33 (2007–2008), p. 50 and pp. 61–63. For such arguments see also Friðriksdóttir (1996, 2003).

[42] Friðriksdóttir (1996), p. 18; Ytterberg (2004), pp. 428–429.

In 1978 a Commission was appointed to analyze and present scientific documentation of homosexuality and to recommend measures aimed at eliminating discrimination of homosexuals. The Commission issued a comprehensive report in 1984. The report rejected the idea of homosexual marriage by referring to the solidly established values in the community concerning marriage as an institution for the formation of families by men and women.[43] The idea of a special registration having corresponding consequences to marriage was also rejected on the grounds that the creation of a new legal institution referring solely to homosexuals would imply an unnecessary stigmatization of a group of people. The Commission was in favor of homosexual cohabitation being equated with legislation already in place for unmarried heterosexual couples and such laws were adopted in 1987.[44]

The Swedish government appointed a new Commission in 1991. This Commission issued a report in 1993 declaring its results to be based on an ideological foundation grounded in human equality, both as between individuals and under the law. The Commission stated that one important way of achieving results was: "[To] establish, as far as possible, legal parity between homosexuals and heterosexuals living together."[45] The Commission recommended the passing of laws on registered partnership similar to the Danish and Norwegian laws, reasoning that:

> The only unquestionable difference between homosexuals and heterosexuals is that homosexuals are emotionally attracted by persons of the same sex. A typical pair relationship between two women or two men is very similar to a pair relationship between a man and a woman. These relationships have the same feelings of love, consideration, tenderness, friendship, loyalty and care. Persons living in homosexual relationships have the same emotional needs to show these feelings both between themselves and outwardly, and to show their desire to live together in a lasting and mutually binding relationship, as persons living in heterosexual relationships [...] We maintain that the parties in a homosexual relationship have the same need for economic and legal security [...] Our proposals imply equating homosexual love with heterosexual love, homosexuals with heterosexuals and, last but not least, the minority with the majority.[46]

In June 1994 the Swedish Parliament adopted law No. 1117/1994 on registered partnership, formulated after the laws in Denmark and Norway.

In 1999 the government appointed a Commission to study and analyze the situation of children in homosexual families, i.e. to scrutinize the justifications underlying legal provisions regarding custody, adoption and reproductive technologies discriminating between same-sex couples and different-sex couples. The

[43] SOU 1984:63 *Homosexuella och samhället* [Swedish Government Official Reports: Homosexuals and society].

[44] Sweden had already adopted law No. 1973:651 on common homes for unmarried couples. The law was replaced by law No. 1987:282 on common homes for cohabitants and law No. 1987:813 on homosexual cohabitation. These laws were later replaced by law No. 376:2003 *Sambolag* [Law on cohabitation] confirming certain rights and obligations on both same-sex and different-sex cohabitants.

[45] SOU 1993:98 *Partnerskap* [Swedish Government Official Reports: Partnership].

[46] *Ibidem*, pp. 27–28.

leading principle of the inquiry was to be the best interests of the child. The Commission issued a comprehensive report in 2001.[47] The Report focused on available research on same-sex parenting and families and conducted some research of its own, aimed at analyzing if and how sexual orientation of parents affected living conditions and the psychological and social development of children. The Commission found that:

> All available research confirms that children growing up with homosexual parents develop psychologically and socially similar to other children. No differences can be found as regards sexual development. Some children may experience conflicts at some stages in their lives related to their parents sexual orientation. [. . .] Research shows that a child's capacity to handle such conflicts depends on the child's relationship with his or her parents. A child growing up in a loving environment, where the child is at the center of its parents love and care, has the capacity to handle such conflicts. The relevant research confirms that there are no differences between homosexual and heterosexual parents' capabilities with regards to providing quality care and support in a child's upbringing.[48]

The report notes that Swedish family law is founded on the general principle of the right of the child to have two parents and that traditionally the best interests of the child had been thought optimal by the child having two parents of opposite sex. In light of current research this was rejected as a justification for restricting the access for same-sex partners to adoption and reproductive technologies.[49] The Commission proposed to repeal all provisions currently in force prescribing different treatment for registered same-sex partners regarding adoption, joint custody and assisted reproduction.[50] The government introduced a bill that was passed in 2002 (entering into force in 2003) implementing the aforementioned proposals in the area of adoption and joint custody.[51] The bill remarked that further analysis on parental status was necessary before repealing the restrictions on the use of reproductive technologies for lesbian partners.[52] These restrictions were then repealed in 2004 (entering into force in 2005) allowing lesbian registered partners and different-sex and same-sex cohabitants access to reproductive technologies.[53]

The government appointed a special investigator in 2005 with the main task of reporting on all the reasons for or against allowing couples of the same sex to enter

---

[47] SOU 2001:10 *Barn i homosexuella familjer* [Swedish Government Official Reports: Children in homosexual families].

[48] *Ibidem*, p. 15.

[49] *Ibidem*, p. 22.

[50] See also Ytterberg (2004), p. 435.

[51] Law No. 2002:603 amending the law on registered partnership and other laws. Contrary to Denmark and Norway no exception was made for step-parent adoption of children adopted from another Country.

[52] Proposition 2001/02:123 [Government bill, Partnership and adoption].

[53] Proposition 2004/05:137 [Government bill, Assisted reproduction and parental status] and law No. 2005:447. The government looked at further aspects of parental status in the report SOU 2007:3 *Föräldraskap vid assisterad befruktning* [Swedish Government Official Reports: Parental status and assisted reproduction].

into marriage. A report was issued in 2007.[54] It notes that while international obligations could not be interpreted as an obligation to make marriage available to couples of the same sex, the relevant conventions could not be deemed to prevent national legislation from also granting the right to get married to same-sex couples. Defining marriage as a union between a man and a woman might thus not be considered discriminatory in light of human rights obligations but it nonetheless implies "a kind of special disfavorable treatment."[55] The report compares marriage and registered partnerships, stating:

> The legal effect of registered partnership does not differ significantly from marriage. However, in my opinion, marriage may be deemed to have a higher symbolic value. Marriage is traditionally considered to represent a lifelong relationship between a couple, founded on love and consideration and on mutual obligations between the spouses. Although the development of society has resulted in a somewhat different view of marriage, registered partnership does not have the same connotation as marriage in the general public consciousness. For homosexual people, marriage is important as a standard of values, both for their own relationships and for the attitude of those around them. With these points of departure there is consequently no reason for making any distinction between homosexual and heterosexual persons as regards the opportunities to be able to enter into marriage.[56]

The report also addresses, among other things, the deeply rooted societal and religious definition of marriage as a union between a man and a woman. The report emphasizes that a particular perception or definition of a social phenomenon cannot last forever. The view of society on homosexuality was a good example of how shifts in opinion and values and social progress advances can pave the way for fundamental changes.[57] The conclusion of the report is that the reasons that had been advanced against marriage for couples of the same-sex were not of sufficient substance and could not outweigh the reasons that supported a statutory amendment extending the right to marriage to same sex couples. A bill for amending the law on marriage and repealing the law on registered partnership was subsequently introduced in the Swedish Parliament in 2009. The law accepting gender neutral marriage came into force on 1st May 2009.[58]

---

[54] SOU 2007:17 *Äktenskap för par med samme kön: Vigselfrågor* [Swedish Government Official Reports: Marriage for person of the same sex, Formalities for entering into marriage].

[55] *Ibidem*, p. 33.

[56] *Ibidem*, at note 55, p. 32.

[57] *Ibidem*, p. 33.

[58] Law No. 253:2009 on amendments to the law on marriage and law no. 260:2009 repealing the law on registered partnership. The treatment of registered partnerships already established in Sweden is similar to the situation in Norway, as described above.

7.2.4.4 Iceland

The Icelandic Parliament passed a resolution in 1992 commanding the government to appoint a Commission to explore the legal, cultural and social situation of homosexuals and to propose measures to abolish discrimination against homosexuals in Iceland. The Commission was appointed in 1993 and issued a report in 1994.[59] The majority of the Commission recommended the adoption of laws similar to those already adopted in Denmark, Norway and Sweden. The minority demanded full equality within family law. In February 1996 the government introduced a bill for registered partnership similar to the laws in the aforementioned Countries.[60] In June 1996 the Icelandic Parliament adopted law No. 87/1996 on registered partnership, formulated after the laws in Denmark, Norway and Sweden.

There was one significant difference with regards to the parental consequences. At this time Iceland began making distinctions between the legal situation of children already living with a homosexual parent/s and the legal possibilities of becoming parents. The Icelandic law thus assumed joint custody of children in homosexual relationships already in 1996.[61]

In 2000 the Government introduced a proposal widening the categories of those able to register their partnership in Iceland. A parliamentary committee further proposed to open up step-parent adoption for same sex couples and the law on registered partnership was subsequently amended.[62]

In 2001 the government introduced a special report in Parliament on the legal status of cohabitants, highlighting the somewhat precarious situation of same-sex cohabitants in Icelandic legislation.[63] Parliament adopted a resolution on further analysis of the legal status of same-sex partners and the government appointed a Commission in 2003. The Commission issued a comprehensive report in 2004 and the government subsequently introduced a bill for several amendments in 2005. The bill emphasized recent positive developments in law and in society for homosexuals and stated that the discussions surrounding the law on registered partnership had facilitated growing acceptance of homosexuality as such and particularly of

[59] *Skýrsla nefndar um málefni samkynhneigðra* (1994) [Official Report from the Commission on homosexual issues].

[60] An actual translation of the terms from Icelandic would be: confirmed partnership. The main reason was to avoid confusion as in Iceland it is possible for unmarried cohabitees to register their cohabitation with the National Registry. In some areas of law such registration is required in order for unmarried cohabitation to have legal effects. In spite of this the official English translation of the Icelandic law used the term registered partnership.

[61] Alþt. 1995–1996, þskj. 564 [Icelandic Parliament 1995–1996, doc. no. 564]. Of the Nordic Countries, Iceland also has the widest scope for legal rights and duties of stepparents. According to the Icelandic laws a stepparent in a homosexual relationship could thus aquire joint custody with the birth parent and retain custody after the death of the birth parent, unless challenged.

[62] Law No. 52/2000 on amendments to the law on registered partnership. Following Denmark and Norway with respect to inter-countries adoptions.

[63] Parliamentary document no. 935: 2000–2001 Report on the legal status of cohabitants.

homosexual family life. The most important issues in the bill were firstly proposals equating same-sex cohabitation with different-sex cohabitation and secondly proposals repealing all restrictions on allowing same-sex partners access to full adoption and to reproductive technologies.[64] The reasoning for accepting same-sex parenting was the same as had facilitated similar changes in Sweden in 2003 and 2005. The bill was accepted into law and came into effect in 2006.[65]

The law on registered partnership was amended again in 2008. After discussions between the government and the Church of Iceland an agreement was reached on opening up the possibility of solemnizing registered partnerships in religious ceremonies. In passing these amendments in Parliament it was noted that the next logical step had to be to amend the law on marriage. A newly formed government in 2009 avowed in its main policy document to propose changes securing a gender neutral marriage, a bill was introduced and accepted in 2010. Law repealing the law on registered partnership and amending the law on marriage making the institution gender neutral, with the explicit aim of securing full equality, came into force in Iceland on June 27, 2010.[66]

7.2.4.5 Finland

The Ministry of Justice in Finland appointed a Commission on family issues in 1991 which issued a report in 1992.[67] The Commission recommended the passing of laws on registered partnerships but the proposal was rejected by the Finnish Parliament.[68] The Government set up another Commission in 1997 which recommended the same in its report from 1999.[69] A bill for registered partnership was introduced in 2000 and in 2001 the Finnish Parliament adopted law No. 950/2001 on registered partnership, formulated after the laws in Denmark, Norway, Sweden and Iceland.[70] The law entered into force in March, 2002.

[64] Members of the aforementioned Commission had debated the latter issues and although they accepted that there were no discernible differences between heterosexuals and homosexuals as parents, relying mostly on the Swedish report from 2001, their proposals had not been unanimous.

[65] Law No. 65/2010 amending the law on registered partnership and several other laws.

[66] Law No. 65/2010 on changes to the law on marriage and others laws. The treatment of registered partnerships already established in Iceland is similar to the that of Norway and Sweden, as described above. It is worth noting that the law on registered partnership in Iceland entered into force on the same date, June 27 1996, symbolic since the Stonewall uprising in 1969, and the same applies to most of the subsequent amendments to the legislation in Iceland.

[67] *Familjekommission betänkande* 1992:12 [Finnish Governement Official Report: The Family Commission].

[68] See further Savolainen (2003), pp. 26–27.

[69] *Justitieministeriets Betänkande* 1999:2 [Ministry of Justice Report].

[70] The law came into force in 2002. Registered partners in Finland can also obtain joint custody of a child.

In May 2002 the government appointed a Commission to investigate the legal rights of registered couples, including the possibility of adoption rights and assisted reproduction.[71] At this time there was no legislation in Finland regulating access to reproductive technologies and private clinics treated lesbian couples and single women.[72] Law on assisted reproduction was passed in 2006, effectively allowing a woman in a registered partnership access to reproductive technologies, though without establishing her partner as the co-parent of the child.[73]

In accordance with the main policy of the Finnish government a bill was introduced in 2008 allowing for step-parent adoptions for registered partners. The main goal was to strengthen the position of children already in same-sex families.[74] The bill was accepted as law which entered into force in 2009.[75]

As mentioned before, proposals for full adoption rights and gender neutral marriage have been introduced in the Finnish Parliament, but such proposals have all been rejected.

7.3 Conclusionary Remarks

When you look at the developments of the recognition of same-sex relationships within family law in the Nordic Countries, one of the most outstanding features is how rights/equality has been furthered step by step exclusively through the legal democratic processes. This resonates with the characteristics of the Nordic model described earlier where values implicit in formal laws are internalized and embedded as social norms and as such are not challenged through the judiciary.[76]

This also relates to the practice of judicial review. The Nordic Countries adopted theories and practices of judicial review in the late Nineteenth or very early in the twentieth century. After the middle of the twentieth century they in general developed a flexible interpretation of their constitutions creating a notable leeway for the legislature to address various issues. The awareness of separate roles of the legislature and the judiciary became evident with a focus on the need for judicial deference to the Parliaments with a high degree of respect for the democratic process of lawmaking.[77] This practice has in many ways been dominant in Nordic

[71] It has been argued that the Finnish gay and lesbian movement focused more on parenthood in their campaign for registered partnership than in any other Nordic Country: see Rydström (2011), p. 123.

[72] Hiltunen and Waaldijk (2004), p. 82.

[73] The issues had been hotly debated for many years as described in the bill, RP 3/2206, which became law No. 1237:2006 on assisted reproduction.

[74] RP 198/2008 [Bill for amending the law on registered partnership].

[75] Law No. 391:2009 amending the law on registered partnership.

[76] Berggren and Trägårdh (2011), p. 19.

[77] Helgadóttir (2006), pp. 251–254.

constitutional law apart from the last few decades when international and regional human rights conventions have had a growing impact on the development of constitutional interpretation. This has to some extent changed the ways Nordic courts exercise judicial review but they have never been known for radical judicial activism.

The expansion of same-sex relationship rights in the Nordic Countries owes much to the presence of strong gay and lesbian organizations cooperating with favorable governments.[78] It has been pointed out that the way this Nordic state/civil society interaction has been institutionalized and routinized may provide useful inspiration to others.[79] This cooperation has most notably been channeled through well prepared and researched government bills and/or government appointed commissions armed with the task of providing practical and theoretical analysis of the situation in society and law and proposing acceptable amendments to the legal order. This approach can be time consuming and the amount of time and energy spent has differed from one Country to another at different points in time. This can partly explain why laws have been amended at different times in the Nordic countries.[80]

Many have recognized the step by step approach in the movement towards full equality, or how certain legal steps pave the way for further and greater recognition. Waaldjik refers to working of the "law of small change" and describes how the recognition of homosexual relationships has been governed by a clear pattern of steady progress according to standard sequences.[81] It is interesting to note how this applies to the development within the Nordic Countries. Within family law the turning point was the acceptance of the legitimacy of homosexual families through the introduction of registered partnership legislation. The next logical step was acknowledging same-sex families already having children, then the acceptance of same-sex partners as legitimate parents and finally gender neutral marriage.

It is also interesting to look at the interaction between the Nordic Countries in this respect. The legal reforms are obviously not the results of formal cooperation between the Countries but the reforms are intrinsically linked together.[82] A

[78] Merin (2010), p. 66. Rydström (2011), p. 168 suggests that a de-radicalisation of the movements is an important factor in explaining why gay marriage became a priority for the national gay and lesbian movements and why it had any chance to be accepted by mainstream society.

[79] Berggren and Trägårdh (2011), p. 27.

[80] Glass et al. (2012), p. 170, compared the extension of marriage rights for same sex couples in five Countries—the Netherlands, Belgium, Norway, Sweden and Spain—and concluded that the single most important factor predicting the extension was the ascension of a strong leftist ruling party or coalition.

[81] Waaldijk (2004) pp. 439–440. Fassin (2004), p. 188 notes how history supports the optimistic narrative. See also Adams, p. 273, and Lund-Andersen (2003), p. 23.

[82] Finland does lag a little behind the other Nordic Countries. One possible reason can by the fact that the Icelandic, Danish, Norwegian and Swedish languages are very closely related and the last three are largely understood in the other Countries. Finnish is of quite another origin and this may hamper successful formal and informal cooperation on legal matters.

government commission in a Nordic Country requested to analyze a certain situation routinely looks closely at the developments in the other Nordic Countries (and also often further abroad). The impact is twofold, firstly the Nordic Countries seek a level of uniformity for practical reasons and secondly accepted theoretical and legal analysis in one Nordic Country can greatly affect understanding and social norms in another.[83] This is obvious when looking at registered partnership. The introduction of registered partnership legislation was a revolutionary step in the development of modern family law.[84] This formulation was the result of a long debate in Denmark and was in many ways a political tactic as a way of securing important rights by steering clear of the most contested issues (direct access to marriage and parenting).[85] The Danish model was relatively quickly followed in the other Nordic Countries without much theoretical debate on the formulation of this (or any other possible) new family law institution.

It is also important to note how the formulation of this new family institution steered the debate well away from a long (and still) contested area of the legal differences between marriage and unmarried cohabitation in society in general. The Nordic Countries have never in any real sense debated whether registered partnership should be available to different-sex partners. Registered partnership was always seen as equivalent to marriage as a starting point, which different-sex partners could choose if they wanted to, with restrictions of rights no one thought conceivable that any different-sex partners would wish for.[86] This is also evident from the fact that Norway, Sweden, Iceland and Denmark have all repealed the laws on registered partnership upon accepting gender neutral marriage laws.

The laws on registered partnership were of tremendous symbolic importance in making same-sex families with children and wishing to have children more visible.[87] The comprehensive Swedish research report from 2001 on same-sex parenting had a clear strong impact in Iceland, Denmark and Norway, paving the way for new accepted values and norms in society and finally in law. The same can be said about the Swedish report from 2007 legitimizing the idea of same-sex marriage. Having repealed, or being in the throes of repealing, all restrictions or differences in treatment of registered partners and married couples, Norway, Sweden, Iceland and Denmark quickly rejected the separate but equal doctrine[88] and embraced gender neutral marriage with almost identical reasoning.

---

[83] Jänterä-Jareborg, p. 148 speaks of the importance of the uniformity of approach.

[84] Scherpe (2007), p. 286.

[85] Adams, p. 273. Rydström (2011), p. 168, suggests that the idea of a separate registration for homosexuals was not orginially Nordic but was discussed in different European gay and lesbian movements in the 1960s.

[86] Fassin (2004), p. 188 uses the term "quasi-marriage". In admitting same-sex partners into a legal realm alongside of marriage, albeit with restrictions, it also became almost self evident that same-sex cohabiting partners would automatically enjoy the same legal rights and protection afforded the less revered institution that cohabiting different-sex partners enjoyed in various areas of law.

[87] Lund-Andersen (2004), pp. 425–426.

[88] Ytterberg (2003), p. 8.

It is quite amazing to see the strong legal reasoning by the governments and Parliaments in Norway, Sweden, Iceland and Denmark for accepting gender neutral marriage, being almost identical to the powerful and reasonable pleas for equality and non-discrimination so thoroughly rejected by the same governments a few decades before.[89] It is theoretically possible that positive outcomes might have come about more speedily through the judicial process at one point or another but the societal and political deliberations ('the learning curve') most certainly were not hampered by the possible stifling effects of a negative judgment in court.

References

Adams B (2003) The defence of marriage act and American exceptionalism: the "Gay Marriage" Panic in the United States. J Hist Sex 12:259–276

Arter D (2006) Democracy in Scandinavia: consensual, majoritarian or mixed? Manchester University Press, Manchester/New York

Berggren H, Trägårdh L (2011) Social trust and radical individualism: the paradox at the heart of Nordic capitalism. In: Shared norms for the new reality: the Nordic way. World economic forum Davos, Stockholm, pp 13–27. http://www.globalutmaning.se/wp-content/uploads/2011/01/Davos-The-nordic-way-final.pdf

Bernitz U (2007) What is Scandinavian law? Scand Leg Stud 50:13–30

Betækning No. 1127/1988 Homoseksuelles vilkår [Official Governmental Report The situation of homosexuals]

Et Danmark – der står sammen (2011) Regeringen, Danmark [A Denmark that stands together, The Government, Denmark]. http://www.stm.dk/multimedia/Regeringsgrundlag_uk_2011.pdf

Familjekommission betänkande 1992:12 [Finnish Government Official Report, The Family Commission]

Fassin E (2004) Sociological questions: an epilogue to "More or less together". In: Waaldijk K (ed) More or less together: levels of legal consequences of marriage, cohabitation and registered partnership for different-sex and same-sex partners. Ined, Paris, pp 187–192

Friðriksdóttir H (1996) The Nordic gay and lesbian "marriage": no children allowed. LLM thesis, Harvard Law School

Friðriksdóttir H (2003) Leyfilegar og óleyfilegar fjölskyldur: Mannréttindi og lagaleg staða samkynhneigða fjölskyldna [Accepted and unaccepted families: human rights and the legal situation of same-sex families]. In: Traustadóttir R, Kristinsson Þ (eds) Samkynhneigðir og fjölskyldulíf [Gays, lesbians and family life]. Háskólaútgáfan, Reykjavík, pp 47–74

Friðriksdóttir H (2010) Ein hjúskaparlög fyrir alla [One marriage laws for all]. In: Heiðursrit Ármann Snævarr 1919–2010 [In honor of Ármann Snævarr]. Codex, Reykjavík, pp 233–258

Friðriksdóttir H (2012) Munur á hjúskap og óvígðri sambúð [The difference between marriage and unmarried cohabitation]. Úlfljótur 65:149–190

Friedman L (1990) The republic of choice. First Harvard University Press, Cambridge

Giczi J, Sik E (2009) Trust and social capital in contemporary Europe. In: Tóth IG (ed) Tárki European Social Report 2009, pp 63–81

Glass CM et al (2012) Toward a European model of same-sex marriage rights: a viable pathway for the US. Berkley J Int Law 29:132–174

Greve B (2007) What characterise the Nordic welfare state model. J Soc Sci 3:43–51

[89] Friðriksdóttir (1996, 2003, 2010).

Helgadóttir R (2006) The influence of American theories of judicial review on Nordic constitutional law. Martinus Nijhoff Publishers, Leiden/Boston

Hiltunen R, Waaldijk K (2004) Major legal consequences of marriage, cohabitation and registered partnership for different-sex and same-sex partners in Finland. In: Waaldijk K (ed) More or less together: levels of legal consequences of marriage, cohabitation and registered partnership for different-sex and same-sex partners. Ined, Paris, pp 79–92

Jänterä-Jareborg M (2003) Registered partnerships in private international law: the Scandinavian approach. In: Boele-Woelki K, Fuchs A (eds) Legal recognition of same-sex couples in Europe. Intersentia, Antwerp/Oxford/New York, pp 137–158

Lund-Andersen I (2003) The Danish registered partnership act. In: Boele-Woelki K, Fuchs A (eds) Legal recognition of same-sex couples in Europe. Intersentia, Antwerp/Oxford/New York, pp 13–23

Lund-Andersen I (2004) The Danish registered partnership act, 1989: has the act meant a change in attitude? In: Wintemute R, Andenæs M (eds) Legal recognition of same-sex partnerships: a study of national, European and international law, 2nd edn. Hart Publishing, Oxford-Portland, pp 417–426

Merin Y (2010) Equality for same-sex couples: the legal recognition of gay partnerships in Europe and the United States. The University of Chicago Press, Chicago

Persson T, Wiberg M (2011), The Nordic model of parliamentary government and its challenges. In: Parliamentary government in the Nordic countries at a crossroads: coping with challenges from Europeanisation and Presidentialisation. Santérus Academic Press, Stockholm, pp 17–40

Rydström J (2011) Odd couple: a history of gay marriage in Scandinavia. Aksant, Amsterdam

Savolainen M (2003) The Finnish and the Swedish partnership acts – similarities and divergences. In: Boele-Woelki K, Fuchs A (eds) Legal recognition of same-sex couples in Europe. Intersentia, Antwerp/Oxford/New York, pp 24–40

Scherpe JM (2007) The Nordic countries in the Vanguard of European family law. Scand Leg Stud 50:265–288

Skýrsla nefndar um málefni samkynhneigðra (1994) Forsætisráðuneytið. Ísland 1994 [Official Report from the Commission on homosexual issues, Office of the Prime Minister, Iceland]

SOU 1984:63 Homosexuella och samhället [Swedish Government Official Reports: Homosexuals and society]

SOU 1993:98 Partnerskap [Swedish Government Official Reports: Partnership]

SOU 2001:10 Barn i homosexuella familjer [Swedish Government Official Reports: Children in homosexual families]

SOU 2007:3 Föräldraskap vid assisterad befruktning [Swedish Government Official Reports: Parental status and assisted reproduction]

SOU 2007:17 Äktenskap för par med samme kön: Vigselfrågor [Swedish Government Official Reports: Marriage for person of the same sex, Formalities for entering into marriage]

Svenson E, Pylkkänen A (2004) Contemporary challenges in Nordic feminist legal studies. In: Svenson et al. (eds) Nordic equality at a crossroads: feminist legal studies coping with difference. Ashgate Publishing Limited, Aldershot, pp 17–46

Waaldijk K (2004) Small change: how the road to same-sex marriage got paved in the Netherlands. In: Wintemute R, Andenæs M (eds) Legal recognition of same-sex partnerships: a study of national, European and international law, 2nd edn. Hart Publishing, Oxford-Portland, pp 437–464

Ytterberg H (2003) All human beings are equal, but some are more equal than others – equality in dignity without equality in rights? In: Boele-Woelki K, Fuchs A (eds) Legal recognition of same-sex couples in Europe. Intersentia, Antwerp-Oxford-New York, pp 1–10

Ytterberg H (2004) From society's point of view, cohabitation between two persons of the same sex is a perfectly acceptable form of family life: a Swedish story of love and legislation. In: Wintemute R, Andenæs M (eds) Legal recognition of same-sex partnerships: a study of national, European and international law, 2nd edn. Hart Publishing, Oxford-Portland, pp 427–436

Chapter 8
A Glorious Revolution? UK Courts and Same-Sex Couples

Aidan O'Neill

Abstract This chapter traces the developing jurisprudence and legislation in the United Kingdom concerning same sex couples. It focuses on the opposing pulls made on this issue as between equality law and human rights law. Equality law is about the State changing society, by legislating to instruct and educate institutions and individuals as to how they might act in their public interactions: thus employers and employees, teacher and pupils, providers of goods and services to the public have now to be blind to differences in race, in gender, in age, in sexuality; they have to uncaring to differences in religion or belief; and they have to be ready to make reasonable adjustments for the differently abled. Human rights law is, by contrast, essentially about limitations being imposed upon the State, to stop it from interfering in how individuals may choose to structure their lives. It may be said to seek to carve out areas of freedom for individuals and voluntary organisation—privacy, free expression, free exercise of religion—which the State should not interfere in (except for very good reason) and if the State does interfere in those freedoms it has to do so only in a manner which does not discriminate on grounds of sex, race, age, religion, social status and the like. So equality law arises from the State not doing enough to protect its citizens and those in its care, whereas human rights law arises from the perception that the State is doing too much in oppressing its citizens and those at its mercy. The fulcrum for the creative tension between these two notions in recent United Kingdom law has been the legalisation of same sex marriage.

A. O'Neill (✉)
Matrix Chambers, London, UK
e-mail: aidanoneill@matrixlaw.co.uk

D. Gallo et al. (eds.), *Same-Sex Couples before National, Supranational and International Jurisdictions*, DOI 10.1007/978-3-642-35434-2_8,

8.1 Introduction: From the Period of Criminalisation to That of Liberalization

Same sex conduct was first criminalised in Britain after the sixteenth century Protestant Reformations in these islands, as part of a conscious ideological shift which wrested issues concerning the regulation of (private) sexual behaviour from the jurisdiction of priests and confessors operating under the canon law of the courts of the Roman Church, and making them instead matters for the royal courts to determine and punish.

In 1533 a statute of the English Parliament made the "detestable and abominable vice of buggery committed with mankind or beast" a capital offence. The criminal law of England (including this statute) was subsequently extended to Ireland when its legal system was adopted in whole the common law of England, particularly after the Act of Union of 1800 between Great Britain and Ireland, which resulted in the abolition of a separate Parliament in Dublin.

Scotland, even after the 1707 Union creating the United Kingdom of Great Britain, retained a separate legal system. In Scotland the criminal law was, in large part, the creation of the judges at common law-judges of the High Court of Justiciary in Edinburgh exercised that court's claimed inherent declaratory power[1] to find and declare all and any same sex conduct between males to be criminal, even in the absence of—or indeed supplementing—specific legislation on this matter.[2] But as recently as 1976, sect. 7 of the Sexual Offences (Scotland) Act 1976 (a consolidating provision) positively re-enacted for Scotland section 11 of the Criminal Law Amendment Act 1885, the "Labouchère amendment" which had been used to convict Oscar Wilde and which made it an imprisonable offence for any male person, in public or in private, to commit an act of "gross indecency" with another male.

For over 400 years in the British Isles, then, same sex sexual acts between men were criminalized (though homosexual acts between women were never specifically made the subject of any criminal legislation).

The first liberalizing change in the law in the UK happened with the passing of the Sexual Offences Act 1967 which, at least in the jurisdiction of England and Wales, decriminalized consensual sexual acts in private between two males, so long as neither of whom were in the Armed Forces or serving in the Merchant Navy and both were aged over 21 and where no other person or persons were present.

Such limited decriminalization of same-sex acts did not formally occur in Scotland until 1980. And, in the face of a campaign of public demonstration organized by local religious leaders to "Save Ulster from Sodomy", same sex

---

[1] See *Grant v. Allen*, 1987 JC 71 per Lord Justice-Clerk Ross: "[T]his court has an inherent power to punish any act which is obviously of a criminal nature".

[2] See for example *McLaughlan v. Boyd*, 1934 JC 19. In *Webster v. Dominick*, 2005 JC 65 a court of five judges decided to abolish the previously recognized crime of "shameless indecency" and replace it with a crime of different scope which they termed "public indecency".

conduct between two consenting adult males was not decriminalized in Northern Ireland until 1982.[3]

There has of course been significant change in the past 40 years (and, more particularly, over the past decade) in the law's approach in the UK to same-sex conduct. But unusually for common law legal systems, which are in so many ways the creation of the judges, the changes which have occurred in the matter of homosexuality has largely resulted from legislation rather than by any activist or progressive decisions from UK judges.

But the decisions and developments to which the national legislatures in the UK have been responding have been European in nature, rather than national. Because the UK has no written constitution, the three distinct legal systems in the UK (English law, Scots law and Northern Ireland law) are remarkably porous to European law. We have the paradox that in the UK we have perhaps the most politically Euro-skeptic of countries but which contains legal systems which are perhaps the most open to European influence.

So, in contrast to other essays in this collection, the case of the UK represents a study in national judicial *in*activism, one where the undoubted radical change in the position of same-sex couples has resulted from decisions of the national legislature, albeit often prompted by developments at a European level. This particular situation justifies an analysis principally founded on the impact of the European legislation and jurisprudence on UK legislation and jurisprudence.

8.2 The UK's Approach to Same-Sex Conduct and Couples: The Interaction Between the European Court of Human Rights and National Courts

The decriminalization of homosexual activity in Northern Ireland in 1982 only occurred as a result of the judgment of the European Court of Human Rights (also further referred to as ECtHR or the Strasbourg Court) in *Dudgeon v. United Kingdom*[4] which found that this continuing criminalization of same-sex conduct was in breach of Art. 8 ECHR right to respect for private life, albeit that the Court allowed that question of what the age of consent for homosexual acts might be (and the possibility of having a differing age of consent between heterosexual and homosexual acts) lay at that stage of European *consensus* on these issues still lay within the margin of the contracting States. There is no doubt, as said in the

[3] The issue of same sex-conduct remains a sensitive one in Northern Ireland. See, for example, *Christian Institute's Application for Judicial Review* [2007] NIQB 66, [2008] NI 86 in which local religious groups successfully challenged, for want of proper consultation, the provisions outlawing harassment on grounds of sexual orientation contained in the Equality Act (Sexual Orientation) Regulations (Northern Ireland) 2006.

[4] *Dudgeon v. United Kingdom*, n. 7525/76, judgment of 22nd October 1981.

Introduction, that the ECtHR was the main motor for the rapid liberalization in the law in the UK relating to same-sex sexual conduct which has occurred thereafter. It is also very important to stress that many of these Strasbourg cases were applications from the UK, which could only be made after all domestic remedies had been exhausted and the national courts had failed to provide any effective remedy to the litigants.[5]

Decisions of the Strasbourg Court became particularly influential after 2 October 2000 when the Human Rights Act 1998—which incorporated into domestic law many of the substantive rights contained in the European Convention—came fully into force in UK. But even before the Human Rights Act 1998 formally required national courts to take account of Strasbourg jurisprudence its influence was spilling over into the decisions of national courts.

8.2.1 Gays Openly in the Military

On 3 November 1995 the Court of Appeal of England and Wales held in *R v. Ministry of Defence, ex parte Smith and Grady, R v. Admiralty Board of the Defence Council, ex parte Lustig-Prean and Beckett*,[6]—a judicial review of the UK Ministry of Defence's "Policy and Guidelines on Homosexuality" which imposed a ban on homosexuals serving in the Armed Forces—held that discrimination on grounds of sexual orientation as such fell outside the scope of the Equal Treatment EC Directive 76/207 and that the appellants had no remedy against their dismissal in UK law. Their remedy had therefore to be sought before the European Court of Human Rights which, on 27 September 1999 in the case of *Lustig-Prean and Beckett v United Kingdom*, found that the investigation of the sexuality, and subsequent dismissal, of homosexual service personnel from the UK Armed Forces on grounds simply of their sexual orientation contravened their Convention rights under Art. 8 ECHR.[7] On 12 January 2000 the Secretary of State for Defence announced in Parliament a change in policy whereby homosexuality was no longer seen as *per se* incompatible with service in the Armed Forces.

[5] On same-sex couples under the ECHR see the Chapters by Crisafulli and Pustorino in this volume.

[6] *R v. Ministry of Defence, ex parte Smith and Grady, R v. Admiralty Board of the Defence Council, ex parte Lustig-Prean and Beckett* [1996] QB 517.

[7] *Lustig-Prean and Beckett v. United Kingdom*, n. 31417/96 and Smith *and Grady v. the United-Kingdom*, n. 33985/96, judgments of 27th September 1999.

8.2.2 *Equalisation of the Age of Consent Between Gay and Straight*

The age of consent was equalized as between same-sex and opposite sex sexual conduct with the coming into force of the Sexual Offences (Amendment) Act 2000. Again this change was by way of legislation passed in the wake of the Report in July 1997 of the European Commission of Human Rights in *Sutherland v. United Kingdom*[8] which found there to be a violation of Art. 14 taken in conjunction with Art. 8 ECHR and affirmed, for the first time in Strasbourg case-law, that the principle of equal treatment of homosexuals and heterosexuals under the criminal law was a principle contained within the European Convention of Human Rights.[9]

8.2.3 *Children and Their Gay Parents*

On 21 December 1999 the European Court of Human Rights held that discrimination in child custody disputes on grounds of the (homo)sexual orientation of the parent contravenes Art. 14 as well as Art. 8 ECHR.[10]

On this issue at least the Strasbourg jurisprudence had already been anticipated in the UK. In fact, in *T, Petitioner*, a decision of 26 July 1996, the Scottish civil appeal court, the Inner House, reversed a decision of the judge at first instance ("the Lord Ordinary") who had refused to permit a severely disabled child to be adopted by single gay man in a committed relationship of some 10 years duration on the grounds that, in the judge's opinion, it could not be in best interests of the child to be adopted into and brought up in a gay household. In reversing the decision of the Lord Ordinary, the first instance judge, the Lord President, Lord Hope, presiding over the Inner House (the Scottish appeal court) made the following observations:

> The Lord Ordinary's position on this matter was expressed by him in these terms:
>
> '... In my view there is a fundamental question of principle as to whether the statutory process of adoption should be sanctioned by the court in circumstances where it is expressly

---

[8] *Sutherland v. United Kingdom*, n. 25186/1997, report of 1st July 1997. The application to the ECtHR in this case was, by consent, struck out by the Court following the coming into force of the Sexual Offences (Amendment) Act 2000: see *Sutherland v. United Kingdom*, n. 25186/94, judgment of 27th March 2001.

[9] See to like effect the Strasbourg Court's judgment in *A.D.T. v United Kingdom*, n. 35765/0, judgment of 31 July 2000, where the ECtHR ruled a prosecution under UK criminal law which differentiated between the criminality of (videoed) group same-sex consensual sexual acts conducted in private, compared to group different-sex consensual sexual acts conducted in private constituted a violation of Art. 8 ECHR.

[10] *Salgueiro da Silva Mouta v. Portugal*, n. 33290/96, judgment of 21st December 1999.

proposed by a single male prospective adopter that the child should be brought up jointly by himself and by a third party with whom he cohabits in a homosexual relationship.'

As I understand these observations, which are expressed in general terms without reference to the particular facts of this case, he saw the question of the petitioner's homosexuality as raising two issues: the first is whether it is within the intendment of the Adoption (Scotland) Act 1978 that a child can be adopted by a person who is homosexual and is cohabiting with a third party in a homosexual relationship; the second is whether, if it is within the intendment of the Act, the court can nevertheless ever be satisfied that the child's welfare can be safeguarded in such circumstances.

In my opinion the short answer to the concerns which the Lord Ordinary has expressed on this point is that the present case raises no such fundamental question of principle. Section 6 of the 1978 Act states that, in reaching any decision relating to the adoption of a child, the court shall have regard to all the circumstances, first consideration being given to the need to safeguard and promote the welfare of the child throughout his childhood. There can be no more fundamental principle in adoption cases than that it is the duty of the court to safeguard and promote the welfare of the child. Issues relating to the sexual orientation, lifestyle, race, religion or other characteristics of the parties involved must of course be taken into account as part of the circumstances. But they cannot be allowed to prevail over what is in the best interests of the child. The suggestion that it is a fundamental objection to an adoption that the proposed adopter is living with another in a homosexual relationship finds no expression in the language of the statute...

Where public policy stands on homosexuality is a matter for the court to determine from the material placed before it and then to apply, so far as it may be relevant, to the facts of the case. So the judge may examine such material as the intendment of the Act and decisions and dicta in other cases in order to discover objectively what, if anything, public policy has to say on the issue. In that exercise he is performing a judicial function on behalf of the court. What he must not do is to permit his own personal views, or his own private beliefs, to affect his judgment.[11]

8.2.4 Death and the Same-Sex Couple

In its decision of 28 October 1999 in *Fitzpatrick v. Sterling Housing Association*[12] the UK's highest court, the Appellate Committee of the House of Lords, reinterpreted an existing UK statute protecting "family members" for the purposes of succession to a statutory tenancy to include same-sex partners. This case may be said to mark the first law relating to same-sex couples in the UK and for the first time shows the UK courts going ahead of Strasbourg jurisprudence in these matters, demonstrating a very interesting interconnection between the UK and Strasbourg jurisprudence.

It was not until its July 2003 decision in *Karner v. Austria*[13] that the Strasbourg Court applied the Convention prohibition against differential treatment on grounds of sexual orientation to landlord and tenant law and found that the decision of the Austrian Supreme Court to the effect that the surviving member of a cohabiting couple was not entitled to be recognised as the "life companion" of his late partner

---

[11] *T, Petitioner*, 1997 SLT 724, IH.

[12] *Fitzpatrick v. Sterling Housing Association* [2001] 1 AC 27, HL.

[13] *Karner v. Austria*, n. 40016/98, judgment of 24th July 2003.

by reason of the fact the parties in the relationship were of the same sex, thereby preventing him from succeeding to his partner's tenancy, constituted a breach of Art. 8 and 14 ECHR. As for other cases previously cited, this case was then followed and applied by the House of Lords in its June 2004 decision in *Ghaidan v. Godin-Mendoza* which held for the first time that a same-sex couple could be regarded by the law as if they were each other's spouses.[14]

8.3 The UK's Approach to Same-Sex Couples: The Influence of EU Law

The other transforming influence on the UK courts and legislature on this issue was the EU legislature, rather than the Court of Justice of the European Union (further referred to as CJEU) which has not been particularly progressive on the issue of sexual orientation discrimination.[15]

The CJEU in *Grant v. South West Trains*[16] had rejected the argument that the prohibition of sex discrimination in EU law extended to discrimination on grounds of sexuality. Further, in *D v. Council* the CJEU held that it considered it lawful under EU law for the Council of Ministers to discriminate in the employment benefits paid to its employees in opposite-sex relationships and those paid to employees in (State-registered) same-sex relationships.[17] And in *MacDonald v. Ministry of Defence*[18] the House of Lords followed this line of CJEU authority to hold that the Sex Discrimination Act 1975 could *not* be interpreted so as to cover discrimination on grounds of sexual orientation.

8.3.1 The EU Legislature Prohibits Sexual Orientation Discrimination in the Workplace

Protection against workplace discrimination on grounds of sexual orientation required legislative intervention from a European level.

On 27 November 2000 Council Directive 2000/78/EC (the Employment Equality Directive)[19] was adopted which outlawed discrimination in the workplace on a

---

[14] *Ghaidan v. Godin-Mendoza* [2004] 2 AC 557, HL.

[15] See the Chapter by Orzan and the one by Rijpma and Koffeman in this volume.

[16] *Grant v. South West Trains*, C-249/96, judgment of 17th February 1998 [1998] ECR I-621.

[17] *D v. Council*, C-122/99P, judgment of 31st May 2001 [2001] ECR I-4319, upholding the decision of the Court of First Instance in case *D v. Council*, T-264/97, judgment of 28th January 1999 [1999] ECR SC I-A-I and II-1.

[18] *MacDonald v. Ministry of Defence* [2003] ICR 937, HL.

[19] Council Directive 2000/78/EC of 27th November 2000 establishing a general framework for equal treatment in employment and occupation, OJ 2000 L 303, p. 16.

number of grounds, including sexual orientation. The Employment Equality Directive laid down minimum requirements as regards legal protection against workplace discrimination on grounds of sexual orientation. The Directive was implemented in the UK by the Employment Equality (Sexual Orientation) Regulations 2003 (SI 2003/1661).

These UK regulations as originally implemented contained broad exceptions allowing for discrimination on grounds of sexual orientation to be lawful in any employment where being of a particular sexual orientation could be said to be "a genuine occupational requirement". And an even wider derogation was allowed in respect of employment "for purposes of an organized religion" where "a requirement related to sexual orientation" was allowed to be a considered to be "genuine occupational requirement".

In the UK, a judicial review challenging to the EU law compatibility of these broad exceptions to the non-discrimination principle was unsuccessful on the basis that the court considered that these derogations were to be read as narrowly as possible such that the apparent exemptions had more symbolic than real value,[20] but the case highlighted a (still unresolved) tension between the right to be free from discrimination on grounds of sexual orientation against the claims of certain institutions and individuals that the free exercise of their religious beliefs requires them to be allowed to discriminate against others on the grounds of the (homo) sexual orientation of those others.

8.4 Same-Sex Couples in the Twenty-First Century: The UK Legislature Becomes the Motor for Change in the UK

The coming into force of the prohibition against discrimination in the workplace on the basis of sexual orientation marked something of a watershed in legal, political and social attitudes towards homosexuality in the UK. Since making the Employment Equality (Sexual Orientation) Regulations 2003, the UK has forged far ahead of the minimum requirements of EU and ECHR law. The overwhelming political consensus in this country appears to be to ensure the full equality before the law for all purposes for everyone in the UK, gay or straight. The main statutory provisions which seek to realize such equality are, currently, the Civil Partnership Act 2004, the Equality Act 2010 and the Marriage (Same Sex Couples) Act 2013 (and its counterpart in Scotland, the Marriage and Civil Partnership (Scotland) Act 2014).

---

[20] *R (on the application of AMICUS–MSF section, NUT and others) v. Secretary of State for Trade and Industry* [2007] ICR 1176 (EWHC, Admin).

8.4.1 *Civil Partnerships and Same Sex Marriages*

The Civil Partnership Act 2004 first made comprehensive provision for the legal recognition of same-sex couples who register their partnership in the UK.

In *Wilkinson v. Kitzinger*[21] Potter P. noted that, in enacting the Civil Partnership Act 2004, the Parliament decided that there should be statutory recognition of a status and relationship closely modeled upon that of marriage that sought to remove the legal, social and economic disadvantages suffered by same-sex couples and made available to civil partners essentially every material right and responsibility arising from marriage (including for all tax matters), with the exception of the form of ceremony and the actual name and status of marriage.

The Civil Partnership Act 2004 was something of a compromise measures designed to reassure the churches and defenders of the "traditional" definition of marriage as a lifelong sexual and faithful union between one man and one woman would not be changed or affected by the extension of certain legal recognition to couples in a same sex relationship. As originally enacted the legislation allowing for the creation of (same-sex) civil partnerships maintained some few distinctions from opposite-sex marriage. The Marriage (Same Sex Couples) Act 2013 has since been rather awkwardly bolted on to the existing legal regime for civil partnerships, in that same sex couples now have the option (denied to opposite sex couples) of entering into (or maintaining their existing) civil partnership or marrying. But there is no substantive difference in the rights and obligations afforded to civil partners as compared to same sex spouses

8.4.1.1 Same Sex Marriages and Civil Partnerships Have Nothing (Expressly) to Do with Sex

Heterosexual sexual intercourse is central to the notion of (opposite sex) marriage under the present law.

Sect. 12 of the Matrimonial Causes Act 1973 provides that an opposite sex marriage shall be voidable if (a) the marriage has not been consummated owing to the incapacity of either party to consummate it or (b) the marriage has not been consummated owing to the willful refusal of one of the parties to it. And the civil contract of marriage brings with it obligations of mutual sexual fidelity of the spouse such that "adultery" constitutes one of the grounds for establishing the irretrievable breakdown of a marriage such as to justify the court in pronouncing a decree of divorce.[22] Both consummation and adultery are understood by the law to refer to acts connected with heterosexual intercourse.[23]

---

[21] *Wilkinson v. Kitzinger* [2006] EWHC 2022 (Fam); [2007] 1 FLR 295.

[22] See, for example section 1(2)(a) of the Matrimonial Causes Act 1973.

[23] See for example *Dennis v. Dennis* [1955] P 153, EWCA and *W. v. W: physical inter-sex* [2001] Fam 111.

By contrast, the Civil Partnership Act 2004 was deliberately drafted to avoid any mention of or reference to any kind of sexual acts, and the Marriage (Same Sex Couples) Act 2013 continues with this same policy of reticence. There is no provision in the legislation for the dissolution of a civil partnership or of a same sex marriage on grounds of its "non-consummation" or on grounds of the "adultery" of one of the civil partners or same sex spouses. Instead there is a general reference to the possibility of seeking a court order mandating the dissolution of a civil partnership or a same sex marriage on the basis of its irretrievable breakdown.[24] But the best measure of how far the law has changed on the matter of same-sex relations is perhaps best seen in the terms of sect. 42 of the Civil Partnership Act 2004 which allows the court to adjourn proceedings for the dissolution of a civil partnerships "if at any stage of proceedings for the order it appears to the court that there is a reasonable possibility of a reconciliation between the civil partners". These provisions are also paralleled within the Marriage (Same Sex Couples) Act 2013 in England and Wales and Marriage and Civil Partnership (Scotland) Act 2013 in Scotland. Same-sex relationships are now something which the State sees it has a role to foster and encourage by pursuing the possibility of reconciliation between estranged civil partners or same sex spouses.

8.4.1.2 Same Sex Marriages and Civil Partnerships and Religious Ceremonies

The law in the UK does not recognize a distinction in 'types' of marriage: 'religious' as opposed to 'civil' marriage.[25] This distinction refers simply to the different formalities which might be gone through, as a matter of law, to achieve the one state of a valid and legally recognized marriage. Thus, the law concerning capacity to marry and impediments to marriage does not differ according to the form by which a marriage is solemnized[26] and the grounds on which a marriage is void or voidable are the same irrespective of the form by which it was solemnized.[27]

Sect. 11(c) of the Matrimonial Causes Act 1973 previously provided that a marriage is void unless the parties are "respectively male and female"[28] but this provision was repealed by the Marriage (Same Sex Couples) Act 2013.

---

[24] See Hayden et al., p. 236, para. 8.112: "The question of what constitutes separation or unreasonable behaviour will be the same as for divorce since the provisions of the Civil Partnership Act 2004 mirror the provisions of the Matrimonial Causes Act 1974 in this respect. The only distinction is that adultery is not a fact on which an applicant can rely in asserting that a [same-sex] relationship has broken down for the purposes of obtaining a dissolution. However there is nothing to prevent the formation by one party of an intimate relationship with another person being cited as evidence of unreasonable behaviour".

[25] See *Hudson v. Leigh* [2009] EWHC 1306 (Fam); [2009] 2 FLR 1129.

[26] See e.g., sections 1 and 2 of the Marriage Act 1949.

[27] See sections 11 and 12 of the Matrimonial Causes Act 1973. On this see Court of Appeal in *R v. Dibdin* [1910] P 57 by Cozens Hardy MR at 109.

[28] *Bellinger v. Bellinger* [2003] UKHL 31 and *Corbett v. Corbett* (*otherwise Ashley*) [1971] P 83.

8.4.1.2.1 Marriage in England and Wales in an Anglican Church

Persons who are otherwise legally eligible to marry one another according to general law of England and Wales have a right to have their marriage solemnized in their local Anglican parish church by clergy of the (established) Church of England and/or of the (formerly established) Church in Wales. This right to be married according to the rites of the Church of England or of the Church in Wales is *not* dependent on the individuals in question being members of the (or, indeed, any) Church.[29] All that is required to exercise this right to a(n) Anglican) Church wedding in England or Wales is that at least one of the prospective spouses possesses the legal qualification of residence in or connection with the Anglican parish.[30] A minister of the Church of England (or Church in Wales) who, without just cause, refuses to marry persons otherwise entitled to be married in his or her church or chapel commits an ecclesiastical offense for which he or she is punishable in the ecclesiastical courts.[31]

Ministers of the Church of England (and the Anglican Church in Wales) are undoubtedly carrying out a "public function" when marrying two individuals who have the requisite residence connection within the relevant geographical area of a parish church.[32] And when carrying public functions (on behalf of the State) the Church—and its clergy—are obliged to act in accordance with the requirements of the general law of the law (including human rights law).

The Marriage (Same Sex Couples) Act 2013 expressly excludes same sex couples (however devoutly Anglican) from this right to be wed in their local Anglican parish, while still maintaining the right of an opposite sex couple (regardless of any religious affiliation or practice) to be married in an Anglican Church in England or in Wales. The 2013 Act provides that a Minister of the Church of England or of the Church in Wales has no legal power to solemnize or conclude a marriage between a same sex couple who would otherwise be eligible to marry under the general law. It would be unlawful for such a Minister to attempt or purport

---

[29] *R v. James* (1850) 3 *Car & Kir* 167, CCR. See too *R.* (*on the application of Baiai*) *v. Secretary of State for the Home Department* [2008] UKHL 53, [2009] 1 AC 287 per Baroness Hale at [37]:

> [T]he Church of England believes itself (with some parliamentary encouragement, for example in sections 57 and 58 of the Matrimonial Causes Act 1857 (20 &21 Vict c 85)) required to marry for the first time anyone who lives in the parish regardless of faith or the lack of it.

[30] *Argar v. Holdsworth* (1758) 2 Lee 515.

[31] *Davis v. Black* (1841) 1 QB 900.

[32] *Aston Cantlow and Wilmcote with Billesley Parochial Church Council v. Wallbank and Another* [2003] UKHL 37; [2004] 1 AC 546 per Lord Rodger of Earlsferry, para. 170.

> For the most part, in performing his duties and conducting the prescribed services, the minister is simply carrying out part of the mission of the Church [of England], not any governmental function of the state. On the other hand, when in the course of his pastoral duties the minister marries a couple in the parish church [of the Church of England], he may be carrying out a governmental function in a broad sense and so may be regarded as a public authority for purposes of the Human Rights Act 1998.

to conduct a same sex wedding. In so enacting the 2013 Act makes new provision for a difference in treatment which is based solely on the sexual orientation (and/or the sex/gender of one) of the couple seeking marriage. This exemption which prohibits same sex marriage but allows opposite sex marriage to be conducted in the Church of England and in the Church in Wales made the scheme discriminatory in breach of art. 14 read together with art. 12.[33] This discrimination, in principle, calls for justification before the Strasbourg Court in order to be lawful. In its decision in *Kozak v. Poland*, the Court went so far as to say that:

> if the reasons advanced for a difference in treatment were based *solely* on the applicant's sexual orientation, this *would* amount to discrimination under the Convention.[34]

And as the Court noted in *Savez Crkava "Rijec Zivota" v. Croatia*[35]:

> [T]he Convention, including its art.9(1), cannot be interpreted so as to impose an obligation on states to have the effects of religious marriages recognised as equal to those of civil marriages.[36] ... It also notes that Croatia allows certain religious communities to provide religious education in public schools and nurseries and recognises religious marriages performed by them. The Court reiterates in this connection that the prohibition of discrimination enshrined in art.14 of the Convention applies also to those additional rights, falling within the wider ambit of any Convention article, for which the state has voluntarily decided to provide.[37] Consequently, the state, which has gone beyond its obligations under art.9 of the Convention in creating such rights cannot, in the application of those rights, take discriminatory measures within the meaning of art.14.[38]

But it would be difficult to justify this difference in treatment of same sex and opposite sex couples seeking marriage in an Anglican church before the Strasbourg Court, even on claimed religious liberty/autonomy grounds,[39] given that this

---

[33] See *R. (on the application of Baiai) v Secretary of State for the Home Department* [2008] UKHL 53, [2009] 1 AC 287 per Baroness Hale:

Article 12 does also envisage national laws governing the capacity to marry, but these must obviously be non-discriminatory and consistent with the fundamental principles of dignity, equality and freedom which underlie the whole Convention. ... The declaration of incompatibility ... should ...make it clear that it is directed solely at the discrimination between civil and Anglican preliminaries to marriage.

[34] *Kozak v. Poland*, n. 13102/02, judgment of 2 March 2010 at [92]. See, to similar effect, *Genderdoc-M v. Moldova*, n. 9106/06, judgment of 12th June 2012, para. 51.

[35] See *Savez Crkava "Rijec Zivota" v. Croatia*, n. 7798/08, judgment of 9th December 2010, paras 56 and 58.

[36] See *X v. Germany*, n. 6167/73, judgment of 18th December 1974; *Khan v. United Kingdom*, n. 11579/85, judgment of 7th July 1986; *Spetz v. Sweden*, n. 20402/92, judgment of 12th October 1994; and *Şerife Yiğit v. Turkey*, n. 3976/05, judgment of 2nd November 2010, para. 102.

[37] See *EB v. France*, n. 43546/02, judgment of 22nd January 2008, para. 48.

[38] See, *mutatis mutandis*, *EB v. France* n. 43546/02, judgment of 22nd January 2008, para. 49.

[39] Religious autonomy is not, in any event an absolute principle under ECHR jurisprudence as is plain from the decision *Sindicatul "Păstorul cel Bun" v. Romania* n. 2330/09, judgment of 9 July 2013 (Grand Chamber) where the Strasbourg Court found that a ban on priests and other employees of the state recognised Romanian Orthodox church from forming and joining trade unions was Convention incompatible. And see *Lombardi Vallauri v. Italy*, n. 39128/05, judgment

universal duty to marry is one imposed/maintained by the State on the Anglican Churches (in England and Wales) by the general law.[40] Indeed, given sections 1[41] and 3[42] of the Submission of the Clergy Act 1533 it would be *ultra vires* for the Church of England or the Church in Wales to seek to modify or revoke this general marriage duty by their own canon law.

8.4.1.2.2 Marriage in a Non-Anglican Church

In England and Wales marriages may also be solemnized according to non-Anglican religious rites[43] within approved religious premises.[44] Express provision is made in both the Civil Partnership Act 2004 and in the The Marriage (Same Sex Couples) Act 2013 to the effect that nothing in these Act places an obligation on religious organisations to host civil partnerships or solemnise same sex marriages if the religious organisation do not wish to do so.[45]

---

of 20th October 2009 holding that, in the circumstances of the non-renewal of the contract of a long-serving legal academic in a private Catholic university, the Italian courts should have required the university (and by necessary implication the supervising Church authorities) to provide full and proper reasons for the claims made against the applicant which led to the decision not to renew his contract. The university's mission to deliver a Catholic education could not, in the Strasbourg Court's view, justify such a basic denial of the applicant's rights to a fair process.

[40] Compare *O'Donoghue v. United Kingdom*, n. 34848/07, judgment of 14th December 2010 where a mirror requirements (that couples subject to immigration control were *obliged* to marry in an Anglican church in order to avoid having to obtain and pay for a certificate of approval from the Secretary of State at a cost to them of £295) was conceded by the UK Government and confirmed by the Court to be Convention incompatible. Through being subject to a regime to which those wishing to marry in the Church of England would not have been subject, the prospective married couple's rights under art.14, taken together with art.9, had been breached.

[41] Section 1 of the Submission of the Clergy Act 1533 provides (in modern spelling) as follows:

[I.] The Clergy shall not make any Constitutions except in Convocation with the King's Assent, &c.

They not any of them from henceforth shall presume to attempt allege claim or put in use any constitutions or ordinance provincial or Synodal or any other canons, nor shall enact promulgate or execute any such canons constitutions or ordinance provincial, by what so ever name or names they may be called in their convocations in time coming, which always shall be assembled by authority of the King's writ, unless the same Clergy may have the King's most Royal assent and licence to make promulgate and execute such canons constitutions and ordinances provincial or Synodal; upon pain of every one of the said Clergy doing contrary to this act and being thereof convicted to suffer imprisonment and make fine at the King's will.

[42] Section 3 of the Submission of the Clergy Act 1533 provides (in modern spelling) as follows:

"III. No Canons, &c. shall be enforced contrary to the King's Prerogative.

Provided always that no canons constitutions or ordinance shall be made or put in execution within this Realm by authority of the convocation of the clergy, which shall be contrary or repugnant to the King's prerogative Royal *or the customs laws or statutes of this Realm*; anything contained in this act to the contrary hereof notwithstanding."

[43] See sect. 26(1)(a) of the Marriage Act 1949.

[44] Sect. 41 of the Marriage Act 1949.

[45] See Regulation 3A of the Marriages and Civil Partnerships (Approved Premises) Regulations 2005.

8.4.1.2.3 Marriage and Civil Partnership in a Non-Religious Civil Ceremony

If an (opposite-sex) couple wished to marry in a purely civil ceremony before a registrar they were prohibited from doing so in religious premises or from using any religious wording or imagery in the wedding ceremony.[46]

Sect. 2(4) of the Civil Partnership Act 2004 similarly provides that "no religious service is to be used while the civil partnership registrar is officiating at the signing of a civil partnership document". Originally civil partnerships could not be celebrated on religious premises but under pressure from certain 'faith groups' (notably Quakers, Unitarian and some Liberal Jewish congregations) who wished their places of worship to be open to and embracing of same-sex couples, civil partnerships, though still without religious rites, may be solemnized in premises which have been duly approved by the registration authorities notwithstanding that these premises are otherwise used solely or mainly for religious purposes.

It should be noted the maintenance of the statutory ban against the use of any religious service at a civil partnership held in religious premises—which, at the request of religious bodies, have been duly approved under the 2005 Regulations—may itself come to be challenged as a discriminatory infringement of the fundamental right to "manifest religion or belief, in worship, teaching, practice and observance" which is protected under both Art. 9 ECHR and Art. 10 CFR amounting to, in effect, illicit State interference in the internal and doctrinal affairs of a religious body.[47] Arguably the Scottish provision Marriage and Civil Partnership (Scotland) Act 2013 which gives an opt-out to individual ministers of religion from being required to celebrate or solemnise same sex marriages even where their church or governing religious body has chosen so to do also constitutes a Convention incompatible interference in the internal affairs of a religious body, contrary to the principle of respect for the autonomy of the churches.

8.4.1.3 Conscientious Objection and the Civil Registrar

In *Ladele v London Borough of Islington*[48] the Court of Appeal ruled that a civil registrar who from reasons of religious conscience refused to officiate at same-sex civil partnership ceremonies could lawfully be dismissed from her employment by her local authority employers. The fact that Ms. Ladele's refusal to perform civil partnership duties was based on her religious view of marriage could not justify the

[46] Sect. 46B(4) of the Marriage Act 1949 provides that "no religious service shall be used at a marriage on approved premises in pursuance of section 26(1)(bb) of this Act".

[47] See *Supreme Holy Council of the Muslim Community v. Bulgaria*, n. 3903/97, judgment of 16th December 2004, para. 96. See too *Fernández Martínez v. Spain*, n. 56030/07, judgment of 15th May 2012, para. 84.

[48] *Ladele v London Borough of Islington* [2010] ICR 532, CA.

non-implementation of her employer's aim to the full, namely that all registrars should perform civil partnership duties as part of its "Dignity for All" policy. Ms. Ladele was employed in a public job and was required to perform a purely secular task pursuant to the policy which sought to avoid discrimination. Her refusal to perform the task involved discriminating against gay people. Her view of marriage was not a core part of her religion, and the council's requirement no way prevented her from worshipping as she wished.

The Court of Appeal observed that the right to manifest religion or beliefs under Art. 9 ECHR was a qualified right and that the employer was acting lawfully in insisting that Ms. Ladele's albeit genuine desire to have her religious views relating to marriage respected should not be permitted to override the council's concern to ensure that all its registrars manifest equal respect for gay people as much as non-gay people. However, at para. 75 of his judgment in *Ladele* in the Court of Appeal, Lord Neuberger observed in passing that:

> some registration authorities have (as I understand to be the case) decided not to designate registrars who shared Ms Ladele's beliefs as civil partnership registrars, and ... such decisions may well be lawful.

But the Strasbourg Court has held that discrimination (whether on grounds of sex or of sexual orientation) cannot be justified, even if based on conscientious and religiously based convictions. This would be a situation directly comparable—on the basis of the law outlawing any discrimination on racial grounds—to that of a registrar seeking to be excused from officiating at mixed race weddings. Any such request would simply not be acceded to by any employer under any circumstances because the request would always be an instance of unlawful discrimination, no matter its motivation.[49] The European Court of Human Rights Grand Chamber has reiterated in *X v. Austria*:

> Sexual orientation is a concept covered by Article 14. The Court has repeatedly held that, just like differences based on sex, differences based on sexual orientation require particularly serious reasons by way of justification or, as is sometimes said, particularly convincing and weighty reasons. Where a difference of treatment is based on sex or sexual orientation the State's margin of appreciation is narrow. Differences based solely on considerations of sexual orientation are unacceptable under the Convention.[50]

In *Eweida and others v. United Kingdom*[51] the European Court of Human Rights upheld the Convention compatibility of the dismissal of Ms. Lillian Ladele as a registrar of births deaths and marriages in response to her conscientious objection seeking to be excused from solemnising same sex civil partnerships.

---

[49] See *R. (on the application of E) v JFS Governing Body* [2010] 2 AC 728, UKSC.

[50] *X and others v. Austria*, n. 19010/07, judgment of 13th February 2013, para. 99.

[51] *Eweida and others v. United Kingdom*, n. 48420/10, judgment of 15th January 2013.

8.4.2 *The Equality Act 2010 and Its Application*

The Equality Act 2010 is largely a consolidating measure which brings into the four corners of one statute the various grounds or characteristics (sex, transgendered identification, married/civilly partnered status, race, disability, age, sexual orientation, and religion or belief) which may form the basis for a claim of unlawful discrimination.

One of the other aims of the statute is avowedly to attempt to simplify and harmonize the approach to equality law across the field by providing, where possible, for the same approach or tests to be applied under reference to all the protected characteristics as regards claims to discrimination, harassment or victimization claims.

In principle, sex discrimination law protects men and women equally. Sexual orientation discrimination law wishes the equality of treatment between gay and straight. But the Equality Act's prohibition on discriminatory treatment against those identifying as trans gives legal protection only to those who would so identify themselves. The Equality Act does give equal protection to a woman making the transition to being a man, as to a man making the transition to being a woman; and it requires equivalent protection for those who have started out on the process of changing their gender with those who have completed the process, at least to their own satisfaction.

8.4.2.1 Marriage and Civil Partnership to Be Treated as of Equivalent Status within the ambit of EU Law

The prohibition in the Equality Act 2010 on married/civilly partnered state discrimination protects only those who are married or civilly partnered[52] and requires that the two states be treated equivalently at last in so far as the treatment at the issue falls within the ambit of EU Law.[53]

Yet while the married and civilly partnered are protected against discrimination because they are married or civilly partnered[54] (rather than simply in a close

[52] Sect. 8 of the Equality Act 2010 specifies 'marriage or civil partnership' as one of the protected characteristics under the Act.

[53] See to like effect under EU law: *Tadao Maruko v. Versorgungsanstalt der deutschen Bühnen*, C-267/06, judgment of 1st April 2008 [2008] ECR I-1757 and *Jürgen Römer v. Freie und Hansestadt Hamburg*, C-147/08, judgment of 10th May 2011 [2011] ECR I-3591.

[54] The categories of sex and marital status discrimination can be interconnected. In *Chief Constable of the Bedfordshire Constabulary v Graham* [2002] IRLR 239 (EAT), a challenge to a police force's policy restricting officers who were married to or in a (opposite-sex) relationship with another officer from working together, was found not to be marital status discrimination but was, instead, discriminatory on grounds of sex, in that a higher proportion of women police officers were found to be in relationships with their male colleagues than the proportion of male constables in relationships with their female fellow officers.

relationship with[55]) to a particular individual,[56] the single—or those cohabiting without benefit of the law, whether gay or straight—are not expressly protected under the Equality Act 2010 against discrimination because unwed,[57] though the treatment of a gay couple who are not civilly partnered may be held to constitute unlawful discrimination against them on grounds of sexual orientation even in situations where an unmarried opposite sex couple would have been treated in the same way[58] on the grounds that the opposite-sex couple might have had the option of marriage to each other open to them whereas the same sex couple do not.[59]

8.4.2.2 Prohibition Against Sexual Orientation Discrimination Extended to Provision of Goods and Services to the Public and to All Functions of a Public Law Nature

It should be noted too that the provisions of the Equality Act 2010 go beyond the requirements of EU law as embodied in the various anti-discrimination directives in that the prohibition against discrimination (on grounds, among others, of sexual orientation) in UK law is not limited to the workplace but extends to the provision of goods and services to the public and the exercise by public bodies of public functions.

The Equality Act (Sexual Orientation) Regulations 2007[60] first made it unlawful for a person concerned with the provision to the public (or a section of the public) of goods, facilities or services to discriminate on the basis of sexual orientation in the way he or she provides those goods, facilities or services. The relevant parts of these Regulations have since been repealed and re-enacted in the Equality Act 2010. These provisions have been found to entail that an adoption agency which has a strong religious ethos (which is evidenced by the terms of its constitutive trust deed)

---

[55] See *Hawkins v. Atex Group Ltd* [2012] ICR 13157, EAT holding that the characteristic protected was the fact of being married. The appropriate comparator would be someone in a relationship akin to marriage, but who was not actually married.

[56] See *Dunn v. Institute of Cemetery and Crematorium Management* [2012] ICR 941, EAT holding that a person who was married, or in a civil partnership, was protected against discrimination on the ground of that relationship and on the ground of their relationship to the other partner.

[57] Though see *In re P (A Child) (Adoption: Unmarried Couples)* [2009] 1 AC 173 where the House of Lords declared that it was contrary to fundamental rights for the Family Division of the High Court of Justice in Northern Ireland to reject the appellants as prospective joint adoptive parents on the ground only that they were cohabiting but not married to one another.

[58] See *Hall and Preddy v. Bull* [2012] EWCA Civ 83; [2012] 1 WLR 2514 (at the time of writing this case was being appealed to the UK Supreme Court).

[59] *Black v. Wilkinson* [2013] EWCA CIV B20, [2013] 1 WLR 2490.

[60] SI 2007/1263.

is nonetheless not permitted to continue to insist on any express or implicit religiously based requirement that it will provide its adoption services only to married opposite sex couples.[61]

8.4.2.3 Duty on Public Sector Bodies Actively to Promote Equality Between Gay and Straight

Further, Sect. 149 of the Equality Act 2010 obliges public authorities in the exercise of their functions to have due regard to the need to:

(a) Eliminate discrimination, harassment, victimization and any other conduct that is prohibited by or under this Act, and
(b) To advance equality of opportunity between persons who share a relevant protected characteristic and persons who do not share it

and also to "tackle prejudice, and promote understanding".

In *R.* (*on the application of Johns*) *v. Derby City Council*[62] the claimant husband and wife sought permission to apply for judicial review to challenge the approach of the defendant local authority to their application to be approved as short-term, respite, foster carers. The claimants were members of the Pentecostalist Church and believed that sexual relations other than those within marriage between one man and one woman were morally wrong. They applied to the local authority to be short-term foster carers.

The local authority considered that the applicants' expressed views on same-sex relationships did not equate with the National Minimum Standards for Fostering Services, which required carers to value individuals equally and to promote diversity. The local authority argued it could lawfully decide not to approve a prospective foster carer who objected to homosexuality and same-sex relationships and was unable to respect, value and demonstrate positive attitudes towards homosexuality and same-sex relationships. In refusing the applicant's permission for judicial review the court observed that the attitudes of potential foster carers to sexuality were relevant when considering an application for local authority approval.

The court made reference to Statutory Guidance on Promoting the Health and Well-Being of Looked-After Children issued under Section 10 of the Children Act 2004 which provided that support in relation to the sexual health of looked-after children should be provided regardless of the children's sexual orientation and should not be affected by individual practitioners' personal views. If children, whether they were known to be homosexuals or not, were placed with carers who

---

[61] See *Catholic Care (Diocese of Leeds) v. Charity Commission for England and Wales* [2012] UKUT 395 (TCC), [2012] *Equality Law Reports* 1119.

[62] *R.* (*on the application of Johns*) *v Derby City Council* [2011] EWHC 375 (Admin); [2011] 1 FCR 493.

objected to or disapproved of homosexuality and same-sex relationships, there might well be a conflict with the local authority's duty to safeguard and promote the welfare of looked-after children.

There might also be a conflict with the National Minimum Standards and the Statutory Guidance. Accordingly the local authority was entitled to explore and have regard to the extent to which prospective foster carers' beliefs might affect their behaviour and their treatment of a child being fostered by them. If it had failed to explore those matters it might very well have found itself in breach of its own guidance and of the National Minimum Standards and the Statutory Guidance and indeed of the public sector equality duty contained in sect. 149 of the Equality Act 2012.

8.4.2.4 Homophobia and Freedom of Expression

In similar tenor is the decision of Lang J. in *Core Issues Trust v Transport for London*[63] upholding the Convention compatibility of a ban on a bus advertisement which referred to the possibility of individuals being "ex gay" or "post gay". This advertisement had been sponsored by Christian groups for display on London buses and was seen to be a response to a previous bus advertising campaign sponsored by LGBT campaigning groups to the effect that "some people are gay; get over it".

The judge upheld the Convention compatibility of the ban on the Christian groups' advertisement, notwithstanding a decision-making process by Transport for London ("TfL") which was found to have been procedurally unfair and in breach of TfL's own procedures in that: TfL failed to consider the relevant issues (including impact upon the claimants' Convention rights) before coming to the decision; TfL did not duly and timeously notify to the claimant the decision and the reasons for it; and TfL took the decision too quickly and without analysis of its own policy and its past practice.

The judge considered that the advertisement was liable to encourage homophobic views[64] and that TfL would be acting in breach of its public sector equality duty under Section 149 of the Equality Act 2010 if it had allowed the advertisement to appear on its buses.[65] In the whole circumstances, the judge considered that TfL's

---

[63] *Core Issues Trust v. Transport for London* [2013] EWHC 651 (Admin), [2013] HRLR 22.

[64] *Ibidem*, para. 142.

"The Trust has the right to express its view. But, as I have already indicated, this advertisement is a confrontational assertion, not a reasoned, informed contribution to a debate. I consider that it is liable to encourage homophobic views, whether intentionally or not, and, in general terms, homophobia places gays at risk."

[65] *Ibidem*, para. 144.

"In my judgment, TfL would be acting in breach of its duty under section 149 if it allowed the Trust's advertisement to appear on its buses, as it encourages discrimination, and does not foster good relations or tackle prejudice or promote understanding, between those with same-sex sexual orientation and those who do not."

refusal to display the advertisement was justified and proportionate, in furtherance of the legitimate aim of protecting the rights of others. It was therefore said not to be in breach of the claimants' rights to free expression under Article 10 ECHR. The claimants' rights to freedom of thought conscience and religion under Article 9 were said not even to be engaged.[66] And the court was of the view that there was no breach of the anti-discrimination provisions of Article 14 ECHR since the claimants (and those who described themselves as ex gay or post-gay[67]) were not a protected group under the Equality Act 2010.

8.4.2.5 Equality of Treatment of Gay and Straight Received by the UK Courts as a General Principle of (Common) Law

In *HJ (Iran) v. Secretary of State for the Home Department*[68] the general principle of equality of treatment as between gay and straight was applied within the context of a claim by a refugee from Iran seeking asylum in the UK from State-sponsored (and religiously inspired) persecution in his country of origin on the basis of his sexual orientation.

The UK Supreme Court (which replaced the Appellate Committee of the House of Lords as the UK's highest court in October 2009) rejected the claim of the Secretary of State that the applicant could "reasonably accommodate" himself to his persecutors and, in effect, choose no longer to be a victim of persecution if, on being returned to Iran, he were to live 'discreetly'.[69] The lead judgment, concurred

---

[66] *Ibidem*, paras 160–162

"In my judgment, Article 9 is not engaged in this case. First, because the rights protected by Article 9 cannot be enjoyed by corporate entities or non-natural persons such as associations (see *Lester & Pannick: Human Rights Law & Practice*, (3 ed.), at 4.9.4; *Vereniging v Rechtswinkels Utrecht v Netherlands* 46 DR 200 (1986) E Com HR). *Article 9 rights may be enjoyed by religious communities and churches, but the Trust is neither of those*. Second, because *the Trust is seeking to express its perspective on a moral/sexual issue, not the manifestation of a religious belief.*

[67] *Ibidem*, paras 153–156:

The Trust submitted that TfL discriminated against ex-gays who are a protected class under the Equality Act 2010, falling within the definition of sexual orientation in section 12, and that ex-gays face hostility and discrimination from both homosexuals and heterosexuals. I do not accept this submission, for two reasons. First, this claim is brought by the Trust, which as a corporate body, has no sexual orientation and therefore is not a victim of any discrimination on the grounds of sexual orientation. Second, ex-gays are not protected under the Equality Act. Section 12 prescribes three categories of sexual orientation protected under the Act: orientation to persons of the same sex (homosexuals); orientation to persons of the opposite sex (heterosexuals); orientation to persons of either sex (bisexuals). There is no fourth category of persons who were previously orientated to persons of the same sex and are now orientated to persons of the opposite sex.

[68] *HJ (Iran) v. Secretary of State for the Home Department* [2011] 1 AC 596, UKSC.

[69] Lord Rodger's analysis in *HJ (Iran)* has since been expressly taken up and followed in the context of the exercise of religious liberty both in the jurisprudence of the CJEU and in the Scottish courts: *Y and Z v. Germany*, joined cases C-71/11 and C-99/11, judgment of 5th September 2012 nyr., concerned a claim for asylum based on fear of persecution for religious beliefs and the

in by all his colleagues, was given by the late Lord Rodger of Earlsferry who in rejecting this submission, expressing founded upon the principle of equality of gay and straight, noting:

> 77 At the most basic level, if a male applicant were to live 'discreetly', he would in practice have to avoid any open expression of affection for another man which went beyond what would be acceptable behavior on the part of a straight man. He would have to be cautious about the friendships he formed, the circle of friends in which he moved, the places where he socialized. He would have constantly to restrain himself in an area of life where powerful emotions and physical attraction are involved and a straight man could be spontaneous, impulsive even. Not only would he not be able to indulge openly in the mild flirtations which are an enjoyable part of heterosexual life, but he would have to think twice before revealing that he was attracted to another man. Similarly, the small tokens and gestures of affection which are taken for granted between men and women could well be dangerous. In short, his potential for finding happiness in some sexual relationship would be profoundly affected. It is objectionable to assume that any gay man can be supposed to find even these restrictions on his life and happiness reasonably tolerable......
>
> 80. ... [A] tribunal has no legitimate way of deciding whether an applicant could reasonably be expected to tolerate living discreetly and concealing his homosexuality indefinitely for fear of persecution. Where would the tribunal find the yardstick to measure the level of suffering which a gay man - far less, the particular applicant - would find reasonably tolerable? How would the tribunal measure the equivalent level for a straight man asked to suppress his sexual identity indefinitely? The answer surely is that there is no relevant standard since it is something which no one should have to endure.[70]

8.4.2.6 Statutory "Ministerial Exemption" from Prohibition on Sexual Orientation Discrimination

Para. 2 of Schedule 9 to the Equality Act 2010 effectively sets out the UK's own statutory "ministerial exemption" clause.[71]

This makes provision, in the context of "employment for the purposes of an organized religion", for the application of occupational requirements relative to

Opinion of 19th April 2012 of Advocate General Bot noted at paras 100, 103–105. And see to similar effect *AHC (Pakistan) v. Secretary of State for the Home Department* [2012] CSOH 147 (11 September 2012) *per* Lord Stewart at [46]: "[I]f a proper respect for human rights entails that individuals should be entitled to live out their sexuality openly, they should be as much entitled to live out their religious faith; and that no one should be expected to veil his or her faith from a motive of self-protection".

[70] *HJ (Iran) v Secretary of State for the Home Department* [2011] 1 AC 596, paras 76–80.

[71] The ministerial exemption is a doctrine developed by the courts in the United States which would exempt religious organisations from general anti-discrimination measures. In *Hosanna-Tabor Evangelical Lutheran Church v. Equal Employment Opportunity Commission and others* 565 US (2012) (12 January 2012) the US Supreme Court held that the "Establishment" and "Free Exercise" Clauses of the First Amendment to the US Constitution bar suits brought on behalf of those employed in any religious capacity against their employing religious organisation claiming that they had suffered unlawful treatment in violation of anti-discrimination statutes.

sex, to issues of gender reassignment,[72] to married/civil partnership status and to sexual orientation. No mention is made of the possibility of such religious genuine occupational requirements relative to race, disability or age. Any requirement imposed on the expressly permitted grounds in para. 2 in relation to "employment for the purposes of an organized religion" need not be shown to be proportionate or necessary, or aimed at some legitimate end.

Instead, the statute requires only that the court be satisfied that the requirement or requirements in question is or are being applied "so as to comply with the doctrines of the religion" (the "compliance principle") or, because of the nature or context of the employment, to "avoid conflicting with the strongly held religious convictions of a significant number of the religion's followers" (the "non-conflict principle").

Thus there might be imposed, under reference to para. 2:

(a) A requirement to be of a particular sex (thereby allowing, for example, for the continuation of a male-only priesthood) (para. 2(4)(a))[73];
(b) A requirement not to be a transsexual person (thereby permitting, for example, the maintenance or imposition of a ban on transsexuals as priests or ministers, or monks or nuns) (para. 2(4)(b));
(c) A requirement not to be married or a civil partner (and so allowing for single status/celibacy requirements to be maintained in relation to priests or monks and nuns) (para. 2(4)(c));
(d) A requirement not to be married to, or the civil partner of, a person who has a living former spouse or civil partner (so allowing for a prohibition on church employees from being married or civilly partnered to the divorced) (para. 2(4)(d));
(e) A requirement relating to the circumstances in which a marriage or civil partnerships came to an end (allowing, perhaps, for ordination for those

[72] Paras 24 and 25 of Schedule 3 to the Equality Act 2010 contains exceptions from the general prohibition of gender reassignment discrimination in section 29 of the Act for the religious solemnisation of marriages allowing, for example a clergyman in the Church of England to indicate to an engaged couple resident in his parish that he will not solemnise their marriage as he reasonably believes that one of the couple has acquired his or her gender under the Gender Recognition Act 2004. This would not be unlawful discrimination because of gender reassignment.

[73] Where a church allows both men and women to be ordained however then this may open up the possibility of sex discrimination claims based on allegations of differential treatment among Ministers by their church on grounds of sex. See *Percy v. Church of Scotland*, 2006 SC (HL) 1, [2006] 2 AC 28. In *President of the Methodist Conference v Preston (formerly Moore)* [2013] UKSC 29 [2013] ICR 833 (15 May 2013) the UKSC by a majority (Lady Hale dissenting) distinguished the decision of the House of Lords in *Percy* and held that, in the absence of some special arrangement having been made with a particular minister, the rights and duties of ministers of the Methodist Church arose entirely from their status in the constitution of the Church and not from any contract. Accordingly, the majority of the court ruled that claimant/respondent, a former minister, had not been an employee of the Church and had not been entitled to bring a claim for unfair dismissal against it.

previously married who are now widowed or whose marriages had been annulled, while maintaining a ban against ordination of the divorced) (para. 2 (4)(e));

(f) A requirement related to sexual orientation (para. 2(4)(f)).

Such religiously justified or mandated requirements may then be applied by the relevant decision-maker within the context of employment for the purposes of an organized religion as the basis for decisions about: to whom to offer, or to refuse, employment, or (not) to recommend for appointment to a personal or public office; promotion within employment or office; dismissal from employment or termination of office. The Explanatory notes to the Equality Act 2010 observe:

> 790. This specific exception applies to employment for the purposes of an organised religion, which is intended to cover a very narrow range of employment: ministers of religion and a small number of lay posts, including those that exist to promote and represent religion. ... This exception would apply to a requirement that a Catholic priest be a man and unmarried. This exception is unlikely to permit a requirement that a church youth worker who primarily organises sporting activities is celibate if he is gay, but it may apply if the youth worker mainly teaches Bible classes. This exception would not apply to a requirement that a church accountant be celibate if he is gay.

The provisions of para. 2 of Schedule 23 EA seem to be inviting the courts to become becoming mired in matters of ecclesiastical sensitivity and/or theological controversy by requiring them to enter into what has otherwise been described as the "judicial no-man's land of religious doctrine and practice".[74]

The court would have to determine and rule to its satisfaction in any such dispute. First, on ecclesiological questions of what constitutes the relevant "religious organization": whether the individual Minister; or the particular congregation of the church; or the Synod or assembly of any larger Church of which that congregation forms part and whether the larger Church is seen as constituted and delimited territorially or whether regard may be had to any transnational communion of which the national Church may be part. Secondly, on doctrinal question so what if any are the actual doctrines of the relevant religious organization once this has been identified and determined by the court. Finally, on sociological question as to what the religious convictions of this religion's followers might be, how strongly these convictions are held and as to what would constitute a "significant number" of this religion's followers.

8.4.2.6.1 UK Ministerial Exemption Incompatible with EU Law?

As we noted above the possibility of (religious) employers being permitted to discriminate on grounds of sexual orientation has a somewhat controversial history.

[74] *Khaira v. Shergill* [2012] EWCA Civ 983 [2012] PTSR 1697 *per* Mummery LJ, para. 24. (At the time of writing this case was under appeal to the UK Supreme Court).

The UK first made provision in regulation 7(3) of the Employment Equality (Sexual Orientation) Regulations 2003 (SI 2003/1661)[75] for religious organizations to be able to impose occupational requirements on their employees specifically relating to sexual orientation, if such sexual orientation requirements could be shown to be required so as to comply with the doctrines of the religion or to "avoid conflicting with the strongly held religious convictions of a significant number of the religion's followers".

A judicial review before the Administrative Court challenging the compatibility of these provisions with the requirements of EU law was unsuccessful,[76] but in a reasoned opinion issued to the UK Government towards the end of 2009 the European Commission formally advised the Government that it considered the UK's national implementation of the provisions allowing for the possibility of lawful discrimination on the basis of sexual orientation in the (religious) workplace on religious grounds contravened the protections against discrimination conferred by the Employment Equality Directive.[77]

Despite having no basis in the terms of Directive 2000/78/EC, these "genuine occupational requirement" provisions allowing for "justified" discrimination on grounds of sexual orientation within the context of employment "for the purposes of an organized religion", were consolidated and, as we have seen, are now contained in para. 2 (specifically para. 2(4)(f)) of Schedule 9 to the Equality Act 2010. The attempt by the Government to amend the Equality Bill during its passage through Parliament to remove the apparent EU law incompatibility of the original implementing provisions in relation to justified religious based discrimination on grounds of sexual orientation in the 2003 Regulations was defeated in the House of Lords.

But the fact that the Government failed in its attempt to remove this provision by reason of its incompatibility with EU law does not mean that no challenge can be brought to it. The principle of the primacy of EU law means that all national courts and administrative authorities are obliged to refuse to apply any provision of national law which is inconsistent with the requirements of EU law.

8.4.2.6.2 Ministerial Exemption for Religious Employers and the Strasbourg Jurisprudence

In any event the Equality Act 2010 has to be read, so far as possible, in a manner compatible with Convention rights.

---

[75] These regulations were revoked with effect from 1 October 2010 by para. 1 of Schedule 27(2) to the Equality Act 2010.

[76] *R (on the application of AMICUS–MSF section, NUT and others) v. Secretary of State for Trade and Industry* [2007] ICR 1176, [2004] IRLR 430 (EWHC, Admin).

[77] See European Commission Reasoned Opinion 226/EC to the UK Government re Infringement No 2006/2450.

In *Bernhard Schüth v. Germany*,[78] the Strasbourg Court considered the lawfulness of the dismissal of a Church employee (the organist and choirmaster in the Catholic parish) on grounds of conduct falling within the sphere of his private and family life, namely the fact that he had separated from his wife in 1994 and in 1995 moved in with a new partner who was then expecting his child. In finding his dismissal from his position by the Church authorities to be incompatible with respect for his Convention rights, the ECtHR found that the German labour courts had failed properly to take into account and balance the applicant's right to respect for his private and family life against the interests of his Church employer. While the Strasbourg Court accepted that in signing the employment contract, the applicant had entered into a duty of loyalty towards the Catholic Church which limited his right to respect for his private life to a certain degree, his signature on the contract could not be interpreted as an unequivocal undertaking to live a life of sexual continence in the event of separation or divorce.[79]

In *Fernández Martínez v. Spain*[80] the Strasbourg Court held that there had been no violation of Article 8 ECHR in a case in which the employment contract of an individual licensed annually by the local Catholic bishop to teach Catholic religion and morals in a State High School was not renewed following the publication of an article about the "Movement for Optional Celibacy" for Catholic priests which reported that Mr Fernández Martínez, a member of the movement, had previously been a priest and rector of a seminary but was now canonically laicized and dispensed from his vows and was married with five children. The newspaper article included comments by a number of participants urging the Catholic ecclesiastical authorities to introduce optional celibacy and the possibility of the laity being involved in the appointment of priests and bishops and indicated their disagreement with the Catholic Church's official positions on abortion, divorce, sexuality and contraception. The terms of a priest's laicization were to the effect that anyone granted such a dispensation was barred from teaching the Catholic religion in public institutions, unless the local bishop decided otherwise "according to his own criteria and provided that there is no scandal". The Spanish courts considered that the bishop was in the circumstances entitled to object to the applicant continuing to teach a religion and morals course and the Strasbourg Court by a majority considered that the domestic courts' decision could not be impugned on Convention grounds.

---

[78] *Schüth v. Germany*, n. 1620/03, judgment of 23 September 2010.

[79] See also the Strasbourg Court's non-admissibility decision in *Pay v. UK*, n. 32792/05, decision of 16th September 2008, upholding the Convention proportionality of the dismissal of a probation officer who worked with sex offenders, once his out-of-work involvement in hedonist and fetish clubs, and in selling bondage and sadomasochism products, had become public and was brought to the attention of his employer.

[80] *Fernández Martínez v. Spain*, n. 56030/07, judgment of 15th May 2012.

In *Lombardi Vallauri v Italy*[81] the Strasbourg Court extended the principle of Article 6 fairness protection even to employment in the private sector by holding that held that in the circumstances of the non-renewal of the contract of a long-serving legal academic in a private Catholic university, the Italian courts should have required the university (and by necessary implication the Church authorities) to provide full and proper reasons for the claims made against the applicant which led to the non-renewal of his employment contract. Had the Italian courts done so, this would have allowed the applicant both to know just what was being said against him and, if so advised, to challenge its accuracy contest any supposed link between the opinions ascribed to him and his teaching activities. The university's mission to deliver a Catholic education could not, in the Strasbourg Court's view, justify such a basic denial of the applicant's rights to a fair process.

These Strasbourg decisions seem to be to the effect that, regardless of question of competence in a particular job, public expressions of views which are seen as contrary to the ethos[82]or values[83] of the particular post for which an individual is employed by a religious employer may be considered by the European Court of Human Rights to justify dismissal from employment, provided that an otherwise fair procedure is followed.

8.5 Conclusions

There has been a revolution within a span of 40 years—with most changes occurring within the first decade of the twenty-first century—in public attitudes to, and the law's treatment of, gay individuals and same-sex couples in the UK. From male homosexuality being criminalised and individuals subject to discrimination for their sexuality, the situation is now transformed into one where there appears to be a genuine commitment in the public sphere to an equality of treatment and between, and equality of regard for, gay and straight.

The issue now to be considered is whether society can or should give time, make allowance, for these apparent laggards to catch up; for example, by making legal

[81] *Lombardi Vallauri v. Italy*, n. 39128/05, judgment of 20th October 2009.

[82] See *Siebenhaar v. Germany*, n. 18136/02, judgment of 3rd February 2011, where the Strasbourg court held that the dismissal of a Catholic kindergarten teacher by Protestant Church for her active commitment to a third religious community—which styled itself the Universal Church/Brotherhood of Humanity—was justified.

[83] See *Michael Obst v. Germany*, n. 425/03, judgment of 23rd September 2010, where the Strasbourg Court accepted the Convention compatibility of the German labour courts' upholding of the lawfulness of dismissal and excommunication of a Mormon individual who had been employed by the Mormon Church as director for Europe of their public relations department, after he had confessed to the church authorities of an adulterous affair.

provision for the reasonable accommodation of these now heterodox though conscientiously held beliefs which would mandate their continued discrimination against others on sexual orientation grounds.

But is our idea for the full and proper realization of the values of pluralism, tolerance, and broadmindedness within a democratic society robust enough to allow for the continued expression within the public square of—and separately for action both within the workplace and the commercial marketplace based on—beliefs on traditional religious beliefs regarding the lack of equivalence between heterosexuality and homosexuality? Or is the revolution still too fragile to allow space for tolerance of the intolerant?

The courts in the UK appear to have set their face against allowing claims by employees in non-religious public employment either that their religiously based beliefs—for example, as to the immorality or sinfulness of same-sex sexual conduct—should be respected such as to allow them to be exempted from any general workplace prohibition against discrimination on grounds of sexual orientation,[84] or that their religious claims might require the modification or non-application to them of a general staff dress code to allow them to wear distinctively religious apparel or adornment at work.[85] As the English Court of Appeal judge, Sir John Laws has robustly observed:

> 24. We do not live in a society where all the people share uniform religious beliefs. The precepts of any one religion – any belief system – cannot, by force of their religious origins, sound any louder in the general law than the precepts of any other. If they did, those out in the cold would be less than citizens; and our constitution would be on the way to a theocracy, which is of necessity autocratic. The law of a theocracy is dictated without option to the people, not made by their judges and governments. The individual conscience is free to accept such dictated law; but the State, if its people are to be free, has the burdensome duty of thinking for itself.
>
> 25. So it is that the law must firmly safeguard the right to hold and express religious belief; equally firmly, it must eschew any protection of such a belief's content in the name only of its religious credentials. Both principles are necessary conditions of a free and rational regime.[86]

[84] See, e.g., *Ladele v. Islington London Borough Council* [2010] ICR 532, CA concerning a marriage registrar who refused to officiate at same-sex civil partnerships because of her religious beliefs; *McFarlane v. Relate Avon Ltd* [2010] IRLR 196, EAT concerning a relationship counsellor who sought to be exempted from work with same-sex couples where specifically sexual issues were involved on grounds of his belief in the immorality of this conduct; and *McClintock v. Department of Constitutional Affairs* [2008] IRLR 29, EAT concerning a magistrate who objected to hearing cases involving the possible placement of children with same-sex couples on ethical grounds to the effect that the placing of children in such an environment was potentially harmful to them.

[85] *Eweida v. British Airways plc* [2010] ICR 890, CA. See too *Azmi v. Kirklees Metropolitan Borough Council* [2007] IRLR 484, EAT upholding the lawfulness of a suspension of a school teaching assistant after she persistently refused to follow an instruction not to wear a full-face veil when in class with pupils, assisting a male teacher.

[86] See *McFarlane v. Relate Avon Limited* [2010] EWCA Civ 880, [2010] IRLR 872, Laws LJ's decision refusing a renewed application for leave to appeal from the decision of the EAT in *McFarlane v Relate Avon Ltd* [2010] IRLR 196.

And yet the Grand Chamber of the ECtHR has itself of late reversed the long established previous case law of the European Commission of Human Rights and has now held—in the light of Art. 10(2) CFR which provides that in the context of EU law that "the right to conscientious objection is recognized, in accordance with the national laws governing the exercise of this right"—that there is also a right of religiously based "conscientious objection" which is implicit within Art. 9 ECHR. In *Bayatyan v. Armenia*[87] the Strasbourg Court found that opposition to military service by a Jehovah's Witness resulted in serious and insurmountable conflict between the obligation to serve in the army and the individuals religiously informed conscience. The court recognized that the individual's failure to report for military service was a manifestation of his religious beliefs. His conviction for draft evasion was therefore found to constitute interference with his freedom to manifest his religion, as guaranteed by Article 9 ECHR. Since no alternative civilian service was available in Armenia at the material time, the claimant had no choice but to refuse to be drafted into the army if he was to stay faithful to his convictions and, by doing so, to risk criminal sanctions. Thus, the existing system imposed on citizens an obligation which had potentially serious implications for conscientious objectors. Such a system failed to strike a fair balance between the interests of society as a whole and those of the religiously informed individual. Therefore, the imposition of a criminal penalty on him, in circumstances where no allowances were made for the exigencies of his conscience and beliefs, was not a measure necessary in a democratic society.

But the Equality Act 2010 made no express provision for there being any duty in UK law of reasonable adjustment to allow individuals to maintain their strongly held religious beliefs in the workplace or in the marketplace.[88] The proper line may

---

[87] *Bayatyan v. Armenia*, n. 23459/03, judgment of 7th July 2011.

[88] See, for example, *Smith v. Trafford Housing Trust* [2012] EWHC 3221 (Ch), [2013] IRLR 86 where an employee was demoted from his position as a manager in a housing association after having posted comments on his private Facebook page describing the move towards allowing same sex couples to marry in the UK as "an equality too far". See too *Haye v General Teaching Council for England* Queen's Bench Division (Administrative Court, King J.) (unreported, 11 April 2013) where the court upheld the proportionality and Convention compatibility of a minimum 2 year ban on being able to work as a teacher which was imposed by the respondent council's professional conduct committee against a teacher who was an avowed Christian. The teacher was found to have been guilty of misconduct in responding to direct questions from pupils—immediately after they had attended a school assembly where they were shown a video on homosexuality—as to his views as a Christian on homosexuality. His answer referred to the Bible. A teaching assistant was present during that discussion and reported it to the teacher's superiors. The school investigated matters and was dismissed from his position. The matter was then referred on to the General Teaching Council whose professional conduct committee then imposed the 2 year minimum prohibition order, finding that the teacher's conduct had fallen significantly below the standards expected of teachers in the English education system. In *R (Raabe) v. Home Office* [2013] EWHC 1736 (Admin) where the court upheld the lawfulness of the dismissal of the claimant, a practising GP, from his position of member of the Advisory Council on the Misuse of Drugs after it came to the attention of the Home Office that Dr Raabe had in 2005 in the context of the campaigning around the legalisation of same sex marriage in Canada co-written an article

be, as the Equality and Human Rights Commission submitted to the European Court of Human Rights in the cases of *Eweida and Chaplin v. United Kingdom*[89] that State services must be provided on an impartial basis and employees cannot expect their public functions to be shaped to accommodate their personal religious beliefs.[90] On the other hand in *Doogan v Greater Glasgow and Clyde Health Board*[91] the Inner House of the Court of Session (the Scottish appeal court) afforded a broad interpretation to the right of medical staff to object on grounds of conscience to their being required by their employers to have any involvement in provision of abortion services. The appeal court noted that legislation such as this should be interpreted in a way which allows those claiming its protection to be true to their beliefs while remaining respectful of the law such that the only circumstance when the conscientious objection could not prevail should be when the termination is necessary to save life or prevent grave permanent injury to the mother.

But whatever happens in these various court challenges, the story isn't over. The tension between the protection sought on human rights grounds by those wishing to give expression or manifestation within the workplace and the marketplace of their conscientiously held religious beliefs, and the claims of equality law to insist on a workplace and a public marketplace where, it appears to the religious that those deemed to be (religiously) intolerant will be granted no toleration and no quarter—will continue.

Reference

Hayden A et al (2012) Children and Same Sex Families: a legal handbook. Family Law, Bristol

called "Gay Marriage and Homosexuality: some medical comments". His co-authorship of this article was to raise concerns over his credibility (though not his ability or willingness) to provide balanced advice on drug misuse issues affecting the lesbian, gay, bi-sexual and transgender (LGBT) community and might impact on the smooth running of the ACMD such as to justify his dismissal.

[89] *Eweida and others v. United Kingdom*, n. 48420/10, judgment 15th January 2013.

[90] See the decision of the Court of Appeal for Saskatchewan in *In the Matter of the Marriage Commissioners appointed under the Marriage Act 1995* [2011] SKA 3 (10 January 2011), para. 97.

[91] *Doogan v. Greater Glasgow and Clyde Health Board* [2013] CSIH 36, 2013 SLT 517, para. 37. At the time of writing this decision was under appeal to the UK Supreme Court.

Chapter 9
Between Recognition and Homophobia: Same-Sex Couples in Eastern Europe

Adam Bodnar and Anna Śledzińska-Simon

Abstract This chapter argues that the recognition of same-sex couples in Eastern Europe can occur either via legislative change or court decisions. Nevertheless, local specificity challenges the theory of incremental changes that, as applied to Western European countries, assumes a step-by-step progress from the decriminalization of sodomy, through the prohibition of sexual orientation and to the recognition of same-sex partnership or marriage. In Eastern Europe, however, some countries have not gone beyond the minimum of decriminalizing sodomy, while others have adopted anti-discrimination laws under the pressure of the EU accession yet object to the institutionalization of same-sex relationships as a matter of their national identity and defence of traditional values. Moreover, the recent tendency in the region is to limit the concept of family to heterosexual relations based on marriage and to exclude the protection of same-sex partnerships. The chapter examines the four jurisdictions of Croatia, Hungary, Slovenia, and Poland in order to demonstrate that the role of courts in the recognition of same-sex couples is contingent on the constitutional limitations and strategic litigation that provides opportunities to challenge the existing *status quo*.

A. Bodnar (✉)
Faculty of Law and Administration, Warsaw University, Warsaw, Poland
e-mail: a.bodnar@wpia.uw.edu.pl

A. Śledzińska-Simon
Faculty of Law, Administration and Economics, Wroclaw University, Wroclaw, Poland
e-mail: a.simon@prawo.uni.wroc.pl

D. Gallo et al. (eds.), *Same-Sex Couples before National, Supranational and International Jurisdictions*, DOI 10.1007/978-3-642-35434-2_9,

9.1 Introduction

This chapter posits that the recognition of same-sex couples either via statutory laws or court decisions is not specific to the Western liberal States, and it can successfully take place in newly-fledged democracies in Eastern Europe.[1] Nevertheless, it tentatively assumes that the legal argument for equating same-sex unions with marriage varies by geographical location due to complex historical, legal, political, and socio-cultural reasons.[2]

On the one hand, the Europeanization process, including the accession to the Council of Europe and the European Union (further referred to as EU), greatly contributed to progress in achieving the minimum standard of protection against discrimination with regard to sexual orientation and decriminalization of sodomy in this region. Anything above this minimum is subject to country-specific political decisions, the prudence of national judicial authorities, and the vibrancy of the LGBT movement. Therefore, the EU conditionality could be considered a factor contributing to the adoption of anti-discrimination laws and the implementation of the EU directives, but not to the recognition of same-sex marriage and partnerships. Since civil *status* generally falls outside the EU competence, some Eastern European EU Member States object to the institutionalization of same-sex relationships as a matter of their national identity and in the defense of their traditional values.

On the other hand, the 'success' of the legal recognition of same-sex couples in some Eastern European countries is undermined by widespread homophobia, intolerance, and low social acceptance of homosexual relationships. Undeniably, reforms that generally concern LGBT rights seldom result in a significant change in social prejudices, including the prevalent view that homosexual relations are sinful, wrong, or unnatural, and that homosexuality is a curable disease. As rightly observed by Renata Uitz, any developments with regard to LGBT rights can be better explained by the role and actual power of veto-players in the political process, rather than by a new societal or political consensus in these countries.[3] In this chapter, we argue that courts are also important veto-players in the processes of recognizing the rights of same-sex couples in Eastern Europe.[4]

While the argument not to legalize same-sex relations is based on morality and the protection of traditional values, it usually derives from a deeply-rooted social belief about marriage as a union between a wife and a husband. In some contexts,

[1] This chapter covers broadly all post-communist countries in Central and Eastern Europe and focuses on four jurisdictions—Croatia, Hungary, Poland and Slovenia—in which the international and national courts played a crucial role in the legal recognition of rights of same-sex couples.

[2] While religion and church attendance seem to be a determining factor in defining societal attitudes towards homosexuality in almost all countries, this correlation is not equal for all religions and all countries.

[3] Uitz (2012), p. 236.

[4] Veto-players are actors that can change the *status quo*: Hönnige (2009), Santoni and Zucchini (2006), and Tsebelis (2002).

however, the argument results from homophobia and hatred against the 'other'.[5] While morality or politics of emotions may be a valid ground for making legislative choices, judicial review is a domain of reason where rationalized analysis should apply. Therefore, it is expected that judges will "extend principles to their logical end"[6] more so than the average person, and that same-sex couples may achieve more rights' recognition before the courts than they would from national legislatures or people's hearts.

9.2 The Eastern European Countries' Approach to LGBT Rights and Same-Sex Couples in Brief

The level of recognition of LGBT rights and the rights of same-sex couples in particular vary greatly across the region of Eastern Europe. Notwithstanding the common past under the communist regime, the Eastern European countries chose differing paths of democratic transition or national independence. Although all countries formally established the rule of law and human rights, their adherence to the principles of liberal democracy is subject to various national interpretations and contingent on pre-existing constitutional traditions. While some countries—such as the Russian Federation or the Ukraine—have never rooted out the elements and methods of an authoritarian regime, others—such as Hungary—have tended recently to restore them. In the 1990s, many Eastern European States enshrined the principle of equal treatment and non-discrimination in their newly adopted or amended constitutions. Still, they differ from each other with regard to grounds of prohibited discrimination and the constitutional concept of marriage and family.

9.2.1 National Constitutions

Among the Eastern European constitutions, only the Constitution of Kosovo explicitly prohibits discrimination on the basis of sexual orientation.[7] The constitutions of Albania,[8] Bosnia and Herzegovina,[9] Croatia,[10] Czech Republic,[11]

[5] In comparison to anti-Gypsism and anti-Semitism, the anti-gay attitude often prohibits promotion of immorality (known as 'no promo homo').

[6] *Lawrence v. Texas*, 539 U.S. 558, 602 (2003) (Scalia, J., dissenting).

[7] Art. 24(2) of Constitution (adopted on 9th April 2008).

[8] Art. 18(2) of the Constitution (adopted on 28th November 1998).

[9] Art. 4 of the Constitution (adopted on 1st December 1995).

[10] Art. 14 of the Constitution (adopted on 22nd December 1990).

[11] Art. 3 of the Charter of Fundamental Rights and Basic Freedoms (adopted on 16th December 1992).

Estonia,[12] Hungary,[13] Latvia,[14] Poland,[15] Montenegro,[16] Romania,[17] the Russian Federation,[18] Slovakia,[19] Slovenia,[20] and the Ukraine[21] contain an open-ended catalogue of prohibited grounds of discrimination. This means that discrimination is prohibited on any grounds, and that constitutional courts have the discretion to create or extend the list of grounds upon which discrimination is prohibited according to their own judicial standards.[22] The constitutions of Bulgaria,[23] Lithuania,[24] Macedonia,[25] Moldova,[26] and Serbia[27] do not enumerate sexual orientation within their close lists of prohibited grounds of discrimination. However, these countries adopted new statutory laws in line with the EU legislation that ban discrimination with regard to sexual orientation in the field of employment or access to goods and services.

The Eastern European countries also differ with regard to the constitutional protection of marriage. Some (Hungary, Latvia, Montenegro, Poland, Romania, Slovakia, Slovenia, Ukraine, and the Bulgaria) guarantee the State protection of marriage in their constitutions, while others refer rather to family, motherhood, or parenthood. Only the Hungarian,[28] Montenegrin,[29] Latvian,[30] Polish,[31] Serbian,[32] Ukrainian[33], and Bulgarian[34] Constitutions define marriage as the union of a man and a woman. Also the Moldovan constitution reaffirms that a family is founded on a marriage between a wife and a husband.[35] It is noteworthy that the Constitution of

[12] Art. 12 of the Constitution (adopted by *referendum* on 28th June 1992).

[13] Art. XV(2) of the Constitution (adopted on 25th April 2011).

[14] Art. 91 of the Constitution (adopted on 15th February 1922).

[15] Art. 32(2) of the Constitution (adopted on 2nd April 1997).

[16] Art. 17(2) of the Constitution (adopted on 19th October 2007).

[17] Art. 16(2) of the Constitution (adopted on 21st November 1991).

[18] Art. 19 of the Constitution (ratified on 12th December 1993).

[19] Art. 12(2) of the Constitution (ratified on 1st September 1992).

[20] Art. 14 of the Constitution (adopted on 23rd December 1991).

[21] Art. 24 of the Constitution (adopted on 28th June 1996).

[22] The Hungarian Constitutional Court considered sexual orientation as a prohibited ground in a number of decisions: e.g., see 20/1999, AB decision, 25th June 1999.

[23] Art. 6(2) of the Constitution (adopted on 12th July 1991).

[24] Art. 29 of the Constitution (adopted by *referendum* on 25th October 1992).

[25] Art. 9 of the Constitution (adopted on 17th November 1991).

[26] Art. 16(2) of the Constitution (adopted on 29th July 1994).

[27] Art. 21 of the Constitution (adopted by *referendum* on 28th/29th October 2006).

[28] Art. L(1) of the Hungarian Constitution.

[29] Art. 71 of the Montenegrin Constitution.

[30] Art. 110 of the Latvian Constitution as amended on 15th December 2005.

[31] Art. 18 of the Polish Constitution.

[32] Art. 62(2) of the Serbian Constitution.

[33] Art. 51 of the Ukrainian Constitution.

[34] Art. 46 (1) of the Bulgarian Constitution.

[35] Art. 48(2) of the Moldovan Constitution.

Albania states that everyone has the right to get married and have a family,[36] following the language of Art. 9 of the EU Charter of Fundamental Rights (further referred to as CFR).[37]

Undeniably, in the transitional period after the fall of communism the various processes of establishing national sovereignty and constitution-making reinforced ideological debates about which fundamental values should be enshrined in the constitutions. For example, the drafters of the 1997 Polish Constitution included a legal definition of a marriage as the union of a woman and a man in the text of the constitution in order to ensure that the introduction of same-sex marriage would not be passed without a constitutional amendment.[38] Moreover, any ratified international agreement, including the EU treaties, would not suffice to change this provision.[39] While the constitutionally embedded protection of a heterosexual marriage does not *per se* exclude the recognition of same-sex partnerships in a statute,[40] opponents of draft laws on civil partnerships recently contested such an interpretation and argued that the constitution excludes the institutionalization of any relationships other than marriage.[41]

A similar controversy was recently decided by the Lithuanian Constitutional Court. It ruled that the Family Policy Concept is contrary to the Constitutional concept of family, which is not restricted to marriage and extends to other relations based on mutual responsibility, emotional attachment, support, and voluntary self-determination.[42] In the Court's view,

> the constitutional concept of family may not be derived solely from the institute of marriage, which is entrenched in the provisions of Paragraph 3 of Article 38 of the Constitution. The fact that the institutes of marriage and family are entrenched in the same Article 38 of the Constitution indicates an inseparable and unquestionable relationship between marriage and family. (. . .) However, this does not mean that (. . .) the Constitution does not protect and defend families other than those founded on the basis of marriage, inter alia the relationship of a man and a woman living together without concluding a marriage.[43]

Notably, the Constitutional Court did not mention same-sex relations as other constitutionally protected family models. The legislation referred to as the Family Policy Concept defined the family as a man and woman's wedlock and was passed with the support of the Conservatives in an attempt to win over a predominantly Roman Catholic electorate. As a result of this law, 'incomplete families' such as

[36] Art. 53(1) of the Albanian Constitution.

[37] OJ 2010 C 83, p. 389.

[38] Judgement of the Constitutional Tribunal of Poland, K 18/04, 11th May 2005.

[39] Notably, both Art. 9 CFR and Art. 12 ECHR guarantee the right to marry in accordance with the national laws governing the exercise of this right.

[40] Art. 18 of the Polish Constitution is not only an expression of constitutional axiology, but also has a normative character. It contains a positive obligation of the public authorities to deny the protected status of a marriage to any de facto same-sex and opposite-sex partnerships. Garlicki (2003), pp. 2–3.

[41] See Sect. 9.5.1.

[42] Judgment of the Constitutional Court of Lithuania, No. 28/2008, 28th September 2011.

[43] *Ibidem*, para. 15.1.

divorcees, widows and widowers, and single parents with children, could not access privileges and benefits reserved for married couples.[44] In 2012, in response to the Court's ruling, the Speaker of the *Seimas*, Irena Degutienė, suggested an amendment to the Constitution that would link family and marriage more closely.

In the wake of a similar tendency to constitutionalize the heterosexuality of marriage, a new constitutional amendment was adopted in Latvia in order to reassert that marriage is only reserved for two persons of opposite sex, notwithstanding the fact that same-sex marriage was already banned by civil law.[45] Similarly, the new constitution of Hungary, which entered into force on 1st January 2012, provided that

> Hungary shall protect the institution of marriage, understood to be the conjugal union of a man and a woman based on their voluntary decision; Hungary shall also protect the institution of the family, which it recognises as the basis for survival of the nation.

Lead by Victor Orban, the Hungarian government initiated further amendments of the Constitution to deny the protection of laws to same-sex families and bypass the Constitutional Court's rulings endorsing a broad concept of family. Hungary's Parliament approved the amendments by a 265/11 vote on 11th March 2013, giving preference to traditional family relationships based on marriage between a man and a woman and the parent–child relationship.[46]

9.2.2 Membership in the Council of Europe

To date, all countries of the region, except Belarus, are Member States of the Council of Europe and parties of the European Convention on Human Rights (further referred to as ECHR). Nevertheless, the Convention does not mandate that the State parties introduce same-sex marriage and leaves them a wide margin of appreciation with regard to the regulation of the civil *status* in their domestic laws. The Strasbourg Court has not (yet) ruled that States have a positive obligation to institutionalize same-sex relationships, which would stem either from Art. 12 or 14 in conjunction with Art. 8 of the Convention.[47] Therefore, the national authorities are free to grant or deny the right to enter into marriage or a civil union to same-sex couples, and States parties that do not provide same-sex couples with access to marriage do not violate the Convention,[48] along with the States giving a different legal *status* to spouses and civil partners.[49] However, it remains an open

[44] Jegelevicius (2001).

[45] Art. 110 of the Latvian Constitution was revised in 2006 and reads as follows: "The State shall protect and support marriage – a union between a man and a woman, the family, the rights of parents and rights of the child."

[46] Human Rights Watch (2013).

[47] *Schalk and Kopf v. Austria*, n. 30141/04, judgment of 24th June 2010, para. 101; see the chapter by Pustorino, in this volume.

[48] *H. v. Finland*, n. 37359/09, judgment of 13th November 2012.

[49] *Gas and Dubois v. France*, n. 25951/07, judgment of 12th March 2012; *X and others v. Austria*, n. 19010/07, judgment of 19th February 2013.

question as to whether the States refusing the recognition of a same-sex marriage concluded in another country are acting within their margin of appreciation or contrary to the Convention.[50]

Importantly, the Convention requires that the states afford same-sex couples the protection of law as a family. In fact, the Court

> considers it artificial to maintain the view that, in contrast to a different-sex couple, a same-sex couple cannot enjoy 'family life' for the purposes of Article 8. Consequently the relationship of (...) a cohabiting same-sex couple living in a stable de facto partnership, falls within the notion of 'family life', just as the relationship of a different-sex couple in the same situation would.[51]

Additionally, the Convention prohibits any discrimination of LGBT persons in their enjoyment of Convention rights. Notwithstanding development in this field, the implementation of judgments of the Strasbourg Court in Eastern European countries often causes problems that undermine the effectiveness of Convention rights on a national level.

9.2.3 *Membership in the EU*

In the past decade, Bulgaria, Croatia, the Czech Republic, Estonia, Hungary, Latvia, Lithuania, Poland, Romania, Slovakia, and Slovenia accessed the EU. The process of accession required that the candidate countries align with the EU *acquis*.[52] Importantly, the evaluation of national human rights standards, and in particular minority protection, has played a major role in making progress in the area of anti-discrimination laws in these countries.[53] Currently, such requirements concern other candidate countries in the region—FYROM and Montenegro. Notably, non-Member or non-candidate States such as Armenia, Azerbaijan, Belarus, Russia, or the Ukraine do not prohibit discrimination with regard to sexual orientation or gender identity in any areas of law either in their constitutions or statutes.[54] Still, the prohibition of discrimination on grounds of racial and ethnic origin under EU law operates across a wider range of areas than the prohibition of discrimination on the ground of sexual orientation, and some Member States including Estonia,

---

[50] *Irina Fet and Irina Shipitko v. Russia* (concerning the refusal of the city civil registration office to register a marriage concluded between two Russian citizens of same sex in Canada), filed in January 2011.

[51] *Ibidem*, note 46, para. 94. See also Hodson (2011).

[52] LGBT Rights thus form an integral part of both the Copenhagen political criteria for accession and the EU legal framework on combatting discrimination. They are closely monitored by the EU commission, which reports annually on the progress made by enlargement countries with regard to the situation of the LGBT community (see EU Observer 2012).

[53] Schimmelfennig and Sedelmeier (2005), p. 20.

[54] ILGA Europe (2013a).

Latvia, Lithuania, and Poland maintain the 'hierarchy of protected grounds' in their national legislation.[55]

Notwithstanding the problems with adequate implementation of the directives, it is also likely that there is a discrepancy between formal implementation of the EU anti-discrimination law and the actual practice of it in the new Member States.[56] For instance, with respect to the Framework Employment Directive prohibiting discrimination with regard to sexual orientation in the field of employment and occupation, a question appeared whether the religious exception provided for in Art. 4(2) authorizes unequal treatment of gays by any church or religious institutions with regard to their organization's ethos.[57] The scope of this exception needs more clarification to secure adequate implementation in countries with strong religious organizations.[58] Similar implementation problems arise with regard to the EU family-related law[59] when Member States refuse to include same-sex marriages, registered partnerships, or *de facto* unions in the notion of 'family' and to recognize civil *status* documents issued by other countries. Lack of mutual recognition of civil *status* based on the principle of country of origin has negative consequences for same-sex couples with respect to employment-related partner benefits and free movement of EU citizens, as well as family reunification of refugees and third country nationals.

A glaring example of resistance of Eastern European Member States to the EU law on moral grounds was the reaction of Poland and the Czech Republic to the CFR. One of the contested provisions of the Charter was Art. 9, which stipulates that

> [t]he right to marry and the right to found a family shall be guaranteed in accordance with the national laws governing the exercise of these rights.

The Polish and Czech government expressed their concern about the indirect introduction of homosexual marriages and attempted to restrict the application of the CFR.[60] As a result, they joined the UK in the so-called

---

[55] FRA Study on Homophobia (2010), p. 19.

[56] *Asociaţia ACCEPT v. Consiliul Naţional pentru Combaterea Discriminării*, C-81/12, judgment of 25th April 2013 nyr (concerning anti-gay comments by Gigi Becali, the main shareholder of the Romanian football team, FC Steaua). On 5th October 2012 also the Supreme Court of Croatia ruled the former president of the Croatian Football Association, Vlatko Marković, to publicly apologize for his discriminatory anti-gay comments.

[57] Council Directive 2000/78/EC of 27th November 2000 establishing a general framework for equal treatment in employment and occupation, OJ 2000 L 303, p. 16; on this and the other EU measures further cited in this essay see the chapter by Orzan, and the one by Rijpma and Koffeman, in this volume.

[58] FRA Study on Homophobia (2010), p. 27.

[59] Council Directive 2003/86/EC of 22nd September 2003 on the right to family reunification [Art. 4(3)], OJ 2003 L 251, p. 12, and Directive 2004/38/EC of the European Parliament and the Council of 29th April 2004 concerning the right of citizens of the Union and their family members to move and reside freely within the territory of the Member States (Art. 2), OJ 2004 L 158, p. 77.

[60] Bodnar (2009a), p. 138; Wyrzykowski (2009), p. 28; Zwolski (2009), p. 191.

"British Protocol".[61] Notably, the British government opposed the guarantees of the Charter (Title IV) for very different (social and economic) reasons.[62] Although the intention of the Protocol was to provide an opt-out option from the Charter's legal applicability in national courts and on national legislation, as well as from the jurisdiction of the European Court of Justice, the latter recent case-law confirms that

> Protocol (No. 30) does not call into question the applicability of the Charter in the United Kingdom or in Poland, a position which is confirmed by the recitals in the preamble to that protocol.[63]

It is important to note that the reach of EU law does not extend to national laws regulating issues of civil *status*[64] and the Charter does not move the field of application of Union law beyond the powers of the Union or establish any new power or task for the Union.

9.3 The Link Between Recognition of Same-Sex Couples and Homophobia

Regarding the level of recognition and protection of LGBT rights and rights of same-sex couples, Eastern European countries can be divided into several categories: (a) countries that recognized rights of same-sex couples in statutory laws—Croatia (2003), the Czech Republic (2006), Hungary (2009), and Slovenia (2006); (b) countries that recognized some rights of same-sex couples as a result of international and national court decisions—Poland; (c) countries that passed the laws prohibiting discrimination with regard to sexual orientation—in addition to the EU member and candidate states, this category includes Albania (2010), Bosnia and Herzegovina (2009), Georgia (2006), and Moldova (2012); (d) countries that recently passed laws decriminalizing sodomy—Armenia (2003), Bosnia and Herzegovina (1998), Belarus (1994), Georgia (2000), Moldova (1995), the Russian Federation (1993), and the Ukraine (1991).

---

[61] Protocol No. 30 on the application of the Charter to Poland and to the United Kingdom, OJ 2007 C 83, p. 313.

[62] Declaration by the Republic of Poland concerning the Protocol on the application of the Charter of Fundamental Rights of the European Union in relation to Poland and the United Kingdom and Declaration by the Republic of Poland on the Charter of Fundamental Rights of the European Union, OJ 2009 C 306, p. 249.

[63] *N.B v. Secretary of State for the Home Department and M. E. and others v. Refugee Applications Commissioner, Minister for Justice, Equality and Law Reform*, C-411/10 and C-493/10, judgment of 21st December 2011 [2012] ECR I-8, para. 119.

[64] *Tadao Maruko v. Versorgungsanstalt der deutschen Bühnen*, C-267/06, judgment of 1st April 2008 [2008] ECR I-1757.

In Poland (2003, 2004, 2011, and 2013) and Slovakia (2012) the registered partnership bills were presented in the Parliament but voted down or not revived after the end of the parliamentary term. In other countries, same-sex marriages or registered partnership bills were considered by the government or groups of MPs, but have not reached the Parliament yet—Albania (2009), Estonia (2008 and 2011), Latvia (1999), and Romania (2008 and 2011). Additionally, some countries recognize isolated rights of same-sex couples. For example, Serbia allows women in same-sex relations to undergo IVF.[65]

Notably, the Czech Republic was the first country in the region to allow registration of same-sex civil unions. Still, registered partnership bills failed four times since 1998 due to lack of parliamentary support. Finally, the Registered Partnerships bill was passed in 2006 by the Lower House and the Senate, but the President, Vaclav Klaus, refused to sign it. However, the Lower House overruled the Presidential veto and the law entered into force on 1st July 2006.[66] It granted same-sex couples rights comparable to the rights of spouses, such as representation in ordinary matters and mutual maintenance obligation, the right to refuse to give testimony in criminal proceedings, and the ability to choose defending counsel for the partner.[67] Unlike opposite-sex couples and marriages, same-sex partners are excluded from access to IVF. They are not able to share or inherit property, receive widow's pension, or even use a common surname. The achieved *status quo* was not changed by any of the veto-players. Contrary to other countries that have recognized same-sex couples, their legal *status* in the Czech Republic has not yet been challenged before the Constitutional Court.[68] Moreover, opinion polls show a growing social support for equating rights of same-sex relationships with heterosexual marriages.[69]

With regard to the last category, it is apparent that although the right to not be discriminated against and the right to marriage have a great importance for individuals, freedom from criminal prosecution for engaging in sexual activity with a same-sex partner is significantly more fundamental.[70] Ideally, decriminalization of sodomy should mark the beginning of a new era of protection of privacy in a legal system. However, the decriminalization would appear from another perspective to be the best that the LGBT community can get in terms of recognized rights when neither the government, nor public opinion, are ready to offer legal affirmation of same-sex relationships.

---

[65] Gay Law Net 2013.

[66] The scope of the rights granted to registered partners is not affected by the new Civil Code, which is supposed to take effect in 2014.

[67] Honuskova and Sturma (2008), p. 31.

[68] The authors are not aware of national case-law with regard to the same-sex couples. It is also not mentioned in any of the FRA studies on homophobia or annual reports.

[69] According to the 2012 annual CVVM poll on gay rights, 75 % support registered partnerships, 51 %—same-sex marriage, and 37 %—adoption of children. CVVM opinion poll (2012).

[70] Aloni (2010), p. 143.

The country-by-country analysis of LBGT rights and the recognition of same-sex couples provide limited relevance to the theory of incremental changes in Eastern Europe.[71] Some countries in the region are likely to remain in their category for longer, and the lack of progress in the recognition of same-sex couples means that changing

> societal understandings of marriage in both law and social practice is quite different from conferring the right to engage in sexual acts and the right not to be discriminated against.[72]

Although changes in the law do have an impact on social attitudes, the fact that many political leaders and members of the society remain homophobic is not easy to change. Therefore, as suggested by Waaldijk, a step-by-step approach is necessary to overcome the politics of disguise.[73] Nevertheless, the Hungarian example teaches us that a country in this region can take a step back when the political majority is able to silence veto-players such as the international community, human rights organizations, and the Constitutional Court.

Further distinctions among countries in the region could be made with regard to the level of popular support for same-sex couples, the reaction of national authorities to gay pride parades, the introduction of legislative proposals banning homophobic speech (or, conversely, banning promotion of homosexuality), and finally, the level of homophobia and hate crimes against LGBT people in a given country. With regard to the reactions of national authorities to gay pride parades, the first case of the European Court of Human Rights (further referred to as ECtHR) to lay down the standards of protection of peaceful assemblies organized by gay rights-activists was *Bączkowski and Others v. Poland.*[74] As a result of this ruling, gay-pride bans in Poland were either not issued or not upheld under instance of appeal. Nevertheless, the judgment has been not fully implemented because the national law still offers only *ex post facto* remedies redressing the illegality of the denial of authorization to organize an assembly after the planned date of the assembly. In other countries of the region, the reactions of national authorities or anti-gay organizations to LGBT marches are often very negative. The ECtHR also ruled against Russia[75] and Moldova[76] with regard to repeated rejections of gay

---

[71] According to 'the theory of small change' or 'incrementalism,' any legal changes concerning homosexuality take three steps—the repeal of sodomy, the adoption of anti-discrimination laws, and finally the legalization of same-sex unions or marriages.

[72] Aloni (2010), p. 109.

[73] Waaldijk (2001), p. 437.

[74] *Bączkowski and Others v. Poland*, n. 1543/06, judgment of 3rd May 2007. The Court held that the ban on gay pride was contrary to freedom of assembly and association (Article 11), right to an effective remedy (Article 13), and prohibition of discrimination (Article 14) in conjunction to Article 11. In the Court's view the decision of national authorities was motivated by the belief that a gay person has the right to assembly as a citizen, but not only as a gay person (para 27). Moreover, the national law did not guarantee effective remedies against the denial of authorization, which would enable the final resolution of the dispute by an administrative court before the date of a planned event.

[75] *Alekseyev v. Russia*, n. 4916/07, 25924/08 and 14599/09, judgment of 21st October 2010.

[76] *Genderdoc-M v. Moldova*, n. 9106/06, judgment of 12th June 2012.

pride parades in Moskow and Chişinău. The Court's docket shows also that LGBT associations encountered problems with registration in the Russian Federation.[77] In contrast, organization of the Baltic Pride in Riga in June 2012 proves that, even though the general public remains hostile to LGBT issues, public authorities and opponents of the LGBT movement can develop a more tolerant approach and refrain from bans and massive protests.[78]

Faced with the spread of homophobia in Eastern Europe, institutions of the EU[79] and the Council of Europe[80] repeatedly call Member States for respect of the rights of sexual minorities and condemn acts or threats of violence against LGBT people. The 2012 Resolution of the European Parliament on the fight against homophobia in Europe[81] lists the examples of criminal and administrative laws against the 'propaganda of homosexuality' that had been enacted in several regions in the Russian Federation and by several cities in Moldova, as well as similar bills put forward in the State *Duma*,[82] the Parliament of Ukraine, the Riga City Council, the Parliament of Hungary, and in the Budapest City Council with the aim of preventing gay pride parades. It also expresses concern about the interpretation of the Lithuanian Law on the Protection of Minors against the Detrimental Effects of Public Information as amended in 2010.[83]

Additionally, the Eastern European countries' approach to anti-discrimination laws and the recognition of LGBT rights and same-sex couples could be characterized by the level of social and legal mobilization of various social organizations. Some authors rightly observe that the dominant position of the Catholic or Orthodox Church in a given country plays a role in slowing down the Europeanization process with regard to anti-discrimination protection.[84] Nevertheless, the influence of the Church's veto power in the Europeanization process depends strongly on the

---

[77] *Zhdanov and Rainbow House v. Russia*, n. 12200/08, pending.

[78] ILGA Europe (2011).

[79] European Parliament Resolution on homophobia in Europe of 26th April 2007, OJ 2008 C 74 E, p. 776; European Parliament Resolution on the increase in racist and homophobic violence in Europe of 15th June 2006, OJ 2006 C 300 E, p. 491; European Parliament Resolution on homophobia in Europe of 18th January 2006, OJ 2006 C 287 E, p. 179.

[80] Recommendation CM/Rec(2010)5 of the Committee of Ministers to Member States on measures to combat discrimination on grounds of sexual orientation or gender identity, 31st March 2010; Recommendation 1915(2010) of the Parliamentary Assembly on discrimination on the basis of sexual orientation or gender identity, 29th April 2010.

[81] European Parliament Resolution of 24th May 2012 on the fight against homophobia in Europe [No. 2012/2657(RSP)], http://www.europarl.europa.eu/sides/getDoc.do?type=TA&reference=P7-TA-2012-0222&language=EN.

[82] The State Duma adopted so-called gay propaganda law on 11th June 2013. It made it illegal for any organisation or individual to publish an article, hold an event, and publicly discuss LGBT issues in the entire country.

[83] In Lithuania Petras Gražulis, a member of the governing coalition, attempted even to introduce the prohibition of 'homosexual propaganda' in the constitution via a national referendum. ILGA Europe (2013b).

[84] Huseby (2009), Ramet (2006), and Byrnes (2002).

government's political strength or weakness. In countries where the government has to compromise with conservative forces within the Parliament or even within its own political supporters, religion is easily employed for political purposes.

9.4 The Interplay Between Courts and Parliaments in Recognition of Same-Sex Couples

The legal situation of same-sex couples in Eastern European countries is to a large extent the result of an interplay between courts and Parliaments in recognition of same-sex couples within a legal system. The recognition is therefore contingent on various domestic factors influencing the political process, including the political power of the government and the opposition in national parliaments, the position of extra-parliamentary supporters and allies, the role of the Constitutional Court, national human rights institutions and equality bodies, human rights organizations, the media, and, finally, the dominant religion and its impact on public life. It also depends on the system of legal remedies available to victims of human rights violations. As noted above, the EU accession process and membership in the Council of Europe are also important external factors that influence the content of the national law and its application. However, the regulation of civil *status* remains within the competence of EU Member States and within the margin of appreciation of ECHR State Parties.

9.4.1 Croatia

On 1st July 2013, after 22 years of independence, Croatia became the 28th member of the EU.[85] It became a candidate country in 2004 when the Croatian Democratic Union government expressed determination to solve the remaining post-war problems regarding the protection of Serbian refugees and the delivery of indicted war criminals to the International Criminal Tribunal for the former Yugoslavia in the Hague. Thus, taking into consideration the history of the Balkan conflicts, the pressure of the EU institutions on the Croatian government in the area of minority rights and anti-discrimination law had a particularly strong moral and legal justification.[86]

In its most recent monitoring report, the European Commission emphasizes that in Croatia "[h]uman rights continue to be generally well respected" and further refers to "the gay pride events in Split and Zagreb (that) took place without major incidents, with strong commitment from the Croatian government to their smooth

[85] Since 1996 Croatia is a member of the Council of Europe.

[86] Huseby (2009), p. 111.

organisation."[87] It stresses, however, that LGBT people suffer discrimination and remain target of hate crimes and attacks. Last year, the U.S. Department of State's human rights report on Croatia noted an increase in societal violence and discrimination against LGBT persons.[88] Other international sources also gathered information about the homophobia and widespread intolerance of LGBT people in Croatia.[89]

In Croatia, the greatest achievements of the LGBT movement was the adoption of various anti-discrimination provisions introducing prohibition of discrimination with regard to sexual orientation,[90] the Same-Sex Unions Act,[91] and the Anti-Discrimination Act.[92] These laws are clearly by-products of the EU-membership project.[93] Nevertheless, the scope of the Same-Sex Unions Act is rather limited, since it only provides same-sex couples with the right to share assets and joint health coverage on the condition that they live together for at least 3 years.[94] The law does not prescribe registration of same-sex couples.

In fact, same-sex unions remain less privileged than spouses in a legal marriage and opposite-sex partners in a common-law marriage.[95] Their situation is not regulated under Croatia's Family Law. In consequence, same-sex partners do not enjoy the *status* of family members for the purpose of receiving social security and other social protection measures, parental leave, unemployment benefits, health insurance or benefits, family benefits, or funeral benefits.[96] Furthermore, the Inheritance Act excludes the right of same-sex partners to become legal successors of the deceased partner, while opposite-sex common-law partners who cohabited for a longer period of time until the testator's death can inherit from each other provided the conditions for a valid marriage existed.[97] In a similar fashion,

---

[87] Commission Staff Working Document: Comprehensive Monitoring Report on Croatia, accompanying the document Communication from the Commission to the European Parliament and the Council: Comprehensive Monitoring Report on Croatia's State of preparedness for EU membership, COM(2012)601 final, 10 October 2010, pp. 7 and 37.

[88] United States Department of State, Croatia, Country Reports on Human Rights Practices for 2011.

[89] Immigration and Refugee Board of Canada, Croatia 2012.

[90] Gender Equality Act (Official Gazette, 82/08), Act on Amendments to Criminal Code (Official Gazette 111/03), Act on Amendments to Labour Act (Official Gazette 114/03), Scientific Work and Higher Education Act (Official Gazette 123/03), Schoolbook Standards (Official Gazette 63/03) and Media Act (Official Gazette 59/04).

[91] Official Gazette 116/03.

[92] Official Gazette 85/08.

[93] Juras (2010), p. 21.

[94] Gay Law Net 2013.

[95] For example family benefits are granted to spouses and common-law partners under the Protection of Patients Act (Official Gazette 169/04) and Public Servants Act (Official Gazette 92/05).

[96] Medical Insurance Act (Official Gazette 94/01), Labour Act (Official Gazette 149/09), Pension Insurance Act (Official Gazette 102/98).

[97] Official Gazette 48/03.

the Medical Insemination Act only grants the right to insemination to a woman who is married or in a common-law relationship with a man. Notably, the Medical Insemination Act was extended to the common-law partners after the intervention of the Ombudswoman, who claimed that their exclusion would constitute discrimination with regard to the marital family *status*.[98] In 2012, the law was amended to allow single women to access in vitro fertilization, yet LGBT parenting remains outside the scope of this law. The Same-Sex Unions Act does not permit that same-sex couples adopt children either.[99]

The advocates of the LGBT rights in Croatia claim that the limited protection of same-sex partners constitutes discrimination with regard to sexual orientation and family *status*. Notwithstanding the great engagement of LGBT organizations, their movement remains rather weak. Many activities proposed to the Office for Gender Equality by the Women's Network of Croatia, Kontra and Iskorak, which related to education on the rights of same-sex couples and hate crimes, were not carried out. On the other hand, individual members of sexual minorities rarely contact the Ombudsman for Human Rights or the Ombudswoman for Gender Equality, and cases of discrimination or hate crimes against them remain un- or underreported.[100] The cooperation between the LGBT organizations and the government concerns rather small-scale projects, such as awareness training of the police. This is largely due to the fact that Croatian NGOs have few resources for defending the rights of sexual minorities, since in the whole country "there are only 10 people who are employed full time, in addition to five associates, such as lawyers or psychologists."[101] Moreover, the equality bodies have only recently begun to collaborate with the LGBT organizations to combat discrimination in the courts.[102] LGBT victims of discrimination or hate crimes have found that State institutions avail them greater (police) protection once they obtain media coverage, involvement of an equality body, or the support of LGBT organizations.[103]

In 2006, Kontra and Iskorak presented the Registered Partnership bill via a group of parliamentarians in order to secure same-sex couples the same rights and

[98] Juras (2010), p. 22. Notably, the Gender Equality Act is an organic act, and the Ombudswoman for Gender Equality is authorised to evaluate harmonisation of the regulations with the mentioned Act and to warn and give recommendations.

[99] According to the Family Law, a child can be adopted by married spouses jointly, by one spouse if the other is the parent of a child or adoptive parent of a child, by one spouse if the other gives consent to adoption, and by a single person if it is of a special benefit to a child.

[100] Juras (2010), pp. 16–20.

[101] Immigration and Refugee Board of Canada (2012).

[102] *Ibidem*.

[103] Juras (2010), p. 19 (referring to the case of Neven Rauk, 2009-XXIX KO-421/09. "In this case, after a criminal complaint had been filed by the associations, a proper investigation was carried out, and the perpetrators were found and convicted. However, it must be emphasized that this case is an exception resulting from the fact that it was covered very widely in the media and a case in which the associations were involved through the offering of legal help and the Ombudswoman for Gender Equality also publicly reacted").

privileges as married couples, except for the right to adoption. It generated a lot of homophobic speech in parliamentary debate and was finally rejected due to a lack of governmental support. The current Prime Minister, Zoran Milanovic, reportedly reconsidered the introduction of registered partnerships in 2012.[104]

To date, legal marriage in Croatia remains restricted to heterosexual unions, while common-law marriage is defined as "a life union of an unmarried woman and an unmarried man." Both legal marriage and common-law marriage are recognized under the Constitution (Art. 61) and the Family Law.[105] Remarkably, in a case concerning the pension insurance system, the Constitutional Court held that the law should not reserve marital rights for widows and widowers while excluding non-marital partners. It reiterated that

> (i)n relation to family the Constitution does not create differences between marital and non-marital union. Both types of unions are recognised by the Constitution and regulated by the law. … The Constitutional Court reports to the Croatian Parliament on the need of amendments to the Pension Insurance Act regarding modification of the legal presumptions for recognition of rights to a family pension of a non-marital widow, or widower of the insured party, as a member of his family.[106]

Notably, the Croatian Constitutional Court has not yet decided any case directly concerning same-sex couples. As long as the Constitutional Court is not given an opportunity to assume a more activist role in protecting the rights of same-sex couples and the Parliament does not grant them protection on equal basis with common-law partners, national courts can continue to discriminate against them. Although the reaction of some judges to LGBT claims may still be biased, there are some optimistic signals that both instance courts[107] and the Supreme Court of Croatia[108] take LGBT rights seriously. Undeniably, the support offered by international human rights organizations helps to litigate LGBT cases more effectively,[109] but their implementation on the national level, in particular in such nationally

---

[104] 2006 Annual Report on Status of Human Rights of Sexual and Gender Minorities, Kontra.

[105] Official Gazette 116/03.

[106] U-X-1457/2007, OG 43/07, 18th April 2007.

[107] In January 2011 Zagreb County Court gave a precedential ruling on hate crime against homosexuals. Verdict reached in country's first gay hate crime case, Croatian Times, 27th January 2011.

[108] In October 2012, the Supreme Court found Vlatko Marković, former president of the football federation, guilty of discrimination for stating that "fortunately football is only played by healthy people. As long as I am president, I won't permit any gay footballer." He had to publish both his apology and the court's ruling in a local newspaper. The ruling overturns the decision of the District Court in Zagreb, which dismissed the lawsuit against Marković filed by the Centre for LGBT Equality and the Centre for Peace Studies as unfounded. Similar lawsuits are pending in other cases.

[109] *Interights v. Croatia*, n. 45/2007, decision of 30th March 2009 of the European Committee of Social Rights. The Committee found violations of Article 11 (2) of the European Social Charter (right to protection of health) with regard to the lack of a comprehensive educational curriculum of sexual education and non-discrimination clause with regard to the discriminatory statements contained in educational material used in the ordinary curriculum.

sensitive area as education, may again be subject to the opposition of veto-players such as the Catholic Church.

9.4.2 *Hungary*

The democratic transition in Hungary took place without bloodshed and the symbolic change of the regime occurred with the amendment of the 1949 Socialist Constitution in October 1989. Until 2011, it was the only constitution in Eastern Europe that remained in force without being repealed by an entirely new document. In 2004, Hungary became a EU member and it was among its 'best pupils' in regard to implementation of anti-discrimination laws.[110] Nevertheless, the interplay between the changing government coalitions and the Constitutional Court in Hungary took place in the context of a strong radicalization movement of the right, with growing homophobia and intolerance towards the 'other'. For the radical forces, the institutions of marriage, family, and the nation soon became a major battlefield.

According to Art. 15 of the Constitution (as amended in 1989) "the Republic of Hungary shall protect the institutions of marriage and the family". Although the Constitution did not define marriage or family, the Constitutional Court held in 1995 that marriage is reserved for heterosexual relations. It found, however, that the exclusion of same-sex couples from common-law civil unions (*élettársak*) violates the principles of equal treatment and human dignity.[111] In the aftermath of this judgment, the Parliament recognized the rights of common-law, unregistered same-sex couples. Under certain conditions, they are also able to inherit property from their partners and receive a deceased partner's pension.[112]

The first attempt to introduce equality of rights between same-sex couples and married couples, with the exception of the name change and adoption, was a partial success. It was submitted by the Hungarian Socialist Party and the Alliance of Free Democrats coalition and passed by the Parliament as the Act No. 184 of 2007 on registered civil unions. Yet, before it even entered into force, the Constitutional Court had annulled the Act on a motion of the right wing parties.[113] The Court held that allowing opposite-sex couples to enter into registered partnerships diminished the value of marriage enshrined in the Constitution. It further argued that the Act

[110] Before the EU accession in 2003 Hungary introduced laws banning discrimination on the basis of sexual orientation and sexual identity.

[111] Judgment of the Constitutional Court of Hungary, 14/1995, AB hat, 13th March 1995 (concerning Art. 685/A. of the Act No. 4 of 1959 on the Civil Code). It was an established approach of the Constitutional Court to read the constitutional protection of human dignity jointly with the equal protection of laws, which requires that all people are treated as subjects with equal dignity. See Uitz (2012), p. 247.

[112] Gay Law Net 2013.

[113] Judgment of the Constitutional Court of Hungary, 154/2008, AB hat, 17th December 2008.

created registered civil unions as an unconstitutional 'concurrence' to marriage.[114] The role of the Constitutional Court in this case was pivotal, since it moved the legislation forward beyond what was originally intended by the drafters. While distinguishing marriage from the registered civil union, the Court mandated the Legislator to recognize same-sex partnerships.[115]

Parliament adopted the Act in response to this decision but, following the Court's suggestions, it allowed only same-sex partners to register for civil unions (*bejegyzett élettársi kapcsolat*). It equalized legal marriage with registered civil unions except in cases of adoption,[116] artificial insemination, other medical support, and the possibility of holding the name of the partner.[117] In addition to the Act of 2005 on equal treatment and on promoting equal opportunities, the Act on registered civil unions prohibits discrimination on the basis of the registered civil union *status*. It became binding on 1st July 2009. In 2010, the Act was again reviewed by the Constitutional Court, which found that registered unions are in conformity with the Constitution provided that they are not equal to marriage.[118] It also concluded that a registrar could not deny the registration of same-sex civil unions on the basis of a conscience clause. Importantly, the legislation concerning same-sex couples was more progressive than the majority of the society, which accordingly remained rather sceptical towards the necessity to regulate homosexual relations in the law.[119]

The disappointment with the left-wing government contributed to the victory of the FIDESZ in the 2010 parliamentary elections and allowed the coalition government not only to make laws, but also to change the Constitution and the cardinal laws with the required two-thirds majority. Given such an opportunity, the government proposed a new constitution that was passed by the Parliament on 18th April 2011 and came into force on 1st January 2012. The new Constitution of Hungary fell short of including sexual orientation among the prohibited grounds of discrimination (Art. XV)[120] and the suspected grounds of persecution in the country of origin with respect to asylum seekers [Art. XIV(3)]. It also preserved a special position of heterosexual marriage. The original version of Art. L(1) as adopted in 2011 provided that

> Hungary shall protect the institution of marriage, understood to be the conjugal union of a man and a woman based on their voluntary decision; Hungary shall also protect the institution of the family, which it recognises as the basis for survival of the nation.

---

[114] Körtvélyesi and Pap (2012), p. 215.

[115] Uitz (2012), pp. 250–251.

[116] Although the 2009 second-parent adoption is excluded, a gay person can theoretically adopt a child as a single applicant while two unrelated applicants cannot adopt the same child.

[117] Still, the same-sex partners can change their names under ordinary rules for change of names.

[118] Judgment of the Constitutional Court of Hungary, 32/2010, AB hat, 25th March 2010.

[119] Special EU Barometer 2009.

[120] In 2000, the Constitutional Court recognized that the Constitutional ban on discrimination based on "other *status*" covers sexual orientation.

Both the process of drafting this constitution and its content raised serious concerns of the international community, including the Venice Commission of the Council of Europe.[121] Nevertheless, the practical implications of the new Constitution became known with the adoption of so-called cardinal—supermajority—laws, implementing its provisions.[122] The opposition and civic organizations were not consulted in either of these processes, since the government used the controversial practice of introducing the laws through private member bills where extensive public consultations and impact assessment were not required.

The most critical Act for the protection of same-sex couples in both registered and unregistered unions was Act No. CCXI of 2011, passed on 23rd December 2011. It expressed the view that a heterosexual marriage is a privileged type of a family and being raised in such a family is more secure than other forms of upbringing. In pursuance of this Act, the definition of a family based on a marriage[123] would apply to all other laws, regardless of their purpose, and exclude all other forms of family relationships, such as cohabitation and registered partnership. Moreover, it ignored the text of the new Constitution and the recent Strasbourg case-law, which separate the notions of marriage and family. The Act also limited the legal succession to persons related through lineal and collateral kinship and spouses. All other persons were entitled to legal succession only in the absence of persons mentioned above. It was expected that these rules, as applied, would endanger the right of same-sex registered partners to inherit from each other. According to critics of the Act, it also over-emphasizes the element of linear descent for the establishment of family ties.[124]

Not surprisingly, the Commissioner for Fundamental Rights initiated the constitutionality review of the Act with regard to the concept of family and the legal succession. On 17th December 2012, the Constitutional Court held the concept of Family as unconstitutional and annulled it.[125] It maintained that the statutory law should not reduce the concept of the family contained in the Constitution, nor reduce or withdraw protection granted to other forms of families based on marriage. The Constitutional Court also declared the legal succession rules, which excluded

[121] Venice Commission, Opinion of the New Constitution of Hungary, 17th–18th June 2011, CDL-AD(2011)016, para. 18, available at: http://www.venice.coe.int/docs/2011/CDL-AD(2011)016-E.pdf.

[122] The Venice Commission expressed its concerns that including family legislation within the list of policy areas requiring a qualified majority is a crucial aspect of democracy. It stressed that "a too wide use of cardinal laws is problematic with regard to both the Constitution and ordinary laws. (. . .) Functionality of a democratic system is rooted in its permanent ability to enact change". *Ibidem*, para. 24.

[123] Art. 7 of the Act on the protection of families states that "(1) Family is the relationship between natural persons in an economic and emotional community that is based on a marriage between a woman and a man, or lineal descent, or family-based guardianship. (2) Lineal descent is established by way of filiation or adoption."

[124] Halmai and Scheppele (2012), p. 21.

[125] Judgment of the Constitutional Court of Hungary, 17th December 2012.

the existing and future registered partners from the group of legal successors, to be null and void. It found them contrary to the provisions of the Civil Code, which secure the right for registered partners to inherit on an equal basis with spouses. The collision between the two set of rules could lead to a situation where the registered partner of the testator could consider her/himself the legal successor under Art. 607(4) of the Civil Code, and a brother or sister of the testator could claim their right to inherit under the Act on the protection of families if the deceased person had no descendants. Thus, for the purpose of legal certainty, Art. 8 of the Act was annulled as well.[126]

In the last episode of the interplay between the Constitutional Court and the right-wing government, the Parliament adopted an amendment to the Constitution reintroducing the concept of family that had been struck down by the Constitutional Court in December. The amendment cuts down the authority of the Constitutional Court to review the substance of laws and to refer to its own decisions taken prior to 1st January 2012. It thus silences the most important veto-player in the area of recognition of same-sex couples and arguably ends the era of democracy based on the principle of checks and balances.[127] The government has displayed blatant disregard for the Constitutional Court. This is in addition to its other decisions violating the separation of powers and the institutional safeguards of fundamental freedoms, including freedom of the press and religion, and calls for an urgent reaction of the EU institutions within the procedure referred to in Art. 7 of the EU Treaty.

9.4.3 Slovenia

Slovenia was the first among the former Yugoslav republics to become a Member of the EU on 1st May 2004. In comparison to other countries analysed in this chapter, it has the smallest territory and population but the highest GDP per capita in the region. Like in Croatia, Hungary, and Poland, the dominant religion is Roman Catholicism, but the society is to a large extent secularized.[128] The Constitution of the Republic of Slovenia was adopted in 1991 and guarantees everyone equal protection of law irrespective of personal circumstances, which also implies protection of sexual orientation. It first adopted anti-discrimination law in the area of employment,[129] and it then implemented the EU anti-discrimination directives outside the field of employment.[130] A number of bodies were established to monitor, prevent, and fight discrimination.[131]

---

[126] Constitutional Court of Hungary (2012).

[127] Abtan (2013).

[128] Only 57.8 % declared their belonging to the Roman Catholic Church in the 2002 census.

[129] Employment Relationships Act 42/02 and 103/07 as amended, 3rd May 2002.

[130] Implementation of the Principle of Equal Treatment Act 93/07, 27th September 2007.

[131] In addition to the Ombudsman, there is the Government Council for the Implementation of the Principle of Equal Treatment and the Advocate of the Principle of Equal Treatment.

Art. 53 of the Constitution offers protection to the family, motherhood, fatherhood, children, and young people. However, the concept of family remains based on a relationship of two people of different sex and it includes the parent-to-child relationship. Nevertheless, by 1998 the government had already considered the introduction of legal same-sex partnerships. The law on the registration of same sex partnership was passed in May 2005.[132] The legitimacy of the majority vote in favour of the bill was tight, since only 47 out of 90 deputies of the National Assembly were present. Although the civic organizations were consulted in the drafting process, their views were not adequately included in the final draft. Regardless, they consider the adoption of the Act as an achievement in the area of human rights (Kuhar 2006).

Art. 2 of the Act defines the registered same-sex union as a legally established union of two women or two men who register their union before the competent authority in a manner determined by the Act. Registered partners gained a set of rights and obligations with regard to joint property, support, and inheritance (albeit limited to joint property acquired throughout the duration of the union). The Act falls short of regulating any family relationships between parents and children. It has been also criticized for not defining the *status* of a ‘relative’ versus the *status* of a registered partner. Consequently, registered partnerships provide fewer rights than marriages. For this very reason, the Act has been challenged in the Constitutional Court by a group of NGOs that claims discriminatory treatment under law of homosexual couples.[133]

The issue under review by the Constitutional Court concerned the compatibility of Art. 22 of the Registration of Same Sex Partnerships Act with Art. 14 of the Constitution (non-discrimination on the ground of sexual orientation).[134] In fact, the law differentiated between common and special possessions of partners so that same-sex partners, unlike spouses, were excluded from having a share in special possessions. The Court found the law contrary to the principle of non-discrimination, since the inheritance rules applicable to same-sex partners were less favourable than those applicable to opposite-sex partners.[135] It also held that the Parliament should remove the challenged provision within 6 months after

[132] Registration of Same-Sex Partnership Act 65/06, 8th July 2005.

[133] Mavcic and Avbelj (2008), pp. 24–25.

[134] Decision No. U-I-425/06-10, 2nd July 2009.

[135] Art. 22 of the Act provides that: “(1) In case of death of a partner the surviving partner has the right to inheritance on the share of common possessions under this act. (2) If the deceased has children, the possessions from the previous paragraph are inherited by the surviving partner and the children of the deceased by equal shares. (3) If the deceased does not have children, the surviving partner inherits the entire share of common possessions of the deceased. (4) Special possessions of the deceased are inherited in accordance with the general rules on inheritance. General rules on inheritance are also used in inheritance of the share of common possessions of the deceased if this act does not stipulate otherwise. (5) The material competency for the inheritance procedures lies within the county courts.”

the publication of its decision. In the justification of this judgment, the Court reiterated that a

> [R]egistered partnership is a relationship which is in content similar to marriage or civil partnership. The stable connection between two persons, who are close to each other, who help and support each other is the key element of both. The ethical and emotional essence of a registered partnership, as stated in Article 8 of RSSPA, according to which the partners have to respect, trust and help each other, is similar to the union between a man and a woman. The legal situation of such partnership is also similar to marriage. RSSPA also ensures mutual rights and obligations to partners, protects a weaker partner, regulates their legal position towards third parties, the State, and the social environment.[136]

The next round in the recognition of same-sex couples came with the Family Law bill, which was put forward by the central-left government in 2009 but stalled until 2011. It aimed to endorse marriage as the union of a man and a woman without equating the concept of family with the concept of heterosexual marriage. The original version of the bill intended to introduce gay marriage and gay adoption, but was compromised in the Labour, Family and Social Affairs Committee under the pressure of conservative groups. The new definition of family covering two persons, regardless of their gender, and a child seems to discriminate against single parents. The bill was passed on 16th June 2011, with a 38/43 vote. It granted all rights of married couples to same-sex couples, except for the right to adopt children. Importantly, the bill included the right to same-sex parent-adoption and laid the ground for the country's first case of a child adoption by the lesbian partner of the child's biological mother.[137] Notably, by 2010 the Supreme Court recognized the U.S. decision authorizing the adoption of a girl by a gay couple. The couple had a dual U.S.–Slovenian citizenship. Pursuant to this ruling, they also became legal parents in Slovenia.[138]

The lobbying group Civil Initiative for the Family and the Rights of Children nevertheless challenged the 2011 Family Law by collecting signatures for a *referendum* to overturn the law. In opposition, another lobby group—the Initiative for All Children, for All Families, for Free Choice, and for Equal Rights—questioned the *referendum*'s legality. The question divided the Constitutional Court, which ruled by a 4/5 majority that the national *referendum* was constitutional. As a result, the *referendum* took place on 26th March 2012. While the voter turnout was very low, 55 % Slovenians decided to reject the new Family Law. The decision meant that a new bill regulating rights of same couples could not be drafted for 1 year after the *referendum*.

The Slovenian case illustrates that the incremental change theory does not fully explain the dynamics of the recognition of same-sex couples' rights in the Eastern European countries, even if they seem to endorse liberal laws and appear to be overtly tolerant towards the LGBT community. Nevertheless, the mobilization of

[136] ERT Summary: Blazic and Kern v. Slovenia.

[137] U.S. Department of State, Slovenia, Country Reports on Human Rights Practices for 2011.

[138] Decision No. II Ips 462/2009-9, 28th January 2010.

opponents to the institutionalization of same-sex marriage and adoption challenged the Family Law and led to a return to the *status quo* of a rather weak legal position of registered partners. Characteristically, all ground-breaking decisions—of the National Assembly, the Constitutional Court, and the *referendum*—were made by narrow vote. Except from showing that same-sex relationships, in particular in a family law setting, are a very divisive issue, it illustrates that Slovenian society still prefers to accept traditional values.

9.5 Judicial Recognition of the Rights of Same-Sex Couples: The Case of Poland

9.5.1 The Emergence of the LGBT Movement and Failures to Recognize Same-Sex Couples in Law

Poland is among the countries in Eastern Europe that still do not have laws regulating same-sex relationships. However, the case of Poland could be considered exemplary for examining the evolution of the recognition of same-sex couples via court decisions. It is at the same time a laboratory of different legal problems concerning same-sex couples. However, before explaining in detail the current problems of same-sex couples, one needs to look at the situation of LGBT people in Poland from a historical perspective.

Poland is one of very few countries to have already abolished penalization for homosexual conduct before the Second World War. Interestingly, by the 1960s and 1970s, the Polish courts had established the legal possibility to change one's gender by virtue of their jurisprudence. These judge-made rules on gender reassignment for transsexuals are still applicable today, since no new legislation has been adopted in this area and Supreme Court case-law shapes current judicial practice.[139] Before 1989, the LGBT minority could not legally organize in the Polish People's Republic. Moreover, the communist party used the knowledge about somebody's homosexuality for blackmail, and it particularly used the networks of collaborators and informers of the secret services to search for this type of information.

After 1989, the LGBT groups emerged in a slow process, and only a small number of persons came out as LGBT. In this initial phase of the LGBT movement, the leaders managed to get the support of the senator Maria Szyszkowska, who introduced the first draft law on same-sex partnerships in 2003.[140] The Senate rejected the law before it had even been presented to the Lower Chamber of the Parliament.

[139] Śledzińska-Simon (2010), p. 5.

[140] The draft law by Maria Szyszkowska is available at: http://www.bezuprzedzen.org/prawo/art.php?art=140.

The breakthrough year for the Polish LGBT community was 2005. The ban on the Equality March in Warsaw, issued by the Mayor of Warsaw, Lech Kaczyński, was a major event that sparked the LGBT movement. Over the following years new, powerful LGBT organizations emerged and, most importantly, the issue of sexual orientation became a part of the public agenda.[141] At the same time, the authorities banned gay pride parades in other cities and the freedom of assembly by the LGBT minority was litigated before the Polish Constitutional Court,[142] the Supreme Administrative Court,[143] and the Strasbourg Court.[144] Furthermore, LGBT people started to take action in courts in the first hate speech cases.[145]

From 2005 to 2007, the LGBT movement concentrated on its fight against discrimination by public authorities. Homophobic remarks by right-wing politicians, proposals to introduce a ban on 'homosexual propaganda' in schools,[146] dismissals of high-ranking officials due to alleged promotion of homosexuality,[147] and bans on gay pride parades were crucial elements of the social and political climate in this period. Notably, the homophobic language permeating the right-wing political speeches replaced, or at least supplemented, that which had traditionally been anti-Semitic rhetoric.[148] It was important, however, that the media actively presented the LGBT people as a discriminated group.[149] Thus, the 'invisible' LGBT got a *status* of a minority whose members were discriminated against.

---

[141] Bodnar (2009b).

[142] Judgment of the Constitutional Court of Poland, K 21/05, 18th January 2008. English summary available at: http://www.trybunal.gov.pl/eng/summaries/documents/K_21_05_GB.pdf.

[143] Judgment of the Supreme Administrative Court, I OSK 329/06, 25th May 2006.

[144] *Bączkowski and Others v. Poland*, n. 1543/06, 3rd May 2007.

[145] In the case called 'Nasza Sprawa' ('Our Cause'), four lesbians accused two members of the Law and Justice of defamation. The case ended with a settlement. On 11th September 2006, the accused politicians publicly apologized for their homophobic comments. See more at http://kobiety-kobietom.com/naszasprawa/art.php?art=3763.

[146] The proposal to introduce a ban on homosexual propaganda was made by the government coalition party—the League of Polish Families. It was never officially discussed in public even though the draft law had been submitted to the Parliament. See http://www.guardian.co.uk/world/2007/mar/20/schools.gayrights.

[147] The leader of the League of Polish Families, the Minister of National Education, Roman Giertych, dismissed the head of the National In-Service Teacher Training Centre (CODN) for publishing the official handbook of the Council of Europe "The Compass – Education on Human Rights". In his opinion, the handbook included statements on homosexuality and same-sex marriages that are contrary to the Polish Constitution. On 30 May 2007, the District Court in Warsaw (VIII P 1028/06) held that the Minister of National Education discriminated against the head of CODN and awarded him a compensation for moral damages in the amount of over 16,000 PLN. It was the first judgment in Poland dealing with discrimination on the ground of private convictions.

[148] Czarnecki (2007).

[149] On the homophobic language in politics see Graff (2010).

The result of the 2007 parliamentary elections in Poland ended the era of illiberal democracy.[150] The pro-EU centrist party—the Civic Platform—and its even more conservative coalition partner—the Polish People's Party—replaced the right-wing coalition government. Nevertheless, even this new political situation did not produce a significant improvement of the legal position of LGBT people. However, it did create opportunities for a dialogue between the LGBT movement and the authorities. In addition to the raising expectations concerning some form of recognition of same-sex partnerships, strategic litigation began before international and national courts by and for same-sex couples living together in Poland.

In 2009, LGBT organizations managed to make nation-wide consultations regarding the future of the registered partnership bill, and the French PACS model seemed to be the favoured option. At the end of the Parliament term, on May 17, 2011, LGBT leaders, associated in so-called Initiative Group on the Registered Partnerships (*Grupa Inicjatywna ds. Związków Partnerskich*), submitted the bill via one of the political parties. The bill was not subject to parliamentary debate before the end of the term. Notably, in the 2011 elections, the Leader of the Campaign Against Homophobia, Robert Biedroń, who had publicly declared his own homosexuality, and the Leader of the *Trans-Fuzja* Foundation, Anna Grodzka, who was a declared M/F transsexual, were elected to the Parliament.[151] Both of them ran on the ticket of Palikot's Movement, a liberal, anti-clerical, and progressive political party established by Janusz Palikot.

During the present parliamentary term, two left-wing parties—Palikot's Movement and the Alliance of the Democratic Left—submitted two separate drafts of the registered partnership laws, albeit with a different set of rights and duties for the partners regarding joint taxation and the possibility to change names and acquire certain social benefits. In response, the Civic Platform responded to these proposals with its own bill on the registered partnership, so-called Dunin's Bill, which provided less partnership rights than the above-mention projects. For example, it excluded the possibility for the registered partners to jointly declare their taxes, arguing that such rights would make registered partnership and marriage too much alike.

The first historical debate in the Polish Parliament devoted to three bills on the registered partnership took place on 25th January 2013. During this debate, members of the Law and Justice party expressed their homophobic opinions, and a major disagreement was revealed between two members of government. Namely, the Prime Minister, Donald Tusk, supported the Dunin's Bill as the government initiative and the Minister of Justice, Jarosław Gowin, objected to it, arguing that the registration of same-sex partnerships is contrary to the Constitution. The Sejm had nonetheless already voted against all of the bills during the first reading, which

---

[150] On the decrease in democratic standards in Poland after the EU accession—see Bodnar (2010a, b).

[151] This historical moment was highly commented by international media. See e.g. http://www.huffingtonpost.com/2011/11/08/anna-grodzkatransgender-w_n_1081636.html.

was considered to be a political failure for the Prime Minister.[152] It is far from clear whether the current Parliament will adopt any law on registered partnership since the ruling party—the Civic Platform—is highly divided on this issue.

The key point of the parliamentary debate on the future statutory regulation of the registered partnership was compliance with Art. 18 of the Constitution, which defines marriage as the union of a man and a woman. According to one view, this provision excludes any alternative to marriage and the constitutional protection covers only relationships between two adult persons of different sex. In this view, the State protection granted to any other personal relationships is an attack against the traditional family and Christian values, and therefore also on the natural order that is referred to in the Preamble of the Constitution. The opponents also use pragmatic arguments, taking into account that most of the rights to be established in the law are, or can be, obtained as a result of court decisions.

On the other hand, the proponents of registered partnerships claim that the Constitution not only permits the partnerships, but it also requires that the legislation regulate other forms of family life outside of marriage. The constitutional protection of human dignity (Art. 30), equality before the law and non-discrimination (Art. 32), and the right to respect of private and family life (Art. 47) read in conjunction a mandate that a minority consisting of approximately 5 % of society is adequately protected by law. The proponents also claim that Art. 18 of the Constitution does not create an obstacle to the regulation of this issue in the marriage statute, and registered partnership and marriage would remain two separate legal institutions. Therefore, Art. 18 of the Constitution should not be read as excluding the possibility to regulate registered partnerships. Finally, there are already numerous examples in Polish law where a legislative provision or case-law challenges the traditional notion of marriage or family. For example, the Polish Family and Guardianship Code allows for 'separation' of spouses in marriage. In addition, substantive case-law and selected statutory provisions regulate the status of cohabiting partners who live out of wedlock.[153]

Those arguments are important to demonstrate that the public debate on same-sex couples in Poland concentrates on two major issues: (a) whether adoption of any legislation on registered partnership is in compliance with the Constitution, and (b) what rights should be granted to registered partners by virtue of such legislation. It is very likely that if any law on the registered partnership is adopted, it will be challenged before the Constitutional Court. Currently, the ruling party is even using the argument that the Parliament should adopt a restrictive law in order to defend it later before the Constitutional Court. However, it seems that such a statement is an excuse for not accepting a more progressive bill on the registered partnership. Thus,

[152] See e.g. http://www.reuters.com/article/2013/01/25/us-poland-homosexuals-idUSBRE90O0LU20130125.

[153] See the opinion of the Committee of the Legal Sciences of the Polish Academy of Sciences, available at http://www.knp.pan.pl/images/stories/KNP_PAN/Pismo_do_Prezesa_PAN_z_23_04_2012.pdf.

the referral to the authority of the Constitutional Court to declare the law null and void is used to chill the work on the bill even if nobody could ever predict what the outcome of such a review would be.

As previously mentioned, Poland serves as a laboratory of different legal problems concerning the *status* of same-sex couples. The lack of statutory regulation combined with rather strong non-discrimination guarantees in the Constitution empowers LGBT persons to litigate their rights in international and domestic courts.

9.5.2 **Kozak v. Poland***: The Right to Enter into a Lease Agreement After a Partner's Death*

One of the most interesting cases on same-sex couples' *status* concerned the right to enter into a lease agreement after the death of one's homosexual partner. Mr. Kozak wanted to stay in the municipal dwelling in Szczecin after his partner died. He particularly relied upon Section 8 (1) of the Lease of Dwellings and Housing Allowances Act of 2nd July 1994, according to which such a possibility should be awarded to persons living in "marital *de facto* cohabitation." However, the social welfare authorities and the domestic court interpreted this provision as being only applicable to heterosexual couples. The Regional Court in Szczecin referred to the legal definition of marriage and found as follows:

> (i)t must be stressed that a de facto marital relationship differs from a marriage only by lack of its legitimisation. For this reason, the subjects actually remaining in marital cohabitation can only be persons who, under the Polish law, are eligible for marriage. Pursuant to Article 1 § 1 of the Family and Custody Code, the fundamental principle of the family in Poland is the difference in sex of a prospective nuptial couple (nupturienci), which means that contracting a marriage between persons of the same sex is inadmissible. Having regard to the fact that de facto cohabitation constitutes a substitute for a marriage, one must consider that its subjects can exclusively be a woman and a man.

Kozak appealed this decision to the Strasbourg Court. From the legal perspective the judgment in *Kozak v. Poland*[154] did not create a new standard, because the European Court had previously decided a similar case, *Karner v. Austria*,[155] where it had found a violation of Art. 8 and 14 ECHR. However, in *Kozak v. Poland* the Strasbourg Court took into account factors related to national legislation. First, there was a new provision in the Civil Code that permitted stepping into a lease agreement. Art. 691 of the Civil Code provides that such a possibility extends, *inter alia*, to "a person who has lived in de facto cohabitation with the tenant." It should be noted that word 'marital' is not included into this notion. Second, the Court

---

[154] *Kozak v. Poland*, n. 13102/02, judgment of 2nd March 2010.

[155] *Karner v. Austria*, n. 40016/98, judgment of 24th July 2003.

found that States have a narrow margin of appreciation in maintaining provisions based on discrimination with regard to sexual orientation.

Third, the Strasbourg Court underlined that States may protect a meaning of traditional marriage in their Constitution or legislation; however,

> in pursuance of that aim a broad variety of measures might be implemented by the State (ibid). Also, given that the Convention is a living instrument, to be interpreted in the light of present-day conditions [. . .] the State, in its choice of means designed to protect the family and secure, as required by Article 8, respect for family life must necessarily take into account developments in society and changes in the perception of social, civil-status and relational issues, including the fact that there is not just one way or one choice in the sphere of leading and living one's family or private life.[156]

The paragraph stating that the domestic authorities "should take into account developments in society" seems to be one of the most important indications by the Court that sooner or later it may need to decide whether the lack of any regulation of same-sex couples' *status* violates the Convention.

The Strasbourg judgment in *Kozak v. Poland* was widely commented on in the Polish media, which also reported on numerous examples of similar cases pending before the Polish courts. In over ten cases, the courts interpreted this provision as applicable to same-sex couples and they consequently declared that a homosexual partner has the right to enter into a lease agreement after the death of the tenant. However, there was one exceptional case pending in the District Court of Warsaw-Mokotów, in which the court refused to rule in favour of the homosexual partner.[157] The court argued that Art. 691 of the Civil Code is applicable only to heterosexual couples in 'de facto cohabitation.' The Regional Court in Warsaw, which heard the appeal of the case, decided to refer the legal question to the Supreme Court and ask whether this provision should be interpreted as extending to homosexual couples in addition to heterosexual couples.

In the judgment of 28th November 2012, the Supreme Court clarified that same-sex couples in *de facto* cohabitation should not be discriminated against under Art. 691 of the Civil Code.[158] In this regard, the Supreme Court took into account principles of non-discrimination contained in Art. 32 of the Constitution. It also referred to the Strasbourg case-law, particularly the case of *Kozak v. Poland*.

On its surface, the judgment of the Supreme Court does not seem to be that of a milestone case, since it merely confirmed the existing case-law of the European Court. However, the national context of Poland must be taken into consideration, in that it is a post-communist country, where courts tend to listen more to the Supreme Court than to an external authority such as one of the European courts. Therefore, this judgment may have a significant impact not only on the problem of lease tenants, but also on many other areas of law where legal provisions use notions of 'the closest person,' and 'living together,' etc., without mentioning marriage. The

[156] *Kozak v. Poland*, para. 98.

[157] Judgment of the District Court for Warsaw Mokotów, no. I C 1447/10, 13th October 2011.

[158] Judgment of the Supreme Court, No. III CZP 65/12, 28th November 2012.

judgment of the Supreme Court may also become a source of interpretation for other areas of law, including the right to refuse testimonies concerning an accused person. In this regard, the Code of Criminal Proceedings in Art. 115, sect. 11 uses the notion of 'the closest person' (*osoba najbliższa*),[159] which provides the right to participate in civil proceedings as a witness. Art. 261 of the Code of Civil Proceedings does not explicitly state that persons living in *de facto* cohabitation as being excluded from the possibility to be a witness. However, one may expect such a development to occur in the future.

One may also consider that the understanding of the notion of 'family' or 'family members' may be extended by virtue of interpretation. For example, Art. 446, para. 3, of the Civil Code provides the right to compensatory claim for 'family members' in case of the death of the person who was the main supporter of the family. The doctrine interprets this provision by referring to Art. 18 of the Constitution and relates the notion of 'marriage' with the notion of 'family.'[160] However, one should not exclude the possibility that a different interpretation may be adopted in the courts' practice.

9.5.3 *The Rights of Same-Sex Couples Exercising Their Freedom of Movement in the EU*

Poland is also an interesting laboratory of cases concerning freedom of movement of EU citizens, where the issue of legally recognizing same-sex couples has raised at least three types of situations. In the first situation, the problem concerned the right of a person who wished to enter into a same-sex marriage or registered partnership in another EU Member State to obtain a non-marriage certificate. The second type of situation regarded the recognition of a registered partnership concluded in another EU Member State. The third scenario concerned the right of a national of a third country who is a same-sex partner of an EU citizen to move to and legally reside in the territory of Poland.

9.5.3.1 The Right to Obtain a Non-marriage Certificate and a Certificate for the Legal Capability to Enter into Marriage

Due to the growing migration within the EU, there are more and more Polish citizens who take advantage of the right to move freely to the territory of another Member State where registered same-sex partnerships or marriage are legal. In order to register their partnership or marriage abroad, they usually need to present a certificate issued by the Civil Status Office (*Urząd Stanu Cywilnego*) stating that the

[159] On the situation of homosexual persons in the criminal law see Płatek (2009).

[160] Strus (2010), p. 39.

person concerned is unmarried. The position of the Ministry of Internal Affairs and Administration was that Polish law does not provide for the issuance of such certificates. However, if a person cannot not obtain a certificate then she or he can make an appeal to the governor (*wojewoda*).

In a landmark judgement concerning the issuance of a non-marriage certificate, the Regional Administrative Court in Gdańsk found that the refusal is contrary to law.[161] The complaint was lodged by a female citizen of Poland who wished to register a partnership with a female citizen of Germany under provisions of German law recognizing same-sex partnerships. The Head of the Civil Status Office refused to issue such a certificate, with the justification that the citizen did not have any legal interest to obtain it. The citizen made an appeal to the Governor, which was also dismissed. Finally, she lodged a complaint to the Regional Administrative Court, which overruled the decisions of the first and the second instance for being grossly contrary to the law. It stated that the law does not allow the examination of where or with whom an applicant wishes to contract marriage, nor test authenticity of her/his intentions. The only role of the administrative organ in charge is to examine if a person fulfilled conditions stipulated by the Polish law that are necessary to get married. Moreover, a citizen is entitled to receive such a certificate without substantiating her/his request, and her/his intentions cannot be prerequisite for the refusal in any case. The court noticed that it would be contrary to the constitutional principle of the democratic State ruled by law if the authorities were to examine the veracity of the most personal intentions of the citizens.

Following the court's decision, the problem of issuing certificates to homosexual persons was broadly commented on in the media. It was also the subject of a massive European campaign organized by the Campaign Against Homophobia. The Campaign reported on numerous cases of persons who faced obstacles while applying to receive the non-marriage certificate in order to register for a same-sex partnership abroad.[162] In general, the problem still persists and concerns not only Poland but also many other countries. Under Polish law, a person may obtain two types of certificates. The first is the non-marriage certificate (i.e. clarifying the civil *status* of a person, as in the case decided by the Regional Administrative Court in Gdansk). There is currently no special problem with obtaining such a certificate. The second type is a certificate on the capability to enter into marriage abroad. In such a case, the applicant needs to fill out a special questionnaire. However, this questionnaire is prepared for heterosexual couples only and Polish Civil Status Offices refuse to use it for purposes of same-sex marriages. However, the Polish authorities announced that this questionnaire will be changed to suit homosexual couples.

Tomasz Szypuła, one of the leaders of the LGBT movement in Poland, is currently litigating his own case concerning issuance of a certificate regarding his capability to marry. The Civil Status Office refused to provide him with the

[161] Judgment of the Regional Administrative Court, No. III SA/Gd 229/08, 6th August 2008.

[162] http://www.kph.org.pl/pl/allnews/15-kph/98-parlament-europejski-zajmie-si-petycj-kph.

certificate for the purpose of entering into a same-sex marriage with a Spanish citizen. Tomasz Szypuła appealed to the District Court in Warsaw, and then to the Regional Court in Warsaw, yet both courts refused to agree with his argumentation. They stated that such a certificate could be issued only with respect to a heterosexual marriage and referred to Art. 18 of the Constitution.[163]

9.5.3.2 The Right to the Recognition of a Same-Sex Registered Partnership or Marriage Concluded in Another Member State

One of the most interesting aspects of the EU integration is a conflict between EU citizens' freedom of movement rights and the possibility to enter into same-sex registered partnership or marriage while residing abroad. The EU Court of Justice has not addressed such cases, although there is one case pending in Austria that has a chance of becoming an EU-wide precedent.[164]

There have been some litigation attempts in Poland concerning this issue. In one case, X and Y entered into registered partnership in Edinburgh according to UK legislation. They did so to take advantage of the UK law that allows all nationals to enter into same-sex registered partnerships on its territory. However, the couple then returned to Poland and wished to have their partnership recognized by the Polish authorities. In the proceedings before the Polish courts (described below) they argued that Polish law should not treat them as persons who are completely alien to each other, and it should not ignore the existence of the legal relationship between them. However, the Polish courts underlined that Polish law does not recognize same-sex registered partnerships and marriages, and it similarly does not recognize any such relationship entered into in another EU Member State.

X and Y also wanted to include a special remark (*wzmianka*) on their registered partnership in the civil *status* act, which reflects the personal and civil *status* of every citizen. However, the Civil Status Office also refused to make such a remark, claiming that it cannot include information regarding an institution that is not recognized under the Polish law. Upon appeal, the administrative courts took a similar approach.

It should be noted that the issue of recognition of same-sex registered partnerships and marriages entered into in other States was heavily discussed during works on the new Law on Private International Law (law governing conflicts of jurisdictions and choice of law). According to some politicians, drafting provisions of this Law created the necessity to recognize the official *status* of same-sex couples coming from other States to Poland. However, this interpretation was, to a great extent, the result of a misunderstanding of the special character of legal provisions

---

[163] On Tomasz Szypuła case see Geitner (2012).

[164] Case of Dutch same-sex marriage seeking for their recognition as a marriage in Austria is currently pending before the Austrian Constitutional Court. It is litigated by the Rechtskommittee Lambda. More information available at http://www.rklambda.at/e/index.htm.

in a case of different cross-border situations. Nevertheless, the debate in the Polish Parliament required an official reaction by the Minister of Justice, who stated that it is legally impossible to recognize same-sex couples in Poland on the basis of Private International Law provisions.

The Minister of Justice has also presented a statement, signed later on behalf of the Government, with respect to the EU Commission's proposal of the Council Regulation on jurisdiction, applicable law, and the recognition and enforcement of decisions regarding the property implications of registered partnerships.[165] In general, Poland protested against an imposed necessity to pass any legislation of that kind at the EU level. It has also expressed critical comments in a situation where some Member States would like to pass the Regulation through the enhanced cooperation under Art. 20 TEU and 326–334 TFEU. The government of Poland therefore emphasized that issues falling under family law are within the exclusive competences of the Member States. Thus, introduction of any regulation that would require the recognition of same-sex partnerships or marriages in Poland would indirectly introduce such institutions into the Polish legal system. Furthermore, the government pointed out a number of difficulties resulting from the multitude of means of regulating registered partnerships or marriages in Europe.

The open refusal by different courts to deal with the issue of recognition of foreign same-sex registered partnerships, and the unanimous stance taken by politicians, suggest that there is a chance to address this problem in favour of the same-sex partners in the near future. It seems that a court would currently rather forego their task than make a preliminary reference under Art. 267 TFEU.

9.5.3.3 The Right to Move and Reside in a Member State by a Third Country National Who Is a Same-Sex Partner of an EU Citizen

Another problem concerning same-sex couples migrating from other States concerns the interpretation of Directive 2004/38/EC on freedom of movement of EU citizens and their family members. According to its provisions, family members of the EU citizens, who are non-EU citizens themselves, are exempt from the obligation to have a visa when entering another EU Member State. The only pre-condition is possession of a valid residence card. This possibility extends to every family member who is in a long-term, registered relationship with the EU citizen, irrespective of whether it is a same-sex or different-sex relationship. When the EU Member State finds the relationship to be long-term and duly confirmed, then it should facilitate entry of such couple into its territory even if it does not recognize an equivalency of marriage and registered partnerships.

[165] Proposal for a Council Regulation on jurisdiction, applicable law, and the recognition and enforcement of decisions regarding the property consequences of registered partnerships of 16 March 2011, COM(2011) 127/2, available at http://ec.europa.eu/justice/policies/civil/docs/com_2011_127_en.pdf.

However, Polish practice indicates that authorities are not aware of guarantees stemming from the Directive 2004/38/EC. In 2012, there were two instances where the Border Guard refused to allow a homosexual partner of an EU citizen to enter Polish territory. Notably, decisions in this case were made without considering legal grounds and even the facts of the case, in particular with regard to the *status* of the family member of the EU citizen. Also, the Border Guard used an argument that Polish law does not recognized same-sex registered partnerships. The first case of this sort concerned a citizen of Dominican Republic, who travelled to Poland with his partner, a UK citizen. The second case concerned a citizen of the Philippines travelling with a Polish citizen. Both cases are currently pending. In the first case, the Regional Administrative Court in Warsaw revoked the decision of the Border Guard refusing entry into Poland, but it was done purely on administrative grounds. The Court did not analyse the compliance of the practice with Directive 2004/38/EC. In the second case, the Regional Administrative Court in Warsaw is currently reviewing the motion to make a preliminary reference to the EU Court.[166]

9.5.4 The Right to the Recognition of Same-Sex Couples in Poland in Light of the ECHR

The lack of statutory laws regulating the legal *status* of same-sex couples in Poland has resulted in the strategic litigation of a case that may lead to changes in the existing case-law of the ECtHR. The facts of the case are as follows—X and Y have lived in a stable lesbian relationship since 2004. They rent a flat together and have a common household. In 2010, they entered into a civil partnership in Edinburgh under the Civil Partnership Act. However, they live permanently in Poland and their civil partnership status is not recognized under Polish law. In 2009, they started a number of proceedings relating to their *status* as a same-sex couple living together. Those proceedings concerned issues such as:

(a) Special allowances for taking care of an ill spouse. One of the partners could not work for 2 weeks in 2009 because she was taking care of the second partner. The Social Welfare Office provides such allowances to spouses in a legal marriage, but not to same-sex partners;
(b) Tax qualification for donations between spouses. Under Polish law, married couples qualify under the first category and any donation between them is almost exempt from taxation. However, same-sex couples living together are treated as though they are not affiliated with one another, and they are placed under the third category of taxation;

[166] The case is litigated within the Program Art. 32 of the Helsinki Foundation for Human Rights. More information: http://www.hfhr.org.pl/dyskryminacja/litygacja/dyskryminacja-ze-wzgledu-na-orientacje-seksualna/.

(c) Joint taxation with regard to personal income tax. In Poland, couples living together, if not joined by marriage, cannot take advantage of submitting joint tax declaration (which would allow them to pay lower taxes).

In the discussed case, the legal proceedings were initiated before the administrative authorities and domestic courts, including the Supreme Administrative Court and the Constitutional Court. In all instances, the courts refused to recognize the *status* of the same-sex couple and grant them the same rights as married spouses. The Constitutional Court argued that it could not decide a case concerning legislative lacuna, and the administrative courts refused to recognize the *status* of the couple as registered under the UK Civil Partnership Act.

Due to the exhaustion of domestic remedies, X and Y decided to submit the application to the ECtHR in August 2012. They argue, in particular, that the lack of any form of legal recognition by Polish law of same-sex couples violates Art. 8 and 14 of the ECHR. They have made a separate argument regarding the lack of recognition of same-sex partnerships concluded in another European State. It is noteworthy that the Helsinki Foundation for Human Rights is representing the applicants *pro bono*.

9.6 Conclusions

This chapter demonstrates that the road to the legal recognition of same-sex relationships is full of obstacles. Even if some rights of same-sex couples are regulated by law, the parliamentary (super)majority can reverse this process through the adoption of constitutional amendments that foreclose (or make extremely difficult) any further changes by a simple majority in the future. On the other hand, in countries that have not legally recognized same-sex couples, one should not expect that courts will readily replace the legislator. Strategic litigation can only provide courts with the opportunity to interpret the existing provisions more progressively. Adjudication has a subsidiary role in civil law countries, where precedential law does not generally apply and where the courts are reluctant to implement international human rights standards or judgments. Nevertheless, precedential cases before courts may help to illuminate problems of same-sex couples living together, both for the government and for the people. Still, much depends on the popular support for LGBT movement in society. Positive attitudes towards gay marriage or adoption can prevent the governments from changing the *status quo*. Although the parliamentary debates on same-sex couples in the region show a great deal of animosity and homophobic stereotypes, it is clear that despite the strong conservative influences of the Catholic Church and the right-win politicians, governments are likely to respond to the views of the majority of society.

Acknowledgment The authors would like to thank Sabrina Rewald for her invaluable help in editing the final version of this chapter.

References

Abtan B (2013) Hungary: to safeguard democracy, Europe must use Article 7! Open Editorial, EGAM. http://egam-eu.blogspot.com/

Aloni E (2010) Incrementalism, civil unions, and the possibility of predicting legal recognition of same-sex marriage. Duke J Gender Law Policy 18:105–143

Bodnar A (2009a) The charter of fundamental rights: differentiated legal character of charter's provisions, their consequences for individuals, courts and the legislator. In: Barcz J (ed) Fundamental rights protection in the EU. C.H. Beck, Warszawa, pp 145–167

Bodnar A (2009b) Shaping the freedom of assembly: counter-productive effects of the Polish road towards illiberal democracy. In: Sajo A (ed) Free to protest: constituent power and street demonstration. Eleven International, Utrecht, pp 165–187

Bodnar A (2010a) Legal study on homophobia and discrimination on grounds of sexual orientation and gender identity. www.fra.europa.eu/sites/.../fra.../1364-LGBT-2010_thematic-study_PL.pdf

Bodnar A (2010b) Poland: EU driven democracy? In: Sadurski W, Morlino L (eds) Democratization and the European Union. Comparing Central and Eastern European post-communist countries. Routledge, London, pp 19–43

Byrnes TA (2002) The challenge of pluralism, the Catholic Church in democratic Poland. In: Jelen TG, Wilcox C (eds) Religion and politics in comparative perspective: the one, the few, and the many. Cambridge University Press, Cambridge, pp 27–44

Constitutional Court of Hungary (2012) Certain provisions of the act on the protection of families held contrary to the fundamental law. www.mkab.hu/sajto/news/certain-provisions-of-the-act-on-the-protection-of-families-held-contrary-to-the-fundamental-law

CVVM Opinion Poll (2012) Postoje veřejnosti k právům homosexuálů – květen 2012. http://cvvm.soc.cas.cz/media/com.../c1/.../ov120710.pdf

Czarnecki GE (2007) Analogies of pre-war anti-semitism and present-day homophobia in Poland. In: Kuhar R, Takacs J (eds) Beyond the pink curtain. Everyday life of LGBT people in Eastern Europe. Mirovni Institut, Ljublana, pp 327–344

ILGA Europe (2011) Registered partnership debate renewed in Latvia – society at large remains homophobic. http://ilga-europe.org/home/guide/country_by_country/latvia/registered_partnership_debate_renewed_in_latvia_society_at_large_remains_homophobic

ILGA Europe (2013a) Country by country. http://ilga-europe.org/home/guide_europe/country_by_country

ILGA Europe (2013b) MP Petras Gražulis promises to fight homosexuals once again. ILGA Europe. http://ilga-europe.org/home/guide/country_by_country/lithuania/MP-Petras-Grazulis-Promises-to-Fight-Homosexuals-Once-Again

Garlicki L (2003) Komentarz do art. 18. In: Garlicki L (ed) Konstytucja Rzeczypospolitej Polskiej Komentarz, 3rd edn. Ksiegarnia, Warszawa, pp 2–3

Geitner P (2012) On gay marriage, Europe strains to square 27 interests, New York Times. http://www.nytimes.com/2012/07/26/world/europe/on-gay-marriage-europe-strains-to-reconcile-27-interests.html?pagewanted=all&_r=0

Graff A (2010) Looking at pictures of gay men. Political uses of homophobia in Poland. Public Cult 22:583–603

Halmai G, Scheppele KL (2012) Opinion on Hungary's new constitutional order: amicus brief for the Venice Commission on the transitional provisions of the fundamental law and the key cardinal laws. http://lapa.princeton.edu/hosteddocs/hungary/Amicus_Cardinal_Laws_final.pdf

Hodson L (2011) A marriage by any other name? Schalk and Kopf v Austria. Hum Rights Law Rev 11:170–179

FRA Study on Homophobia (2010) European Union Agency for Fundamental Rights, Homophobia, transphobia and discrimination on grounds of sexual orientation and gender identity. Comparative legal analysis. http://fra.europa.eu/en/publication/2012/homophobia-transphobia-and-discrimination-grounds-sexual-orientation-and-gender

Hönnige C (2009) The electoral connection: how the pivotal judge affects oppositional success at European constitutional courts. West Eur Polit 35:963–984

Honuskova V, Sturma P (2008) Legal study on homophobia and discrimination on grounds of sexual orientation – Czech Republic. www.fra.europa.eu/sites/default/files/.../369-FRA-hdgso-part2-NR_CZ.pdf

Human Rights Watch (2013) Hungary: constitution changes warrant EU action. Government Action to Bypass Court Undermine Rule of Law, 12th March 2013. http://www.hrw.org/news/2013/03/12/hungary-constitution-changes-warrant-eu-action

Huseby DO (2009) The Catholic Church and the Europeanization of anti-discrimination protection – the cases of post-communist Poland and Croatia. West Balkans Secur Obs 14:102–119

Immigration and Refugee Board of Canada (2012) Treatment of sexual minorities by society and government officials; laws, state protection and support services. http://www.unhcr.org/refworld/docid/4fc4abab2.html

Jegelevicius L (2001) Challenged definition of family has sent tremors throughout the conservative landscape. The Baltic Times, 12th October 2011. http://www.baltictimes.com/news/articles/29789/

Juras S (2010) Study on homophobia, transphobia and discrimination on grounds of sexual orientation and gender identity, legal report: Croatia. www.coe.int/t/Commissioner/Source/LGBT/LGBTStudy2011_en.pdf

Körtvélyesi Z, Pap AL (2012) National report: Hungary. Am Univ J Gender Soc Policy Law 19:211–220

Kuhar R (2006) The impracticability of active citizenship beyond the closet in Slovenia. In: Weyembergh A, Carstocea S (eds) The gays' and lesbians' rights in an enlarged European Union. Editions de l'Université de Bruxelles, Bruxelles, pp 147–168

Mavcic AM, Avbelj M (2008) Legal study on homophobia and discrimination on grounds of sexual orientation in Slovenia. http://www.pedz.uni-mannheim.de/daten/edz-b/ebr/08/FRA-hdgso-NR_SI.pdf

Płatek M (2009) Sytuacja osób homoseksualnych w prawie karnym. In: Wieruszewski R, Wyrzykowski M (eds) Orientacja seksualna i tożsamość płciowa. Aspekty prawne i społeczne. Instytut Wydawniczy EuroPrawo, Warszawa, pp 49–82

Ramet SP (2006) Thy will be done: the Catholic Church and politics in Poland since 1989. In: Byrnes TA, Katzenstein PJ (eds) Religion in an expanding Europe. Cambridge University Press, Cambridge, pp 117–147

Santoni M, Zucchini F (2006) Legislative output and the constitutional court in Italy. Constitut Polit Econ 17:165–187

Schimmelfennig F, Sedelmeier U (2005) Introduction: conceptualizing the Europeanization of Central and Eastern Europe. In: Schimmelfennig F, Sedelmeier U (eds) The Europeanization of Central and Eastern Europe. Cornell University Press, New York, pp 1–28

Śledzińska-Simon A (2010) Prawa osób transseksualnych w Polsce. Rozwiązania modelowe a sytuacja w Polsce. Wolters Kluwer, Warsaw

Strus Z (2010) Zadośćuczynienie w razie śmierci osoby najbliższej. In Strus Z, Ortyński K, Pokrzywniak J (eds) Zadośćuczynienie po nowelizacji art. 446 Kodeksu cywilnego na tle doświadczeń europejskich, Polska Izba Ubezpieczeń. http://www.piu.org.pl/public/upload/ibrowser/WU/spec_zadosc/zadoscuczynienie_WU.pdf.

Tsebelis G (2002) Veto players. How political institutions work. Princeton University Press, Princeton

Uitz R (2012) Lessons from sexual orientation discrimination in Central Europe. Am J Comp Law 60:235–264

United States Department of State (2011) Croatia, country reports on human rights practices for 2011. www.state.gov/j/drl/rls/hrrpt/humanrightsreport/index.htm#wrapper

Waaldijk K (2001) Small change: how the road to same-sex marriage got paved in the Netherlands. In: Wintemute R, Andenaes M (eds) Legal recognition of same-sex partnerships: a study of national, European, and international law. Hart Publishing, Oxford, pp 437–464

Wyrzykowski M (2009) Introduction: limitations of power and limits of interpretation. In: Barcz J (ed) Fundamental rights protection in the EU. C.H. Beck, Warszawa, pp 25–38

Zwolski K (2009) Euthanasia, gay marriage and sovereignty: the Polish ratification of the Lisbon Treaty. J Contemp Eur Res 3:489–497. http://www.jcer.net/ojs/index.php/jcer/article/view/248/173

Chapter 10
Same-Sex Couples in France and Belgium: The Resilient Practice of Judicial Deference

Philippe Reyniers

Abstract The recognition and institutionalization of same-sex couples in France and Belgium are mainly political questions. But courts are not insignificant actors: they frame the terms of the democratic debate. In legal systems where courts have no formal law-making powers, questions of recognition are quickly transformed into institutional questions in which the responsibility of the legislator remains central. The French and Belgian cases, in that respect, fit the expectations of a civilist model of legislative supremacy. It does not mean however that fundamental rights play no role. On the contrary, the Belgian case shows that courts can be responsive to right-claims when these concern discrete, easily isolated questions of discrimination on the ground of sexual orientation or of family status. The practice of judicial deference then allows for a piecemeal recognition of same-sex couples by multiple judgments of moderate effects, and not by landmark judicial decisions.

10.1 Political and Institutional Contexts

Both French and Belgian institutional contexts are comparable in respect of the rights of same-sex couples. Both are countries of civil law in which legislative supremacy is central. Both include constitutional rights to equality that are interpreted in terms of consistency, and which provide the ground for a seemingly thin rationality review. Both consider that same-sex relationships are ultimately questions of personal status that are central to the *Code civil*, which itself is the foundation of their national legal cultures. Jean Carbonnier, an eminent figure of French legal scholarship, wrote that the Code formed the actual French constitution[1]: it embodies political principles applied in the private sphere.

[1] Carbonnier (1997).

P. Reyniers (✉)
Department of Law, European University Institute, Florence, Italy
e-mail: philippe.reyniers@eui.eu

D. Gallo et al. (eds.), *Same-Sex Couples before National, Supranational and International Jurisdictions*, DOI 10.1007/978-3-642-35434-2_10,

Politics, on the other hand, are very different. Whereas the French legal system is the mirror of a unitary and centralized Republican State, Belgium is a Federal Monarchy fragmented along linguistic and ideological lines. Whereas Belgium is pluralist and prompt to recognize cultural differences, France stands firmly on its principle of *laïcité* and its assimilating implications. That does not mean that religious conceptions are less capable of framing the public debate on same-sex couples in France than in Belgium. French Catholicism is politically conservative (or reactionary), while Belgian Catholicism is humanist and liberal. Historically, both France and Belgium have an exceptionally permissive approach to homosexuality. In the wake of the Revolution, the French criminal code of 1791 no longer incriminated homosexual relationships. The *Code pénal* of 1810 enacted by Napoleon also considered that the law did not have to regulate a behaviour that did not contravene public order. In the following sections, the key rulings on same-sex couples are analysed in the different stages of recognition: from repression to tolerance, to equal status.

10.2 France

10.2.1 Overcoming Homosexuality as a Deviant Conduct

The authoritarian and collaborationist regime of Vichy suppressed the liberal customs of the nineteenth century. A law of 6th August 1942 criminalized acts "against nature" involving minors. This text allowed the deportation of thousands of homosexuals to Germany.[2] It was maintained after the war, only to be modified by a discriminatory distinction. Homosexual lewd acts were punishable against a minor under the age of 21, while heterosexual acts were punishable under the age of 15. This distinction was kept through the many reforms of criminal law. The *Conseil constitutionnel* validated the distinction in 1980, considering that equality before the law did not bar differentiations made between "acts of different nature."[3]

At the same period nevertheless, the French legislator undertook to abolish a number of penalizing and stigmatizing measures against homosexual people. The beginning of the pandemic of HIV/AIDS also jump-started a burgeoning social movement.[4] As the virus disproportionately struck gays, claims for recognition of same-sex couples took importance, and were not well received by judges. The *Cour de cassation* refused a social advantage to the partner of an homosexual worker, considering that the term "spouse" (*conjoint*) had to be understood for persons

[2] Sibalis (2002).

[3] "Le principe d'égalité devant la loi pénale (...) ne fait pas obstacle à ce qu'une différenciation soit opérée par la loi pénale entre agissements de nature différente." Decision n° 80-125 of 19th December 1980 (*Journal Officiel*, 20 December 1980, p. 3005).

[4] Caballero (2010), p. 279.

engaged in a stable and continuous relationship having appearance of a marriage "therefore between a man and a woman."[5] It also prevented the transmission of a lease between homosexual tenants in case of death.[6] For the law and for French courts thus, same-sex couples did not exist. In this context, their recognition seemed impossible and requires the intervention of the Legislator. Again, this caused the Legislator to respond and enact a number of specific measures, such as the prohibition of discrimination on the ground of sexual orientation on the labour market. The process culminated at the end of the 1990s by the vote of the *Pacte civil de solidarité* (PACS),[7] a registered partnership that comported personal and patrimonial rights similar to the ones of the marriage. The PACS was the first legal recognition of same-sex couples. Yet, legal scholars, in general, harshly criticized the decision of the Legislator. The root of the opposition is to be found in the resilience of idea of homosexuality as deviance. For some, the idea itself of same-sex couple is a "negation of the familial order"[8] and the legislation is the monstrous child of a Legislator[9] dominated by demagogical considerations.[10] As a leading scholar, proponent of the law, wrote,

> all the branches of the law were mobilized to stress the imperfections and demonstrate the incongruities of a 'mediocre', 'one-sided' law that animates 'perplexity' and triggers 'doubt' and 'uncertainty'.[11]

10.2.2 Early Recognition of Same-Sex Couples

The PACS was controversial, and the debate in the French assemblies surrounding its adoption took a legal turn before the *Conseil constitutionnel*.[12] The claims before that jurisdiction adopted all the dimensions of the critique expressed by the political and academic opponents to the project. The *Conseil* validated the law by rejecting claims relating to competences, equality before the law, and a number of general principles stemming from constitutional provisions.[13] What is remarkable in this decision is that it went quite far in analysing the intention of the

---

[5] F. *Cour de Cassation Soc.*, 11th July 1989, *X c. Air France* (*Recueil Dalloz* 1990, p. 589, note Malaurie).

[6] F. *Cour de Cassation Civ.*, 17th December 1997, *Vilela c. Mme Weil* (*Recueil Dalloz* 1998, p. 111, note Auber).

[7] Loi No. 99-944 du 5 novembre 1999 relative au Pacte civil de solidarité (*Journal Officiel*, 16th November 1999, p. 16959).

[8] Malaurie (1997).

[9] Malaurie and Fulchiron (2008).

[10] Terré (1999).

[11] Borillo (2001), p. 185.

[12] Note that the *Conseil*, until recently, is called to review the constitutionality of legislation preventively: it intervenes before the law is published.

[13] Decision No. 99-419 DC, 9 November 1999 (*Journal Officiel*, 16th November 1999, p. 16962).

Legislator and operated a frank constructive interpretation of the provisions of the law. Doing so, it actually redefined the purpose itself of the PACS. Constrained by the political necessity of creating a regime substantially distinct from the marriage, the French Legislator avoided resorting to language evoking the institutional aspects of the (same-sex) relationships recognized by its legislation. It did centrally define the PACS as a "contract concluded by two major natural persons, of different sex or same sex, for organizing their common life".[14] If it's a contract, it is not a matter of affective relationship, even less a question of family. And the law gave no precision on the concept of 'common life', and thus allowing the partnership to be open to relations of friendship or convenience. The *Conseil* nevertheless 'sexualised' the contract. It saw that no contract can be concluded between members of the same family, that a common residence must be established, and that a mutual obligation of material assistance must be respected by the parties. It concluded that, under the light of the parliamentary debates, the PACS was not strictly a community of interests of two persons living under the same roof: the partnership required a life as a couple (*vie de couple*).[15]

The *Conseil* nevertheless, by referring to the terms of *vie de couple*, did not create an obligation of marital fidelity between the parties of a PACS and refused to identify in the regime created by the Legislator anything that touches upon personal status.[16] What the *Conseil* did was to strengthen the *sui generis* character of the partnership as a specific contract of family law.

Why did the Court proceed to such an interpretive operation? The legislation voted by the French Parliament is short and leaves open many questions concerning the nature and extent of the obligations of mutual assistance between the parties, the effect of the contract on parental rights, its mode of termination. The allegation of the claimants concerned the lawful exercise by the Legislator of its constitutional competence in matters of private law (Art. 34 of the French Constitution). For them, the absence of precise and clear rules on the questions mentioned amounted to a violation of the constitutional competence to the extent that it left discretion to other institutions (the executive and the judiciary) for determining the content of the regime itself. The *Conseil* rejected the argument by imposing reserves of interpretation.[17] What mattered to the *Conseil* was clearly not a question of substance or recognition: the formal characters of the law, legal certainty and institutional balance are the reasons which lead the Court to affirm the specific nature of the contract, and the personal and affective relationships it is expected to protect. Nevertheless, as narrow as the grounds of the judgment are, the decision remains a form of acceptation of same-sex relationships and sexuality at the apex of the French judicial hierarchy.[18]

---

[14] Art. 515-1 of the *Code civil*.

[15] See para. 26 of the Decision.

[16] It seems however that the decision of the *Conseil* and the traditional contractual principles of the *Code civil* provide the basis for an obligation of loyalty that implies the sanction of infidelity.

[17] Drago (1999).

[18] Caballero (2010), p. 285.

10.2.3 Same-Sex Marriage

The vote of the PACS had a considerable chilling effect on the politics of same-sex couples in France. The bill, as progressive as it was, double-edged: it constituted a form of recognition of same-sex couples forced by the legal formalism of the *Conseil constitutionnel*, but was also a confirmation a political attachment to a traditional order of family and sexuality. The debate remained blocked amid the wave of acceptation of same-sex marriage taking place in Europe and beyond. It did not dissuade gay rights lobbying and activism however. Some of these actions were deployed at local level, and mainly consisted in celebrating the same ceremony of marriage for the conclusion of registered partnerships.

The most emblematic case concerned the celebration of a marriage of two male partners by the mayor of Bègles, a commune of Bordeaux. The mayor, a strong proponent of same-sex marriage and a green member of the French assembly named Noël Mamère, responded to a call of the jurist Daniel Borrillo and philosopher Didier Eribon.[19] The celebration and consequent litigation had, it seems, no other purpose than kindling the political debate on the question of same-sex marriage. Yet, it gave the opportunity to the *Cour de cassation* to affirm that the definition of marriage in French law, as it stood, can only be understood as the union of a man and a woman.[20] This conclusion, it declared, was not contradicted by the European Convention of Human Rights (further referred to as ECHR), nor by the EU Charter of fundamental rights, which was, at that time, not a binding instrument.

Doctrinal commentators welcomed the decision of the Court. They considered, in the greatest majority, that judicially opening the marriage to same-sex partners cannot be solved by a traditional operation of interpretation: this entails a redefinition of the concept of marriage. For Hugues Fulchiron, the obstacle is the procreative "function" expected from a married couple.[21]

The *Conseil constitutionnel* in a decision delivered a few years later adopted the same position in the case of *Corinne C*.[22] Invited by the *Cour de cassation* to rule on the constitutionality of the provisions of the *Code civil* that incidentally refer to a man and a woman as the parties to a marriage, the *Conseil* espoused the views expressed by the *Cour de cassation*: the ordinary meaning of marriage is heterosexual. The court was also required to determine whether this definition was in breach of the constitutional right to lead a normal family life, as protected by the preamble of the French constitution of 1946. It considered that this right did not include the right to marry for homosexual couples, which could already benefit from the PACS or from the provisions applicable to *de facto* relationships (*concubinage*). It also rejected claims based on equality: the legislator could validly

---

[19] Paternotte (2008).

[20] Fr. *Cour de cassation*, 13th March 2007 (*Recueil Dalloz*, 2007, p. 935, note Gallmeister).

[21] Fulchiron (2007).

[22] Decision No. 2010-92 QPC, 28 January 2011 (*Journal Officiel*, 29th January 2011, p. 1894).

considered that same-sex couples are not in the same situation than heterosexual couples. The *Conseil* nevertheless emphasised that the competence of the legislator was not restrained by the constitutional principle of freedom to marry. Doing so, the *Conseil* considered that a judgement of opportunity must be made, and that it could not make a decision in this respect in place of the legislator.

On the 23rd of April 2013, the French national assembly and senate voted the law No. 2013-404 granting the right to marry to same-sex couples.[23] The project of "*Mariage pour tous*" was initiated in autumn 2012 by the then-newly elected president François Hollande. The piece of legislation, which allows both marriage and adoption, was debated in a heated political context, with multiple popular demonstrations organised by Catholic and right wing groups. The *Conseil constitutionnel* was called to verify the validity of the act and rendered a considerably longer decision on 17th of May, which permitted the law to be finally promulgated.[24] The bill was attacked on many procedural and substantive grounds, but the jurisdiction was particularly careful in rejecting claims relating to the definition of marriage. For the applicants (all elected members of the houses of the French parliament), the socialist majority misrecognised the "natural roots" of civil law, which posit sexual otherness as the foundation of marriage. For the *Conseil*, tradition and "nature" do not constitute fundamental principles of the law of the French republic. This position is in line with the decision of 2011: the legislator has the sole competence to legally define the law of marriage as long as constitutional provisions are respected. The *Conseil* is compelled to adopt a more substantive stance in matters of filiation and adoption. As in the Belgian case, the presumption of paternity does not apply to married same-sex couples, which means that the female partner of a mother is not presumed to be the co-parent of her child. The French bill leaves the presumption untouched and causes the spouses who are not the biological authors of the child to establish filiation by mechanisms of adoption. The court validates this situation, as it accepts that in matters of procreation, same-sex couples are not in a similar situation to heterosexual families. For the applicants, the possibility to establish filiation for same-sex couples contravened the right of the child to lead a normal family life. The position of the *Conseil* is here twofold. First, the legislator is simply institutionally competent in these matters and is allowed to imposed its views. Secondly, adoption and filiation correspond to the best interests of the child, which are constitutionally protected (para. 53). The Court here neutralises the concept of "normal family life" brought up by the applicants: this "normality" does not entail the secret of family origins or the heterosexuality of parents.

[23] Loi No. 2013-404 du 17 mai 2013 ouvrant le mariage aux couples de personnes de même sexe (*Journal Officiel*, 18th May 2013, p. 8253).

[24] Decision No. 2013-669 DC, 17 May 2013 (*Journal Officiel*, 18th May 2013, p. 8281).

10.3 Belgium

The Belgian case is in many respects similar to the French case. To the extent that it shares with France the same civilist legal culture, Belgian law nourishes a similar anxiety towards the power of judges.

Formally, the judiciary does not enjoy law-making powers. If they embraced rights-based judicial review recently, courts hesitate to contemplate the transformative potential of fundamental rights. An advocate general to the *Cour de cassation*, recently considered that the application of the law often required a purposive interpretation that entails law-making and creative dimensions. Yet, novel interpretations and constructions in case law are explained and justified by the pursuit of a secular value: the reparation of damage.[25] This is approach and the model of restorative justice it implies[26] is inadequate to questions of recognition, and the question of recognition of same-sex couples in particular.

Nevertheless courts are participants in a democratic culture shared by all public institutions and social actors. They thus contribute to its evolution, in collaboration or opposition with the legislator. Like in the previous chapter, the role of courts can be analysed during the historical stages of the law of same-sex couples: repression, recognition, and marriage.

10.3.1 Overcoming the Conception of Homosexuality as Deviant Conduct

Belgium is also similar to France in the stages of the politics of homosexuality. The historical background is filled with events expressing outright prejudice against sexualities that are consistently described as behaviors "against nature". Like in France, Belgian criminal law included between 1965 and 1985 a discriminatory provision on age of consent. The *Cour de cassation* saw no issue of validity on this differentiated treatment, considering that if the law constituted indeed an interference in the right to private life guaranteed by Art. 8 ECHR, this interference was justified by the public interest in order and morals.[27] The judgment was delivered in a context of revision of the law on the question of homosexuality.

---

[25] Opinion of Advocate General Henkes before B. *Cour de Cassation*, 7th December 2007, Pas., para 40: "En fin de compte, par le recours à des constructions juridiques inédites, la Cour, à chaque fois fait le choix d'étendre à de nouvelles applications une valeur séculaire – la réparation d'un dommage par celui qui l'a causé ou qui doit l'assumer – traduite dans des textes de droit parfaitement muet sur ces applications voire longtemps considéré comme étrangers à ces nouvelles applications."

[26] For example, see Suk (2006).

[27] B. *Cour de Cassation*, 7th December 1982 (in Pasicrisie 1983, p. 437).

Before 1965, the law knew no specific rules on homosexual conduct. Homosexuality was punishable only if it constituted a lewd act committed with violence or an affront to public decency. Then, the Belgian Legislator adopted measures for the protection of minors,[28] and the basis for the distinction was openly scientific, not moral. As a measure of protection, the Legislator considered that adolescents are psychologically vulnerable to "seduction" that ultimately leads to a "conversion" to homosexuality. Protection was needed since, in the view of medicine and psychology, homosexuality was considered a pathology. This view, shared by the Legislator and medical professionals for long, was later rejected. In the early 1980s, the scientific foundation of the incrimination of same-sex activities of minors was dismissed and the Legislator admitted the negative effects of the repression on young homosexual adults. The Legislator abolished this provision of the criminal code, and broadly considered that consensual same-sex activities were not harmful and should thus not be condemned.

The abolition did however not amount to the public acceptation of same-sex relationships. The debates in the Assembly made clear that some amalgamated homosexuality with paedophilia, sadism or exhibitionism, and that the vote could not amount to a form of recognition. Homophobia is culturally ingrained, and criminal courts are not alien to its promotion, even in a context of depenalization. Françoise Tulkens exposed that courts used the crime of debauchery (as an open-ended notion) to repress gay gatherings and venues.[29] Debauchery was then given the meaning of any dysfunction of sexuality, which included homosexuality.[30] Was then condemned on that ground Michel Vincineau, a Law professor from the Université Libre de Bruxelles. As in France, the 1980s are a transition period that included a growing toleration or acceptance of homosexuality as a conduct and the beginnings of a social movement carrying the claim of gay rights. Like anywhere else, the context of AIDS pushed the agenda for legal protection of same-sex relationships, which came in the form of a registered partnership[31] (with substantially less content than the French PACS) adopted by the Belgian Legislator in 1998. Courts are thus not the authors of the first legal recognition of same-sex couples.

[28] *Loi du 8 avril 1965 relative à la protection de la jeunesse*, Moniteur Belge, 15th April 1965.

[29] Tulkens (1986).

[30] "Si l'homosexualité n'est pas en elle-même constitutive d'infraction, il n'en demeure pas moins qu'elle constitue une forme de dérèglement de la sexualité par cela même qu'elle méconnait la finalité de l'existence de deux sexes différents, finalité dont l'abandon généralisé mènerait à l'extinction de l'espèce humaine (...) que celle seule considération suffirait déjà à permettre se supposer que le législateur a voulu (...) empêcher la propagation de l'homosexualité précisément en ne lui Assurant pas la sécurité ailleurs qu'au domicile des particuliers." *Tribunal correctionnel de Bruxelles*, 29 mai 1985, *Journal des procès*, 27th December 1987.

[31] *Loi du 23 novembre 1998 instaurant la cohabitation légale* (Moniteur Belge, 12th January 1999).

10.3.2 Early Recognition of Same-Sex Relationships

It does not mean however that Belgian courts were not confronted to cases involving same-sex relationships over the same period. But decisions were diverse. Two kinds of approaches can be identified. The first is the case law of civil jurisdictions, which have worked to preserve a heterosexual definition of couples in matters of family law. The second case law concern labour courts, which were ready to redefine the notion of household and to protect same-sex couples for the purposes of social security legislation.

The cases of family law on the question of same-sex relationships may seem absurd to many. Adultery is a legal cause of divorce, and a line of case law considered that adultery was not constituted if it was committed with a person of the same sex.[32] The *Cour de cassation* decided in 1998 that the law did not require a condition of heterosexuality in the legal definition of adultery.[33] The judgment is remarkable in declaring, "Everyone is entitled to the respect of their private life, without distinction, such as sex".

Against this affirmation of a fundamental right, the decision is striking in placing on an equal footing hetero- and homosexuality. These cases do not concern the protection of same-sex relationships, and the judgment of the *Cour de cassation* will not be the foundational recognition of homosexual couples. As it adapts the definition of adultery to more accurate circumstances, the decision nevertheless constitutes the acknowledgement of the diversity of sexualities, and simply proceeds to draw the appropriate conclusions from it.

The role of labour courts is more proactive. A diverse number of pieces of social security legislation referred to the notion of household for the calculation of benefits. Royal decrees adopted in execution of these legislations have repeatedly defined this notion as the cohabitation of persons of different sexes. Labour courts have overwhelmingly considered this definition to be illegal because that it constituted a discrimination on the ground of sexual orientation or of family status.[34] The Constitutional court (then called *Cour d'arbitrage*) confirmed this case law in 2000. The case[35] concerned a mode of calculation of family benefits which applied in an equal manner to cohabitants of different sexes and to same-sex cohabitants of the same family, but not to same-sex cohabitants *simpliciter*. The Court saw less a discrimination on the ground of sexual orientation than a lack of consistency in the determination of the personal scope of the royal decree. The decision is short but

[32] For example, *Cour d'appel de Mons*, 29th March 1989 (*Revue Trimestrielle de Droit Familial*, p. 385).

[33] *B. Cour de Cassation*, 17th December 1998 (Pasicrisie 1998, p. 527).

[34] See *Cour du travail de Bruxelles*, 22nd January 1996 (*Journal des Tribunaux* 1996, p. 263); Arbeidsrechtbank Gent, 4th April 1996 (Sociaalrechtelijke Kronieken 1996, p. 407). See also, in a case of social aid, Arbeidsrechtbank Brugge, 8th March 1999 (Rechtskundig Weekblad 1999–2000, p. 565).

[35] *Cour d'arbitrage*, Case n° 80/2000, 21 June 2000 (Moniteur Belge 2000, p. 30028).

notable, to the extent that it protects homosexual households with children on equal terms with traditional families. Note that if same-sex couples benefit directly from the decisions of labour (and constitutional) courts, these cases go beyond the question of homosexuality as they include both relations of affection and relations of care.

Should we thus consider that courts contributed to the recognition of same-sex couples? We know already that the main mode of recognition was and remained political and that the Legislator played the leading role. But the answer must certainly be positive. There was however, no frontal case. Courts resolved a series of discrete or isolated questions of inequality. They were not summoned to affirm generally and solemnly the equal moral standing of same-sex couples. The technique of these courts also remains usual for the Belgian legal-formalist culture. Questions of equality become tractable once they are framed in terms of rationality and consistency, not in terms of the fundamental right to equal dignity. Plainly, cases of discrimination are easier to deal with so long as they do not tackle directly the questions of *status* organized by the Code civil, which are not only symbolically more potent, but which have comprehensive legal consequences with respect to personal rights and obligations, contractual liability, parental authority and fiscal treatment.

10.3.3 Same-Sex Marriage

The question of marriage is, again, political. In 1999, the federal elections resulted in a governmental coalition that did not comprise Christian-democrats parties supported by relatively conservative electorate. More progressive policies took shape. Against the background of the bill on the *cohabitation légale*, whose weaknesses were already apparent at the time of its adoption, the coalition agreement of the new liberal-socialist-green majority announced a general law on discrimination and a "véritable régime légal de vie commune".[36] The legislative project defended by the government included the following motivation:

> In our contemporary society, the marriage is experienced as a (formal) relationship, the principal purpose of which is the creation of a durable life together (communauté de vie). The marriage offers to both partners the possibility of affirming publicly their relationship and their mutual feelings. Attitudes and mindsets have evolved – today, the marriage is used to affirm the intimate relationship of two persons and loses is procreative character. There are no more reasons not to open the marriage to persons of the same sex. This opening will signify that same-sex couples will exercise the fundamental right to marry. The foundation of the present draft bill is the equal right to marry for homosexual and heterosexual couples.[37]

[36] Arend-Chevron (2002).

[37] *Projet de loi ouvrant le marriage aux personnes de même sexe et modifiant certaines dispositions du Code civil*, Doc. Parl., Chambre, 2001–2002, n° 1692/001.

The very definition of marriage as *communauté de vie* turned out to be extremely problematic for lawyers, and for a jurisdiction in particular.

The *Conseil d'Etat* is the court entrusted with the review of the acts of the Belgian administration. Its *Section législation* functions as an advisory body for the legislative and executive branches of the State. It delivered an opinion on the draft bill of the government, which considered that objective differences remain between heterosexual and homosexual couples.[38] These differences concern "the nature of things". Only heterosexual couples are able to give birth to children, and as such, they have a different social utility than homosexual unions. The *Conseil d'Etat* concluded that, contrary to the view adopted by the government, there is no (legal) discrimination between hetero- and homosexual couples in the access to marriage. It nevertheless considered that if there were no obligation for the Legislator to give the right to marry to same-sex couples, it can be viewed as a question of opportunity. But for the *Conseil d'Etat*, the project remains incoherent on that level too. The single concept of marriage cannot be reduced to a question of *communauté de vie* since it is legally organized for filiation, parentage and descent.

The opinion of the *Conseil d'Etat* was very badly received, both in the political and public spheres. Many considered that the jurisdiction overstepped its mandate and expressed unacceptable moral views the draft bill was meant to combat. It was nevertheless well received and defended by prominent academic figures who contended, like the *Conseil d'Etat*, that the governmental project was incoherent.[39]

The draft bill of the government is indeed founded on equality, but the regimes proposed therein are not equal since they maintain rules of filiation for heterosexual couples and excludes their application in cases of homosexual couples. For Jean-Louis Renchon, the only way to guarantee legal coherence was to reshape completely the institution of marriage and discard all its rules on filiation for different sex couples first. It would indeed be

> fictitious to assimilate an homosexual union that cannot generate a double filiation of a child to a heterosexual marriage is not (yet) reduced to a simple partnership and which is and remains a social organization allowing to structure the parentage of children.[40]

Despite the typically legal criticism of incoherence, a large majority in the two Houses of Parliament promptly voted the law as proposed by the government.[41] The equalization (or assimilation) then concerned the modes of conclusion and dissolution of marriage, the effects on alliance, mutual rights and obligations between spouses, and social and fiscal rights and obligations between spouses and the state. Filiation finds no application here.

The idea of difference in the "nature of things" between heterosexual and same-sex couples persisted legally. Still today, the spouse of the mother of a child is not

---

[38] B. *Conseil d'Etat*, Opinion n° 32.008/2, 12th November 2001.

[39] Renchon (2002, 2004).

[40] Renchon (2004), pp. 184–185.

[41] *Loi du 13 février 2003 ouvrant le mariage à des personnes de même sexe*, Moniteur Belge, 28th February 2003.

the child's second mother: there is no legal parentage established between the two. And *a fortiori*, the husband of the father of a child is not the father of that child, regardless of the identity of the child's mother.

The Constitutional court validated the law opening marriage to same-sex couples against that background. In a judgment[42] delivered on a direct action in annulment, the *Cour d'arbitrage* considered that the difference between heterosexual and same-sex couples was "not such" that the latter should be excluded from the right to marry.[43] The argument of the claimants was founded on the constitutional guarantee of equality: as the law treated identically two allegedly objectively different situations without reasonable justification, it contradicted the Constitution. It is difficult to understand which is the objective difference between couples that the Court perceived but deemed irrelevant. It nevertheless is reminiscent of the views of the *Conseil d'Etat* for which same-sex couples are not in a comparable situation with heterosexual couples that there is the acknowledgement of a difference, again, in the "nature of things" between the two categories. But the Constitutional court remains deferent to the choices of the Legislator: if it wishes to universalize the right to marry despite objective differences, it is free to do so as long as these differences, "natural" or "socially constructed", are not important.

10.3.4 Same-Sex Parenthood

In 2006, the Belgian legislator extended the law of adoption to same-sex couples.[44] The same logic of equality is thus applied in matters of adoption. To a certain extent, the Legislation is an attempt to solve the issue raised by the problem of filiation in the context of a same-sex marriage.

The Constitutional court had to review certain of its provisions that disadvantaged same-sex parents, especially in respect of the transmission of surnames.[45] But the judgments of the *Cour constitutionnelle* in these cases are hardly addressed same-sex couples as such. Judges were more concerned with the interest of the child, not the claim of equality associated with homosexual parenthood.[46]

---

[42] *Cour d'arbitrage*, Case No. 154/2004, 16 June 2004 (Moniteur Belge, 2nd August 2004).

[43] See para. B.4.7.: "Au regard d'une telle conception du mariage (la création d'une communauté de vie durable), la différence entre, d'une part, les personnes qui souhaitent former une communauté de vie avec une personne de l'autre sexe et, d'autre part, les personnes qui souhaitent former une telle communauté avec une personne de même sexe n'est pas telle qu'il faille exclure pour ces dernières la possibilité de se marier."

[44] *Loi du 18 mai 2006 Loi modifiant certaines dispositions du Code civil en vue de permettre l'adoption par des personnes de même sexe*, Moniteur Belge, 20th May 2006.

[45] *Cour constitutionnelle*, Case No. 104/2010, 16th September 2010 (Moniteur Belge, 17 November 2010); Case No. 26/2012, 1st March 2012 (Moniteur Belge, 11 June 2012).

[46] Art. 22*bis* of the Belgian Constitution provides that in all decision that concerns her or him, the interest of the child is taken into account and is of primordial importance.

In an important decision delivered in the context of the debate on same-sex marriage, the Court considered discriminatory the impossibility to dissociate the exercise of parental authority and parentage in the case of a same-sex household.[47] It declared that the interest of the child in maintaining a bond with the same-sex partner of their mother or father must prevail against the legal impossibility to grant parental authority to a person who is not a parent. The discrimination established by the Court concerns distinctions made between children with and without a parentage with the persons who have a particular relationship of care with them.[48] It is not a question of sexual orientation, although the two categories obviously overlap in facts, and the case is of major instance of the recognition of same-sex household and "homoparentalité".

The case knew a follow-up in the context of same-sex marriage. As we saw, the rules of same-sex marriage do not automatically create the filiation between a child and the same-sex partner of their parent. The law of 2006 allows the establishment of this filiation by adoption. But the law requires the consent of both partners, except in specific situation of abandonment. In a case where the refusal to consent to the adoption by one spouse was claimed to be abusive, the *Cour constitutionnelle* ruled that there is a prevailing interest of the child to obtain a double bond of filiation (both with her parent and with their same-sex partner) despite the absence of consent of both partners to the adoption.[49] The decision of 2012 deserves to be read in the light of the judgment of 2003: the best interest of the child ultimately enhances the *status* of same-sex couples even if the latter are not the object of concern for the Court. Quite remarkably, the same-sex nature of the household seems to be of the least importance in the treatment of the case.

Perhaps a benign indifference to homosexual relationships has become prevalent for the Belgian constitutional court. It remains that differences of regimes subsist even if they are explained, for the Legislator and for the doctrine, by *la nature des choses*. The *Cour constitutionnelle* will have to address them in the future. The absence of filiation, the need for adoption and the inapplicability, for instance, of the presumption of paternity/maternity/parenthood in the case of same-sex couples will remain problematic. It is possible that Belgian courts, and probably the *Cour constitutionnelle*, will prompt the Legislator to reform the law of filiation radically and to equalize and unify the regimes completely.

---

[47] *Cour constitutionnelle*, Case No. 134/2003, 8th October 2003 (Moniteur Belge, 19th January 2004).

[48] The judgment mentions the "relations personnelles entre un enfant et la personne qui justifie d'un lien d'affection particulier avec celui-ci" and the necessity to legally enable the effects of that bond for the person who would offer to guarantee care and protection for the child. See para. B.6.

[49] *Cour constitutionnelle*, Case No. 93/2012, 12th July 2012 (Moniteur Belge, 18th October 2012).

10.4 Conclusion

In many respects, the topic of the roles of courts in the recognition of an equal status to same-sex couples in France and Belgium cannot be adequately treated by focusing on a small number of decisions of the higher courts, even of these landmark rulings establish the main lines of fault. Both systems fit the expectations of a civilist institutional arrangement, where the final word is actively given to a political authority. There is no grand narrative of emancipation and human dignity here: only the resilient practice of judicial deference is to be found.

References

Arend-Chevron C (2002) La loi du 13 février 2003 ouvrant le mariage à des personnes de même sexe. Courrier hebdomadaire du CRISP 1780

Borillo D (2001) Fantasmes des juristes *vs Ratio juris*: la *doxa* des privatistes sur l'union entre personnes de même sexe. In: Borillo D, Fassin E, Iacub M (eds) Au-delà du PaCS: l'expertise familiale à l'épreuve de l'homosexualité. Puf, Paris, pp 160–175

Caballero F (2010) Droit du sexe. L.G.D.J., Paris

Carbonnier J (1997) Le Code civil, Les lieux de mémoire. In: Nora P (dir) La Nation. Gallimard, Paris

Drago G (1999) La Constitution "en réserves", commentaire de la décision du Conseil constitutionnel du 9 novembre 1999 portant sur la loi relative au pacte civil de solidarité. Droit de la famille 13:46

Fulchiron H (2007) Un homme, une femme: la Cour de cassation rejette le mariage homosexuel. Dalloz 20:1375–1376

Malaurie P (1997) Le mariage et les homosexuels. Recueil Dalloz, Paris

Malaurie P, Fulchiron H (2008) La famille, 3rd edn. Defrénois, Paris

Paternotte D (2008) Les lieux d'activisme: le «mariage gai» en Belgique, en France et en Espagne. Can J Polit Sci 41:935–952

Renchon J-L (2002) Mariage et homosexualité. J des Tribunaux 505–514

Renchon J-L (2004) L'avènement du mariage homosexuel dans le Code civil belge. Revue de droit international et de droit comparé 81:169–207

Sibalis M (2002) Homophobia, Vichy France, and the "Crime of Homosexuality": the origins of the ordinance of 6 August 1942. GLQ: J Lesbian Gay Stud 8:301–318

Suk J (2006) Antidiscrimination law in the administrative state. Univ Illinois Law Rev 2006:405–473

Terré F (1999) Histoire d'une loi. Droit de la Famille 7:28–29

Tulkens F (1986) Egalité et discrimination en droit pénal belge. Revue international de droit pénal 57:63–89

Chapter 11
At the Crossroads Between Privacy and Community: The Legal *Status* of Same-Sex Couples in German, Austrian and Swiss Law

Giorgio Repetto

Abstract The *status* of same-sex couples in German, Austrian and Swiss law reveals many similarities, from both the substantial (with regard to parental and material rights, particularly in the field of social benefits) and the institutional perspective (with regard to the shared powers between the central authority and the member States and to the dialectics between the Legislator and the judiciary). In the three jurisdictions examined, the traditional resistance toward same-sex marriage has not prevented the national Legislators from adopting, over the past decade, a regulation introducing same-sex registered partnerships. The main common features of these provisions are admittance to registered partnerships only for same-sex couples, a regulatory framework imitating the basic structure of marriage, and a progressive inclusion of registered partners within the social security schemes. This common model, which could per se be referred to a 'separate but equal' rhetoric, is undergoing some significant transformations in the field of parental rights, whose increasing enjoyment by registered partners (above all in Germany) is broadening the legal and symbolic relevance of same-sex relationships.

11.1 Introduction

The inquiry into the legal *status* of same-sex couples in the countries examined in this contribution moves from the assumption of the common features lying behind the different national models. Germany, Austria and Switzerland indeed have a largely common historical and cultural background, which reflects the different regulations concerning the legal treatment of same-sex couples. According to a

G. Repetto (✉)
University of Perugia, Perugia, Italy
e-mail: Giorgio.Repetto@unipg.it

D. Gallo et al. (eds.), *Same-Sex Couples before National, Supranational and International Jurisdictions*, DOI 10.1007/978-3-642-35434-2_11,

recent classification,[1] these three countries—despite the different solutions given in some areas—share a common approach regarding both the substantive questions surrounding same-sex couples and the institutional ones.

By "substantive questions" I mean, with Bamforth, "the content of the legal rights afforded to those in same-sex partnerships in the jurisdiction concerned" and, in this vein, they encompass both material and parental consequences of same-sex partnerships. For this aspect, the problems raised in the German, Austrian and Swiss jurisdiction are taken into account from the perspective of the constitutional background that has biased the recognition of rights to marriage and cohabitation for same-sex couples, as well as from the most significant judicial decisions that have marked the evolution of this topic in the national fields. Constitutional background is meant to operate as a matrix shaping judicial as well as legislative decisions and, in this way, it reflects the deepest underpinnings of the different models sketched out in these pages.[2] On this basis, special attention is thus given to the questions arising from the social security benefits granted to same-sex couples in respective jurisdictions, since the three countries taken into consideration have a highly complex and evolved Welfare State system, whose basic inclusive premises have for the most part accepted granting some basic benefits to (registered) same-sex couples. Another aspect highlighted in the following pages concern parental rights, traditionally a hotly debated issue when the *status* of same-sex couples is at stake: in this case, the three models examined show partially different solutions, in particular with regard to the extension of adoption rights, and to access to medically assisted reproduction.

Substantive questions are nonetheless not the only ones that merit examination: behind these, institutional questions arise, "concerning the proper roles and powers of different state institutions in resolving the substantive questions". From this perspective, it must be stressed that the Federal character of the three countries concerned has influenced the evolution of the *status* of same-sex couples, both from the political point of view (in particular when member States show a more traditional approach to these issues) and moreover because of the legislative and administrative powers that fall within their powers, particularly in the field of social security and of family issues procedure (e.g. name, ceremony). Another, although less evident, institutional question concerns the division of powers between the Legislator and the courts, in particular constitutional courts (at least for Germany and Austria, whereas Switzerland lacks a proper system of constitutional judicial review on federal law).

Among the three countries examined in this contribution, Germany is given much more attention because of the scholarly and judicial attention given in recent years to the topic in question and, above all, since its system of registered

[1] Bamforth (2011), p. 551.

[2] A general overview about the problems raised by the constitutional family law in a comparative perspective is that of Marella and Marini 2012, p. 747. Specifically on the comparative legal treatment of same-sex relationships see Sáez (2011), p. 1.

partnership (adopted in 2001) has served as a model for the subsequent Swiss (2004) and Austrian (2010) legislation, that raised until now a narrow judicial litigation.

11.2 The *Status* of Same-Sex Couples in German Law

11.2.1 Constitutional Background

According to a widespread trend in comparative constitutionalism, the explicit granting of family rights in the Constitution is a relatively new phenomenon in German law.[3]

Whereas the Art. 119 of the Weimar Constitution (1919) enshrined a program of State protection for the family by considering it a relevant element in safeguarding the basic tenets of the society, the *Grundgesetz* of 1949 (Basic Law, BL) embodied in Art. 6 a set of directly enforceable guarantees, which aimed at protecting marriage (para. 1), the rights and duties of parents (paras 2 and 3), the role of the mother (para. 4), and the removal of every discrimination toward children born out of wedlock (para. 5).

The provision of Art. 6 BL most relevant to same-sex relationships is obviously that enshrined in its para. 1, according to which "Marriage and family shall enjoy the special protection of the State". According to the prevailing literature and the longstanding case-law of the Constitutional Federal Tribunal (further referred to as CFT), the constitutional notion of marriage is marked by three necessary elements: it requires State recognition, it must be basically not limited in time, and it requires the different sex of the partners.[4] The influence of Art. 6 BL on the establishment of a system of guarantees for same-sex couples is therefore deeply biased by the traditional arrangements of family law, which historically has been forged upon the model of heterosexual couples, because of their openness to children and to the consequent creation of a "family", which enjoys the rights embodied in the other paras of Art. 6.[5] Before dealing with the concrete *status* homosexual couples can have in German law, it bears mentioning the interpretive developments affecting Art. 6, in order to assess its contribution to the most recent evolution concerning homosexual marriage and registered partnership.

The CFT has stated from the early stage of its activity that Art. 6, para. 1, BL embodies a three-fold guarantee, since marriage and family cannot be reduced to a plain individual right, not only because marriage and family are institutions that the law inherits from social practices, but also because they are deeply shaped by these

[3] For the historical evolution see Ipsen (2009), p. 432.

[4] Gröschner (2004), Artikel 6, para. 39. The leading cases of the CFT in this field are BVerfGE 10, 59 (66), 49, 286 (300) and 62, 323 (330).

[5] Papier (2002), p. 2129.

practices and by individual (religious, cultural, ethical) beliefs.[6] Their protection and enforcement therefore imply a wider range of constitutional protection, which must take into account, at the same time, both the individual dimension of marriage and its social embeddedness. At an initial stage, the right to marriage is thus deemed to encompass a sphere of private autonomy which protects individuals from State intervention (*Abwehrrecht*): according to this function of right to marriage, Art. 6 ensures that both individuals that decided to marry and spouses should not be deprived of their freedom by the State—a freedom needed to reserve to individuals the basic decisions concerning whether, when, how and with whom to marry and to establish a family. In this light, the fundamental right empowers individuals to react against external, i.e. public, pressure on their free will, that they are called to exercise responsibly in order to freely shape their matrimonial and familiar choices.[7]

At a second stage, the right to marriage must be considered a guarantee of the institution of marriage (*Institutsgarantie*), in that it protects the "core" of the public regulation of marriage and family law against a reshaping which may threaten their basic tenets.[8] This peculiar mode of protection of fundamental rights related to deeply-rooted social institutions, which German legal doctrine inherited from the Weimar period and which reflects the enmeshment of constitutional provisions and basic choices made over time by the Legislator, is intended to protect individuals not only from State interventions, but also to ensure them and society a substantial continuity in the discipline of the legislative basic ordering (*Ordnungskern*) of marriage: individual rights are infringed whether the legal framework of marriage is abolished or, more plausibly, whenever a legislative choice imperils an element of this basic ordering, whereas in other cases Parliament is free to regulate marriage.[9] It bears stressing that the institutional guarantee had great relevance for the questions concerning same-sex couples, since it was deemed to set a limit against any effort to recognize the union between homosexuals—be it marriage or registered partnership—by reason of the heterosexual structure of marriage enshrined in the legislation.

At the third and final stage, the right to marriage is understood as an objective value (*objektive Wertentscheidung or Grundsatznorm*): in this sense, Art. 6, para. 1, establishes a duty for the Legislator to protect and support marriage and family, as well as a value system, which influences other areas of law (such as tax law or social law) in order to provide a favourable treatment for people that have decided to marry and to establish a family. According to this third way of conceiving the right to marriage, this is thus detached from its individual component and operates

[6] So BVerfGE 31, 58 (83).

[7] BVerfGE 6, 55 (71). For further references on this aspect see Sanders (2012), p. 917.

[8] BVerfGE 76, 1 (49).

[9] BVerfGE 31, 58 (69). For an insightful overview of the right to marry as a guarantee of institution see Pieroth and Kingreen (2002), p. 224.

as a general policy directive, which aims to favour the legislative conditions that encourage and sustain people entering wedlock.[10]

11.2.2 The Emergence of Same-Sex Relationships Issues and the Right to Marriage: The Different Cohabitation Regimes

Before dealing with the enjoyment by same-sex couples of the fundamental rights to live together, it is worth noting that homosexuals acts were generally criminalized in Germany until 1969, when the crime of sodomy (*Unzucht*) was narrowed in its application to male sexual relationships involving a partner under 21 years of age, with the aim of "protecting young men". In 1974 the age limit was even reduced to 18 and the crime was labelled as "sexual acts" (*sexuelle Handlungen*). Only in 1994 was any differential treatment between heterosexual and homosexual relationships abolished in the Criminal Code. It thus appears clear that all debate concerning the *status* of same-sex couples has been deeply influenced, at least until a certain period, by the widespread criminalization of homosexual practices.

11.2.2.1 Same-Sex Marriage

As noted above, the traditional interpretation of Art. 6 BL has described marriage as the relationship that necessarily involves, among other things, two persons of different sex. Notwithstanding this, several efforts have been made in order to broaden the scope and the field of application of the right to marriage to same-sex couples, although neither the Parliament nor the CFT have until now accepted, each one within its own agency, introducing same-sex marriage.

The main critical opinions against this resistance can be summarized in that a similar reading of Art. 6 BL ignores the potential stemming from the anti-discrimination clause enshrined in Art. 3, para. 3 BL, according to which "No person shall be favoured or disfavoured because of sex ...". Although the notion of "sex" calls into question the male/female dichotomy and not the sexual orientation as such (which is *per se* neutral *vis-à-vis* biological divide), it has been held that it is not sufficient to retain that Art. 6 is a special law applicable only to couples of mixed sex,[11] since the similarities between sex and sexual orientation should call upon the CFT to use very weighty reasons in denying same-sex couples access to marriage.[12]

---

[10] BVerfGE 87, 1 (35). For further insights see von Coelln (2011), Artikel 6, paras 34–51.

[11] As the CFT lastly did in its admissibility judgment of 4. October 1993 in NJW 1993, 3058, on the basis of its precedents: BVerfGE 10, 59 (66); 49, 286 (300); 53, 224 (245); 87, 234 (264).

[12] Sanders (2012), p. 931 and, even more expressly, Möller (2005), p. 65.

On the other side, beyond the wording of Art. 6 BL, the most relevant question concerning the introduction of same-sex marriage seems to rely upon the possibility of furthering an evolutive interpretation of the right to marriage. Although the CFT has not excluded the possibility of a future overruling—if and when the socially accepted notion of marriage evolves toward accepting same-sex matrimonial relationships[13] and, moreover, the impossibility of procreation is devaluated to an incidental element of marriage, in that the relative decision is safeguarded by the protection of intimacy both for heterosexual and for homosexual couples[14]—the prevailing literature (even that stemming from the progressive wing) has emphasized the unsuitability of an interpretation of Art. 6 BL aimed at bringing same-sex marriage within its field of application.[15]

The contribution arising from the constitutional debate on the legitimacy of same-sex marriage can be seen in the legal evaluation of the discrepancy between the shared meaning of the Art. 6 BL, traditionally referred to heterosexual couples, and social evolution, which has been progressively shown, in Germany, a growing acceptance toward other models of partnerships. In this light, while the majority of scholars recall originalist and essentialist arguments in order to exclude even for the future the constitutionality of same-sex marriage[16] and a minority fosters an over-interpretation of Art. 6 grounded on shared social practices in order to render it applicable to other forms of partnerships,[17] a more nuanced and convincing line of reasoning is that supporting a reading of Art. 6 BL according to which it does not protect same-sex marriage *per se*, but does not rule out that other forms of partnership could be introduced and permitted by the Constitution.[18]

Moreover, in Germany, the strict ban on same-sex marriage has seen a significant exception of relevance for the future chances of broadening the constitutional meaning of marriage. In 1978, the CFT[19] recognized that a post-operative transsexual is admitted to marriage with a person of the opposite gender, although the spouses share the same biological sex. Although this exception to the strictly biological heterosexual paradigm has been justified by the fact that transsexual couples do not call into question the classical social schemes, in that they accept playing the roles of wife and husband and, in so doing, they reinforce tradition, on the other hand this decision is noteworthy since it openly calls into question the potential to procreate as a constitutive aspect of marriage. In the same vein, in 2008 the CFT upheld Art. 8, para. 1, of the law regulating transsexualism (*Transsexuellengesetz*), in that it imposed divorce upon married couples consisting of a partner who, at a certain time, has decided to change his or her gender and become

---

[13] Sanders (2012), p. 931.

[14] Gröschner (2004), Artikel 6, para. 44.

[15] Pieroth and Kingreen (2002), p. 220.

[16] Among others see Burgi (2000), p. 487 and Robbers (2010), Artikel 6, para 45.

[17] See the authors cited *supra*, note 12, and also Ott (1998), p. 117.

[18] Pieroth and Kingreen (2002), p. 222.

[19] BVerfGE 49, 286.

transsexual.[20] The CFT explicitly recognizes that the aim of the challenged provision was to preserve the heterosexual structure of marriage[21] so that its unconstitutionality in the light of Art. 6, paras 1 and 2 BL can be considered another step toward the erosion of the conceptual hegemony of heterosexuality in marriage issues.

11.2.2.2 *De Facto* Homosexual Couples

If marriage can be considered the main road to the legal recognition of same-sex couples, their *de facto* union can be considered the lesser binding and relevant one, since they do not enter into a specified legal regime. Despite this, same-sex couples that are engaged in a factual relationship (as well as heterosexual couples) are not deprived of a minimum standard of rights.

Although their relationship is not entitled to enjoy rights and benefits accorded to married couples (because in their case a public recognition is lacking), it is still protected by Art. 2 BL, according to which:

> Every person shall have the right to free development of his personality insofar as he does not violate the rights of others or offend against the constitutional order or the moral law.

In the jurisprudence of the CFT as well as in the literature, it has been held that *de facto* couples should not be favoured over married couples, nor could they in any way be equated,[22] although the Legislator is not prescribed to refuse them every kind of legal recognition.[23] The problem is rather whether and to what extent same-sex couples are entitled to enjoy the same rights as heterosexual couples: the equivalence is hotly debated, since some scholars emphasize that even in *de facto* relationships the requisite of opposite sex should be respected—and in this light a difference is drawn between "non-matrimonial community of life" and "community of life similar to registered partnership"[24],—while for others there is no reason to distinguish between sexual orientations of *de facto* partners, since in the light of Art. 2 BL they are both deemed to exercise a "free development of personality".[25]

Apart from this debate and the underlying discrimination profiles, another resource for *de facto* same-sex couples are the so-called "partnership contracts" (*Partnerschaftsverträge*), which are agreements aimed at regulating mutual economic assistance. Even if partnership contracts are freely available to same-sex couples, it must be stressed that their sphere of regulation is closely bound by

---

20 BVerfGE 121, 175.

21 BVerfGE 121, 175 (193).

22 BVerfGE 9, 20 (35).

23 BVerfGE 82, 6 (15) and 87, 234 (267).

24 von Coelln (2011), Artikel 6, para. 48.

25 Schüffner (2007), p. 374.

economic matters, since every agreement aimed at intervening in personal or lifestyle aspects must be considered void according to Art. 134 and 138 of BGB (contrast with good morals).

11.2.2.3 Registered Partnerships (*Lebenspartnerschaft*)

In Germany, the most important legal instrument same-sex couples can refer to in order to recognize their union is registered partnership (*Lebenspartnerschaft*: literally "life-partnership"), introduced in 2001. The Act on registered partnerships (*Lebenspartnerschaftsgesetz*, further referred to as LPartG) was approved by a coalition of social-democrats and the Green Party despite huge resistance stemming both from the broad areas of the population more sensitive to opposition by the two leading religious groups (Catholics and evangelicals), and from the more conservative executives of the *Länder*. For this reason, the parliamentary majority decided to split the Act into two different regulations, since many articles needed to be approved by the *Bundesrat*, whose majority was represented by hostile *Länder* members. The first one, LPartG, was published on 16 February 2001 as a part of a broader legislative intervention aimed at ending all discrimination toward same-sex couples,[26] while the more controversial aspects (concerning tax law and public employment law) were delayed to a later time and were approved only in 2004,[27] after the CFT had ruled on the constitutionality of LPartG in 2002.[28]

The regulation model of LPartG reflects the constitutional constraints which led to its approval in 2001, under which the necessity was invoked to preserve a "principle of distance" (*Abstandsgebot*) with respect to marriage. Many scholars argued that the protection of marriage enshrined in Art. 6 BL implied that no other family regime, be it heterosexual or homosexual, could be afforded an equal, or even similar, protection and *status*. For this reason, the legislator in 2001 created a model of registered partnership which was centred upon the special nature of the subjects involved therein and upon a limited equivalence with marriage, in particular in the most debated fields of social benefits of registered partners and their relationships with children.

For the first aspect, LPartG reserves access to partnership exclusively to same-sex couples: if opposite sex partners were allowed to engage in a registered partnership, according to the leading opinion, this regime would concur with marriage and thus the "principle of distance" would be imperilled with the consequent violation of Art. 6 BL. Although this policy choice has been strongly criticized, since in so doing it ignores many other relationships that deserve protection without fitting into the "same-sex relationship" cluster, this special

[26] BGBl. I 2001, p. 266.

[27] Gesetz zur Überarbeitung des Lebenspartnerschaftsgesetzes of 15.12.2004 (BGBl. I p. 3396).

[28] See paragraph 11.2.3.1.

regime has remained unchallenged until now and represents, as we shall see in the next paragraph, one of the core reasons used by the CFT in order to justify the constitutionality of LPartG.

Despite this, upon deeper analysis LPartG shows evident similarities among the basic tenets of marriage and registered partnership. According to § 1, the relationship is assumed to be life-long and it cannot in any way be subject to particular conditions or terms. Moreover, according to § 2, partnership is considered as a community of life within which life-partners are compelled to mutual care and support as well as to common life-planning, and are involved in a shared responsibility. They can even choose a common family name (§ 3). All these elements, together with other relevant aspects, lead to the conclusion that the legal framework of registered partnership in Germany has derived from marriage those basic elements concerning mutual engagement and shared responsibility that are not a strict consequence of the heterosexual paradigm: in this vein, it has been correctly held that marriage and registered partnership are "separate but equal".[29]

For the aspects not strictly related to the structure and requisites of partnership, in particular in the social and childcare fields, the choices of 2001 were marked by an outstanding prudence and only in subsequent years, thanks to the joint action of the legislator and of the CFT, were some restrictions eliminated. As we shall see,[30] it has been up to the CFT (also under pressure from the EU Court of Justice) in recent years to erode some discrimination concerning the enjoyment of social benefits by same-sex couples, whose awarding was initially denied both for constitutional reasons and due to political resistance, since social rights often involve executive competences of the *Länder*.[31]

11.2.2.3.1 Constitutional Review of Registered Partnership and the Right to Marriage: The Overcoming of the Principle of Distance (*Abstandsgebot*)

After the stark criticism that accompanied the approval of LPartG on both formal and material grounds, the first decision by the CFT on its constitutionality marked a real turning point, whose reasons and effects deeply influenced the evolution of the issue in subsequent years. Called upon to decide on the claims raised by the governments of some *Länder* according to the procedure of "abstract control" (*abstrakte Normenkontrolle*), the CFT rejected the several grounds of unconstitutionality aimed at ascertaining the violation, among others, of Art. 6 BL, since the institute of *Lebenspartnerschaft* was deemed to threaten the constitutional protection of marriage, which deserves a "special" protection and is thus infringed whenever another family law regime is given the same (or almost equal) *status* and protection.

[29] Grünberger (2010), p. 208.

[30] See paragraph 11.2.3.2.

[31] Scherpe (2011), p. 156.

The heart of the decision lies in the solution given by the Karlsruhe Tribunal to the relationship between the legislative measure afforded by LPartG and the "special protection" granted to marriage. The problem is taken into account by separating the different dimensions of the constitutional right to marriage sketched above: as an individual freedom, as a guarantee of the institution as such, and as an objective value reference.

In the form of individual freedom to marry, Art. 6 BL is not infringed by the creation of registered partnership: every person able to marry is not limited in her or his intention by the entry into force of LPartG, since marriage is reserved for heterosexual couples just as registered partnership is reserved to homosexual ones.[32]

Even the guarantee of marriage as an institution is not violated by LPartG: although the concept of marriage has to be drawn mainly by the evolution of social structures, it still involves the basic elements that were highlighted above, under which the sexual difference of the spouses has a cornerstone relevance. This has led the CFT to rule that registered partnerships are excluded from the sphere of protection of Art. 6 BL, in that the Legislator has introduced them in order to safeguard the free expression of personality and the prohibition of discrimination toward homosexuals enshrined in Art. 2 and 3 of the Basic Law. The different sphere of application, which reflects the different personal elements that characterize the legal regimes at stake, means that the right to marriage in not endangered by the possible devaluation afforded by the introduction of registered partnerships.[33]

However, the most controversial question, one that had been hotly debated before the CFT's judgment, regarded the possible infringement of the right to marriage in the established terms of an objective value choice (*objektive Wertentscheidung*). Given that Art. 6 BL assigns to marriage a "special protection", this was meant to establish a "principle of distance" from other forms of cohabitation, i.e. a principle according to which both non-matrimonial heterosexual and same-sex relationships should be treated less favourably than marriage, whose structure and basic elements are deemed to be exclusively referred to it and should not be extended to other forms. This "principle of distance", drawn literally from the reference to the "special protection", also implied in its most extreme strains that marriage should be positively accorded a preference over other forms of relationship: in this wider acceptation, LPartG should have been even more evidently unconstitutional, since LPartG expressly draws from the legal framework of marriage some basic features, such as life-long engagement, mutual support, shared responsibility and so on.[34]

---

[32] This assertion is all the more true in that a performed partnership is not a limit per se on a person involved in it marrying a person of the opposite sex, even though in such cases the public officer celebrating the marriage is entitled to evaluate the actual will of the spouses to engage in a conjugal relationship: BVerfGE 105, 313 (342).

[33] BVerfGE 105, 313 (345–6).

[34] Among others Burgi (2000), p. 487.

In its 2002 judgment, the CFT rejected these extreme conceptions and stated that, from the constitutional mandate to promote and support marriage, no principle aimed at treating other forms of relationships like registered partnerships less favourably can be drawn: their recognition and promotion does not endanger its significance, which could be threatened only if these other forms concurred with marriage in that partners would enjoy the same rights but would be subject to fewer duties. However, this risk is not run in the case of registered partnerships, since this concurrence is excluded a priori by the different subjects these institutions refer to: "because of this difference, registered partnership is not a marriage under a false label, but a completely other thing" (*ein aliud zur Ehe*).[35] In other words, the constitutional right to marriage is not violated by LPartG because it can still fulfil its functions without any limitation on or prejudice to its basic tenets, while registered partnership—by reason of its functional and structural difference from marriage—does not conflict with Art. 6 BL, even though its introduction is not considered mandatory under the Constitution.[36]

The significance of this decision is undoubted, and has paved the way to the enlargement of guarantees and benefits accorded to registered partners, as shown by the approval in 2004 of the Act containing the provisions in the social field that had been excluded for political reasons in 2001. In this light, it is worth noting that the arguments used by the CFT provide a meaningful account of the constitutional framework that distinguishes registered partnerships from marriage.

The CFT has refused to measure the constitutionality of the 2001 provision moving from a comparison with marriage and, on the contrary, has highlighted the even symbolic difference between the two regimes: while marriage is deemed to operate as a constitutionally mandatory regime, which implies rights and duties whose balance is not generally at the political majorities' disposal, registered partnership operates as a "simple" family law regime,[37] whose significance should not be symbolically overestimated as a "second-choice marriage" and whose main features remain in the hands of the legislator, since it enjoys only the constitutional protection offered by Art. 2 and 3 BL.

One might say that, in so doing, the CFT has devalued the constitutional significance of same-sex relationships, particularly because it has left its introduction in the simple hands of the Legislator, although bound by the freedom to express their personality and the right to equality and non-discrimination. On the other hand, it is to be said that with its judgment, the CFT has weakened the criticisms against registered partnership as a "lesser marriage", which for opposite reasons could have imperilled the autonomy and persistence of LPartG. On the one hand, the drastic distinction drawn by the CFT erodes every effort to conceive of registered partnership as an institution aimed at threatening the centrality of

[35] BVerfGE 105, 313 (351).

[36] For a similar reading of Art. 6 BL see Pieroth and Kingreen (2002), p. 241 and Gröschner (2004), Artikel 6, para. 49.

[37] Robbers (2001), p. 782.

marriage. On the other hand, the pragmatic approach used by the CFT ends up rendering same-sex relationships something even symbolically different from marriage, in that they can deploy a proper symbology and a rhetoric that is not blatantly forged upon marriage and its heterosexual paradigm.[38]

11.2.2.3.2 The *Status* of Registered Partners in the Social Field

Since the constitutionality of the Act introducing registered partnership was affirmed in 2002, its legitimacy has remained unchallenged until now. Moreover, grounding its legislative action upon the outcomes of the 2002 judgment, since 2004 the Legislator has introduced a wider range of social provisions, aimed at progressively enacting the principle of equal treatment between marriage and registered partnerships. For example, several dispositions of the Code of Social law (*Sozialgeseztbuch*) have been modified by Art. 3 of the Act revising LPartG in order to grant benefits like compulsory social insurance (*gesetzliche Rentenversicherung*) or the widower's pension (*Hinterbliebenenversorgung*) not only to spouses, but to registered partners as well. In the same vein, Art. 4 of the same Act extended measures in the field of social assistance provided by Federal law (*Bundesversorgung*). The Federal legislation was however not completely free to regulate the social matter, since in the field of pensions and other state benefits many legislative powers fall within the competence of the German States, which have correspondingly not made uniform provisions in this area.[39]

Since 2004, federal and local interventions in the social field—each within its own realm—and judgments by the CFT have alternated, and, in so doing, a certain overlapping has been created, although it should be recognized that the regulative stream now flows steadily toward a progressive widening of social guarantees ensured to same-sex registered partners. This stream has moreover been corroborated by the constitutional reform concerning federalism of 2006, which clarified the separation of powers between the Federation and the States, often by strengthening the position of the former over the latter.

Within this framework, the CFT's decisions have helped steer the interpretation of constitutional guarantees concerning the matter at hand, and have influenced the enactment of local and federal provisions aimed at granting a wider spectrum of social benefits to same-sex partners.

The point of departure is represented by two decisions of 2007 and 2008, in which the CFT was called upon to decide whether the denial of a family allowance to registered partners violated Art. 3 BL and the principle of non-discrimination

[38] An example, among others, of this virtuous approach lies for example in the recognition that registered partners, unlike spouses, are not legally compelled to engage in a sexual relationship: BVerfGE 105, 313 (317). This fact should not necessarily be regarded as a deficiency with respect to marriage, but rather as a difference that qualifies same-sex relationships and makes them able to develop a proper constellation of values and symbols.

[39] For an overview see Hußmann (2010), p. 194.

enshrined therein. In both cases, the Karlsruhe Tribunal provided a traditional interpretation of the non-discrimination clause against same-sex couples, mainly referring the notion of "sex" to the differential treatment grounded on biological sex and not sexual orientation. Since this factor rests outside the realm of Art. 3 BL, registered partners are not infringed in their rights to enjoy such benefits granted to married couples. Moreover, the CFT stresses that the preference accorded to married couples is to be drawn from the duty to promote marriage over other forms of partnership as vested in Art. 6 BL (*Förderungspflicht*). This restrictive interpretation of the principle of non-discrimination appears to narrow the chances for a fuller enjoyment of social benefits by same-sex couples if one considers that in the 2008 judgment, the CFT was called upon to decide also on the basis of a preliminary ruling by the European Court of Justice (further referred to as ECJ),[40] which had stated in the same year that the denial of a widower's pension to a German registered partner infringed Directive 2000/78/EC, which prohibits discrimination grounded on sexual orientation.[41]

Even though it was devalued in 2008, the contribution of the ECJ's *Maruko* ruling played a key role in 2009 when the CFT had to deal with the refusal to recognize the widower's pension to a registered partner as had been provided for by the organizational norms of the main pension agency for public officers (*Versorgungsanstalt des Bundes und der Länder*—VBL). On this occasion, the CFT reversed its interpretive principles. On the one hand, it stated, in accordance with a trend emerging in European law,[42] that discrimination grounded on sexual orientation should be encompassed among those prohibited in Art. 3 BL, since it is at any rate centred upon a personal trait that should render the scrutiny of the judge much more strict and severe.[43] On the other hand, the equation in this field between married couples and registered partners is not prevented by the "special protection" afforded to marriage, which in this case was connected, according to the first-instance judges, with the objective of the widower's pension to support the family as a whole, i.e. the surviving spouse and the couple's children. The CFT upheld this established interpretation by ruling that the presence of children is not necessary in order to grant the benefit in question and therefore the discrimination is not justified, because the legislative aim to support couples engaged in a life-long relationship, in mutual support and in a shared responsibility should regard married as well as

[40] *Tadao Maruko v. Versorgungsanstalt der deutschen Bühnen*, C-267/06, judgment of 1st April 2008 [2008] ECR I-1757. The principles enshrined in *Maruko* are at the core of the following decision *Jürgen Römer v. Freie und Hansestadt Hamburg*, C-147/08, judgment of 10th May 2011, ECR I-3591.

[41] See the Chapter by Orzan in this volume.

[42] Michael (2010), p. 3539.

[43] BVerfGE 124, 199 (220). The same argument has recently been used by the CFT in order to reverse its previous case-law concerning family allowance, whose denial to registered partners is unconstitutional: see Second Senate Decision of 19 June 2012 (2BvR 1397/09).

same-sex registered couples.[44] In this light, the enjoyment of the widower's pension finds its *raison d'être* not in the furtherance of a given social role played by the heterosexual family (which is deemed per se open to procreation), but rather in a partnership which engages in a community of life, in which a basically common set of rights and duties is accepted. In such a framework, the partner's sexual orientation loses its discriminatory potential.[45]

11.2.2.3.3 The *Status* of Registered Partners and Children

The first version of LPartG in 2001 was very hesitant with regard to the rights of registered partners toward children, since the only provision in this field concerned "small parental custody", which implies the right of a member of the couple to take decisions concerning the everyday life of the other member's child and to intervene in case of emergency (§ 9, paras 1 and 2, LPartG). However, this provision does not create a family bond, with the consequence that between the child and the other registered partner, no legal parenthood is established. This lack of recognition has been considered a disadvantage for the child, because, should the only legal parent die, the other partner would not be entitled to take care of him or her or to let him or her benefit from the parental *status* (e.g. for succession, maintenance, or social benefits). For these reasons, the Act revising LPartG introduced the step-child adoption (§ 9, para. 7, LPartG), according to which a life partner may solely adopt a child of his or her partner.[46]

The issue of constitutionality raised against this provision was declared inadmissible by the CFT in 2009 on formal grounds.[47] A recent decision adopted by the CFT has on the contrary declared this provision partially unconstitutional, in that it forbids the adoption by a life partner of the child previously adopted by the other (successive adoption).[48] It bears emphasizing that the grounds of unconstitutionality on this occasion have been found in the discrimination suffered by the child adopted by a single involved in a life partnership as compared with the child adopted by a single before marriage, who can be freely adopted by the other spouse after the establishment of the marriage bond. Notwithstanding this, the CFT has not seen in the prohibition of successive adoption made by § 9, para. 7, LPartG for life partners a violation of Art. 6 LF, since a similar right is considered to rest outside the core-content of the right to family, and therefore it is deemed to fall within Legislator's discretion.

---

[44] BVerfGE 124, 199 (226). In the same vein, the CFT has declared unconstitutional on 7 May 2013 the impossibility for registered couples to benefit of the regime of separate taxation (income splitting) which was available only to married couples (so called *Ehegattensplitting*, 2 BVR 909/06).

[45] Classen (2010), p. 411.

[46] Critical insights toward an enlargement of partners' adoption rights in Gärditz (2011), p. 932.

[47] Decision of 10.8.2009, 1BvL 15/09.

[48] Decision of 19.2.2013, 1 BvL 1/11, 1 BvR 3247/09.

11.3 The *Status* of Same-Sex Couples in Austrian Law

11.3.1 Constitutional Background and the Introduction of Registered Partnerships in 2010

The acceptance of same-sex couples in Austrian law has taken more time and met more resistance than in Germany or even in Switzerland.

The main feature concerning Austria lies in the influence that the European Convention on Human Rights, thanks to its constitutional ranking, has deployed in internal law in these matters. The hostility toward a legal recognition of same-sex couples, which also stems from the narrow space for equalization left open by constitutional rights concerning anti-discrimination and in the absence of a constitutional clause granting the right to marriage and family life,[49] has only in recent years been broadly dismantled due to the interventions of the Strasbourg Court, which has held on two occasions that Austrian same-sex couples are entitled to enjoy a legal *status* assuring them a set of rights and guarantees that takes account of their enduring relationship.[50]

In *Karner v. Austria*,[51] the European Court of Human Rights (further referred to as ECtHR) was called upon to decide whether the inability of a homosexual to succeed in the rent contract of his *de facto* same-sex partner with whom he cohabited was in violation of Art. 8 (Right to respect for private and family life) and 14 (Prohibition of discrimination) of the European Convention on Human Rights (further referred to as ECHR). On that occasion, the necessity to protect the family in the traditional sense was deemed too abstract a goal for justifying a denial that impinges directly upon the sexual orientation of the applicant without any reasonable justification.

Seven years later, in *Schalk and Kopf v. Austria*,[52] Strasbourg judges had to decide whether the impossibility for same-sex couples to access marriage established by Art. 44 of the Austrian Civil Code, which explicitly reserves marriage to "persons of opposite sex", conflicted with Art. 8, 14 and 12 (Right to marry) of the ECHR. In this case, the ECtHR stated that the ban on same-sex marriage did not conflict with the Convention's rights, mainly because marriage issues, given their deep rootedness in society's basic value choices, fall within the state's margin of appreciation and, secondly, because Austria had in the meantime enacted a federal act introducing registered partnership. Although this provision should not be considered fully satisfactory for the applicant's claims, the spaces for

[49] The Austrian Constitutional Court has held in two occasions, with a sharply brief motivation, that same-sex marriage is unconstitutional: in Case B 777/03, 12th December 2003 and in Case B 1512/03, 14th October 2004.

[50] On the ECtHR jurisprudence see the Chapters by Crisafulli and Pustorino in this volume.

[51] N. 40016/98, judgment of 24th July 2003.

[52] N. 30141/04, judgment of 24th June 2010.

legal recognition it opens reduce, to a certain degree, the harm and distress suffered by same-sex couples living in an entirely *de facto* relationship.

The Registered Partnership Act,[53] which now provides a complete regulation of the *status* of same-sex registered couples, entered into force on 1st January 2010. According to its § 2,

> A registered partnership may be formed only by two persons of the same sex (registered partners). They thereby commit themselves to a lasting relationship with mutual rights and obligations.

The rules on the establishment of registered partnership, its effects and its dissolution, resemble the rules governing marriage: like married couples, registered partners are expected to live together as spouses in every respect, to share a common home, to treat each other with respect and to provide mutual assistance (§ 8(2) and (3)). As in the case of spouses, the partner who is in charge of the common household and has no income has legal authority to represent the other partner in everyday legal transactions (§ 10). Registered partners have the same obligations regarding maintenance as spouses (§ 12). The Registered Partnership Act also contains a comprehensive range of amendments to existing legislation in order to provide registered partners with the same *status* as spouses in various other fields of law, such as inheritance law, labour, social and social insurance law, fiscal law, the law on administrative procedure, the law on data protection and public service, passport and registration issues, as well as the law on foreigners.[54]

The recent entry into force of the EPG has yet to raise significant judicial litigation, both at the constitutional and ordinary levels. A noteworthy exception concerns a decision of 22nd September 2011 by the Constitutional court,[55] ruling on the constitutionality of reserving registered partnership only to same-sex couples and not to heterosexual couples. The applicants claimed infringement of Art. 8 and 14 of the ECHR as well as of the constitutional clauses on equality (Art. 2 of the Fundamental law on citizen's rights and Art. 7 of the Federal Constitutional Law). The Constitutional court dismissed the application with reference to both parameters, since neither from the ECHR nor from the Constitution should a principle of equal treatment between same-sex (registered) couples and heterosexual (married or non-married) couples be drawn: marriage and registered partnership are placed on a different—although in certain aspects equated—scale, and the legitimacy of the EPG rests upon the different subjects that can be involved therein. Access by heterosexual couples to registered partnership, as well as by same-sex couples to marriage, imperils this separation of areas and, in so doing, threatens the preference accorded to marriage as the cornerstone of family law. Moreover, in a recent decision,[56] the Constitutional court decided to declare unconstitutional those

[53] Federal Law Gazette (Bundesgesetzblatt) vol. I, no. 135/2009 (further referred to as EPG).

[54] Further elements in Aichberger-Beig (2010), p. 68.

[55] Case B 1405/10-11.

[56] Case B 125/11-11, 12.12.2012.

provisions of the EPG that discriminated registered partners with respect to spouses as to the place of the ceremony (since partnership ceremony was performed according to the EPG before the District Administrative Authority whereas marriage is concluded before the Office of personal *status*).

11.3.2 The Enjoyment of Social Rights by Registered Partners

Despite the even symbolic distance that in some aspects pervades marriage and registered partnerships (e.g., spouses share a "family name" whereas partners have a "last name") and the significant exclusion of parental rights for same-sex couples (as we will see in the next paragraph), vast fields of ordinary legislation have been modified by the EPG in order to equate partners' and spouses' rights, with particular respect to social benefits. A significant example of such an equivalence concerns the widower's pension, which has been extended to registered partners under the same terms prescribed for spouses.[57]

11.3.3 The Enjoyment of Parental Rights by Registered Partners

However, the most significant restriction on registered partners' rights concerns parental rights, as they are not allowed to adopt, nor is a partner allowed to adopt the other registered partner's child (step-child adoption) pursuant to § 8(4) of the EPG. Only in 2013 the prohibition of step-child adoption has been declared contrary to Art. 8 and 14 by the European Court of Human Rights, since it infringes the rights of registered partners not to be discriminated in comparison with unmarried different-sex couples, in which one partner is entitled to adopt the other partner's child, whereas a similar discrimination is not found by the Court with regard to married couples.[58] Despite of this recent decision, the restrictive vein of the Austrian legislation is however plain to see in § 2(1) of the Federal law on medically assisted reproduction,[59] that indirectly prohibits access to artificial procreation by same-sex partners, be they registered or not, because such a right is attributed exclusively to "married couples or marriage-like relationships".

---

[57] See §§ 216 and 259 of the General Law on Social Security (Allgemeines Sozialversicherungsgesetz, in BGBl. I Nr. 116/2009).

[58] Grand Chamber, *X and others v. Austria*, n. 19010/07, judgment of 19th February 2013. For further insights see the Chapters by Crisafulli and Pustorino in this volume.

[59] Fortpflanzungsmedizingesetz (BGBL. I 1992, 1299).

11.4 The *Status* of Same-Sex Couples in Swiss Law

11.4.1 Constitutional Background and the Introduction of Registered Partnership in 2007

The constitutional background concerning the rights of same-sex partners in Switzerland shares many features with Germany and Austria. Even in this case, a constitutional tradition which is basically hostile to full recognition of the same-sex relationship in the form of marriage has been able to establish a legal framework aimed at regulating registered partnerships. This outcome was made possible after the entry into force in 1999 of the new Federal Constitution, which contains some basic rights whose introduction has paved the way to the recognition of same-sex relationships. In this light, it must be emphasized that Art. 14 of the Constitution states that "The right to marry and to found a family is guaranteed" without linking the access to marriage to a necessary heterosexual relationship, and that Art. 8 (2) Const., containing a general principle of equality which prohibits—among others—discrimination grounded on "sex" and "way of life", is deemed to enshrine a general clause prohibiting discrimination grounded upon sexual orientation.[60]

Despite this, according to the long-standing case law of the Federal Tribunal (*Bundesgericht*), same-sex marriage is not protected by the Constitution since it infringes the basic tenets of public order and its legitimacy cannot be drawn by an evolutive interpretation of Art. 8 and 12 ECHR,[61] because the Strasbourg Court has held, as we already know, that the right to allow same-sex couples to marry falls within the state's margin of appreciation and its denial is not a violation of conventional rights. Nevertheless, the wording of Art. 14 is significant in that it should not hinder the Legislator from introducing same-sex marriage without modifying the text of the Constitution: this perspective is, however, unlikely for the moment,[62] although a significant exception to the heterosexual paradigm concerns, as in Germany, post-operative transsexuals, who can marry a person of their same (biological) sex.

In this framework, in 2004 the Swiss Parliament adopted the "Federal Act concerning same-sex registered partnerships",[63] which was approved by a 58 % majority of Swiss voters in a *referendum* held on 5th June 2005, entering into force on 1st January 2007. In its quality as Federal law, PartG has a derogatory force toward Cantonal law, with the effect that it has quashed several Cantonal regulations that already provided a basic structure for registered partnership, which in

---

[60] Ziegler and Bueno (2012), p. 41.

[61] ATF 119 II 264 and ATF 126 II 425.

[62] Peters (2011), p. 310.

[63] Bundesgesetz über die eingetragene Partnerschaft gleichgeschlechtlicher Paare—Loi fédérale sur le partenariat enregistré entre personnes du même sexe (RS 211.231, further referred to as PartG).

several cases had a wider sphere of application, e.g. as in Zürich, where partnership had been introduced before 2005 with the possibility to establish homosexual as well as heterosexual registered partnerships.

The Swiss model of registered partnership has much in common with the German and the Austrian models: partnership is reserved exclusively to same-sex couples and establishes a community of life with mutual rights and duties (Art. 2, paras 1 and 2), and partners must give reciprocal assistance and take mutual care (Art. 12), also by contributing, with their own resources and capacities, to the community's maintenance (Art. 13).

On the basis of requisites of this kind, registered partnerships are deemed to establish a long-standing relationship and, in so doing, they are open to those benefits and privileges that are granted to married couples, such as those in the areas of succession, taxes, hospital visitation, and property rights.[64] In this way, a strengthened approach to the anti-discrimination principle is seen at work, since equalization with marriage in mainly economic fields is considered a consequence of the similarly strong and persistent mutual commitment by partners.

Notwithstanding this, in other fields a full equalization has been considered in contrast with a persisting preference accorded to marriage, such as in the field of citizenship, for whose achievement registered partners do not enjoy the preferred position accorded to spouses but are, on the contrary, bound to the limits valid for everyone. Along with other minor differences of treatment in the field of work benefits,[65] the other main area in which registered partners are not equated with spouses, with even more severe restrictions than in Germany, concerns parental rights.[66]

To sum up, the quest for equalization of rights between married couples and registered partners stems from the different interpretations of the above-mentioned principle of equality: whether it is limited to the centrality accorded to marriage pursuant Art. 14 Const. or whether it should discern more strictly the differences in treatment that are justified because of the involvement of children: in all other cases, a full equalization should be targeted by both the legislator and judges.[67]

11.4.2 The Enjoyment of Social Rights by Same-Sex Couples

The 2004 PartG has not provided detailed regulation in the social field, also because many competences pertaining to social benefits fall within the power of Cantons, which have adopted a multifarious, although progressively inclusive, legislation concerning registered partnership. In the absence of systematic intervention by

[64] Peters (2011), p. 313.

[65] Examples in Ziegler and Bueno (2012), p. 44.

[66] See paragraph 11.4.3.

[67] Further insights in Ziegler and Bueno (2012), p. 43.

Parliament and judges, it is worth noting that one of the most relevant benefits accorded to spouses, i.e. the widower's pension, is granted to registered partners with no discrimination, and to non-registered partners, whether homosexual or heterosexual, if the surviving partner has significantly contributed to the widower's maintenance or has lived with him or her for 5 years.[68]

11.4.3 The Enjoyment of Parental Rights by Registered Partners

The more severe limitation of registered partners' rights concerns their relationship with children. Art. 27 PartG prescribes the duty for the partner to contribute appropriately to the other partner's child maintenance, albeit with due respect for the rights of natural parents. The partner is entitled, in case of separation, to be granted the right to visit the child. It should be evident that, in this way, partners are not equipped with an instrument similar to the *kleines Sorgerecht* existing in German law, and their contribution to the child's upbringing is strictly limited to contribution duties.

Even more clearly, Art. 28 PartG stated that:

> Persons living in a registered partnership are admitted neither to adoption nor to medically assisted reproduction.

In relation to the latter, PartG only reaffirmed the limits already established in the Federal law on medically assisted reproduction (Art. 3, para. 3)[69] according to which only married couples are entitled to access these techniques, for the sake of protecting the child's best interest.

In the field of adoption, the denial enshrined in Art. 28 PartG for registered partners is much more debated, since pursuant to Art. 264b of the Swiss Civil code single persons are entitled to adopt. This raises a discrimination which has not been challenged for the moment,[70] even if a decision recently taken by the European Court of Human Rights in the case *E.B. v. France*[71] may have an effect on internal law. On that occasion, the Strasbourg Court declared the violation of the

[68] Art. 19a and 20a, para. 1, a) of Bundesgesetz über die berufliche Alters-, Hinterlassenen- und Invalidenvorsorge—Loi fédérale sur la prévoyance professionnelle vieillesse, survivants et invalidité (RS 831.40). On the interpretation of the latter provision see the Bundesgericht decision of 3.2.2012, 9C_676/2011.

[69] Bundesgesetz über die medizinische unterstützte Fortpflanzung—Loi fédérale sur la procréation médicalement assistée (of 18.12.1998—RS 810.11).

[70] An interlocutory decision is that of Bundesgericht of 5.5.2011 (ATF 137 III 241), in which the Supreme Tribunal refused to deal with the legitimacy of Art. 28 in a case concerning step-child adoption, since the registered couple did not have the requisites demanded by the Civil Code for married couples.

[71] Grand Chamber, n. 43546/02, judgment of 22nd January 2008.

Convention in that French law admits single persons to adopt with the exception of homosexuals. Even if the ECtHR recently had a more severe approach in the case *Gas and Dubois v. France*[72] (concerning adoption by a registered partner of a child born after artificial procreation with an anonymous donor), it bears mentioning that in March 2012 the Council of States (the branch of Parliament representing Cantons) asked the Federal Council (the federal Executive organ) to modify Art. 28 PartG and the norms of the Civil code prohibiting adoption even to heterosexual unmarried couples, with the aim of allowing step-child adoption, when necessary for the child's best interest.

11.5 Conclusions: The "Central European" Model of Same-Sex Partnership at the Crossroads Between Symbols and Reality

The common refusal of same-sex marriage and the introduction of an exclusively homosexually framed model of registered partnership is the main common aspect that emerges from the analysis. Behind the solution given by Legislators, the common approach that arises in the three countries examined mainly concerns the constitutional justification of registered partnerships with respect to rights and principles traditionally centred upon the preference accorded to marriage and (heterosexual) family (at least in Germany and Switzerland) and the discriminatory potential of "sex" intended as biological sex (i.e. running through the male/female divide) and not as "sexual orientation" (i.e. running through the homosexual/heterosexual divide). In this regard, the common approach of German, Austrian and Swiss legislations on registered partnership moves from the assumption of a radical symbolic difference between it and marriage, whose justification rests on different principles (family rights for the latter and personality rights for the former, community versus privacy[73]). In this way, same-sex partnerships are conceptually built outside the symbolic realm of family.

Despite this, the concrete aspects concerning the legal relationship between partners, moving from their mutual rights and duties, the requisites for admittance to partnership, and the limits to its dissolution and the economical consequences thereof, show in the three jurisdictions concerned strong similarities with marriage. In the same vein, the public side of the regulation of same-sex couples (first of all in the field of social security) has progressively moved toward a full equalization of

[72] N. 25951/07, judgment of 15th March 2012. On these cases see the Chapter by Crisafulli in this volume.

[73] The difference between communitarian and privacy models of family law has been recently re-elaborated by Marella and Marini (2012), pp. 485 and 489.

the benefits granted to partners with respect to spouses, and the still persisting discrepancies are often connected to the presence of children and to the capacity of spouses to procreate.

The only legal area in which this difference is at the moment more debated is that of parental rights in their different sub-aspects: right to custody, adoption (either in the form of step-child adoption or of successive adoption, whose legitimacy is currently before the German CFT), and access to medically assisted reproduction. The *status* of same-sex couples' parental rights lies at the crossroads of the divergent interests that have until now characterised the model sketched out in these pages: on the one hand since their enlargement risks threatening the symbolic centrality of marriage and the effort to relegate registered partnership to the totally different domain of the free expression of the partners' personality, and on the other hand because the substantial equivalence attained in the different legislations implies almost logically a wider access to parental rights. For this reason, the initial (and still persisting) resistances of the Austrian and Swiss legislation and the recent openness of the German legal system may reveal a significant path of evolution.

References

Aichberger-Beig D (2010) Registered partnership for same-sex couples. In: Verschraegen B (ed) Austrian law – an international perspective. Jan Sramek, Wien, pp 63–77

Bamforth N (2011) Legal protection of same-sex partnerships and comparative constitutional law. In: Ginsburg T, Dixon R (eds) Comparative constitutional law. Edward Elgar, Cheltenham/ Northampton, pp 551–567

Burgi M (2000) Schützt das Grundgesetz die Ehe vor der Konkurrenz anderer Lebensgemeinschaften? Der Staat 39:487–508

Classen CD (2010) Der besondere Schutz der Ehe – aufgehoben durch das BVerfG? JuristenZeitung 65:411–412

Gärditz KF (2011) Gemeinsames Adoptionsrecht Eingetragener Lebenspartner als Verfassungsgebot? JuristenZeitung 66:930–939

Gröschner R (2004) Artikel 6. In: Dreier H (Hrsg) Grundgesetz Kommentar, 2. Aufl., Band I. Mohr Siebeck, Tübingen, pp 751–825

Grünberger M (2010) Die Gleichbehandlung von Ehe und eingetragener Lebenspartnerschaft im Zusammenspiel von Unionsrecht und nationalem Verfassungsrecht. Familie Partnerschaft Recht 5:203–207

Hußmann W (2010) Die Behandlung von Lebenspartnern im Sozialrecht. Familie Partnerschaft Recht 5:194–196

Ipsen J (2009) Ehe und Familie. In: Isensee J, Kirchhof P (eds) Handbuch des Staatsrechts, 3. Aufl., Band VII. C.F. Müller, Heidelberg, pp 431–476

Marella MR, Marini G (2012) Famille. In: Troper M (dir) Traité international de droit constitutionnel, Tome 3. Dalloz, Paris, pp 472–519

Michael L (2010) Lebenspartnerschaften unter dem besonderen Schutze einer (über-) staatlichen Ordnung. Neue Juristische Wochenschrift 63:3537–3542

Möller K (2005) Der Ehebegriff des Grundgesetzes und die gleichgeschlechtliche Ehe. Die öffentliche Verwaltung 58:64–71

Ott S (1998) Die Begriffe "Ehe und Familie" in Art. 6 I GG. Neue Juristische Wochenschrift 51:117–119

Papier HJ (2002) Ehe und Familie in der neueren Rechtsprechung des BVerfG. Neue Juristische Wochenschrift 55:2129–2133

Peters A (2011) National report Switzerland. Am Univ J Gend Soc Policy Law 19:309–314

Pieroth B, Kingreen T (2002) Funktionen des Ehegrundrechts am Beispiel des Lebenspartnerschaftsgesetzes. KritV 85:219–241

Robbers G (2001) Eingetragene Lebenspartnerschaften. Verfassungsrechtliche Überlegungen. JuristenZeitung 56:779–786

Robbers G (2010) Artikel 6. In: von Mangoldt H, Klein F (eds) Kommentar zum Grundgesetz, 6th edn. Vahlen, München, pp 683–755

Sáez M (2011) Same-sex marriage, same-sex cohabitation and same-sex families around the world: why "same" is so different. Am Univ J Gend Soc Policy Law 19:1–52

Sanders A (2012) Marriage, same-sex partnership, and the German constitution. German Law J 13:911–940

Scherpe J (2011) National report Germany. Am Univ J Gend Soc Policy Law 19:151–186

Schüffner M (2007) Eheschutz und Lebenspartnerschaft. Eine verfassungsrechtliche Untersuchung des Lebenspartnerschaftsrechts im Lichte des Art. 6 GG. Duncker & Humblot, Berlin

von Coelln C (2011) Artikel 6. In: Starck C (Hrsg) Grundgesetz Kommentar, 6. Aufl., Band I. Beck, München, pp 352–394

Ziegler AR, Bueno N (2012) La protection constitutionnelles des gays et lesbiennes. In: Ziegler AR et al. (eds) Droit des gays et lesbiennes en Suisse/Rechte der Lesben und Schwulen in der Schweiz (Partenariat enregistré, communauté de vie de fait, questions juridiques concernant l'orientation sexuelle et l'identité de genre des personnes LGBT), 2e édn. Staempfli, Berne

Chapter 12
Judicial Restraint and Political Responsibility: A Review of the Jurisprudence of the Italian, Spanish and Portuguese High Courts on Same-Sex Couples

Tiago Fidalgo de Freitas and Diletta Tega

Abstract The chapter states that on a topic like that of same-sex couples, that stirs and divides public opinion and about which there is no consensus among political actors, courts refuse to act as *avant-garde* actors. In the jurisdictions under analysis—Italy, Spain and Portugal—the judiciary chose to give precedence to the Legislator, stating it was the province of the latter to regulate the issue. The main argument put forward was that the Constitutions at stake do not mandate same-sex marriage and therefore there is no constitutional right to perform it. Simultaneously, nonetheless, they also acknowledged, to a certain extent, that the Legislator is free to choose which type of legal protection to afford to same-sex couples, from civil partnerships to same-sex marriage (except for the Italian Constitutional Court, which seems to have implied that same-sex marriage could only be allowed after a constitutional amendment). While doing so, a substantial part of the majority reasonings are packed with references to comparative law and to the Strasbourg's jurisprudence as a way to seek external legitimation.

The first author drafted Sects. 12.1, 12.3, and 12.4, whereas the second author drafted Sect. 12.2. The first author would like to thank Spyridon Drosos and Rita de Brito Gião for their invaluable comments; the usual disclaimer applies, though.

T.F. de Freitas (✉)
Law Department, European University Institute, Florence, Italy

Faculty of Law, University of Lisbon, Lisbon, Portugal
e-mail: tiago.freitas@eui.eu

D. Tega
Department of National and International Juridical Science, University of Milano Bicocca, Milan, Italy
e-mail: diletta.tega@unimib.it

D. Gallo et al. (eds.), *Same-Sex Couples before National, Supranational and International Jurisdictions*, DOI 10.1007/978-3-642-35434-2_12,

12.1 Introduction

Italy, Spain and Portugal share important ties at several levels; they are rather close in cultural terms and they all have, to a greater or lesser extent, transformative post-World War II Constitutions which are grounded in the tradition of enhanced fundamental rights and the principles of human dignity and equality. Although the Catholic religion is deeply embedded in the social fabric and the nation's consciousness, the principle of separation of Church and State is in force in the three legal orders.

All three jurisdictions have one very central aspect in common: Constitutional Courts have refused to be the agents of change and to invalidate Civil Code norms which only give the right to marry to opposite-sex couples. That was considered to be the province of the Legislator. Indeed, at different points in time, the three Constitutional Courts reached the conclusion that their Constitutions do not mandate same-sex marriage and therefore there is no constitutional right to perform it. At the same time, however, they also acknowledged that the Legislator can recognise same-sex civil partnerships and marriage. The difference is that whereas the Spanish and Portuguese Constitutional Courts have stated that there is a duty to protect same-sex couples, but the legislator is free to choose which type of legal protection to afford them, the Italian Constitutional Court, while stating the need (or even duty) of introducing a discipline for same sex partnership, seems to have implied that same-sex marriage could only be allowed after a constitutional amendment.[1] Another shared feature of the rulings of the three Constitutional Courts is that they extensively (and unusually) resort to international, supranational and foreign law elements. This happens both when the Courts agree with those jurisdictions and change the national legal order, thereby seeking external validation, and when the majorities choose to differ, thus providing reasons for the discrepancy in the solutions reached.

As for the differences that set these three legal systems apart, the one that stands out is that whereas the Spanish and later the Portuguese Legislators chose to approve same-sex marriage and civil partnerships, the same did not happen with the Italian one, which still does not even recognise same-sex (or, for that matter, different-sex) civil partnerships.

This paper expounds the way Italian, Spanish and Portuguese Courts—especially those entrusted with constitutional jurisdiction—have addressed the legal status of same-sex couples,[2] especially focusing on the issue of same-sex marriage.

---

[1] Part of the scholars noted that this was a groundless judgment (decisione di infondatezza) and that the considerations on the fact that the Italian Constitution enables or excludes same-sex marriage were not required and, above all, that are contained in an *obiter dicta*, as such not binding.

[2] For an overview, see González Beilfuss (2012), pp. 41–53.

12.2 Italy

12.2.1 Introductory Remarks

The Italian Parliament has recognised neither same-sex marriage nor same-sex[3] civil partnerships (or different-sex ones, in fact). Nevertheless, with regard to opposite-sex couples, both the legislative and judicial sides tend to equate *more uxorio* partners with spouses.

The Italian legal system does not entitle unmarried individuals, regardless of their sexual orientation, to adopt. Only heterosexual couples married for at least 3 years can adopt.[4] Quite recently, the Court of Cassation[5] declared that the idea that the custodial parent's homosexual orientation would be dangerous for the minor's well-balanced growth was a mere prejudice and therefore inadmissible. The sexual orientation of the custodial parent is irrelevant in evaluating parental aptitude in that case, whereas the harmfulness of the family setting has to be proved.[6]

The Italian Constitution declares under Art. 29 that the Republic recognises the rights of the family as a natural society founded on marriage, without explicitly stating that spouses have to belong to different sexes. The framers unquestionably used the terms "spouses" referring to a man and a woman.[7] This provision places

---

[3] Part of the Italian scholars believe that same-sex marriage should not be considered a 'new right', but rather the removal of a discrimination banned by the Constitution; see Pugiotto (2010). Others, on the contrary, consider same sex marriage as a 'new right'; see Romboli (2012).

[4] See Art. 6 of Law No. 149/2001.

[5] Decision of the Italian Court of Cassation No. 601, of 11th January 2013.

[6] Similarly, see Decision of the Italian Court of Cassation No. 16593, of 18th June 2008; and Decision of the Court of Naples of 28th June 2006, confirmed by the Decision of the Court of Appeal No. 1067, of 11th April 2007.

[7] The Italian Constitutional Court stated in Decision No. 138 of 2010 (para. 9) that the concepts of 'family' and 'marriage' cannot be considered to have been "crystallised" with reference to the time when the Constitution entered into force, because they are endowed with the flexibility that is inherent to constitutional principles; they are therefore to be interpreted taking into account not only the transformations within the legal system, but also the evolution of society and customs. However, such an interpretation cannot go so far as to impinge upon the core of the provision, modifying it in such a way as to embrace situations and problems that were not considered at all when it was enacted. In fact, as is clear from the *travaux préparatoires*, the question of same-sex unions remained entirely unaddressed within the debate conducted within the Assembly, even though homosexuality was by no means unknown. When drafting Art. 29 of the Constitution, the delegates discussed an institution with a specific configuration and which was regulated in detail under civil law. Therefore, absent any different references, the inevitable conclusion is that they took account of the concept of marriage defined under the Civil Code which entered into force in 1942 and which, as noted above, specified (and still specifies) that married couples must be comprised of persons of different sex. The second paragraph of the same Article also makes provision to this effect, in asserting the moral equality of the married couple, focused in particular on the woman's position. See Biondi (2013).

marriage at the core of 'family', defined as a "natural association".[8] This expression was used to stress that the contemplated concept of 'family' had original rights which pre-existed the State, and which the latter was obliged to recognise, as may be inferred from the Constituent Assembly's *travaux préparatoires*. The majority of constitutional scholarship holds that a constitutional amendment of Art. 29 would be required for the Parliament to adopt legislation recognising same-sex marriage.[9] The meaning of the constitutional rule could not be set aside through mere interpretation, because doing so would not involve a simple rereading of the system or the abandonment of a mere interpretative practice, but rather the implementation of a 'creative' interpretation. This is the reason why the bills brought before Parliament during recent legislatures concerned exclusively the recognition of both same-sex and different-sex civil partnerships—and at any rate, they did not pass.

On 8th February 2007, the Italian Government brought before the Parliament a draft bill on the rights and duties of people who cohabit permanently (*Diritti e doveri delle persone stabilmente conviventi*, hereinafter DICO). The draft bill, which eventually was not approved, made no mention of the sexual orientation of the "two adults who, joined by mutual emotional ties, cohabitate permanently, helping each other morally and materially" who would be entitled to the recognition of the DICO. Couples should register at the municipalities' registry offices, and rights and duties would follow factual cohabitation. The content of the bill was particularly cautious: no manifestation of will before public officials was required; the accompanying explanatory report stressed that there was no intention of establishing a new legal institution or administrative instrument harmful to family rights or able to create a sort of para-marriage; there was no mention of property rights. To the contrary, the bill recognised the right to give assistance to the other person in case of illness, the right to take decisions concerning healthcare assistance or in case of death; the reduction of taxation on testate succession; regions had to take account of this kind of cohabitation in assigning council house buildings; 3-year cohabitation entitled partners to employment facilities and to succession in leasing agreements in the event of death or end of cohabitation; a 9-year cohabitation entitled partners to intestate succession. The main duty consisted of providing alimony to the cohabitant in need after a 3-year cohabitation (see in particular Art. 4, 5, 7–9, 11). The majority of scholars, despite having underlined the draft bill's ambiguities and contradictions, agreed on its compatibility with the Constitution and criticised the opposition expressed by the permanent Episcopal Council

[8] As the Italian Constitutional Court affirmed in Decision No. 138 of 2010, which has given rise to a lively debate within the academic literature that is still on-going.

[9] In the opposite direction, see, among others, Bin (2000), p. 1067 and Veronesi (2008), p. 584, who consider the expression 'family as a natural society' as the emotional and mutually supportive union of two persons, perceived as a need for the personal fulfilment of its members. The adjective 'natural' is intended by these authors in a way that emphasises the partners' natural inclinations.

in a note of 28th March 2007 on the family based on marriage. To the contrary, the catholic-inspired doctrine pointed out, correctly, that the implicit goal of the DICO would have been recognising same-sex partnerships with no assumption of the underlying political responsibility.[10]

Faced with the failure of legislative recognition of same-sex partnerships, almost thirty town councils decided to create 'civil partnerships registers'. The aim of these registers is to allow opposite-sex and same-sex couples to publicly express their *status*. Registers of this kind have no legal value because they are not to be confused with those established by General Registry Offices. The administrative judges have already affirmed that 'civil partnerships registers' have exclusively a strong symbolic value, and may be considered as a tool to improve the performance of the municipalities' duties, without adding any legal value.[11]

12.2.2 Decision No. 138 of 2010 of the Italian Constitutional Court

For the first time in its history, in 2010 the Italian Constitutional Court dealt with a question concerning the constitutionality of Art. 93, 96, 98, 107, 108, 143, 143a and 156*bis* of the Civil Code with reference to Art. 2, 3, 29 and 117(1) of the Constitution, "insofar as, interpreted systematically, they do not allow homosexual individuals to celebrate marriage with persons of the same-sex".[12]

The Courts of Venice and Trento based their referral orders to the Constitutional Court on Art. 117(1) of the Italian Constitution, which states that

> Legislative powers shall be vested in the State and the Regions in compliance with the Constitution and with the constraints deriving from EU legislation and international obligations;

Art. 29 of the Constitution, already quoted above; Art. 2 of the Constitution, which states that

> The Republic recognises and guarantees the inviolable rights of the person, both as an individual and in the social groups where human personality is expressed. The Republic expects that the fundamental duties of political, economic and social solidarity be fulfilled;

Art. 3, which contains, alongside other bans on discrimination, the prohibition of discrimination on the basis of sex; on Art. 8 (right to respect for private and family life), 12 (Right to marry), and 14 (prohibition of discrimination) of the European Convention on Human Rights (further referred to as ECHR), as well as a well-known

---

[10] See Violini (2007).

[11] See Decision No. 1041, of 11 June 2001, of the Administrative Regional Tribunal of Florence, sect. I.

[12] There is ample doctrine on that decision. *Ex multis*, see Bin et al. (2010), Romboli (2010), Pezzini and Lorenzetti (2011), Paladini (2011), and Biondi (2013).

judgment of the Strasbourg Court in *Goodwin v. UK* of 2002[13]; and on Art. 7 (respect for private and family life), 9 (Right to marry and right to found a family) and 21 (non-discrimination) of the Charter of Fundamental Rights of the European Union (further referred to as CFR).

In this case, the Constitutional Court considered the provisions of the Civil Code governing marriage. Several same-sex couples sought judicial recognition of their right to marry following refusals by the civil registrar to publish the notice of their intention to marry. These courts referred the cases to the Constitutional Court, stating that since same-sex marriage is neither expressly permitted nor prohibited under Italian law, there would be a gap in the legal system which the Constitutional Court should fill in. In particular, the Court of Venice rightfully underlined that on the basis of the European Court of Human Rights' (further referred to as ECtHR) precedents, private life and the protection of personal identity would not be limited to the individual sphere, but would also encompass relationships, thus raising a positive duty of State intervention to remedy the shortcomings that impede personal fulfilment.[14]

The Constitutional Court rejected the questions raised on the grounds that they were seeking to obtain a substantive judgment not required under constitutional law, and that it was up to the Parliament to determine the particular form of the guarantees required under Art. 2. Moreover, all the provisions of international and supranational law referred to are clear in reserving the detailed regulation of such matters for the discretion of the national authorities, namely Parliaments.

The Court recalled (para. 8) that Art. 2 of the Constitution provides that the Republic recognises and guarantees the inviolable rights of man, both as an individual as well as in social groupings in which he or she expresses his or her personality and requires compliance with the mandatory duties of political, economic and social solidarity. It continues by affirming that according to Art. 2, the social grouping must be deemed to include all forms of simple or complex communities that are capable of permitting and favouring the free development of the person through relationships, within a context that promotes a pluralist model. This concept must also include same-sex unions, understood as the stable cohabitation of two individuals of the same-sex, who are granted the fundamental right to live freely as a couple, and to obtain the legal recognition thereof along with the associated rights and duties, according to the time-scales, procedures and limits specified by law.[15]

However, the Court found that the aspiration to this recognition—which would necessarily postulate legislation of a general nature aimed at regulating the rights

[13] This is *Christine Goodwin v. United Kingdom*, n. 28957/95, judgement of 11th July 2002, in which the Court held that the prohibition of marriage for (post-operative) transsexuals with persons of their original sex was contrary to the Convention.

[14] See Ninatti (2010).

[15] Official Translation provided by the Constitutional Court, at http://www.cortecostituzionale.it/documenti/download/doc/recent_judgments/S2010138_Amirante_Criscuolo_EN.pdf.

and duties of the members of the couple—could not be achieved solely by rendering same-sex unions equivalent to marriage. It would be sufficient in this regard to examine—even not exhaustively—the legislation of the countries that have recognised the aforementioned unions in order to ascertain the diversity among the legislative choices made.

It followed that, for the purposes of Art. 2 of the Constitution, it would be for the Parliament to determine—exercising its full legislative discretion—the forms of guarantee and recognition of the aforementioned unions, whilst the Constitutional Court would only have the possibility to intervene in order to protect specific situations, as it had already occurred for unmarried cohabitees.[16] It may in fact be the case that, in particular circumstances, there is a need to treat different-sex married couples and same-sex couples equally, which the Constitutional Court may guarantee by reviewing the provision's reasonableness.

The Court (para. 9) moved to consider Art. 29 of the Constitution, which has given rise to a lively debate within the academic literature that is still ongoing, and that places marriage at the core of the legitimate family, defines it as a "natural association" (as it may be inferred from the *travaux preparatoires* of the Constituent Assembly, by using this expression the intention was to stress that the family contemplated under the provision had original rights which pre-existed the State, and which the latter was obliged to recognise). In view of the above the Court stated that it is true to say that the concepts of family and marriage cannot be considered to have been "crystallised" with reference to the time when the Constitution entered into force, because they are endowed with the flexibility that is inherent within constitutional principles, and are therefore be interpreted taking account not only of the transformations within the legal system, but also the evolution of society and customs. However, such an interpretation cannot go so far as to impinge upon the core of the provision, modifying it in such a manner as to embrace situations and problems that were not considered at all when it was enacted. In fact, as is clear from the *travaux preparatoires* cited above, the question of homosexual unions remained entirely unaddressed within the debate conducted during the Constituent Assembly, even though homosexuality was by no means unknown. Therefore, absent any different references, the inevitable conclusion is that they took account of the concept of marriage defined under the Civil Code which entered into force in 1942 and which, as noted above, specified (and still specifies) that married couples must be comprised of persons of the opposite sex. The second para. of the Article also makes provision to this effect, in asserting the principle of the moral equality of the married couple, focused in particular on the position of the woman to whom it wishes to guarantee equal dignity and rights within the marital relationship.

This meaning of the constitutional rule cannot be set aside through interpretation, because to do so would not involve a simple re-reading of the system or the abandonment of a mere interpretative practice, but rather the implementation of a

[16] See Decisions of the Italian Constitutional Court No. 559, of 12th December 1989, and No. 404, of 24th March 1988.

creative interpretation. It must therefore be reasserted that the provision did not take account of homosexual unions, but rather intended to refer to marriage within the traditional meaning of that institution.

In what the principle related to Art. 117(1) of the Italian Constitution is concerned, it is pointed out that, in asserting the right to marry, Art. 9 CFR (like Art. 12 ECHR) refers to the national laws governing its exercise.[17] Therefore, except for the express reference to men and women, the observation that the cited legislation also does not require the application of the rules put in place for marriages between men and women on a fully equivalent basis to homosexual unions is in any case decisive. On the basis of the above considerations, the Court ruled inadmissible the questions raised by the referring tribunals with reference to Art. 2 and 117(1) of the Constitution, and groundless the one raised with reference to Art. 3 and 29. The Constitutional Court chose not to open up a dialogue with the ECtHR's precedents. This attitude could be interpreted in a way that, in my opinion, has been confirmed by the latter in *Schalk and Kopf v. Austria*[18]: in the light of the heterogeneity of national disciplines and the lack of a Europe-wide consensus, the international jurisprudence has no voice in dealing with a Constitution that does not explicitly recognise same-sex marriage.[19] To sum up, the constitutional justices decided that the question raised with reference to Art. 3 and 29 of the Constitution was groundless, and the ECtHR ruled there was no violation of Art. 14 and 12 of the ECHR.[20]

12.2.3 The ECtHR's Judgement in **Schalk and Kopf v. Austria**

In June 2010, a few months after the Italian Constitutional Court's decision, the ECtHR delivered its judgment in the case *Schalk and Kopf v. Austria*. This ruling is based on a similar reasoning to the former and demonstrates harmony in the solutions adopted; indeed, after all, the approaches of an international court and a national constitutional court on divisive topics are not necessarily in conflict.

Without going too deep into the decision,[21] it is worthwhile recalling that the Strasbourg judges unanimously declared that the choice made by the Austrian legislature of not recognising marriage for same-sex couples was not in breach of

[17] The Court recalled that the Explanations relating to the Charter of Fundamental Rights drawn up under the authority of the Praesidium of the Convention which drafted the Charter (which, while not having the status of law, undoubtedly constitute an instrument of interpretation), clarify, with respect to Art. 9 (*inter alia*) that "This article neither prohibits nor imposes the granting of the status of marriage to unions between people of the same-sex".

[18] *Schalk and Kopf v. Austria*, n. 30141/04, judgment of 24th June 2010.

[19] On this case see extensively the chapter by Pustorino in this volume.

[20] Crivelli (2012), pp. 35–71.

[21] See Danisi (2010).

the ECHR. The national legal system's choice does not violate Art. 12 of the ECHR, because there is no common European consensus shared by most of the countries in the Council of Europe.[22] The ECtHR acknowledges that Art. 12 could also be applied to same-sex couples on the basis of an 'evolutive' interpretation. However, the ECtHR is clear in affirming that the choice of wording in Art. 12 must be regarded as deliberate: even if, in literal terms, the Article grants the right to marry to "men and women", the French version states "*l'homme et la femme ont le droit de se marier*". Moreover, regard must be had to the historical context in which the Convention was adopted: in the 1950s, marriage was clearly understood in the traditional sense of being a union between partners of different sexes.[23]

The Court observed that marriage has deep-rooted social and cultural connotations which may differ largely from one society to another. The Court reiterates that it must not rush to substitute its own judgment for that of national authorities, which are best placed to assess and respond to the needs of society.

Nor is the Austrian legislation held to violate (this time, four votes against three) Art. 14 read together with Art. 8. The ECtHR considers that the relationship of the applicants, a same-sex couple living in a stable *de facto* partnership, falls within the notion of "family life", just as the relationship of a different-sex couple in the same situation would. And it recognises there is a growing tendency within the Member States of the Council of Europe towards the legal and judicial recognition of stable *de facto* partnerships between same-sex couples. Nonetheless, given the existence of little common ground among the Contracting States, the Court admits that this is an area in which they still enjoy a wide margin of appreciation.[24] The ECtHR chose, in the end, not to anticipate solutions that would not be shared by the majority of national legal systems as a way not to lose its own legitimacy. At the same time, however, this decision represented a step forward and lead to others on the same topic by the ECtHR.

The dissenting opinion in favour of declaring a breach of Art. 14 and 18 of the ECHR[25] and the concurring opinion[26] reveal two different attitudes that reflect at least two of the positions into which the national debate on the Convention is divided. The former used the ban against discrimination to foster the thesis that once same-sex couples are considered to be a form of 'family', the absence of a legal *status* assuring them, at least partially, the same rights or benefits pertaining to married couples requires a robust justification in order to invoke the State margin of appreciation.[27] The concurring opinion, on the contrary, focused on the 'evolutive' interpretation of the right to marry within the ECHR, stating that it is not possible to

[22] See para. 58.

[23] See paras 54 and 55.

[24] See paras 89–94.

[25] Judges Rozakis, Spielmann and Jebens.

[26] Judges Malinverni and Kovler.

[27] I recall that Austria, on 1 January 2010, passed a law that recognises same-sex unions. While this legislation bans access to adoption and to medically assisted procreation to same-sex couples, it

force the text of the Convention to make it affirm a right that was not provided when the Convention was proclaimed.

12.2.4 Decision No. 4184 of 2012 of the Italian Supreme Court of Cassation

The Supreme Court of Cassation Decision no. 4184 of 2012[28] ruled for the first time on whether two same-sex Italian citizens, married abroad, were entitled to record their marriage certificates at the Italian Civil Registry Office. While doing so, it referred profusely to the Constitutional Court Decision no. 138 of 2010 and to the ECtHR's *Schalk* case.

The previous Supreme Court of Cassation case-law addressing the question held that the different sex of the married couple's members was one of the indispensable prerequisites for the existence of marriage.[29] Italian judges agreed in considering the Registry Office's refusal to record a marriage celebrated abroad as legitimate. In support of that position, the judges point to four arguments. To start with, a constitutional interpretation that recognises family as a natural society founded on marriage between two persons of different sex. Secondly, it would be inferred from the Civil Code provisions that the difference of sexes is an essential element of the institution of marriage in the Italian legal system (Art. 89, 143 bis, 156 bis, 231, 235, 262). Furthermore, the Court[30] had already considered that the manifestation of will expressed by two persons of different sex before a public official would be a necessary requisite for the existence of marriage. Finally, unlike family, marriage was not considered to be a pre-juridical right endowed by the Fundamental Law to each individual by the Italian Constituent Assembly. The judges also stressed the need for the Parliament to recognise new family *status*, thus eschewing the possibility of taking the legislature's place.

It therefore came as no surprise that the Supreme Court of Cassation overruled the request of the petitioning same-sex couple. At the same time, the ruling shows the irresistible charm of the multilevel protection of human rights. Indeed, the conclusion is strongly based, in my opinion, on its interpretation of the *Schalk* case. Proof of this is that the Court of Cassation reaffirms, in the first part of the decision, that the impossibility of recording the marriage at the Registry Office is not due to its contrariety to public order but due to its non-recognisability as a

grants to the latter the application of the same taxation and succession regimes, as well as grounds for dissolving marriage, rights and duties.

[28] Available at www.forumcostituzionale.it.

[29] See Decisions No. 7877 of 2000, No. 1304 of 1990, and No. 1808 of 1976, of the Italian Supreme Court of Cassation. See also the Decision of the Court of Latina of 31st May 2005, confirmed by the decision of the Court of Appeals of Rome of 13th July 2006, which contributed to fuelling the debate (in line with the Court of Appeals of Florence of 30th June 2008).

[30] See Decision No. 7877 of 9th June 2000 of the Italian Supreme Court of Cassation.

marriage certificate in the Italian legal system. In other words: two Italian same-sex citizens cannot register a marriage celebrated abroad, not because that marriage is non-existent or invalid for the Italian legal system, but because same-sex unions are unsuited to giving rise to any legal effects therein.

The second half of the (long) decision is devoted to determining whether "the Italian Constitution recognises the fundamental right to marry to same-sex couples or if EU law and international law do so [. . .]".

The Court focuses on the latter option, devoting unusually detailed attention to it. First, it correctly interprets EU law, and in particular of the CFR and Art. 6 TEU: considering Art. 9 of the Charter and its attached explanations, no justification for recognising same-sex marriage can be found. Likewise, it must surely be admitted that same-sex marriage clearly lies outside the EU's purview. Second, it recalls that it is up to the Strasbourg Court to interpret the ECtHR, in a fashion which is not unconditionally binding upon national judges. It then states that the Strasbourg Court in the *Schalk* decision brought down the implicit condition underpinning marriage: the different sexes of the persons getting married. This is to say, according to the Italian Supreme Court of Cassation, the ECtHR would have removed the obstacle that prevented the recognition of same-sex marriage, reserving the guarantee of the said right to the free choices by national parliaments. Here, I believe that the Italian Court has the Strasbourg Court say that the right to marry enshrined in the ECHR, read jointly with Art. 9 of the EU Charter, also includes same-sex marriage. The truth, however, is that the ECtHR stated something different, interpreting Art. 9 of the Charter[31] and affirming that

> no longer [. . .] the right to marry enshrined in article 12 must in all circumstances be limited to marriage between two persons of the opposite sex. Consequently, it cannot be said that article 12 is inapplicable to the applicant's complaint.

In the end, it is submitted that the Italian Supreme Court of Cassation, correctly recalling the possibility of constitutional justices to intervene through the reasonableness check to protect specific situations, is ambiguous in configuring it as a role for common judges. The trouble, though, is that the Italian Constitutional Court, in Decision No. 138 of 2010, did not recognise them as having one such responsibility.[32]

---

[31] The ECHtR at para. 60 states that "The commentary to the Charter, which became legally binding in December 2009, confirms that Art. 9 is meant to be broader in scope than the corresponding articles in other human rights instruments". Only in a second moment does it recall the harsh disputes around the Article at the time of the proclamation of the Charter, or that the lack of any reference to the different sexes of the spouses and to the national legislations is explained in the name of the special features and the differences between various Member States in recognising same-sex marriages, and not for other reasons.

[32] Indeed, the Court of Cassation affirms (p. 71) that the members of the homosexual couple can go to the court in order to assert their right to the same treatment as that accorded to a married heterosexual couple and in that situation, where applicable, raise objections on the grounds of constitutional illegitimacy. I believe that that part of the decision accords the judges more than the Constitutional court stated.

Altogether, this means that the unusual attention the Court paid to EU and international law did not result in a positive decision for the petitioners. So what, in the end, did the Italian Supreme Court of Cassation say with its decision? It is submitted that, on the one hand, it underlined statements in favour of same-sex unions made by the ECtHR and the Italian Constitutional Court. On the other hand, it sent a message to the Italian Legislator which is the *dominus* of the national choices on this topic.

12.2.5 Concluding Remarks

The *Schalk* decision did not remove the obstacles to same-sex marriage, as the Italian Supreme Court of Cassation seemed to state, for the simple reason that it is not up to the ECtHR to remove them—as the Strasbourg Court clearly affirms.

To be sure, the Grand Chamber in *Schalk* tried to remove the obstacle to same-sex marriage which concerns Art. 12 of the Convention (with two judges dissenting). Quite recently indeed, in the case of *H v. Finland*[33] decided on 13 November 2012, the Court (§ 1) reiterated that Art. 12 of the Convention is the *lex specialis* for the right to marry. It secures the fundamental right of a man and a woman to marry and to establish a family. Art. 12 expressly provides for regulation of marriage by national law. The Court points out that Art. 12 of the ECHR enshrines the traditional concept of marriage as being between a man and a woman. While it is true that some contracting States have extended marriage to same-sex partners, this reflects their own vision of the role of marriage in their societies and does not flow from an interpretation of the fundamental right as laid down by the contracting States in the Convention in 1950.

At the same time, the Italian Supreme Court of Cassation's understanding of the issue cannot be seconded. It is not accurate to say that, in the Italian legal system, the mentioned reading of Art. 12 ECHR is no longer adequate because the conception that the different sex of the partners is an indispensable requirement for the existence of marriage has become radically outmoded. In the end, it seems that, at least in part, the Italian Supreme Court of Cassation manipulated the decision of the ECtHR. For those who fear the danger of a so-called judiciary colonialism, the

[33] The applicant, H., was a Finnish national who was born in 1963 and lives in Helsinki. Having undergone male-to-female gender reassignment surgery in 2009 and having previously changed her first names, H. wished to obtain a new identity number that would indicate her female gender in her official documents. However, in order to do so, her marriage to a woman would have had to be modified into a civil partnership, which H. refused to accept. She complained that making the full recognition of her new gender conditional on the transformation of her marriage into a civil partnership violated her rights under Art. 8 (right to respect for private and family life) and 14 (prohibition of discrimination). The Court held that there has been no violation of Art. 8 of the ECHR or of Art. 14 read together with Art. 8; and that there is no need to examine the case under Art. 12 of the ECHR.

interpretation of the *Schalk* decision put forward revealed the intent to impose a "liberal" attitude on legal systems that did not choose that option. The responsibility of such an attitude must not fall on the multilevel protection of fundamental rights, but on the use that the national legal interpreter decides to make of it. In particular, it seems that the Supreme Court of Cassation is doing politics, rather than law. Even if such position is shared by many, it is doubtful whether it is up to judges to develop it.

In conclusion, it is here argued that the Italian Legislator has the possibility to recognise same-sex partnerships (not marriages) without modifying the Constitution. Not only through *ad hoc* legislation, but also through single interventions, treating married couples and opposite-sex and same-sex couples similarly. The point is that it does not want to do so.

In any case, it appears to be the case that, throughout the last decades, Italy has had Legislators affected by a general—and for this reason even more serious—cultural and political backwardness, and a substantial incapacity of developing, at least, a competent, mature and serious political debate on the topic.

12.3 Spain

12.3.1 Introductory Remarks

Before having become the first Southern European State to allow same-sex marriage, the Spanish Civil Code's Art. 44(1) plainly stated that:

> Men and women are entitled to marry in accordance with the provisions of this Code.

At the same time, Art. 32 of the Spanish Constitution determined that:

> 1 – Men and women have the right to marry with full legal equality.
> 2 – The law shall make provision for the forms of marriage, the age and capacity for concluding it, the rights and duties of the spouses, the grounds for separation and dissolution, and their effects.

During the period that preceded the approval of the same-sex marriage act,[34] the Constitutional Court delivered its ruling in Case No. 222/1994. A constitutional complaint was filed, by the widower of a deceased same-sex partner, to request the award of a widow's pension. The law, however, reserved access to this benefit only to opposite-sex married couples. Granting this right would amount to extending, without a previous statute and directly based on the Constitution, the effects of same-sex civil unions to those of different-sex marriages. This request was dismissed with the argument that there is no constitutional protection of (either

[34] On the evolution of anti-discrimination measures in Spain, see Platero (2007). For a reference to the legislation of the Autonomous Communities, see González Beilfuss (2012), pp. 45–52.

different or same-sex) *more uxorio* unions. In a later ruling—Case n. 198/2012—the Constitutional Court said it followed from this decision that the Legislator was free to restrict marriage to different sex couples, but not that that would be the only constitutionally valid option.

12.3.2 Law No. 13/2005 and Case No. 198/2012 of the Constitutional Court

Law No. 13/2005, of 1st July 2005, introduced several changes to the Civil Code, the most relevant of which were the addition of a paragraph to Art. 44, according to which "marriage will have the same requisites and effects when both spouses are of the same or different sex", and the introduction of the possibility of joint adoption by same-sex couples.[35] Its preamble stated that it was aimed at the

> promotion of effective equality of citizens in the development of their personality [Art. 9 (2) and 10(1) of the Constitution], the preservation of freedom of living together [Art 1 (1) of the Constitution], and the implementation of real equality in the enjoyment of rights without any discrimination based on sexual orientation.

After its approval,[36] 71 centre/right-wing MPs lodged a complaint before the Constitutional Court asking it to quash the new law as unconstitutional.[37] The Court came to deliver its judgement on 6th November 2012, more than 7 years later. During this time, however, the law was fully in force and not suspended, thereby allowing same-sex couples to perform marriage.[38] With a majority of right Justices in favour of its constitutionality and only three against, the Court upheld it.

The applicants claimed that the principle of equality was violated to the extent that granting the right to marry to same-sex couples amounted to discrimination (of different-sex couples) for lack of differentiation.[39] The Court held, however, that assertion to be without any merit: in the Court's opinion, there is no subjective right to different legal treatment and hence inequality for excess of equality does not constitute a valid reason to invalidate the statute.

[35] See para. 7 of the single Art. of Law No. 13/2005 of 1st July 2005. For an overview, see Bazán (2009).

[36] On the conflictive procedure of approval of the bill, see Rodríguez Ruiz (2011), pp. 76–78; Santos (2009), pp. 165–179.

[37] The MPs were backed by a report of the General Council of the Judiciary—see Consejo General del Poder Judicial (2005), available at http://www.poderjudicial.es/cgpj/es/Poder_Judicial/Consejo_General_del_Poder_Judicial/Actividad_del_CGPJ/Informes/Estudio_sobre_la_reforma_del_Codigo_Civil_en_materia_de_matrimonio_entre_personas_del_mismo_sexo.

[38] Ahumada-Ruiz (2013), p. 429.

[39] See Art. 1(1), 9(2), and 14 of the Spanish Constitution.

The applicants also invoked the principle of equality in its dimension of prohibition of arbitrariness.[40] The Court dismissed this argument: the different treatment is not the result of normative discrimination (as mentioned, it is a case of a non-objectionable excess of equality) and the measure at stake does not lack a rational explanation (it pursues a legitimate goal, which is clearly stated in the statute's preamble).

The Court next underlined that marriage and family are two distinct constitutional goods. On this note, the Court reminded that all children, whether born in or out of wedlock, are afforded the same legal treatment. Consequently, a violation of Art. 32 does not necessarily imply a violation of Art. 39. The Court quoted the ECtHR to support its position.[41]

Art. 32 is included in Section II ("Citizens' rights and duties") of Chapter II ("Rights and freedoms") of Title I ("Fundamental rights and duties") of the Spanish Constitution. Its diction is inspired by, among many other cited texts, Art. 16 of the UDHR. According to settled constitutional case-law, this Article creates both an 'institutional guarantee' and a constitutional right.

An 'institutional guarantee' requires the "safeguarding of an institution in such terms that the general social conscience would be able to recognise it throughout time and space". The Legislator enjoys ample discretion when giving it a concrete shape, as it would only be necessary that it would be identifiable. Alongside with the autonomy of municipalities, the autonomy of universities, or the *habeas corpus*, marriage would be one such 'institutional guarantee'.

As the Legislator fully assimilated different-sex and same-sex marriages, the Court conceded that it modified the institution of marriage.[42]

The applicants brought forward three arguments on how Law n. 13/2005, of 1st July, had changed the essential core of marriage, thus disrespecting the 'institutional guarantee'. First, a literal reading of Art. 32, which refers to "men and women", would indicate that only different-sex marriages enjoy constitutional protection.[43] Moreover, from a systematic perspective, all other constitutional provisions that make explicit (Art. 39) or implicit (Art. 58) reference to marriage and the relevant international law conventions [Art. 10(2)] would confirm this. Lastly, the *travaux préparatoires* of the Constitution, namely the debate in the Constituent Assembly, would buttress that literal reading.

The Court acknowledges that in 1978, when Art. 32 was enacted, marriage was primarily perceived as an institution for different-sex couples. The issues that were debated in the Constituent Assembly were those related to the conceptual distinction of family and marriage, to the rights to separation and divorce, and to the equality of spouses. This does not mean, however, that the Constitution rejected

---

[40] See Art. 9(3) of the Spanish Constitution.

[41] Namely cases *X, Y and Z v. UK*, n. 21830/93, judgement of 22nd April 1997, and *Van Der Heijden v. The Netherlands*, n. 42857/05, judgement of 3rd April 2012.

[42] See Rodríguez Ruiz (2011), pp. 83–86; Martín Sánchez (2010), pp. 257–259.

[43] See Díez-Picazo (2007), pp. 10–12.

(or, for all that matters, accepted) same-sex marriage. Indeed, even a strictly literal interpretation of Art. 32 shows that it only identifies the rights holders ("men and women") and not with whom may one celebrate it. The Court quotes the ECtHR's reasoning in *Schalk and Kopf v. Austria* to reinforce its argument.

The Court then sketches a theory of evolutionary constitutional interpretation, based on the idea of legal culture that sees law as a social phenomenon bound to the reality in which it is embedded. According to the Court, constitutional interpretation must evolve so as to accommodate modern life realities and circumstances and thence guarantee the very relevance and legitimacy of the Constitution itself. For this, the observation of the pertinent social reality, the opinions of legal scholars and consultative bodies, foreign law, and the case-law of international bodies would be elements to take into account when interpreting a Constitution.[44] According to this theory of evolutionary constitutional interpretation, as set up by the Court, the institution of marriage would not have become unrecognisable after the enlargement of its subjective scope by Law n. 13/2005, due to the evolution of the concept of marriage in the Spanish society. The essential elements of marriage are: the equality of spouses, the free nature of the consent to celebrate marriage with the chosen person, and the necessity to demonstrate the consent. These three elements still are present after the approval of Law No. 13/2005 in all types of marriage.

It was also deemed necessary to determine how integrated same-sex marriage had become in the Spanish legal culture to decide whether the institution of marriage encompasses it or not. Foreign law would show that the assimilation of different sex and same-sex marriage has consolidated in Western legal culture: such would be the cases of the Netherlands, Belgium, Norway, Sweden, Denmark, Portugal, Iceland, Canada, several States of the United States of America, Mexico, Argentina, or South Africa; as well as that of Slovenia and Finland, where similar legislative projects exist. Other States have chosen civil unions: France, Germany, Finland, Luxembourg, the United Kingdom, Andorra, the Czech Republic, Switzerland, Austria, or Liechtenstein, as well as Iberoamerican States such as Colombia, Uruguay, Ecuador, or Brazil. This new socio-legal reality would stand in sharp contrast to that of the 1980s, when no State had granted any right to same-sex unions.

The case-law of international bodies would show a similar openness to same-sex marriage. That would be, in particular, the case of the ECtHR (quoting, again, *Schalk*).

Likewise, in Spain there has been ample social acceptance of same-sex marriage. On the one hand, according to one of several quoted polls, same-sex marriage has achieved an approval rate of 66.2 %, significantly above the EU average (56 %). On the other hand, 22,124 same-sex marriages have been celebrated since the entry into force of Law n. 13/2005, of 1st July.

Lastly, the Court held that the fact that married same-sex couples benefit (and are burdened by) the same regime applicable to different sex couples—be it, e.g., in

[44] Which would also be a requirement of Art. 10(2) of the Spanish Constitution.

terms of succession law, tax law, social security law, or criminal law—causes no malfunction or distortion whatsoever to the latter.

Altogether, this led the Court to the conclusion that the Legislator had not exceeded the freedom it had to shape the 'institutional guarantee' of marriage, enshrined in Art. 32 of the Spanish Constitution, when approving Law No. 13/2005. Among the several options at hand, the Legislator chose to fully assimilate the legal *status* of different-sex and same-sex couples for marriage purposes. In doing so, the Court considers that "the Legislator seems to have followed the logic according to which two equivalent relationships which have similar effects should share the same title"—a statement which seems to convey the idea that the chosen path (marriage instead of civil partnership) is the most faithful to the Constitution. It concludes this paragraph, however, by saying that "the previous statement does not consider or exclude the constitutionality of the other alternative the Legislator had".[45]

From a subjective standpoint, the Legislator was bound to respect the 'essential core' of the right to marry.[46] The definition of 'essential core' of a right provided by the Court was similar to that of 'institutional guarantee' it had earlier relied upon. The scope of freedom enjoyed by the Legislator in regulating it would also be comparable.

After providing an overview of the constitutional case-law related to the right to marry, the Court asserts that Law n. 13/2005, of 1st July, changed the forms of exercise of the right to marry, not its holders. In doing so, it followed the general tendency to assimilate the legal status of homosexual and heterosexual persons, also shown in the case-law of the ECtHR. This modification neither restricted the right of different-sex couples to marry, nor did it convert or denaturalise the right. It represented, however, a step forward in the guarantee of human dignity and of the free development of personality, promoting the conditions so that the individual's freedom and equality are real and effective.[47]

The applicants also argued that allowing the joint adoption of minors by same-sex couples would violate Art. 39(2) of the Spanish Constitution, according to which "the public authorities [...] ensure full protection of children". The Court also dismissed this argument by stating that the children's interest is defended by a thorough scrutiny of the adopters, regardless of their sexual orientation. And the adoption laws in force all had as its main guiding principle that of the best interests of the child. Quoting a previous decision, which was later confirmed by the ECtHR,

---

[45] Urías Martínez (2008), pp. 896–897, is of the opinion that Art. 32 does not guarantee the fundamental right to same-sex marriage, but that the Legislator would be allowed to enlarge the subjective scope of the existing fundamental right.

[46] See Art. 53(1) and (2) of the Constitution. On this topic, see Rodríguez Ruiz (2011), pp. 79–83; Martín Sánchez (2010), pp. 259–269.

[47] See, respectively, Art. 10(1) and 14 of the Spanish Constitution.

> what is not constitutionally admissible is to assume the existence of a risk of modification of the minor's personality merely due to the sexual orientation of one or both parents.[48]

12.3.3 Concluding Remarks

It was unanticipated that the Spanish Constitutional Court took 7 (long) years to deliver the judgment in this case. All the more surprising if one considers that the decision was not taken by one or two votes: there was a clear majority outvoting the dissenters, which shows that the cause of the delay was not an internal impasse. And even more unexpected if one considers that, according to the data provided by the Court itself, public opinion was favourable to Law n. 13/2005, of 1st July, thereby excluding the risk of a social backlash against the ruling. Among the strong points of the decision is the fact that it addresses all the arguments put forward by the applicants, one by one, and in a structured way. It may be true that the Court's reasoning is not very developed in some points and not particularly abundant in references, but it is authoritative in the fashion it settles the issue.

12.4 Portugal

12.4.1 Introductory Remarks

Art. 36 of the Constitution of the Portuguese Republic of 1976, entitled "Family, marriage and parentage", establishes that

1. Everyone shall have the right to found a family and to marry on terms of full equality.
2. The law shall regulate the requirements for and the effects of marriage and its dissolution by death or divorce, regardless of the form in which it was entered into. [. . .]

At the same time, its Art. 13(2) determines, since the 6th constitutional amendment (2004), that

> No one shall be privileged, favoured, prejudiced, deprived of any right or exempted from any duty on the basis of [. . .] sexual orientation.[49]

[48] See Rodríguez Ruiz (2011), pp. 78–79; Martín Sánchez (2010), pp. 270–277.

[49] The other two potentially relevant provisions are Art. 26(1), according to which "Everyone shall have the right to a personal identity, to the development of their personality, to civil capacity, [. . .] to protect the privacy of their personal and family life, and to legal protection against any form of discrimination", and Art. 67(1), which reads as follows: "As a fundamental element in society, the family shall possess the right to protection by society and the State and to the effective implementation of all the conditions needed to enable family members to achieve personal fulfillment".

The Portuguese Civil Code was approved in 1966 and entered into force in the following year. According to its original version:

> marriage is the contract celebrated between two persons of different sex who intend to start a family through a full communion of life, in accordance with this code.

A marriage celebrated between same-sex persons was deemed to be legally non-existent.[50]

The Constitution only entered into force 10 years later, after the fall of the right-wing dictatorship that ruled Portugal for almost half a century. It was then determined that the Civil Code should be reviewed, to make it compatible with the Constitution, which was achieved within 1 year.[51] The majority of the changes proposed by the appointed reviewing Commission were on matters of Family Law, especially related to the *status* of the wife and children born out of wedlock.[52] From the entry into force of the Constitution until the Constitutional Court first had the opportunity to decide on same-sex marriage, the most relevant legislative development was the approval of same-sex civil partnerships by Law n. 7/2011, of 11th May.[53]

12.4.2 Case n. 359/2009 of the Constitutional Court

On February 2006, two women, Teresa Pires and Helena Paixão, decided to approach the Registrar of Births, Marriages and Deaths and request their marriage to be celebrated. As the Civil Code did not allow same-sex marriages, the Registrar refused to perform it. The brides then contested this refusal in a court of law, which maintained the decision, and appealed to the Lisbon Court of Appeals, which also upheld it. Before these courts, the applicants incidentally invoked the unconstitutionality of the Civil Code Articles that denied them the right to marry. As there is no constitutional complaint that can provide direct access of private parties to the Constitutional Court for violations of fundamental rights in the Portuguese legal system, this was the only way of bringing a case to the Constitutional Court, which exercises its jurisdiction in concrete review.[54] Together with their pleadings, the applicants filed four *pro bono* legal opinions[55] adding further arguments in the defence of their petition.

[50] See Art. 1577 and 1628(e) of the original version of the Portuguese Civil Code.

[51] See Decree-Law No. 496/77, of 25 November.

[52] For a survey, see Duarte Pinheiro (2008), pp. 51–59.

[53] For an overview, see Martins (2008), pp. 194–211; see also Duarte Pinheiro (2010), pp. 713–760.

[54] For a more detailed report, see Santos (2009), pp. 60–72.

[55] Which have been published afterwards: see Pamplona Côrte-Real (2008), Moreira (2008), Duarte d'Almeida (2008) and Múrias (2008).

The question that the Court, sitting in chambers of five justices, had to answer was whether same-sex marriage was a constitutional obligation and therefore the existing Civil Code provision prohibiting it was unconstitutional. It started by analysing at length the statutory framework and the constitutional case-law of several national jurisdictions—namely, but not exclusively, the United States of America (going through the jurisprudence of the Supreme Courts of Hawaii, Vermont, Massachusetts, New Jersey, California, Connecticut, and Iowa), Canada (encompassing the case-law of the Supreme Court of Canada, the British Columbia Court of Appeal, and the Court of Appeal for Ontario), South Africa, and Germany—and international or supranational instruments and courts—such as the ECHR and the ECtHR, the CFR and the ECJ. This comparative exercise (unexpectedly) takes up to 2/3s of the actual decision of the Court.

In the end, the Court overruled the applicants' request by a difference of one vote only, having concluded that there was no constitutional obligation to establish same-sex marriage. To reach this result, the Court started by putting forward a historical-systematic argument. It recalled that the Civil Code had been reviewed after the entry into force of the Constitution and that its Art. 1577 and 1628(e) had never been modified, not even after the introduction of the suspect category of 'sexual orientation' in Art. 13(2) of the Constitution.[56] The Court seems to presuppose that for one such constitutional provision to be fully effective, ordinary law would have to have been modified in accordance to it. This is clear when the Court says that what the prohibition of discrimination based on sexual orientation requires is merely that the Portuguese constitutional order be "sexual orientation-blind". And it goes further: it says that for one such prohibition of discrimination to be fully consequential, Art. 36 of the Constitution should have been modified in accordance with it. One such position cannot be seconded: the very prohibition of discrimination according to sexual orientation necessarily has an impact in the constitutional concept of 'family'.[57]

The Court then moves forward to determine the constitutional concept of 'marriage'. When Art. 36(2) of the Constitution, without providing a definition of its own, deferred to the ordinary law the establishment of "the requirements for and the effects of marriage and its dissolution", it did not intend to question the "common, socially rooted" meaning of 'marriage' as a contract celebrated between two different sex persons. At the same time, however, Art. 36(2) of the Portuguese Constitution would not establish the immutability of the concept of 'marriage' as it existed in the Civil Code in the moment the Constitution was approved, thereby excluding the legal recognition of other forms of life-communion among people. Although the Court writes that 'institutional guarantees' should be read from the

[56] This is also the backbone of the argument of Medeiros (2010), pp. 819–820. Pamplona Côrte-Real (2008), pp. 18–19, considers this to be a *petitio principii*.

[57] See Miranda (2010), p. 433—who, nonetheless, moves away from this argument, and puzzlingly says that "one thing is to grant a homosexual the right to constitute a family and to marry, another thing is the right to marry with a same-sex person"; similarly, and equally unexpectedly, cf. Nogueira de Brito (2008), pp. 54N–57N.

Constitution and not from the ordinary law, the ambiguous interpretation it puts forward clearly downplays the paramount character of the Constitution. The referral to the ordinary law, as any referral to the ordinary law made by the Constitution, necessarily requires a solution that is consistent with the latter. And, within the Constitution, not only Art. 36(1) makes reference to "everyone" being the rights holders, without any distinction, but Art. 13 also lists 'sexual orientation' as a suspect factor for the principle of equality control.[58]

The conciliatory reading of Art. 36(2) of the Portuguese Constitution makes room for the Court's key (institutional) argument: that changing one such concept, rather than representing the removal of a restriction to the exercise of a right, would amount to a full-fledged change of the legal order. Now, according to the Court, the competence to do this would lie within the sphere of competence of the organs that represent the popular will. It would be up to the Legislator to make such changes in matters over which there are diverse worldviews within the society, while the Court would only retain the power to control those changes negatively if the legislature would subvert the axiological matrix of the Constitution.[59] The fact that in some (common law) legal orders the judiciary assumed that role does not, in the Court's judgement, contradict the previous statement, as the respective Constitutions would be structurally different and did not contain norms similar to Art. 36 and 67 of the Portuguese Constitution.[60]

But the Court adds another (substantive) reason. Although it *prima facie* denies its competence, also based on institutional premises, to opt between the conception of "marriage as a socially relevant union between a man and a woman aimed at procreation" and that of "marriage as a purely private relationship between two adults", the Court undoubtedly chooses the former. Indeed, and without the support of any statistics, it states that marriage is the legal institution through which the State diffuses certain societal values:

> a way to involve a generation in the creation of the generation that will succeed it, and the only of such means to ensure a child the right to know and be brought up by his/her biological parents.[61]

---

[58] Cf. the dissent of Justice M. J. Antunes, as well as Múrias (2008), pp. 17S–19S.

[59] Similarly, but defending the need for a referendum, see Machado (2010), pp. 9–37.

[60] It is at this point that the overview of foreign and international law proves instrumental to the decision. See Violante (2012), pp. 227–228. The arguments that explain the difference between the Portuguese system and the jurisdictions where courts extended the right to marry to same-sex couples are not entirely convincing, though. If anything, the diction of Art. 36 of the Portuguese Constitution, considering that the rights holders would be "everyone", would strengthen the judicial role. And a common law system is not a synonym of an activist (constitutional) court. For a stronger version of the same arguments, which still does not frame the issue in its entirety, as the Author acknowledges in footnote 68, see Violante (2012), pp. 236–237.

[61] Strongly seconding this interpretation, cf. Miranda (2010), p. 437, who also anchors it in the need to ensure the sustainability of the welfare State; de Oliveira Ascensão (2011), p. 403. Considering that the association between marriage and parentage can only be justified from a religious catholic perspective, see Raposo (2009), pp. 175–177; the Author further adds that

In other words,

> a complete union between a man and a woman oriented towards the joint education of the children they might have.

The two dissents are particularly (and rightfully, it seems) confrontational in their reaction to this line of reasoning. It is argued that

> the Court resorts to traditional arguments related to 'procreation and offspring education' that have not even been raised in the original version of the Civil Code of 1966.[62]

At the same time, it is clearly demonstrated that the conception of marriage the Court uses does not stem from the Constitution, which enshrines the right to constitute a family as a right that is different from the right to marry, the principle of non-discrimination of children born out of wedlock, and the constitutional protection of family, of maternity and paternity.[63] What is more: not even the ordinary law provides any support for such conception.[64]

Finally, the Court goes back to the principle of equality, only to refuse applying it to the case at stake. The argument is, yet again, that assessing its violation would require choosing between the two mentioned conceptions of marriage. Moreover, a ruling considering Art. 1577 of the Civil Code to be under-inclusive and expanding its subjective scope would not be in accordance with the practice of the Court.[65]

12.4.3 *Law No. 9/2010 and Case n. 121/2010 of the Constitutional Court*

In the aftermath of the Constitutional Court's decision, the centre/left-wing Government decided to present a legislative proposal to the Assembly of the Republic to legalise same-sex marriage.[66] In January 2010, Prime-Minister Sócrates presented it to the Members of Parliament as follows:

> This law aims to unite the Portuguese society, rather than divide it. This is a law of agreement and social harmony [. . .]. This law will constitute everyone's victory, because that is what happens with laws of freedom and humanist laws [. . .]. What is properly

Portugal has remnants of a confessional State (pp. 173–174); disagreeing with the latter view, see Nogueira de Brito (2008), pp. 26N–38N.

[62] Cf. the dissent of Justice G. Galvão.

[63] See, respectively, Art. 36(1), Art. 36(1) first part, Art. 67, and Art. 68 of the Portuguese Constitution. Cf. the dissent of Justice M. J. Antunes.

[64] Definitely settling the issue, see Duarte Pinheiro (2004), pp. 299–300; Múrias (2008), pp. 39S–41S; Duarte d'Almeida (2008), pp. 68–69.

[65] According to the court, this type of ruling would only be legitimate if the case was that of the elimination of special or exceptional norms that would result in the extension of a general regime, or that of a constitutionally mandatory more favourable regime.

[66] For a socio-political analysis of the process that lead to the approval of Law n. 9/2010, of 31st May, see Brandão and Machado (2012), pp. 666–670.

> expected from a humanist is to feel humiliated with the humiliation of others; to feel excluded with the exclusion of others [. . .]. That is why, when we pass a law that will make more people happy, it is our own happiness that we are taking care of. [. . .] This is a law that will honour the best tradition of tolerance and mutual respect, ethical foundations of pluralist democracies such as the Portuguese democracy [. . .].[67]

It was approved with 125 (out of 230) votes in favour, all from centre/left and left wing parties. The bill that became Law n. 9/2010, of 31st May, consisted of only five Articles. The first stated its object, the second modified three provisions of the Civil Code, the third determined that the law did not imply the admissibility of adoption by same-sex married couples, the fourth revoked Art. 1628(e) of the Civil Code, and the last one determined that every legal provision related to marriage and its effects should be interpreted in accordance with it.[68]

After its approval, the President of the Republic requested the Constitutional Court to review the constitutionality of all the provisions in the law in *ex ante* abstract review, except for the one that excluded adoption. The explanation for this seems to have been that, being himself ideologically conservative, he was afraid that the Court would declare it unconstitutional, thereby giving same-sex marriages the right to adopt children. Whereas in the previous case the Court had to decide whether same-sex marriage was a constitutional obligation, in this case, in plenary session, it had to determine if the Constitution permitted it. The majority, with 11 Justices, voted in favour, whereas 2 Justices voted against.

Once again, now noting the universality of the issues at stake, the Court went through the same national and international cases, even with more detail, and included some new ones.[69] This time it distinguished from the beginning the legal orders in which same-sex marriage or civil partnership had been approved by the Legislator from those in which it was the result of judicial decisions.[70]

The first issue the Court faced was whether the suppression of one of the elements of the traditional concept of marriage (the difference of sexes) would put at stake the preservation of the essential core of the 'institutional guarantee' of marriage. Even though only family is protected as such,[71] the Court understood that the institution of 'marriage' was, too, for otherwise it would not make sense to award the right to marry and at the same time allow the Legislator to suppress or disfigure the concept of 'marriage'.[72] Indeed, as the right to marry is a fundamental right, the Legislator cannot suppress 'marriage' from the Portuguese legal order.

---

[67] See Santos (2013), pp. 59–60.

[68] Criticising the Legislator for not having introduced the necessary modifications to the Code of Register of Births, Marriages and Deaths, see Duarte Pinheiro (2010), pp. 431–437.

[69] See Violante (2012), pp. 229–230.

[70] Cf. the dissenting vote by Justice B. Rodrigues, who considers this type of *excursus* to be futile, bearing in mind that the Portuguese Constitution is a rigid one.

[71] See Art. 67 of the Portuguese Constitution.

[72] Similarly, see Gomes Canotilho and Moreira (2007), pp. 567–568. Defending a much broader interpretation of the institutional guarantee of 'marriage', cf. de Oliveira Ascensão (2011), pp. 398–402. See also Pereira Coelho and de Oliveira (2008), pp. 113–114, 203–204.

This is why it focuses its analysis on the concept of 'guarantee of institute' (a modality of the concept of 'institutional guarantee' *lato sensu*): the complex of norms and legal relations structured and sedimented in the infra-constitutional legal order through a process of historical development.

The Court recognises that such concept was formed when the Weimar Constitution was in force and the Legislator was neither directly bound to the Constitution nor were fundamental rights directly applicable; to this extent, banning the Legislator from modifying the content of Private Law institutes was a way of actually ensuring fundamental rights. But nowadays, with constitutional supremacy, the direct applicability of fundamental rights, and judicial review, it would make no sense for that this device to maintain its historical function. The Court asserts, however, that the concept can still be used to verify if individual and collective goods to which the right to marry are instrumental would be limited in their essential core.[73]

These goods would be twofold. On the one hand, the Court admits that Art. 16 (1) of the UDHR only protects marriage between a man and a woman, but rejects that this could be invoked to restrict the scope of a constitutional right.[74] On the other hand, the Court examines the historical and systematic interpretation of the constitutional concept of 'marriage', always lumping together the notions of family and parentage, to determine whether the difference in the spouses' sex was part of the concept's essential core.

The majority claims that when the Constitution enshrined the concept of 'marriage' in Art. 36(2), it had been a stable concept for centuries.[75] The more pressing social needs at the time the Constitution was drafted were related to the reformation of the rules on divorce, the equality of the spouses, or the distinction between children born in and out of wedlock. Same-sex marriage was not discussed at that

[73] Justice C. Sarmento e Castro, in her concurring opinion, claims that even though the existence of the right to marry presupposes the corresponding private law institute of marriage, the latter must be read in accordance with the Constitution.

[74] See Art. 16(2) of the Portuguese Constitution, according to which "The provisions of this Constitution [. . .] concerning fundamental rights shall be interpreted and construed in accordance with the Universal Declaration of Human Rights". In disagreement with the majority's view, see Miranda (2011), p. 178; de Oliveira Ascensão (2011), pp. 403–404; and the dissenting vote by B. Rodrigues. Raising the bar, Barroso (2010), pp. 59–60, claims that Art. 16(1) of the UDHR is a *ius cogens* norm that would prohibit same-sex marriages. Based on this assumption, the Author considers the South African Constitutional Court case *Minister of Home Affairs v. Fourie* be null and void—without having even read it (the case is quoted *apud*, note 14)—as well as Law n. 9/ 2010, of 31st May. A quick survey of International Law materials would have spared the Author from incurring in such a mistake—see, for instance, the decision of the UN Human Rights Committee in the case *Joslin v. New Zealand* regarding Art. 23(2) of the ICCPR; see also Joseph et al. (2005), p. 453. On the HRC case-law on same-sex couples, see the chapter by Paladini in this volume.

[75] This would only be true if one disregards aspects which are central to the constitutional concept of 'marriage' such as the equality between the spouses. In his dissent, Justice B. Rodrigues goes even further back and considers the concept has been stable for at least 7 millennia.

time—in reality, what was then discussed about homosexuality were aspects related to its repression, such as whether it should be criminalised.

After explicitly rejecting a necessary connection between marriage and parentage (by demonstrating that, albeit in the initial Civil Code draft one such connection was actually indispensable, it was abandoned in the version which was approved), the Court once again counterintuitively claims that a marriage which makes reproduction possible,[76] at least theoretically, is more relevant from the societal perspective.[77] The consequence of this would be that same-sex marriage would not be constitutionally imposed.[78]

Bearing in mind the open and plural nature of the society, the Court admits "reasonable divergence" in what the essential elements of the concept of 'marriage' are. As 'marriage' is an open concept, it would be up to the Legislator to make the connection between the law and social reality.[79] Two additional grounds would support this conclusion: the right's holders are "everyone", instead of "men and women",[80] and the fact that the Constitution explicitly defers to the Legislator the definition of its requisites and effects. In a nutshell, this would mean that the Legislator would be competent for modifying the law in accordance with the dominant social conceptions at each moment in time.

Once again, however, the Court limits the conclusion it reaches, by asserting that this would not mean that the concept of 'marriage' would be devoid of any fixed meaning and therefore freely shaped by the Legislator. 'Marriage' is taken to refer to the

> communion of life between two people, celebrated by means of an official act and with legally binding effects, which is free, not subject to any condition or deadline

and which would tend to be everlasting. One such communion of life and mutual assistance would also be at the disposal of same-sex couples who so wish in accordance with the free development of their personality.[81]

Having settled the issue of whether the essential elements of the institute guarantee of 'marriage' were respected, the Court moves on to other issues.

---

[76] The Court goes on to claim that different sex marriage "makes possible the generation of citizens and its maintenance in useful activity within the society – not only as individuals of a specific biological species, but as balanced, useful and responsible citizens". Justice B. Rodrigues, in his dissenting vote, also summons the "laws of Nature".

[77] Disagreeing with this assertion, cf. the concurring votes of Justices C. Sarmento e Castro and J. Cura Mariano.

[78] This is clearly a *non sequitur*. Justice C. Sarmento e Castro, in her concurring opinion, argues that the principle of human dignity, the principle of equality, the right to personal identity and the right to the free development of personality [Art. 1, 13, 26(1), and 36(1) of the Constitution], would result in the constitutional right of same-sex couples to marry.

[79] Miranda (2011), p. 179, refuses that social transformations might impact constitutional interpretation with such a magnitude.

[80] See Art. 36(1) of the Portuguese Constitution.

[81] Justice B. Rodrigues, in his dissenting opinion, considers that it is not possible for a same-sex couple to have a full communion of life. Differently, see Duarte d'Almeida (2008), pp. 70–71.

On the one hand, it argues that allowing same-sex couples to marry would not impinge upon the protection of family as a "fundamental element of society" (Art. 67 of the Constitution). The reason for this is that the Constitution would have adopted an open and pluralistic concept of family, based on the disjunction between the right to constitute a family and the right to marry (Art. 36) and according to the right to the free development of one's personality [Art. 26(1) of the Constitution]. On the other hand, it affects neither the freedom of opposite-sex couples to marry, nor the rights and duties that arise from marriage for those couples. Neither would it amount to a loss of the symbolic value or source of social commitment of (different sex) marriage in itself, for this conjecture would rest on a constitutionally illegitimate premise: sexual orientation [citing Art. 13(2) of the Constitution].

Lastly, the Court rejects the idea that there is a violation of the principle of equality. Even though biologically, sociologically and anthropologically same-sex and different-sex marriage are different realities, there is no arbitrariness. The Legislator would be allowed to assimilate them to maximise its symbolic effect and optimise its anti-discriminatory social outcome. And, in any case, the Legislator would be institutionally better equipped and democratically legitimised to modify the legal order in accordance with the understanding that one constitutional principle has at each point in time.[82]

The dissenters base their divergence on originalist grounds and refuse that the Constitutional Court has legitimacy to modify one such interpretation based on the countermajoritarian character of judicial review, i.e. the idea that the purpose of the constitutional jurisdiction is to protect the constitutional order from "occasional legislative majorities". Only by means of constitutional amendment would it be possible to validly approve same-sex marriage. As none of the seven constitutional amendments modified the constitutionally presupposed concept of 'marriage', the law at stake would be unconstitutional.[83] This is, however, a clear misrepresentation (or misunderstanding) of what the 'countermajoritarian difficulty' is. Bickel's theory is positive, not teleological: constitutional courts do decide against democratically elected majorities and that is the starting point for (the quest for) a theory of judicial review and not a theory in itself.[84]

After the Constitutional Court's decision, the President of the Republic could still politically veto the law. However, the Parliament would be able to overcome it if it confirmed it by a vote by absolute majority. In this case, the President would then be obliged to promulgate the bill[85]—in other words, a veto would only prolong the discussion and would not avoid the entry into force of the law. Even disagreeing

[82] In their concurring opinion, Chief Justice R. Moura Ramos and Justice M. L. Amaral add that they consider that this concrete legislative option (same-sex marriage) is reversible by the democratic Legislator.

[83] Cf. the dissenting votes by Justices J. Borges Soeiro and B. Rodrigues.

[84] Cf. Bickel (1986), pp. 16–23. For its analysis, see Friedman (2002). Among Portuguese scholars, see Reis Novais (2012), pp. 143–145, and Reis Novais (2006), pp. 14–17.

[85] Cf. Art. 136(1) and (2) of the Constitution.

with the law and considering that a middle-ground solution (such as a civil partnership with the full effects of marriage, but with a different name) would better promote consensus within the Portuguese society,[86] the President made clear that he chose to promulgate it only so as to allow the country to focus on more pressing issues, such as the economic and financial crisis it was then facing. The President of the Republic's ambiguous position finds shelter in the Courts' assertion that there is no social consensus about same-sex marriage. In any case, a political stalemate was averted.

12.4.4 Concluding Remarks

Bearing in mind the political and social backdrop against which the Portuguese Constitutional Court decided, it is unequivocal that both decisions are a victory for the civil rights. Indeed, in 2008, still 41.9 % of the Portuguese considered homosexual behaviour to be "always wrong" and only 28.9 % deemed it as "never wrong".[87]

They are not, however, free of criticism. To start with, and in contrast with the Spanish Constitutional Court decision, neither of the two decisions of the Portuguese Constitutional Court has a clear and neat structure that guides the reader and chains the arguments. This results in some logical leaps and gaps in the majority's reasoning, as well as in an abundance of unnecessary side-comments which are not all compatible with one another.

Another aspect that negatively stands out in the Court's decisions, now from a substantive point of view, is the insistence on the idea that different-sex marriage is valued more than any other type of union between two persons (be it different-sex or same-sex civil partnerships, be it same-sex marriage) because it supposedly fosters procreation. Apart from the (religious?) assumptions underlying such statement, the most problematic issue is that the Court is not backed by any statistics that confirm this statement—and even if it were, it is doubtful what part should this data play.[88]

Even so, what impresses the most in both rulings is that the Portuguese Constitutional Court completely disregards the subjective element of the fundamental right to marry. The majority almost focuses the entirety of its analysis on the concept of 'institutional guarantee' and what is, and is not, part of the immutable

[86] See President of the Portuguese Republic (2010), available at http://www.presidencia.pt/?idc=22&idi=41152.

[87] See Brandão and Machado (2012), p. 667.

[88] On the potential catalytic role that Constitutional Courts may assume on fundamental rights issues that do not gather social consensus, more specifically on the principle of equality and same-sex relationships, see de Brito Gião (2012), pp. 71–74.

essential core of the concept of 'marriage'. The notion of 'institutional guarantee'[89] becomes a sort of natural law hologram over which content it is impossible to reach any consensus and which is, for that reason, exposed to the subjectivism-trap, (yet again) to logical leaps and gaps (which happened more than once) and to arguments of authority or from sheer prejudice.[90] At the same time, the majority does not take into account the central standing of the principle of equality, either by resorting to formal arguments to put it aside or by severely narrowing down its scope of application. All in all, the truth is that even if the 'institutional guarantee' objective dimension would be relevant, the starting point should be that of the right to marry and the control of the legitimacy of its limitation[91] in relation to the principles of proportionality and equality.[92]

The President of the Commission which reviewed the Civil Code of 1966 to make it fully compatible with the Portuguese Constitution of 1976 wisely recalled that many of the changes it brought about—such as the equality of spouses or the possibility of divorce—"are nowadays *ius commune*, but were new and maybe even daring in 1977".[93] It will be a good sign if, in a not so distant future, the same will be said of Law No. 9/2010, of 31 May.

References

Ahumada-Ruiz M (2013) Spain. Constitutional Court rejects challenge to same-sex marriage. Public Law 1:428–430

Antunes Varela J (1999) Direito da família. Petrony, Lisbon

Barroso IM (2010) Casamento civil entre pessoas do mesmo sexo: um "direito fundamental" à medida da lei ordinária. Lex familiae 13:57–82

---

[89] Considering that this concept no longer makes sense for the legal science, see Nogueira de Brito (2007), pp. 754–794; see also Múrias (2008), pp. 27S–30S; Pereira Coutinho (2004), pp. 106–108; Reis Novais (2003), pp. 61–62. Disagreeing, and still seeing some conceptual utility in this notion, cf. Sérvulo Correia (2002), pp. 89–98; de Melo Alexandrino (2006), pp. 155–156. In general, with references, see d'Oliveira Martins (2007), pp. 105–202.

[90] It is the case of Santos (2009), pp. 324–341, who considers that it is not possible to achieve a full life-communion in same-sex couples. Leite de Campos (2004), p. 42, considers that "catholic marriage is, in the Portuguese society, the foundation of family". Pulido Adragão (2006), pp. 530 and 533, claims this issue is a "civilisational matter" and compares the constitutional relevance of homosexuality to that of philately or fishing. Antunes Varela (1999), p. 181, classifies it as a "morbid" perversion and a "sexual aberration".

[91] Medeiros (2010), p. 819, somewhat ambiguously states that "the principles of human dignity, the prohibition of discrimination according to sexual orientation, the right to personal integrity, and the right to the development of the personality *impede* that a gay person *may be prevented from* living in a civil union with a same-sex partner, or punished for that reason" (italics added).

[92] With a rights-based approach, see Raposo (2009), pp. 177–184; Moreira (2008), pp. 36–52; Múrias (2008), pp. 44S–52S.

[93] See de Magalhães Collaço (2004), p. 40.

Bazán J-L (2009) Report on the impact of Spanish same-sex marriage act in the national law. http://www.academia.edu/1550436/Report_on_the_Impact_of_the_Spanish_Same-Sex_Marriage_Act_in_National_Law
Bickel AM (1986) The least dangerous branch. The Supreme Court at the bar of politics, 2nd edn. Yale University Press, New Haven
Bin R (2000) La famiglia: alla radice di un ossimoro. Studium Iuris 1067–1071
Bin R et al (eds) (2010) La società naturale e i suoi nemici. Sul paradigma eterosessuale del matrimonio. Giappichelli, Torino
Biondi F (2013) Famiglia e matrimonio. Quale modello costituzionale. http://www.gruppodipisa.it/wp-content/uploads/2013/05/BIONDI.pdf
Brandão AM, Machado T (2012) How equal is equality? Discussions about same-sex marriage in Portugal. Sexualities 15:662–678
Crivelli E (2012) La tutela dell'orientamento sessuale nella giurisprudenza interna ed europea. Edizioni scientifiche italiane Napoli, pp 35–71
d'Oliveira Martins M (2007) Contributo para a compreensão da figura das garantias institucionais. Almedina, Coimbra
Danisi C (2010) La Corte di Strasburgo e matrimoni omosessuali: vita familiare e difesa dell'unione tradizionale. Quaderni costituzionali 870–873
de Brito Gião R (2012) New governance mechanisms and international human rights law: moratoriums in law and practice. Unpublished (on file with author)
de Magalhães Collaço I (2004) A Reforma de 1977 do Código Civil de 1966. Um olhar vinte e cinco anos depois. In: AA VV (ed) Comemorações dos 35 anos do Código Civil e dos 25 Anos da Reforma de 1977, I. Coimbra editora, Coimbra
de Melo Alexandrino J (2006) A estruturação do sistema de direitos, liberdades e garantias na Constituição portuguesa, II. Coimbra editora, Coimbra
de Oliveira Ascensão J (2011) O casamento de pessoas do mesmo sexo. Revista da ordem dos advogados 71/II:391–411
Consejo General del Poder Judicial (2005) Estudio sobre la reforma del código civil en materia de matrimonio entre personas del mismo sexo
Díez-Picazo LM (2007) En torno al matrimonio entre personas del mismo sexo. http://www.jus.unitn.it/cardozo/Review/2007/picazo.pdf
Duarte d'Almeida L (2008) Casamento civil e "sexo diferente". Sobre a inconstitucionalidade das normas expressas pelos artigos 1577.° e 1628.°, alínea e), do Código civil. In: Pamplona Côrte-Real C et al (eds) O casamento entre pessoas do mesmo sexo. Almedina, Coimbra, pp 55–79
Duarte Pinheiro J (2004) O núcleo intangível da comunhão conjugal. Os deveres conjugais sexuais. Almedina, Coimbra
Duarte Pinheiro J (2008) O ensino do direito da família contemporâneo. AAFDL, Lisbon
Duarte Pinheiro J (2010) O direito da família contemporâneo, 3rd edn. AAFDL, Lisbon
Friedman B (2002) The birth of an academic obsession: The history of the countermajoritarian difficulty, part five. Yale Law J 112:153–259
Gomes Canotilho JJ, Moreira V (2007) Constituição da república portuguesa anotada, I. Coimbra editora, Coimbra
González Beilfuss C (2012) All or nothing: the dilemma of Southern jurisdictions. In: Boele-Woelki K, Fuchs A (eds) Legal recognition of same-sex relationships in Europe: national, cross-border and European perspectives. Intersentia, Cambridge
Joseph S, Schulz J, Castan M (2005) The International Covenant on civil and political rights: cases materials and commentary. Oxford University Press, New York
Leite de Campos D (2004) Eu-tu: o amor e a família (e a comunidade) (eu-tu-eles). In: AA VV (ed) Comemorações dos 35 anos do Código Civil e dos 25 Anos da Reforma de 1977, I. Coimbra editora, Coimbra
Machado J (2010) A (in)definição do casamento no Estado constitucional. In: de Oliveira G et al (eds) Família, consciência, secularismo e religião. Coimbra editora, Coimbra

Martín Sánchez M (2010) El derecho constitucional al matrimonio homosexual en España. Revista iberoamericana de derecho procesal constitucional 13:241–275
Martins R (2008) Same-sex partnerships in Portugal. From *de facto* to *de jure*? Utrecht Law Rev 4:194–211
Medeiros R (2010) Artigo 36.°. In: Miranda J, Medeiros R (eds) Constituição portuguesa anotada, I, 2nd edn. Coimbra editora, Coimbra, pp 802–843
Miranda J (2010) O Tribunal Constitucional em 2009. O direito 142/II:405–460
Miranda J (2011) O Tribunal Constitucional em 2010. O direito 143/I:151–218
Moreira I (2008) Da inconstitucionalidade das normas resultantes da leitura conjugada do artigo 1577.° do Código civil e da alínea e) do artigo 1628.° do mesmo código, nos termos das quais duas pessoas do mesmo sexo não podem contrair casamento e, se o fizerem, é o mesmo tipo por inexistente. In: Pamplona Côrte-Real C et al (eds) O casamento entre pessoas do mesmo sexo. Almedina, Coimbra, pp 35–54
Múrias P (2008) Um símbolo como bem juridicamente protegido. Sobre o casamento entre pessoas do mesmo sexo. In: Múrias P et al (eds) Casamento entre pessoas do mesmo sexo. Sim ou não? Entrelinhas, Lisboa, pp 9s–55s
Ninatti S (2010) Adjusting differences and accommodating competences: family matters in the European Union, Jean Monnet Working Paper 06/10. http://centers.law.nyu.edu/jeanmonnet/papers/10/100601.pdf
Nogueira de Brito M (2007) A justificação da propriedade privada numa democracia constitucional. Almedina, Coimbra
Nogueira de Brito M (2008) Casamento civil e dignidade dos homossexuais. In: Nogueira de Brito M et al (eds) Casamento entre pessoas do mesmo sexo. Sim ou não? Entrelinhas, Lisboa, pp 9n–59n
Paladini L (2011) Le coppie dello stesso sesso tra la sentenza della Corte costituzionale n. 138 del 14 aprile 2010 e la pronuncia della Corte europea dei diritti dell'uomo del 24 giugno 2010 nel caso Schalk and Kopf v. Austria. Diritto Pubblico Comparato ed Europeo 137–151
Pamplona Côrte-Real C (2008) Da inconstitucionalidade do Código civil – artigos 1577.°, 1628.°, alínea e), e disposições conexas – ao vedar o acesso ao instituto do casamento a casais do mesmo sexo. In: Pamplona Côrte-Real C et al (eds) O casamento entre pessoas do mesmo sexo. Almedina, Coimbra, pp 11–33
Pereira Coelho F, de Oliveira G (2008) Direito da família, I, 4th edn. Coimbra editora, Coimbra
Pereira Coutinho LP (2004) As faculdades normativas universitárias no quadro do direito fundamental à autonomia universitária. Almedina, Coimbra
Pezzini B, Lorenzetti A (2011) (eds) Unioni e matrimoni same-sex dopo la sentenza 138 del 2010: quali prospettive? Jovene editore, Napoli
Platero R (2007) Love and the state: gay marriage in Spain. Feminist Legal Stud 15:329–340
President of the Portuguese Republic (2010) Declaração do Presidente da República sobre o diploma da Assembleia da República que permite o casamento entre pessoas do mesmo sexo
Pugiotto A (2010) Una lettura non reticente della sent. n. 138/2010: il monopolio eterosessuale del matrimonio. www.forumcostituzionale.it
Pulido Adragão P (2006) Casamento: entre pessoas do mesmo sexo? Pressupostos fundamentais da questão. In: Miranda J (ed) Estudos em homenagem ao Professor Doutor Marcello Caetano no centenário do seu nascimento, II. Faculdade de Direito da Universidade de Lisboa, Lisbon, pp 527–533
Raposo VL (2009) Crónica de um casamento anunciado (O casamento entre pessoas do mesmo sexo). Revista do ministério público 120:157–190
Reis Novais J (2003) As restrições aos direitos fundamentais não expressamente autorizadas pela Constituição. Coimbra editora, Coimbra
Reis Novais J (2006) Direitos fundamentais: Trunfos contra a maioria. Coimbra editora, Coimbra
Reis Novais J (2012) Direitos fundamentais e justiça constitucional em Estado de direito democrático. Coimbra editora, Coimbra

Rodríguez Ruiz B (2011) Matrimonio, género y familia en la Constitución española: Transcendiendo la familia nuclear. Revista española de derecho constitucional 91:69–102

Romboli R (2010), Il diritto "consentito" al matrimonio ed il diritto "garantito" alle coppie omosessuali in una pronuncia in cui la Corte dice "troppo" e "troppo poco". Giurisprudenza costituzionale 1629–1642

Romboli R (2012) Il matrimonio tra persone dello stesso sesso ed il diritto ad una vita familiare per le coppie omosessuali. In: D'Elia G, Tiberi G, Viviani Schlein MP (eds) Scritti in memoria di Alessandra Concaro. Giuffrè, Milano

Santos D (2009) Mudam-se os tempos, mudam-se os casamentos? O casamento entre pessoas do mesmo sexo e o direito português. Coimbra editora, Coimbra

Santos AC (2013) Are we there yet? Queer sexual encounters, legal recognition and homonormativity. J Gender Stud 22:54–64

Sérvulo Correia JM (2002) Direitos fundamentais. AAFDL, Lisboa

Urías Martínez J (2008) Artículo 32: El régimen constitucional del matrimonio. In: Casas Baamonde ME, Rodríguez-Piñero, Bravo-Ferrer M (dir.) (eds) Comentarios a la Constitución española. XXX aniversario. Wolters Kluwer, Madrid

Veronesi P (2008) Costituzione, "strane famiglie" e "nuovi matrimoni". Quaderni costituzionali 577–602

Violante T (2012) *Judicial dialogue* e casamento entre pessoas do mesmo sexo. In: AA VV (eds) 35.° aniversário da Constituição de 1976, II. Coimbra editora, Coimbra, pp 211–238

Violini L (2007) Il riconoscimento delle coppie di fatto: praeter o contra constitutionem? Quaderni costituzionali 392–395

Chapter 13
The Legal Situation of Same-Sex Couples in Greece and Cyprus

Spyridon Drosos and Aristoteles Constantinides

Abstract This chapter explores in depth the question of the legal recognition of same-sex couples in Greece and Cyprus. The chapter begins by presenting and critically examining the (narrow reading of) existing law in both countries, and concludes that, according to the dominant view, same-sex couples are excluded from both civil marriage and civil unions. The picture is further complemented by an analysis of the most consequential judicial rulings, both already delivered and pending. As evidenced through the discussed case-law and reports of independent authorities, there is room for optimism in these two countries regarding the future developments in the legal protection of same-sex couples. Interestingly, any change in the law in both countries will bear the stamp of Strasbourg and Brussels.

13.1 Introduction

The legal situation of same-sex couples in Greece and in Cyprus[1] is discussed in parallel in this chapter because the two countries share very close ties and a number of common (ethnic and other) characteristics: the Greek language, the Greek

[1] Cyprus remains *de facto* divided since the Turkish invasion of 1974. The chapter will not discuss the situation in the Turkish-occupied northern part of Cyprus, which illegally proclaimed independence in 1983 as the 'Turkish Republic of Northern Cyprus' (TRNC) and is not recognized by any state other than Turkey. The Republic of Cyprus retains sovereignty but does not exercise effective control over that part (36.2 %) of the island, which has also been exempted from the application of the EU *acquis* when Cyprus joined the EU in 2004. UN-sponsored talks to reunite the island have been fruitless. There is not much to report on same-sex marriage in the TRNC,

S. Drosos (✉)
Department of Law, European University Institute, Florence, Italy
e-mail: spyridon.drosos@eui.eu

A. Constantinides
Department of Law, University of Cyprus, Nicosia, Cyprus
e-mail: ariscons@ucy.ac.cy

D. Gallo et al. (eds.), *Same-Sex Couples before National, Supranational and International Jurisdictions*, DOI 10.1007/978-3-642-35434-2_13,

Orthodox religion espoused by the large majority of the population, popular culture, traditions etc. What is more, Greece and Cyprus have been quite reluctant to introduce same-sex marriage for similar reasons. Both are Member States of the European Union (Greece since 1981, the Republic of Cyprus since 2004) and parties to the European Convention on Human Rights (further referred to as ECHR) and all major instruments of international human rights law.[2]

Political and social developments in Greece are extensively covered in Cyprus on a daily basis and exert influence on developments in the island although there are many considerable differences in various aspects of public life. Thousands of Cypriots study or work and live in Greece and thousands of Greeks work and live in Cyprus. The Greek Orthodox Church is quite influential in both countries. Art. 3 (1) of the Greek Constitution states that "[t]he prevailing religion in Greece is that of the Eastern Orthodox Church of Christ". In Cyprus, Church reaction was the main reason why (male) homosexuality was only decriminalized as late as 1998, 5 years after the Strasbourg Court ruled in *Modinos v. Cyprus* that the relevant legislation was in violation of the right to private life[3] (there was no provision in the law addressing female homosexuality).

This background is reflected in public opinion polls, which portray a similar societal attitude towards homosexuality and same-sex marriage in both countries. Thus, in the 2006 Eurobarometer, which examined attitudes toward same-sex marriage in each EU Member State, the findings for Greece and Cyprus were almost identical. Forty-four percent of EU citizens thought that such marriages should be allowed throughout Europe; the figure was 15 % in Greece and 14 % in Cyprus (Netherlands scored the highest with 82 % and Romania the lowest with 11 %). With regard to adoption by same-sex couples, the level of acceptance decreased in all Member States (32 %) as well as in Greece (11 %) and Cyprus (10 %) (Netherlands again scored highest with 69 %, while Poland and Malta polled the lowest with 7 %).[4] The situation has certainly changed since 2006 for a variety of reasons but it is common ground that both Greece and Cyprus are among the conservative countries in Europe with regard to same-sex couples and the legal recognition of their rights. This is indeed reflected in the analysis that follows.

---

since the criminal ban on (male) homosexuality (a legacy of the British colonial era) still holds at the time of writing and has actually been enforced in recent years, even though the authorities have reportedly promised to lift the ban.

[2] For an overview of the political structure and the legal framework for the protection of human rights in both countries see UN Doc. HRI/CORE/1/Add.121 of 7th October 2002 (Greece) and UN Doc. HRI/CORE/CYP/2011 of 2 September 2011 (Cyprus).

[3] N. 15050/89, judgment of 22nd April 1993.

[4] European Commission, 'Eurobarometer 66: Public Opinion in the European Union' (2006), pp. 43–46, http://ec.europa.eu/public_opinion/archives/eb/eb66/eb66_en.pdf.

13.2 Legal Framework

13.2.1 Greece

The Greek Constitution protects family and marriage as two distinct institutions. Art. 21(1) does not leave any room for any competing interpretations as its clear wording provides that

> [f]amily, being the cornerstone of the preservation and advancement of the Nation, as well as marriage, motherhood and childhood, shall be under the protection of the State.

Several variations of family life, regardless of their grounding in a marriage, civil union or free union, come within the scope of the provision. There is, however, sharper disagreement among Greek scholars on the correct interpretation of the term "marriage". On the one hand, the constitutional term "marriage" is taken to refer to the permanent and freely established partnership of two persons of the opposite sex that is recognized by law and based on the equality of spouses.[5] This reading of the term identifies the difference in sex as a constitutive element of the institution of marriage.

Taking this opinion a step further, the ordinary Legislator is prevented by the Constitution from extending marriage to same-sex couples as that would interfere with the constitutional meaning ascribed to this institution. The Legislator, too, is not under any positive obligation to provide for alternative institutions to marriage for same-sex couples. At the other end of this spectrum lies the claim that the core immutable elements of marriage are the (official) form of celebration and the enhanced treatment *vis-à-vis* free unions.[6] According to this opinion, the term marriage should be in agreement with other ever-evolving constitutional principles, like the principles of equality and non-discrimination. To this regard, Art. 4 of Constitution provides that: "1. [a]ll Greeks are equal before the law; 2. Greek men and women have equal rights and equal obligations". On these two constitutional provisions rests the prohibition of discrimination in account of sex. Excluding same-sex couples from the institution of marriage and, at once, not affording them any legal recognition would be at odds with the above principle.

Turning to ordinary legislation, the original provisions of the IV Book (Family Law Book) of the Greek Civil Code (further referred to as GCC) envisioned a family model which has been dismissed as conservative even by the standards of the post World War II era of its drafting (the Code entered into force in 1946).[7] Following the enactment of a new progressive Constitution in 1975 and pursuant to shift in the moral values and social attitudes of the Greek people, the IV Book of the

---

[5] Dagtoglou (2005), para. 502.

[6] Papadopoulou (2008), pp. 418–422.

[7] Fessas (2011), p. 195.

GCC has undergone a series of amendments,[8] most recently by virtue of Law No. 3719/2008 which, amongst else, introduced into the domestic legal order the institution of the civil union.

Art. 1350–1360 GCC lay down the requisites of marriage, distinguishing between impediments and positive conditions. The difference of the sex of the spouses is not listed under either category of conditions. Notably, the chosen diction of Art. 1350, providing that "[t]he agreement of the future spouses is required for the celebration of marriage", does not shed light on the sex-difference condition as the Greek word for "future spouses" (= *μελλόνυμφοι*) is sex-neutral.

The dominant view in Greek scholarship maintains that the not sex-specific word "future spouses" can only refer to a different-sex couple. This opinion rests on the teleological interpretation that the draftsman of the GCC could not have anything else in his mind at that time,[9] certainly not the pressing need for the protection of same-sex relationships, as well as on the systematic interpretation of the IV Book of the GCC. Until the decisions 114 and 115/2008 of the Rhodes three-member Court of first instance, no other domestic court had ever dealt with the interpretation of this term.

The non-compliance with the statutorily provided requisites can lead to a non-existent, void, or voidable marriage. According to the dominant view, the violation of the sex-difference condition results in an *ipso iure* non-existent marriage, which does not produce any legal effects.[10] Although no judicial ruling is required to ascertain the non-existence of a marriage, any one with a legal interest is entitled to seek a declaratory court judgment.

In a nutshell, the vast majority of Greek theoreticians would concur that the GCC, in its present form, does not leave any room for same-sex marriages. A minority view has argued that the amendments of the family law provisions of the Civil Code have done away with the difference in sex as a fundamental component of spousal relations, and therefore (and as there is no express prohibition) marriage is already available to same-sex couples.[11]

Despite the inertia of the Legislator to clarify the sex-difference condition in the institution of the civil marriage, there has been as of recently intense mobility with regard to alternative legal institutions of partnership. In specific, in 2004, following

---

[8] The Constitution of Greece has been amended three times since its enactment, in 1986, 2001 and, most recently, 2008. The IV Book received a major overhaul with Laws No. 1250/1982 and No. 1329/1983 which introduced much-needed amendments, amongst which were the possibility to celebrate one's marriage before the mayor (where only a religious ceremony was previously available); the equality of man and woman in their rights and duties as parents and spouses; the introduction of divorce by consent; the equal legal treatment of children born in and outside wedlock. Law No. 2447/1996 introduced further amendments in matters of adoption and legal guardianship, and Law No. 3089/2002 regulated in detail filiation in the context of medically assisted reproduction.

[9] Papachristou (2005), p. 37.

[10] *Ibidem*, p. 55.

[11] Vidalis (1996), pp. 73–74.

an invitation submitted from the Lesbian and Gay Community of Greece (*ΟΛΚ*), the National Commission for Human Rights opined that rights ought to be extended to same-sex couples. In the same Opinion the Commission urged the Ministry of Justice to put together a working group with the mandate to explore the legal recognition of same-sex partnerships and lift discrimination against same-sex couples in the fields of succession, taxation, insurance, health, pensions, welfare and labour.[12] In 2006, the Ministry of Justice initiated a discussion on a cohabitation pact that would include same-sex couples. However, in 2008, the Minister of Justice introduced in the Parliament a bill on the cohabitation pact, which left same-sex couples outside of its scope. The introductory report to the bill neither made any reference to same-sex couples nor did it attempt to justify their exclusion from the scope of the proposed institution, but only summarily stated that "[t]he present bill exclusively refers to the free union of persons of the opposite sex".[13] In the Parliament, the Minister of Justice explained that the bill reflected "the social acceptance of certain principles and values" and that, given the lack of support from the society, "we should not proceed with the establishment of a pact for same-sex couples".[14]

The bill was passed on 17th November 2008. With regard to the cohabitation pact, Law No. 3719/2008 requires that the adult opposite-sex partners wishing to enter into a cohabitation pact sign the pertinent notarial deed before filing a copy thereof with the competent registry.[15] The pact confers a set of rights on the cohabitants. In specific, they are free to regulate the ownership of the property acquired during cohabitation; in the absence of an agreement to the contrary, the party who has contributed to the increase of the other party's property is entitled to seek recovery of that contribution.[16] A claim to maintenance can be agreed in the case of termination of the cohabitation, on the condition that the party seeking maintenance lacks the ability of self-support; however, this maintenance may not be claimed from the heirs of a deceased cohabitant.[17] Regarding children born in cohabitation, the same paternity presumption rule applies as to children born in wedlock. The nullity or annulment of the pact does not influence the parentage of the offspring.[18] Finally, the pact establishes rules of intestate succession, whereby the surviving party is entitled to one-sixth or one-third or the whole of the

[12] National Commission for Human Rights, *Annual Report 2004* [in Greek], pp. 183–210, available at: http://www.nchr.gr/category.php?category_id=103.

[13] Introductory report to the bill on the amendments for the family, the child, society and other provisions (09 October 2008).

[14] Fessas (2011), note 77.

[15] Law 3719/2008, Art. 1. For a lengthy discussion of the new institution, see Papachristou et al. (2009).

[16] Law No. 3719/2008, Art. 6.

[17] *Ibidem*, Art. 7.

[18] *Ibidem*, Art. 8.

decedent's estate, depending on the surviving relatives.[19] Regrettably, same-sex couples have been excluded from the exercise of all the foregoing rights. The Grand Chamber of the Strasbourg Court is expected to decide, by the end of 2013, an application complaining that the law on the cohabitation of opposite-sex couples has breached the right of same-sex couples to respect for their private life and the principle of non-discrimination.[20]

Despite the increasing protection afforded to opposite-sex couples in free unions, same-sex couples in alike living arrangements find themselves, once again, beyond the scope of protection. For instance, in awarding monetary compensation to the surviving party of a free union for the emotional pain suffered from the wrongful death of the other party, the Court of Cassation described free union in limiting terms as "the cohabitation outside marriage between a man and a woman".[21] In similar vein, the protection afforded through the rules on domestic violence are inapplicable insofar the relevant Law 3500/2006, in Art. 1, employs gendered terms when delimiting the subjective scope of application which extends to "the man's [female] permanent partner or the woman's [male] permanent partner ... on the condition they cohabit" [= *μόνιμη συτροφος του άντρα, μόνιμος συτροφος της γυναίκας*].

The above *tour d'horizon* shows beyond doubt that same-sex couples are not meaningfully recognized in the eyes of the Greek Legislator, while at once suffering monetary and non-material damages from this comprehensive discrimination.

13.2.2 Cyprus

Cyprus is generally considered as having a comprehensive legal framework for safeguarding equality and combating discrimination.[22] The 1960 Constitution is largely modeled on the ECHR and in some instances it even expands upon the rights and liberties enshrined in the Convention. Fundamental rights and freedoms are generally safeguarded to all persons without differentiating between citizens and non-citizens. Art. 28 of the Constitution on equality and non-discrimination does not specifically mention sexual orientation but this should be deemed to fall within the open-ended wording ("or on any other grounds") of the provision. Sexual orientation is explicitly included among the prohibited grounds of direct or indirect discrimination in Art. 6 of Law No. 42(I)/2004, which implemented the EU Racial

---

[19] *Ibidem*, Art. 11.

[20] *Vallianatos and Mylonas v. Greece* and *C.S. and Others v. Greece*, n. 29381/09 and 32684/09 (pending before the Grand Chamber); see Statement of Facts published by the Court on 8th February 2011.

[21] Court of Cassation, judgment 434/2005, *EllDni* 2005, p. 1060.

[22] See the European Committee against Racism and Intolerance (ECRI) Report on Cyprus, CRI (2011)20, p. 7 (adopted on 23rd March 2011 and published on 30th May 2011). For a critical account see: Trimikliniotis and Demetriou (2008a).

Equality Directive 2000/43/EC. Significantly, the Cyprus Constitution was amended in 2006 to give supremacy to EU laws. Other legal instruments also provide protection against discrimination since Cyprus is a party to all major universal human rights instruments and has transposed all relevant EU directives. However, this legal framework co-exists with a post-colonial legacy of illiberal laws, some of which are still in force.[23]

Art. 22 of the Constitution guarantees the right to marry and to found a family for all persons of marriageable age but refers to ordinary legislation for detailed regulation. Section 3 of the Marriage Law 104(I)/2003 defines marriage explicitly as a union between a man and a woman.[24]

In terms of institutions, the Office of the Commissioner for Administration (Ombudsman) was appointed as the national equality body in 2004. Under Law No. 42(I)/2004, two separate authorities were set up within the Ombudsman's office: the 'Equality Authority' and the 'Anti-discrimination Body', together comprising the Cyprus Equality Body under the Ombudsman. The Ombudsman, in her capacity as 'Anti-discrimination Body',[25] investigates complaints of maladministration and discrimination from public bodies towards individuals. Under certain conditions specified in the law, the Ombudsman is vested with the power to issue Orders or impose fines; however, the Ombudsman does not have the power to refer the non-complying party to court. In practice, the Ombudsman has rarely, if at all, made use of the powers to issue orders and impose fines when acting as Authority against Racism and Discrimination. Resort was almost invariably made to recommending measures aimed at the cessation of the discriminatory behavior or practice.

13.3 Case-Law

13.3.1 Greece

13.3.1.1 The Meaning of 'Marriage' Under the Greek Civil Code

In the meantime, while the Parliament was debating a cohabitation pact that would exclude same-sex couples, the mayor of the Dodecanese island of Tilos officiated on 3rd July 2008 the first same-sex wedding ceremonies ever to have been performed on Greek soil,[26] between two gay men and two gay women. The

[23] Trimikliniotis and Demetriou (2008b), p. 17, note 54.

[24] For an overview of the Marriage Law see Emilianides (2011), pp. 219–221.

[25] Both the incumbent holder of the position (Ms Eliza Savvidou, serving since March 2010) and her predecessor (Ms Eliana Nicolaou, who served from 1999–2010) are women.

[26] A qualification could be entered here, if one is to subscribe to late historian John Boswell's thesis that a precedent to contemporary same-sex marriages is the rite of *adelphopoiesis* as

prospective officiation had been leaked to the national press, and the Court of Cassation Prosecutor instructed prosecutors to take immediate action against any mayor that would accept declarations for the celebration of marriage by persons of the same sex, on grounds of a committed act of misconduct.[27] Despite the threatened action, the mayor of Tilos proceeded to perform the two marriages, and the prosecutor at the Rhodes Court of first instance reacted by bringing two actions against each of the couples and the mayor, seeking before the competent court the judicial declaration of the marriages as non-existent.

Decisions 114 and 115/2008 of the Rhodes three-member Court of first instance (Court hereinafter) are the first judgments by a Greek court to address same-sex marriage domestically.[28] Before delving into the substance of the dispute, the Court addressed two preliminary objections raised by the defendants who argued that the action had been brought inadmissibly against the defendant mayor and that the prosecutor had no legal standing to sue. As these objections exceed the scope of the present survey, suffice it is to say that the Court pronounced the action inadmissible with regard to the mayor. The Court further found that the prosecutor both enjoyed discretionary power to seek the declaration of the marriage as non-existent,[29] in light of the increased interest of the State in family affairs, and could represent himself in the audience without counsel.

The substantive point of the dispute asked whether the ambiguous, sex-neutral term “future spouses” covered same-sex spouses, too (Art. 1350 GCC). Essentially, the Court was called on to decide whether same-sex marriage was allowed in the Greek legal order, given that the difference of sex was not amongst the positive conditions of marriage, as explicitly enumerated in the Greek Civil Code.

In the Court’s opinion, the Civil Code cannot be readily relied on as the issue of same-sex marriage had not been anticipated by the draftsman back in the 1950s. It should be noted as an aside that the draftsman of the Draft Civil Code had actually considered same-sex marriages when suggesting that, in cases of fraud as to the sex of one of the spouses, the marriage between two persons of the same sex should be declared as non-existent.[30] Then, to no avail, the Court sought guidance in international human rights documents such as the ECHR (Art. 12) and the ICCPR) (Art. 23). However, both these documents neither prohibit nor require same-sex marriage, and they leave the determination of the marriage conditions to the

celebrated in Eastern Orthodoxy during the late Byzantine period. See Boswell (1994). For an eloquent critique of this thesis (aimed at a lay audience, and pointing out several fallacies in Boswell’s argumentation), see Mendelsohn (2009), pp. 289–321.

[27] See Instruction 5/2008 by the Court of Cassation Prosecutor, *EfAD* 2008, pp. 1073–1074.

[28] Judgment 114/2008, *ChrID* 2009, p. 617; Judgment 115/2009, *EfAD* 2009, p. 690.

[29] According to Article 608 para. 2 of the Code of Civil Procedure: “[an] action [on the existence, non-existence or nullity of marriage] by the prosecutor or any other interested person is to be brought against both spouses and, if one of them is deceased, against his decedents; otherwise it is denied as inadmissible”.

[30] Balis (1962), p. 42.

discretion of the parties.[31] Without finding any foothold on contemporary legal instruments, the Court unexpectedly turned to the definition of marriage provided by the Roman jurist Modestinus around 250 CE, according to which marriage is "the union of male and female and the sharing of life together, involving both divine and human law".[32] The Court explained why it resorted to this bygone point of reference by arguing that this is the departing point of analysis taken by most Greek scholars in family law. Undoubtedly, this is an outdated definition and the Court should have fleshed out in more detail how this definition bodes with, or why it should even be relevant, for the Greek legal order.

It is to a certain extent befuddling that the Court uncritically adopted a definition that actually refers to divine law, as if the 1982 amendment of the IV Book (of the GCC) had not once and for all removed the metaphysical or religious aspects from the institution of civil marriage. Then, the Court performed a leap in its reasoning and arrived all too hastily at the conclusion that, according to the standing Greek laws, the difference in the sex of the spouses-to-be is an implicit condition for the existence of the marriage. A violation of that condition renders the marriage non-existent.

To reinforce the soundness of its verdict, the Court mentioned that the ordinary Legislator, as recently as in 2008, decided purposely to confer the right of entry into civil unions only to opposite-sex couples:

> a fact that, regardless of the counterargument that one could raise, represents the expressed will of the internal legal order, which is taken to reflect the moral and social values and traditions of the Greek people.

There are two claims hidden in the court's reasoning. First, as the Court reminds, the Greek Legislator, when very recently called upon to regulate same-sex partnerships, chose to explicitly exclude those couples from the newly minted institution of civil union. In this clearly stated normative preference of the Legislator, the Court reads an *a fortiori* exclusion from the traditional institution of civil marriage; if the Legislator has decided to shut same-sex couples out of the cohabitation pact, then the same should hold true about the more comprehensive institution of civil marriage. This line of reasoning is unpersuasive and it could easily be reconstructed as an argument in favour of sex-neutral civil marriage. In specific, according to the reverse form of the Court's argument, while the ordinary Legislator has chosen, for the time being, to place an explicit sex-difference condition for the access to the institution of civil-union, the Legislator never did the same with regard to civil marriage, not even during the 2008 amendment of the IV Book of the GCC.

[31] Art. 12 ECHR reads: "[m]en and women of marriageable age have the right to marry and to found a family, according to the national laws governing the exercise of this right", and Art. 23 ICCPR provides that "[t]he right of men and women of marriageable age to marry and to found a family shall be recognized". See the chapters by Pustorino on ECHR and Paladini on ICCPR in this volume.

[32] Translated from "nuptiae sunt coniunctio maris et feminae et consortium omnis vitae, divini et humani iuris communicatio".

A contrario, from the ongoing silence of the ordinary Legislator on civil marriage, notwithstanding the arisen opportunities for amendment and clarification, one could infer that the Civil Code indeed does not prescribe the difference in the sex of the spouses as a condition of marriage.

Second, the Court seems to imply that the civil union institution, even if discriminatory, only reflects the mores and shared attitudes of the majority of Greek people. On this point, the European Court of Human Rights has unconditionally held that references to traditions, general assumptions or prevailing social attitudes in a particular country are insufficient justification for a difference in treatment on grounds of sex.[33] This particular ruling bodes well with the gay-rights strategy to reframe the exclusion of same-sex couples from the institution of marriage as sex discrimination as, in this form, the grievance would potentially mandate a higher degree of judicial scrutiny (at least in jurisdictions with no protection against discrimination on grounds of sexual orientation but with laws against sex-discrimination).[34]

It should be reminded that the Greek judicial system is primarily one of incidental and diffuse review of the constitutionality of the laws. Regardless of one's agreement or disagreement with the conclusion reached on the substance of the case, it is regrettable that the Court failed to seriously review the constitutionality objections that the applicants (and many legal scholars) had raised.[35] The Court held that the constitutional principle of equality does not mandate the same legal treatment of same- and opposite-sex couples as, in its judgment, these are two dissimilar categories; therefore, different treatment is allowed. This is a very narrowly constructed understanding of equality. The Court also found that sexual freedom, namely a person's right to conduct their sexual life in whichever way they please, does not include a claim to have those freely chosen relationships protected.

An unexpectedly welcome part of the judgment, albeit mostly just sugar-coating the pill, is the concluding *obiter dictum* where the court emphasizes that the domestic legislation is constantly progressing, all the more through its interaction with EU and other Member States' laws (naming countries where cohabitation pacts are in place), to reflect the changing social attitudes and contemporary needs. On this note, the Court suggests that these ambiguities in the Greek legal order about the rights of same-sex couples ought to be resolved through legislative amendments.

[33] *Konstantin Markin v. Russia*, n. 30078/06, judgment of 22nd March 2012, para. 127.

[34] Koppelman describes this strategy of emphasizing the sex discrimination defects of anti-gay laws not as the only meaningful path but as one arrow in the quiver. See Koppelman (1994); Koppelman (2002), pp. 53–70; Green (2011).

[35] Papadopoulou (2008), pp. 418–422.

13.3.1.2 The Exclusion of Same-Sex Couples from Civil Unions Before the Strasbourg Court

The question on the alleged unlawful discrimination against same-sex couples in Greece has recently moved beyond the national borders and a case is at the moment of writing pending before the Grand Chamber of the Strasbourg Court. In specific, on 6th May 2009, four same-sex couples, residents in Athens, relying on Art. 8 ECHR, taken alone and in conjunction with Art. 14, lodged a complaint before the European Court of Human Rights (further referred to as ECtHR) claiming that the Law No. 3719/2008, which limits civil unions exclusively to adults of the opposite sex, breaches their right to respect for their private life and the principle of non-discrimination.[36] On 11th September 2012, the Chamber relinquished jurisdiction in favour of the Grand Chamber,[37] and the hearings were held on 16th January 2013. This much-awaited decision is expected by the end of 2013.

Since the case is still pending at the time of writing, the section here will look closer at the arguments of the applicants and of the respondent government, as delivered at the oral hearings.

A first issue that was raised before the Grand Chamber concerned the admissibility of the application in view of the applicant's apparent failure to exhaust any domestic remedies.[38] The Government brought forward the fact that the four couples had not pursued any legal action in Greece. They had thus deprived the authorities of the possibility to deal internally with the complaint, before seeking recourse to an international tribunal like the ECtHR. The government proceeded to enumerate a series of national remedies that the applicant could have pursued to seek damages, and asked the Court to declare the case inadmissible in line with Art. 35(1) ECHR.[39]

In response, the applicants relied on the Court's well-established case-law that the rule of exhaustion of domestic remedies requires that domestic remedies be both available and effective; otherwise, the applicants are exempt from this obligation.[40] In light of the absence of a constitutional review remedy in the Greek legal order,

---

[36] *Vallianatos and Mylonas v. Greece* and *C.S. and Others v. Greece.*

[37] Jurisdiction was relinquished in accordance to Art. 30 ECHR, which provides that "[w]here a case pending before a Chamber raises a serious question affecting the interpretation of the Convention or the protocols thereto, or where the resolution of a question before the Chamber might have a result inconsistent with a judgment previously delivered by the Court, the Chamber may, at any time before it has rendered its judgment, relinquish jurisdiction in favour of the Grand Chamber, unless one of the parties to the case objects".

[38] See also Statement of Facts cited earlier, Question 1 and Question 3.

[39] Art. 35, para. 1, on admissibility criteria "The Court may only deal with the matter after all domestic remedies have been exhausted, according to the generally recognized rules of international law, and within a period of six months from the date on which the final decision was taken".

[40] See in particular *Burden and Burden v. UK*, n. 13378/05, judgment of 12th December 2006. For an up-to-date collection of the Court's case-law on the rule of exhaustion of domestic remedies see in particular Jacobs et al. (2010).

the applicants underlined that they could not seek an *in abstracto* judicial review of the impugned legislation. In addition, the applicants argued that there is no available and effective domestic remedy to seek redress for non-pecuniary damages caused by a legislative piece or the absence thereof.

With regard to the merits of the grievances, the first point of contestation revolved around the rationale of the impugned law. In particular, the Greek government argued that same-sex couples had been lawfully excluded from the scope of the law, because the new institution of civil union aims at addressing the pressing social need of the parentage of children born by parents who do not wish to get married. According to the government, the said rationale of this new institution lies in sects. 8–10 of Law No. 3719/2008, which respectively regulate the presumption of paternity when a child is to be born, the surname, and the sharing of the guardianship. This societal need, the argument continued, could not possibly be of concern to same-sex couples for pragmatic, biological reasons, and therefore these citizens have been excluded from the scope of the law in light of this objective and reasonable justification. In their intervention, the applicants suggested that it was the first time the Greek government had identified this problem of parentage as the driver behind this new institution and that this argument should not be taken at face value. However, a more careful reading reveals that the Introductory Report to the Draft Bill of the impugned law does in fact include the argument raised by the government. Furthermore, the applicants also suggested that only 16 same-sex couples had signed the cohabitation pact; a too small figure which, in the applicants' view, indicated the non-existence of this societal need. The source of that figure is not clear from the oral hearings. According to the most recent official data, as published by the Ministry of Interior in March 2013 (3 months after the oral hearings), at least 775 different-sex couples have signed the cohabitation pact under Law No. 3719/2008.[41]

Notably, this "parentage justification" has been a recurring theme in the defence of anti-gay policies. For instance, following the decision of the Obama Administration to not defend in courts (as discriminatory) the Defense of Marriage Act, the House of Representatives Bipartisan Legal Advisory Group (BLAG) stepped in and, in similar vein to the Greek government's argument, submitted in its written observations to the case *United States v Windsor* that

> [t]he link between procreation and marriage itself reflects a unique social difficulty with opposite-sex couples that is not present with same-sex couples—namely, the undeniable and distinct tendency of opposite-sex relationships to produce unplanned and unintended pregnancies.[42]

[41] The Ministry of Interior disclosed this figure in March 2013. See: http://www.ekathimerini.com/4dcgi/_w_articles_wsite1_1_29/03/2013_490797.

[42] See the Bipartisan Legal Advisory Group of the U.S. House of Representatives Brief on the merits for Respondent in the case United States v. Windsor (pending before the Supreme Court of the US), p. 44.

This position of the Greek government appears disingenuous on at least two grounds. First, the claim to an "objective justification" does not really hold much water as different-sex couples who are for their own reasons disinclined or biologically unable to procreate are still entitled to sign a cohabitation pact and enter into a civil union. Had the new institution aimed only at the regulation of the parentage of children born out of wedlock, it would then only be available to those couples with children—or at least to those capable of producing a positive fertility test. The government's line of reasoning is even less convincing in light of a 2013 Eurostat report stating that Greece has the lowest share of children born outside marriage, at a rate of 7 %, a far cry from the EU-27 average of 40 %.[43] Arguably, the Greek government invokes a barely existing social reality as the thin justification of the present law without explaining why the rights of same-sex couples do not constitute a similarly pressing social need. More importantly, there are already rules in place to address the parentage of children born out of wedlock, as well as legal means that are available to unmarried opposite-sex parents who wish to safeguard the interests of the child.

To return to the merits of the case, a second line of argumentation before the Grand Chamber considered whether alternative legal tools were available to same-sex couples for the management of their financial affairs. According to the Greek government, same-sex couples could rely on contractual freedom mechanisms in order to manage their estate as if they were married. Therefore, according to the government, same-sex couples do not suffer any damages as a result of their exclusion from the institution of cohabitation. As demonstrated immediately below, this assertion could not be further from the truth.

The applicants first claimed that same-sex couples are excluded symbolically from the scope of the impugned law; per the wording of the representing counsellor, same-sex partners "are in a legal no man's land on grounds of their sexual orientation only; they have lost the symbolic right to be seen as a fully fledged citizen, they are second-class citizens". This idea turns on the potential of legislation to shift socially backward attitudes.

More to the point, the applicants persuasively counter-argued that same-sex couples are not afforded the same legal protection as granted to their heterosexual counterparts, including in financial affairs. For instance, same-sex partners are not legally empowered to present themselves as a couple in the eyes of the administration and have to face insurmountable obstacles regarding the management of their shared estate. The applicants reinforced their latter point by explaining the state of affairs in the hypothetical scenario of the passing of one partner of a same-sex couple. They correctly identified that Greek law requires that, notwithstanding a valid will, a significant portion of one's estate be reserved for the surviving

[43] Eurostat, *Report on demography*, 49-2013, 26th March 2013, available at: http://epp.eurostat.ec.europa.eu/cache/ITY_PUBLIC/3-26032013-AP/EN/3-26032013-AP-EN.PDF. According to the same report, the second lowest share belongs to Cyprus at 17 % while the highest to Estonia at 60 %.

relatives, to the detriment of the decedent. By contrast, the inheritance rights of the different-sex partners of a civil union are explicitly regulated and protected under sect. 11 of Law No. 3719/2008. Furthermore, Greek courts have denied inheritance rights to beneficiaries who, according to the language used by the Greek Courts, might have abused the sexual weaknesses of the deceased or which would reflect situations contrary to accepted standards of behaviour.[44] Naturally, such judicial precedents, all the more when handed down by superior courts, foster a climate of uncertainty regarding the finances of a same-sex couple. The applicants did not refer in detail to other discriminatory practices; by way of illustration, they did not elaborate financial losses suffered by same-sex couples due to their ineligibility to receive social welfare benefits and tax cuts. Naturally, contractual freedom could not help same-sex couples obtain those tax cuts that are readily available to opposite-sex couples.

It should be noted that the discrimination under scrutiny is unique in kind inasmuch Greece is the only Member State of the Council of Europe that has established a civil union institution that is open only to opposite-sex couples. In maintaining two institutions with corresponding rights for opposite-sex couples and no institution for same-sex couples, Greece has taken a regulatory approach without any precedent among the Member States of the Council of Europe, which will hopefully find no imitators. The Greek government has attempted to defend in Court a policy decision that essentially transforms the single exclusion of same-sex couples from marriage into a double exclusion from both marriage and civil union.

It should also be reminded that the Court has been increasingly vigorous when dealing with questions of discriminatory practices on account of sexual orientation. In its most recent judgment in *Vejdeland and others v. Sweden,* it underlined that 'discrimination based on sexual orientation is as serious as discrimination based on "race, origin or colour"'.[45] In this vein, the counsellor for the applicants incisively pointed out that

> limiting a new legal institution to different-sex couples only is just as unacceptable in Europe as limiting it to white couples only or Christian couples only.

As per the adage, "definitions belong to the definer, not the defined". The Greek Legislator would only need to delete the words "of different sex" in sect. 1 to change the definition of the rights-holder, while leaving the rest of the text intact.[46]

---

[44] Court of Cassation 981/2006. In this recent judgment the Court of Cassation uses unacceptable and, in my view, nearly hateful language when referring to the decedent's homosexuality, which the Court perceives as a "disorder that aggravated to the point of pathology", and when presenting gratuitous details of his personal life, such as the fact that the decedent "had displayed, since his childhood, tendencies of passive homosexuality [sic] and engaged in casual erotic same-sex relationships".

[45] Case of *Vejdeland and others v. Sweden*, n. 1813/07, judgment of 9th February 2012, para. 55; see also *Smith and Grady v. the United Kingdom*, n. 33985/96 and 33986/96, judgment o 27th September 1999, para. 97, cited by the Court in the same judgment.

[46] In December 2010, the Committee, established by the Minister of Justice, for the preparation of an Introductory Report to the Draft Bill for the amendment of Family Law rules recommended the

Sections 8–10 would require no amendment, as the already chosen diction, referring to a mother and a man, does not leave room for misunderstandings. The ease of this amendment, that would scrub the discrimination tarnish from the new institution, highlights the disproportionality of the exclusion of same-sex couples from the protective scope of this new instrument.

In the profoundly queer film Victor/Victoria, there is a soft-shoe number called "You and Me", where a gay male couple, performed by Julie Andrews and Robert Preston, sings "we don't care that tomorrow comes with no guarantee, we've each other for company". However moving and sentimental this lyric in its depiction of dignified suffering, however vigorously it resonates with the experiences of numerous same-sex couples in Greece, it is high time that these citizens also obtained the rights and guarantees that their different-sex counterparts rightfully enjoy.

13.3.2 Cyprus

13.3.2.1 Reports of the Ombudsman: Discrimination Against Same-Sex Couples

The first complaint was filed in July 2007 and concerned the rejection by the Civil Registry and Migration Department (CRMD) of a request by Mr. N.V., a national of India, to be granted a residence permit as a family member of Mr. B.J.G., an EU (UK) citizen who was permanent resident of Cyprus.[47] N.V and B.J.G. had entered into a civil partnership in the UK in June 2006. N.V.'s request to the CRMD relied on Directive 2004/38/EC on the right of citizens of the Union and their family members to move and reside freely within the territory of the Member States.[48] The request was rejected on the ground that the law of Cyprus did not recognize same-sex marriage.

Art. 2(2)b of the Directive treats any

> partner with whom the Union citizen has contracted a registered partnership on the basis of the legislation of a Member State" as a family member "if the legislation of the host Member State treats registered partnerships as equivalent to marriage.

When incorporating the Directive in the legal order of Cyprus by Law No. 7(1)/2007, the Parliament did not include either opposite-sex or same-sex partners, that is, relationships falling short of traditional marriages, in the category of 'family members'. Art. 3(2)b of the Directive states that the host Member State shall, in accordance with its national legislation, facilitate entry and residence of "the

same solution to the Minister (p. 25 of the Report; available [in Greek] at: http://www.isotita.gr/var/uploads/POLICIES/NOMOPARASKEBASTIKES%20EPITROPES/EISIGITIKI-EKTHESI-OIKOGENEIAKO.pdf).

[47] Complaint No. 68/2007.

[48] On same-sex couples under EU law see the chapter by Rijpma and Koffeman in this volume.

partner with whom the Union citizen has a durable relationship, duly attested" by undertaking an extensive examination of the personal circumstances and by justifying any denial of entry or residence to these people.

In a report of 23rd April 2008, the Ombudsman reviewed the European legal framework on same-sex marriage and made extensive analysis of the Strasbourg Court's case-law on the evolving notion and meaning of 'family' and 'marriage' and on same-sex couples; she also made particular reference to Recommendation No. 1470 (2000) of the Parliamentary Assembly of the Council of Europe (PACE).[49] Although the Ombudsman admitted that the CRMD's position was not in direct conflict with the Directive and the national implementing legislation, since the matter was left at the discretion of national authorities, she opined that the Directive set the minimum level of protection and that the exercise of national discretion should not conflict with the principles, values and rights recognized and protected by the broader international and domestic legal framework. This line of analysis led the Ombudsman to conclude that the exclusion of same-sex spouses or partners from the notion of 'family members' was problematic in terms of fully respecting the Community principle of free movement of persons; it also discriminated against homosexual partners of EU citizens and against same-sex couples on the basis of sexual orientation in a way that could not be justified in objective and reasonable terms. In addition, according to the Ombudsman, the adverse implications of such discrimination on the private and family life of same-sex couples did not seem to accord with the principle of proportionality. She expressed the view that the introduction of same-sex partnerships in the legal order of Cyprus should become a matter for public debate and study in the light of international and European practice and expressed her intention to issue a Recommendation to the competent authorities to that effect. She also forwarded her Report to the Director of the CRMD, the Minister of Interior and the Attorney-General of the Republic.

The Ombudsman's report was followed by a complaint filed in July 2008 by Mr. S.S., a Cypriot citizen, on behalf of his Canadian spouse, Mr. T.C.[50] The couple had got married in Ontario, Canada in July 2006 and moved permanently to Cyprus in July 2007. T.C. requested a residence permit as a 'family member' of S.S. in accordance with Directive 2004/38/EC. His request was rejected by the CRMD on the ground that he was not considered a family member of a Cypriot citizen because their marriage was not recognized by Cypriot legislation. Both S.S. and T.C. filed an application before the Supreme Court, which is examined in Sect. 13.3.2.3.

T.C. was granted a temporary residence permit as a visitor for 1 year. On 21st October 2008, S.S. filed a fresh complaint on behalf of T.C. concerning the latter's

---

[49] "Situation of gays and lesbians and their partners in respect of asylum and immigration in the member states of the Council of Europe", adopted on 30th June 2000.

[50] Complaint No. 159/2008. It is noteworthy that the facts and legal issues raised in the complaint were virtually identical to the case of *Tadeucci and McCall v. Italy*, which was pending before the ECtHR at the time of writing.

visitor's permit.[51] As a visitor, T.C. did not have the right to work or open his own bank account (he could only have a special bank account for visitors), which was a source of numerous problems in his daily life.

The Ombudsman's report of 10th December 2008 referred to the EC rules on discrimination against homosexuals, including the Proposal for a Directive of 2nd July 2008 on implementing the principle of equal treatment between persons irrespective of religion or belief, disability, age or sexual orientation (which has however remained a Proposal at the time of writing).[52] She also referred to the comparative legal analysis of homophobia, transphobia and discrimination on grounds of sexual orientation and gender identity published by the EU Fundamental Rights Agency in June 2008, and emphasized that 18 out of the 27 EU Member States had introduced measures that went beyond the minimum standard required under EU legislation on combating discrimination on the ground of sexual orientation in labor, access to goods and services, housing and social benefits. She finally referred to the conclusions of the study that the rights and privileges accorded to married couples, including those rights relating to freedom of movement and family reunification, should be extended to same-sex couples.

In her own conclusions, the Ombudsman felt the need to clarify that regulation of same-sex marriage in Cyprus fell within the exclusive competence of the legislature. That said, she held the view that the complainant did not receive equal treatment because his right to work was directly linked with the non-recognition of same-sex marriage under Cyprus law. She added that the Cypriot legal order, as part of the EU legal order, should grant full protection to homosexuals; a blanket exclusion of same-sex partners from the rights granted to different-sex spouses of EU citizens as 'family members' was an unjustified discrimination on the ground of sexual orientation and a clear discrimination against same-sex couples. Consequently, the Ombudsman held that the denial of Mr. T.C.'s right to work was an unjustified adverse treatment that was directly linked to his sexual orientation and recommended that the CMRD reexamine his request with a view to granting him the right to work.

Similar arguments and conclusions were reiterated in a third report dated 3rd August 2009, which was triggered by two fresh complaints and by the negative reaction of the CMRD to the Ombudsman's previous reports. In particular, the CMRD insisted that their interpretation of the Directive was correct and that they had acted within the law; hence, the Ombudsman should have refrained from addressing any recommendation to the Department to act in a different way. The CMRD also invoked a Legal Opinion issued by the Law Office of the Republic of Cyprus in July 2008, which had similarly concluded that the Republic had no legal obligation but mere discretion to receive the (non-EU nationals) same-sex partners of persons legally residing in Cyprus.

---

[51] Complaint No. 213/2008.

[52] COM(2008) 426.

In the third report, the Ombudsman remained firm in her reading of the Directive within the broader legal framework, as articulated in her previous reports. In addition, she referred to the European Parliament Resolution of 2nd April 2009 on the application of Directive 2004/38/EC,[53] which, *inter alia*,

> call[ed] on member states to fully implement the rights granted under [the Directive] not only to different sex spouses, but also to the registered partner, member of the household and the partner, including same-sex couples recognized by a Member State, irrespective of nationality and without prejudice to their non-recognition in civil law by another Member State, on the basis of the principles of mutual recognition, equality, non-discrimination, dignity, and private and family life

and

> call[ed] on member states to bear in mind that the Directive imposes an obligation to recognize freedom of movement to all Union citizens (including same-sex partners) without imposing the recognition of same-sex marriages.[54]

In line with this Resolution, the Ombudsman reiterated that the CMRD's restrictive interpretation of all relevant provisions was to the detriment of EU citizens who had registered partnerships—especially same-sex ones—in their country of origin. Such restrictive interpretation would make it virtually impossible for this category of EU citizens to exercise their freedom of movement and establishment. She concluded that the blanket exclusion of same-sex partners of EU citizens from the rights deriving from the EU *acquis* on the mere ground that same-sex marriage was not recognized in Cyprus amounted to an unjustified discrimination and was incompatible with the spirit of the Directive and basic principles of EU Law; at the very least, there should have been some examination of the individual circumstances surrounding each case.

13.3.2.2 Reports of the Ombudsman: Recommending the Introduction of Civil Partnership for Both Opposite-Sex and Same-Sex Couples

The first three reports aimed at urging the State to adopt measures towards equal treatment of same-sex couples and full respect of their right to private life, but fell short of linking such measures to recognition of same-sex marriage or partnership in the legal order of Cyprus. The Ombudsman was indeed cautious to keep the two issues apart. However, in a fourth report dated 31st March 2010 she moved a step further towards recommending that Parliament introduce civil or registered partnerships for both opposite-sex and same-sex couples. The report was triggered by two complaints concerning the legislative gap on the civil marriage or registered

[53] P6_TA(2009)0203.

[54] Art. 2.

partnership of same-sex couples.[55] One of the complainants had received a clear reply by the Ministry of Interior informing him that the Cypriot law only provided for marriage between persons of different sex; since same-sex marriage was not recognized, any such marriage celebrated abroad had no legal basis in Cyprus.

The Ombudsman identified a gap in the law of Cyprus since cohabitation outside of marriage of either different-sex or same-sex couples, even if long and stable, did not give rise to any rights for the partners and was not subject to any regulation whatsoever. She stressed that new types of living together and cohabitation between such couples were a reality that required revisiting the traditional concept of marriage and the introduction of legal rules that would fill in the gap. The Ombudsman was cognizant that societal consensus would be broader for the legal recognition of different-sex partnerships outside of marriage than for same-sex ones, but she was also mindful of everyone's right not to be subjected to discrimination on the ground of sexual orientation. In her view, the continuing legal non-recognition of the social reality of same-sex partnerships reinforced negative stereotypes and prejudices against homosexuals and deprived them of the possibility to claim their rights. On the other hand, legal recognition would be a realistic response to an existing social need and essential for the realization of equal treatment. It would also bring Cyprus fully in line with the fundamental EU principle of free movement of persons.

The Ombudsman also underlined that legal regulation of civil unions would not undermine traditional marriage, which would continue to be the prevalent basis for establishing a family. In any case, the legitimate aim of protecting traditional marriage and family should not be achieved by ignoring or refusing to regulate existent (same-sex) partnerships. The State should secure the same respect and protection to all citizens irrespective of their sexual orientation. It thus fell on Parliament to introduce relevant legislation. In doing so, Parliament could be guided by the legislative provisions of other European countries as well as by the obligations of states under European and international law to eliminate any form of discrimination.

These views were reiterated in a Position Paper issued on 22nd December 2011 in the Ombudsman's capacity as Equality Authority. The Ombudsman stressed once again that there was a legal gap in regulating cohabitation outside marriage of both different-sex and same-sex couples, and that Cyprus was one of the few EU Member States that had not introduced civil partnerships. She also noted that there was no constitutional obstacle for doing so since this was an issue to be regulated by the legislature. Finally, she pointed out that legal recognition of civil partnerships would have a positive impact on public attitudes towards same-sex couples and would contribute to eliminating negative stereotypes against them, as experience in other countries has shown.

The publicity given to this series of reports in the local press and media, as well as the growing number of other initiatives and public debates in mass and social

[55] No. 142/2009 of 15th December 2009 and No. 16/2010 of 29th January 2010.

media have raised some public awareness in an issue that was considered taboo until less than a decade ago. Such initiatives and the on-going integration of Cyprus in the EU seem quite likely to counterweight—to some extent at least—deeply embedded negative public attitudes and stereotypes, including sporadic homophobic statements by prominent figures of public life. This improved climate has made it easier for a small group of parliamentarians stemming from various political parties to initiate informal discussions within Parliament with a view to introducing civil partnerships, including for same-sex couples. It is noteworthy, however, that neither the Ombudsman nor any other public figure has suggested the extension of marriage to same-sex couples; they have invariably called for introducing civil partnership/union for both opposite-sex and same-sex couples and keeping marriage for opposite-sex couples. Indeed, any other proposal would be extremely unlikely to find wider public support.

13.3.2.3 The Supreme Court Decision in *Correia and Or v. Republic*

This case was a follow-up to Complaint No. 159/2008 examined by the Ombudsman and mentioned in Sect. 13.3.2.1. The petitioners, the Cypriot Savvas Savva and his Canadian spouse Thadd Correia, claimed that the CMRD letter/reply of 25th July 2008 (stating that Mr Correia was not considered a family member of a Cypriot citizen because his marriage with Mr Savva in Canada was not recognized by Cypriot legislation) was null and void, illegal and without legal effect, for being contrary to the EU Law, the ECHR as well as Art. 15 (right to private life), 22 (right to marry) and 28 (right to equal treatment) of the Cyprus Constitution. The petition was rejected on procedural grounds,[56] mainly because under Cypriot administrative case-law the impugned act—the CMRD letter of 25th July 2008—was held to be of an informative nature and not an enforceable act of administration. Nonetheless, the Court went on to discuss the merits of the petitioners' claim (albeit not as fully as it would have done had the petition not been dismissed).

The Court rejected the arguments of the petitioners and held as follows: (a) Directive 2004/38/EC and national implementing legislation did not apply to EU nationals who wished to reside in an EU Member State of which they were a national, such as Mr Savva who wished to reside in his native Cyprus; (b) facilitation of entry and residence could take many forms but did not amount to recognition of marriage celebrated abroad; (c) there was no question of violating Art. 22 and 28 of the Constitution since the law in Cyprus did not provide for same-sex marriage but only for marriage between persons of different-sex; (d) the Strasbourg case-law has not advanced to the point of ruling that non-recognition of same-sex marriage was in violation of the right to private and family life; on the contrary, it has acknowledged that the right to marry and regulation of same-sex marriage fell within the discretion of the ECHR States parties, which could decide

[56] Judgment of 22nd July 2010, Case No. 1582/2008.

on the meaning of marriage in accordance with their own legislation and social views; the fact that some States decided to extent the right to marry to persons of same-sex reflected their own views on the role of marriage in their societies and did not give rise to any legal principle or interpretation of the Convention that could affect the traditional concept of marriage; (e) the Strasbourg case-law on the right of transsexuals to marry could point to an extension of that right to persons of same-sex in the future; (f) the Strasbourg jurisprudence on the right of same-sex couples to private life did not help the petitioners in the instant case; the protection of traditional family was a valid ground for justifying distinctions in treatment.[57]

This was a narrow reading of the same legal provisions that were construed more liberally by the Ombudsman. Admittedly, the Ombudsman had more leeway to make extensive use of non-binding instruments such as the relevant PACE recommendations and resolutions of the European Parliament. This was among the factors that led to different legal determinations and conclusions than the Supreme Court.

The legal issues raised in this case were virtually identical to the ones in *Tadeucci and McCall v. Italy*,[58] which was brought before the Strasbourg Court and was pending at the moment of writing. The outcome of this case as well as the cases pending against Greece is expected to influence related developments in Cyprus.

13.4 In Lieu of Conclusion: Towards Introducing Same-Sex Civil Unions in Both Greece and Cyprus (?)

The above analysis of the legal situation of same-sex couples in Greece and Cyprus presents an interesting case study of how social changes and human rights improvements can be gradually brought about 'from above' when supranational actors empower local ones to overcome the unwillingness and reluctance of conservative constituencies and make necessary changes in law (and society). In many respects, the issue of same-sex marriage (or, rather, civil union in the case of Greece and Cyprus) is not much different than similar changes that have occurred in the past in these two countries and elsewhere (decriminalization of homosexuality, rights of transsexuals etc). The slow and gradual process followed is indeed a *déjà vu*. In Greece, legislative change is expected to come as the result of Strasbourg's verdict in *Vallianatos and Mylonas v. Greece*. In Cyprus, the Ombudsman's reports were triggered by complaints concerning the rights of non-Cypriot partners/spouses of Cypriot or EU nationals under EU law, as a result of the evolving integration of Cyprus in the EU. Following past experience, there is little doubt that such change

[57] Reference was made to *Mata Estevez v. Spain*, n. 56501/00, decision of 10th May 2001; *Kerhoven and Hinke v. Netherlands*, n. 15666/89, decision of 19th May 1992; *Kozak v. Poland*, n. 13102/02, judgment of 2nd March 2010.

[58] App. No. 51362/09.

will sooner or later eventually transpire in both Greece and Cyprus. By the time these lines are written, this is not the case yet. It will hopefully (and more likely than not) be the case by the time these lines are read. Thus, in lieu of conclusion, the remainder of this chapter will briefly present fresh developments unfolding by the time of writing.

The prospects of the legal recognition of same-sex couples in Greece look at the moment of writing more auspicious. On the one hand, the ECtHR is reviewing a complaint on the alleged violation of the right to private life of same-sex couples, and the decision is expected to be delivered by the end of 2013. On the other hand, responding to a parliamentary question, the Greek Minister of Justice announced in February 2013 that he was planning to formally restart dialogue on the extension of the cohabitation pact to same-sex couples.

Similarly, prospects look more positive in Cyprus. During their last meeting before the presidential elections of February 2013, the outgoing Council of Ministers endorsed a draft law for submission to Parliament, which would lead to the introduction of civil partnership in Cyprus for both opposite-sex and same-sex couples. Such a development was in line with public statements made by the new President. Initial reactions by the Ministry of Interior also seem to be positive. It could still be the case, however, that the process can be affected and delayed by contingent factors, such as the unfolding sovereign debt crisis.

If these evolving initiatives eventually succeed, this chapter will have shown that/how narrow readings of legislation can be defeated, and the principle of non-discrimination will have scored yet another victory in the long and enduring battle for equality for all.

Acknowledgments The authors wish to thank Zinaida Onoufriou and Nasia Dionysiou of the Office of the Cyprus Ombudsman for their kind help.

References

Balis G (1962) Family law. Sakkoulas, Athens

Boswell J (1994) Same sex unions in premodern Europe. Villard Books, New York

Dagtoglou PD (2005) Human rights, vol A. Sakkoulas, Athens

Emilianides A (2011) Religion and law in Cyprus. Kluwer, Alphen aan den Rijn

Fessas AG (2011) National report: Greece. Am Univ J Gender Soc Policy Law 19:187–209

Green L (2011) Sex-neutral marriage. Curr Legal Probl 64:1–21

Jacobs F, White R, Ovey C (2010) The European convention on human rights. Oxford University Press, Oxford

Koppelman A (1994) Why discrimination against lesbians and gay men is sex discrimination. N Y Univ Law Rev 69:197–287

Koppelman A (2002) The gay rights question in contemporary American law. The University of Chicago Press, Chicago

Mendelsohn D (2009) How beautiful it is and how easily it can be broken. Harper Perennial, New York

Papachristou T (2005) Manual of family law. Sakkoulas, Athens

Papachristou T, Koumoutzis N, Tsouka C (2009) Cohabitation pact. In: Kotzambasi A (ed) Cohabitation pact and family law amendments. Sakkoulas, Athens

Papadopoulou L (2008) Same-sex marriage? DtA (Δικαιώματα του Ανθρώπου) 38:405–489

Trimikliniotis N, Demetriou C (2008a) Evaluating the anti-discrimination law in the Republic of Cyprus: a critical reflection. Cyprus Rev 20:79–116

Trimikliniotis N, Demetriou C (2008b) Thematic legal study on homophobia and discrimination on grounds of sexual orientation – Cyprus. http://fra.europa.eu/sites/default/files/fra_uploads/315-FRA-hdgso-NR_CY.pdf

Vidalis T (1996) The constitutional aspect of power in marriage and family. Civil liberties and institutional changes. Sakkoulas, Athens

Post Scriptum

On 7 November 2013, the ECtHR handed down its much-awaited decision in *Vallianatos and Others v Greece*, and delivered the first major win for gay rights in Greece. In an exemplary ruling, the Grand Chamber of the Court held the Greek Government to be in violation of Article 14 (prohibition of discrimination) taken in conjunction with Article 8 (respect for one's private and family life). The applicants had complained against the exclusion of same-sex couples from the scope of Law 3719/2008 on civil unions, which extended that right only to different-sex couples.

The Court reminded that, according to its case-law, same- and different-sex couples are in comparable situation in what regards their need for legal recognition and protection of their relationship (*Schalk and Kopf v. Austria*, no. 30141/04, ECHR 2010, para. 99). The Court reiterated that the protection of the family in its traditional sense as well as the interests of the child are both legitimate aims that could in principle justify a difference in the treatment of similar situations. However, the Court entered certain caveats; first, there is a broad range of measures capable of protecting the family in the traditional sense; second, given that the Convention is a living instrument which should be interpreted in present-day conditions, any State, regulating family affairs, ought to take into account societal developments, "*including the fact that there is not just one way or one choice when it comes to leading one's family or private life*" [emphasis added] (para. 84). As previously established in the Court's case-law, sexual orientation is protected under Article 14, and Parties enjoy a narrow margin of appreciation; thus, the different treatment of similar situations on grounds of sexual orientation requires "particularly convincing and weighty reasons" by way of justification.

The Court, then, proceeded to address the flimsy argument of the Greek Government that the raison d'être of the impugned Law is to strengthen the legal status of children born outside marriage. In the mind of the Greek government, the "biological difference between different-sex and same-sex couples, in so far as the latter could not have biological children together, justified limiting civil unions to different-sex couples" (para. 67). Going into the nitty-gritty details of the Law in question, and echoing the arguments put forward by the applicants at the stage of the oral hearings, the Court concluded that this Law was designed first and foremost with the idea of providing a legal alternative to the traditional institution of marriage, and was not confined to the protection of children born outside of marriage. To this end, the Court adduced the fact that the Law allowed different-sex couples without children to enter into a civil union, without extending the same right to childless same-sex couples. Of equal importance was the fact that various sections of the Law regulate the living arrangements between the different-sex partners in a civil union, such as their financial relations and the maintenance obligations as well as the right to inherit, regardless of the existence or not of a child. The Court also held that the Government had failed to demonstrate how the interests of children born outside marriage would have been compromised, had same-sex couples been brought within the scope of the law.

In a separate concurring Opinion, three judges, amongst whom the Greek judge, drew a clear line between the clear-cut trend across the Parties in making civil unions available to same-sex couples and the thorny question of adoption by gay partners which, in their view, still remains controversial.

At the time of writing, there has been neither any coverage in the mainstream Greek press on the ramifications of the Court's ruling nor any official statement by the Government. It remains to be seen when and how and whether the present Greek (coalition) Government will remedy the existing incompatibility, as found by the Court, between the Law no. 3719/2008 and the prohibition of discrimination taken with the right to one's private and family life. It is regrettable that back then the Greek government opted, in full knowledge, to adopt a clearly discriminatory law instead of shouldering the political costs of extending rights to gay people; 5 years later, it is high time that the Greek legislature repaired, without any delay, the injustice done to an already discriminated segment of its population.

Chapter 14
The Law Applicable to the Formation of Same-Sex Partnerships and Marriages

Roberto Virzo

Abstract Several States that have legalized same-sex marriages and/or registered partnership have adopted conflict of laws rules. Among the many issues of private international law that may come into play, this chapter focuses on the law applicable to the formation of same-sex unions. If, indeed, we wish to understand which categories of same-sex couples are allowed to enter into a partnership or marriage, surely we need to look at the legislative policy of the individual countries concerned, whether they have chosen to adopt specific conflict rules or to apply private international law rules originally conceived for other legal institutions.

14.1 Preliminary Remarks

In addition to the necessary substantive provisions, several States that have legalized same-sex marriage and/or registered partnerships have also adopted conflict of laws rules. Indeed, it is not uncommon that at least one of the partners wishing to formalize their relationship in a given State is neither a national nor a resident of that State. And it is also not uncommon that the competent authorities of the same State are asked to recognize gender-neutral marriages or partnerships contracted abroad.

Among the many issues of private international law that may come into play, this chapter will only focus on the law applicable to the formation of same-sex unions. After all, the specific issues concerning the recognition of marriages or registered partnerships contracted abroad will be discussed in the next chapter.[1] Moreover,

[1] See the chapter by Biagioni in this volume.

R. Virzo (✉)
Department of Law, Economics, Management and Quantitative Methods, University of Sannio, Benevento, Italy
e-mail: roberto.virzo@unisannio.it

D. Gallo et al. (eds.), *Same-Sex Couples before National, Supranational and International Jurisdictions*, DOI 10.1007/978-3-642-35434-2_14,

when compared to other aspects of private international law, the question of the applicable law deserves to be given special attention in this collection of essays.

Indeed, based on the legislative policy choices made in this field by the States concerned—both those whose legislations entail the adoption of specific conflict of laws rules and those that opt for the application to the legal institutions at issue of private international law rules originally conceived for other situations—it will be possible to determine which categories of same-sex couples are actually allowed to enter into a partnership or marriage.

14.2 Private International Law Issues Concerning the Formation of Same-Sex Registered Unions

14.2.1 Applicability of the Conflict of Laws Rules on Contractual Obligations

With regard to the private international law issues surrounding registered unions,[2] the first point to be made is that the question of the law applicable to their formation is interwoven with that of their qualification. In short, it is the classical problem of determining which juridical category is appropriate in order to establish which private international law rules could be applied in a given case.

As is well known, there are vast differences between the national laws of the States that have recognized registered unions.[3] In some cases, the term 'contract' is expressly used to define this institution, as in Art. 515-1 of the French Civil Code:

> Un pacte civile de solidarité est un contrat conclu par deux personnes physiques majeures, de sexe différent ou du même sexe, pour organiser leur vie commune.

As a consequence, it has been argued in the literature[4] that the conflict of laws rules on contractual obligations must necessarily apply.[5]

Such an argument is vulnerable to several objections.

To begin with, we should note that, with regard to contractual obligations, some of the States in question have to apply Regulation (EC) No. 593/2008 of the European Parliament and the Council of 17 June 2008, also known as the 'Rome I Regulation'.[6] In addition to "questions involving the status or legal capacity of

---

[2] In this respect, and for further bibliography, see Kessler (2004) and Tonolo (2007).

[3] See Jessurun d'Oliveira (2000), p. 297.

[4] See, among others, Revillard (2000), p. 337.

[5] According to this approach, the application of the conflict of laws rules on contractual obligations to the French *pacte civile de solidarité* (*PACS*) is justified also by Art. 515-1 of the French Civil Code, where the emphasis is on a contract concluded *between* two persons, rather than *by* a couple, who wish to organize their life in common. See the chapter by Reyniers in this volume.

[6] France, moreover, has no specific legislation in this area. As noted in Audit (2008), p. 678, "[il n'existe] aucune disposition législative d'ensemble consacré aux conflits de lois en matière de contrats".

natural persons", excluded also in the Rome Convention of 19 June 1980, this Regulation excludes from its material scope of applications[7] two sets of obligations that are particularly relevant to the topic discussed here: those

> arising out of family relationships and relationships deemed by the law applicable to such relationships to have comparable effects

and, most importantly,

> obligations arising out of matrimonial property regimes, *property regimes of relationships deemed by the law applicable to such relationships to have comparable effects to marriage*, and wills and succession.[8]

Even if one still wished to apply the Rome I Regulation to registered partnerships, there would a number of problems to be faced. The acknowledgement of party autonomy as a connecting factor in Art. 3 of the Regulation, for instance, does not per se rule out, on the one hand, the possibility that a couple will eventually subject their contract to the law of a State which does not regulate or recognize registered unions, and, on the other hand, the risk that one of the partners will have the law applied that is most favourable to his or her position.

But there is more. As noted by others,[9] in the absence of choice of law by the parties, it would be difficult to apply the connecting factor of habitual residence as per Art. 4(2), which provides that:

> the contract shall be governed by the law of the country where the party required to effect the characteristic performance of the contract has his habitual residence.[10]

In fact, from the point of view of their legal status, the performance of both partners is equally essential and characteristic.

Last but not least, even considering to apply Art.4(3) of Rome I Regulation ("Where it is clear from all the circumstances of the case that the contract is manifestly more closely connected with a country other than that indicated in paragraphs 1 or 2, the law of that other country shall apply"), the argument in favour of the applicability of the conflict of law rules on contractual obligations cannot be accepted because, in fact, it is the differences, and not the similarities, between registered unions and contracts that should be emphasized. Contractual obligations usually govern economic relationships, whereas registered unions are

---

[7] Since it is focused on the States whose legislation provides for the recognition of registered partnerships, this chapter will not cover Art. 57 of Law No. 218/1995, which overhauled the Italian system of private international law. Amply discussed in the literature, that Article provides that: "in all cases, contractual obligations are governed by the Rome Convention of 19 June 1980 [now the 'Rome I Regulation'] on the law applicable to contractual obligations." On the meaning of the expression "in all cases" see, among others, Villani (2000), pp. 57–61; Mosconi and Campiglio (2010), pp. 371–380.

[8] Regulation (EC) No. 593/2008, Art. 2(2), subparas (a), (b) and (c). Emphasis added.

[9] Rossolillo (2003), p. 387; Seraglini (2005), p. 124; Scaffidi Runchella (2012), p. 266.

[10] Regulation (EC) No. 593/2008, Art. 4(2).

based on the intention on the part of two people to have a life in common.[11] As a result, these unions are subject to limitations that do not apply to contracts. It is not permitted, for instance, to "enter two partnership simultaneously".[12] In addition to these limitations, typical marriage restrictions also apply: for example, entering into a registered partnership if one of the partners is married or registering an incestuous union is not allowed.

14.2.2 Applicability of the Conflict of Laws Rules on Marriage

Following from the above, the question may arise as to whether, in a State that has adopted substantive law rules covering the different forms of civil unions between people of the same sex, the conflict of laws rules on marriage, rather than those on contractual obligations, may apply to the formation of registered partnerships between persons connected to more than one legal system. For sure, this option would be more consistent with the conflict of law rules of the forum,[13] since the purpose of two persons registering a partnership, like that of people entering into a marriage, is to build a life in common based on their emotional relationship with each other. Even so, it cannot be regarded as an ideal solution.

In the first place, as emphasized in the literature,

> the intervention of many legislators when adopting legislation on partnership was precisely meant to create something different from marriage.[14]

This holds true not only for the States that have passed a law on same-sex marriage, but also those which, in order not to undermine the institution of heterosexual marriage, have chosen to provide same-sex couples only with access to 'lighter' forms of registered unions.

A second problem specifically concerns the law applicable to the formation of a registered partnership and the capacity of couples to access this institution.

As is well known, with regard to the formation of marriage various systems of private international law use the technique of *dépeçage*.[15] As for the formal validity

[11] With specific regard to France, it must be noted that Art. 515-1 forms part of Book I, "Of Persons", of the Civil Code.

[12] As emphasised by Harnois and Hirsch (2008), p. 23: "The exclusivity requirement is almost universal [. . .]. All jurisdictions having legislated with respect to registered partnership follow the first principle, i.e., that the partnership is to be registered between only two persons, exclusive of any others. Thus they have all refused to create a new institution that would sanction an equivalent to the concept of polygamy" (for a list of relevant provisions, see *ibid.* footnote 186).

[13] Rossolillo (2003), p. 383.

[14] Wautelet (2012), p. 153.

[15] A notable exception is the Uruguayan General Law on Private International Law, whose Art. 22 provides that: "La ley del lugar de la celebración del matrimonio rige la capacidad de las personas para contraerlo, la forma, la existencia y la validez del acto matrimonial".

of a marriage, in most systems, that is determined under the *lex loci celebrationis*, which is applied exclusively or, if the legislation in question accepts the principle of *favor validitatis*, in conjunction with other laws. The *lex loci celebrationis* rule is laid down also in Art. 2 of the Hague Marriage Convention,[16] according to which formal requirements are "governed by the law of the State of celebration".

Essential validity, on the other hand, is determined by personal connecting factors, and the legal capacity to marry of each future spouse usually depends on the law of the State of which he or she is a national.

In this perspective, applying the conflict of laws rules that govern the essential requirements for marriages also to the capacity to enter into a partnership would mean, in many cases, using the nationality of each partner as a connecting factor. Now, with regard to the registration of a same-sex partnership, that could give rise to several disadvantages.

For example, if at least one of the members of the couple were a citizen of a State that has no laws on the subject or that recognizes only heterosexual marriage, relying on the national law of each partner would make it impossible for the couple to register their union. To put it differently: in that situation, there would be an impediment not only in the State of origin, but also in the State of registration, which would be led to exclude certain categories of homosexual couples from access to the type of registered partnership recognized in its laws—and, as rightly noted in the literature, this would cause significant discrimination within the same social community.[17] A same-sex couple residing in a State that recognizes registered unions between people of the same sex and whose members are citizens of Luxembourg, for instance, would be allowed to register their union, whereas a same-sex couple residing there but whose members are Italian citizens would not.[18]

14.2.3 *Special Conflict of Laws Rules and* lex loci registrationis *as a Connecting Factor*

In order to avoid the problems outlined above, some States provide that the formation of a same-sex union and the conditions for registering it with domestic authorities must be governed by domestic legislation. When this provision is embodied in a specific conflict of laws rule, it may entail either the direct

---

[16] Hague Convention on Celebration and Recognition of the Validity of Marriages. Developed by the Hague Conference of Private International Law, the Convention was concluded on 14 March 1978 and entered into force on 1 May 1991.

[17] Scaffidi Runchella (2012), p. 226.

[18] On the Italian situation, see, among others, Boschiero (2007), p. 50; Scaffidi Runchella (2012), *passim*.

application of the *lex fori*[19] or the use of the connecting factor of the *lex loci registrationis*.[20] In the latter case, the conflict of laws rule applies also to unions registered abroad.

With reference to both formal and essential requirements in a State that has legalized same-sex unions, it must be noted, first of all, that the application of domestic law has the advantage of reducing, and sometimes eliminating, discrimination against categories of same-sex couples wishing to register as partners.

Of course, whether discrimination is reduced or eliminated depends on the legislative policy choices of individual States. In order to prevent the phenomenon of 'registration shopping', which occurs for instance when same-sex partners travel abroad for a vacation and get registered there during their short stay, some countries permit the registration of a partnership only if the couple in question have a significant connection with them.

The nature of this connection varies from country to country.[21] In Slovenia, for example, at least one of the two partners must be a national of that State.[22] The Czech Registered Partnership Law also lays down a similar requirement.[23] While Andorran law requires that at least one party be a national or a permanent resident of the Principality.[24]

Nationality or residence in the State of registration is required also under the laws of some Scandinavian countries but with some differences. Scandinavian countries permit registration for two categories of same-sex couples. The first consists of couples where at least one member, in addition to residing in the State of registration, is a citizen of (a) the State of registration, or (b) another Scandinavian state, or (c) a State that has passed a registered partnership law which is recognised as being equivalent to its Scandinavian counterpart; the second consists of partners who have both resided in the State of registration for a certain period of time.[25]

The legislations of other States, such as Belgium[26] and Switzerland,[27] provide that both partners must have taken up residence in the State of registration, while under the UK Civil Partnership Act couples can register as civil partners in England

[19] Art. 11 of the Finnish Partnership Act, for instance, provides as follows: "The right to the registration of partnership before a Finnish authority shall be determined in accordance with the laws of Finland".

[20] For an in-depth analysis of the application of this connecting factor to the formation of same-sex registered unions, and for further bibliography, see Kessler (2004), pp. 120–150.

[21] For a detailed discussion, see: Harnois and Hirsch (2008), pp. 40–51; Scaffidi Runchella (2012), pp. 217–234; Wautelet (2012), pp. 151–158.

[22] Slovenian Law on Registered Same-Sex Partnership, Art. 3(2).

[23] Czech Registered Partnership Law, Art. 5. On Eastern European countries see the chapter by Bodnar and Śledzińska-Simon in this volume.

[24] Andorran Registered Partnership Law, Art. 1.

[25] On this point, see Lung-Andersen (2012), pp. 3–17.

[26] Belgian Civil Code, Art. 1476. See the chapter by Reyniers in this volume.

[27] Swiss Registered Partnership Law, Art. 5. See the chapter by Repetto in this volume.

or Wales if both parties have resided for at least seven days "in the area of the same registration authority".[28]

By contrast, another group of legislations, while establishing that a registered partnership must be formed in accordance with the *lex loci registrationis*, do not require that same-sex couples have a personal connection (by way of nationality, residence or domicile) to the State of registration. A case in point is, for instance, Art. 17b of the Introductory Act to the German Civil Code.[29]

Finally, in other States the laws are even less restrictive. Under the Nevada Domestic Partnership Act,[30] for example, two persons wishing to register as domestic partners must share a common residence, but they do not have to live in Nevada or even visit Nevada to register their partnership. In other words, they can also register by mail.[31]

As suggested by this brief overview, by applying the law of the State of registration to both the formal and substantive requirements for the formation of registered unions,[32] it is possible to reduce, even when the essential requirements are very strict, the discrimination that may arise if the nationality of each partner is used as a connecting factor to determine the law applicable to the conditions for access to a registered union.

Indeed, when the capacity to enter into a partnership is governed by the law of the State of registration, rather than by the nationality or residence of each member of the couple, the result is quite different. Under Art. 3(2) of the aforementioned Slovenian Law on Registered Same-Sex Partnership, for example, a national may register a partnership in Slovenia regardless of whether his or her partner is a citizen of Iceland or Italy. On the other hand, if nationality were used as a connecting factor for both partners, that same Slovenian citizen would be entitled to registration with a partner from Iceland, but not with one from Italy. In the same way, under Art. 1476 of the Belgian Civil Code (also mentioned above), all same-sex couples residing in Belgium can register their civil partnerships in that State. By contrast, if the connecting factor of nationality applied to each partner, there would be a discrimination among same-sex couples residing in Belgium, since, in that case, registration would be allowed only for residing partners who are both nationals of a State which recognizes this type of unions.

---

[28] UK Civil Partnership Act, Section 8(1)(b). See the chapter by O'Neill in this volume.

[29] On this point see Martiny (2012), pp. 196–197.

[30] Nevada Domestic Partnership Act, Section 6. See the chapter by Romeo in this volume.

[31] The Practical Guide for Domestic Partnerships in Nevada (available at www.acluvnv.org) specifies as follow: "Individuals wishing to register as domestic partners must file a one-page Domestic Partnership Declaration Form with the Nevada Secretary of State. The form must be filled out completely and the signatures of each partner notarized separately. The completed form and registration fees must be mailed to, or dropped off at, the Secretary of State's office in Las Vegas or Carson City."

[32] The application of the law of the State of registration may be determined, in this case, by: (a) a substantive law rule; (b) a conflict rule establishing the *lex fori* principle; (c) a conflict rule providing for the use of *lex loci registrationis* as a connecting factor.

Applying the law of the State of registration has also additional advantages with regard to the great diversity of national forms of gender-neutral partnerships.

Firstly, since partnerships are created in accordance with the form provided by the law of the country where they are registered, recourse to the domestic law offers "ease of application" from "the perspective of the practitioner", which

> is particularly relevant in an area where rapid growth and change of legislations makes it more difficult for authorities to verify compliance with requirements of national law.[33]

Secondly, creating a partnership under the national law of the State of registration seems more consistent with the reasonable expectations of the parties, for registration in one of the States where a couple is allowed access to that institution may well be the result of a specific choice on the part of that couple. In this respect, it has been rightly noted that:

> deux partenaires suédois résidant en France, par exemple, pourraient enregistrer un partenariat suédois ou un PACS. La teneur de leur engagement ne sera pas la même dans les deux cas: s'ils choisissent la première voie, ils seront liés par un lien contraignant proche du mariage; s'ils choisissent la seconde, ils ne feront l'objet que d'un simple statut contractuel.[34]

The expectations of a couple who have chosen a specific type of registered union and who, for whatever reason, need to seek its recognition in a foreign State that has introduced a similar institution in its legal system, are further protected by conflict of laws rules that, like Art. 515-7-1 of the French Civil Code, do not subject the application of the *lex loci registrationis* to any condition. Said Article provides as follows:

> Les conditions de formation et les effets d'un partenariat enregistré ainsi que les causes et les effets de sa dissolution sont soumis aux dispositions matérielles de l'État de l'autorité qui a procédé à son enregistrement.[35]

This provision applies not only to PACS registered in France, but also to partnerships registered abroad. With regard to the latter, the purpose of the French *legislator* is to ensure, rather than undermine, their validity and effects in the event that the two partners decide to take up residence in France.

This approach differs from that of other legal systems, where foreign partnerships are recognized but subjected to certain restrictions or even to modifications that, based on the literature, can be classified under the following *categories*: "conversion",[36] "revision"[37] or "replacement".[38]

---

[33] Wautelet (2012), p. 156.

[34] Kessler (2004), p. 136.

[35] On Art. 515-7-1 of the French Civil Code, see, among others, Hammje (2009), pp. 483–491; Péroz (2010), pp. 399–410.

[36] Wautelet (2012), p. 173.

[37] Scaffidi Runchella (2012), p. 232.

[38] Hammje (2009), p. 488.

An example of the first category can be found in the German system, where Art. 17b(4) of the Introductory Law to the Civil Code provides that the legal effects of a partnership registered abroad can never exceed those arising under the German law on *Lebenspartnerschaften*.[39]

As for the second category, a notable example is the UK Civil Partnership Act, whose Section 215(1) provides that:

> Two people are to be treated as having formed a civil partnership as a result of having registered an overseas relationship.

This section aims at assimilating unions registered outside the UK to the domestic model of civil partnership, with the result, for instance, that

> two persons having concluded a PACS under French Law will be deemed to have entered a civil partnership

and

> [t]he relationship will generate the same effects as a Civil Partnership concluded in England.[40]

Finally, always with regard to the scope of the conflict rules (if any) on the law applicable to registered partnerships and, thus, also to their formation, Art. 17b (3) of the Introductory Act to the German Civil Code covers the case of a partnership registered in more than one country. In this case, the solution is to consider applicable the law of the State of last registration (obviously from the time of the last registration onwards).

14.3 Private International Law Issues Concerning the Formation of Same-Sex Marriages

Turning now to the formation of gender-neutral marriages, it is worthwhile to consider how the States that have legally recognized them apply and adapt their conflict rules on heterosexual marriage to the new institution.

In this regard, a first observation is that relying on the conflict-of-law rules already in place for opposite-sex marriage, rather than laying down specific provisions, seems consistent with the legislative policy of the States concerned, which is aimed at allowing same-sex couples to access the institution of marriage.[41]

---

[39] See Art. 17b(4) of the Introductory Act to the German Civil Code: "Die Wirkungen einer im Ausland angetragenen Lebenspartnerschaft gehen nicht weiter als nach den Vorschriften des Bürgerlichen Gesetzbuchs und des Lebenspartnerschaftsgesetzes vorgesehen". Gruber (2013) has argued that "[c]ette disposition marque une sorte de 'plafond'. Selon la conception du législateur, il s'agit d'une clause spéciale d'ordre public".

[40] Wautelet (2012), p. 173.

[41] Orejudo Prieto de los Mozos (2006), p. 300; Scaffidi Runchella (2012), p. 235; Wautelet (2012), p. 146.

If discrimination is to be eliminated, the conflict of laws rules on marriage must be made applicable to all categories of couples, and thus also to all marriages with foreign elements, regardless of the sexual orientation of the couple. When same-sex marriage was introduced in Sweden in 2009, for instance,

> the ideology of the reform was to subject all marriages to the same rules, and this was in principle achieved by making the existing provisions gender-neutral.[42]

Nevertheless, if this helps to prevent discrimination between heterosexual and same-sex couples, some connecting factors used in private international law with regard to the formation of marriage may be discriminatory towards certain categories of same-sex couples.

This problem does not arise when the connecting factor is the *lex loci celebrationis*. Such is the case, for example, of Argentine law[43] and Uruguayan law. Regarding the latter, two provisions are especially relevant: Art. 22 of the *Ley General de Derecho Internacional Privado*, cited above,[44] and Art. 1 of Law no. 19.075 of 3 May 2013, which amends Art. 83 of the Civil Code and provides that

> el matrimonio civil es la unión permanente, con arreglo a la ley, de dos personas de distinto o igual sexo.

Reading the two provisions together means that the formation of marriage and the capacity of spouses, whether heterosexual or same-sex, are governed by the law of the place where the marriage is celebrated. If the *lex loci celebrationis* rule is applied to all civil marriages, then also same-sex non-resident foreign nationals will be able to get married in Uruguay.[45]

On the other hand, if the conflict of laws rules in force in a State that has legalized gender-neutral marriage provide that the capacity to marry and other relevant requirements are governed by the national law of each spouse, or by the law of the State of residence of each spouse, certain categories of same-sex couples may be denied access to marriage. Indeed, it may happen that same-sex marriage is not recognized under the substantive provision applicable by virtue of the conflict rules of the legal system to which the connecting factor refers.[46] This possibility is

---

[42] Bogdan (2009), p. 253.

[43] Art. 159 of the Argentine Civil Code provides as follows: "Las condiciones de validez intrínsecas y estrínsecas del matrimonio se rigen por el derecho del lugar de su celabración, aunque los contrayentes hubieren dejado su domicilio para sujetarse a las normas que en él rigen". See the analysis of Grosman and Herrera (2011).

[44] *Supra*, note 15.

[45] After the entry into force of the law, practice will provide information as to whether there is a risk of 'marriage shopping' and whether the competent Uruguayan authorities will take actions to discourage 'limping marriages', that is, marriages between nationals of countries which have not opened up marriage to same-sex partners, or between people in a relationship who wish or have to live in said countries.

[46] Of course, the substantive provision in question may be that of a third legal system, if the relevant conflict rule of the system to which the connecting factor used by the State of celebration

not unlikely, since, to date, only a few States have legalized same-sex marriage or recognized the legal effects of gender-neutral marriages contracted abroad.

As a consequence, some States that use personal connecting factors to determine the essential validity of marriages with foreign elements have developed specific solutions to make gender-neutral marriage, which they have institutionalized, more available to same-sex couples.

The first of these solutions is to include in the conflict of laws rule on essential validity a set of alternative connecting factors. As is well known, the use of alternative connecting factors always serves a specific legislative purpose, which in this case is to extend the categories of couples legally entitled to enter into a marriage (whether heterosexual or same-sex).[47] This solution has been adopted in the Netherlands, which in 2000 became the first State to institutionalize gender-neutral marriage. Indeed, Art. 2 of the *Wet Conflictenrecht Huwelijk* provides as follows:

> A marriage is contracted [. . .] if each of the prospective spouses meets the requirements for entering into a marriage set by Dutch Law and one of them is of Dutch nationality or has his [or her] habitual residence in the Netherlands, or [. . .] if each of the prospective spouses meets the requirements for entering into a marriage of the State of his [or her] nationality.[48]

By contrast, States such as Belgium, Spain and Portugal have adopted limitations, namely, an *ad hoc* limitation in the case of Belgium and the public policy exception in that of Spain and Portugal. Such limitations apply, in different ways and with different effects, when the personal connecting factor specified in the conflict rule relating to the capacity of future spouses refers to a foreign law that does not allow same-sex marriage.

As mentioned above, a specific provision applies under Belgian law. After establishing, in the first paragraph, that the capacity to marry of each future spouse is governed by the law of the State of which he or she is a national, Art. 46 of the *Loi portant le Code de droit international privé* specifies that:

> l'application d'une disposition du droit désigné en vertu de l'alinéa 1er est écartée si cette disposition prohibe le mariage de personnes de même sexe, lorsque l'une d'elles a la nationalité d'un Etat ou a sa résidence habituelle sur le territoire d'un Etat dont le droit permet un tel mariage.

Quite clearly, this limitation is not related to public policy: when the foreign law provision determined by the personal connecting factor set out in para. 1 prohibits

originally referred provides for transmission to a third system. Another possibility is the remission to the law of the State of celebration, which instead should be favourable to the conclusion of the same-sex marriage. On the problem of '*renvoi*' in private international law see Davì (2012).

[47] See, among others, Picone (1996) pp. 301–304.

[48] A similar solution has been adopted in Sweden. As summed up by Bogdan: "Chapter 1, section 1 para. 2 of Act (1904:26) on Certain International Marriage and Guardianship Relations stipulates that if none of the parties is a Swedish citizen or habitual resident, each of them must, in addition to possessing marriage capacity according to Swedish law, fulfil the requirements pursuant to the law of at least one country of which he or she is a citizen or habitual resident" (Bogdan 2009, pp. 256–257).

same-sex marriages, that provision will be ignored if (and only if) the law of nationality or residence of the other spouse allows gender-neutral marriage. In other words, there is no manifest conflict[49] with Belgian public policy here, so Art. 21 of the *Loi portant le Code de droit international privé*—which provides that a manifest conflict with public policy prevents the application of foreign law, unconditionally and in all circumstances—does not apply. The limitation set out in Art. 46, para. 2, appears to be 'in favour' of same-sex marriages. Indeed, it precludes the application of a provision of the national law of one of the spouses if that law prohibits same-sex marriage, but only when the law of nationality or residence of the other spouse, which *allows* gender-neutral marriage, can still be applied. As noted by others, when there is a relative impediment to same-sex marriage in the national law of one of the spouses, the Belgian legislation makes it possible to apply the law of nationality or residence of the other spouse, thus "unlocking" access to marriage.[50] Therefore, according to some scholars, the solution contained in Art. 46 of the *Loi belge portant le Code de droit international privé* reflects the so-called '*tesis anti-bloqueo*'.[51]

As already noted, Spanish law provides instead for a general public policy exception. More specifically, it is clear from Art. 40 and 57 of the Civil Code that only habitual residents of Spain are entitled to marry there. The capacity to contract marriage is thus determined on the basis of the national law of each future spouse.[52] However, as made clear by the *Dirección General de Registros y del Notariado* (Directorate General for Registries and Notaries),[53] if the national law of the spouse who habitually resides in Spain prohibits same-sex marriage, the public policy exception set out in Art. 12(3) of the Civil Code applies.

On the other hand, Portuguese law does not require future spouses to be habitual residents and provides a solution allowing all foreign same-sex couples to marry. Also in this case, the national law of each spouse governs the capacity to marry[54]; however, if the foreign law in question prohibits same-sex marriages, the public policy exception set out in Art. 22 of the Civil Code applies. As a consequence, the capacity to marry will be determined, for instance, by Spanish law in the case of a Spanish same-sex couple, but by Portuguese law if the couple are Italian citizens.

---

[49] Under Art. 21(2), this manifest incompatibility must be determined based on "l'intensité du rattachement de la situation avec l'ordre juridique belge" and "la gravité qui produirait l'application de ce droit étranger".

[50] Mosconi and Campiglio (2012), p. 308.

[51] See Calvo Caravaca and Carrascosa Gonzàlez (2005), p. 37, who note that the Belgian provision "desbloqua el matrimonio entre personas del mismo sexo [...] haciendo que, cuando deben aplicarse de modo distributivo las Leyes nacionales a las respectivas capacidades matrimoniales de los contrayentes no se aplique la 'Ley más restrictiva', sino que se aplique la 'Ley más favorable' al matrimonio. La tesi potencia el *jus connubii* y encaja con el *favor matrimonii*".

[52] Spanish Civil Code, Art. 9. See the chapter by Fidalgo de Freitas and Tega in this volume.

[53] For a list of the *Resoluciones* adopted in this field by the *Dirección General de Registros y del Notariado*, see Mosconi and Campiglio (2012) p. 308.

[54] Portuguese Civil Code, Art. 25.

By contrast, domestic law rather than private international law applies in other countries. Notable examples are the laws of Norway and the State of Vermont in USA, which, in their turn, differ from each other in their approach to this subject. The Norwegian Marriage Act provides that, in addition to Norwegian citizens, foreign nationals who are 'lawfully' (even if not 'permanently') resident in Norway[55] may contract marriage. On the other hand, under bill S.115 (7 April 2009)[56] both residents and non-residents may marry in Vermont.

To conclude, we can say that, despite their differences, all the legislative models examined in this chapter provide solutions that serve the same purpose: namely, not to limit the possibility for citizens to access same-sex marriage. Those solutions are thus based on the principle of non-discrimination between not only heterosexual and homosexual couples, but also—as we have often pointed out—between categories of same-sex couples.

At the same time, the pursuit of that purpose may give rise to complex issues as far as the recognition of foreign same-sex marriages is concerned. This question will be discussed in detail in the next chapter,[57] but at least one remark seems appropriate here.

With regard to some laws of States that have legalized gender-neutral marriage, the risk of favouring 'marriage shopping' and that of creating 'limping relationships' (i.e., not recognized in the State of nationality or residence of one or both of the foreign spouses, or in third States), even if not negligible, may be lower than commonly thought. Indeed, these phenomena are more likely to occur in countries that, like Argentina and Uruguay, apply the connecting factor of the place of celebration or, like Portugal and Vermont,[58] that do not require residence in the State where the marriage is to be celebrated. In other words, these phenomena occur in countries whose laws make same-sex marriage available, in practice, to all foreigners who simply meet the other formal and substantive conditions provided for in the domestic law of the State of celebration.

---

[55] Norwegian Marriage Act, sections. 5a and 7 (subpara. h). Based on the fact that foreign spouses are **not** required to be permanent residents, Wautelet argues that "in Norway the *favor matrimonii policy* is also present" (Wautelet 2012, p. 148).

[56] "An Act to Protect Religious Freedom and Recognize Equality in Civil Marriage".

[57] See the chapter by Biagioni in this volume.

[58] In the case of Vermont, before the Judgment of the Supreme Court of 26 June 2013, United States v. Windsor, the problem was further complicated by the federal Defence of Marriage Act (DOMA, entered into force on 21 September 1996), whose Section 2 provides that: "No State, territory, or possession of the United States, or Indian tribe, shall be required to give effect to any public act, record, or judicial proceedings of any other State, territory, possession, or tribe respecting a relationship between persons of the same sex that is treated as a marriage under the laws of such other State, territory, possession or tribe, or a right or claim arising from such relationship". On this point, and for further bibliography, see, among others, Silberman (2005), pp. 2209–2212; Simson (2010), pp. 35ff.; Solimine (2010), pp. 105ff.; Winkler (2011), pp. 93ff.

However, we should not forget that, sometimes, it is precisely a State's prohibition against same-sex marriage, which is mainly due to socio-cultural factors,[59] that leads a couple not only to get married in another State where they are allowed to do so, but also to move there permanently.[60]

References

Audit B (2008) Droit international privé, 5th edn. Economica, Paris

Bogdan M (2009) Private international law aspects of the introduction of same-sex marriages in Sweden. Nordic J Int Law 78:235–261

Boschiero N (2007) Les unions homosexuelles à l'épreuve du droit international privé italien. Rivista di diritto internazionale 90:50–131

Calvo Caravaca A-L, Carrascosa Gonzàlez J (2005) Derecho internacional privato y matrimonio entre personas del mismo sexo. Anales de Derecho Univ Murcia 23:11–70

Davì A (2012) Le renvoi en droit international privé contemporain. Recueil des cours 352:3–521

Grosman CP, Herrera M (2011) Family, pluralism and equality: marriage and sexual orientation in Argentine law. In: Atkin B, Banda F (eds) The international survey on family law, 2011th edn. Jordan Publishing, Bristol

Gruber UP (2013) Le mariage homosexuel et le droit international privé allemand. Revue critique de droit international privé 102:65–73

Hammje P (2009) Réflexions sur l'article 515-7-1 du Code civil. Revue critique de droit international privé 93:483–491

Harnois C, Hirsch J (2008) Note on development in international law and private international law concerning cohabitation outside marriage, including registered partnership. In: Hague Conference on Private International Law, Preliminary Document No 11 of March 2008 for the attention of the Council of April 2008 on General Affairs and Policy of the Conference, The Hague

Jessurun d'Oliveira HU (2000) Registered partnership. Pacses and private international law. Some reflections. Rivista di diritto internazionale privato e processuale 36:293–312

Kessler G (2004) Les partenariat enregistrés en droit international privé. LGDJ, Paris

Lung-Andersen I (2012) The Nordic countries: same direction, different speeds. In: Boele-Woelki-K, Fuchs A (eds) Legal recognition of same-sex relationships in Europe. National, cross-border and European perspectives, 2nd edn. Intersentia, Antwerp, pp 3–17

Martiny D (2012) Private international law aspects of same-sex couples under German law. In: Boele-Woelki K, Fuchs A (eds) Legal recognition of same-sex relationships in Europe. National, cross-border and European perspectives, 2nd edn. Intersentia, Antwerp, pp 189–223

[59] Calvo Caravaca and Carrascosa González define it as follows: "una prohibición que persigue reforzar la institución del matrimonio entre personas de distinto sexo. Esta prohibición, a diferencia de otras prohibiciones, come el límite de edad nupcial o los impedimentos de parentesco, no persigue la protección de los contrayentos" (Calvo Caravaca and Carrascosa Gonzàlez 2005, p. 41).

[60] As a consequence, "los Estados cuyas Leyes nacionales ostentan los cónyges no se ven afectados por este matrimonio entre personas del mismo sexo", for it is clear that "cuando dos personas del mismo sexo y de nacionalidad extranjera, unidas en matrimonio, residen habitualmente en un Estado, en el que trabajan, pagan impuestos, conviven, adoptan hijos, y desarollan, en definitiva, su vida profesional y personal, dicho matrimonio entre personas del mismo sexo sólo afecta a la sociedad de dicho Estado" (Calvo Caravaca and Carrascosa Gonzàlez 2005, p. 42).

Mosconi F, Campiglio C (2010) Diritto internazionale privato e processuale. Parte generale e obbligazioni, 5th edn. Utet, Turin

Mosconi F, Campiglio C (2012) I matrimoni tra persone dello stesso sesso: livello "federale" e livello statale in Europa e negli Stati Uniti. Rivista di diritto internazionale privato e processuale 48:299–316

Orejudo prieto de los Mozos P (2006) Private international law problems relating to the celebration of same-sex marriages. Yearbook Private Int Law 8:229–306

Péroz H (2010) La loi applicable aux partenariats enregistrés. Journal du droit international 137:399–410

Picone P (1996) La teoria generale del diritto internazionale privato nella legge italiana di riforma della materia. Rivista di diritto internazionale 79:289–364

Revillard M (2000) Le pacte civil de solidarité en droit international privé. Rép Defrénois 37124:330–345

Rossolillo G (2003) *Registered partnership* e matrimoni di persone dello stesso sesso: problemi di qualificazione ed effetti nell'ordinamento italiano. Rivista di diritto internazionale privato e processuale 39:363–398

Scaffidi Runchella L (2012) Il riconoscimento delle unioni *same-sex* nel diritto internazionale privato italiano. Jovene, Naples

Seraglini C (2005) Les nouvelles formes de conjugalité: nouveau "jouet" pour la doctrine de droit international privè? In: Flauss-Diem J, Fauré G (eds) Du Pacs aux nouvelles conjugalités: où en est l'Europe? PUF, Mayenne, pp 115–146

Silberman L (2005) Same-sex marriage: refining the conflict of laws analysis. Univ Pa Law Rev 153:2195–2214

Simson GJ (2010) Religion, same-sex marriage, and the Defence of Marriage Act. Calif West Int J 41:35–46

Solimine ME (2010) Interstate recognition of same-sex marriage, the public policy exception and clear statement of extraterritorial effect. Calif West Int Law J 41:105–141

Tonolo S (2007) Le unioni civili nel diritto internazionale privato. Giuffré, Milan

Villani U (2000) La Convenzione di Roma sulla legge applicabile ai contratti, 2nd edn. Cacucci, Bari

Wautelet P (2012) Private international law aspects of same-sex marriages and partnership in Europe. Divided we stand? In: Boele-Woelki K, Fuchs A (eds) Legal recognition of same-sex relationships in Europe. National, cross-border and European perspectives, 2nd edn. Intersentia, Antwerp, pp 143–188

Winkler MM (2011) Same-sex marriage negli Stati Uniti: le nuove frontiere del principio di uguaglianza. Politica del diritto 42:93–121

Chapter 15
On Recognition of Foreign Same-Sex Marriages and Partnerships

Giacomo Biagioni

Abstract The traditional problem of 'limping relationships' in private international law is emerging more and more often with regard to same-sex couples. In fact, the question of validity under the applicable choice-of-law rules is seldom raised in the State of registration of the partnership or in the State of celebration of the marriage, but can come to light when the couple moves to another country. However, it is often argued that this can amount to a violation of principles concerning fundamental rights and granting a cross-border continuity of *status* and familial relationships. The chapter examines in turn the type of proceedings in which the question of validity of the same-sex relationship instituted abroad can actually arise and the solutions resorted to by national courts in order to deal with that question. The chapter outlines the different attitudes of States in that connection, depending on whether they grant same-sex couples access to marriage or to civil unions only, or they do not recognise same-sex relationships as legal. The latter case obviously proves to be the most troublesome, since national courts feel forced to refuse recognition of foreign same-sex relationships, regarded either as non-existent for the lack of an essential requirement (the opposite sex of the spouses/partners) or as contrary to the public policy of the State concerned.

15.1 Preliminary Remarks

In the context of legal literature about same-sex couples the word 'recognition' occurs very often and is mainly used to mean that under national law same-sex relationships are lawful and can produce legal effects. Accordingly, recognition concerns the entitlement of same-sex couples to a legal *status* and same-sex relationships are said to be recognized in the sense that national legal systems

G. Biagioni (✉)
Department of Social Sciences, University of Cagliari, Cagliari, Italy
e-mail: biagioni@unica.it

D. Gallo et al. (eds.), *Same-Sex Couples before National, Supranational and International Jurisdictions*, DOI 10.1007/978-3-642-35434-2_15,

allow same-sex couples to enter into a marriage or into some kind of civil union and thus confer them a legal basis within that State. Those issues are extensively dealt with in other chapters; this chapter will be devoted to the different issue of recognition of same-sex couples in private international law.

In the context of private international law the word 'recognition' bears a different meaning. In broad terms, recognition implies that a relationship established under the law of one State ('State of origin') can produce legal effects in another State ('host State'). However, as a matter of principle, States are not under an obligation to recognize legal relationships established abroad, but can regard such cross-border relationships as non-existent.

Whether a relationship can be recognized in the host State or not will thus depend on its choice-of-law rules. When those rules do not lead to the application of the law of the State of origin, it can happen that the applicable law does not recognize the *status* established in the State of origin. Such a situation occurs when the applicable law does not provide for the legal institution on which the *status* is based (for example, divorce[1]) or when some conditions are missing, under the applicable law, for the *status* to be validly established (for example, under-age marriage[2]). Accordingly, national choice-of-law rules can give rise to a limping family *status*, because rights acquired in one country cannot be enforced in another country.

However, it must be pointed out that private international law rules are not bound to a complete neutrality and do not require a merely mechanic application. It is now widely recognized that those rules can often be reflective of general values of the legal system they belong to and are strongly affected by social and ethical considerations.[3] On the other hand, the application of private international law rules suffers increasing limitations due to the primacy of fundamental principles stemming from national constitutions and international human rights conventions, as well as from cooperation through regional integration systems. For this reason, more and more often private international law rules have been subject to scrutiny before national supreme courts and supranational courts.

Especially conflict of laws rules pertaining to personal *status* fit into that scheme, because they involve directly the enjoyment of fundamental individual rights.[4] Building on this reasoning line, in several occasions it has been argued that the application of private international law rules cannot lead to interferences with a

[1] For this reason a number of conventions have been concluded in order to ensure recognition of divorce judgments and avoid the creation of limping statuses: see, e.g., Bellet and Goldman, Explanatory Report on the 1970 Hague Divorce Convention, p. 2.

[2] A direct parallel between underage marriage and same-sex marriage is drawn by Adams (1996), pp. 111–115, who recalls how in common law the distinction between choice-of-law rules concerning formal and essential validity was developed in order to avoid evasion of age requirements.

[3] In general, see Gannagé (2001) and Kinsch (2005).

[4] See Marchadier (2007), pp. 24–41.

status established under a foreign law, insofar as the creation of a limping *status* can result into a violation of fundamental rights.

Thus, in *Wagner v. Luxembourg* the Strasbourg Court held that there had been a violation of Art. 8 of the European Convention on Human Rights (further referred to as ECHR), since the Contracting State had not recognized a filial relationship created by an adoption order issued by Peruvian authorities[5]. Even though the case had been originated by a denial of *exequatur* of a foreign judgment (as the subsequent case *Negrepontis v. Greece*[6]), the Court underlined the need for consideration of the social and familial ties effectively established and made it clear that the respect due to family life under Art. 8 demands that the actual *status* acquired under foreign law not be disregarded. Accordingly, when a family *status* is at stake, States are called upon to preserve, through their private international law rules, what has been called "cross-border continuity".[7]

Of course, such an approach describes only a general aim of contemporary private international law—'cross-border continuity of personal and familial status'—and shows that a significant transformation of the traditional choice-of-law method and of the rules concerning recognition of foreign judgments has taken place.[8] However, it says nothing about the most suitable mechanisms to be recurred to in order to pursue that aim and therefore they must be still identified within national (and, when available, supranational) conflict of laws systems.

National jurisdictions are, of course, the main actors in that process. They are called upon more and more frequently to deal with cases involving matters of recognition of cross-border relationships. However, since in most cases traditional choice-of-law rules appear inadequate to cope with those unprecedented problems, they will be often forced to depart from statute law and to envisage new solutions and inclined to take special features of single problems into account.[9]

As far as same-sex couples are concerned, the above mentioned problems of recognition will often come into play and are far from being settled. In general, recognition of cross-border same-sex relationships can be hampered by several factors.

First, many national legal systems did not pass any substantive legislation about same-sex couples, as yet; as a consequence, it is also unlikely that their private international law rules are consistent with the need for recognition of cross-border same-sex relationships. Such is the case, for instance, with the Italian Statute on Private International Law, that does not provide for any specific choice-of-law rule

[5] *Wagner and J.M.W.L. v. Luxembourg*, n. 76240/01, judgment of 28th June 2007.

[6] *Negrepontis-Giannisis v. Greece*, n. 56759/08, judgment of 3rd May 2011.

[7] The expression is borrowed from Franzina (2011), p. 611.

[8] D'Avout (2010), p.170.

[9] As soon as civil unions began to appear in the legislation of some States, some scholars pledged for the necessity of an original approach to that institution in conflict of laws, suggesting that neither the choice-of-law rules regarding contracts nor those regarding marriage would lead to convincing results: see, e.g., Fulchiron (2000), p. 889.

about civil unions.[10] For the same reasons, in those States the application of conflict of laws rules about marriage can be extended to same-sex marriages only with some difficulty.

Secondly, even when States ensure a legal basis to same-sex relationships, they can establish different regimes for same-sex couples: while some States grant them access to marriage, many others merely allow them to enter into a civil union. In addition, national legislation about civil unions can vary significantly from State to State.

Those divergences are often closely reflected in national conflict of laws rules. Accordingly, conflict of laws systems can entail some limitations to the recognition of civil unions registered abroad or of marriages celebrated abroad, especially if the local regime is intended to be exclusive, e.g. for nationals of that State or for couples resident in that State.[11]

The present chapter will analyze those problems, as they emerged in the recent practice, and the solutions resorted to by national jurisdictions in order to achieve the cross-border continuity of the *status* of partner/spouse in a same-sex couple.

15.2 Cross-Border Mobility and Private International Law Implications of Same-Sex Marriages and Civil Unions

Issues of private international law about same-sex couples arise mainly as a consequence of cross-border mobility, after the marriage has been entered into or the civil union has been instituted. Nevertheless, conflict of laws rules are meant to apply also in the State of celebration or of registration, in order to establish its validity of the future marriage or civil partnership. Theoretically, the application of those rules can lead to the conclusion that the parties are not allowed to enter into a same-sex relationship and to a refusal of celebration or of registration.

To this regard it must be borne in mind that, when the validity of a marriage is at stake, a distinction is often drawn between formal and substantive requirements, the former being usually subject to the *lex loci celebrationis*, the latter to the law of the home jurisdiction (alternatively, the national law or the law of habitual residence or the law of domicile), to be determined separately for each spouse.[12] That distinction, though deeply criticized,[13] is supposed to apply to same-sex marriages as well. Since the requirement concerning the gender of the spouses is undoubtedly a substantive one, a same-sex marriage can be considered valid when both the applicable laws to the capacity of each spouse permit it.

---

[10] Tonolo (2007), pp. 144–150.

[11] Requirements of residence must be met especially for the registration of civil unions in most States: see Wautelet (2012), p. 158.

[12] Calvo Caravaca and Carrascosa Gonzàlez (2005), pp. 26–27; Fulchiron (2006), p. 423.

[13] Adams (1996), pp. 114–115.

However, a different framework can be found in U.S. conflict of laws system, which follows the rule of *lex loci celebrationis* and considers foreign marriages valid unless they are repugnant to public policy principles or prohibited under statutory provisions.[14]

Yet, the validity of a cross-border same-sex marriage is not often questioned before the celebration, with regard to the national law of the spouses or to the law of the State of their habitual residence.

In some States this is due to the application of private international law rules, that avoid referring to foreign law. For instance, in the Netherlands, pursuant to Art 3(1) of the 1978 Hague Convention on Celebration and Recognition of the Validity of Marriages, only internal law will be taken into account for marriages—either opposite-sex or same-sex—celebrated in that State, if one of the spouses has its nationality or resides there.

Other States introduced specific conflict of laws rules for same-sex marriages, based on a strong policy-oriented approach.[15] Therefore, Art. 46(2) of the Belgian Code of Private International Law provides that a foreign law denying access to same-sex marriage must be dismissed because it violates public policy. The same line of reasoning was followed in Spain by some resolutions of the *Dirección General de los Registros y de Notariado*, one of which actually concerning a refusal of celebration of a marriage between a Spanish citizen and a foreigner and, more recently by a French National Court in order to discard a bilateral convention with Morocco, prohibiting same-sex marriages.[16,17]

However, even in States where similar rules have not been enacted, refusals of celebration of same-sex marriages for reasons involving private international law issues are not reported to have occurred. It is worth noting that, quite paradoxically, such a question arose in Canada in the context of a divorce proceeding. A US citizen residing in Florida and a British citizen residing in England entered into a marriage under Canadian law in 2005 and applied for divorce in 2009 in Canada, since the marriage was not recognized in their home jurisdictions. Surprisingly, the Attorney General argued that the marriage was invalid under Canadian law because the spouses did not meet the substantive requirements for marriage under the laws of their respective domicile.[18] As a consequence, a bill was introduced in the Canadian Parliament in order to grant retroactively validity to same-sex marriages of non-residents already performed in Canada and to ensure non-resident same-sex couples access to divorce.[19]

---

[14] See *Jessica Port v. Virginia Anne Cowan*, No. 69, September Term, 2011 (Court of Appeals of Maryland); *Paula Christiansen v. Victoria Lee Christiansen*, 2011 WY 90, 253 P.3d 153.

[15] The approach was criticized, as concerns Belgium, by Renchon (2004).

[16] For an appraisal of the resolutions see Orejudo Prieto de los Mozos (2006).

[17] See Tribunal de grande instance Chambery, judgement of 11 October 2013, reported at conflictoflaws.net. Accessed 23 October 2013.

[18] The answer of the Attorney General is available, in its entirety, at http://www.cbc.ca/news/canada/story/2012/01/12/pol-harper-same-sex-marriage.html. Accessed 20th January 2013.

[19] The bill is now law, having been granted royal assent. See Bill C-32: An Act to Amend the Civil Marriage Act at http://www.parl.gc.ca. Accessed 23 October 2013.

For civil unions such an issue is much more unlikely to arise. The reason can be found in the fact that in most legal systems the validity of civil partnerships is determined by the law of the State of registration. Of course, such a conflict rule—incorporated as well in the 2007 Munich Convention on the Recognition of Registered Partnerships, not yet in force[20]—can avoid the puzzling conclusion that the union is invalid even in the State where it was entered into.

Nonetheless, private international law issues for same-sex couples are most likely to be debated in a State different from the State of celebration of the marriage or the State of registration of the partnership.

As has been noted by many scholars, two situations can be envisaged, depending on whether a previous connecting factor between the State of celebration of the marriage (or of establishment of the union) and the concerned couple exists or not.[21]

In the first scenario—which can be described in short as ‘change of residence after marriage’—the same-sex couple enters into marriage or into a civil union in the State of habitual residence (or in the national State) of at least one of the spouses/partners and subsequently moves to another country, where they seek recognition of the *status* acquired in the State of origin.

A second scenario—for the sake of brevity, ‘marriage shopping’—has thus far proved to be more common, especially with regard to same-sex marriages. Since only few States have legalized that form of marriage, a same-sex couple can leave the country where they are habitually resident, because the local law denies them access to marriage, and move out temporarily to a country where they can acquire the *status* of spouses, subsequently returning to the first country in order to seek recognition of their new *status*.

The crucial question in order to distinguish those two situations is that, while in the one case the spouses/partners are in some way linked to the State of celebration (or of registration) before the establishment of the *status*, in the other they have no actual connection with that State. As we shall see, several national jurisdictions argued that the absence of any connecting factor appears to be a clear indication that the marriage is entered into abroad exactly in order to circumvent the law of the couple’s home country.

Sometimes, such situations are ruled out by provisions requiring that the spouses/partners have some connection to the territory of the State of celebration. In this regard, the most significant link is usually the residence of the parties, which is commonly used as a connecting factor in family matters, even though private international law rules still leave some room for the nationality of the spouses or for their domicile in common law systems.[22]

---

[20] For an appraisal of the Convention, see Marchisio (2009).

[21] Silberman (2005), pp. 2198–2208, distinguishes an “evasion scenario” and a “mobile marriage scenario”; such a distinction would be relevant in U.S. interstate conflict of laws also in terms of validity of the marriage, according to the author.

[22] Under Article 2 of the Dutch Wet Conflíktenrecht Huwelijk same-sex couples are eligible for marriage only if at least one of the spouses is resident in the Netherlands or possesses Dutch nationality or if each of the spouses meets the requirements of his/her national law. Under Article

However, since most States grant every couple access to marriage, irrespective of their residence or of their nationality, the 'marriage shopping' scenario may well take place.[23]

On the other hand, the host State will hold true that its law must apply to a couple residing or domiciled in its territory and/or possessing its nationality. Such a conclusion will be usually supported by traditional choice-of-law rules, insofar as they designate the national law of (each of) the spouses or the law of their habitual residence as the law applicable to the capacity of acquiring a matrimonial *status*. This can lead to conflicting qualifications of the same-sex marriage or civil partnership and to divergent views as to the validity of the new *status* acquired.

Accordingly, the 'marriage shopping' context—even though for many couples it represents the only chance of access to marriage or to a civil union—can result in an entangled situation for the concerned couple and in challenging disputes for the recognition of the *status*.

15.3 Proceedings Involving Recognition of Same-Sex Relationships Before National Courts

Even though the two situations envisaged above are likely to entail different consequences, the nature of the proceedings aiming at recognition of the *status* acquired abroad is very similar in both cases. An outline of some general characteristics of those proceedings can prove to be very useful at this stage, since national jurisdictions are also likely to follow different approaches when the couple seek recognition of the marriage or of the civil union, in order to enjoy the rights flowing from the marital *status* (or from the establishment of a partnership) in the host State or when they pursue a different goal (for example, dissolution of the marriage or of the partnership).[24]

46 of the Belgian Code of Private International Law a couple may enter into same-sex marriage if at least one of the spouses resides in or is national of a State whose law allows such a marriage. Under Article 5 of the Norwegian Marriage Act access to marriage is restricted to nationals or residents in Norway. In Sweden only Swedish law applies to the requirements for marriage if at least one of the spouses has his/her residence in Sweden or is a Swedish national; otherwise, each of the spouses must meet the requirements under his/her national law or the law of the State where he/she resides. In Canada same-sex marriage is open also to non-domiciled couples only when it is valid under the law of domicile of each spouse.

[23] Wautelet (2012), p. 149, recalls that "in most countries, it seems that the fact that the marriage will not be recognized in the country of one of the spouses, is not taken into account".

[24] As concerns U.S. interstate practice, a similar classification can be found also in Cossman (2008), pp. 158–161.

15.3.1 Proceedings for Registration of Same-Sex Relationships

When same-sex couples enter into the host State, they usually require updating of civil records and the Registrar is thus called upon to scrutinize if the registration of a foreign same-sex marriage or civil union is allowed under the local law. Of course, the Registrar must take also private international law rules into account to that aim, even though that may involve complex findings, subject to subsequent judicial review.

Actually, some court cases had their origin in a denial of registration of same-sex marriages or civil partnerships created abroad. For instance, at least two cases concerning filed before Italian courts originated from issues concerning registration of foreign same-sex marriages.

In the very first case two Italian citizens required registration of the marriage they had entered into in the Netherlands and lodged a complaint against the refusal of the administrative authority. Their case was ultimately rejected by the *Corte di Cassazione*;[25] we will revert later to the analysis of some features of the decision stemming from the Italian Court of last resort.

The second case, filed before the *Tribunale* of Treviso, concerned a marriage entered into by an Italian citizen and a French citizen in California. At first the marriage had been registered; however, after the Registrar was informed by the Italian Consulate in California that the spouses were of the same sex, the Public Prosecutor brought a successful action for annulment of the registration.[26]

Reportedly, also the Israeli Supreme Court had occasion to deal with the issue of registration of same-sex marriages entered into abroad: even though it held that registration was in itself admissible, it assumed that it served exclusively statistical purposes and consequently a future challenge as to the validity of the marriage was not precluded.[27]

While it may hold true for Israeli legal system, in most States updating of the civil records and registration of a foreign marriage or civil union will amount to a recognition of the *status* and imply attribution of legal effects. More rarely, the spouses/partners will seek for a judicial declaration of validity of their marriage/ partnership to the same purpose: up to date, the only example is provided by *Wilkinson v. Kitzinger*, a case concerning a marriage entered into in Canada and filed before the English High Court.[28]

---

[25] *Corte di cassazione*, judgment of 15th March 2012 No. 4184 (in Rivista di diritto internazionale privato e processuale, 2012, pp. 747–767).

[26] *Tribunale* of Treviso, judgment of 19th May 2010 (in Diritto di Famiglia, 2011, p. 1236).

[27] The judgment is cited in Einhorn (2008), p. 227, fn. 20.

[28] *Wilkinson v Kitzinger* [2006] EWHC 2022 (Fam).

15.3.2 Claims by Same-Sex Couples for Benefits Recognized to Opposite-Sex Couples

A second set of cases concerning recognition of foreign same-sex marriages and partnerships had its roots in a request of the couple concerned for benefits provided by the legislation of the host State. Granting preferential treatment to married couples with regard to several issues of internal law (tax law, property law, etc.) is commonplace in many legal systems; however, that treatment is not automatically extended to same-sex spouses and/or partners. While it is reported that in some States the Governments instructed all public agencies to recognize same-sex marriages,[29] in other States the administrative authorities denied such a recognition and those issues were submitted to the national courts.

In *Zappone and Gilligan v. Revenue Commissioners* two Irish citizens, after entering into marriage in Canada, filed an application to the High Court of Ireland requesting that the treatment of married couples under Irish Tax Code be extended to them.[30] A similar case was referred to the Supreme Court of the State of New York, when the employee of a local college requested spousal health care benefits after entering into a same-sex marriage in Canada (the case was adjudicated before the State of New York legalized same-sex marriages).[31] In another case the U.S. Supreme Court held that the survived spouse of a same-sex marriage entered into in Canada is entitled to the application of the preferential treatment due to opposite-sex spouses in matters of inheritance taxes.[32]

Of course, the existence of a marital *status* can have relevance also in migration law, when one of the spouses/partners is not entitled to reside in the territory of the host State:[33] thus, on the basis of the right to family reunification an Italian court of first instance ruled in favour of a non-EU spouse of an Italian citizen who had been refused a long-term residence permit, so recognizing incidentally the validity of a same-sex marriage entered into under Spanish law.[34] Similar proceedings were

---

[29] La France reconnaît le mariage d'un couple d'hommes néerlandais. http://www.lemonde.fr/europe/article/2008/09/05/la-france-reconnait-le-mariage-d-un-couple-d-hommes-neerlandais_1091846_3214.html. Accessed 15th January 2013.

[30] Other national jurisdictions were confronted with similar issues in tax law: see e.g. *Tribunal administratif du Grand-Duché de Luxembourg*, 8th August 2007, http://www.ja.etat.lu/22355.doc. Accessed 7 January 2013. However, the application was declared inadmissible for procedural reasons.

[31] *Martinez v County of Monroe*, 2008 NY Slip Op 00909 [50 Ad3d 189].

[32] For the decision of the Court of Appeals see *Windsor v United States*, No. 12-2335-cv(L), slip op (2d Cir. 18th October 2012). The Supreme Court affirmed the decision in June 2013: see http://www.supremecourt.gov/opinions/12pdf/12-307_6j37.pdf. Accessed 23 October 2013.

[33] Soto Moya (2009), pp. 697–702.

[34] *Tribunale* of Reggio Emilia, order of 13th February 2012, at http://www.asgi.it/public/parser_download/save/tribunale_reggio_emilia_decreto_13022012.pdf. Accessed 5 January 2013. For a different case in migration matters, concerning a *de facto* partnership between an Italian citizen

instituted by other same-sex couples before German[35] and Luxembourgish[36] courts, though with divergent results.

15.3.3 Proceedings for Divorce or Dissolution of Same-Sex Relationships

Thirdly, the issue of recognition of a same-sex couple may arise when an action for the dissolution of a marriage or a civil partnership is brought in the host State. Previous recognition of the existence and validity of the same-sex relationship is obviously necessary to that aim: as it was made clear by the Wyoming Supreme Court in the context of a divorce proceeding concerning a Canadian same-sex marriage, the recognition of the existence of a valid marriage is 'a condition precedent to granting a divorce'.[37]

In this regard it is worth noting that the necessity of assessing existence and validity of the marriage as a preliminary question in divorce proceedings emerged also in the EU Regulation No. 1259/2010 implementing enhanced cooperation in the area of the law applicable to divorce and legal separation. Under Article 13 thereof national courts are not obliged to pronounce a divorce according to the law applicable under the Regulation, when, *inter alia*, the *lex fori* does not deem the marriage in question valid.

While same-sex divorce gave rise to the largest group of cases, at least in the U.S., it seems to be also in some ways the most puzzling, because it will often raise the issue of jurisdictional competence for dissolution proceedings.

When registration of the same-sex marriage or partnership is sought in the host State or when a same-sex couple apply for the concession of a benefit provided by the local law, the jurisdictional competence of the courts of the host State is not questionable. The existence of a head of jurisdiction can be far more uncertain when the action concerns the dissolution of the same-sex marriage or partnership.

As a preliminary issue, national jurisdictions will have to identify the rules governing their international competence in the subject-matter, since no State has enacted special rules for same-sex relationships. Of course, as far as dissolution of a same-sex marriage is concerned, one might be tempted to take provisions on jurisdictional competence about opposite-sex marriages into account.[38] This

and a New Zealander, though certified by the authorities of New Zealand, see *Corte di cassazione*, judgment of 17th March 2009 No. 6441 (in Foro italiano, 2009, I, 2076).

[35] VG Karlsruhe, 9 September 2004, in *IPRax*, 2006, p. 284.

[36] *Tribunal administratif du Grand-Duché de Luxembourg*, 3rd October 2005, http://www.ja.etat.lu/19509.doc. Accessed 7th January 2013.

[37] *Paula Christiansen v Victoria Lee Christiansen*, 2011 WY 90, 253 P.3d 153.

[38] The approach is consistent with the idea that same-sex marriage is not a different legal institution from opposite-sex marriage and that similar rules should therefore apply. See Orejudo Prieto de los Mozos (2006), p. 300.

seems to be the attitude of the U.S. courts in interstate divorce proceedings; the same position seems to have prevailed in Canada. In Europe, as well, some scholars claim for the application of EU Regulation No. 2201/2003,[39] underlining that it refers to marriage in a neutral way and does not set forth a definition in terms of male/female marriage.[40]

Nevertheless, the recourse to ordinary jurisdictional competence rules on divorce is not without problem, as they will often impose a residence—or domicile—requirement. As a matter of fact it means that in the majority of cases cross-border same-sex couples will not be able to get divorced, or to have their partnership dissolved, in the State of celebration and will be forced to institute proceedings in the host State. On the other hand, if that State does not recognize same-sex marriages or partnerships, it will neither grant divorce or dissolution since it considers the legal relationship to be completely void.

If this happens, same-sex couples may find it impossible to obtain divorce or dissolution of the civil partnership.[41] As we shall see, the U.S. practice shows that exactly the existence of such a risk induced some courts to accept recognizing same-sex marriages exclusively for the purpose of divorce proceedings.

However, when the courts of the State of habitual residence (or of domicile) are not inclined to recognize a same-sex marriage, even for the limited purpose of divorce proceedings, a solution is left only insofar that the courts of the State of celebration are conferred jurisdictional competence by way of exception[42]. Such a head of jurisdiction should apply regardless of traditional connecting factors, like residence and nationality, and would operate as a forum of necessity when no other forum is available to the spouses.[43] In the EU, should the Regulation No. 2201/2003 apply to same-sex marriages, the State of celebration of marriage could have jurisdictional competence over divorce, irrespective of the nationality and of the residence of the spouses, under Articles 7 and 8 of the Regulation only when the defendant is neither a EU national nor habitually resident in a EU Member State and the law of the State of the *forum* provides for such a head of jurisdiction.

Jurisdictional competence over proceedings for dissolution of a civil partnership will be often governed by the same rules concerning marriages: in some States this is the consequence of statutory provisions, such as Section 219 of the English Civil Partnership Act 2004, while in other States those rules were extended to civil unions by national courts reasoning by analogy. Of course, since reference has to be made to habitual residence or domicile in order to establish jurisdictional competence, the

[39] It is worth noting that a reference to the rules contained in the Regulation is made by regulations adopted under Section 225 of the Civil Partnership Act 2004 (Part 3) for Scotland, as regards civil partnerships (see Carruthers 2006, p. 8). The Regulation is also supposed to apply to proceedings for divorce and for dissolution of civil unions in the Netherlands (Curry-Sumner 2007, p. 11).

[40] Boele-Woelki (2008), p. 1972.

[41] See Joslin (2011), pp. 1713–1715.

[42] Tarasen (2012), pp. 1601–1606.

[43] A provision of this kind was introduced in Canada by the above mentioned legislative bill amending the Civil Marriage Act (*supra*, note 20).

above mentioned hurdles are likely to arise also when the dissolution of a cross-border civil partnerships is at stake.

15.4 Recognition of Foreign Same-Sex Unions in National Courts. . .

The attitude of national courts towards foreign same-sex unions is influenced by the circumstances above outlined (nature of the proceedings in which the issue of recognition arises; existence of connecting factors with the State of celebration or of registration). In addition, it must be borne in mind that in every single system the case law often reflects the position of same-sex relationships as enshrined in municipal law: however, that does not merely mean that the courts of States allowing same-sex unions show to be more willing to recognize or to grant some legal effect to foreign same-sex marriages or partnerships. Rather, in most cases, even when national legal systems are inclined to grant recognition to foreign same-sex unions, they often do so using their own legal framework as a yardstick.

One can assume that the reason for such a principled approach can be traced back to the sensitivity of the subject, since same-sex unions are supposed to point to the very cornerstones of each legal order. Accordingly, technical considerations as to the functioning of private international law rules and to the relevance of possibly applicable foreign law tend to be overlooked. Instead, national courts usually find arguments for recognition of foreign same-sex unions in the doctrine of marriage equality, which refers to the principle of non-discrimination and to the universal right to family life; on the other hand, when recognition is refused, special emphasis is attached to natural law and to the traditional concept of marriage.

In the light of the foregoing, it seems here appropriate to classify the relevant case law with regard to whether the concerned legal systems recognize same-sex marriages, civil partnerships or neither in municipal law.

15.4.1 . . .In States Which Grant Same-Sex Couples Access to Marriage

Recognition of a foreign same-sex marriage can be sought in a State whose law grants, as well, same-sex couples access to marriage; such a situation does not seem to give rise to significant difficulties. The characterization of foreign same-sex marriages will be unproblematic; on the other hand, the rules of private international law, largely inspired to the principle of *favor validitatis*, will not impede the recognition of foreign same-sex marriages.

It is worth noting that up to date no case law from those States is known. Presumably, a same-sex married couple can expect that, when moving to a country where same-sex marriage is legal as well, the administrative authorities and the courts of the host State will simply treat them as a local married couple and recognize entirely the *status* validly acquired abroad.

It can be added that such a situation will not usually be the consequence of a marriage shopping scenario, as above outlined, except for the case that the host State did not consider same-sex marriage legal at the time when it was entered into. However, when it is subsequently legalized in municipal law, no obstacle to the recognition of previous foreign marriages, as well, should arise.[44]

As concerns civil unions, if the host State grants same-sex couples access to marriage only, two different approaches can be conceived. For instance, under Belgian law all foreign civil unions are recognized as marriages (the so-called "adapted recognition"), unless in the State of origin distinct regimes are established for same-sex marriages and civil unions.[45] In other States the same result is likely to be achieved by the judiciary, especially if the foreign civil union resembles marriage in its features and effects;[46] such a conclusion seems to be most suitable for Scandinavian countries, that repealed legislation on same-sex partnerships when the same-sex marriage was legalized. On the contrary, Spanish authorities have taken the view that civil partnerships present distinguishing traits and cannot be deemed to correspond fully to marriage.[47]

The first occurrence can be considered an example of characterization of the civil union according to the *lex fori*, even though on the grounds of a policy-oriented approach. In other words, States granting couples access to marriage only do not refuse to recognize foreign civil unions as unknown to their legal order or affecting fundamental principles; rather, they support marriage equality by treating foreign civil unions in the same manner as marriages.

As a matter of principle, the other approach is more consistent with the need to ensure correct application of the foreign law and exact recognition of the *status* acquired abroad, unless it is conflicting with overriding principles of the host State. However, since in most cases the 'adapted recognition' proves to be more satisfactory for same-sex couples, no substantial problem can be expected to arise; suffice here to say that no case law is reported on that issue.

---

[44] See e.g., in Spain, the Resolution of the Direcciòn General de los Registros y de Notariado of 29th July 2005, available at http://www.boe.es/boe/dias/2005/08/08/pdfs/A27817-27822.pdf. Accessed 18th January 2013.

[45] For the meaning of the expression see Boele-Woelki (2008), p. 1967.

[46] Such a solution is envisaged, for Sweden, by Bogdan (2009), p. 259.

[47] *Supra*, note 43. For a criticism see Álvarez Gonzàlez (2006), p. 58.

15.4.2 …In States Which Grant Same-Sex Couples Access to Civil Unions

When recognition of foreign same-sex partnerships is sought in States that passed legislation on the matter, it usually will not take place as undisputedly as illustrated in the previous section about recognition of foreign marriages.

In particular, since legislation on civil partnerships may differ significantly in every single State, some national jurisdictions raised the issue of characterization. For instance, in a South African case concerning the dissolution of a union established under English law the Western Cape High Court did recognize that it could be characterized and considered valid as a civil partnership in that State and as such be subject to the South African Divorce Act. It is, however, worth noting that recognition was granted only after careful examination of the characteristics of the foreign partnership and also conformity to South African *ordre public* was evaluated.[48]

In some States statutory provisions were dictated in order to pave the way for automatic recognition of foreign civil unions. Nonetheless, techniques for achieving that result may vary. The New Zealand Civil Union 2004 was implemented by Regulations prescribing types of overseas relationships that are recognized in New Zealand as civil unions: such a mechanism has been severely criticized as 'suspiciously limited'[49]. The UK Civil Partnership Act 2004, too, contains a Schedule 20 listing foreign relationships that can be recognized as civil unions, but it allows national courts to recognize other relationships as well, provided that they meet certain general requirements. Accordingly, characterization of a foreign institution as a civil union must be made following the guidance of those statutory provisions.[50]

Article 515-7-1 of the French Civil Code, as amended in 2009, stipulates that a civil union registered abroad is governed by the law of the State of registration: the amendment was passed in order to facilitate recognition of foreign civil unions (especially, English civil partnerships) before national courts. However, as the case law developed immediately after the entry of the new rule into force demonstrates,[51] French courts still deem it necessary to proceed to characterization of foreign civil unions.

It follows that a wide range of discretion is enjoyed by national jurisdictions as concerns the characterization of foreign civil unions, to be effected according to the *lex fori* or, at least, to some general principles enshrined in the municipal law (for instance, it is usually expected that the civil union be exclusive, in the sense that, unless it is dissolved, the partners cannot get married or register a civil union with

[48] The judgment is summarized at http://conflictoflaws.net:80/2011/recognition-and-proprietary-consequences-of-a-uk-civil-partnership-in-south-africa/. Accessed 16th January 2013.

[49] McK Norrie (2009), p. 353.

[50] For similar provisions in Dutch and Belgian law see Wautelet (2012), pp. 171–172.

[51] *Tribunal de grande instance de Bobigny*, 8th June 2010 (unpublished).

another person). It is then possible that, when a civil union does not meet the general requirements imposed by the law of the forum, recognition will be denied on the grounds of the insurmountable divergence of national legislations.

When recognition of a same-sex marriage is sought in a country which allows same-sex couples only to establish a civil union, characterization will prove to be even more difficult. A *prima facie* characterization would obviously lead to consider a foreign same-sex marriage as a marriage. However, that option brings about further problems. To begin with, recognition of a foreign marriage can take place only if the marriage is deemed to be valid: as we have already pointed out, traditional choice-of-law rules require that the validity be examined according to the national law of each of the spouses or to the law of the State of the habitual residence. Of course, there is a serious risk that a marriage entered into abroad, especially in what we have called the 'marriage shopping' scenario, will result to be void.

In the second instance, if a marriage entered into by a same-sex couple is to be characterized as a marriage, it can be found to be in violation of underpinning social, moral or religious principles of the host State and thus disregarded on public policy grounds. That course of reasoning was followed, *inter alia*, by the English High Court in *Wilkinson v. Kitzinger*, where it was stated that an English court will decline to recognize or apply what might otherwise be an appropriate foreign rule of law, when to do so would be against English public policy.

It is worth noting that in that case the existence of public policy grounds was made clear by several statutory provisions: in particular, the High Court relied on the section 215 of the Civil Partnership Act 2004, under which an overseas registered same-sex relationship can be considered as a civil partnership in England, irrespective of its characterization under the law of the State where it was entered into.[52] That provision does give rise to the so-called "downgrade" recognition of the same-sex marriage.[53]

That option was also recently supported by a German administrative court: dealing with a marriage entered into in Canada by a German citizen and a Spanish citizen, the Verwaltungsgericht Berlin ordered its registration in Germany as a "*Lebenspartnerschaft*".[54]

Such a course of reasoning is recurred to as a remedy against the conclusion, supposed to be otherwise unavoidable, of the invalidity or non-existence of the same-sex marriage. Nonetheless, the remedy is worse than the disease for at least three reasons.

---

[52] Section 215 of the Civil Partnership Act 2004 can be coupled with Article 45.3 of the Swiss Private International Law Act, which reads "Un mariage valablement célébré à l'étranger entre personnes du même sexe est reconnu en Suisse en tant que partenariat enregistré".

[53] Boele-Woelki (2008), p. 1968.

[54] VG Berlin, 15 June 2010, 23 A 242.08, in *IPRax*, 2011, p. 270. Some scholars had already argued that such a solution could be reached even in the silence of art. 17b EGBGB: see Mankowski (2003), pp. 820–821.

First, it does not avoid creating a limping *status* for the same-sex couple: they will be spouses in the State of origin and partners in the host State. Even though it can be argued that civil unions, especially in States where same-sex marriage is not legal, do not differ significantly from marriage as to their legal effects, it is impossible to take for granted that the downgrade recognition will not give rise to any difficulty.

On the other hand, as the English High Court expressly stated, the downgrade recognition relies on the opinion that proper recognition of the same-sex marriage in the host State would lead to a violation of public policy principles of that State. However, it is far from clear how same-sex marriage can infringe public policy, when the host State grants same-sex couples access to civil unions. Since these unions—to be characterized as such—usually show quasi-matrimonial features and do entail effects similar to marriage, it cannot be said that recognition of a same-sex relationship is *per se* a violation of public policy. As far as we can see, the application of foreign law can be considered against public policy if it produces a completely (and repugnantly) different result from the application of municipal law. When the application of foreign law only entails slight differences (mainly concerning the *nomen juris* of the relationship), public policy should not come into play.

A third reason is that in the reported cases national courts did not elaborate on the factual background in order to construe the foreign same-sex marriage as a so-called 'evasion marriage' (which have would been probably possible in *Wilkinson v. Kitzinger*). However, it can be argued that, only when the spouses entered into marriage abroad just in order to circumvent the law of their home State, the latter has a substantial interest in not recognizing the relationship so established. In other words, such a situation could fit into the scheme of "*fraude à la loi*" and then justify downgrade recognition of the *status* acquired abroad, limiting it to the same extent that could be achieved under the law of the recognizing State.

15.4.3 . . .In States Which Do Not Recognize Same-Sex Unions as Legal

Of course, the most challenging situation concerns States where same-sex unions cannot be established either in the form of marriage or of civil union. If this is the case, the difference between the two kinds of relationship seems to fade out; since both are unknown to the legal order of the host State. However, thus far national jurisdictions had occasion to deal mainly with cases concerning foreign same-sex marriage and one can only build on these decisions in order to envisage how foreign civil unions would be treated.

Another preliminary remark is necessary. In most cases the foreign same-sex marriage whose recognition was sought was the consequence of a 'marriage shopping' scenario and the circumstance may have had some relevance, at least implicitly, in the reasoning of the courts.

When national courts have dismissed the cases filed by same-sex couples, they have mostly relied upon two arguments, namely non-existence of the same-sex marriage and public policy exception. Those two arguments are quite different from each other, even though sometimes they have been recalled altogether[55]: if a personal *status* does not exist (that is, has never been acquired by the persons concerned), obviously it cannot produce any effect; only if a personal *status* does exist (that is, has been actually acquired by the persons concerned), it can deploy its effects, that would undermine public policy principles. Accordingly, the two arguments cannot concur: either the *status* exists and can be considered in violation of public policy or it does not exist at all.[56]

Such a different background brings about also a clear divergence in terms of conflict of laws approach: when national courts have disregarded foreign same-sex marriages as non-existent, they have done so implicitly stating that the issue had to be adjudicated according to the *lex fori* as applicable law. On the contrary, recourse to public policy exception implies that foreign law is the applicable law but its application must be discarded as its effects would undermine fundamental principles of the State of the *forum*. However, it is worth noting that in some cases the conflict of laws dimension was completely overlooked or very briefly touched and national courts focused only on principles of municipal law.[57]

Having clarified the different starting point of the two arguments envisaged, we will now briefly examine both in turn.

15.4.3.1 Non-Existence of a Foreign Same-Sex Marriage

The non-existence argument has been developed mainly by European courts, since under traditional choice-of-law rules essential validity of marriage is governed by the national law or the law of the State of habitual residence (or domicile, in UK and Ireland) of each of the spouses. Accordingly, when at least the capacity to marry of one of the spouses is governed by the *lex fori*, national courts must refer to their own legal system in order to evaluate whether same-sex marriages can be deemed legal.

Thus far, that argument has been deployed in the Irish case *Zappone and Gilligan v. Revenue Commissioners*, where the High Court elaborated mainly on the notion of 'marriage' under Irish Constitution and under the Civil Registration

---

[55] For instance, *Tribunale* of Latina, decree of 10th June 2005 (in Foro italiano, 2006, I, p. 287).

[56] See also Winkler (2011), p. 1244.

[57] For instance, in *Zappone and Gilligan v. Revenue Commissioners* the High Court confines itself to recalling that both the spouses have their domicile in Ireland and are Irish citizens. In its judgment of 15th March 2012 No. 4184 the *Corte di cassazione* recalled in general terms that under Article 27 of the Italian Statute on Private International Law the capacity to marry is governed by the national law of each of the spouses, but did not elaborate on the subject with reference to the factual background of the case.

Act 2004, and in Italy by the *Corte d'Appello* of Rome, that relied upon the statement that a same-sex marriage is non-existent since it lacks one of the essential requirements, that is the opposite sex of the spouses.[58]

More recently, the Italian *Corte di Cassazione* adjudicated the same case and, while accepting that a foreign same-sex marriage could not be regarded as non-existent according to the European Court of Human Rights (further referred to as ECtHR) case law and to the EU Charter of Fundamental Rights, stated that it is incapable of producing legal effects as a marriage in the Italian legal order.[59] That judgment shows a clear intent of drawing a very sophisticated (but unexplained) distinction between a non-existent marriage and a marriage that does not produce legal effects; but it is clear that, according to the Italian court, same-sex marriage does not have, as yet, a place in the national legal framework.

On the other hand, even when an Italian lower court rejected the non-existence argument and recognized a Spanish same-sex marriage for the purposes of migration law, it did so on the ground of a (different) national notion of 'marriage', developed through the interpretation of the EU Directive 2004/38/EC[60] and of the Italian implementing legislation.[61] It must be added that such a notion of "marriage" was carefully limited to the field of migration law, supporting explicitly the point of view that in one legal order two concurrent notions of "marriage" could coexist.

As far as EU Member States' courts are concerned, an objection to this line of reasoning can however be raised. It is now commonplace that national choice-of-law rules must be consistent with EU fundamental principles in matters of freedom of circulation of persons. However, a conflict can be envisaged in case of non-recognition of a *status* acquired abroad as a consequence of the application of a national choice-of-law rule, especially when the latter relies on the citizenship of the parties as a connecting factor.

Even if in a different legal context, in *Garcia Avello*[62] and *Grunkin-Paul*[63] the European Court of Justice held that a Member State cannot deny recognition to a personal *status* (such as the right to bear a certain surname) validly acquired in another EU Member State. As a result, a State can be forced to derogate from its private international law rules, when they would lead to the application of the so-called State of origin, in order to pursue the stability of the *status* in all Member States and to avoid interfering with freedoms of circulation.[64]

[58] *Corte d'Appello* of Rome, decree of 13th July 2006 (in Foro italiano, 2008, I, 3695).

[59] *Corte di cassazione*, judgment of 12th March 2012 No. 4184.

[60] Directive 2004/38/EC of the European Parliament and the Council of 29th April 2004 concerning the right of citizens of the Union and their family members to move and reside freely within the territory of the Member States (Art. 2), OJ 2004 L 158, p. 77. On this Directive see the chapter by Rijpma and Koffeman in this volume.

[61] *Tribunale* of Reggio Emilia, order of 13th February 2012.

[62] *Garcia Avello*, C-148/02, judgment of 2nd October 2003 [2003] *ECR* I-11613.

[63] *Grunkin and Paul*, C-353/06, judgment of 14th October 2008 [2008] *ECR* I-7639.

[64] Tomasi (2007), pp. 81–87.

Can the same approach apply to issues of private international law concerning same-sex marriages? Of course, as no judgment of the ECJ is available yet, one can but speculate on the possible outcome of a preliminary ruling.

In that context it must be borne in mind that, according to *Grunkin and Paul*, the obstacle to the freedom of circulation of persons would arise as a consequence of a discrepancy in surnames, as this discrepancy leads to different entries in registers, documents, certificates etc. and thus may cause serious inconvenience to the person concerned.[65] In the light of the foregoing, there is no doubt that a limping *status* as to marriage is likely to cause even greater inconveniences to the parties and to deter them from exercising the freedom of circulation. On the other hand, given the fact that the ECJ always set a high bar for justification of restriction to freedom of circulation,[66] it seems very difficult to conceive a ground for asserting the non-existence of the foreign marriage, given also the very narrow definition of "abuse of the freedom of circulation".[67]

In addition, it must be borne in mind that, since same-sex marriage appears to be within the scope of application of Art. 8 and Art. 12 ECHR,[68] also the risk that the non-recognition of the *status* of same-sex spouses can result into a violation of those provisions should be taken into account. Certainly, an obligation of granting in each and every case recognition of the *status* of same-sex spouses does not exist and to this regard *Zappone and Gilligan v. Revenue Commissioners* still seems convincing. However, in some cases the actual circumstances can lead to the conclusion that a violation of rights to marry and to family life has taken place,[69] wherever the *status* has been acquired, as *Wagner v. Luxembourg* demonstrates.[70]

15.4.3.2 Public Policy

While in European countries only in one case a national jurisdiction invoked public policy exception with regard to the recognition of foreign same-sex marriages,[71] in the US reference to the public policy exception is far more common. The different approach can be explained recalling that in that conflict of laws system the validity of the marriage is governed by the law of the State of celebration and US courts usually recognize foreign marriages, provided that they are valid under that law and

[65] *Grunkin and Paul*, judgment of 14th October 2008, para 23–28.

[66] Honorati (2009), pp. 388–391; Meeusen (2010), pp. 194–201.

[67] *Akrich*, C-109/01, judgment of 23rd September 2003 [2003] *ECR*, I-9607.

[68] *Schalk and Kopf v. Austria*, n. 30141/04, judgment of 22nd November 2010. On this judgment see the chapter by Pustorino in this volume.

[69] Franzina (2011), p. 613, stresses, as well, the need for a case-by-case assessment of the circumstances that could result into a violation of rights protected by the ECHR.

[70] See also Pirrone (2009).

[71] *Tribunale* of Latina, decree of 10th June 2005.

unless the marriage is deemed to be repugnant to public policy or is expressly prohibited by statutory provisions.[72]

Leaving aside the latter case and the issues raised by the Federal Defense Of Marriage Act and the DOMAs enacted by single States,[73] we will focus on the public policy exception. The case law shows a clear tendency to a narrow interpretation of the exception, even though for different reasons. In *Paula Christiansen v Victoria Lee Christiansen* such an approach was justified on the ground that the parties did not claim to entertain their same-sex relationship in Wyoming, but requested to have their marriage dissolved. In *Jessica Port v Virginia Anne Cowan* the Court of Appeals of Maryland refused to uphold the public policy exception, since several statutes had been enacted in that State in order to support same-sex couples, even though they were not granted access to marriage. In *Martinez v County of Monroe* the legislative framework in the recognizing State was again taken into account in order to reject the public policy exception.

As far as we can see, the public policy exception can constitute a weak ground for the non-recognition of same-sex marriages except in a small number of cases. It must be recalled in that connection that public policy plays an important role especially when the circumstances show that the case is closely linked to the State of the forum according to the theory of the so-called *ordre public de proximité*[74]. On the other hand, it produces only a 'weakened' effect when the State is called upon to recognize judgments or acts that have already produced legal effects in the State of origin.[75] Such an approach found the most effective field of application in family matters,[76] affecting for instance the recognition of foreign polygamic marriages.

How can such characteristics of the public policy affect same-sex marriages? To this regard, the distinction to be drawn between the 'change of residence after marriage' scenario and the 'marriage shopping' scenario seems to be crucial. In the former the host State has only a poor connection with the same-sex marriage, which has been entered into abroad and does not concern persons linked significantly with the host State. In that case recourse to the public policy exception as a ground for non-recognition of the *status* acquired abroad can be avoided, since the State does not have a substantial interest in superimposing its underpinning principles and the parties can be better protected in their reasonable expectations.

---

[72] All the judgments in matters of foreign same-sex marriages agree on this course of reasoning: see *Paula Christiansen v Victoria Lee Christiansen*, 2011 WY 90, 253 P.3d 153; *Martinez v County of Monroe*, 2008 NY Slip Op 00909 [50 Ad3d 189]; *Jessica Port v Virginia Anne Cowan*, No. 69, September Term, 2011 (Court of Appeals of Maryland).

[73] For a comparison between the situation in the United States after the DOMAs and the situation in the European Union, see Mosconi and Campiglio (2012), pp. 311–316.

[74] See, among others, Kropholler (2006), pp. 244–259.

[75] For a critical description of the functioning of the so-called *effet attenué de l'ordre public*, see Bucher (1993), pp. 47–52.

[76] An appraisal of recent French case-law based on that approach can be found in Feraci (2012), pp. 14–19.

The ‘marriage shopping’ scenario is completely different. Even though the personal *status* is established abroad, it is precisely in order to circumvent the substantive rules of the home country of the same-sex couple. The couple must then be aware of the risks of non-recognition in their home country and the need for a protection of their situation seems weaker, while the State has a deeply-rooted interest in reaffirming the applicability of its law. However, as usual, before the public policy exception can actually come into play, it is necessary to evaluate the substantial effects of the recognition of the same-sex marriage. Only when it is demonstrated that it would imply a real and serious infringement of public policy, recognition should be dismissed; in other cases, accepting the position of Supreme Court of Wyoming in *Paula Christiansen v Victoria Lee Christiansen*, requiring a case-by-case assessment, seems advisable.

References

Adams WA (1996) Same-sex relationships and Anglo-Canadian choice of law: an argument for universal validity. Canadian Yearbook Int Law 114:103–136

Álvarez Gonzàlez S (2006) El impacto de la admission del matrimonio entre personas del mismo sexo en el derecho español: perspectiva internacional. In: Navas Navarro S (ed) Matrimonio Homosexual y Adopciòn. Reus, Madrid, pp 45–73

Boele-Woelki K (2008) The legal recognition of same-sex relationships within the European Union. Tulane Law Rev 82:1949–1981

Bogdan M (2009) Private international law aspects of the introduction of same-sex marriages in Sweden. Nordic J Int Law 78:253–261

Bucher A (1993) L’ordre public et le but social de lois en droit international privé. Recueil des Cours 239:9–116

Calvo Caravaca A-L, Carrascosa Gonzàlez J (2005) Derecho internacional privado y matrimonio entre personas del mismo sexo. Anales de la Universidad de Murcia - Derecho 23:11–70

Carruthers JM (2006) Scots rules of private international law concerning homosexual couples. Electronic J Comp Law 10:1–16

Cossman B (2008) Betwixt and between recognition: migrating same-sex marriages and the turn toward the private. Law Contemp Probl 71:153–169

Curry-Sumner I (2007) Private international law aspects of homosexual couples. The Netherlands report. Electronic J Comp Law 11:1–16

D’Avout L (2010) Droits fondamentaux et coordination des ordres juridiques en droit privé. In: Dubout E, Touzé S (eds) Les droits fondamentaux: charnières entre ordres et systèmes juridiques. Pedone, Paris, pp 159–192

Einhorn T (2008) Same-sex family unions in Israeli law. Utrecht Law Rev 4:222–235

Feraci O (2012) L’ordine pubblico nel diritto dell’Unione europea. Giuffré, Milan

Franzina P (2011) Some remarks on the relevance of Article 8 of the ECHR to the recognition of family status judicially created abroad. Diritti umani e diritto internazionale 5:609–616

Fulchiron H (2000) Réflexions sur les unions hors mariage en droit international privé. Journal de droit international 127:889–913

Fulchiron H (2006) Mariage et partenariats homosexuels en droit international privé français. Revue international de droit comparé 58:409–438

Gannagé L (2001) La hiérarchie des normes et les méthodes du droit international privé: étude de droit international privé de la famille. L.G.D.J, Paris

Honorati C (2009) Free circulation of names for EU citizens? Il diritto dell'Unione europea 14:379–401
Joslin CG (2011) Modernizing divorce jurisdiction: same-sex couples and minimum contacts. Boston Univ Law Rev 91:1669–1721
Kinsch P (2005) Droits de l'homme, droit fondamentaux et droit international privé. Recueil des Cours 318:9–332
Kropholler J (2006) Internationales Privatrecht, 6th edn. Mohr Siebeck, Tübingen
Mankowski P (2003) Artt. 13-17b EGBGB. In: von Staudinger J (ed) Kommentar zum BGB. de Gruyter, Berlin, pp 1–901
Marchadier F (2007) Les objectifs généraux du droit international privé à l'épreuve de la CEDH. Bruylant, Brussels
Marchisio M (2009) Les conventions de la Commission internationale de l'État civil. In: Bariatti S, Venturini G (eds) Liber Fausto Pocar. Giuffré, Milan, pp 659–673
McK Norrie K (2009) Recognition of overseas same-sex relationships in New Zealand. N Z Universities Law Rev 23:339–367
Meeusen J (2010) The Grunkin and Paul judgment of the ECJ, or how to strike a delicate balance between conflict of laws, union citizenship and freedom of movement in the EC. Zeitschrift für europäisches Privatrecht 18:189–201
Mosconi F, Campiglio C (2012) I matrimoni tra persone dello stesso sesso: livello "federale" e livello statale in Europa e negli Stati Uniti. Rivista di diritto internazionale privato e processuale 48:299–316
Orejudo Prieto de los Mozos P (2006) Private international law problems relating to the celebration of same-sex marriages. Yearbook Private Int Law 8:299–306
Pirrone P (2009) Limiti e 'controlimiti' alla circolazione dei giudicati nella giurisprudenza della Corte europea dei diritti umani: il caso Wagner. Diritti umani e diritto internazionale 3:151–168
Renchon J-L (2004) L'avènement du mariage homosexuel dans le Code civil belge. Revue belge de droit international et comparé 81:169–207
Silberman L (2005) Same-sex marriage: refining the conflict of laws analysis. Univ Pa Law Rev 153:2195–2214
Soto Moya M (2009) Matrimonio, orinetaciòn sexual y integraciòn del extranjero. In: Sanchez Lorenzo S (ed) La integraciòn de los extranjeros. Un analisis trasversal desde Andalucìa. Atelier, Barcelona, pp 685–715
Tarasen N (2012) Untangling the knot: finding a forum for same-sex divorces in the state of celebration. Univ Chic Law Rev 78:1585–1626
Tomasi L (2007) La tutela degli status familiari nel diritto dell'Unione europea. CEDAM, Padua
Tonolo S (2007) Le unioni civili nel diritto internazionale privato. Giuffré, Milan
Wautelet P (2012) Private international law aspects of same-sex marriages and partnerships in Europe – Divided we stand? In: Boele-Woelki K, Fuchs A (eds) Legal recognition of same-sex relationships in Europe. Intersentia, Mortsel, pp 143–223
Winkler MM (2011) Ancora sul rifiuto di trascrizione in Italia di same-sex marriage straniero: l'ennesima occasione mancata. Diritto di Famiglia 39:1239–1253

Chapter 16
Same-Sex Families Across Borders

Matteo M. Winkler

Abstract The chapter examines the impact of the transnational movement of same-sex families on private international law mechanisms at the national level. The chapter approaches this topic by using a fundamental right standard evaluation. Every time a same-sex family moves from a country to another, in fact, it triggers the protection of fundamental rights in terms of the right to respect of private and family life, the freedom of marriage and the protection of the children's best interest. By investigating the extension of these rights, continuous references to case-law are made to support the existence of said standard.

16.1 Introduction

There is perhaps no more conflictual issue in contemporary society than same-sex marriage. States deeply differ in the level and intensity of recognition of same-sex unions, "vary[ing] from almost equivalent to marriage to giving relatively limited rights."[1] States also differ in the legal treatment and recognition of gay parenting.[2] In this respect, the possibilities for registered partners to undergo medically assisted

[1] *Schalk & Kopf v. Austria*, n. 30141/04, judgment of 24th June 2010, paras 27–30 (concluding that "[a]ccording to the information available to the Court, the vast majority of the [European] States concerned have introduced the relevant legislation in the last decade"). On same-sex couples under the ECHR see the chapters by Crisafulli and Pustorino in this volume.

[2] The expression 'gay parenting' is actually multifaceted. There are actually two macro-categories of gay parenting (1) the families composed by children and their parents who came out before or after breaking up with and divorcing from a different-sex spouse; (2) the families formed *ab initio* by same-sex parents and their children through joint adoption, medically assisted procreation or surrogate motherhood.

M.M. Winkler (✉)
Department of Law, Bocconi University, Milan, Italy
e-mail: matteo.winkler@unibocconi.it

D. Gallo et al. (eds.), *Same-Sex Couples before National, Supranational and International Jurisdictions*, DOI 10.1007/978-3-642-35434-2_16,

insemination or to foster or adopt children vary greatly from one country to another.[3]

All such differences entail extremely heavy consequences on the transnational movement of families. When a family moves to a country that is "still stuck on the image of the two-heterosexual-parent-nuclear-family of the late nineteenth century,"[4] the latter's courts will most likely declare the same-sex unions established abroad be null and void in all instances. Situations of this kind, which are not merely theoretical but come out of current practice, incidentally impact the legal *status* of same-sex parents vis-à-vis their children. This chapter aims at analyzing the private international law aspects of same-sex parental issues, a topic that, surprisingly, has been mostly ignored.[5] This chapter tries to make a point against non-recognition that typically follows a same-sex family's contact with countries that do not recognize same-sex marriage and unions. In developing such a point, it uses international law norms, general legal principles, and common sense in favor of the permanence of same-sex families' legal *status* beyond national borders. It consists of three Sections; one is dedicated to the general aspects of the topic (Sect. 16.2); the subsequent one examines the conflict-of-law issues (Sect. 16.3); a short conclusion finally follows.

16.2 Same-Sex Families in a Transnational Context

There are three ways for a same-sex couple to access parenthood. First, certain States allow registered partners to retrieve medically assisted procreation ("MAP").[6] MAPs, which put at the center of the picture not the sexual intercourse, but rather the procreational project, aim at responding to the interest of the couple to become parents.[7] Second, in some States and under certain circumstances, married

---

[3] *Schalk & Kopf v. Austria*, para. 33.

[4] Schwenzer (2007), p. 147.

[5] Scholars have explored this topic only recently. *See* Grammaticaki-Alexiou (1999), p. 1113 (noting that "extremely little attention has been paid to the problems created by reproductive technologies in a world where the everyday private life of individuals, due to their mobility, may be linked with more than one jurisdiction"). For further remarks on the topic see Winkler (2011), pp. 115–120.

[6] The term refer to "a range of procedures that vary in complexity [that] have one thing in common: [they do] not include reproduction through sexual intercourse." Knaplund (2012), p. 903. On the legal issues arising out of MAP see Shapo (2006), p. 468.

[7] See Hurwitz (2000), p. 128 (noting that "surrogacy allows the fracturing of the intention to become a mother from the biological aspects of mothering: the gestational and sometimes genetic aspects"). See also Herring (2010), p. 368, pointing out that "[t]he mother is the woman who gives birth to the child even if she became pregnant using donated eggs. So even though the woman does not have a genetic link to the child, the fact she has carried the child through pregnancy and given birth entitles her to be the mother." Moreover, "[o]vulation, gestation, birth, and lactation matter, [...h]owever, just as their absence does not deprive someone of the status of 'mother,' their

or registered same-sex couples can adopt a child (joint adoption). In this case, adoption realizes the child's interest to have a family. Third, a limited number of States regulates surrogacy (or surrogate motherhood), a special MAP technique through which a couple entrusts a woman to carry and give birth to a child under the agreement that the child will be subsequently delivered to the commissioning couple, whose members will in turn become legally parents following an appropriate court order.[8] Surrogacy realizes both the couple's interest to become parents and the child's interest to have a family, precisely the commissioning one.

Cast in a multi-jurisdictional context, all those techniques raise several private international law issues. First, the main question regarding MAPs is the recognition of second-parenthood on the non-biological mother. In fact, while most national regulations that recognize same-sex marriage and unions provide the non-biological mother with the benefit of "spousal presumption," moving to another country might cause her legal relationship with the child to dissolve. Second, the main conflict-of-law problem of foreign joint same-sex adoption concerns its recognition, which would permit both same-sex parents to be legally acknowledged as the child's parents in a State that rejects same-sex adoptions. Finally, surrogacy stimulates a debate about whether to favor the planned parenthood in place of the *mater semper certa* principle and, as a result, to assign the child to the family that really wants her, rather than to the parturient and her husband.

The phenomenon generated by such a collision of jurisdictions was characteristically named by Andrew Koppelman, a prominent scholar that investigated this issue, a "blanket rule of non-recognition."[9] According to this rule, any obligation created by a same-sex marriage would evaporate the instant the affected party set foot within the border of such a State.[10] Put differently, "[c]rossing the border [...] can mean the difference between losing and retaining custody or being able to adopt as a gay or lesbian couple".[11] Koppelman also correctly observed that "events of this kind are not far-fetched [and] occur with some regularity."[12] One could also predict that cases like this would exponentially multiply in the future along with the current increase of transnational movement of families and, in parallel, the progressive recognition of same-sex couples in more and more countries.

The blanket rule deserves the strongest criticisms for at least four reasons. First, methodologically speaking there is a patent misunderstanding in considering the issue at stake. In fact, the question does not regard the relationship of the parents between them, but rather their respective relationship with the child, the former

presence does not *make* someone a mother." Rosenblum (2012), p. 71. In general, see Zgonjanin (2005).

[8] Under a surrogacy contract, "a woman agrees to bear and give birth to a child so that another person or couple may raise it as legal parent(s)." Gruenbaum (2012), p. 479.

[9] See Koppelman (2006), p. 70.

[10] *Ibidem*.

[11] Polikoff (2001) p. 153. In addition, *see* Anderson (2006), p. 1.

[12] Koppelman (2006), pp. 73–74.

operating merely as an incident or a preliminary question in respect of the latter.[13] In solving such preliminary question, one should wonder whether, even if the State does not recognize same-sex marriage or unions, there appear any reason why the child should be deprived of one parent just because the couple is formed by two people of the same gender. Therefore, no surprise if some courts tend to confuse these two planes, as the practical operation of the blanket rule of non-recognition clearly demonstrates.

Second, the rule is contrary to the preminent interest of the child. If the child has two parents in one State, misrecognition of same-sex parenthood in another State would amount to a "limping situation" which inherently harms the child in her daily relationship with the society, as she would have different parents in different countries.[14] In this respect,

> [c]hildren receive a wide array of emotional and financial protections based on the existence of a legally recognized parent–child relationship. [. . .] As a result, if a court refused to enforce an out-of-state order recognizing a person as a legal parent, the child may be completely cut off from one of the only two parents she has even known. It is not hard to imagine how harmful this would be to the individual child involved.[15]

Third, the rule entails a discrimination based on sexual orientation. Treating the child as legally bound to one parent only would constitute a discrimination as much as the same rights and obligations are normally recognized by local courts to straight parents. Moreover, as a general principle, children may not be discriminated against based on their parents' *status*, which implicitly includes sexual orientation.[16] In fact, States have a duty to combat and monitor any form of discrimination for children that have been born "in circumstances that deviate

---

[13] Such a decision would actually precede any principal judgment on the claimed rights. On the debate on the preliminary questions concerning same-sex unions, see Boschiero (2007), pp. 62–70. In fact, "[i]n the majority of cases, the dispute concerns one of these incidents, rather than the validity of marriage for all purposes. The validity of marriage is simply a preliminary or 'incidental' question, whose answer may—or may not—determine the answer to the principal question of whether the claimed incident exists." Actually, "[t]he decision of whether or which incidents to accord depends on the strength of the forum's public policy with regard to the particular incident, the nature and the context of the particular issue, and, of course, the equities of each case." Symeonides (2008), pp. 236–237.

[14] The European Court of Human Rights examined the consequence of limping situations in *Wagner and J.M.W.L. v. Luxembourg*, n. 76240/01, judgment of 28th June 2007, para. 110.

[15] Joslin (2009), p. 590. In addition, "[a] child could be permanently stripped from receiving motional support from a person who, not only was relied upon by the child as a parent, but who also had been adjudicated to be a parent by a court of another state."

[16] In fact, under the Convention on the Rights of the Child, which has been signed by 140 States, States Parties are obliged to "take all appropriate measures to ensure that the child is protected against all forms of discrimination or punishment on the basis of the status, activities, expressed opinions, or beliefs of the child's parents, legal guardians, or family members." Convention on the Rights of the Child, Signed in New York on 20th November 1989 and entered into force on 2nd September 1990, 1577 U.N.T.S. 3 (1999), Art. 2(2).

from traditional values."[17] From this standpoint, non-recognition of parent *status* performed abroad entails a violation of both the parents and children's rights, and this would be contrary to the principle of non-discrimination.

Finally, the blanket rule represents an illegitimate intrusion in family life. In particular, lesbian couples with children have a right to respect of their family life, free from the State's illegitimate interference. Such an intrusion needs to be justified under strict reasons, which in this case do not exist at all.[18]

The following paragraph describes in depth the three issues above, trying to focus on the need to reject the blanket rule of non-recognition in respect of each of them. The main vehicle exploited by local courts to enforce such a rule is public policy. Generally, the non-recognition occurs because courts confront the domestic legal system with the foreign one, and makes the former prevail over the latter. We will propose a solution that looks beyond this self-limited approach and tries to take into consideration all aspects involved.

16.3 Crossing the Border: Conflict-of-Law Aspects of Same-Sex Families

16.3.1 Access to Medically Assisted Procreation

A quick comparative overview of MAP regulations throughout the world confirms that domestic legislators are influenced by culture, religion, history and politics, and that, as a result, their regulations vary deeply depending on the interaction of all such factors.[19] This is true, in particular, for same-sex couples.

States that recognize to same-sex couples the right to marry or establish a civil partnership also grant them, with various declinations, the right to access MAP in order to ensure their procreative autonomy.[20] Also, they tend to entitle the

[17] Convention on the Rights of the Child, General Comment No. 7 (2005), CRC/C/GC/7/Rev. 1 (20th September 2006), para. 12.

[18] Under the case-law of the European Court of Human Rights the relationship between same-sex parents and their child is protected under the right to respect of family life. See *Gas and Dubois v. France*, n. 25951/07, judgment of 12th March 2012), para. 37 (holding that "examination of the applicants' specific case leads to the conclusion that they have a 'family life' within the meaning of Article 8 of the Convention"). See once again the chapter by Crisafulli in this volume.

[19] See Knoppers and LeBris (1991), p. 333 (noting that this is an area "in which countries, due to cultural, social, economic and religious differences have little or no common ground").

[20] For a comparative analysis of national regulations that recognize to gay and lesbians access to MAP, see Wardle (2006), pp. 424–431 (comparing the various national laws on the matter). Moreover, "[o]nce it is recognized that both married and unmarried persons have a liberty right to reproduce, including the right to use different ART combinations when infertile or when necessary to ensure a healthy offspring, there is no compelling reason for denying that right to persons because of their sexual orientation." Robertson (2004), p. 330.

non-biological mother to a "spousal presumption" very similar to the marital one.[21] In Queensland (Australia), for example, *de facto* or registered same-sex partner of the woman who underwent a MAP procedure is presumed to be the "parent" of the child, and such presumption is irrefutable.[22] Vermont (US) follows a similar rule.[23]

Typical multi-jurisdictional cases of MAP involve a breaking-up lesbian couple or its sudden dissolution for one partner's death. Would the non-biological mother in the former case enjoy custody and visitation right to the child? What happens to the child in the latter? In both incidents, would the child be considered as having two parents according to the law of the place of marriage or birth, or will she have one parent only, and therefore remain without life support and assistance forever?[24]

The *Miller–Jenkins* litigation in the U.S. is illustrative in this respect. Lisa Miller and Janet Jenkins entered into a civil union under the laws of Vermont.[25] They soon

---

[21] The application of the presumption of fatherhood to same-sex couples requires a neutral approach as to the gender of the biological mother's partner. From this standpoint, "[w]ithout a gender-blind (or sexual-orientation-blind) presumption, the lesbian spouse who becomes pregnant by an anonymous donor is the only legal parent to that child, depriving the child of having two legal parents, even if the non-biological spouse is ready, willing, and able to care for and support that child." Lopez (2011), p. 913. Advocates against same-sex marriage stress the importance of marital presumption in different-sex couples, like the New York Supreme Court did in *Hernandez v. Robles*, 805 N.Y.S.2d 354 (8th December 2005), aff'd, 855 N.E. 2d 1 (App. N.Y., dec. 6th July 2006), according to which (at 360) marriage "provides a basis for the legal and factual assumption that a man is the father of his wife's child via the legal presumption of paternity plus the marital expectations of monogamy and fidelity."

[22] In this respect, sect. 19C(3) of the *Status of Children Act 1978*, amended in 2010, establishes that "[t]he woman's de facto partner is presumed, for all purposes, to be a parent of any child born as a result of the pregnancy." This Section applies also to children born before 2010. In this event, parenthood results from joint application to the Registry of Births, Deaths and Marriages.

[23] In this respect, for instance, Vermont's law on civil unions, enacted in 1999, established that "[t]he rights of parties to a civil union, with respect to a child of whom either becomes the natural parent during the term of the civil union, shall be the same as those of a married couple, with respect to a child of whom either spouse becomes the natural parent during the marriage." *An Act Relating to Civil Unions*, 15 Vt. Stat. Ann. § 1204(f) (1999). For an analysis of the consequences of legal recognition of same-sex marriage from the standpoint of gay parenting, see McGuire (2004).

[24] For some cases, see Joslin (2005), pp. 689–690. Clearly, in a State both parents are legally the child's parents for the sole fact of being parties to the procreational project, to the extent that this is recognized by the law. National regulations of same-sex marriage and unions tend to provide for a spousal presumption in lesbian couples. Therefore, lesbian couples who have married or entered into a civil partnership under the laws of such State would preserve the horizontal "alliance" between them and the vertical effect on the child, who will be linked to each of them and, at the same time, to both. The aspect of parenthood relating to the "alliance" is highlighted by Cadoret (2008), pp. 48–50 (discussing the opportunity of recognizing the non-biological parent from a perspective of the alliance in the family).

[25] Vermont enacted a law on civil unions in 1999 after a ruling of the State Supreme Court in *Baker v. Vermont*, 744 A.2d 864 (Vt., dec. on 20th December 1999). See *An Act Relating to Civil Unions*, 15 Vt. Stat. Ann. 1204 (1999). Ten years later, the State legislature passed a law on same-sex marriage, overriding the Governor's veto through qualified majority.

moved to Virginia where, through MAP, Lisa gave birth to a child, Isabella. Back to Vermont, in 2003 they broke up[26] and began litigating their separation before Vermont courts, which awarded custody to Lisa and visitation to Janet.[27] Subsequently, Lisa fled to Virginia with Isabella, seeking a declaration from local court that their union was null and void under Virginia law—which categorically refused to recognize same-sex unions—and that, as a result, Janet was not entitled to any visitation or custody right towards Isabella.[28] Vermont and Virginia courts confronted on the issue and, although Lisa and Isabella are currently untraceable, eventually Janet won her legal battle in both States.[29] Even transplanted out of U.S. context, the case epitomizes how transnational movement of same-sex families could result in a loss of parental bond and rights, especially for the non-biological parent.[30]

The *Miller–Jenkins* litigation is a good case of the perverse effects of the blanket rule of non-recognition. Relating to that, recognizing the result of a foreign MAP implies local courts to defer to the planned aspect of procreation over the gestational one in a situation that is actually centered on the former—an implication that sounds neither revolutionary nor actually shocking.

Moreover, nothing prevents domestic court to consider that, when a lesbian couple decided to access MAP in a foreign country, it did it in light of a procreational project which was consensually planned and deliberated by both women together. Therefore, the non-biological mother may reasonably expect that the partner would not withdraw the project at will, based on the misrecognition

[26] The divorce of same-sex couples has evident transnational implications, for seldom States that do not recognize same-sex marriage are asked to pronounce divorce. On this problem, *see* Oppenheimer (2011), p. 78 (noting that "same-sex divorce is just beginning to receive attention in the popular press").

[27] For a summary of the case, *see* Symeonides (2007), pp. 302–303.

[28] See Dye (2007).

[29] See in this respect *Miller-Jenkins v. Miller-Jenkins*, 180 Vt. 441, 465 (Vt. Sup. Ct., dec. 4th August 2006) (holding that Janet is Isabella's parent because, "first and foremost, [. . .] Janet and Lisa were in a valid legal union at the time of the child's birth, [. . .i]t was the expectation and intent of both Lisa anche Janet that Janet would be [Isabella]'s parent, Janet participated in the decision that Lisa would be artificially inseminated to bear a child and participated actively in the prenatal care and birth. Both Lisa and Jane treated Janet as [Isabella]'s parent during the time they resided together, and Lisa identified Janet as a parent of [Isabella]") with *Miller Jenkins v. Miller-Jenkins*, 49 Va. App. 88 (App. Va., dec. 28th November 2006) (rejecting Lisa's claim that Virginia law prohibited recognition of Janet as a parent in light of Virginia's refusal of recognizing same-sex couples).

[30] This is a quite different phenomenon than forum shopping for straight couples, where the race to foreign courts usually aims at seeking more favorable conditions in custody and visitation. Here, instead, the defendant is allegedly denied her *status* as a parent, based upon the union's gender qualification. Actually, unlike previous cases, where parents "sought the court of a second state to issue a more favorable allocation of custody and visitation, [i]n this new wave of same-sex parent cases, the litigants seek to persuade a court to declare that a person previously held to be a parent by the court of another state is, in face, not a parent at all". See Joslin (2009), p. 565.

of the union by the *forum*'s courts.[31] In some case-law, a shared home and shared expenses and contributions during pregnancy and thereafter were considered relevant elements in support of an estoppel-like argument against the biological parent's claim of exclusivity in the exercise of parental rights.[32] Good faith in the couple's life and leading decisions should matter in cases like these, especially when it is the biological mother who tries to challenge the partner's *status* in order to obtain a privileged position in the child's custody or visitation.

From this standpoint, it is also noteworthy that national laws providing access to MAP to straight couples only, usually establish that the husband or partner who consented to the MAP cannot subsequently challenge the paternity of the child. Indeed, this seems a common principle among national regulations. Once the law of the *forum* contemplates such an absolute presumption of fatherhood, deciding that the non-biological partner in a same-sex union is not entitled to the same consideration represents not only an unjustified discrimination based on sexual orientation, but also a completely illogical step. As a result, there seem to be no obstacle in applying the same principle to lesbian couples with children as well. Such an estoppel-like argument could lead domestic judges towards a set of rulings which is consistent both with the child's interest to have two parents and with the parents' interest to preserve their union when they confront odd situations like breaking-up or death. The blanket rule of non-recognition clearly does not fit this picture.

16.3.2 Joint Adoption by Same-Sex Couples

In certain countries same-sex couples can adopt.[33] When they move to other States, however, the blanket rule of non-recognition normally cuts the family bond and denies the parents their legal *status* as adopters vis-à-vis the child.

It is the case of Italy. In 2006, in fact, an Italian court denied the recognition of a child adoption by a gay couple performed in California.[34] As a justification, the court admitted that to establish a parental relationship between the minor and two

---

[31] By this argument, one can use "estoppel to argue that the child's biological mother is estopped from denying the former partner's parental status." Shapo (2006), p. 470. See also O'Bryan (2010), p. 1133 (noting that certain domestic courts "found that the biological parent had ceded over a measure of parental authority and autonomy to the non biological parent and that the non biological parent had a strong parent–child bond with the children"). See also Saladino (2011), p. 4 (arguing in favor of voluntary acknowledgment of paternity to lesbian co-parents).

[32] Larson (2010), p. 880.

[33] While a human right to adopt does not exist in general, same-sex couples may present themselves with the competent authorities to receive entitlement in this respect. In the European context, same-sex couples can adopt in Belgium, United Kingdom, Spain, Denmark, Iceland and Sweden. See Kipiani (2012), para. 36.

[34] Tribunale dei Minori di Brescia, 26th September 2006, No. 2/2006, 74.

same-sex parents collides with "[the nation's] ethical and social fundamental principles".[35]

The same approach was adopted—actually not without hesitation—by the French Supreme Court, that ruled on the matter in 2012. In a single decision incorporating two lawsuits, one pertaining to an English and a French gay men residing in the UK and the other regarding two French–Canadian men residing in Canada, the Court stated that, while the fact of reserving adoption to married couples does not trigger a public policy exception, on the other hand it is contrary to public policy that the transcription of the foreign judgment on the French civil *status* registries would imply that the child was registered as born by two parents of the same sex.[36] In other words, the requirement of gender difference must be considered a "fundamental principle of French law" and, therefore, foreign adoptions by same-sex couples are contrary to French public policy.[37] This recent decision contradicts a previous judgment of 2010, where the same chamber of the same Court, annulling a ruling of the Court of Appeals of Paris, held that the *adoption simple* by the female partner of the biological mother was not contrary to French public policy.[38] The contradiction lies in the different treatment of very similar situations, where the only material variance between the two cases is represented by the effects of the adoption, which does not cut the links with the previous family in case of *adoption simple*, as opposed to *adoption plénière* (full adoption), where such links are definitely cut off.[39]

The practical consequences of the refusal of transcription are hardly negligible, especially for the child. First, she would have two different personal *status* in two countries, having two parents in Canada or the UK and being an orphan in France. Second, if litigation arises domestically, French courts will be unable to grant him/her maintenance or alimony rights vis-à-vis the members of the couple.

---

[35] *Ibidem.*

[36] Cass. Civ., Ch. Ire, 7th June 2012, No. 755 and No. 756 (11-30,261 and 11-30,262), *reversing* CA Paris, 24th February 2011. As the Court simply put it, Art. 346 of the French *Code Civil*, establishing that "[n]o person can be adopted by two people if they are not married," "does not consecrate an essential principle of private law." *Ibidem.*

[37] In particular, "[i]t is because [French] filiation law requires that the child has a maternal and a paternal link that the transcription of the [foreign] judgment of *adoption plénière*, which corresponds to a birth certificate, is prohibited." Azincourt (2012), p. 1314.

[38] Cass. Civ., Ch. Ire, 8th July 2010, No. 791 (08-21,740), according to which "the denial of *exequatur* of a foreign decision, based on contrariety to French international public policy, requires it include provisions that conflict with essential principles of French law; this is not the case concerning the decision that the parental authority be shared between the child's mother and the adopting woman."

[39] Likewise Neirinck (2012), p. 1, noting that "the reasoning, which is identical in both rulings, is material and supports the different treatment applied between the simple adoption judgment and the full adoption one."

Finally, the same child would be an alien in France, thus be treated as such in all respects. One could barely see how this interference in the family life could be legitimate in light of any goal that domestic courts are pursuing in resorting to fundamental principles of French law. Moreover,

> it is not certain that the application of fundamental principles of French law in the context of public policy exception would resist the impact of [human rights law].[40]

Fortunately, these negative implications have been considered by the French *Assemblée Nationale*, which legislated on same-sex marriage in May 2013.[41] Prospectively, and in a sense suitably, the enactment of same-sex marriage in France would likely impact the concept of French international public policy, and then solve the issue in favor of the child. This last consideration seems to require, on a more general standing, that recognition of same-sex couples' right to marry would have positive effects on the consolidation of same-sex family, and damage none.

16.3.3 Surrogate Motherhood

Except for a few countries, "[t]he sole procedure that has elicited almost uniform disapproval is that of surrogate motherhood."[42] In Europe, only the UK and Ukraine permit surrogacy agreements and enforce them. In particular, in the former a distinctive regulation establishes strict conditions for the validity of surrogacy agreements and mandates local courts to scrutinize whether such conditions have been met. If it is so, the court would issue a parental order and establish filiation on the commissioning couple, through a regime that "attempts to perpetuate an ideal family form".[43] After the introduction of the Civil Partnership Act in 2005, surrogacy was made available to same-sex couples.[44] As to Ukraine, a one-shot norm of its family law assigns parenthood to the commissioning couple.[45] Outside Europe,

---

[40] Moissinac Massenat (2012), p. 5.

[41] Loi du 17 May 2013 ouvrant le mariage aux couples de personnes de meme sexe, n. 2013-404, JO 18th May 2013. On the development of this bill, especially concerning the aspects relating to filiation (MAP and adoption), see Hauser (2012).

[42] Venturatos Lorio (1999), p. 263.

[43] Probert (2004), p. 277.

[44] Under Section 54(2)(b) of the *Human Fertilisation and Embryology Act 2008*, 2008 c. 22, amending the previous regulation of 1985, the applicants for a parental order regarding a child born through surrogacy "must be [. . .] civil partners of each other, or [] two persons who are living as partners in an enduring family relationship and are not within prohibited degrees of relationship in relation to each other." For an critical overview of the law, see Anderson (2010), at 37.

[45] See Art. 123(2) of the Family Code of Ukraine, which states that "[i]n case of implantation of embryo, which was conceived by spouses, in a body of another woman, the parents of the child are considered the spouses."

apart from China, India and Thailand, one common venue for surrogacy is the US,[46] where the picture is actually multicolored.[47]

In the last two decades, the demand of surrogacy by couples residing in countries where it is illegal created a transnational surrogacy market.[48] Surrogacy-friendly countries became the destination of the so-called "procreative tourism"—an expression which is probably misleading, as here the "tourism" is neither voluntary nor pleasant. Many same-sex couples, both lesbian and gay, seek fertilization and surrogacy in said countries, where commercial agencies exist to assist them in the process. The primary reason for such a procreative traveling is that their own country does not grant them access to surrogacy, prohibits it or limits it to such conditions which render it either economically expensive or psychologically burdensome. Once back in their own countries after completion, said couples claim recognition of the child's double-parenthood.

A typical illustration of the problems arising out of foreign surrogacy comes from the *In re X* case, decided by the High Court of England and Wales in 2008.[49] A British different-sex couple attempted to procreate through surrogacy in Ukraine. The twin children that resulted were born in Ukraine but they were not Ukrainian, as under local family law their gestational mother and her husband were not legally the parents. On the other hand, UK law provided for transfer of parenthood in favor of the commissioning couple only after the issuing of appropriate parental order by the court, so in light of UK law, and until then, the twins' parents were the Ukrainian couple, while the UK couple could not claim any right over them. In addition, UK law limits the validity and enforceability of surrogacy agreements to the requirement that no payment was made in favor of the surrogate mother. Apparently, the commissioning parents had instead paid a price to the Ukrainian mother and her husband. While the parental order should not be granted, the interaction of the two countries' conflict-of-law rules generated a perverse consequence, that the babies were "stateless and parentless."[50] The English judge, quite unsatisfied by the method and yet obliged to protect the interests of the twins, granted the parental order, noting nevertheless that

---

[46] In fact, "India seems to be actively vying to be the international surrogacy capital. In 2002, India became the first country to explicitly allow commercial surrogact. The Indian government provides tax breaks to hospitals treating international patients. India has state of the art medical facilities and technical capabilities, combined with lower costs than fertility tourists may experience in their home country." See Mohapatra (2012), p. 193.

[47] Davis (2012), p. 123.

[48] See Brugger (2011), p. 668 (noting that "[t]he decision to go abroad to these reproductive services often is triggered by substantive differences in national laws," while "[t]he trend towards surrogacy tourism in a few favorable—and inexpensive—parts of the worlds, has raised concerns about the need to develop and implement measures on a global level").

[49] *In re X and Y (Children) (Parental Order: Foreign Surrogacy)*, [2008] EWHC 3030 (Fam), [2009] Fam 71 (9th December 2008).

[50] *Ibidem*, p. 75 (noting that "[t]he effect of all this was of course that these children were effectively legal orphans and, more seriously, stateless").

> I feel bound to observe that I find this process of authorization most uncomfortable. What the court is required to do is to balance two competing and potentially irreconcilably conflicting concepts. Parliament is clearly entitled to legislate against commercial surrogacy and is clearly entitled to expect that the courts should implement that policy consideration in its decisions. Yet it is also recognized that as the full rigour of that policy consideration will bear on one wholly unequipped to comprehend it let alone deal with its consequences (i.e., the child concerned) that rigour must be mitigated by the application of a consideration of that child's welfare.[51]

In re X reveals how conflict of laws may generate limping situations that impact the child in its daily life and fundamental rights. Here, even in absence of an intervention by national legislators, a problem remains if different private international law regulations are not coordinated, or if international law remains silent on the topic. Furthermore, one should move beyond the transnational or the commercial aspects of the case, and focus on the family formation element. Clearly, "[f]amily and commerce mix in many different ways"[52] but, not surprising yet, insufficient attention has been given to the former. It might happen, abstractly speaking, that a reflection on the family formation issues of surrogacy, combined with the need to establish a certain filiation bond in respect of the child, would lead to a solution that, as a general principle, uphold the validity of the surrogacy agreement and declare the commissioning couple to be the child's legal parents.

A hot topic in international surrogacy is doubtlessly public policy. Under a public policy exception, countries that prohibit surrogacy as a matter of domestic law would be tempted to deny effect to a foreign parental order, because it would amount to a recognition of the surrogacy performed abroad. The question, however, is very narrow, as

> the point is obviously not the force of the norm as a matter of domestic law, but rather whether the prohibition of surrogacy agreements reflects so fundamental a principle within a legal system that it is encompassed by the narrow circle of international ordre public. This is a difficult issue.[53]

Public order was the subject of a decision rendered by an Italian court in 2009, where an English-Italian mother, who filed for divorce, sought recognition in Italy of two parental orders released by English courts in her favor in 1998 and 2000.[54] Initially, the government reasoned that the orders could not be recognized in light of public policy. However, the court rejected such a defence and responded that the recognition of the parental orders was mandated by the need

> to protect the vested rights of filiation, as [surrogacy] must be considered as a mere incident, deprived of material consequences [. . .] as now what is really essential is to continue to grant [the children] the parents that they has since their birth.[55]

---

[51] *Ibidem*, p. 81.

[52] Ikemoto (2009), p. 278.

[53] Gruenbaum (2012), p. 495.

[54] Corte d'Appello di Bari, 13th February 2009, *I.M. v. G.A.J.R.*, Famiglia e minori, No. 5/2009, 50. For some comments, *see* Campiglio (2009) and Baruffi (2009).

[55] *Ibidem*, p. 54.

The case concerned a family with a long and well-established bond between the parents and the children. However, the ruling seems to express a more general principle, signally that the public policies surrounding the prohibition of surrogacy agreements in the *forum*, whatever reason supports it, should step back and let the principle of the best interest of the child to operate in the spot.[56] Therefore, the *In re X* court was right in stating that

> it is almost impossible to imagine a set of circumstances in which by the time the case comes to court, the welfare of any child (particularly a foreign child) would not be gravely compromised (at the very least) by a refusal to make an order.[57]

It is therefore not surprising at all that this case was lately certified as a precedent, indeed as a leading case for future decisions in parental proceedings concerning a foreign surrogacy. As a consequence of *In re X*, parenthood was granted even if the domestic requirement had not been strictly observed by the applicants.[58] As everyone can see, the blanket rule of non-recognition is completely inadequate to solve litigation of this kind in a way that sounds just and fair for all the subjects involved.

16.4 Conclusion

In a modest attempt this chapter tried to examine how the global movement of same-sex families impact individual rights and responsibilities. Interestingly, private international law can play an important role in regulating and settling the litigation coming out from it. As mentioned at the beginning of this chapter, it also makes the point that same-sex families deserve recognition even outside the

[56] Accordingly, "[t]he Italian court concluded that the prohibition of surrogacy under Italian law was not per se an indicator that the recognition would be against Italian (international) public policy." Gruenbaum (2012), p. 497.

[57] *Supra*, note 49, at 81. It followed that "[i]f public policy is truly to be upheld, it would need to be enforced at a much earlier stage than the final hearing of a Section 30 application. In relation to adoption this has been substantially addressed by rules surrounding the bringing of the child into the country [. . .]. The point of admission to this country is in some ways the final opportunity in reality to prevent the effective implementation of a commercial surrogacy agreement. It is, of course, not for the court to suggest how (or even whether) action should be taken, I merely feel constrained to point out the problem." *Ibidem*. Actually, "[a]s it is necessary for the child to be living with the applicants, it is rarely the case that the removal of the child from its settled home will promote its welfare." Anderson (2010), p. 40.

[58] For an application of *In re X*, reference could be made to *In re IJ* (*a child*) (*Overseas Surrogacy*: *Parental Order*), [2011] EWHC 921 (Fam), [2011] All ER (D) 241 (Apr) (19th April 2011), maintaining that, in light of *In re X*, "it was crystal clear that the best interests of IJ required the making of the Parental Order sought by the applicants;" *In re L* (*a child*) (*Surrogacy*: *Parental Order*), [2010] EWHC 3146 (Fam) (8th December 2010), noting that "The effect of that must be to weight the balance between public policy considerations and welfare (as considered in *Re X and Y*) decisively in favour of welfare."

country where their procreational project was founded, i.e. in countries that do not actually recognize same-sex marriage and unions.

What emerges from this analysis is what a few decades ago Horatia Muir Watt called "the seditious function of comparative law".[59] In fact,

> comparison is engaged against dogmatism, against the stereotypes, against ethnocentrism, i.e., against the diffuse belief (regardless of the nation concerned) that national categories and concepts are the only one conceivable.[60]

Comparison with other countries' legal system and social structures stresses not only the common aspects, but also the differences of approaches to same-sex families, and ultimately imposes scholars to evaluate the justifications which lay behind certain regulations. After due reflection, in fact, it seems difficult to find a policy supporting the disruption of same-sex families for the only reason of the passing of a physical border. This is perhaps the most simple principle which could lead domestic judge to solve complex cases involving same-sex families in a way that resembles justice most.

References

Anderson LS (2006) Protecting parent–child relationships: determining parental rights of same-sex parents consistently despite varying recognition of their relationship. Pierce Law Rev 5:1–30

Anderson P (2010) An evaluation of surrogacy law and its potential development in the UK; is there a clear war forward? Kings Stud Law Rev 2:37–50

Azincourt J-D (2012) Quel Ètat Civil en France por l'Enfant Adopté à l'Ètranger par un Couple Homosexuel? La semaine juridique (Not. & Imm.), No. 35

Baruffi MC (2009) Maternità Surrogata e Questioni di Status nella Giurisprudenza Italiana ed Europea. Int'l Lis 20–25

Boschiero N (2007) Les Unions Homosexuelles À l'Épreuve du Droit International Privé Italien. Rivista di Diritto Internazionale 90:50–131

Brugger K (2011) International law in the gestational surrogacy debate. Fordham Int Law J 35:665–697

Cadoret A (2008) Genitori Come gli Altri. Omosessualità e Genitorialità. Feltrinelli, Milan

Campiglio C (2009) Lo stato di figlio nato da contratto internazionale di maternità. Rivista di diritto internazionale privato e processuale 589–604

Davis E (2012) The rise of gestational surrogacy and the pressing need for international regulation. Minn J Int Law 21:120–144

Dye BE (2007) Expanding parental rights for lesbian couples. Law Sex Rev Lesbian Gay Bisex Transgender Leg Issues 16:169–180

Grammaticaki-Alexiou A (1999) Artificial reproduction technologies and private international law. La Law Rev 60:1113–1122

Gruenbaum D (2012) Foreign surrogate motherhood. *Mater Semper Certa Erat*. Am J Comp Law 60:475–506

[59] Muir Watt (2000).

[60] *Ibidem*, p. 506.

Hauser J (2012) Le Projet de Loi sur le Mariage des Personnes de Meme Sexe. Le Paradoxe de la Tortue d'Achille. La Semaine Juridique, No. 44, Doctr. 1185
Herring J (2010) Medical law and ethics. Oxford University Press, Oxford
Hurwitz I (2000) Collaborative reproduction: finding the child in the maze of legal motherhood. Conn Law Rev 33:127–180
Ikemoto LC (2009) Reproductive tourism: equality concerns in the global market for fertility services. Law Inequality J Theory Pract 27:277–310
Joslin CG (2005) The legal parentage of children born to same-sex couples: development in the law. Fam Law Q 39:683–706
Joslin CG (2009) Interstate recognition of parentage in a time of disharmony: same-sex parent families and beyond. Ohio State Law J 70:563–618
Kipiani P (2012) Mariage Homosexuel et Adoption par un Couple Homosexuel: D'une Revendication en Droit Français A une Reconnaissance en Droit Belge. Droit de la famille, No. 1/2012, Ètude 3
Knaplund K (2012) Children of assisted reproduction. Univ Mich J Law Ref 45:899–936
Knoppers BM, LeBris S (1991) Recent advances in medically assisted conception: legal, ethical and social issue. Am J Law Med 17:329–361
Koppelman A (2006) Same-sex, different states. When same-sex marriages cross state lines. Yale Univ. Press, New Haven & London
Larson M (2010) Don't know much about biology: courts and the rights of non-biological parents in same-sex partnerships. Georgetown J Gend Law 11:869–886
Lopez WM (2011) Artificial insemination and the presumption of parenthood: traditional foundations and mother applications for lesbian mothers. Chic-Kent Law Rev 86:897–924
McGuire L (2004) Parental rights of gay and lesbian couples: will legalizing same-sex marriage make a difference? Duquesne Law Rev 43:273–284
Mohapatra S (2012) Achieving reproductive justice in the international surrogacy market. Ann Health Law 21:190–202
Moissinac Massenat V (2012) Ordre Public International Versus Droits de l'Homme en Matière de Filiation. Union International des Avocats (UIA), Dresde/Allemagne 31 Octobre–4 Novembre 2012
Muir Watt H (2000) La Fonction Subversive du Droit Compare. Revue Internationale du Droit Comparé 52:503–527
Neirinck C (2012) Homoparentalité et désexualisation de l'état civil. Droit de la famille, No. 7, Juillet 2012, Rep. 6
O'Bryan KM (2010) Mommy and daddy and me: a contract solution to a child's loss of the lesbian or transgender nonbiological parent. DePaul Law Rev 60:1115–1168
Oppenheimer E (2011) No exit: the problem of same-sex divorce. N C Law Rev 90:73–124
Polikoff ND (2001) Lesbian and gay couples raising children: the law in the United States. In: Wintemute R, Andenaes M (eds) The legal recognition of same-sex partners: a study of national, European and international law. Hart Publishing, Oxford, pp 153–168
Probert R (2004) Families, assisted reproduction and the law. Child Fam Law Q 16:273–288
Robertson JA (2004) Gay and lesbian access to assisted reproductive technology. Case West Reserve Law Rev 55:323–372
Rosenblum D (2012) Unsex mothering: towards a new culture of parenting. Harv J Law Gend 35:57–116
Saladino J (2011) Is a second mommy a good enough second parent?: Why voluntary acknowledgments of paternity should be available to lesbian co-parents. Mod Am 7:2–11
Schwenzer I (2007) Convergence and divergence in the law on same-sex partnerships. In: Antokolskaia M (ed) Convergence and divergence of family law in Europe. Intersentia, Antwerpen/Oxford, pp 145–157
Shapo HS (2006) Assisted reproduction and the law: disharmony on a divisive social issue. Northwestern Univ Law Rev 100:465–480

Symeonides SC (2007) Choice of law in American Courts in 2007: twenty-first annual survey. Am J Comp Law 56:243–320

Symeonides SC (2008) American private international law. Wolters Kluwer, London

Venturatos Lorio K (1999) The process of regulating assisted reproductive technologies: what we can learn from our neighbors—what translates and what does not. Loyola Law Rev 45:247–268

Wardle LD (2006) Global perspective on procreation and parentage by assisted reproduction. Cap Univ Law Rev 35:413–478

Winkler MM (2011) Friends to our children: omogenitorialità e diritto internazionale privato. In: Schuster A (ed) Omogenitorialità. Filiazione, Orientamento Sessuale e Diritto. Mimesis, Milan, pp 115–136

Zgonjanin S (2005) What does it take to be a (lesbian) parent? On intent and genetics. Hastings Womens Law J 16:251–280

Part II
Supranational and International (and *Quasi*-) Jurisdictions

Section 1 Human Rights Law Issues

Section 2 EU Law Issues

Section 3 International Labour Law Issues and Quasi-Jurisdictional Bodies

Chapter 17
Same-Sex Couples Before the ECtHR: The Right to Marriage

Pietro Pustorino

Abstract This chapter analyses the jurisprudence of the European Court of Human Rights on the recognition of the right to marriage for same-sex couples. It focuses on the Court's 2010 judgment in the well-known case *Schalk and Kopf*, referring also to other cases on the subject. The discussion highlights important aspects of the evolutive approach of the Court and the limits of the decision of 2010, particularly with regard to the absence of a European consensus on same-sex marriages among the States Parties to the ECHR. The conclusion provides some observations on recent and future developments, both in the case law of the Court and in the legislation of the Member States.

17.1 Introduction

The European Court of Human Rights (ECtHR) has decided several cases concerning the rights of same-sex couples or individuals in a homosexual relationship. The issues examined in this and the following chapter were referred to the Court following individual complaints against States whose laws, acts or decisions were considered by the applicants as contrary to the ECHR.

The specific provisions invoked in the cases discussed here are Articles 8, 12 and 14 ECHR. The first, on the protection of private and family life, reads:

1. Everyone has the right to respect for his private and family life, his home and his correspondence.
2. There shall be no interference by a public authority with the exercise of this right except such as is in accordance with the law and is necessary in a democratic society in the interests of national security, public safety or the economic well-being of the country, for the prevention of disorder or crime, for the protection of health or morals, or for the protection of the rights and freedoms of others.

P. Pustorino (✉)
Department of Political and International Sciences, University of Siena, Siena, Italy
e-mail: pietro.pustorino@unisi.it

D. Gallo et al. (eds.), *Same-Sex Couples before National, Supranational and International Jurisdictions*, DOI 10.1007/978-3-642-35434-2_17,

The second, on the right to marriage, states that:

> Men and women of marriageable age have the right to marry and to found a family, according to the national laws governing the exercise of this right.

And the third, on the prohibition of discrimination,[1] provides that:

> The enjoyment of the rights and freedoms set forth in this Convention shall be secured without discrimination on any ground such as sex, race, colour, language, religion, political or other opinion, national or social origin, association with a national minority, property, birth or other status.

The above provisions have been invoked either alone or in combination—e.g., Art. 8 in conjunction with Art. 14.

This chapter will focus on the issues related to the application to same-sex couples of Art. 12 on the right to marry, while the application of the other two provisions of the ECHR to same-sex couples or individuals in a homosexual relationship will be discussed in Chap. 18.

17.2 *Schalk and Kopf*: The Proceedings Before the National Courts

As is well known, the ECtHR's case law on the extension of the right to marry to same-sex couples consists primarily of one case, *Schalk and Kopf v. Austria*,[2] which was decided by the Court on 24 June 2010.

In this judgment, the First Section of the Court found that the Austrian Government had breached neither Art. 12 nor Art. 14 taken in conjunction with Art. 8 ECHR. The choice of the First Section not to relinquish its jurisdiction in favour of the Grand Chamber has been strongly criticized.[3] At any rate, the five-judge panel of the Grand Chamber rejected the applicant's request to review the judgment of the First Section.[4]

---

[1] Originally, Art. 14 was not a free standing provision and it could be invoked only in connection with a substantive ECHR provision. After the entry into force of Protocol 12, the prohibition of discrimination stands as an autonomous right and it can be invoked also separately from other substantive rights protected by the Convention. However, since only 18 out of the 47 States Parties to the ECHR have ratified Protocol 12, *de facto* Art. 14 cannot yet be considered a free-standing provision.

[2] *Schalk and Kopf v. Austria*, n. 30141/04, judgment of 24th June 2010. On this judgment, see Buyse (2010), Johnson (2010), Milanovic (2010), Peroni (2010), Ragni (2010), Repetto (2010), Timmer (2010a), Timmer (2010b), Wiemann (2010), Winkler (2010), Graupner (2011), Magi (2011), Paladini (2011), Waaldijk (2011), Cozzi (2012), Vitucci (2012) and Scherpe (2013).

[3] Thienel (2010). In this regard, and in connection with very recent developments in the case law, see the last paragraph of this chapter.

[4] Registrar of the ECtHR, press release of 29 November 2011.

The facts of the case are quite well known. The applicants created a same-sex couple living in Vienna. In 2002, they requested the Office for matters of Personal Status to proceed with the formalities to enable them to contract marriage. The Office refused their request based on the Austrian legislation (Art. 44 of the Austrian Civil Code) and national case law on the subject, which restricted the right to marry to opposite-sex couples only. Following the decision of the Vienna Regional Governor in 2003, which confirmed the refusal, the applicants lodged a constitutional complaint.

In its judgment of 12 December 2003, the Constitutional Court dismissed the complaint as ill-founded. With regard to the ECHR, it observed that the concept of marriage enshrined in Art. 12 should not be extended to homosexual relationships, and that "the fact that same-sex relationships fall within the concept of private life and as such enjoy the protection of Art. 8 ECHR" did not "give rise to an obligation to change the law of marriage."[5]

17.3 The ECtHR's Judgment in *Schalk and Kopf*: The Reference to Transsexual Cases

Before examining the arguments that led the ECtHR to conclude that there had been no violation of Arts. 8, 12 and 14 ECHR, we should emphasize that the Court, at the outset of the judgment in *Schalk and Kopf*, acknowledged a connection between cases concerning the right to marry of same-sex couples and its own case law on the rights of transsexuals, observing that "certain principles might be derived from [the] Court's case-law relating to transsexuals".[6] Among the principles applied in the case of transsexuals, the Court referred to the distinction between the right to marry and the right to found a family, which, based on the wording of Art. 12, are closely linked to each other.

The connection between marriage and family, which was certainly justified at the time when the provision was drafted, had already been established by the Court in *Christine Goodwin v. The United Kingdom.*[7] In that judgment, the Court found that there had been a violation of Arts. 8 and 12 with regard to the rights claimed by a female transsexual. The decision was based on an evolutive interpretation of Art. 12 and expressly overruled the Court's conclusions in previous cases concerning transsexuals. In particular, the ECtHR observed that Art. 12 secured the fundamental right to marry and to found a family, but added that

[5] *Schalk and Kopf v. Austria*, paras 7–14.

[6] *Ibidem*, para. 50.

[7] *Christine Goodwin v. the United-Kingdom*, n. 28957/95, judgment of 11th July 2002 (Grand Chamber).

> the second aspect is not however a condition of the first and the inability of any couple to conceive or parent a child cannot be regarded as *per se* removing their right to enjoy the first limb of the provision.[8]

17.4 The Reasoning of the European Court in *Schalk and Kopf*

Some of the arguments used by the Court in *Schalk and Kopf* as regards the interpretation of the right to marry and the right to private and family life, in conjunction with the principle of non-discrimination, were inspired by the need to apply an evolutive approach to the interpretation of the ECHR, whereas other arguments seemed more cautious and in line with its previous case law.

Concerning the application of Art. 12, the Court overruled its previous interpretation—according to which the provision referred "to the traditional marriage between persons of opposite biological sex"[9] and stated that "it cannot be said that Article 12 is inapplicable to the applicants' case".[10]

Even though the negative form of the statement may be vulnerable to criticism (a positive form establishing the applicability of the provision would have been more appropriate), the meaning does not change: Art. 12 applies to the situation of a same-sex couple claiming to have a right to marry. However, as noted in the literature,[11] the Court did not specify the circumstances in which Art. 12 may be applied to same-sex couples.

The Court's reasoning seems to reflect the position adopted by an authoritative member of the former European Commission of Human Rights, Mr. Schermers, in his partially dissenting opinion in the Commission's report of 7 March 1989 on the case of *W. v. The United Kingdom*, which concerned a transsexual. Considering that the right to live in a family is of paramount importance for the individual, Schermers observed that

> the fundamental right underlying Article 12 should also be granted to homosexual and lesbian couples. They should not be denied the right to found a family without good reasons.[12]

As regards the application of Art. 8 ECHR, the Court, referring to a large number of cases concerning discrimination based on sexual orientation, stated very clearly that it was "undisputed" in this case that "the relationship of a same-sex couple

[8] *Ibidem*, para. 98.

[9] *Rees v. the United Kingdom*, n. 9532/81, judgment of 17th October 1986, para. 49.

[10] *Ibidem*, para. 61.

[11] Hodson (2011), p. 173.

[12] *W. v. United Kingdom*, n. 11095/84, report of 7th March 1989.

like the applicants' falls within the notion of 'private life' within the meaning of Article 8".[13]

In addition to confirming its approach that the sexual relationship of a same-sex couple has to be qualified as "private life" within the meaning of Art. 8, the Court also noted that a rapid evolution of social attitudes towards same-sex couples had already taken place in many member States of the ECHR.

For this reason, the Court had no hesitation in observing that it was "artificial" to "maintain the view that, in contrast to a different-sex couple, a same-sex couple cannot enjoy 'family life' for the purposes of Article 8."[14]

In terms of the application of Art. 8 to same-sex couples, the recent approach of the Court fits into the broader context of a wide interpretation of the notion of "family life" contained in the provision. For quite a long time now, the Court has recognized *de facto* stable family relationships between persons of the opposite sex,[15] specifically protecting the *de facto* relationships of these persons with their children. From this point of view, the *Schalk and Kopf* judgment can be regarded as a further and relevant development of the substantial equivalence between *de jure* and *de facto* relationships.

Finally, the Court answered the question regarding the combined application of Arts. 14 and 8 ECHR. Establishing that the legal situation of opposite and same-sex couples is comparable also in this respect, the Court stated that the applicants were "in a relevantly similar situation to a different-sex couple as regards their need for legal recognition and protection of their relationship."[16]

In light of the foregoing, some of the criticisms made against the conclusions of the Court seem rather excessive. In particular, the judgment has been defined as "particularly underdeveloped"[17] and "hasty and unsatisfactory for its lack of reasoning".[18] On the contrary, we believe that there are many positive aspects to the evolutive interpretation of the ECHR in *Schalk and Kopf*, and that these aspects are likely to be taken up and developed in future cases.

All the same, we need to comment on the fact that, according to the Court, Art. 12 ECHR cannot be interpreted in the sense of establishing the right to marry of a same-sex couple.

The main reason that led the Court to conclude that the Convention did not protect the right claimed by the applicants was the absence of a "European consensus regarding same-sex marriage". According to the Court, at the time of the judgment only 6 of the 47 States Parties to the Convention allowed same-sex marriages.[19] This is not the appropriate place to focus on the nature and meaning of

[13] *Schalk and Kopf v. Austria*, para. 90.

[14] *Ibidem*, para. 94.

[15] *Keegan v. Ireland*, n. 16969/90, judgment of 26th May 1994, para. 44.

[16] *Schalk and Kopf v. Austria*, para. 99.

[17] Johnson (2013a), p. 149.

[18] Hodson (2011), p. 175.

[19] *Schalk and Kopf v. Austria*, para. 58.

the expression "European consensus", which is often used by the Court to take account of the developments of legal and social issues relevant to the interpretation of the ECHR. In particular, the question arises whether European consensus necessarily corresponds to a general principle of European Union law, or whether, as we believe, it may be a lower and less established legal standard, which gives the Court a wider margin of appreciation in terms of an evolutive interpretation of the ECHR. In any case, what it is necessary is to clearly identify the trends followed by the majority of the States Parties to the ECHR, in order to avoid abuses about evolutive interpretation of the ECHR based on an European consensus which simply does not exist or is only in phase of initial formation. In *Schalk and Kopf,* the absence of a European consensus led the Court to rule out the possibility of an evolutive interpretation of Art. 12 in the sense suggested by the applicants.

The Court also excluded that Art. 9 of the Charter of Fundamental Rights of the European Union (proclaimed on 7 December 2000 and 12 December 2007, and entered into force on 1 December 2009) (further referred to as CFR) could lead to an interpretation favourable to the applicants. Art. 9 which has dropped the reference to men and women, provides that: "The right to marry and to found a family shall be guaranteed in accordance with the national laws governing the exercise of these rights." Moreover, the Commentary of the CFR states that Art. 9 "neither prohibits nor imposes the granting of the status of marriage to unions between people of the same sex."[20]

Since Austrian legislation did not recognize the right to marry for same-sex couples, the Court ruled out a conflict with Art. 9 CFR, which could have been relevant to an evolutive interpretation of Art. 12 ECHR.

To sum up, it is my opinion that, at the time of the judgment, it was not so easy to take a different decision on the merits. In the absence of an adequate legal criterion based on a European consensus, a different decision would have meant applying just a "creative" interpretation of Art. 12, rather than an evolutive interpretation of the provision. As correctly noted by others, the main question at stake in *Schalk and Kopf* concerned the limits of the 'living instrument approach',[21] i.e., the extension of the evolutive method in interpreting the Convention. Even though the Court has progressively extended the limits on the use of the evolutive method, it would have been very difficult to decide in favour of the applicants when there was just an emerging European consensus on the right to marry for same-sex couples.

This observation seems to be confirmed by the criticisms raised in the Concurring Opinion of Judge Malinverni joined by Judge Kovler. According to the two judges, the rules on the interpretation of international treaties laid down in the Vienna Convention on the Law of Treaties of 23 May 1969 precluded "Article

[20] Explanations Relating to the Charter of Fundamental Rights, OJ 2007 C 303, p. 17.

[21] Thienel (2010).

12 from being construed as conferring the right to marry on persons of the same-sex."[22]

Moreover, the judges even seemed to hold that the Court could not retrospectively change its approach by using an evolutive interpretation of Art. 12:

> the Court cannot, by means of an evolutive interpretation "derive from [it] a right that was not included therein at the outset".[23]

This second part of the concurring opinion is not in line with the importance of evolutive interpretation in the jurisprudence of the Court, which does not hesitate to accept interpretations that are very far from the ordinary meaning of the provisions of the ECHR, if a clear European consensus on the right to marry of a same-sex couple will emerge.

17.5 Effects of the Decision in *Schalk and Kopf* and Future Developments

It seems reasonable to assume that the *Schalk and Kopf* case led the Austrian legislature to pass the Registered Partnership Act on 1 January 2010, which establishes, to some extent, rules very similar to those governing marriages in Austria.[24] Although it is difficult to assess to what extent a simple application to the European Court can induce the respondent State to change its legislation prior to the judgment of the Court—especially in area in which there is no precedent similar to that of the application and when the provision at stake (Art. 12) does not recognize the right to marry for same-sex couples—there is no doubt that in some cases it has happened. This clearly shows that the ECHR and the jurisprudence of the Strasbourg Court have an influence on national legal systems.

To conclude, we will make some final observations on whether future developments in the interpretation of Art. 12 will lead to the recognition of the right to marry for same-sex couples.

In my opinion, the time is not ripe yet for to the rapid formation of a European consensus in that direction. Moreover, it must be noted that the European Court has recently confirmed that "Article 12 does not impose an obligation on the Contracting States to grant same-sex couples access to marriages", and that the individual right to marriage cannot be derived from Art. 14 in conjunction with Art. 8.[25] As already emphasised in the literature, the fact that the ECtHR has

[22] Concurring Opinion of Judge Malinverni joined by Judge Kovler, attached to the judgement (*supra*, note 2).

[23] *Ibidem.*

[24] See, in this volume, the chapter by Repetto in this volume.

[25] *X. and Others v. Austria*, n. 19010/07, judgment of 19th February 2013 (Grand Chamber), para. 106. On this judgment, see the chapter by Crisafulli in this volume.

confirmed its interpretation of Art. 12 in *Schalk and Kopf* "is a clear sign that the Court intends no evolution in its case law on same-sex marriage in the near future."[26]

However, the changes in national legislations, case law and social perceptions after 2010, which are amply discussed in this volume, suggest that the margin of appreciation of the States Parties to the ECHR has been further reduced in recent years. As a consequence, we believe that, in order to pass the test of conformity with the Convention, the States Parties to the ECHR are obliged to more strictly justify national measures distinguishing between different and same-sex couples for the purposes of the right to marry or to register civil unions.

In other words, in the absence of a European consensus on this subject, it is still difficult to maintain that the right to marry under Art. 12 already includes same-sex couples. However, it is certainly easier now than a few years ago to assess situations of discrimination for which there is insufficient justification. Certainly, the progressive assessment of violations of ECHR provisions that are due to discrimination between opposite- and same-sex couples is likely to facilitate the formation of a European consensus in the future, and its eventual recognition by the ECtHR. The current problem is, therefore, to understand the extent to which the discretion of the States Parties to the European Convention to approve national measures distinguishing between same- and different-sex couples for the purposes of certain human rights has been reduced.

From this point of view, a number of cases currently pending before the Court can help determine the actual extent of that reduction and, at the same time, whether the Court intends to usher in a new approach in its case law, as it did in the past with regard to the rights of transsexuals.

Two cases are especially noteworthy: *Vallianatos and Mylonas v. Greece* and *C. S. and Others v. Greece*.[27] They both concern the Greek legislation on civil unions (Law no. 3719/2008, entered into force in November 2008), which allows only different-sex adults to register their civil unions by means of a notarial instrument. The applicants rely on Art. 8 and 14 ECHR, complaining that the Greek law breaches their right to respect for their private life and the principle of non-discrimination.

These applications were lodged with the European Court on 6 may 2009, but on 11 September 2012 the Chamber relinquished jurisdiction in favour of the Grand Chamber. Thus, unlike what happened in the *Schalk and Kopf* case, it is the Grand Chamber that will decide this very delicate issue.

[26] Johnson (2013b).

[27] Applications n. 29381/09 and n. 32684/09. On the development of the cases, see Registrar of the Court, press release ECHR 015 (2013), 16 January 2013. For a national perspective on these cases, see the chapter by Drosos and Constantinides in this volume.

References

Buyse A (2010) ECtHR judgment: states not obliged to allow homosexual marriages. http://echrblog.blogspot.com

Cozzi AO (2012) Articolo 12. In: Bartole S, De Sena P, Zagrebelsky V (eds) Commentario breve alla Convenzione europea dei diritti dell'uomo. Cedam, Padova, pp 450–458

Graupner H (2011) Gay rights. Max Planck encyclopedia of public international law, www.mpepil.com

Hodson L (2011) A marriage by any other name? Schalk and Kopf v. Austria. Hum Rights Law Rev 11(1):170–179

Johnson P (2010) An essentially private manifestation of human personality. Hum Rights Law Rev 10(1):67–97

Johnson P (2013a) Homosexuality and the European Court of human rights. Routledge, Abingdon

Johnson P (2013b), X. and Others v Austria. http://www.echrblog.blogspot.it

Magi L (2011) La Corte europea dei diritti dell'uomo e il diritto alla vita familiare e al matrimonio fra individui dello stesso sesso. Rivista di diritto internazionale XCIV(2):396–421

Milanovic M (2010) No right to same-sex marriage under the ECHR, 24 June 2010. www.ejil.org

Paladini L (2011) Le coppie dello stesso sesso tra la sentenza della Corte costituzionale n. 138 del 14 aprile 2010 e la pronuncia della Corte europea dei diritti dell'uomo del 24 giugno 2010 nel caso Schalk and Kopf v. Austria. Diritto Pubblico Comparato ed Europeo 1:137–151

Peroni L (2010) Gay marriage: unlocking the door but keeping it closed? (25th June 2010). http://strasbourgobservers.com

Ragni C (2010) La tutela delle coppie omosessuali nella recente giurisprudenza della Corte europea dei diritti umani: il caso Schalk e Kopf. Diritti umani e diritto internazionale 4(3):639–643

Repetto G (2010) Il matrimonio omosessuale al vaglio della Corte di Strasburgo, ovvero: la negazione "virtuosa" di un diritto. Rivista dell'Associazione Italiana dei Costituzionalisti. http://www.associazionecostituzionalisti.it

Scherpe JM (2013) The legal recognition of same-sex couples in Europe and the role of the European Court of human rights. Equal Rights Rev 10:83–96

Thienel T (2010) Gay marriage and the ECHR. http://invisiblecollege.weblog.leidenuniv.nl/2010/03/02/gay-marriage-and-the-echr

Timmer A (2010a) Same-sex marriage case should go to the Grand Chamber: more on Schalk and Kopf v. Austria, 1st July 2010. http://strasbourgobservers.com

Timmer A (2010b) 2010: year of "profound moral views"?, 20 January 2011. http://strasbourgobservers.com/2011/01/20/2010-the-year-of-"profound-moral-views"/

Vitucci MC (2012) La tutela internazionale dell'orientamento sessuale. Jovene, Napoli

Waaldijk K (2011) Same-sex partnership, international protection. Max Planck encyclopedia of public international law. www.mpepil.com

Wiemann RM (2010) Die Rechtsprechung des EGMR zu sexueller Orientierung. Europäische Grundrechte-Zeitschrift 37:408–414

Winkler M (2010) Le famiglie omosessuali nuovamente alla prova della Corte di Strasburgo. La nuova giurisprudenza civile commentata 1137–1154

Post Scriptum

On 7th November 2013, the ECtHR decided applications no. 29381/09 and no. 32684/08 referred to in para. 17.5 of this chapter. In the judgement, the Court reiterates its considerations in *Schalk and Kopf* on the application of Article 8 to same-sex couples, stating that the relationship of same-sex couples falls within both the notion of "private life" and the notion of "family life", but also interestingly adding that a lack of cohabitation between the two partners does not deprive the relationship of the stability necessary to form a real couple (para. 73). On the merits, the core of the observations of the Court lies in the application of the principle of proportionality, in order to analyze the respect of the margin of appreciation recognized to the State in the treatment of same-sex couples. Even though the Court correctly takes note that there is no uniformity on the subject among the legal systems of the ECHR States parties, it also confirms that "a trend is currently emerging with regard to the introduction of forms of legal recognition of same-sex relationships". On the specific discrimination between same-sex and opposite-sex couples in the matter of accessing to civil unions, as in the case of the Greek legislation at stake, it is noteworthy to underline that the Court, in considering all the pertinent national legislations, observes that "Lithuania and Greece are the only ones to reserve it exclusively to different-sex couples" (para. 91). For these reasons, the Court found a violation of Article 14 taken in conjunction with Article 8. The decision, as stressed in this chapter, confirms the trend to reduce the State's margin of appreciation in order to enact legislations which discriminate same-sex from opposite-sex couples in the enjoyment of identical rights. It is also interesting to note that the "Court continues to use the weapon" of the European trend as the most important parameter to analyze the conformity of national measures to the ECHR, assessing not only the existence of a general trend towards forms of legal recognition of same-sex relationships, but even a sub-level of this trend (formed by just 19 of the 47 States member of the Council of Europe) which becomes essential to find a violation in the present case. Thus, it seems that the only way to enhance the protection of the same-sex couples in the framework of the ECHR is the very flexible application of the method of the European consensus, which implies the appreciation of not particularly wide trends. Maybe this is the only possibility to "open the doors" of the ECHR to same-sex couples, but the problem to limit the use of this evolutive method of interpretation of the ECHR still remains, waiting for a future modification of the Convention that would expressly consider gay people's rights and interests.

Chapter 18
Same-Sex Couples' Rights (Other than the Right to Marry) Before the ECtHR

Francesco Crisafulli

Abstract This chapter offers a general overview on the case-law of the Strasbourg Court concerning the rights of homosexuals and same-sex couples under the European Convention on Human Rights. It covers five main areas: freedom of sexual intercourse, definition of private life and family life in the context of homosexual relationships, patrimonial rights, parental rights and expulsion of aliens.

18.1 Introduction

The European Court of Human Rights in Strasbourg (further also referred to as the Court) has been dealing for quite a long time with various aspects of the legal condition of homosexuals and same-sex couples. Additionally, it has repeatedly been called upon to address issues concerning sexual identity and orientation, and problems faced by transsexual or transgender people.[1] A distinct set of problems, indeed, certainly different from that concerning homosexuality, but still closely related to it (as proved by the very fact that the Court itself would frequently quote its own judgments on cases concerning transsexuals when adjudicating on homosexuality cases),[2] at least because some definitions (such as the definition of 'sex', or that of 'family') are obviously relevant for both.

---

[1] See the case of *Christine Goodwin v. the United-Kingdom*, n. 28957/95, judgment of 11th July 2002 (Grand Chamber). The judgment deals with an operated transsexual's rights. For a quick overview of the main case-law on issues related to sexual life and orientation, see Leach (2005), p. 306, and van Dijk et al. (2006), p. 678.

[2] In the recent case of *Schalk and Kopf v. Austria*, n. 30141/04, judgment of 24th June 2010, which concerns same-sex marriage and is discussed at length in the chapter by Pustorino in this volume, for instance, the Court has felt the need to recall some principles first affirmed in *Christine Goodwin*.

F. Crisafulli (✉)
Court of Rome, Rome, Italy
e-mail: francesco.crisafulli@giustizia.it

D. Gallo et al. (eds.), *Same-Sex Couples before National, Supranational and International Jurisdictions*, DOI 10.1007/978-3-642-35434-2_18,

The provisions of the European Convention on Human Rights (further also referred to as ECHR) and its Protocols, against which the Court checked the legislation and practice of the contracting States by which the applicants felt their rights to be impaired, are essentially Art. 8 (right to respect for private and family life) and 12 (right to marry) of the Convention and, to a lesser extent, Art. 1 of Protocol No. 1 (protection of property). Additionally, Art. 14 ECHR, which prohibits discrimination in the enjoyment of other conventionally protected rights, was—and still is—frequently, though not always, invoked by the applicants.

In this context, the decisions and judgments of the Court addressed a number of different issues, ranging from the very basic right not to be subject to investigations in one's sexual life and not to suffer discriminatory treatment in employment context,[3] to the right to marry or have access to some alternative recognition, and including the enjoyment of certain connected freedoms and rights.[4]

18.2 Homosexuality and Sexual Intercourse

The leading case on what can be seen as the basic essence of the right, for any homosexual man (or woman)[5] to normally lead his (or her) sentimental and sexual life according to his (or her) tendencies, is the judgment of *Dudgeon v. the United Kingdom*,[6] followed (a few years later) by *Norris v. Ireland*.[7]

The *Dudgeon* case is by no means the first one to have brought the prohibition of sexual intercourse between consenting male homosexuals to the attention of the Convention institutions in Strasbourg; it is, however, the first one in which a Court judgment was issued. Three other cases of a similar kind had already been

[3] See, e.g., the judgments concerning investigations into the homosexuality of male and female members of the armed forces in the UK and their subsequent discharge on the sole ground of their sexual orientation: *Smith and Grady v. the United-Kingdom*, n. 33985/96 and 33986/96, and *Lustig-Prean and Beckett v. the United-Kingdom*, n. 31417/96 and 32377/96, judgments of 27th September 1999. In the literature, Mowbray (2001), p. 349.

[4] For a comprehensive in-depth study of the issue of fundamental rights for homosexuals, see Johnson (2013), *passim*. See also Graupner (2011), *passim*.

[5] As can be seen in the cases which will be discussed presently, the legal treatment of male and female homosexuality was not identical in the national legislations.

[6] N. 7525/76, judgment of 22nd October 1981. Comments in McLoughlin (1996).

[7] N. 10581/83, judgment of 26th October 1988. Along the same lines, see also the rather shorter judgment in the case of *Modinos v. Cyprus*, n. 15070/89, judgment of 22nd April 1993.

examined by the former Commission of Human Rights[8] with varying (but on the whole negative for the applicants) results.[9]

The first application, registered under n. 104/55,[10] was rejected as inadmissible on the grounds that legislation prohibiting or limiting homosexual acts, while constituting an interference with the individual rights guaranteed by Art. 8 of the ECHR, was nevertheless legitimate under the second paragraph of the same provision, as directed to protect public health or morals.

In a case of *X v. the Federal Republic of Germany*,[11] the applicant complained about the German legislation criminalizing homosexual acts with a man under 21 of age, which he thought to constitute an interference in his private life, contrary to Art. 8, and to be discriminatory in that only male (and not female) homosexuality was punishable. The Commission dismissed the whole application as being manifestly ill-founded. As for the first limb of the complaint, it found that the interference in the applicant's private life was justified

> by the need to protect the rights of children and adolescents and enable them to achieve true autonomy in sexual matters.

Turning to the determination of the proper age of valid consent, the Commission acknowledged the differences of views existing among Member States on this issue and came to the conclusion that the age limit of 18–21, although "relatively high", did not exceed the "reasonable margin" within which each Member State was entitled to set it. Having said that, it also noted, in addition, that "at all events" the applicant had been convicted for having had homosexual relationships with adolescents under 16: a consideration that the Commission seems to mention merely *ad abundantiam*, although it might have been sufficient alone to reject the application, since 16 was—in Germany as well as in several other European countries—the lowest minimum age of valid consent for any kind of hetero- and homosexual intercourse. As for the second limb of the application, the Commission upheld the view of the German legislator about the different degree of dangerousness between masculine and feminine homosexuality and found that this was both a "reasonable" and an "objective" criterion justifying, under Art. 14 of the Convention, combined with Art. 8, the difference in treatment that the applicant complained of.

---

[8] The Commission, originally vested with the competence to rule on the admissibility of applications, and to issue an opinion on their merits, in view of the final decision to be taken by the Committee of Ministers of the Council of Europe (in what was known as a *quasi-judicial* procedure), or to refer the cases to the Court for adjudication, was abolished, as known, in 1999 by the amending Protocol No 11 to the Convention, which, *inter alia*, established the now existing permanent Court and granted direct access to it to any individual claiming to be a victim of a breach of the conventional rights.

[9] A critical summary of the main case-law on the subject can be found in van Dijk et al. (2006), p. 678.

[10] The case is quoted in the third decision discussed here (cf. note 1) as follows: No. 104/55, Yearbook 1, pp. 228–229; however, it cannot be found in the database of the Court.

[11] N. 5935/72, decision on admissibility of 30th September 1975.

The third application[12] was lodged by a British national who had been sentenced to a term of imprisonment on account of his having entertained homosexual relationships with two men of 18 years of age. The defendant Government had relied on the two cases summarized above, but the Commission did not follow. As for the first precedent,

> taking into account the development of moral opinion in recent years concerning State interference with the private, consensual sexual lives of adults,

it found that the impugned British legislation could not be *prima facie* justified under Art. 8(2), as being "for the protection of health or morals". As for the second, the Commission picked up what had originally been used as a side-argument (namely the particularly young age of the adolescents with whom the applicant had homosexual intercourse in the German case) and posthumously promoted it to the role of primary and decisive ground for the dismissal of the previous application, thus stressing the factual differences between the two cases. This allowed the Commission to elegantly depart from its finding that an age limit of 18–21 was reasonably within the margin of appreciation allowed to domestic authorities and to come to the conclusion that the issue of "whether 18 year olds ought to be considered as 'young people' in need of protection" deserved further consideration both under Art. 8 taken alone and under Art. 14 combined with Art. 8. As a result, the application was declared admissible as far as undue interference in the applicant's private life and prohibited discrimination of male homosexuals *vis-à-vis* female homosexuals and heterosexuals were complained of.

However, in its report to the Committee of Ministers on the merits of the case, the Commission concluded that neither Art. 8 taken alone, nor Art. 14 taken in conjunction with Art. 8 had been violated. In its reasoning, it conceded that "the age limit of 21 may be regarded as high in the present era", that "current trends throughout Europe in relation to private consensual homosexual behaviour tend to emphasise tolerance and understanding as opposed to the use of criminal sanctions", and that "it may be seen as inconsistent to have an age of majority applicable to voting and other legal transactions, which is lower than the age of consent for homosexual behavior".

Nevertheless, heavily relying on its findings in *X v. the Federal Republic of Germany* (the arguments of which it had seemed to reject in the decision on the admissibility of the British case) according to which

> on account of the social reprobation with which homosexuality is still frequently regarded a minor involved in homosexual relationships with an adult might in fact be cut off from society and seriously affected in his psychological development,

the Commission gave preponderant weight to the Government's argument that

[12] *X v. the United Kingdom*, n. 7215/75, decision on admissibility of 7th July 1977, report to the Committee of Ministers of 12th October 1978.

> given the controversial and sensitive nature of the question involved, young men in the eighteen to twenty-one age bracket who are involved in homosexual relationships would be subject to substantial social pressures which could be harmful to their psychological development.

In addition, it also took into account the various occasions in which the impugned legislation had been (and currently was, at the time of the adoption of the report) amended or proposed for amendment (an argument, the pertinence of which in respect of the compatibility of such legislation with fundamental rights was at least questionable, an will actually be repelled in a later decision).

In *Dudgeon*, the applicant—a male homosexual activist living in Belfast—complained about criminal sanctions imposed in Northern Ireland, at the time when the application was lodged (and also in England and Wales, until 1967), on consenting adults who performed, either in public or in private, certain sexual acts defined as "buggery" or "gross indecency".[13] Admittedly, at the relevant time, the impugned legislation was seldom applied, and generally—if not always—in particular cases involving minors, mental patients or prisoners[14] (that is to say, individuals whose need for special protection could have, at any rate, justified, according to the Convention, the intervention of the public authorities, irrespective, though, of the sex and sexual orientation of the persons involved).[15] The applicant himself had not been prosecuted—let alone convicted—for homosexual offences, although he had undergone police questioning and investigation (including seizure of personal items such as diaries and letters) in connection with his sexual tendencies and activities.

At the end of a quite elaborate reasoning—rather clearly revealing the caution with which the delicate issue required to be tackled at the time—the Court found the UK in breach of Art. 8 of the Convention.

It started by upholding the applicant's claim that he was a "victim" of the alleged violation, within the meaning of Art. 34 (formerly Art. 25) ECHR. To this effect, it did not underestimate the police investigation that the applicant had undergone, but put the main stress on the legislation itself: in the Court's own words,

> the very existence of this legislation continuously and directly affects [the applicant's] private life [...]: either he respects the law and refrains from engaging – even in private with consenting male partners – in prohibited sexual acts to which he is disposed by reason of his homosexual tendencies, or he commits such acts and thereby becomes liable to criminal prosecution.[16]

---

[13] Examples are given in the Court's judgment. Buggery, consisting *inter alia* in sexual penetration *per anum*, could involve male as well as female individuals and could be perpetrated also by heterosexual couples; gross indecency, by contrast, only concerned male homosexuals.

[14] The relevant legislation was: the Offence against the Person Act, of 1861, and the Criminal Law Amendment Act, of 1885. An overview of the legislation in Northern Ireland and in the rest of the United-Kingdom, including subsequent reforms and attempted reforms is given in paras 14–28 of the judgment. The following paras 29–31 provide an outline of the law enforcement practice in Northern Ireland between 1972 and 1981.

[15] It should be noted, however, that the minimum age of consent was different for male homosexuals (21) and girls (16 or 17).

[16] *Dudgeon*, n. 7525/76, judgment of 22nd October 1981, para. 41.

A similar approach was followed in *Norris v. Ireland*, where the applicant had suffered no concrete interference at all by the authorities in his individual rights, but could nevertheless claim to be a victim because of the threat represented by the existing legislation *per se*.[17]

The Court then found, accordingly, that there had been an interference in Mr. Dudgeon's right of respect for his private life, as guaranteed by Art. 8 of the Convention, and went on to ascertain whether such interference was a legitimate one in the light of para. (2) of that provision.

Admittedly, the interference was "in accordance with the law" (i.e., the domestic law); more than that: the interference *was* the law, and vice-versa. The first condition set out by the second paragraph of Art. 8 was therefore met.

The Court also found that the second requirement was equally fulfilled: the interference pursued the legitimate aim of protecting both the morals, "in the sense of moral standards obtaining in Northern Ireland",[18] and the rights and freedoms of others, namely by affording "safeguards for vulnerable members of society, such as the young, against the consequences of homosexual practices".[19]

This last—somewhat surprising—statement (it is indeed unclear why homosexual practices should create a risk, for vulnerable people, greater than that represented by any other form of sexual intercourse) is better expressed when the Court includes it in its very cautious examination of the third requirement (proportionality) of Art. 8(2) ECHR. While conceding that

> some degree of regulation of male homosexual conduct, *as indeed of other forms of sexual conduct*, by means of the criminal law can be justified as 'necessary in a democratic society'[20] (emphasis added),

and that "the contested measures must be seen in the context of Northern Irish society" where there is

> a genuine and sincere conviction shared by a large number of responsible members of the Northern Irish community that a change in the law would be seriously damaging to the moral fabric of society,[21]

the Strasbourg judges stressed that the impugned legislation affected "an essentially private manifestation of the human personality".

They pointed out that

> As compared with the era when that legislation was enacted, there is now a better understanding, and in consequence an increased tolerance, of homosexual behaviour to the extent that in the great majority of the member States of the Council of Europe it is no

[17] The question of the *locus standi* of the applicant had been addressed, already, with equally affirmative conclusions, by the former Commission, in the above-cited *X v. the UK* case (report of 12th October 1978).

[18] *Dudgeon*, para. 46.

[19] *Ibidem*, para. 47.

[20] *Ibidem*, para. 49.

[21] *Ibidem*, paras 56–57.

> longer considered to be necessary or appropriate to treat homosexual practices of the kind now in question as in themselves a matter to which the sanctions of the criminal law should be applied,

taking into account "the marked changes which have occurred in this regard in the domestic law of the member States"

as well as the fact that even

> in Northern Ireland itself, the authorities have refrained in recent years from enforcing the law in respect of private homosexual acts between consenting males over the age of 21 years capable of valid consent

and that

> no evidence has been adduced to show that this has been injurious to moral standards in Northern Ireland or that there has been any public demand for stricter enforcement of the law,

they concluded that there was no "pressing social need" to make homosexual acts between consenting male adults a criminal offence.[22] In view of its detrimental effects on the conventional rights of the applicant, the interference was therefore disproportionate and constituted a breach of Art. 8 ECHR.

Unlike Mr. Norris in the Irish case (where the Court reached the same conclusion about the breach of Art. 8 on almost identical grounds and through extensive reference to the 'indistinguishable' *Dudgeon* case), Mr. Dudgeon had also complained, under Art. 14 combined with Art. 8, of a prohibited discrimination *vis-à-vis* male homosexuals in other parts of the UK, and *vis-à-vis* heterosexuals and female homosexuals in Northern Ireland. However, the Court decided, in the light of the conclusion already reached on the previous complaint, that it was not necessary to separately address the discrimination issue.

The question of whether the different age limit set by the legislation for consent to gay sexual intercourse, on the one hand, and for lesbian or heterosexual relationships, on the other, amounted to a prohibited discrimination—indeed an essentially theoretic and abstract issue, in the light of the Court's findings in *Dudgeon* and *Norris*, later confirmed in *Modinos v. Cyprus* and now become a well-established case-law widely integrated in the national legal orders of all member States—was later resolved by the former Commission, by its report on the case of *Sutherland v. the United Kingdom*.[23]

Having declared the application admissible,[24] the Commission did not in fact, explicitly resolve the question of the alleged breach of Art. 8 in itself, but preferred to examine the case in the light of Art. 14 combined with Art. 8, in accordance with the focus placed by the applicant as well as the defendant Government on the issue of alleged discrimination.

---

[22] *Ibidem*, para. 60.

[23] N. 25186/94, report of 1st July 1997.

[24] By a decision of 21st May 1996.

The applicant, who at the time had recently reached majority, had entertained homosexual relationships, since he was 16, with two males of the same age. As the Commission noted, prior to the 1994 reform of the relevant statute, and until his 18th birthday, this had been an illegal conduct which made the applicant liable to criminal punishment: a fact that—according to the *Dudgeon* case-law—was sufficient to grant him the *status* of potential "victim" of the alleged violations of his fundamental rights.

The Commission took note of the unquestioned similarity between the applicant's situation and that of any young man of 16 or 17 who would have wanted to engage in a sexual relationship with a girl of the same age. It then recalled—and indeed confirmed—its own and the Court's previous findings on the legitimacy of some legal control, notably in the form of age limits, over "particular types of sexual behaviour" and especially

> over homosexual conduct "notably in order to provide safeguards against the exploitation of those who are specially vulnerable by reason, for example, of their youth".

While also bearing in mind the national margin of appreciation

> in assessing whether and to what extent differences justify a different treatment ("a margin, though, which must be particularly narrow and rest on specially serious reasons when 'intimate aspects of private life' are at stake and a difference of treatment [is] based exclusively on the ground of sex")

the Commission openly departed from its report in the case of *X v. the United Kingdom*—which, it noted, was by then nearly 20 years old and deserved reconsideration in the light of the scientific, social and political developments that had taken place in the meantime—as from the rest of its case-law.[25] After rejecting the arguments that the Government derived from the fact that the democratically elected Parliament had recently lowered the age limit to 18 but had refused to equal it to that prescribed for heterosexual (or lesbian) activities, as well as from the contents of the parliamentary debate itself, the Commission thus came to the conclusion that, first, it was not

> a proportionate response to the need for protection to expose to criminal sanctions not only the older man who engages in homosexual acts with a person under the age of 18 but the young man himself who is claimed to be in need of such protection

and, second, that

> no objective and reasonable justification exist[ed] for the maintenance of a higher minimum age of consent to male homosexual, than to heterosexual, acts.

[25] Following *X v. the UK*, and prior to the case of *Sutherland*, the Commission had rejected some three similar (but by no means identical, as far as factual circumstances were concerned) applications, as being manifestly ill-founded: *Johnson v. the United Kingdom*, n. 10389/83, decision of 17th July 1986; *Zukrigl vs Austria*, n. 17279/90, decision of 13th May 1992; *H.F. v. Austria*, n. 22646/93, decision of 26th June 1995.

There was, accordingly, a discriminating treatment to the detriment of the applicant in the exercise of his right to respect for his private life and a breach of Art. 14 combined with Art. 8 of the Convention.[26]

18.3 Private Life and Family Life

For a number of years, both the former Commission and the Court have consistently held that homosexual relationships, albeit stable, do not constitute "family life" within the meaning of Art. 8 of the Convention. This, however, did not prevent those same conventional organs from holding that Art. 8 can nevertheless be applicable to such relationships under another of its various limbs.

Among the different rights protected by Art. 8, the one that is most frequently used by the Convention institutions is that of "private life", which can be unlawfully interfered with by legislation or other measures prohibiting, or excessively limiting, homosexual intercourse. This applicability of Art. 8, under its "private life" aspect, is directly derived from the case-law on sexual intercourse between consenting male adults, as described above, as a natural extension of its underlying logic from the single individual sphere to that of the stable couple. This is clearly the pattern of thought that led the former Commission to the conclusion—mainly based on a reference to the *Dudgeon* judgment—that Art. 8 was applicable to the case of *X and Y v. the United Kingdom*,[27] as well as to several other similar cases.[28]

In other cases, it was the right to respect for one's home that triggered the applicability of Art. 8.[29]

For a long time, the Court did not depart from the Commission's conclusions. It explicitly upheld it in the decision whereby the *Mata Estevez* application was found inadmissible.[30] In its judgments in the cases of *Karner v. Austria*[31] and *J.M. v. the*

---

[26] The conclusion was adopted by a majority of 14 votes to 4. To the report are annexed one concurrent opinion (which focuses on the difference of treatment between male and female homosexuals) and three dissenting opinions. The minority members essentially questioned the accuracy of the assumption that there was a common standard among the majority of the member States; they stressed the importance of the margin of appreciation and the better ability of a national Parliament to determine what best suits the society it democratically represents.

[27] N. 9369/81, decision on admissibility of 3rd May 1983.

[28] See, e.g., *C. and L.M. v. the United Kingdom*, n. 14753/89, decision on admissibility of 9th October 1989; *Kerkhoven and Hinker v. the Netherlands*, n. 15666/89, decision on admissibility of 19th May 1992.

[29] See, e.g., *S. v. the United Kingdom*, n. 11716/85, decision on admissibility of 14th May 1986.

[30] *Mata Estevez v. Spain*, n. 56501/00, decision on admissibility of 10th May 2001: "As regards establishing whether the decision in question concerns the sphere of 'family life' within the meaning of Article 8 § 1 of the Convention, the Court reiterates that, according to the established case-law of the Convention institutions, long-term homosexual relationships between two men do not fall within the scope of the right to respect for family life protected by Article 8 of the Convention [. . .]".

[31] N. 40016/98, judgment of 24th July 2003.

United Kingdom,[32] it was able to openly avoid to tackle the issue, thanks to the fact that, for the purpose of determining the applicability of the principle of non-discrimination (Art. 14 ECHR), the right at stake could however be attracted into the applicability sphere of Art. 8, in the former case, via the protection of "home",[33] and, in the latter case, in that of Art. 1 of Protocol n. 1, via the protection of property.[34]

It is only in *Schalk and Kopf* that the Court finally accepted that homosexual long-term relationships could enjoy the protection afforded to "family life" under Art. 8.[35]

It remains uncertain, however, whether—and, in the affirmative, how—this new approach will alter the outcome of future applications. The notion of "private life" is in fact broader in scope than that of "family life", but the material content of the rights enjoyed by the individual and the corresponding obligations (negative or positive) weighing on the State authorities are indeed very similar, if not identical.[36] The Strasbourg case-law offers several examples where both aspects of the "right to respect of private and family life" are treated jointly and indifferently.[37] In particular, as far as same-sex couples are concerned, it appears that the distinction between them does not always play a decisive role in the process of adjudication.[38]

[32] N. 37060/06, judgment of 28th September 2010.

[33] "The Court does not find it necessary to determine the notions of 'private life' or 'family life' because, in any event, the applicant's complaint relates to the manner in which the alleged difference in treatment adversely affected the enjoyment of his right to respect for his home guaranteed under Article 8 of the Convention [. . .]" (*Karner v. Austria*, para. 33).

[34] "[. . .] having regard to its conclusion that the case in any event falls within the ambit of Article 1 of Protocol No. 1 to which the Court considers that it most naturally belongs, the Court does not find it necessary to decide whether the facts of the case, which are virtually contemporaneous with those in the Mata Estevez case itself, also fall within the ambit of Article 8 of the Convention in its family life aspect. Nor does it find it necessary to decide whether the case falls within the ambit of that Article in its private life aspect" (*J.M. v. the United Kingdom*, para. 50). It is worth noting that the judgment fell on 28th September 2010, 3 months after the *Schalk and Kopf* judgment which had just given a sharp turn to the previous case-law.

[35] *Schalk and Kopf*, paras 90–95, where the Court, *inter alia*, finds that I would be "artificial to maintain the view that, in contrast to a different-sex couple, a same-sex couple cannot enjoy 'family life' for the purposes of Article 8". This finding was reiterated, shortly afterwards, in the case of *P.B. and J.S. v. Austria*, n. 18984/02, judgment of 22nd July 2010, and is now to be taken as a well-established principle. On this issue, see Scherpe (2013).

[36] *Contra*, Levinet, in Sudre et al. (2009) p. 567; it is however disputable whether the example given by the A. purports his opinion.

[37] See, e.g., *Üner v. the Netherlands*, n. 46410/99, judgment of 18th October 2006 (Grand Chamber). For further references, Gouttenoire, in Sudre et al. (2009), pp. 532–533.

[38] For an example of the role that the acknowledgment of "family life" between same-sex partners (and their relatives) may play in the Court's approach, see *X. v. Austria*, para. 127. The judgment will be discussed below, in this chapter.

At any rate, the *Schalk and Kopf* judgment will bear consequences also on heterosexual couples' rights, for it contains indeed the first explicit recognition of a protected family life in a childless unmarried couple.[39]

18.4 Patrimonial Rights

In 1984, following the death of the tenant of a house belonging to it, the Harrogate Borough Council brought possession proceedings against Ms. S., who had been living there with the deceased "in a lesbian relationship as 'man and wife'" for the last 3 years or so. Having unsuccessfully exhausted all available remedies at domestic level, Ms. S. applied to the European Commission in Strasbourg complaining, *inter alia*, that her inability, under applicable domestic regulations, to succeed to her companion in the tenancy, and her subsequent eviction from what had been their joint home, amounted to an unjustified interference with her right to respect for private and family life and was the result of a discrimination, based on sex or sexual orientation, *vis-à-vis* the surviving member of a heterosexual couple.[40]

The Commission relied on previous case-law—in particular, on the decision in the already cited case of *X and Y v. the United Kingdom*—and held (quite coherently) that, as well as gay relationships, lesbian ones also fell outside the scope of "family life". As for private life, the Commission noted that the applicant was now living alone and that her private life had never been previously interfered with, as long as she had been living with her partner. It therefore took the view that the complaint must be considered under still another limb of Art. 8: namely, the right to respect for "home".

Having so decided, the Commission dismissed the complaint on two alternative grounds. It first argued that "the applicant was occupying the house, of which her partner had been the tenant, without any legal title whatsoever", that "on the death of the partner, under the ordinary law, [she] was no longer entitled to remain in the house" while "the local authority was entitled to possession", and that, for those

---

[39] According to a well-established Strasbourg case-law, a *de facto* marital life may constitute a family for the purposes of Article 8 (see, among others, *Johnston v. Ireland*, n. 9697/82, judgment of 18th December 1986, *Keegan v. Ireland*, n. 16969/90, judgment of 26th May 1994); but in all cases adjudicated up to date the couples had given birth to children, and the case-law offered no example of "family life" protection actually afforded to a childless *de facto* couple.

[40] *S. v. the United Kingdom*, n. 11716/85, decision of 14th May 1986. The applicant also complained about unlawful interference with her rights under Art. 1 of Protocol n. 1, but the Commission quite reasonably found that she had no contractual right over the house in question, which could therefore hardly be considered as a "possession" within the meaning of that Art. Finally, she also maintained that no effective remedies were available under domestic law, but the contention was found to be manifestly contradicted by the very fact that she had been able to bring appeal proceedings against the eviction order.

reasons, "the house could no longer be regarded as 'home' for the applicant within the meaning of Article 8".[41]

A somewhat tautological reasoning indeed, the fulcrum of which could in fact be translated as follows: since the domestic legislation (which was, actually, the impugned legislation, at the bottom of the alleged violation) did not consider the house in question as the applicant's home, and consequently did not grant her any rights on it, then the said house was not (or no longer) her home and she had no rights on it; in even shorter terms: if a domestic rule deprives you of a conventional right, then you do not have that conventional right!

The Commission's second (and subsidiary) argument is less startling, but it shows which of the competing interests weighed more on the Commission's balance:

> even if the applicant's right to respect for her home [...] could be regarded as having been interfered with [...], such interference was clearly in accordance with the law and was also necessary for the protection of the contractual rights of the landlord to have the property back at the end of the tenancy.[42]

The decision was probably defendable, given that the applicant had not been living in the house for quite a long time and should have had to pay the rent for it just as for any other home. Nevertheless, one would have welcomed some explicit reference to such particular circumstances in the decision, rather than a very broad and general statement that was bound to apply to a number of possibly very different cases.

The Commission then turned to the discrimination issue and found that "the aim of the legislation in question was to protect the family" and that this was "a goal similar to the protection of the right to respect for family life guaranteed by Article 8 of the Convention".

It therefore held that "the family (to which the relationship of heterosexual unmarried couples living together as husband and wife can be assimilated) merits special protection in society" and that there was "no reason why a High Contracting Party should not afford particular assistance to families".

In sum, the Commission accepted

> that the difference in treatment between the applicant and somebody in the same position whose partner had been of the opposite sex can be objectively and reasonably justified.[43]

The same reasoning was subsequently followed by the Commission in the case of *Röössli v. Germany*,[44] where the applicant—a male homosexual who had been living with his companion for some years in a flat rented by the latter—complained of a discrimination prohibited by Art. 14 (taken in conjunction with Art. 8) ECHR because of his inability, under German law, to succeed in the tenancy contract after

[41] *Ibidem*, para. 4.

[42] *Ibidem*, para. 4, *in fine*.

[43] *Ibidem*, para. 7.

[44] N. 28318/95, decision of 15th May 1996.

the death of the original contractor. Noting that Mr. Röössli was no heir to his late companion and considering that the notion of "family member" in the relevant legal provisions, while including (according to the interpretation given to it) also members of other (unmarried) couples, could only apply to heterosexual relationships, the domestic Courts had upheld the landlady claims for termination of the tenancy and evicted Mr. Röössli from the apartment. The Commission shared, in substance, the domestic Courts' approach and declared the application manifestly ill-founded.

In 1998, an Austrian national, placed in a situation virtually identical to that of Mr. Röössli, also lodged a similar application in Strasbourg.[45] At domestic level, his claim to be entitled to succeed to his late same-sex partner, in the tenancy of the flat where they had been living together in Vienna, had been upheld at first instance by the Austrian Favoriten District Court (*Bezirksgericht*), as well as in the appeal proceedings brought by the landlord before the Vienna Regional Civil Court (*Landesgericht für Zivilrechtssachen*), but the Supreme Court (*Oberster Gerichtshof*) had finally quashed the judgement and ruled that the legal notion of "life companion" did not include same-sex partners.

Following the entry into force of Protocol No. 11,[46] the application skipped the Commission's preliminary ruling on admissibility and went directly to the Court, who found in favor of the applicant.

While still refusing to take a clear stand on the applicability of the notions of "private" and "family" life to same-sex couples, the Strasbourg judges held that, at any rate, the impugned domestic decisions "adversely affected the enjoyment of [the applicant's] right to respect for his home": Art. 8 was therefore applicable to the relevant facts and, as a consequence, a discrimination issue did arise within the meaning of Art. 14.

Departing from the Commission's precedents, the Court recalled the relevant principles governing the application of Art. 14: namely, that

> a difference in treatment is discriminatory if it has no objective and reasonable justification, that is, if it does not pursue a legitimate aim or if there is not a reasonable relationship of proportionality between the means employed and the aim sought to be realised

that

> very weighty reasons would have to be put forward before the Court could regard a difference in treatment based exclusively on the ground of sex as compatible with the Convention

and that "[j]ust like differences based on sex, differences based on sexual orientation require particularly serious reasons by way of justification".[47]

The Court did accept that "protection of the family in the traditional sense is, in principle, a weighty and legitimate reason which might justify a difference in treatment", but found that the requirement of proportionality was not met by the

---

[45] *Karner v. Austria*. See also *Kozak v. Poland*, n. 13102/02, judgment of 2nd March 2010.

[46] Protocol N. 11 entered into force on 1st November 1998.

[47] *Karner v. Austria*, para. 37.

domestic interpretation and application of the relevant provisions of Austrian law. It elaborated as follows:

> In cases in which the margin of appreciation afforded to States is narrow, as is the position where there is a difference in treatment based on sex or sexual orientation, the principle of proportionality does not merely require that the measure chosen is in principle suited for realising the aim sought. It must also be shown that it was necessary in order to achieve that aim to exclude certain categories of people—in this instance persons living in a homosexual relationship—from the scope of application of section 14 of the Rent Act.[48]

In conclusion, it held that Art. 14, taken in conjunction with Art. 8, had been violated.

Occasionally, the Court has dealt with issues raised by alleged discriminatory regulations affecting same-sex couples within ambits other than that of private or family life or home. This was the case in *J.M. v. the United Kingdom*, where Art. 14 was examined in conjunction with Art. 1 of Protocol n. 1 (right to peaceful enjoyment of possessions) and was found to be breached by the unjustified exclusion of the applicant (a divorced mother, whose children were in their father's care, living in a lesbian relationship with another woman) from the benefits she would have enjoyed, had she lived with a man, in the calculation of her financial liability, as an absent parent, to contribute to the cost of her children's upbringing, in accordance with the applicable regulations on child maintenance.

The case-law examined so far deals essentially with economic rights and obligations between private persons,[49] but the Court was also called upon to adjudicate on allegedly unconventional regulations concerning social allowances and benefits at the State's expenses or taxation matters.

In the already cited *Mata Estevez* case, the applicant was denied a survivor pension, following the death of his homosexual companion, with whom he had been living for more than 10 years, on the ground that he had not been married to him and could therefore not be legally considered as his surviving spouse for the purposes of the relevant Spanish regulations. According to the legislation and practice in force at the material time in Spain, the award of a survivor's pension was conditional on the existence of a lawful marriage between the deceased and the claimant. However, exceptions were made for unmarried heterosexual couples who had been unable to marry each other because they were already married to someone else and divorce was not allowed before 1981. By contrast, no exception was permissible for same-sex couples, in spite of the fact that homosexual marriage was also prohibited.

---

[48] *Karner v. Austria*, paras 40–41.

[49] Notwithstanding the crucial role lent (perhaps disputably) by the Court to the State authorities, which triggered the applicability of Art. 1 of Protocol No. 1, this is also true for the *J.M.* case, which concerned the obligation of an absent parent to contribute to the children's upbringing, and the corresponding rights of the children themselves (to obtain maintenance from their parents) and of the other parent (to share with the applicant the corresponding financial burden).

The applicant relied on such factual grounds to argue that he had been discriminated, because of his sexual orientation, against both married couples and, subject to their inability to get a divorce, unmarried heterosexual ones.

The Court accepted that the applicant's emotional and sexual relationship with his late companion fell within the "private life" (not the "family life") limb of Art. 8, but considered—quite unnecessarily, indeed, for Art. 8 had not been invoked as such—that

> *even supposing* that the refusal to award the applicant the right to a survivor's pension following his partner's death did constitute an interference with respect for his private life, that interference was justified under paragraph 2 of Article 8 (emphasis added).

It is, then, on the mere assumption (not the positive finding) that the refusal to award the pension to the applicant might have been considered an interference with his rights, that the Court, after recalling that no right to a pension is granted as such by the Convention, came (rather abruptly) to the conclusion that the detrimental treatment complained of by the applicant, although definitely different from that which he would have been entitled to if his partner had been a woman, did not exceed the margin of appreciation allowed to the State authorities and did not amount to a breach of Art. 14.

In *Courten v. the United Kingdom*,[50] the applicant complained about the refusal, by the British authorities, to grant him exemption from the inheritance tax as the heir of his late male companion, with whom he had been living for more than 25 years. Before the European Court, as previously before the domestic authorities, Mr. Courten argued that he had been unable to get married to his companion, because same-sex marriage was not allowed; therefore, refusal to grant him an exemption, equivalent to that which would have been allowed to a spouse, because of his *status* of unmarried partner in a *de facto* relationship, amounted to a discrimination contrary to Art. 14 of the Convention and Art. 1 of Protocol No. 1. In the course of the Strasbourg proceedings, he further argued—in response to the Government's contention that his situation was not analogous to that of a married person or a person bound by a civil partnership—that, at the relevant time, such an alternative was unavailable for it had been introduced only in 2004 and its effects had been extended to taxation matters only as of 2005.

The Court found the application manifestly ill-founded. In so doing, it relied essentially on the "margin of appreciation" doctrine, combined with the reaffirmed legitimacy of the special *status* (and special protection) afforded to marriage. On this basis, the Strasbourg judges unanimously held that, on the one hand, unmarried couples, or couples who have entered some kind of legally binding agreement as permitted by law, cannot be equated to married (or otherwise legally bound) ones, irrespectively of the partners' sex; on the other hand, that, given the margin of appreciation open to member States "in the area of evolving social rights where

[50] N. 4479/06, decision on admissibility of 4th November 2008.

there is no established consensus" the respondent Government could not be criticized for not having allowed same-sex registered partnerships at an earlier date.

Mr. Courten's contentions before the Court relied significantly on a previous Grand Chamber judgment that, although it does not concern a same-sex couple, deserves consideration because of some principles expressed in it, which are quoted and confirmed in *Courten*.

The reference is to *Burden and Burden v. the United Kingdom*,[51] a case brought to Strasbourg by two elderly sisters who had been living "together, in a stable, committed and mutually supportive relationship" in a jointly owned house, built on a land inherited from their parents, and who also owned other movable and immovable properties of a considerable value. Before the Court, they argued

> that when one of them died, the survivor would face a significant liability to inheritance tax, which would not be faced by the survivor of a marriage or a civil partnership

and claimed that this amounted to an unlawful discrimination, prohibited by Art. 14 taken in conjunction with Art. 1 of Protocol n. 1.

Aside from stressing that

> the relationship between siblings is qualitatively of a different nature to that between married couples and homosexual civil partners

the Court seized this opportunity to set out some principles derived from earlier case-law.[52] Among these, the most relevant for the purposes of this study is the definition of the factor that makes the difference between cohabiting couples, on the one hand, and couples bound by marriage or by civil partnerships on the other. On this issue, the Court elaborated as follows:

> [...] marriage confers a special status on those who enter into it and remains an institution which is widely accepted as conferring a particular status on those who enter it

Similarly,

> the legal consequences of civil partnership [...], which couples expressly and deliberately decide to incur, set these types of relationship apart from other forms of co-habitation.

Indeed,

> [r]ather than the length or the supportive nature of the relationship, what is determinative is the existence of a public undertaking, carrying with it a body of rights and obligations of a contractual nature.

This is the decisive reason why

> there can be no analogy between married and Civil Partnership Act couples, on one hand, and heterosexual or homosexual couples who choose to live together but not to become husband and wife or civil partners, on the other hand.[53]

[51] N. 13378/05, judgment of 28th April 2008.

[52] *Shackell v. the United Kingdom*, n. 45851/99, decision on admissibility of 27th April 2000, with further references to the Commission's case-law.

[53] *Ibidem*, paras 62–63.

In *Courten*, because the applicant and his late partner did not (had not been able to) enter (albeit through no choice of their own) a civil partnership, this principle was used—as has been shown above—to support the finding that Art. 14 had not been breached. But it would be arguable, *a contrario*, that whenever some form of "public undertaking", distinct from marriage and alternative to it, is open to couples, the consequences of such undertaking, in the field of taxation, must be equal to those of marriage, in order to avoid any unlawful discrimination.

In this reasoning, the sex or gender of the concerned parties is clearly an immaterial factor: under the impugned British law, entitlement to taxation benefits was dependent on the marital *status* of the partners, not on their sex.[54] It seems, therefore, that the Court's reasoning in *Burden* and in *Courten* has driven it (perhaps in a not entirely conscious and voluntary way) to implicitly depart from the principle—repeatedly affirmed in several judgments—that any forms of legal and social commitment alternative to marriage need not entail consequences equal to those stemming from marriage.

18.5 Parental Rights

The European Court has recently found, in the case of *X. v. Austria*,[55] that the inability, for a woman living in a stable same-sex couple, to adopt the biological child of her partner, without severing the existing mother-child legal relationship, resulted in a breach of Art. 14, combined with Art. 8 of the Convention.

In Austrian law, an exception to the otherwise necessarily joint adoption by married couples is provided for the adoption (under certain conditions) of one spouse's child by the other spouse (so-called "second-parent adoption"). In such an event, the legal tie between the child and its biological parent belonging to the same sex of the adopting parent is severed, while the similar tie with the biological parent of the opposite sex is preserved. Identical consequences derive from the adoption of a child by a single person (which is also permitted by Austrian law), irrespective of his or her living alone or in an unmarried couple. As of 1st January 2010, with the entry into force of the Registered Partnership Act, an explicit prohibition of joint adoption and second-parent adoption by registered partners

[54] In *Shackell*, the complaint, analogous to that of Mr. Courten, concerned the refusal to grant widow's benefits to an unmarried lady whose late (male) companion had died after 17 years of common life *more uxorio*. No question was raised in relation to alternative forms of "registration" of couples and the applicant only claimed to be discriminated *vis-à-vis* a widow. The claim was dismissed on the grounds that "marriage remains an institution that is widely accepted as conferring a particular status on those who enter it" and that "the promotion of marriage, by way of limited benefits for surviving spouses, cannot be said to exceed the margin of appreciation afforded to the respondent Government".

[55] N. 19010/07, judgment of 19th February 2013 (Grand Chamber).

was introduced into the legislation.[56] However, this legislation had not been in force at the relevant time and was therefore not applicable to the applicants' case.

The first applicant's request to adopt her lesbian partner's child had been rejected because, in the very words of the Austrian Supreme Court (as reported and translated in the Court's judgment), "a person who adopts a child on his or her own does not take the place of either parent at will, but only the place of the parent of the same sex", since the adoption by a single person could only replace the legal tie with the biological parent belonging to the same gender, it clearly appeared that the legislation did not allow second-parent adoption by the same-sex partner of the biological parent. Indeed, in such case, the alternative would have been between preserving the legal tie with the biological parent of the same sex (which was prohibited by law) or severing that tie (which would have run contrary to the child's—and also the parents'—interest).

The case-law on which the parties mainly built their respective cases consists of three judgments concerning France: *Fretté*[57] and *E.B.*,[58] on the one hand; *Gas and Dubois*,[59] on the other.[60]

In the first case, a single homosexual man complained about the dismissal of his application for preliminary authorization to adopt a child.[61] He claimed that the decision of the French authorities was motivated by his avowed homosexuality and was therefore in violation of Art. 14 combined with Art. 8 of the Convention. The Court found that Art. 14, taken together with Art. 8, was applicable but had not been infringed.

On the applicability issue, the Court acknowledged that—according to a well-established case-law—"the Convention does not guarantee the right to adopt as such" and that "the right to respect for family life presupposes the existence of a family and does not safeguard the mere desire to found a family".

It therefore concluded that

[56] It should be noted that, in Austrian law, registered partnership is open to same-sex partners only.

[57] *Fretté v. France*, n. 36515/97, judgment of 26th February 2002.

[58] *E.B. v. France*, n. 43546/02, judgment of 22nd January 2008 (Grand Chamber).

[59] *Gas and Dubois v. France*, n. 25951/07, judgment of 15th March 2012.

[60] Extensive reference is made, in these judgments, to an older precedent, *Salgueiro da Silva Mouta v. Portugal*, n. 33290/96, judgment of 21st December 1999. The facts of that case, however, were significantly different, because they concerned the refusal, by the Portuguese authorities, to grant custody of a child to its biological father, who was separated from the mother, on the sole ground of his homosexuality.

[61] In French law, individuals and couples who plan to adopt a child must, as a general rule (and save some exceptions), undergo an administrative enquiry aimed at verifying their suitability (psychological, emotional, economical, etc.) as prospective adoptive parents. The positive outcome of this enquiry is a prerequisite for subsequently applying for adoption of a specific child. The administrative decision on the preliminary authorization can be challenged before the administrative Courts.

> the decision to dismiss the applicant's application for authorisation could not be considered to infringe his right to the free expression and development of his personality or the manner in which he led his life, in particular his sexual life.

Nevertheless, since French law (Art. 343-1 of the Civil Code) allowed adoption by single persons, the Court considered that "there was a difference in treatment based on the applicant's sexual orientation, a concept which is undoubtedly covered by Art. 14 of the Convention"; in other words, the different treatment undergone by Mr. Fretté was motivated by the "decisive factor" of his homosexuality (his "choice of lifestyle", in the wording of the domestic authorities): because such treatment amounted to an infringement of his "right under Art. 343-1 of the [French] Civil Code, which fall[ed] within the ambit of Art. 8 of the Convention", then Art. 14, taken in conjunction with Art. 8, was applicable.[62]

Having said this, and despite the fact that, admittedly, sexual orientation is considered to be an aspect of the concept of "sex", and "sex" is one of the grounds on which Art. 14 explicitly prohibits discrimination, the Court concluded that the applicant's rights had not been violated. Given the lack of "common ground" among the contracting States (and within the scientific community) on the desirability of allowing adoption by homosexuals, the domestic authorities enjoyed a wide margin of appreciation in taking the impugned decision, aimed at the protection of the "health and rights" of the children eligible for adoption, and they did not exceed that margin.[63]

As judge Costa, joined by judges Jungwiert and Traja, noted in his separate opinion appended to the judgment, the Court's reasoning is rather unconvincing both on the admissibility issue and on the merits. As for the admissibility test, the Court acknowledged that Art. 8 ECHR does not guarantee a right to adopt children or to form a family, and that French law merely allows single persons to apply for authorization to adopt (without granting a positive right to obtain such authorization or to actually adopt a child), but did not explain in what way the impugned domestic could be seen as interfering with a conventional right (that, admittedly, does not exist) or with a right (that is also not guaranteed, as such, by the domestic law) falling within the scope (or "ambit") of a conventional provision. As for the merits, once Art. 14 had been (however disputably) found to be applicable, the arguments put forward by the applicant seemed to have been rather expeditiously disposed of by the majority, in finding no violation of the Convention.

---

[62] *Fretté v. France*, paras 32–33.

[63] *Ibidem*, para. 42, *in fine*: "[...] the national authorities [...] were legitimately and reasonably entitled to consider that the right to be able to adopt on which the applicant relied under Article 343-1 of the Civil Code was limited by the interests of children eligible for adoption, notwithstanding the applicant's legitimate aspirations and without calling his personal choices into question. If account is taken of the broad margin of appreciation to be left to States in this area and the need to protect children's best interests to achieve the desired balance, the refusal to authorise adoption did not infringe the principle of proportionality".

Some 6 years later, the findings of *Fretté* were partly confirmed (on the admissibility issue) and partly overturned[64] (on the merits) by the Grand Chamber in the case of *E.B. v. France*.

The case concerned a homosexual woman who wished to adopt a child as a single parent. The applicant was living in a stable relationship with a same-sex partner, but the adoption plan was not a shared one: the applicant's partner, whilst not opposing it, admittedly did not feel committed in it. The requested authorization for adoption had been refused by the French authorities on a number of grounds, among which featured the lack of a paternal role model or referent in the household and the ambiguous attitude of the applicant herself and her partner (who lived together in a couple but refused to think of themselves as forming one) towards the adoption project; to these two main grounds, the authorities added the peculiar attitude of the applicant herself (who showed an attitude of rejection of men—which is by no means a necessary or natural consequence of feminine homosexuality—and, according to the psychological reports, possible unsuitable motivation of her desire to adopt a child and lacunae in her educational skills).

On the admissibility issue, the Grand Chamber went at some length to develop and explain the finding according to which Art. 14 was applicable, which had been rather scantily motivated by the Chamber in *Fretté*. However, as will be shown presently, it is open to doubt whether the Court's efforts were crowned by success in this respect.

Having reiterated that Art. 8 ECHR does not guarantee a right to adopt, and that such a right was not to be found in French law either (nor in other international instruments), the Grand Chamber started by noting that, since the applicant's complaint was based on Art. 14 combined with Art. 8 (and did not involve the latter provision as such), the Court was not "called upon to rule whether the right to adopt [...] should or should not fall within the ambit of Art. 8 of the Convention taken alone".[65] It went on by recalling that, according to a well-established case-law, Art. 14 "only complements the other substantive provisions of the Convention and the Protocols thereto" and "has no independent existence" of its own; that "application of Article 14 does not necessarily presuppose the violation of one of the substantive rights protected by the Convention"; that for Art. 14 to be applicable "it is necessary but it is also sufficient for the facts of the case to fall "within the ambit" of one or more of the Articles of the Convention"; that this "ambit"

[64] As was rightly pointed out by Judge Costa, joined by Judges Türmen, Ugrekhelidze and Jočienė, in the dissenting opinion appended to the judgment, despite the unconvincing efforts made by the Court to distinguish E.B. from *Fretté*, the relevant factors were substantially similar in both cases, and the judgment of 2008 is in fact, as far as the merits are concerned, an overruling of the previous case-law. It might be added that, insofar as some factual differences between the two cases actually did exist, the majority of these should have weighed in favor of confirming, rather than overturning, the conclusions reached in *Fretté* (para. 71). At any rate, it is significant that the Grand Chamber itself later acknowledged that E.B. had actually overturned Fretté: see *X. v. Austria*, para. 103.

[65] *E.B. v. France*, paras 41–46.

encompasses not only the rights that the Convention itself requires each contracting party to grant, but also any additional right, "falling within the general scope of any Convention Article" that a member State may have decided to provide on its own free will.[66]

Having noted that French law *permits* adoption by single persons as well as by couples (under similar conditions, and subject to prior authorization), and grants a *right* to apply for authorization to adopt a child, but not a *right to adopt* as such, the Grand Chamber came to the conclusion—of a rather questionable consistency with the starting point and the further development of the reasoning—"that the facts of this case undoubtedly [fell] within the ambit of Article 8 of the Convention"[67] and that Art. 14 was therefore applicable.

Turning to the merits of the case, the Court noted that the impugned decisions of the domestic authorities (both administrative and judicial) were based on two main grounds[68]: the lack of a "referent" of the opposite sex in the household or the applicant's "immediate circle of family and friends"[69] (a core issue also in *Fretté*) and the "attitude of the applicant's partner", who, despite her being "the long-standing and declared partner of the applicant", "did not feel committed by her partner's application to adopt".[70]

As for the first ground, the Grand Chamber shared and reiterated the finding of the Chamber in *Fretté*: namely, that the requirement that there be a "referent" in the applicant's household or "among her immediate circle of family and friends" (a requirement that, as the Court also noted, was not expressly stated in the relevant French statute) was bound to seriously affect—and possibly to neutralize—the very possibility for a single person (whether homosexual or not) to adopt a child. One cannot but agree with the Court's argument and its undeniable logic. Nevertheless, it was hardly an argument suitable to assess the applicability—let alone the violation—of Art. 14. The lack of a clear legal basis for this requirement, combined with its rather irrational character, could have better served a finding of violation of Art. 8 taken alone, had the Court considered (which it did not) that this provision encompassed a conventional right to adoption, but it does not seem to reveal any

---

[66] *Ibidem*, paras 47–48.

[67] *Ibidem*, para. 49. A conclusion, indeed, on which, just a few lines before, the Court had deemed useless to dwell. But the main flaw in the reasoning lies on the use that the Court makes of its case-law on the applicability of Art. 14. The undisputable fact that French law treats equally couples and single persons as regards the possibility to adopt children does not entail, in itself, any legal definition of that "possibility": is it a right or a mere privilege? Admittedly, no right to adopt is provided either by the Convention or by the national law: the Grand Chamber itself acknowledges this in the judgment. It follows that none of the alternative preconditions for applying Art. 14 is met.

[68] *Ibidem*, para. 72. Other reasons given by the experts and/or relied on by the authorities (such as the psychologically dubious motivations of the applicant) are completely overlooked by the judgment.

[69] *Ibidem*, para. 73.

[70] *Ibidem*, para. 75.

difference of treatment between comparable situations that would trigger the applicability of Art. 14.

As for the non-committed attitude of the applicant's partner towards the adoption plan, the Court quite soundly stated that this was "not without interest or relevance in assessing [Ms E.B.'s] application".

Indeed, in the Court's very words,

> where a male or female applicant, although unmarried, has already set up home with a partner, that partner's attitude and the role he or she will necessarily play on a daily basis in the life of the child joining the home set-up require a full examination in the child's best interests. It would moreover be surprising, to say the least, if the relevant authorities, having been informed of the existence of a *de facto* couple, pretended to be unaware of that fact when assessing the conditions in which the child would be given a home and his future life in that new home. The legal status of a person seeking to adopt is not incompatible with an examination of his or her actual situation and the subsequent finding of not one but two adults in the household.[71]

Once again, this second ground relied upon by the national authorities (besides being legitimate in itself) did not reveal any problem as regards prohibition of discrimination: as the Court noted, "there [was] no evidence to establish that the ground in question was based on the applicant's sexual orientation".

On the contrary,

> this ground, which [had] nothing to do with any consideration relating to the applicant's sexual orientation, [was] based on a simple analysis of the known, *de facto* situation and its consequences for the adoption of a child.[72]

Nevertheless, the Grand Chamber found that these two grounds, on which the ultimate domestic decisions where built, formed a single, complex reason and must be seen as a whole. Therefore, according to the Court, the illegitimacy of the first one contaminated the whole decision-making process and its outcome.[73] At this point of its reasoning, the Court introduced the key-element of its finding of a violation: the reference to the applicant's "choice of lifestyle".[74]

The majority judges disregarded the fact that, objectively, the lack of a "referent of the opposite sex" had nothing to do with the applicant's homosexuality: it was indeed an obstacle that the domestic authorities would have raised (or been able to raise) against any single person who applied for authorization to adopt a child without providing such a "referent" in his/her household or "immediate circle of family and friends". They also disregarded the explicit statements, by both the

[71] *Ibidem*, para. 76.

[72] *Ibidem*, para. 78.

[73] *Ibidem*, para. 80. Judges Loucaides and Mularoni, in their dissenting opinions, criticized the "contamination theory" followed by the majority. They pointed out that, at least in French administrative law (but one would say that this is a general principle that stems from sheer logic) it is enough for one reason given by an authority to be legal and well-founded, in order to have the decision stand, notwithstanding any concurrent additional reason that might, instead, be wrong or unlawful.

[74] *Ibidem*, para. 82.

Administrative Court of Appeal and the *Conseil d'Etat*, that reference to the applicant's "choice of lifestyle" did not entail "a position of principle" against it, and that, although the homosexual relationship in which the applicant was living "had to be taken into consideration in the needs and interests of an adopted child", the lower Court

> neither based its decision on a position of principle in view of the applicant's sexual orientation nor breached the combined requirements of Articles 8 and 14 of the European Convention for the Protection of Human Rights and Fundamental Freedoms; nor did it breach the provisions of Article L. 225-2 of the Criminal Code prohibiting sexual discrimination.[75]

Quite to the opposite, the majority of the Strasbourg judges considered that

> the inescapable conclusion [was] that [the applicant's] sexual orientation was consistently at the centre of deliberations in her regard and omnipresent at every stage of the administrative and judicial proceedings.

In their opinion, "the reference to the applicant's homosexuality was, if not explicit, at least implicit" and "was a decisive factor leading to the decision to refuse her authorisation to adopt".[76]

Hence, the finding of a violation of Art. 14 combined with Art. 8.

This is the background against which the third French judgment was issued, in 2012. The facts in *Gas and Dubois* are virtually identical to those in *X. v. Austria*. The applicants are two women living in a stable homosexual couple since 1989. During their relationship, Ms. Dubois underwent medically assisted insemination by an anonymous donor and gave birth to a daughter. In 2006, Ms. Gas, with the consent of her partner, with whom she had meanwhile entered a registered civil partnership, applied for "simple adoption"[77] in respect of the then 6 year-old child. The request was dismissed, as the competent jurisdictions found that, according

[75] See the findings of the domestic Courts as quoted and translated in *ibidem*, para. 25.

[76] *E.B. v. France*, paras 88–89. It should be noted that the notion of 'lifestyle' is much broader than that of sexual orientation and encompasses, for instance, the attitude of 'rejection' of men (which is not an inescapable consequence of feminine homosexuality and goes much further than the mere desire not to have sex with men), or the choice to live in a stable relationship (whether homosexual or not) without considering oneself as part of a couple (an attitude which might mean, for instance, a sexual promiscuity which might well be deemed unsuitable for the growth of a child also among heterosexuals).

[77] In French law, there are two types of adoption: "full adoption" and "simple adoption". Full adoption replaces entirely the relationship between the child (who must be still minor of age) and the family of origin, while "simple adoption" (which can also concern adult children) only creates an additional legal tie, without severing the original one. Nevertheless, if the adoptee is a minor, "simple adoption" results in removing all rights and duties associated with parental responsibility from the biological parent and vesting them in the adoptive one. The sole exception to this rule is provided by Art. 365 of the French Civil Code, which allows joint parental responsibility and, if the biological parent agrees, joint exercise of such responsibility, only if the adoptive parent is the spouse of the biological one.

to French law, since Ms. Gas and Ms. Dubois were not married (and Art. 365 of the French Civil Code was accordingly not applicable to them[78]), adoption by the applicant would have deprived Ms. Dubois of all her parental rights and duties towards her daughter: a consequence that was neither intended by the applicants, nor compatible with the paramount consideration of the best interest of the child itself.

The European Court ruled the application admissible, but rejected the applicants' contention that they had been discriminated for reasons related to their sexual orientation.

On admissibility, the Court made, *en passant*, a very short reference to the *E.B.* judgment and found that, in the instant case, there was a *de facto* family life which could enjoy the protection of Art. 8 ECHR; moreover, Art. 8 also protected the personal sphere, within which sexual orientation is encompassed: therefore, the facts of the case did fall within the "ambit" of that provision.

On the merits, the Strasbourg judges held that the applicants could not complain of a discrimination either *vis-à-vis* a married couple or *vis-à-vis* an unmarried heterosexual couple (who would, or not, have entered a registered civil partnership). As for the first limb of the complaint, it recalled its case-law to the effect that marriage, which is a right protected by Art. 12 of the Convention, "confers a special status on those who enter into it" and "gives rise to social, personal and legal consequences". As for the second limb, they noted that

> any couple [whether homosexual or not] in a comparable legal situation by virtue of having entered into a civil partnership would likewise have their application for a simple adoption order refused

and therefore did not "observe any difference in treatment based on the applicants' sexual orientation".[79]

In sum, no violation of the Convention was found, and the application was dismissed.

The radically different conclusion which the Court reached in the Austrian case of *X.* (where Art. 14 combined with Art. 8 was held to have been breached) should not be construed as an overruling of the *Gas and Dubois* judgment. Indeed, the

---

[78] In *Gas and Dubois v. France*, para. 19, Art. 365 of the French Civil Code is translated as follows: "All rights associated with parental responsibility shall be vested in the adoptive parent alone, including the right to consent to the marriage of the adoptee, unless the adoptive parent is married to the adoptee's mother or father. In this case, the adoptive parent and his or her spouse shall have joint parental responsibility, but the spouse shall continue to exercise it alone unless the couple make a joint declaration before the senior registrar of the *tribunal de grande instance* to the effect that parental responsibility is to be exercised jointly. [...]".

[79] *Ibidem*, paras 68–69. This finding appears to be confirmed by the judgment in *Emonet v. Switzerland* (n. 39051/03, judgment of 13th December 2007), where an unmarried heterosexual couple and the adult daughter of the woman complained about the automatic severing of the legal tie between the mother and the daughter as a consequence of the latter's adoption by the mother's partner.

comparison between the two judgments shows that the core element which explains the apparently opposite rulings lies in a factual difference between French and Austrian law.

In *X. v. Austria*, the Court followed a path of thought similar to that of the French precedent. It began by comparing the applicants' situation to that of a married couple. Under this respect, it reiterated and confirmed its own findings in *Gas and Dubois*: namely, that the prospective adopting parent and the biological mother of the child were not "in a relevantly similar situation to a married couple in respect of second-parent adoption". The Court then turned to the comparison with an unmarried heterosexual couple and noted that (unlike the French Civil Code) Austrian law (Art. 182(2) of the Austrian Civil Code) allowed adoption of the biological child of one member of an unmarried couple by his or her partner; the adoption would then severe the legal tie between the child and the biological parent belonging to the same sex as the adopting parent, but not that between the child and the other parent, of the opposite sex.[80]

The Court held that this provision (which the domestic Courts consistently interpreted as preventing adoption by the homosexual partner of the child's biological parent) gave rise to a difference of treatment between unmarried couples, depending on the sex and sexual orientation of their members. Having reiterated that

> the prohibition of discrimination enshrined in Article 14 extends beyond the enjoyment of the rights and freedoms which the Convention and the Protocols thereto require a State to guarantee

and "applies also to those additional rights, falling within the general scope of any Convention Article, for which the State has voluntarily decided to provide" and having noted that, notwithstanding the lack of a positive obligation "under Article 8 of the Convention to extend the right to second parent adoption to unmarried couples", Austrian law did in fact allow second-parent adoption in unmarried different-sex couples, but not in homosexual couples,[81] it concluded that—unlike France—Austria had breached Art. 14 of the Convention, combined with Art. 8.

[80] *X v. Austria*, para. 114: "Austrian law allows second-parent adoption by an unmarried different-sex couple. In general terms, individuals may adopt under Article 179 of the Civil Code, and nothing in Article 182(2) of the Civil Code, which regulates the effects of adoption, prevents one partner in an unmarried heterosexual couple from adopting the other partner's child without severing the ties between that partner and the child".

[81] *Ibidem*, para. 142: "The Court would repeat that Article 182(2) of the Civil Code contains an absolute, albeit implicit, prohibition on second-parent adoption for same-sex couples".

18.6 Expulsion of Aliens

Between 1981 and 1989, three applications were lodged with the former Commission of Human Rights, by which non-European nationals complained about being denied long-term residence permits, or being struck by deportation orders, pursuant to the domestic legislation, irrespective of their living in stable and long-term homosexual relationships with citizens of the hosting country.[82]

All three applications were found inadmissible.

In the leading case of *X and Y v. the United Kingdom*,[83] the Commission took the view that stable relationships between two same-sex (male, in the instance) partners did not fall within the scope of the protection of "family life". Nevertheless, it accepted—following the Dudgeon judgment—that "certain restraints on homosexual relationships could create an interference with an individual's right to respect for his *private* life" (emphasis added) and acknowledged that

> the applicants' relationship [was] a matter of their private life and the question [arose] whether the deportation order of 13 October 1982, requiring the first applicant to leave the United Kingdom, constituted an interference with the applicants' right under Article 8

without further indication of the specific right at stake. Moving from such a start-point, the Commission found appropriate to "draw a parallel" with previously examined deportation cases (not involving same-sex couples at all) and to apply similar criteria for scrutiny and adjudication, namely (a) that no right for aliens "to enter or remain in a particular country [is] guaranteed as such by the Convention"; (b) that an issue under Art. 8 (without specification) may arise from the deportation of a "close member of a family" from the country where that family lives; (c) that, however, respect for "family life" does not go as far as implying a right to choose the "geographical location of that family life"; (d) that, therefore, it is necessary to "examine the facts of each case in order to find the extent of the claimed family links and also the ties with the country concerned". The decision was then the result of the application of those principles, as recalled by the Commission, "to the applicant's right to respect for their *private* life" (emphasis added).

Finally, the application was dismissed on the grounds that the British authorities had given "careful consideration to the applicants' claims, including that concerning the difficulties they might face in living together in the first applicant's country of origin", that the applicants were "professionally mobile" and that it had not been shown "that the applicants could not live together elsewhere than the United Kingdom, or that their link with the United Kingdom [was] an essential element of the relationship".

---

[82] *X and Y v. the United Kingdom*, n. 9369/81, decision of 3rd May 1983; *W.J. and D.P. v. the United Kingdom*, n. 12513/86, decision of 13th July 1987; *C. and L. M. v. the United Kingdom*, n. 14753/89, decision of 9th October 1989.

[83] The decision is published in DR 32, p. 220; extracts can be found in .pdf format on the Court's website.

The two other decisions followed a partly similar path of thought, but with additional stress laid on the preeminence of the States' right to control immigration and permanence of aliens on their territory, over the competing right of those aliens (and their partners) to enjoy respect for private and family life. The main leading principles (namely that same-sex partnerships fall within the ambit of *private* life but not of *family* life) are duly reiterated, and the Commission's reasoning shows the usual tendency (although somewhat diluted) to assimilate the right to respect for private and for family life as two limbs of one and the same right. But the essential argument for dismissing the complaints is that expulsion of an alien inevitably "result[s] in a disruption of his private life" that "cannot, in principle, be regarded as an interference with the right to respect for private life, ensured by Article 8". It is only in "exceptional circumstances" that the right to respect for private life can override the State's right to set the rules for allowing the permanence of aliens on its territory and to apply those rules to any given situation.

The applicants in the *C. and L.M.* and *W.J. and D.P.* cases also complained of a discrimination on grounds of their sexual orientation, contrary to Art. 14 of the Convention, against heterosexual couples. They maintained that, had their respective partners belonged to the opposite gender, their long-term relationships would have constituted valid grounds for granting the foreign partner indefinite leave to stay in the country, under the applicable immigration rules.

This contention was also rejected by the Commission, on the somewhat disputable grounds—derived from previous case-law concerning housing—that

> the family (to which the relationship of heterosexual unmarried couples living together as husband and wife can be assimilated) merits special protection in society and [the Commission] sees no reason why a High Contracting Party should not afford particular assistance to families.[84]

In this respect, it may be expected that the recent recognition of a "family life" between same-sex partners, coupled with the now long-standing (and lately reiterated) statement that ability to procreate is not an essential element of the "founding of a family", will lead to the conclusion that different treatment of heterosexual and homosexual partnerships is no longer justified under Art. 14 of the Convention.

In such event, however, the difficulties of same-sex couples, where one of the partners is a non-EU member State national, will not be automatically solved, for the case-law of the Strasbourg Court (and of the EU Court of Justice) allows contracting parties to remove aliens, irrespective of their family ties (however "traditional"), when for so doing there are serious reasons that overweight, in the balance struck between competing private and public interests, the individual rights enshrined in Art. 8.

[84] See W.J. and D.P., para. 5. In fact, this conclusion was already implicit in the finding that "the absence in United Kingdom Immigration Rules of settlement rights for non-nationals in respect of their stable, private relationships, other than family relationships, does not, of itself, disclose any appearance of a violation of Article 8 of the Convention" (para. 4).

References

Graupner H (2011) Gay rights, Max Planck encyclopedia of public international law. www.mpepil.com

Johnson P (2013) Homosexuality and the European court of human rights. Routledge, New York

Leach P (2005) Taking a case to the European Court of human rights, 2nd edn. Oxford University Press, Oxford/New York

McLoughlin MT (1996) Crystal or glass?: A review of Dudgeon v. United Kingdom on the fifteenth anniversary of the decision. Murdoch Univ Electronic J Law. http://worldlii.austlii.edu.au/au/journals/MurUEJL/1996/36.html

Mowbray A (2001) Cases and materials on the European convention on human rights. Butterworths, London/Edinburgh/Dublin

Scherpe JM (2013) The legal recognition of same-sex couples in Europe and the role of the European court of human rights. http://www.equalrightstrust.org/ertdocumentbank/ERR10_sp1.pdf

Sudre F et al (2009) Les grands arrêts de la Cour européenne des droits de l'homme, 5th edn. PUF, Paris

van Dijk P et al (2006) Theory and practice of the European convention on human rights. Intersentia, Antwerpen/Oxford

Chapter 19
Same-Sex Couples Before the Inter-American System of Human Rights

Laura Magi

Abstract This chapter explores the protection granted to the rights of lesbian, gay, transsexual, bisexual and inter-sex persons (LGTBI) in the Inter-American system of human rights protection. It takes into consideration all the measures adopted in such a framework to combat violence and discrimination against LGTBI individuals, paying special attention to the adoption of precautionary measures and the establishment of a Special Unit charged with consultative and monitoring powers in the field of sexual orientation, gender identity and gender expression. A thorough analysis is devoted to cases brought before the Inter-American Commission on Human Rights and to the case-law of the Inter-American Court on Human Rights. The analysis highlights that important legal development have been taking place on a continent where violence suffered by homosexuals is still very significant and where cultural suspicion and ostracism toward them is still widely practiced.

19.1 Introduction

The recognition of and respect for the rights of lesbian, gay, transsexual, bisexual and inter-sex persons (further referred as LGTBI),[1] have only periodically received consideration in the Inter-American system of human rights protection in the past.[2]

[1] This is the acronym usually adopted by the Inter-American Commission on Human Rights.

[2] In its 1999 Annual Report to the OAS General Assembly (OEA/Ser.L/V/II.106, Doc. 6 rev., April 13, 1999), the Commission condemned the arbitrary arrests of homosexuals in Ecuador in the context of a state of emergency (see Chapter IV, para. 46). In the Annual Reports of 2005 and 2006 the Commission limited itself to acknowledging that no improvements had been recorded with respect to the material and legal inequality faced by groups traditionally subjected to discrimination, such as homosexuals (see OEA/Ser.L/V/II.124, Doc. 5, 27 February 2006, Introduction, para. 3; OEA/Ser.L/V/II.127, Doc. 4 rev. 1, 3 March 2007, Introduction, para. 5). In its 1983 Country

L. Magi (✉)
Department of Economics, University of Florence, Florence, Italy
e-mail: laura.magi@unifi.it

D. Gallo et al. (eds.), *Same-Sex Couples before National, Supranational and International Jurisdictions*, DOI 10.1007/978-3-642-35434-2_19,

Only in recent years have the Inter-American Commission on Human Rights (further referred as IACHR) and the Organization of American States (further referred as OAS) General Assembly paid more attention to them.

Since 2008, IACHR Annual Reports to the OAS General Assembly,[3] as well as IACHR Country Reports,[4] have denounced systemic problems faced by LGTBI persons in the Americas, in particular the high rate of violence against them and the widespread impunity granted to perpetrators (being either State organs or private individuals).[5] But also the continuing criminalization of LGTBI sexual behavior,[6] the arbitrary arrest and detention of LGTBI individuals, their summary trials[7] and the widespread discrimination they suffer in the access to health and education services, in the labor sector as well as in political participation, have been frequently denounced. The data collected in the Reports mentioned above show how intolerance and violence towards individuals because of their sexual orientation still represents a serious problem in the framework of several civil societies of the American States.

Report on the situation of human rights in Cuba, the Commission denounced, among other things, that homosexuals were conscripted into forced labor for the Government (see OEA/Ser.L/V/II.61, Doc. 29 rev. 1, 4 October 1983, Chapter VII, para. 27). In the 1993 Country Report on the situation of human rights in Colombia, IACHR reported that homosexuals had been victims of social cleansing in the past decade (see OEA/Ser.L/V/II.84, Doc. 39 rev., 14 October 1993, Chapter VII). A similar conclusion was reached in the 2001 Country Report concerning the situation of human rights in Guatemala (see OEA/Ser.L/V/II.111, Doc. 21 rev., 6 April 2001, Chapter V, paras 32 and 41).

[3] IACHR is entitled to adopt such reports under Art. 41, lett. g, of the American Convention.

[4] They are adopted according to Art. 18, letter (c), of the IACHR Statute.

[5] Serious concern was expressed by the Commission concerning the increase in the number of assaults by the police and armed forces against LGTBI persons in Venezuela and Honduras (see IACHR, 2011 Annual Report of the Inter-American Commission on Human Rights, OEA/Ser.L/V/II., Doc. 5, rev. 1, 7 March 2011, Chapter IV, paras 390–392 and 522–525).

[6] "The Commission was disturbed to find that one of the most serious problems in the region when defending the rights of LGTBI persons is that in some countries of the hemisphere, any sexual orientation other than a heterosexual one continues to be criminalized as offenses labeled "sodomy" (or "buggery"), "gross indecency", "unnatural crimes" and so on. While during the follow-up period the Commission was pleased to learn that some countries like Nicaragua had decriminalized homosexuality, it nonetheless observes that in many Caribbean countries crimes of this kind are still on the books, with the result that the right of association for purposes of promoting and defending the rights of LGTBI persons is prohibited, the argument being that their organizations and activities are "illegal." Laws criminalizing behavior based on non-heterosexual orientation have been adopted in Antigua and Barbuda, in the Bahamas, Barbados, Belize, Dominica, Grenada, Guyana, Jamaica, St. Kitts and Nevis, Saint Lucia, Saint Vincent and the Grenadines and Trinidad and Tobago: see the Second Report on the Situation of Human Rights Defenders in Americas, OEA/Ser.L/V/II, Doc. 66, 31 December 2011, para. 334.

[7] IACHR, 2011 Annual Report, para. 272 concerning the LGTBI situation in Cuba. The Commission particularly stigmatizes the use of the legal concept of "pre-delictive dangerousness" to convict and sentence young Cuban homosexuals to prison.

Taking into account such an alarming record of violence, the OAS General Assembly has approved four resolutions,[8] under the single title of "Human Rights, Sexual Orientation and Gender Identity", which condemn discrimination, acts of violence and other human rights violations committed against individuals by reason of their sexual orientation, and which urge States to adopt the necessary measures to prevent, punish, and eradicate such practices, to investigate them, to ensure due judicial protection for victims and to bring the perpetrators to justice. The General Assembly has also urged States to ensure adequate protection of LGTBI defenders, and has requested that IACHR pay particular attention to the LGTBI situation.[9]

19.2 Measures Adopted to Combat Violence and Discrimination Against LGTBI Individuals

Except for the recommendations of the General Assembly cited above and those contained in IACHR Annual and Country Reports,[10] the most significant measures adopted in the framework of the Inter-American system of human rights protection are two. The first is the adoption of precautionary measures, and the second is the establishment of a Special Unit within IACHR devoted entirely to dealing with LGTBI protection.

---

[8] See the Resolutions No. 2435 (XXXVIII-0/08), No. 2504 (XXXIX-0/09), No. 2600 (XL-0/10), and No. 2653 (XLI-0/11).

[9] On same-sex couples in Mexico, Central and South America see the chapter by Cabrales Lucio in this volume.

[10] In its reports the Commission does not ignore the opportunity to urge States to take measures to prevent and respond to human rights abuses against LGTBI, including the adoption of public policy measures as well as amendments to the laws to bring them in keeping with the American Convention on Human Rights. The Commission also constantly monitors those States that have made progress in this field in order to grant that such improvements (especially law reforms and judgments in favor of LGTBI persons' rights) are being concretely applied. See IACHR, 2001 Annual Report, paras 143–145, concerning Colombia in which the Commission notes that observance of the rights of LGTBI has improved since 1980, when homosexuality was decriminalized through a reform of the Criminal Code. It also takes note that between 2007 and 2008 Colombia's Constitutional Court granted same-sex couples the same pension benefits, social security benefits and property rights that heterosexual couples enjoy. Moreover, in 2009 the Constitutional Court decided to amend provisions that appeared in several laws in order to provide same-sex civil unions the same rights that cohabiting heterosexual unions enjoy. However, the Commission denounces that although the Colombian Constitution and Colombia's laws recognize the rights of LGTBI persons and provide for a number of remedies, access to those remedies and their effectiveness are limited in practice by the discrimination that LGTBI persons have traditionally experienced.

19.2.1 Precautionary Measures

According to the Rules of Procedure of IACHR[11] (Art. 25), in serious and urgent situations, the Commission may, on its own initiative or at the request of a party, request that a State adopt precautionary measures to prevent irreparable harm to persons or to the subject matter of the proceedings in connection with a pending petition or case (para. 1), as well as to persons under the jurisdiction of the State concerned, independently of any pending petition or case (para. 2). As clarified by the Rules of procedure, the measures may also be of a collective nature to prevent irreparable harm to persons due to their association with an organization, a group or a community with identified or identifiable members (para. 3) Pasqualucci (2003).

Several times the Commission has granted precautionary measures in favor of individuals of homosexual orientation, their defenders and, more generally, of members of associations or groups representing them.[12] In each case the Commission has taken into account the fact that such individuals have suffered aggressions, attacks, threats of death and harassment on account of their sexual orientation.

Usually the State is asked to adopt measures necessary to ensure their lives, to investigate the facts that gave rise to the adoption of the precautionary measures, and to inform the Commission about the measures adopted to respond to facts that placed the beneficiaries of the measures at risk. In one case the Commission even asked Honduras to immediately release individuals who had been arbitrary detained because of their sexual orientation and to be informed of others whose whereabouts were unknown.[13]

IACHR makes use of various tools to monitor the outcome of the precautionary measures. In particular, it convenes work meetings during IACHR's sessions or follow-up meetings during its on-site visits or those of Country *Rapporteurs*. It is not easy to estimate to what extent the precautionary measures the Commission has ordered for LGTBI individuals have been applied by the Contracting States. Data collected by the Commission refers in general to all the precautionary measures ordered by it (not just those in favor of LGTBI individuals). It provides conflicting answers. If on the one hand the Commission has recently welcomed the Contracting States' positive response to the precautionary measures it had wholeheartedly

[11] Rules of Procedure of the Inter-American Commission on Human Rights, approved by the Commission at its 137th regular period of session held from 28th October to 13th November 2009 and modified on 2nd September 2011 (available at http://www.oas.org/en/iachr/mandate/Basics/rulesiachr.asp).

[12] Many precautionary measures have been granted in 2012: a detailed list is at http://www.oas.org/en/iachr/decisions/precautionary.asp.

[13] See Honduras: Amplification of Precautionary Measures, PM 196-09.

ordered,[14] on the other hand the Commission's practice has recorded the national authorities' failure to implement the precautionary measures.[15]

19.2.2 IACHR Special Unit

Following the General Assembly recommendations already mentioned, IACHR included in its Strategic Plan the Plan of Action 4.6.i, through which it specifically committed itself to pay attention to the rights of LGTBI persons, and to prioritize petitions alleging discrimination based on sexual orientation. In November 2011, IACHR decided to create a specialized Unit within its Executive Secretariat in order to carry out this commitment.

The Special Unit has started working recently; it is too early to evaluate the impact of its activity in protecting LGTBI's rights. Its mandate is ambitious and the monitoring role it is expected to perform is significant. The Unit's mandate consists of (a) processing petitions and cases, and providing advice to IACHR with respect to requests for precautionary measures and submission of requests for provisional measures before the Inter-American Court that are related to sexual orientation, gender identity and gender expression; (b) providing technical assistance to OAS Member States and OAS political organs on this area; (c) and preparing reports and evidence-based studies that can establish the extent of discrimination and violence towards members of these communities, and containing recommendations addressed to OAS Member States concerning their legislation, public policy, and judicial interpretation of rights of LGTBI persons.

19.3 Case Law of the Inter-American Court on Human Rights Concerning LGTBI Individuals

In 1999, for the first time, a lesbian reported to IACHR the violation of her rights, as protected by the American Convention, because of her sexual orientation. But prior to 2012, no petitions were brought before the Inter-American Court—among those IACHR had declared admissible—that concerned discriminations or the denial of rights each individual is entitled to according to the American Convention because of sexual identity.

---

[14] IACHR, 2011 Annual Report, Chapter III, para. 25.

[15] See, for instance, the Country Report adopted in 2009 concerning Honduras (Honduras: Human Rights and the *Coup d'État*, OEA/Ser.L/V/II, Doc. 55, 30th December 2009, paras 39–41). It is reported that during its on-site visit and thereafter, the Commission was informed that when some beneficiaries of the precautionary measures asked the competent authorities to implement them, they become the targets of attacks and threats. Other beneficiaries were forced to sign documents waiving the protection granted under the precautionary measures.

19.3.1 Cases Brought Before IACHR

The first case in which the Commission dealt with an alleged discrimination suffered by the petitioner because of her sexual orientation is the *Giraldo* case.[16]

The petitioner alleged that her honor and her right to equal protection before the law as granted in Art. 11(1) and 24 respectively had been violated by the Colombian prison authorities' decision not to authorize the exercise of her right to intimate visits of her same sex-partner. In particular, the petitioner argued that in the Colombian legislation there were no provisions allowing a distinction to be made between the right of a heterosexual prisoner to intimate visits and that of a homosexual. She argued, therefore, that the penitentiary authorities engaged in discriminatory treatment that was not authorized by domestic law.

In its decision on the admissibility of the case the Commission found that the claim was referred to facts that could have involved a *prima facie* violation of Article 11(2) of the American Convention,[17] in so far as they could have constituted an arbitrary or abusive interference with the petitioner's private life. The petition never reached the merits phase, in which the Commission could have determined what constituted an arbitrary or abusive interference with an individual's private life.[18]

Afterwards, in 2001, the Commission received another petition concerning the alleged violation of rights granted by the Convention suffered by an individual because of his sexual orientation (case *Pérez Meza v. Paraguay*).[19] The petitioner had asked the Paraguayan authorities to recognize his *de facto* marriage with a deceased individual of the same sex. Such recognition would have enabled their partnership to guarantee him rights similar to those of marriage. In so doing, the petitioner sought to prevent the seizure of the couple's common goods by the heirs of the deceased. The Commission declared the petition inadmissible, among other reasons, because the petitioner had failed to exhaust internal remedies. Before the national tribunals the petitioner had only requested the recognition of his union with a partner of the same-sex as a *de facto* marriage without claiming that the domestic law was discriminatory against homosexuals because it did not allow the recognition of unions between same-sex partners as a *de facto* marriage.

In 2010 the Commission declared admissible a petition concerning the alleged violation of the right to equality before the law established in Art. 24 of the

---

[16] Report No. 71/99, Case 11.656, *Giraldo v. Colombia*, 4th May 1999.

[17] "No one may be the object of arbitrary or abusive interference with his private life, his family, his home, or his correspondence, or of unlawful attacks on his honor or reputation."

[18] It is presumed that the petitioner had desisted from her petition according to Art. 41 of IACHR's Rules of Procedures. Had she not done so the Commission would have had to initiate the petition on the merits (see Art. 36(2) of the Rules of Procedures).

[19] Report No. 96/01, Petition 19/99, *Pérez Meza v. Paraguay*, 10th October 2001.

American Convention in connection with Art. 1(1) of the same treaty[20] against the Ecuadorian State for the discharge of an officer of the Military Police of the Ecuadorian Armed Forces who had been accused of engaging in homosexual conduct in the workplace.[21] The alleged violation of such provisions was denounced on the basis of two different reasons. Firstly, it was argued that the State had adopted a discriminatory policy in sanctioning only homosexual acts as professional misconduct. Secondly, it was claimed that the Ecuadorian Armed Forces maintained a discriminatory policy in regard to heterosexuals and homosexual relationships within a military facility. While Art. 87 of the Rules of Military Discipline condemned engagement in "illegitimate sexual acts within military facilities" as a maximum sanction of 30-day suspension,[22] Art. 117 of the same Rules expressly established that the members of the Armed Forces who were surprised in acts of homosexuality on duty or off duty were subject to the provision of Art. 87(i) of the Law on Personnel of the Armed Forces, which sanctioned such behaviour as grounds for discharge. The Commission declared the petition admissible in regard to the argument put forth in relation to Article 24 (in conjunction with Art. 1(1)), but it has not adopted a merits report yet.

Recently, in 2011, the Commission declared admissible the petition brought before it by the *Comisión Colombiana de Juristas and Germán Humberto Rincón Perfetti* on behalf of Mr. Duque.[23] They alleged the responsibility of Colombia for Mr. Duque's inability to gain access to the pension of his deceased partner because the provision that regulated the right to social security excluded same-sex couples from that benefit. The petitioners alleged that the State was responsible for violating several rights protected by the Convention, among which the right to equality before the law (Art. 24) in conjunction with Art. 1(1) of the American Convention. The Commission declared the petition admissible,[24] but it has not adopted the merits report yet. The Commission's decisions on the merits concerning the last two cases, and perhaps the Court's judgments, are expected to shed light on that topic Vitucci (2012), pp. 61–73.

---

[20] According to it, "[t]he States Parties to this Convention undertake to respect the rights and freedoms recognized herein and to ensure to all persons subject to their jurisdiction the free and full exercise of those rights and freedoms, without any discrimination for reasons of race, color, sex, language, religion, political or other opinion, national or social origin, economic status, birth, or any other social condition."

[21] Report No. 1/10, Petition 2723-02, *Homero Flor Freire v. Ecuador*, 15th March 2010.

[22] In the petitioners' view the terms "unlawful sexual acts" were referred to sexual relationships between heterosexual individuals in the absence of or outside of marriage.

[23] Report No. 150/11, Petition 123-05, Admissibility, *Duque v. Colombia*, November 2, 2011.

[24] It is worth noting that the Commission applied Art. 46(2)(a), of the Convention concerning the exception to the rule of the prior exhaustion of domestic remedies, concluding that Colombian domestic law did not provide for appropriate remedies to protect the right of a homosexual to succeed in the pension of his deceased partner.

19.3.2 *The Court Judgment in* Atala Riffo and Daughters v. Chile

In September 2010 the Inter-American Commission on Human Rights filed an application with the Inter-American Court on Human Rights (further referred also as IACtHR or the Court) in the case *Atala Riffo and daughters v. Chile*[25] concerning the alleged discriminatory treatment Ms Atala and her children had suffered due to Ms Atala's sexual orientation. The petition also concerned the arbitrary interference in the private and family life of Ms Atala and in the family life of her daughters still due to Ms Atala's sexual orientation.[26] Such violations occurred within the framework of a legal process for the custody of three children following the dissolution of the marriage between Mr. Lopéz Allende and Ms Atala.

In particular, the petitioners claimed the discriminatory treatment and the abusive interference in their private and family lives by the Juvenile Court of Villarica and the Supreme Court of Chile, which had granted custody of the girls to the father. In particular, the Supreme Court had founded its conclusion on Art. 225 of the Chilean Civil Code. It provides that, when parents live separately, the personal care of the children falls to the mother. But the provision admits that in exceptional circumstances, when necessary to protect the interests of the child, whether because of mistreatment, neglect, or *another just cause*, the judge may transfer the care of the child to the other parent. In the case at stake, the Supreme Court, taking into account the best interest of the three daughters, had declared that a 'justified cause' existed that made it essential to grant custody to the father.

The IACtHR adopted its judgment the 24th February 2012,[27] substantially upholding the Commission's conclusions and even going beyond it.

19.3.2.1 General Remarks

The judgment surely represents the most significant measure so far adopted to protect homosexuals' rights in the framework of the Inter-American system of human rights protection. It is not an exaggeration to say that the judgment is of historical reach on a continent where violence suffered by homosexuals is still very significant and where cultural suspicion and ostracism toward them is still widely practiced.

The seriousness of the situation might partially explain the approach the Court has followed. The Court has widely referred to the European Court of Human Rights' jurisprudence as well as to the reports and communications so far adopted

[25] IACHR, *Application before the Inter-American Court of Human Rights in the Case of Karen Atala and daughters* (Case 12.502) *against the State of Chile*, 17th September 2010.

[26] The case was referred to the Inter-American Court because IACHR concluded that the State had not complied with the recommendations contained in its Merits Report No. 139/09.

[27] IACtHR, *Atala Riffo and Daughters v. Chile*, judgment of 24th February 2012.

by the human rights treaty-based monitoring bodies in the matter of sexual orientation, in order to justify an evolutionary interpretation of the American Convention. This has prompted the Court to declare the responsibility of Chile for the infringement of the right of the family life that had been established between the same-sex couple and Ms Atala's daughters. The Court might not have obtained the same result had it stated that the Convention imposed on the Contracting States the obligation to protect family life on the grounds of an investigation concerning the level of protection the Contracting States' legal orders guaranteed to same-sex couples.

This approach results in a certain uniformity among different international tribunals' jurisprudence, in such a way as to facilitate (treaty) interpretations otherwise difficult to justify. It is a desirable outcome when international tribunals are called upon to interpret and apply human rights treaties. Nevertheless, questions concerning the efficacy of such a method are left open if it is not associated with the enhancement of those laws (although still few) of the Contracting States which provide for protection to same-sex couples.

Given the impact this judgment may have it is appropriate to devote to it a thorough analysis in the context of this study.

19.3.2.2 Violation of the Right of an Equal Treatment Before the Law

The Inter-American Court has established that the Chilean State had violated the right to the equal treatment before the law contained in Article 24 of the American Convention, in conjunction with Art. 1(1) of the same treaty, toward Ms Atala and her daughters.

To reach such a conclusion, the Court, for the first time, held that sexual orientation is one of the grounds for discrimination covered by the category "any other social condition" provided in Art. 1(1). It consequently concluded that no domestic regulation, decision, or practice of the State Parties may diminish or restrict, in any way whatsoever, the rights of a person on the basis of her/his sexual orientation.[28]

The Court, although in a hasty and rather unclear way, endorsed the Commission's opinion, according to which sexual orientation is also a suspect category of distinction. In its Report on the *Atala* case, the Commission, following the Court's previous case law, had repeated that in order to exclude the discriminatory nature of a specific action, a Contracting State had to prove that it was reasonable and objective, that is to say that it pursued a legitimate goal, and was a fitting means for attaining that legitimate goal—that, in short, a logical means-to-end relationship existed between the goal sought and the distinction made—, that no alternatives existed and that it was proportional. Moreover, in the Commission's opinion, in deciding whether an action had been based on certain suspect justifications (sexual

[28] *Ibidem*, para. 91.

orientation included), a *consensus* existed that the test used to quantify the reasonableness of the discriminatory treatment had to be particularly strict. Thus, in the Commission's opinion, only "weighty reasons" could be invoked as a justification. As the Commission's Report itself had recalled, this strict analysis served to guarantee that the distinction was not based on prejudices or stereotypes.[29]

The consequence which the Commission and the Court inferred by this reasoning is that an action based on a suspect category of distinction is presumed to be incompatible with the American Convention. They consequently concluded that the defendant State had to prove that *weighty reasons* existed to justify that conduct based on sexual orientation issues was not discriminatory.[30]

On this assumption the Court examined whether the justification given by the State for the custody decision (that is, the protection of the children's best interest from the alleged damage the girls might have suffered as a consequence of their mother's sexual orientation) Feria Tinta (2008) could have justified the treatment granted to the petitioners. It concluded negatively. In the Court's opinion, the protection of the best interests of the child is more than a legitimate goal: it is an imperative.[31] Nevertheless, it found that the State had not proved that Ms. Atala's cohabitation with her partner had a negative effect on the girls' best interest. That conclusion was based on a *real and concrete harm test* the Court has not always applied in the same scrupulous way.

The Court decided that the determination of whether the child's best interest was being threatened, in cases involving the care and custody of minors, had to be based on an assessment of specific parental behavior and its negative impact on the well-being and development of the child. In the Court's view such an evaluation had to take into account any real and proven damage or risk to the child's well-being, and none that were merely speculative or imaginary.[32]

The Court used such a test to verify whether the decision to deprive Ms Atala of the custody of her daughters was in keeping with the aim of protecting the well-being of the children. Among other things, having excluded the appropriateness of the measure under examination (as mentioned below), the Court also indirectly denied that it was based on rigorous and weighty reasons.

The Court rebutted three of the four threats the State claimed for the children's development, applying the *real and concrete damage test* rigorously.

Concerning the alleged social discrimination they might have suffered within their social environment due to their mother's cohabiting with a partner of the same sex, and the confusion of sexual roles they might have been affected by due to their living with their mother and her partner, it held that the custody decision had been

[29] IACHR, *Application before the IACtHR in the Case of Karen Atala*, paras 86 and 88.

[30] IACtHR, *Atala Riffo and Daughters v. Chile*, paras 124–125.

[31] *Ibidem*, para. 108.

[32] "Speculations, assumptions, stereotypes, or generalized considerations regarding the parents' personal characteristics, or cultural preferences regarding the family's traditional concepts are not admissible": *ibidem*, para. 109.

based only on *potential and abstract risks* and on the application of a *speculative and imaginative damage test*. In other words, in the Court's view the Chilean judicial organs at stake had not made an assessment of specific parental behavior and its negative impact on the well-being and development of the children. Rather, they had based their decisions on stereotypes associated with the preconception that children raised by homosexual couples would necessarily have difficulties.[33] For this reason, the Court concluded that the judicial decisions regarding custody had not defined in a specific and concrete manner the connection of causality between the mother's behavior and its alleged impact on the children's development. In the Court's opinion, these were sufficient grounds for concluding in favor of a lack of appropriateness between the goal sought (the protection of the girls) and the measure adopted (their custody to the father). On such grounds the Court concluded that those decisions constituted discriminatory treatment against Ms. Atala and her daughters.[34]

As far as the other alleged prejudice the children might have suffered is concerned, namely the damage due to the fact that the mother had put her own interests before those of her daughters in deciding to live with a same-sex partner, the Court acknowledged that no evidence had been found of any harm caused to the three girls. Thus, it established that the differences prohibited under the Convention were not restricted to homosexuality *per se*, but also included its expressions, such as the petitioner's decision to live together with her partner.[35] The IACtHR also found that both sexual orientation and its exercise were relevant aspects of an individual's private life.[36] On the basis of such arguments it concluded that it was not reasonable to require Ms. Atala to put her life and family projects on hold in order to protect her daughters.[37]

The Court's approach was less punctual when it dealt with the claim concerning the prejudice the children might have suffered because of their living in a non-traditional family. The Court mainly followed an abstract and theoretical reasoning, instead of the *real and concrete harm test*, in order to rebut such a claim. It limited itself to stating that the claim reflected a stereotyped perception of

[33] *Ibidem*, paras 115–131. What the Court has to say about the argument that the child's best interest might be affected by the risk of rejection by society is very effective: "[the] potential social stigma due to the mother or father's sexual orientation cannot be considered as a valid "harm" for the purposes of determining the child's best interest. If the judges who analyze such cases confirm the existence of social discrimination, it is completely inadmissible to legitimize that discrimination with the argument of protecting the child's best interest": para. 121.

[34] *Ibidem*, paras 122 and 131–132.

[35] *Ibidem*, para. 133.

[36] *Ibidem*, paras 133–139.

[37] *Ibidem*, paras 139–140. The Court went beyond what was necessary when it stated that "to require the mother to limit her lifestyle options implies using a "traditional" concept of women's social role as mothers, according to which it is socially expected that women bear the main responsibility for their children's upbringing and that in pursuit of this she should have given precedence to raising her children, renouncing an essential aspect of her identity": para. 140.

the concept of family, which had no basis in the Convention. It did not analyze whether the State had demonstrated that the well-being of the girls was at risk because of their living in a non-traditional family.[38]

19.3.2.3 Violation of the Right to a Private and Family Life

The Court judgment is not very innovative when it states that an individual's sexual orientation is part of his/her private life.[39] In its case law on sexual rapes the Court had already asserted that the concept of private life was a wide-ranging term, which could not be defined exhaustively, but included, among others, the sexual life of an individual.[40] I don't want to deny the relevance of such a conclusion. It should not be forgotten that this is the first time that the Court has found that interference occurring in the private life of a petitioner because of his/her sexual identity was not legitimate. To be precise, the Court judged it inappropriate and disproportionate for achieving the legitimate goal of protecting the best interests of the three girls. In the Court's opinion, the Chilean domestic courts should have limited themselves to examining the parental behavior towards the daughters without exposing and scrutinizing Ms. Atala's sexual orientation.[41]

The fact remains that such a conclusion would have been foreseeable if the Court's previous jurisprudence above-mentioned had been taken into account. Rather, what is surprising is that the Court had adopted a *standard test* to justify an interference in the right to privacy on the basis of the sexual identity of an individual while rigorous and weighty reasons had been sought in order to justify a different treatment given on the basis of sexual orientation considerations. Moreover, since the reason given by the Chilean courts for interfering in Ms. Atala's private life was the same one used to justify the discriminatory treatment, namely the best interests of the three girls, it also appears not completely justifiable that the Court expressly excluded the condition that the State, in order to evaluate whether its interference in the private life of Ms Atala was legitimate, had to adduce real and concrete evidence showing that there was a real threat to the well-being of the girls.[42]

Rather, the Court's conclusion regarding the alleged violation of the petitioners' family rights is really innovative, even if it also raises some criticism.

---

[38] *Ibidem*, para. 145.

[39] *Ibidem*, para. 165.

[40] IACtHR, *Rosendo Cantú* et al. *v. Mexico*, judgment of 31st August 2010, para. 119, and IACtHR, *Fernández Ortega* et al. *v. Mexico. Preliminary Objection, Merits, Reparations, and Costs*, judgment of 30th August 2010, para. 129.

[41] IACtHR, *Atala Riffo and Daughters v. Chile*, paras 164–166.

[42] The Court also ruled that the disciplinary investigation carried out by the Chilean judicial authority against Ms. Atala had been performed in such a way as to violate her privacy and discriminate against her on the grounds of her sexual orientation: *ibidem*, paras 225–230.

The Inter-American Commission had been more prudent than the Court in its avoidance of taking a stand on the nature of the family relationship on the notion of family in the case law of IACtHR Quiroga CM (2009), pp. 557–572 between the petitioners and the same-sex partner of Ms Atala. The Commission had stated that the right to a private life also included Ms Atala's right to develop family relationships on the basis of that identity, even if it was not accepted or tolerated by a majority within Chilean society.[43]

Since the decision to deprive Ms Atala of the custody of her daughters was based on her sexual orientation, the Commission had concluded that such a decision also abusively impinged on her family life plans with a partner of the same sex. In this way, the Commission had only indirectly asserted that under Art. 11(2) of the Convention cohabitation with a same-sex partner was a form of family relationship. Only at a later time, and in a distinct section of its Report, had the Commission established that another family—comprising Ms Atala and her daughters—had been created following the dissolution of the marriage with the petitioner's husband. Thus, it had found that Art. 11(2) had been violated also because the decision to separate the girls from their mother had impinged on their rights to develop a relationship with their family members.[44] It may be asserted that, in dealing with such violations of Art. 11(2) separately, the Commission carefully avoided qualifying the relationship between Ms Atala, her same-sex partner and her daughters as a family relationship.

On the contrary, the Court did not hesitate to consider the relationship between Ms Atala, her daughters and her same-sex partner as a family unit.[45] Thus, it came to the conclusion that the decision to separate the girls from their family environment was in violation of Art. 11(2) and 17(1) of the Convention in regard to all the petitioners.[46] While the first Article, as already seen, protects individuals from arbitrary or abusive interference in a person's family life, the second one protects the family unit, obliging States which are parties to the Convention to adopt measures that protect the family.[47]

---

[43] IACHR, *Application before the IACtHR in the Case of Karen Atala*, para. 116.

[44] *Ibidem*, para. 122.

[45] IACtHR, *Atala Riffo and Daughters v. Chile*, paras 176–177.

[46] *Ibidem*, para. 178.

[47] In his *partially dissenting opinion* annexed to the judgment, Judge Alberto Pérez Pérez criticized the Court's choice to rule that Art. 17(1) had been violated. The Judge seems to hold that only the notion of family in Art. 11(2) should encompass families composed by same-sex partners, while he did not consider it prudent to do the same in regard to Art. 17. In his opinion this could be taken as an implicit pronouncement on the interpretation of different provisions of Art. 17(18 and 24). He states that Art. 17 could be interpreted in a way that presupposes that the family is based on a heterosexual marriage or *de facto* union: para. 18. It is not totally clear which risks the Judge wanted to exclude. Maybe that the door was open to an interpretation of Art. 17(2)—the provision protecting the right to marry—in the sense that it imposes an obligation to Contracting States to grant this right also to same-sex partners. Whatever the Judge's opinion may be, it does not seem reasonable to assume that under the Inter-American Convention two notions of family may exist, the one protected, pursuant to Art. 17, and the other in accordance with Art. 11(2). This is so mostly because, according to Art. 27(2) of the Convention, States are not allowed to depart from

The questionable point is the way in which the Inter-American Court reached such conclusion; it followed an approach different from the one adopted by the European Court of Human Rights (further referred as ECtHR).

In the *Schalk and Kopf* case[48] the ECtHR, modifying its previous case law, which only accepted that the emotional and sexual relationships of a same-sex couple constituted "private life" for the purposes of Art. 8 of the European Convention on Human Rights (further referred as ECHR), had established that a cohabiting same-sex couple living in a stable *de facto* partnership fell within the notion of 'family life' according to the same Article. In order to justify such a conclusion, the Court had inquired into the existence of a *consensus* among the Contracting parties of the ECHR, seeking the adoption by a majority of them of legislation granting to same-sex couples a legal recognition of their unions in order to assert that Art. 8 of the European Convention covered the right to family of same-sex couples.[49]

The Inter-American Court did not look for such a *consensus*. To be precise, it did not attempt to check whether a *consensus* in favor of the recognition that stable unions between same-sex individuals as families could be said to be formed among the States Parties to the Inter-American Convention. It only recalled the opinion of various human rights organs created by treaties, which state that there is no single model for a family, but many variations of it. Among them, it mainly made reference to the judgments of the ECtHR in the case of *Schalk and Kopf v. Austria*, and in the case of *X, Y and Z v. The United Kingdom*.[50]

It is not completely clear why the Inter-American Court has not substantially followed the method indicated by the ECtHR. At first glance it might be supposed that it did not agree with it.[51] But the approach followed by the Inter-American Court might also be partially explained by taking into account the fact that the Court was aware of not having been able to prove the existence of such a *consensus*. It is necessary to remember that in several Contracting States of the American Convention, national legislations either discriminate against LGTBI individuals or

---

the rights protected under Art. 17. The adoption of two different notions of family would tend to suggest that the heterosexual family (married or *de facto*) may receive greater protection than the other.

[48] *Schalk and Kopf v. Austria*, judgment of 24th June 2010, paras 92–95. See the chapter by Pustorino in this volume.

[49] *Ibidem*, paras 27–34.

[50] ECHR, *X, Y and Z v. The United Kingdom*, judgment of 22nd April 1997. See the chapters by Crisafulli and Pustorino in this volume.

[51] One might be under such an impression after reading the part of the judgment where the Court is asked to judge whether the custody decision was apt to protect Ms Atala's daughters from the social discrimination they might have suffered because of the mother's sexual orientation. Indeed, the Court states: "While it is true that certain societies can be intolerant toward a person because of their race, gender, nationality, or sexual orientation, States cannot use this as justification to perpetuate discriminatory treatments. States are internationally compelled to adopt the measures necessary "to make effective" the rights established in the Convention, as stipulated in Art. 2 of said Inter-American instrument" (para. 119).

criminalize their sexual behavior. The framework at stake might have convinced the Court it was not useful to search for a *consensus* of this kind. On the contrary, an effort to determine whether the legal recognition of same-sex unions is granted in at least some Contracting States would have been important. An analysis of the legal status and rights recognized for homosexuals in the Contracting States of the American Convention would have enabled the Court to justify its decision on the evolution of social behavior and cultural sensitivity in the Contracting States, if it had determined that at least in some States LGTBI's rights had been receiving protection and recognition.[52]

Furthermore, one may wonder whether the reference to the ECtHR's judgments already quoted was appropriate in justifying the conclusion that between Ms Atala, her partner and her children a family life existed.

Indeed, in the case of *X, Y and Z v. The United Kingdom*, the ECtHR had considered that a *de facto* family tie linked the three applicants (a transsexual, his female partner and a child that was born by means of artificial insemination from the latter).[53] But this does not seem a legitimate basis for justifying the conclusion that, *mutatis mutandis*, a family relationship was established between Ms Atala, her partner and the three girls. In its jurisprudence on transsexuals, the ECtHR took stands not always in keeping with its jurisprudence on same-sex couples. For instance, while it expressly recognized the existence of an obligation by the Contracting States to grant transsexuals the right to marry,[54] it clearly excluded that such an obligation should exist towards same-sex couples.[55]

---

[52] The quest for a *consensus* among the Contracting States would have been expected. Indeed scattered references to internal legislations and case law of national judges of the Contracting States appear in the judgment (especially in the footnotes). See, for instance, para. 19, which quotes the Constitution of Ecuador as recognizing the stable union between same-sex individuals as a family union. See also footnote No. 113, where the Court recalls that the Constitutions of Bolivia and Ecuador explicitly prohibit discrimination based on sexual orientation and that the national legislations of Argentina and Uruguay grant homosexuals the same rights as heterosexuals. Several references to the case law of the Contracting States' national courts are also made in the judgment. For instance, in footnote No. 114 the Court recalls that the Constitutional Court of Colombia declared unconstitutional a provision that considered homosexuality in the armed forces as a disciplinary infraction. In paragraph 136 of the judgment the Court also quotes the judgment of the Supreme Court of Justice of Mexico, which considered sexual orientation as an expression, among others, of the free development of an individual's personality. See the chapter by Cabrales Lucio in this volume.

[53] ECHR, *X, Y and Z v. The United Kingdom*, para. 37.

[54] Since the cases *Christine Goodwin v. The United Kingdom*, judgment of 11th July 2002, paras 100–104 and *I. v. The United Kingdom*, judgment of 11th July 2002, paras 80–84, the Court held that individuals who had undergone operations to perform sex change and entertained an emotional relationship with a person of the opposite biological (or chromosomal) sex—identical to their original sex—also had the right to marry under Art. 12 of the Convention. In the Court's opinion, the law of a Contracting State which had allowed them to marry only persons of opposite biological sex seriously jeopardized their right to marriage.

[55] See ECHR, *Schalk and Kopf v. Austria*, paras 27 and 58 and, more recently, *Gas and Dubois v. France*, judgment of 15th March, 2012, para. 66.

Even the reference to the *Schalk and Kopf* case does not seem to be an appropriate basis for justifying the conclusion reached by the IACtHR. The reference to this judgment is only relevant for arguing that between Ms Atala and her partner a family life existed. On the contrary, it is not appropriate to conclude that a family life could also be said to exist between them and Ms Atala's daughters. It would have been more appropriate for the Inter-American Court to have made reference to the decision on the admissibility adopted by the European Court in the *Gas and Dubois v. France* case.[56] Here the European Court has qualified as family life, under Art. 8, not only the relationship between two women who had concluded a *pacte civil de solidarité*, but also the relationship between them and the biological daughter of one of them, born by artificial insemination during their relationship. The European Court observed that both women had wanted the child, and that

> [l]es requérantes élèvent A. depuis sa naissance, et s'en occupent conjointement et activement, comme l'ont reconnu les juridictions nationales. Dans ces conditions, la Cour estime que les relations entre les requérantes et A. s'analysent en une "vie familiale" au sens de l'article 8 de la Convention.[57]

19.3.2.4 Reparations

As far as the reparation measures granted by the IACtHR are concerned, it is worth noting that they have not been limited to requiring the State to pay monetary compensation for pecuniary and non-pecuniary damages suffered by the petitioners. It has also obliged the State to provide for medical and psychological or psychiatric care, free of charge, through its specialized public health institutions, to hold a public act of acknowledgment of international responsibility with regard to the facts of this case, and finally to continue to implement permanent education programs and training courses directed at public officials, and particularly judicial officials at all levels of the Judicial Branch. Such redress is definitely in keeping with the Inter-American Court case law on reparations. It goes without saying that the measures ordered, especially those of general scope, play an important role in promoting an inclusive and non-discriminatory culture. The role the Court can play in this regard is incisive and goes far beyond the redress of the specific case under its examination Burgorgue-Larsen, Ubeda de Torres (2010).

Nevertheless, it is not unreasonable to wonder whether in the case at stake the Court could have asked the State of Chile to make the custody decision null and void and to re-open the custody proceedings as a form of reparation despite the fact that neither the Commission nor the petitioners' representatives had asked the Court for such a measure Antkowiak (2008).

[56] *Gas and Dubois v. France, Decision on the Admissibility*, 31st August, 2010.

[57] *Ibidem* p. 12. Surprisingly, the Court did not repeat this assertion in its merits judgment.

In its previous jurisprudence, the Court did not hesitate to order the responsible State to grant retrials,[58] even specifying in certain cases how the national law should have been applied. It has also obliged the State to abstain from executing death sentences.[59] Furthermore, it has asked the State to nullify its criminal convictions[60] and to expunge criminal records.[61] Finally, it has even ordered the cancellation of fines already imposed.[62]

The answer to that question may vary, depending on whether one believes that in this way the Court would have substantially taken a stand in favor of the mother, determining indirectly that she would have offered the three girls a better home or, on the contrary, whether one may believe that the Court would have only asked the Chilean judicial organs to decide on the custody of the girls on the grounds of real facts (that is to say, the existence of a real risk to the detriment of the three girls, due to their cohabiting with a same sex couple), and not on prejudices and stereotypes.

In the first case, it is obvious that the Court, due to its subsidiary nature, would not have had the competence to issue a decision that was, essentially, a ruling on the custody of the three girls.

Nevertheless, it does not seem unreasonable to maintain that, had the Court asked Chile to re-open the custody proceedings by taking into account its international obligation not to discriminate on the grounds of the petitioner's sexual identity, it would not have acted as a "fourth instance" court, nor would it have overreached its subsidiary and complementary role with regard to the Chilean national courts.

References

Pasqualucci JM (2003) The practice and procedure of the Inter-American court of human rights. Cambridge University Press, Cambridge

Antkowiak TM (2008) Remedial approaches to human rights violations. the Inter-American court of human rights and beyond. Columbia J Transnatl Law 46:351–419

Feria Tinta M (2008) The landmark rulings of the Inter-American court of human rights on the rights of the child. Martinus Nijhoff, Leiden, Boston

---

[58] IACtHR, *Fermin-Ramirez v. Guatemala*, 20th July 2005, para. 130, lett. a; IACtHR, *Hilaire v. Trinidad & Tobago*, 21st July 2002, para. 214; IACtHR, *Castillo Petruzzi v. Peru*, 30th May 1999, para. 221.

[59] *Ibidem*, *Fermin-Ramirez v. Guatemala*, para. 130, lett. c.

[60] IACtHR, *Herrera-Ulloa v. Costa Rica*, 2nd July 2004, para. 195.

[61] IACtHR, *Acosta-Calderon v. Ecuador*, 24th June 2005, para. 165; IACHR, *Cantoral-Benavides v. Peru*, 3rd December 2001, para. 78.

[62] E.g., IACtHR, *Berenson-Mejia v. Peru*, 25th November 2004, para. 239; IACtHR, *Suarez-Rosero v. Ecuador*, 20th January 1999, para. 76.

Quiroga CM (2009) Family members and the Inter-American court of human rights. In: Liber Fausto Pocar. Diritti individuali e giustizia internazionale, vol 1. Giuffré Editore, Milano, pp 557–572

Vitucci MC (2012) La tutela internazionale dell'orientamento sessuale. Jovene Editore, Napoli, pp 61–73

Burgorgue-Larsen L, Ubeda de Torres A (2010) The Inter-American court of human rights: case-law and commentary. Oxford University Press, Oxford

Chapter 20
Free Movement Rights for Same-Sex Couples Under EU Law: What Role to Play for the CJEU?

Jorrit Rijpma and Nelleke Koffeman

Abstract EU law as it stands fails to provide same-sex couples legal certainty as regards their right of free movement under the EU Treaties. This chapter analyses in detail the situation in which a Member State refuses entry and residence to the same-sex spouse or (registered) partner of an EU citizen invoking free movement rights. Although the EU does not have the competence to harmonise Member States' family laws, the primacy and full effectiveness of EU law require these laws to respect both the fundamental right to free movement of persons, as well as fundamental rights. This chapter argues that it is for the CJEU, as the EU's "Supreme Court" and constitutional adjudicator, to guarantee these freedoms. An approach based on mutual recognition of the relationship status of Member States would allow for an inclusive definition of family, whilst respecting the division of competences between the EU and its Member States.

20.1 Introduction

Across the European Union (further referred to as EU) there are widely diverging attitudes towards homosexuality. Generally, acceptance is high in Western and Northern European Member States, whilst it is lowest in Central and Eastern European Member States.[1] Attitudes towards 'gay marriage' largely follow a similar pattern.[2] On the one hand an increasing number of EU Member States has

[1] Special Eurobarometer 393, Discrimination in the EU in 2012 (November 2012), p. 41.

[2] The term 'same-sex marriage' will be used throughout this chapter. The authors however stress that this term is descriptive. Legally speaking there is no such thing as a same-sex or gay marriage, only civil marriage, which in six Member States has been opened to people of the same sex. Reference to he/his/him should be read so as to include she/her.

J. Rijpma (✉) • N. Koffeman
Europa Institute, Leiden University, Leiden, The Netherlands
e-mail: j.j.rijpma@law.leidenuniv.nl; n.r.koffeman@law.leidenuniv.nl

D. Gallo et al. (eds.), *Same-Sex Couples before National, Supranational and International Jurisdictions*, DOI 10.1007/978-3-642-35434-2_20,

opened civil marriage for people of the same sex and a majority of Member States provides some form of formal recognition of same-sex relationships. On the other hand a number of Member States have sought to define marriage as exclusively between a man and a woman in their Constitution or in domestic legislation. In the European context the question of equal marriage rights is rarely described in terms of a culture war. One could nevertheless qualify it as such, considering that few issues are as divisive and polarized at both EU and Member State level, even in countries which generally are considered as accepting of homosexuality.[3]

This chapter will look at the way in which the Court of Justice of the European Union (further referred to as CJEU), more specifically the Court of Justice (further referred as CJ or the Court) may be called upon to play a role in the debate on the rights of same-sex couples. More specifically it will analyze the way in which the Court may address the obstacles that same-sex partners encounter when trying to assert rights of free movement on the basis of EU law. These obstacles flow from a lack of recognition of same-sex relationships and arise mainly in areas of the law in which different-sex spouses traditionally enjoy certain benefits: immigration, adoption, pension, inheritance and tax.[4] The focus of this chapter will be on the first area of law, namely the right of entry and residence under EU law of same-sex partners, in particular of EU citizens. This is certainly not a new question, but it remains pressing in view of the increasingly diverging levels of recognition accorded to same-sex relationships across the EU.

It is important to note that this discussion is to some extent speculative. So far, the CJ has not been asked to pronounce itself in cases concerning the free movement rights of same-sex couples. Still, this analysis can draw on existing case-law in the area of free movement, in particular the free movement of persons, as well as the Court's judgments relating to same-sex couples in other areas of EU competence, for example in the field of employment.[5] In addition, any discussion of the rights of same-sex couples under EU law must take into account the level of protection of fundamental rights granted by the Strasbourg Court under the European Convention on Human Rights (further referred to as ECHR). Finally, inspiration may be drawn from other jurisdictions in which similar questions have arisen.

This chapter will examine in detail the situation in which a Member State refuses a right of entry and residence to a same-sex couple, which claims migration rights on the basis of EU law. At the outset, a brief discussion of the nature of EU legal order and the CJEU's role within that legal order, will help to understand the function the EU judges may play in the debate on legal recognition of same-sex relationships (Sect. 20.2). Because of the general importance of fundamental rights in the EU legal order, an overview of the relevant fundamental rights is given in Sect. 20.3. This will be followed by an analysis of the EU rules on the free

[3] As evidenced by the massive protests in favour and against preceding the introduction of same-sex marriage in France in 2013.

[4] Waaldijk (2011).

[5] Art. 19 TFEU. See the chapter by Orzan in this volume.

movement of persons in both secondary (Sect. 20.4), and EU primary law (Sect. 20.5). The position of same-sex couples in which both partners are third-country nationals (i.e. non EU citizens) will be examined in Sect. 20.6. Section 20.7 will briefly examine possible legislative avenues to address obstacles to the free movement of same-sex couples.

20.2 Delineating the Jurisdiction of the CJEU

The importance of the CJ for European integration cannot be overestimated. It was the Court that held that the EU, then still the European Community, constituted a new legal order for the benefit of which Member States had carried over part of their sovereign rights. By attributing direct effect to provisions of EU law, as known, the Court allowed individuals to rely directly on the rights conferred upon them by EU law in national courts.[6] The Court's doctrine of supremacy means, moreover, that any national law of whatever standing must be in conformity with EU law and is otherwise inapplicable.[7] In principle, this includes rules of a constitutional nature, although the respect for national identity due under Art. 4(2) TEU raises new questions on the relation between EU law and national constitutional provisions.[8] It is nevertheless clear that the principle of supremacy considerably limits the importance of yet another principle of EU law, the principle of conferral, under which the Union can only exercise the powers that have been conferred upon it.[9] After all, Member States are under a duty to comply with EU law, even when exercising powers that have not been transferred to the EU level. This duty is reinforced by the principle of sincere cooperation which obliges Member States to ensure the effectiveness of EU law.[10]

The Court's constitutional role is reinforced by the fact that the review of the legality of acts by the Union and its bodies goes further than ensuring compliance with the Treaties. As Art. 19 TEU states, the CJEU ensures that in the interpretation and application of the Treaties the law is observed. Its powers of review extend to ensure respect for the general principles of EU law, which have the status of primary law. They act as an aid to interpretation and a ground for judicial review. Fundamental rights form an integral part of these general principles which the Court

[6] *Van Gend and Loos*, Case 26/62, judgment of 5th February 1963 [1963] ECR 1.

[7] *Costa v. ENEL*, Case 6/64, judgment of 15th July 164, [1964] ECR 585, 539; *Internationale Handelsgesellschaft*, Case 11/70, judgment of 17th December 1970 [1970] ECR 1125, para. 3; *Melloni*, C-399/11, judgment of 26th February 2013 nyr., para. 59. See De Witte (2011).

[8] See Sect. 20.5.2.2.

[9] Lenaerts (2010), p. 1340.

[10] Art. 4(3) TFEU.

is bound to uphold.[11] As a matter of EU law, fundamental rights are binding not only upon the Union, but also upon the Member States when they act within the scope of EU law. This is the case where they implement or enforce EU rules,[12] but also when they derogate from EU law.[13] In those situations there is a sufficient link to bring the factual situation within the scope of EU law. If however there is no obligation to act or EU measure from which to derogate, fundamental rights do not apply.[14]

With the entry into force of the Lisbon Treaty the status of the EU's own human rights' catalogue, the Charter on Fundamental Rights (further referred to as CFR) was elevated to that of primary law.[15] The Charter binds the institutions, bodies and agencies of the Union, as well as the Member States, but only when they are 'implementing Union law'.[16] The CJ has recently clarified that the rights laid down in the Charter must be respected in all situations in which national legislation falls within the scope of EU law, and that hence '[t]he applicability of European Union law entails applicability of the fundamental rights guaranteed by the Charter.'[17]

However, as Advocated General (AG) pointed out in her opinion to the *Zambrano* case, it is increasingly difficult to establish when a factual situation provides a sufficient cross-border element in order to trigger the applicability of EU law and hence the protection of fundamental rights as a matter of EU law.[18] It comes as little surprise that in many of the cases that were hailed for the Court's

[11] *Internationale Handelsgesellschaft*, para. 4. The Court identified the Member States common constitutional traditions, as well as international human rights treaties which involved the Member States as a source of these right (*Nold*, Case 4-73, judgment of 14th May 1974 [1974] ECR 491, para. 13). The Court has attributed specific significance to the ECHR: *Rutili*, Case 36–75, judgment of 28th October 1975 [1975] ECR 1219, para. 32 and subsequent cases such as *Omega*, C-36/02, judgment of 14th October 2004 [2004] ECR I-9609, para. 33.

[12] *Wachauf*, Case 5/88, judgment of 13th July 1989 [1989] ECR 2609, paras 17–19.

[13] *ERT* Case 260/89, judgment of 18th June 1991 [1991] ECR I-2925, para. 43.

[14] *Annibaldi*, C-309/96, judgment of 18th December 1997 [1997] ECR I-7493, paras 21–25. See also *Dereci*, C-256/11, judgment of 15th November 2011 nyr., para. 71 and *Iida*, C-40/11, judgment of 8th November 2012 nyr., paras 78–79.

[15] Art. 6(1) TEU.

[16] Art. 51(1) CFR. It has been a matter of much debate whether this limits the scope of the Charter as compared to the general principles. See i.e. Besselink (2012a), p. 108 and Groussot et al. (2011), p. 19. Many authors have convincingly argued it does not, see recently: Lenaerts (2013), pp. 385–386.

[17] *Akerberg*, C-610/11, judgment of 26th February 2013 nyr., para. 21.

[18] Opinion of AG Sharpston of 30th September 2010 in *Zambrano*, C-34/09, judgment of 8th March 2011 [2011] ECR I-1177, paras 156–177. See also the references for a preliminary ruling from the Council of State (Netherlands), lodged on 10 October 2012—Minister voor Immigratie, Integratie en Asiel and O; other party: B (Case C-456/12) and S and Minister voor Immigratie, Integratie en Asiel; other party: G (Case C-457/12), both pending. See Gallo (2012).

emphasis on fundamental rights, it went to great length to establish a link with the fundamental Treaty freedoms.[19]

It may seem to be stating the obvious, but it is important to stress that the EU is not a human rights organization, nor is the CJ a human rights court. Unlike AG Jacobs proposed in *Konstantinidis*, the Court has never adopted a *civis europeus sum* approach, meaning that the mere fact that a European citizen is affected by national law would suffice to subject that national law, or acts based upon it, to review on the basis of EU fundamental rights.[20] It is clear that fundamental rights, be it as general principles or laid down in the Charter, do not constitute free standing rights which can be invoked to challenge national measures in whatever situation.[21] Any interpretation of the scope of EU law to this effect would require

> both an evolution in the case law and an unequivocal political statement from the constituent powers of the EU (its Member States) pointing at a new role for fundamental rights in the EU.[22]

In which different situations may the Court be seized of a case requiring it to pronounce itself on the legal recognition of same-sex relationships? In relation to the EU institutions, the Court has jurisdiction in the very specific field of staff cases.[23] In that context, it has had to rule on the entitlement of same-sex partners to benefits available to married partners under the EU's staff regulations.[24] As regards Member States, is will be clear that in the absence of a sufficient link with EU law, EU citizens cannot challenge Member States' rules on civil status on the basis of EU law. Powers in the field of family law have remained almost exclusively within the competence of the Member States.[25] Unlike Supreme Courts from jurisdictions like the US, Canada and South Africa, the Court will not be in the position to

---

[19] *Carpenter*, C-60/00, judgment of 11th July 2002 [2002] ECR I-6279; *Baumbast*, C-413/99, judgment of 17th September 2002 [2002] ECR I-7091 and *Garcia-Avello*, C-148/02, judgment of 2nd October 2003 [2003] ECR I-11613.

[20] Opinion of AG Jacobs of 9th December 1992 in *Konstantinidis*, C-168/91, [1993] ECR I-1191, para. 46.

[21] Groussot et al. (2011), pp. 23–24. See *Akerberg*, C-610/11, judgment of 26th February 2013 nyr., para. 22.

[22] Opinion of AG Sharpston of 30th September 2010 in *Zambrano*, para. 173.

[23] Art. 270 TFEU.

[24] Regulation No. 31 (EEC), 11 (EAEC), OJ 1962 L 45, p. 1385. See for instance *D. and Sweden v Council*, Joined Cases C-122/99 P & C-125/99 P, judgment of 31st May 2001 [2001] ECR I-4319. The Staff Regulations were amended in 2004, in order to accommodate non-married partners, including same-sex partners: Council Regulation (EC, Euratom) No. 723/2004 of 22nd March 2004 amending the Staff Regulations of officials of the European Communities and the Conditions of Employment of other servants of the European Communities, OJ 2004 L 124, p. 1. See the chapter by Orzan in this volume.

[25] The Treaty of Lisbon did introduce the competence to adopt measures concerning family law with cross-border implications (Art. 81(3) TFEU), but legislative progress in this area has been slow. See also Sect. 20.7.

pronounce itself on the validity of legislation either providing for, or banning same-sex marriages.

Nonetheless, where a factual situation is found to fall within the scope of EU law, and where a conflict between domestic law and EU law arises, the principle of supremacy applies, also in areas in which the Member States have remained competent. As such, the Court has been asked to interpret the EU Directive on equal treatment in employment and occupation as it applies to the pension rights of same-sex partners.[26] Moreover—returning to the topic of this chapter—the Court would have the competence to decide to what extent the rules on the free movement of persons oblige a Member State to recognize the same-sex spouse or registered partner of an EU citizen in a cross-border situation. Likewise, the Court would have jurisdiction to rule on the position of non-EU same-sex couples under the legislation regulating the status of third-country nationals.

In theory, the Court could be seized of a question concerning the compatibility of national rules on the recognition of same-sex relationships with EU law through infringement proceedings. These could be initiated either by the Commission or a Member State, if they were to believe that (non-) recognition would amount to a violation of EU law.[27] However, infringement proceedings initiated by Member States are extremely rare for their political implications. Likewise, the Commission has discretion to initiate infringement proceedings and is unlikely to do in such a sensitive area.[28] It is therefore more probable that a case would reach Luxembourg by way of a preliminary reference from a national judge, who in domestic proceedings is confronted with a case in which a same-sex couple challenges the non-recognition of their relationship on the basis of EU law.[29]

Before examining in detail how the applicable rules of secondary and primary law on the free movement of persons should be interpreted if such a case were to make its way to the CJ (Sects. 20.4 and 20.5), a look will be had at the role of fundamental rights. As established above, EU law commands the respect for fundamental rights of the EU institutions and the Member States when acting within the scope of EU law. This means not only that the CJ has to interpret EU law in accordance with these rights, but also that it has to ensure that Member States comply with these rights to the extent that they apply as a matter of EU law. This begs the question which fundamental rights are at stake in cases of non-recognition of same-sex relationships and what the substance of these rights is. Hence, a brief overview of the state of the law is in order.

[26] *Maruko*, C-267/06, judgment of 1st April 2008 [2008] ECR I-1757 and *Römer*, C-147/08, judgment of 10th May 2011 nyr. See the chapter in this volume by Orzan.

[27] Art. 258 TFEU.

[28] The words of Commissioner of Justice seem to confirm this: 'We have to advance cautiously, because what we do not want – and I believe all those who have spoken here of their experiences, from their hearts, understand this too – is [not] to be too harsh.' Speech by Commissioner Reding of 7th September 2010, Strasbourg (PV 07/09/2010—17 CRE 07/09/2010—17).

[29] Art. 267 TFEU.

20.3 The Rights of Same-Sex Partners as Fundamental Rights

At the outset, it must be noted that in as far as the ECHR and the CFR contain corresponding rights, these rights have in principle the same meaning and scope.[30] However, this does not prevent EU law from granting more protection[31] and hence would not prevent the CJ from reading additional obligations into the rights of the CFR as regards same-sex couples.

The right to private life has in the past served to strike down the criminalization of homosexual activity.[32] It has been argued that now the case for the public recognition of same-sex relationships could be made on the basis of a "right to relate" included in the same right to private life.[33] At the same time, rights that are more frequently invoked are the right to marry and to found a family,[34] the right to respect for family life,[35] the prohibition on discrimination[36] and the right to human dignity.[37] In case a same-sex couple has parental rights, this does not only add an extra dimension to the right to family life, but also brings the rights of the child into the equation.[38]

Both the ECHR and the CFR provide that the right to marry and to found a family is guaranteed in accordance with domestic laws governing the exercise of this right. Because of this reference to national law and because "marriage has deep-rooted social and cultural connotations which may differ largely from one society to another", the European Court of Human Rights (further referred to as ECtHR) in the 2010 landmark case of *Schalk and Kopf* left States a wide margin of appreciation in regard to access to marriage for same-sex couples.[39] Although the Court no longer considered that the right to marry under the Convention was in all circumstances limited to marriage between two persons of the opposite sex, it held that a prohibition on same-sex marriage did not constitute a violation of Art.

---

[30] Art. 52 (3) CFR.

[31] Art. 52 (3) CFR, last sentence.

[32] Art. 8 ECHR and Art. 7 CFR. See e.g. *Dudgeon v. the United Kingdom*, n. 7525/76, judgment of 22nd October 1981 and *Norris v. Ireland*, n. 8225/78, judgment of 26th October 1988.

[33] See in detail: Waaldijk (2012).

[34] Art. 12 ECHR and Art. 9 CFR.

[35] Art. 8 ECHR and Art. 7 CFR.

[36] Art. 14 ECHR and Art. 21 CFR.

[37] Art. 1 CFR.

[38] Art. 24 CFR. An extensive discussion of this right would however be beyond the scope of this chapter. See on the best interest of children under EU law the recent judgment in Joined Cases *O*, *S*, C-356/11 and *L*, C-357/11, judgment of 6th December 2012, nyr.

[39] *Schalk and Kopf v. Austria*, n. 30141/04 judgment of 24th June 2010, paras 61–62. In cases like *Serife Yigit v. Turkey* (GC), n. 3976/05, judgment of 2nd November 2010, and *Van der Heijden v. the Netherlands* (GC), n. 42857/05, judgment of 3rd April 2012, the ECtHR also gave considerable protection to the traditional values that marriage is deemed to protect. On same-sex couples under the ECHR see the chapters by Crisafulli and Pustorino in this volume.

12 ECHR.[40] Art. 9 CFR states that the right to marry and to found a family shall be guaranteed in accordance with national law. Although the explanations make it clear that the scope of this article is broader than that of its ECHR-counterpart, covering also "cases in which national legislation recognizes arrangements other than marriage for founding a family", Art. 9 "neither prohibits nor imposes the granting of the status of marriage to unions between people of the same sex".[41] Hence, under the current state of European human rights law (EU and ECHR) same-sex couples would not be able to claim a right to legal recognition of their relationship on the basis of the right to marry and to found a family. The story may be different for the right to respect for family life.

In *Schalk and Kopf*, the ECtHR ruled that cohabiting same-sex couples living in a stable *de facto* partnership enjoy not only the right to respect of their private life, but also the right to respect for their family life.[42] The Court's wording in this judgment, as well as the fact that the Convention is a 'living instrument',[43] make it plausible that at some point the ECtHR will interpret the right to family life so as to entail a positive obligation to provide at least some form of legal recognition for same-sex partners.[44] It would have the opportunity to do so in a number of pending cases. In the case of *Vallianatos* it is argued that the fact that the Greek registered partnership is open only to couples of the opposite sex amounts to a violation of Art. 8 (family life) and Art. 14 (non-discrimination).[45] A violation of the same articles is claimed in *Taddeucci* in which an Italian–New Zealand same-sex couple complain about "the inability to live together in Italy on account of the Italian authorities' refusal to issue the [New Zealand] applicant with a residence permit because the national immigration legislation does not allow unmarried partners to obtain a family member's residence permit".[46] An indication that the Court may eventually rule that the respect for family life requires Member States to recognize a marriage that was legally concluded elsewhere can be found in *Wagner*. This case however

[40] *Schalk and Kopf v. Austria*, n. 30141/04, judgment of 24th June 2010, paras 61 and 63.

[41] Explanation on Art. 9 CFR, OJ 2007 C 303, p. 21. See also Declaration 61 on the CFR which was annexed to the *Lisbon* Treaty by Poland: "The Charter does not affect in any way the right of Member States to legislate in the sphere of public morality, family law, as well as the protection of human dignity and respect for human physical and moral integrity".

[42] *Schalk and Kopf v. Austria*, n. 30141/04, judgment of 24th June 2010, para. 94.

[43] *Tyrer v. the United Kingdom*, n. 5856/72, judgment of 25th April 1978, para. 31.

[44] The Court stressed that there was *not yet* a majority of States providing for legal recognition of same-sex couples (para. 105) and States are *still* free, to restrict access to marriage to different-sex couples (para. 108). The Court furthermore held that States must enjoy a margin of appreciation in the *timing* of the introduction of legislative changes' (para. 105) and that they enjoy 'a certain margin of appreciation as regards the exact status conferred by alternative means of recognition' (para. 108). Emphases added. See also Melcher (2012), pp. 1080–1081.

[45] *Vallianatos and others v. Greece*, n. 29381/09 and 32684/09, pending. In this case the Chamber relinquished jurisdiction to the Grand Chamber.

[46] *Taddeucci v. Italy*, n. 51362/09, pending. The case was communicated to the Italian government in September 2009.

concerned a single-parent adoption on which the Court found a European consensus to exist.[47]

The prohibition of discrimination in Art. 14 ECHR can only be invoked in conjunction with another substantive ECHR-right. It is standing case-law that only 'very weighty reasons' can justify discrimination on grounds of sexual orientation.[48] So far the ECtHR has taken a very formalistic approach in cases brought under Art. 8 and 14, in which same-sex couples have complained that they could not enjoy the entitlements and benefits given to married couples—such as for instance survivor's pension—because they were not allowed to marry. According to the Strasbourg Court the difference in treatment in those cases was based exclusively on the civil status and not on the sexual orientation of the applicants.[49] Consequently, the Court declared the complaints inadmissible. However, in doing so it ignored that the difference in civil status is grounded in the unequal access to marriage of same-sex and opposite-sex partners and hence constitutes a form of (indirect) discrimination on grounds of sexual orientation. In more recent decisions, including *Schalk and Kopf*, the Court did recognize that same-sex couples are in a relevantly similar situation to different-sex couples as regards their need for legal recognition and protection of their relationship, but also stated that evolving practice left Member States with a wide margin of appreciation.[50]

Inspiration may be drawn also from the CJ cases of *Maruko* and *Römer*. Here the Court ruled that if under German national law surviving spouses and surviving registered partners (German 'life partners') were in a comparable situation so far as a survivor's benefit was concerned, a pension scheme which granted such benefits to spouses only—while access to marriage was open to different-sex couples only—would constitute direct discrimination on grounds of sexual orientation in violation of Directive 2000/78.[51] Of course this would still leave same-sex partners, who are unable to formalize their relationship in any way under national law, without remedy. Yet it is important to note that unlike Art. 14 ECHR, Art. 21 CFR which prohibits discrimination, including on grounds of sexual orientation, is a freestanding provision. As long as there is a sufficient link with EU law, a broad interpretation of Art. 21 CFR could be invoked to challenge unequal treatment which, although in form based on civil status, is in substance based on sexual orientation. Moreover, in its interpretation of the Staff Regulations, in *W. v. Commission* the Court has paid considerable understanding not only for the legal, but also the practical, impossibility to marry.[52]

---

[47] *Wagner and J.M.W.L. v. Luxembourg*, no 76240/01, judgment of 28th June 2007.

[48] *Karner v. Austria*, n. 40016/98, judgment of 24th July 2003, para. 37; *E.B. v. France*, n. 43546/02, judgment of 22nd January 2008, para. 91; *Kozak v. Poland*, n. 13102/02, judgment of 2nd March 2010, para. 92.

[49] E.g. *Mata Estevez v. Spain*, n. 56501/00, decision of 10th May 2001 and *Manenc v. France*, n. 66686/09, decision of 21st September 2010.

[50] *Schalk and Kopf v. Austria*, paras 99–108 and *Eweida and others v. the United Kingdom*, n. 48420/10, 59842/10, 51671/10 and 36516/10, judgment of 15th January 2013, para. 105.

[51] OJ 2000 L 303, p. 16. See the chapter by Orzan in this volume.

[52] *W. v. Commission*, F-86/09, judgment of 14th October 2010, nyr.

Finally, attention must be paid to the right to human dignity.[53] This right has been criticized for lack of a broadly shared definition, meaning different things in different contexts, but at the same time praised for

> providing a language in which judges can appear to justify how they deal with issues such as the weight of rights, the domestication and contextualization of rights, and the generation of new or more extensive rights'.[54]

Human dignity is at the basis of the rights contained in the ECHR.[55] Within the CFR it is mentioned as self-standing right, prominently placed as the first article of the CFR. In earlier case-law the right to human dignity had already been identified by the Court as a general principle of EU law.[56]

Both the CJ and the ECtHR have referred to the human dignity of transgender persons, but have not done so specifically in relation to the rights of gay people.[57] In other jurisdictions however, human dignity has played an important role in granting rights to gay people, initially in striking down so-called "sodomy laws" and more recently in the context of claims to the right of same-sex partners to marry.[58] The Court of Appeal for Ontario (Canada), as well as the South African Supreme Court relied at least in part on human dignity when striking down national laws preventing same-sex couples from getting married.[59] The Spanish Constitutional Court in upholding the law opening civil marriage to same-sex spouses qualified it as "an important step in guaranteeing personal dignity and personal development".[60] Also the 9th District Court of Appeals of California referred to human dignity when it held that Proposition 8 ('Prop. 8'), which by popular vote ended the possibility to marry for same-sex couples, was unconstitutional for infringing the Equal Protection Clause.[61] It held that Proposition 8 had no other purpose or effect than to

---

[53] See already Clapham and Weiler (1993), p. 42.

[54] McCrudden (2008), p. 724.

[55] *Pretty v. the United Kingdom*, n. 2346/02, judgment of 24th April 2002, para. 65: "[t]he very essence of the Convention is respect for human dignity and human freedom".

[56] Most explicitly in *Omega*, para. 34.

[57] See e.g. *P v. S and Cornwall County Council*, C-13/94, judgment of 30th April 1996 [1996] ECR I-2143, para. 22 and *Christine Goodwin v. the United Kingdom*, n. 28957/95, judgment of 11th July 2002, paras 90–91.

[58] McCrudden (2008), p. 691.

[59] Court of Appeal for Ontario, *Halpern v. Attorney General* (2003) 65 OR (3d) 161, para. 5; Constitutional Court of South Africa, *Minister of Home Affairs and Another v. Fourie and Another*; *Lesbian and Gay Equality Project and Others v. Minister of Home Affairs and Others* [2005] ZACC 19, para. 78 *per* Sachs J. See the chapter by Mostacci in this volume.

[60] Spanish Supreme Court 198/2012 of 6th November 2012 (Complaint of Unconstitutionality 6864-2005), BOE no 286, 28th November 2012, p. 168 at p. 199. On same-sex couples under Spanish law see the chapter by Fidalgo de Freitas and Tega in this volume.

[61] Part of the 14th Amendment to the US Constitution. *Perry v. Brown*, Nos. 10-16696, 11-16577. On same-sex couples under US law see the chapters by D'Aloia and Romeo in this volume.

> lessen the status and human dignity of gays and lesbians in California, and to officially reclassify their relationships and families as inferior to those of opposite-sex couples.[62]

Whilst the Court refused to engage with the larger question whether gay couples may be denied the right to marry, the case supports the argument that once equal marriage rights have been granted, to withdraw them could amount to a violation of human dignity.[63]

European human rights law as it stands does not require Member States to allow same-sex couples to marry. As was already noticed, such a case would be outside the jurisdiction of the CJ in any case. However, it is clear that in situations falling within the scope of EU law, same-sex stable partners deserve protection under the right to family life, the prohibition of discrimination and the right to human dignity as a matter of EU law. In view of the Charter's obligation not only to protect, but also to promote these rights,[64] it is argued that where necessary the CJ should provide for more protection than is currently awarded under the ECHR. It should in any case be careful not to allow Member States to distinguish between EU citizens who use their free movement rights under the EU Treaty on the basis of their sexual orientation. This is especially the case where the EU citizen's home-Member State has formally recognized same-sex relationships. It would infringe the principle of non-discrimination if those same-sex couples would upon using their right of free movement were to be treated differently from opposite-sex couples of the same nationality. It would moreover violate their human dignity if their relationship were to be stripped of the formal recognition granted in their home Member State.

This interpretation of European human rights law of itself already advocates the recognition of same-sex couples who make use of migration rights that have been conferred upon them by EU law. This would in particular be true for same-sex couples that have been able to formalize their relationship in their country of origin. However, it is likely that the CJ will first try to solve the question on the basis of the rules on the free movement of persons, where necessary interpreting these in line with fundamental rights, before resorting to the application of EU fundamental rights in their own right. These rules will now be examined in detail.

20.4 The Rights of Same-Sex Partners of EU Citizens Under EU Secondary Law

The right to free movement of EU citizens is laid down in general in Art. 21 TFEU. Specific provisions for workers, service-providers and the self-employed can be found in Arts. 45, 49 and 56 TFEU respectively. The free movement of persons has

---

[62] *Ibidem*, *per* Judge Reinhardt, p. 5.

[63] A petition for a hearing *en banc* was rejected. On 7th December 2012 the US Supreme Court granted petition in this case (*Hollingsworth v Perry*, Docket no 12-144).

[64] Art. 51(1) CFR.

been worked out in secondary legislation, most importantly Directive 2004/38 regulating the right of EU citizens to move and reside freely within the territory of the Member States ('Citizens Directive').[65] Following the 'Tedeschi principle', substantive Treaty rules are applied only in the absence of secondary legislation.[66] In order to determine what the rights of same-sex couples are under EU law, it is therefore necessary to start by looking at the relevant secondary legislation. Although third-country nationals cannot claim free movement rights on the basis of the Treaty, they may be able to claim derived free movement rights as family members of EU citizens.

20.4.1 Directive 2004/38/EC

The Citizens Directive grants EU citizens a general right of entry and stay of three months. After three months the residence right is maintained if the EU citizen can prove to be economically active or is either a student or a person of independent means.[67] Importantly, the directive lays down the rights of family members of the EU citizen to join him in the host Member State. Being one of the fundamental Treaty freedoms, the Court has always interpreted the freedom of movement of persons broadly and the exceptions to it narrowly.[68] This is particularly true also for the provisions of the Citizens Directive, which has as its goal to facilitate the exercise of the fundamental right to free movement of EU citizens.[69]

Already at an early stage it was clear to the Union legislator that if an EU citizen's right to move were to be effective, he should be allowed to be joined by his relatives. Since this right was not written expressly in the Treaty, it was laid down in secondary legislation.[70] The Court held that once exercised, the right remains effective also upon return to the home state.[71] In addition, the Court has held that the possibility for an EU worker to be joined by his long-term stable partner who does not fall within the definition of 'family' as laid down in secondary legislation, may constitute a social advantage to the worker, requiring at least equal treatment as regards the right of entry and residence of long-term partners of nationals of the host Member State.[72]

---

[65] OJ 2004 L 158, p. 77.

[66] *Tedeschi*, Case 5/77, judgment of 5th October 1997 [1977] ECR 1555.

[67] Art. 6(1) and 7 Directive 2004/38.

[68] *Orfanopoulos and Oliveri*, Joined Cases C-482/01 and C-493/01, judgment of 29th April 2004 [2004] ECR I-5257, paras 64–65.

[69] *Metock*, C-127/08, judgment of 25th July 2008 [2008] ECR I-6241, para. 89.

[70] Regulation 1612/68 now 492/2011 which repealed Art. 10, Council Directive 73/148 now repealed by Directive 2004/38.

[71] *Surinder Singh*, C-370/90, judgment of 7th July 1992 [1992] ECR I-4265, para. 21.

[72] *Reed*, Case 59/85, judgment of 17th April 1986 [1986] ECR 1283, para. 28.

More recently, in line with a less economic-oriented approach to citizenship, the rights of family members have increasingly been placed in the light of the right to family life, although strictly speaking the right to family life entails only in very limited circumstances a right to family reunification.[73] Indeed, the rights of family members remain first and foremost instrumental to the right of free movement of the EU citizen. They are derived rights, which exist only by virtue of the EU citizen's right of free movement and the family tie between him and his relative.

Since the free movement rights are really rights of the EU citizen, the nationality of the family member is irrelevant. It is obvious that the recognition as "family member" within the meaning of Directive 2004/38 becomes vital in case the relative of an EU citizen cannot himself claim free movement rights. In fact, most free movement cases that have been brought before the Court regarding the right of family members of EU citizens have concerned third-country national relatives. The right of an EU citizen to be joined by his close relatives does not depend on a prior right of residence of these family members in the home Member State.[74]

In examining the question whether same-sex partners of EU citizens are to be considered as family member within the meaning of the Directive, it is necessary to distinguish between three situations: same-sex spouses, same-sex registered partners, and non-married same-sex partners in a durable relationship. Art. 2(a) and (b) of the Citizens Directive provides that the term "family member" covers both the "spouse" and "registered partner." The registered partner is, however, only recognized if the host Member State's laws treat registered partnership as equal to marriage.[75] Provision has also been made for unmarried and unregistered partners, or indeed, registered partners moving to a Member State which does not recognize the registered partnership: on the basis of Art. 3(2)(b) the host Member State has an obligation "to facilitate entrance" of "the partner with whom the Union citizen has a durable relationship, duly attested." In addition Art. 3(2)(a) provides for a similar obligation as regards "members of the household of the Union citizen having the primary right of residence." These three distinct situations will now be discussed in turn.

[73] COM(2001) 257 final, Proposal for a European Parliament and Council Directive on the right of citizens of the Union and their family members to move and reside freely within the territory of the Member States, p. 5. See Case C-540/03 *Parliament v. Council* [2006] I-5769, para. 53 and the reference to the case-law of the ECtHR therein.

[74] *Metock*, para. 58.

[75] The term "family member" furthermore covers the direct descendants who are under the age of 21 or are dependents and those of the spouse or partner and the dependent direct relative in the ascending line and those of the spouse or partner (Art. 2(c) and (d) Directive 2004/38).

20.4.1.1 Same-Sex Spouses

The term 'spouse' under Art. 2(2)(a) of Directive 2004/38 has not been defined in the Directive. In the absence of a definition provided for by the legislator, it would be for the CJ to construe this term. This could result in the Court providing the concept autonomously or it could defer to national law, either the law of the host Member State or that of the home Member State. It is settled case-law that

> terms of a provision of [Union] law which makes no express reference to the laws of the Member States for the purpose of determining its meaning and scope must normally be given an independent interpretation which must take into account the context of the provision and the purpose of the relevant rules.[76]

The question is however whether this provision lends itself for autonomous interpretation.

In the absence of a reference to the sex of the spouse in Art. 2(2)(a), a grammatical interpretation provides limited guidance.[77] Under a systematic interpretation the Court could take into account that whilst for registered partnerships the legislator made an explicit choice to refer to the laws of the host Member State, this solution was not adopted as regards marriage and should therefore be excluded. At the time of adoption of the Directive already two Member States provided for the possibility of same-sex couples to marry (The Netherlands and Belgium), so the issue was not simply unforeseen.

A historical interpretation seems to point in a different direction. The basic assumption of the original Commission proposal was that marriage did not cover persons of the same sex.[78] It relied heavily on the Court's case-law in other areas of EU law—such as employment law and the EU staff Regulations—which concerned non-marital partnerships.

In *Reed* the Court had ruled that a long-term stable partner could not be considered as a spouse, because this word only referred to a marital relationship.[79] In *Grant* the Court held that according to the state of the law in the Community at the time, a stable relationship between two persons of the same sex could not be regarded as equivalent to marriage. Adding insult to injury it stated that also a stable relationship outside marriage between people of the opposite sex was different from a stable relationship between same-sex partners.[80] In *D. v. Council* the Court was asked if the term "married official" within the meaning of the EU Staff Regulations could be interpreted as covering an official who had contracted a registered partnership with a person of the same sex. The Court replied in the negative, noting

[76] *Ekro*, Case 327/82, judgment of 18th January 1984 [1984] ECR 107, para. 11.

[77] The word "spouse" is gender neutral, other language versions only refer to the male spouse, which could not however be interpreted as to exclude the female spouse.

[78] COM(2001) 257 final.

[79] *Reed*, Case 59/85, judgment of 17th April 1986 [1986] ECR 1283, para. 15.

[80] *Grant*, C-249/96, judgment of 17th February 1998 [1998] ECR I-621, para. 35. See for a scorching critique: McInnes (1999).

that according to the definition generally accepted by the Member States, the term "marriage" referred to a union between two persons of the opposite sex.[81]

The original Commission proposal for Directive 2004/38 did try to accommodate to some extent the developments observed by the Court in *D. v. Council*, namely the increased recognition of same-sex relationships by way of statutory arrangements, as well as the increased existence of *de facto* relationships outside marriage. Alongside "spouses" it proposed to grant a right of residence and entry to unmarried partners, if the legislation of the host Member State would treat unmarried couples "as equivalent to married couples and in accordance with the conditions laid down in any such legislation".[82] The definition of "family member" proved to be an important point of contention in the subsequent negotiations. The Parliament proposed to recognize univocally as "family member" the same-sex spouse, the registered partner according to the law of the home member state and the non-married partner in accordance with the law of the home member state.[83] The Commission did not accept these amendments and its amended proposal even limited the rights of the unmarried partner to registered partners.[84] As a compromise in the Council, and between Parliament and Council, the final text introduced an obligation on the Member States to "facilitate" the entry of certain categories of family members that would not be covered by the definition of "family member". This includes the unmarried partner in a durable and duly attested relationship.[85]

In *Reed*, the Court held that a dynamic—and in fact autonomous—interpretation of the term spouse on the basis of social developments which would have effect in all Member States, would have to take into account the situation in the whole Community.[86] Also in *D. v. Council* the Court referred to the views prevailing within the Community as a whole.[87] Still, the undeniable divergences in national legal systems should not automatically rule out the recognition of a legal principle supported in a minority of Member States, "if such a legal principle is of particular significance [for the project of European integration], or where it constitutes a growing trend."[88] In this regard, it must be noted that there is an undeniable and rapid movement towards the opening of civil marriage to same-sex couples in a significant part of the EU. As yet seven Member States have opened marriage to

[81] *D. and Sweden v Council*, Joined Cases C-122/99 P & C-125/99 P, judgment of 31st May 2001 [2001] ECR I-4319, para. 34.

[82] Art. 2(2)(b) of COM(2001) 257 final.

[83] Amendment 14, Report EP (Rapporteur Giacomo Santini), 23rd January 2003, A5-0009/2003.

[84] COM(2003) 199 final.

[85] Common Position adopted by the Council on 5th December 2003 (Council Doc 13263/3/03).

[86] *Reed*, para. 13.

[87] *D. and Sweden v Council*, para. 59.

[88] Lenaerts and Gutierrez-Fons (2010), pp. 1634–1635.

same-sex couples[89] and at least nine Member States authorize the entry and residence of same-sex spouses for the purposes of Directive 2004/38.[90] At the same time, one should also acknowledge developments in the opposite direction, such as the incorporation of a definition of marriage as only between a man and a woman in some Member States constitutions and legislation.[91]

In *Roodhuijzen* the General Court came to the conclusion that in *D. v. Council* the CJ had already given an autonomous definition of marriage, defining it as a union between two persons of the opposite sex.[92] Under this definition, irrespective of national legal classifications, a same-sex marriage would not create "spouses" in the meaning of the Citizens Directive.[93] However, at the time that case was decided, none of the Member States had opened civil marriage to same-sex partners. The key question in *Roodhuijzen* was, much as it had been in *D. v. Council*, *Reed* and *Grant*, whether a stable partnership or registered partnership should be brought within the definition of marriage. This is different from whether a marriage between two people of the same sex legally contracted in one of the Member States is to be recognized as a legally valid marriage in other Member States. *Roodhuijzen* therefore merely confirms standing case-law that a registered partnership or stable relationship cannot be brought under the definition of marriage, but is not good authority for an interpretation of the term "spouse" under the Citizens Directive.[94]

It is submitted that in view of the legislative developments in the Member States since *D. v Council*, the CJ is no longer in the position to identify in EU law or in the general principles of Union law criteria enabling it to define the meaning and scope

[89] The Netherlands, Belgium, Portugal, Spain, Denmark, Sweden and France. Note that also Norway and Iceland, both applying Directive 2004/38 in the context of the EEA Agreement, have introduced same-sex marriage in their national legislation. In May 2013 the House of Commons for England and Wales approved a bill on same-sex marriage. Similar legislation is anticipated in Luxembourg. The legislative committee of the Finish Parliament rejected a bill for marriage equality by a narrow majority in March 2013.

[90] In 2010, the EU Fundamental Rights Agency (FRA) reported that eight Member States did not distinguish between a same-sex or an opposite-sex spouse for the purposes of entry and residence (Belgium, Denmark, Finland, the Netherlands, Portugal, Spain, Sweden, and the UK): FRA 2010, p. 46. In 2012 Italy could be added to this list (Ministry of the Interior, Administrative Guideline n. 8996 of 26th October 2012). While it would be somewhat circular to ground the definition of an EU law term on the implementation of that same EU provision at national level, this nonetheless evidences a social and legal development toward recognition. The report is available at http://fra.europa.eu/sites/default/files/fra_uploads/1286-FRA-LGBT-report-update2010.pdf.

[91] E.g. Art. L of the Fundamental Law of Hungary (25th April 2011), see also Decision of the Hungarian Constitutional Court no. 154/2008 (XII. 17); Art. 46 of the Constitution of the Republic of Bulgaria (12th July 1991); Art. 18 of the Constitution of the Republic of Poland (2nd April 1997); Art. 110 of the Constitution of the Republic of Latvia (as amended on 15th December 2005) and Art. 38 of the Constitution of the Republic of Lithuania (25th October 1992).

[92] *Roodhuijzen*, T-58/08 P, judgment of 5th October 2009 [2009] ECR II-3797, para. 79.

[93] *Bertolete and Others*, Joined Cases T-359/07 P to T-361/07 P, judgment of 20th February 2009, Reports of Cases 2009 FP-I-B-1-00005; FP-II-B-1-00021, para. 46.

[94] *Roodhuijzen*, para. 75.

of marriage by way of independent interpretation.[95] It should therefore defer to the relevant rules of national law as interpreted by national courts.[96] The question that remains is whether in that case reference should be made to the rules of the home or the host Member State. Taking the home Member State's rules as decisive, would be in line with the principle of mutual recognition as is generally applied in the area of free movement. It would be consistent with the Directive's objective of promoting free movement, as it would facilitate the free movement of EU citizens in a same-sex marriage. It would also serve the interest of legal certainty. Normally mutual recognition carries the risk of creating a regulatory gap. It is invoked in order to set aside the rules of the host Member States. Here it could be argued such a gap is actually avoided since same-sex couples would not be left without the protection of their civil status when moving to a Member State that does not provide for same-sex marriage.

Support for the position that a marriage is to be recognized as long as it has been validly concluded in another Member State can be found in the *Metock* case, in which the Court ruled that opposite-sex spouses qualify as family members under the Citizens Directive, irrespective of when and where the marriage took place.[97] Costello argues that this "seems to remove marriages from the normal realms of private international law on recognition of legal relationships contracted elsewhere".[98] Also the Commission, by mouth of Commissioner Reding for Justice, seems to have changed its stance.[99] It has even argued that "in principle" the principle of mutual recognition would apply also outside the EU context, by holding that marriages "validly contracted anywhere in the world" should be recognized.[100] In the absence of EU legislation on this matter, one could however argue that the recognition of marriages concluded outside the EU is to be left to the domestic rules of private international law, and that only if the marriage has already been recognized by the home Member State, there would be an obligation under EU law to recognize the marriage concluded outside the EU.

Yet another approach has been advocated by Lenaerts, who has argued that the term "spouse" would not automatically exclude same-sex partners, but would have

[95] *Díaz García*, T-43/90, judgment of 18th December 1992[1992] ECR II-2619 para. 36 and *Khouri*, T-85/91, judgment of 18th December 1992 [1992] ECR II-2637, para. 32.

[96] *Meinhardt*, Case 24/71, judgment of 17th May 1972 [1972] ECR 269, paras 6, 7 and 12; *Díaz García*, T-43/90, judgment of 18th December 1992 [1992] ECR II-2619, paras 37–41; *Khouri*, T-85/91, judgment of 18th December 1992 [1992] ECR II-2637, paras 33–41; *M v. Court of Justice*, T-172/01, judgment of 21st April 2004 [2004] ECR II-1075, paras 72–75 and 112.

[97] *Metock*, para. 99.

[98] Costello (2009), pp. 615–616.

[99] Speech by Commissioner Reding of 7th September 2010, Strasbourg, PV 07/09/2010—17 CRE 07/09/2010—17.

[100] Communication from the Commission to the European Parliament and the Council on guidance for better transposition and application of Directive 2004/38/EC on the right of citizens of the Union and their family members to move and reside freely within the territory of the Member States, COM(2009) 313, p. 4.

to be defined on the basis of a case-by-case analysis.[101] Member States would be allowed to invoke overriding reasons of general interest in order to justify a refusal to recognize a same-sex marriage of a moving EU citizen. At the same time they would be bound to general principles, including proportionality and fundamental rights. In a similar way, it has been argued that the US Constitution's Full Faith and Credit clause (Art. 5, sect. 1), which obliges States to respect the "public acts, records, and judicial proceedings of every other state", would still allow states to deny recognition to out-of-state marriages as a matter of public policy.[102]

The advantage of the case-by-case approach would be that the CJ does not have to tackle the thorny issue by taking a principled position and could more gradually clear the ground for a broader obligation to recognize. An individual assessment would however lead to conceptual confusion, legal uncertainty and unnecessary litigation. It is also unclear whether such an approach would mean that the Directive applies in principle to all same-sex spouses, but that depending on the particulars of the case the public policy exception in Art. 27 could be invoked. Or would it introduce a preliminary assessment of the free movement rights of the EU citizen under EU primary law, essentially creating an additional hurdle to the application of the Directive to same-sex couples? It is submitted that a case-by-case assessment would ignore the fundamental status of EU citizenship. It would also infringe the general principle of equal treatment if the Directive were to apply to some EU citizens and their same-sex spouses and not to others.

While there are strong arguments in favour of adopting the home state principle or principle of mutual recognition when it comes to recognizing the validity of same-sex marriages concluded by the EU citizen in his home-Member State, the clear wording of the Directive seems to indicate differently for same-sex registered partners.

20.4.1.2 Same-Sex Registered Partners

Art. 2(2)(b) of Directive 2004/38 defines the term "registered partner" as

> the partner with whom the Union citizen has contracted a registered partnership, on the basis of the legislation of a Member State, if the legislation of the host Member State treats registered partnerships as equivalent to marriage and in accordance with the conditions laid down in the relevant legislation of the host Member State.

---

[101] Lenaerts (2010), pp. 1360–1361.

[102] Barrington Wolff (2005), p. 2215. Others have argued that the Full Faith and Credit Clause must be construed in light of other constitutional norms, including those underlying the Commerce Clause, the constitutional right to travel, the Takings Clause, the First Amendment, and the fundamental right to marry, thus requiring recognition: Singer (2005), p. 35. Interestingly, the appeals at the US Supreme Court challenging national and Federal Defense of Marriage Acts (DOMA) do not evolve around the Full Faith and Credit Clause but around the 5th Amendment (Due Process) and 14th Amendment (Equal Protection). On the US see the chapters by D'Aloia and Romeo in this volume.

The explicit choice of law in this article leaves little doubt that the recognition of registered partnerships is to be determined by the law of the host Member State.[103] Only if the host state provides for a registered partnership equivalent to marriage, and the couple fulfils the conditions of the host Member State's legislation, it must authorize the entry and residence of the registered couples. However, because of the wording of the Directive, the recognition of a registered partnership concluded outside the EU seems excluded.[104]

Where a host Member State does not provide for a form of registered partnership equivalent to marriage for same-sex couples, EU law does not seem to require the recognition of the registered partner of a migrant EU citizen as "family member" within the meaning of the Citizens Directive, although a Member State would be free to do so.[105] In case of non-recognition of a same-sex registered partnership, the registered partner would presumably fall within the category of stable partner in a "durable relationship", duly attested by virtue of his registered partnership, whose entry is merely to be facilitated.[106]

The exact meaning of the term "equivalent to marriage" is unclear. There is a wide variety of formal partnerships across the Member States. Some registered partnerships constitute a fully-fledged alternative to civil marriage, often open only to same-sex couples.[107] Others provide for much weaker rights and obligations. There is, for instance, much debate whether the French PACS (*Pacte Civile de Solidarité*), essentially an instrument of contract law, meets the "equivalent to marriage" threshold.[108] If a French couple were able to "boost" its PACS by moving to a Member State that provides for a stronger registered partnership, the question is whether they could subsequently retain stronger partnership rights upon return to their home Member State.[109] It is also unclear whether Member States that do not recognize same-sex marriages, are required to consider the same-sex spouse as a registered partner under Art. 2(2)(b) if their legislation provides for a registered partnership equivalent to marriage. It is submitted that the national judge would be

---

[103] Commissioner Reding's position that host Member States would have to recognize registered partners from migrating EU citizens, regardless of their own national laws, seems difficult to reconcile with the wording of the Directive and the Court's case-law on non-marital partnerships (see Sect. 20.4.1.2).

[104] Fallon (2007), p. 175.

[105] In fact this is the case in Member States such as Portugal, Belgium, Sweden and Denmark.

[106] Or alternatively as 'member of the household' of the EU citizen: Art. 3(2) Citizens Directive. Bell concludes that there are therefore two zones of migration for registered partners within the EU. An inner zone with free movement in Member States with registered partnership and an outer zone where admission and residence is left to the Member States. Bell (2004), p. 624.

[107] Examples are the German Registered Partnership (*Eingetragene Lebenspartnershaft*) as introduced by Act of 16th February 2001 (BGBl. I S. 266) and the UK Civil Partnership, as introduced by the Civil Partnership Act 2004 (c 33).

[108] Art. 515-1 to 515-7 French Civil Code, introduced by Act n° 99–944 of 15th November 1999, JORF No. 265 of 16 November 1999 p. 16959; see the chapter by Reyniers in this volume.

[109] Toner (2012), pp. 288–289.

in the best position to answer whether a national registered partnership must be considered as equivalent to marriage under the guidance of the CJ.[110]

Hence, in cross-border situations involving same-sex registered partners, it is clear that the CJ, bound by the text of the Directive, will have to apply the host State principle. The actual application of that principle, however, raises questions. In situations where a same-sex registered partner of an EU citizen is left without entry and residence rights, Art. 3(2) nonetheless creates some obligations for the host Member State.

20.4.1.3 Same-Sex Partners

Same-sex partners who do not enjoy an automatic right of entry and residence in the host Member State as ‘family members’ within the meaning of Art. 2(2) may fall within the scope of Art. 3(2) of Directive 2004/38. Following this provision the host state has an obligation “to facilitate entrance” of “other family members” who are members of the household of the EU citizen in the State of origin and of “the partner with whom the Union citizen has a durable relationship, duly attested”.

Implied in this provision is the duty for the host Member State to undertake an extensive examination of the personal circumstances and to justify any denial of entry or residence to these stable partners or members of the household.[111] The host Member State must take into consideration their relationship with the Union citizen or any other circumstances, such as their financial or physical dependence on the Union citizen.[112] Member States cannot adopt a blanket policy of not admitting unmarried partners, as this would run counter to the wording of the Directive and precludes an individual assessment. Importantly, Member States must respect fundamental rights when applying the Directive.[113] Recital No. 31 specifically mentions that discrimination, including on grounds of sexual orientation, is not allowed. The refusal of a genuine long-term stable partner, on the mere fact that the couple is of the same sex would therefore be forbidden.[114]

---

[110] Cf. *Maruko* and *Römer*.

[111] Communication from the Commission to the European Parliament and the Council on guidance for better transposition and application of Directive 2004/38/EC on the right of citizens of the Union and their family members to move and reside freely within the territory of the Member States, COM(2009) 313 final, p. 4.

[112] Recital 6 and Art. 3(2) Directive 2004/38.

[113] This is also true where Member States apply discretionary clauses, see *N.S.* and *M.E.*, Joined Cases C-411/10 and C-493/10, judgment of 21st December 2011, nyr, para. 69.

[114] In response to an inquiry and negotiations by the Commission Malta amended its law implementing Art. 3(2) of the Citizens Directive under which same-sex partners could not qualify as durable, duly attested partners. See: European Union Nationals and their Family Members (Amendment) Order, 2011 (L.N. 329 of 2011).

The wording of Art. 3(2) has been criticized for being insufficiently precise.[115] So far there has been one judgment by the CJ interpreting this provision, which has provided only limited guidance. In 2012, the CJEU ruled in *Rahman* that exactly because of its imprecise formulation the provision could not be relied on directly against a Member State.[116] The Court held that the article confers a certain advantage on the relative of the EU citizen, compared with applications for entry and residence of other nationals of third countries. The Court furthermore ruled that because of the lack of more specific rules in the Directive itself and the reference to national legislation, each Member State has a wide discretion as regards the selection of the factors it takes into account to assess the individual's personal circumstances. Nonetheless, the criteria should be consistent with the normal meaning of the term "facilitate" and should not deprive the provision of its effectiveness.[117]

The Commission's Guidelines state that national rules on durability of the partnership could refer to a minimum amount of time as a criterion for whether a partnership can be considered as durable. However, other relevant aspects, such as a joint bank account or children, should also be taken into account.[118] It is submitted that a host Member State that does not provide for any form of legal recognition of same-sex relationships, must accept that the condition that the relationship is duly attested is fulfilled in case the partners have entered into a registered partnership or marriage in another State. Interestingly, this requirement is not explicitly mentioned as regards the 'members of the household', but in view of the discretion left to the Member States in *Rahman* could probably be used as a relevant criterion.

20.5 The Rights of Same-Sex Partners of EU Citizens Under EU Primary Law

If the CJ were to interpret the term "spouse" under the Citizens Directive autonomously so as to include only different-sex partners, this would leave same-sex married couples deprived of recognition of their marital status under EU law. Requiring recognition only when the host Member State does, or on the basis of a case-by-case assessment, could leave a considerable number of couples without recognition. Already, same-sex registered partners forego recognition in Member States that do not provide for a registered partnership in their domestic legislation.

---

[115] A 2010 FRA report qualified the 'duty to facilitate' as 'a vague expression which does not necessarily translate into practical consequences in the absence of specific and inclusive yardsticks.' FRA 2010, p. 50. See also Toner (2012), p. 289.

[116] *Rahman*, Case C-83/11, judgment of 5th September 2012, nyr., paras 21 and 24. This case did not involve a partner, but a half-brother and a nephew.

[117] *Ibidem*, paras 21 and 24.

[118] COM(2009) 313 final, p. 4.

In all those cases in which the Directive provides the same-sex married partners of EU citizens merely with the right to have their entry and residence "facilitated", it is argued that same-sex couples may have recourse to the general provisions on the free movement of persons, as long as at least one of the partners is an EU citizen and there is a cross-border element to their case. This should even apply for registered partners, notwithstanding the Citizens Directive's explicit choice for the host country principle. It may well be possible that, the application of secondary law results in an unjustified restriction of the fundamental Treaty freedom found in primary law, in which case the conflict should be resolved either through a harmonious interpretation of secondary law or by applying directly the Treaty freedom.[119]

20.5.1 The Existence of a Restriction

As early as *Reed*, the Court held that

> the possibility for a migrant worker of obtaining permission for his unmarried companion to reside with him, where that companion is not a national of the host Member State, can assist his integration in the host state and thus contribute to the achievement of freedom of movement for workers.[120]

This was confirmed by the Court in *Commission v. Germany*, where it underlined

> the importance for the worker, from a human point of view, of having his entire family with him and, secondly, the importance, from all points of view, of the integration of the worker and his family into the host Member State.[121]

Admittedly, in both cases the Court interpreted the concept of "social advantage" in Art. 7(2) of Regulation 1612/68 (Now 492/2011), looking at whether or not the host Member State treated the unmarried partners of EU nationals differently from its own nationals. However, the importance of this ruling lies in the Court's acknowledgement of the fact that the possibility for an EU citizen to be joined by his partner, whatever the legal status of their relationship, is instrumental to the free movement of persons. From there, it is a small step to conclude that when the EU citizen is not allowed so, this may constitute a restriction of his right to free movement.

The Court has long moved away from an exclusive discrimination approach in free movement cases, by holding that also national rules which hinder free movement or make the use of free movement rights less attractive are incompatible with the Treaties. In the area of free movement of workers the *Bosman* case forms a clear

[119] See in more detail: Ensig Sørensen (2011), pp. 321–339.

[120] *Reed*, para. 28.

[121] *Commission v Germany*, Case 249/86, judgment of 18th May 1989 [1989] ECR 1263, para. 11.

example of this.[122] Interestingly, in the *Dafeki* case, on the recognition of birth certificates, the Court held that

> the exercise of the rights arising from freedom of movement for workers is not possible without production of documents relative to personal status, which are generally issued by the worker's State of origin.[123]

Therefore, Member States were obliged to accept such documents, unless their accuracy was seriously undermined in an individual case. Still, in this case the dispute revolved around the question of the validity of a civil status document (posterior rectification of a birth certificate), whereas the civil status itself was not contested. It would therefore go too far to read in this judgment an—albeit qualified—obligation to accept marriage certificates from same-sex couples issued in other Member States. It does, however, underline the importance of civil status and the documents attesting such status for the exercise of free movement rights.

The restrictions approach is also visible in other areas of free movement. As regards the freedom to provide services (Art. 56 TFEU), the clearest example can be found in the *Carpenter* case. Here the Court held that this freedom could not be fully effective if the EU citizen would be deterred from exercising it "by obstacles raised in his country of origin to the entry and residence of his spouse".[124] As regards the freedom of establishment, the prohibition on restrictions is clearly spelled out in article 49 TFEU. In *Konstantinidis* the Court held that the misspelling of an EU citizen's name could create an inconvenience to such a degree that it would interfere with his freedom to exercise the right of establishment.[125] Also in *Gebhard* and *Kraus*, the Court adopted a clear restrictions approach.[126] In relation to legal persons, the Court held in cases such as *Centros* and *Überseering*, that the failure to recognize the legal personality of a company set up under the laws of another Member State could amount to a violation of the freedom of companies to move their business elsewhere within the EU.[127] Legal personality is, like marriage, a construct of national law and by analogy also the non-recognition of a marriage could be considered to constitute a restriction of a fundamental freedom.[128]

Finally, in the case of non-economically active citizens, the refusal to recognize a same-sex relationship could be considered an infringement of the "most fundamental status of the nationals of the Member State" under Art. 20 TFEU. In the *Zambrano* case the Court held that Art. 20 TFEU does not allow an EU citizen to be deprived of "the genuine enjoyment of the substance of the rights conferred by

[122] *Bosman*, C-415/93, judgment of 15th December 1995 [1995] ECR 4921.

[123] *Dafeki*, C-336/94, judgment of 2nd December 1997 [1997] ECR I-6761, para. 19.

[124] *Carpenter*, para. 39.

[125] *Konstantinidis*, para. 15.

[126] *Kraus*, C-19/92, judgment of 31st March 1993 [1993] ECR I-1663, para. 32 and *Gebhard*, C-55/94, judgment of 30th November 1995 [1995] ECR I-4165, para. 37.

[127] *Centros*, C-212/97, judgment of 9th March 1999 [1999] ECR I-1459, para. 22 and *Überseering*, C-208/00, judgment of 5th November 2002 [2002] ECR I-09919, para. 82.

[128] Melcher (2012), p. 1081.

virtue of the status of citizen of the Union."[129] One of these rights is the directly effective right to move and reside freely within the territory of the Member States.[130]

Admittedly, in the subsequent cases of *McCarthy*, *Dereci* and *O, S and L* the Court ruled that the fact that a Member State denies its own nationals the possibility of family reunification with a third-country national family member does not mean that the EU citizen will be forced to leave the Union. Hence the EU citizen would not be deprived of the genuine enjoyment of the substance of his citizen's rights.[131] Likewise, the non-recognition of an EU-citizens' same-sex marriage would not force the EU-citizen to leave Union-territory. However, the *post*-Zambrano cases all concerned EU citizens which invoked Art. 21 TFEU without having made us of their free movement rights.[132] An EU citizen who wishes to use his free movement rights, but is effectively confined to the territory of those Member States that recognize his same-sex marriage or registered partnership, is effectively deprived of the "genuine enjoyment" of his citizenship rights in part of the EU territory.

It is difficult to deny that, in particular in the case of economically active EU citizens, the refusal to recognize a marriage or same-sex partnership constitutes a restriction to the free movement rights of the EU citizens. As was pointed out earlier, the fact that the determination of civil status remains within the exclusive competence of the Member States does not mean that these rules are not bound to comply with EU law on the basis of primacy. The question then becomes which grounds may be invoked in order to justify such a restriction.

20.5.2 Possible Justifications

The Treaty itself provides for three grounds for justification of restrictions to the free movement rights: public policy, public security and public health.[133] Since the non-recognition of same-sex marriages would amount to a restriction that does not differentiate on the basis of nationality, additional overriding reasons of public interest could also be invoked.[134] The focus here will be on the public policy argument, which is the broadest ground for justification and the one most likely to be invoked in this context by Member States.

---

[129] *Zambrano*, C-34/09, judgment of 8th March 2011 [2011] ECR I-1177, para. 42.

[130] *Baumbast*, para. 84. Art. 20(2)(a) and 21(1) TFEU.

[131] *McCarthy*, C-434/09, judgment of 5th May 2011, nyr., para. 49; *Dereci*, para. 68; *O, S and L*, para. 52.

[132] Toner (2012), p. 304.

[133] For the sake of completeness it is pointed out that homosexuality was finally declassified by the WTO as a disease in 1992.

[134] *Gebhard*, para. 35.

20.5.2.1 Public Policy

Although public policy and public security are separate criteria, they both require an individual's conduct to pose a genuine, present and sufficiently serious threat.[135] The element of personal conduct constituting an individualized threat is, however, absent when the Court evaluates the compatibility of general rules which may restrict the free movement of EU citizens.[136] The Court has consistently underlined that the concept of public policy as justification for a derogation from a fundamental freedom must be interpreted strictly, so that its scope cannot be determined unilaterally by each Member State without any control by the EU institutions.[137]

Public morality is not a separate ground for justification of a restriction of the free movement of persons, as it is with regard to the free movement of goods. This does not mean that a morality argument could not be brought under the heading of public policy.[138] In this regard the Court has held that, although EU law does not impose a uniform set of values as regards the assessment which conduct is contrary to public policy, conduct may not be considered to be of a sufficiently serious nature if the host Member State does not adopt genuine and effective measures to combat similar conduct by its own nationals.[139] Non-discrimination on grounds of nationality is therefore key.

There would however be an important difference between the situation in which a Member State refuses to recognize a same-sex relationship on the basis of public policy and existing internal market cases in which a public policy argument is brought on the basis of moral objections. In those cases generally the EU citizen would move to a Member State to exercise an activity which raises moral objections in the home Member State, but is considered perfectly legal in the host Member State.[140] Here the situation is reversed. Non-recognizing Member States could therefore argue that the obligation to recognize a same-sex relationship would allow Member States to "export"—so to say—their own value system to other Member States. This would run counter to the Court's case-law, which held that the concept of public policy may vary from one Member State to another and from one era to another and that the competent national authorities must be allowed a margin

---

[135] *Rutili*, para. 28 and *Bouchereau*, Case 30/77, judgment of 27th October 1977 [1977] ECR 1999, para. 35.

[136] *Omega*, para. 30 and *Sayn-Wittgenstein*, C-208/09, judgment of 22nd December 2010 [2010] ECR I-13693, para. 86.

[137] *Omega*, para. 30 and *Jipa*, C-33/07, judgment of 10th July 2008 [2008] ECR I-5157, para. 23.

[138] *Contra*, see Kochenov (2009), p. 203.

[139] *Adoui and Cornuaille*, Joined Cases 115/81 and 116/81, judgment of 18th May 1982 [1982] ECR 1665, para. 8.

[140] See, for instance, with regard to abortion, *Grogan*, Case C-159/90, judgment of 4th October 1991 [1991] ECR I-4685, para. 20; with regard to lotteries, *Schindler*, Case C-275/92, judgment of 24th March 1994 [1994] ECR I-1039, para. 32; and with regard to prostitution, *Jany*, Case-268/99, judgment of 20th November 2001 [2001] ECR I-8615, paras 56–57.

of discretion.[141] The Court has also underlined that there does not have to be consensus amongst Member States as to the way in which a restrictive measure may serve a fundamental right or legitimate interest, and that rather the necessity and proportionality of a measure is not excluded simply because a Member State has chosen a system of protection which differs from that in other Member States.[142]

Although opposition against same-sex marriage or same-sex registered partnership is all too often fed by moral objections and homophobic sentiments, the arguments against the legal recognition of same-sex relationships is rarely presented as opposing homosexuality as such, but rather in defense of the institution of marriage and traditional family values, in the interests of the child, and to protect the moral and religious order of a society. Although all of these interests are worthy of protection, either as public policy argument or as public interest requirement, the non-recognition of a same-sex relationship in cross-border situations would not pass the proportionality test. It is neither suitable, nor the least restrictive means to serve any of these objectives.

The recognition of same-sex relationships by the host Member State would not in any way affect the validity or legal effect of civil marriage in that country, nor would it force a Member State to change its rules on civil marriage. As Melcher has argued, the reverse discrimination resulting from recognition of foreign relationships may create "serious pressure" on these States to change their domestic family law, but in the end a decision on the matter would be left to the national political process.[143] Non-recognition cannot change the fact that throughout the EU people of the same sex enter into durable and committed relationships, constituting families in which often children are being raised. Not only is this perfectly legal in all EU Member States, these forms of family life are also protected under Art. 8 ECHR.[144] It is difficult to maintain that the recognition of a same-sex relationships would contradict family values, rather than reinforce them. It would at the same time ensure respect for the general principle of equal treatment and the CFR's right not to be discriminated against. The fact that discrimination on grounds of sexual orientation is forbidden in Art. 21(1) of the CFR and is explicitly referred to in Art. 19 TFEU would justify equal treatment of all couples using their free movement rights under EU law, independent of the sex of the partners. Finally, non-recognition cannot be automatically considered proportionate where a Member State grants a right of entry and residence to the same-sex partner on a different

---

[141] *Omega*, para. 31 and *Sayn-Wittgenstein*, Case C-208/09, judgment of 22nd December 2010 [2010] ECR I-13693 para. 87. Compare with the approach under the ECHR: *Handyside v. the United Kingdom*, n. 5493/72, judgment of 7th December 1976, para. 48.

[142] *Omega*, paras 37–38.

[143] Melcher (2012), p. 1085.

[144] See Sect. 20.3.

legal basis, especially if this legal basis confers weaker rights than those based on EU citizenship.[145]

20.5.2.2 National Identity

An important question is what value the Court would attribute to an argument against recognition of same-sex relationships based on a Member State's national identity. National identity was first referred to in the *Groener* case, in which the promotion and conservation of the Irish language was recognized as an expression of national identity and culture, which justified a restriction to free movement.[146] In *Commission v. Luxembourg* the Court held that the preservation of national identity "is a legitimate aim respected by the Community legal order" which could in principle justify a restriction to the free movement provisions.[147]

Since the Maastricht Treaty the national identities of the Member States have made their way into the Treaty. Respect for Member States national identities "inherent in their fundamental structures, political and constitutional" is now prescribed in Art. 4(2) TEU. The German Constitutional Court held in its Lisbon judgment that Art. 4(2) TEU "ensures that the primacy of application of Union law only applies by virtue and in the context of the constitutional empowerment that continues in effect."[148] The Polish Constitutional Court even called the duty to respect national constitutional identity "the principal axiological basis of the European Union."[149] Different authors have seen the article as a means of fostering a constitutional dialogue, endorsing a "pluralistic vision of the relationship between EU law and domestic constitutional law".[150]

Art. 4(2) TEU has featured in a number of cases. In *Sayn-Wittgenstein* and *Runevič-Vardyn* the CJ held that rules regarding the composition and spelling of surnames constituted justified restrictions on the basis of national identity.[151] In *Sayn-Wittgenstein* the Court ruled that the Austrian prohibition to use titles of nobility as part of the surname could be saved on the basis of the public policy exception. The rule formed part of the country's constitutional identity as a

[145] See however *Iida*, para. 75, in which the CJ appears to have attached considerable importance to the fact that the applicant who claimed residence rights under Directive 2004/38, could in all likelihood claim rights of residence under Directive 2003/109 (Long Term Residents Directive) OJ 2004 L 16, p. 44.

[146] *Groener*, C-379/87, judgment of 28th November 1989 [1989] ECR 03967.

[147] *Commission v. Luxembourg*, C-473/93, judgment of 2 July 1996 [1996] ECR I-3207, para. 35.

[148] German Federal Constitutional Court, judgment of 30th June 2009, BVerfG, 2 BvE 2/08, p. 240.

[149] Polish Constitutional Tribunal, judgment of 24th November 2010 (K 32/09 (Traktat z Lizbony), 2010 No 229).

[150] Van der Schyff (2012), p. 583 and Von Bogdandy and Schill (2011), p. 3.

[151] *Sayn-Wittgenstein*, judgment of 22nd December 2010 [2010] ECR I-13693 and *Runevič-Vardyn*, C-391/09, judgment of 12th May 2011, nyr.

Republic and implemented the fundamental constitutional objective of equality before the law. In *Runevič-Vardyn* the Court allowed a Lithuanian rule under which the spelling of names in official documents would have to comply with the rules governing the spelling of the official national language.

At first sight, the two cases do not seem to augur well for the recognition of same-sex relationships in Member States which ground their opposition to legal recognition of such relationships on national identity.[152] Yet, national identity should not be allowed to be used as a trump card undermining the principle of primacy of EU law.[153] National identity is a limited concept, which should be defined as national constitutional identity.[154] This then does not mean that every rule of a constitutional nature could qualify for protection under Art. 4(2) TEU.[155] When invoked to justify an exception to a fundamental freedom, the principle should be interpreted restrictively. Hence, the definition of marriage as a union between two people from the opposite sex in a Member State's constitution would not *per se* qualify as part of the constitutional core making up national identity. A constitutional provision that would designate a Member State's national religion probably would, but it would still need to assessed to what extent the application of the fundamental treaty freedoms in full would affect the constitutional core of that identity.

Once it is established that a rule forms part of a Member State's constitutional identity any restrictive measure would still have to comply with the principle of proportionality. Interestingly in *Sayn-Witgenstein* the Court exercised a—very light—proportionality test itself, while in *Runevič-Vardyn* it referred back to the national court, hinting at the disproportionality of at least part of the measure.[156] It is submitted that in both cases the Court, rather than doing justice to the plurality of the EU's internal market, was overly receptive for Member States' sensitivities. To allow a Member State to oblige an EU citizen who has used his free movement rights to change his name seems disproportionate for two reasons. First, civil status documents are of great importance for the free movement of persons, as acknowledged by the Court in *Dafeki*. Secondly, a person's forename and surname are a constituent element of his identity and of his private life, a fact to which the Court had displayed considerably more sensibility in earlier case-law.[157]

---

[152] See in this respect also Declaration 61 on the CFR which was annexed to the Lisbon Treaty by Poland.

[153] Opinion of AG Maduro of 8th October 2008 in *Michaniki*, C-213/07, judgment of 16th December 2008 [2008] ECR I-9999, para. 33, with reference to *Internationale Handelsgesellschaft*, Case 11/70, judgment of 17th December 1970 [1970] ECR 1125, para. 3.

[154] Van der Schyff (2012), pp. 567–568.

[155] Opinion of AG Maduro of 8th October 2008 in C-213/07 *Michaniki*, para. 33. See *O'Brien*, C-393/10, judgment of 28th July 2010, nyr., para. 49 as regards the status of a Member State's judiciary and the Opinion of AG Bot of 2nd October 2012 in *Melloni*, para. 142 as regards fundamental rights included in national constitutions.

[156] Besselink (2012b), p. 692.

[157] *Garcia-Avello* and *Grunkin Paul*.

The denial of free movement rights as a result of the non-recognition of same-sex relationships—especially when assessed in the light of fundamental rights—is even more disproportionate. It should also be recalled that in *Sayn-Wittgenstein* the constitutional rule was held to protect not only constitutional identity, but also pursued the principle of equality, which is recognized as a general principle of EU law as well. To uphold a constitutional ban on same-sex marriage would not seem to serve any EU objective other than to protect an ill-defined concept of national identity to the detriment of a sexual minority.

20.5.3 The Implications of Mutual Recognition

So far it has been argued that the non-recognition of a same-sex relationship in cross-border situations can be considered a restriction of the free movement rights of EU citizens. It may even be argued that such non-recognition deprives EU citizens of the genuine enjoyment of the substance of these rights. It would be difficult for a non-recognizing Member State to prove that a restriction of these rights could be justified on the basis of public policy or in any case that such restriction would be proportionate. However, the new Treaty provision on constitutional identity may prove to be a tool in the hands of non-recognizing Member States.

One may well point out that in practice the non-recognition of same-sex marriages or registered partnerships of EU citizens would not automatically mean that same-sex partners are prevented from moving to another Member State. Same-sex partners with the nationality of a Member State may rely on their independent free movement rights and in the least favourable scenario Art. 3(2) of the Citizens Directive may provide a solution. Leaving aside principled arguments and ignoring the CJ's restrictions approach, this could then be used as an argument both in favour and against requiring Member States to recognize formalized same-sex relationships in cross-border situations.

The real "problem" for many non-recognizing Member States may however lie in the fact that the mutual recognition of civil status or the adoption of an inclusive definition of "spouse" has implications going beyond an initial right of entry and residence. These flow from the fact that civil status by its very nature has effects in a broad range of areas of law, from tax law to social security law and from inheritance law to the law on criminal procedure.

As Member States that have introduced same-sex marriage can testify, a relatively straightforward legislative amendment to open civil marriage to partners of the same sex can require significant adaptations in administrative practices and in some specific areas of law, such as filiation law, even substantive legal amendment. So even if Member States cannot be required to provide for same-sex marriage or civil partnership themselves, they will nonetheless have to accommodate the recognition of these foreign institutions in their national legal system, often in areas of law which are strictly speaking outside EU competence. This is however true for many fields of EU law and should not of itself affect the interpretation and application of the fundamental Treaty freedoms to same-sex couples.

The key question is whether the obligation of equal treatment on the basis of nationality flowing from Art. 21 TFEU and Art. 24 of the Citizens Directive means that all social and fiscal benefits available to spouses and registered partners in a Member State that does not itself provide for same-sex marriage or registered partnership must be extended to same-sex partners from other EU Member States once they have been recognized for the purpose of entry and residence under EU law. Here, it must be argued that anything but full recognition of the status of family member would constitute a further restriction on the right to free movement. Moreover, once a same-sex marriage or registered partnership has been recognized for the purpose of entry and residence, the couple is firmly drawn within the scope of EU law, at which point general principles and fundamental rights apply as a matter of EU law. It therefore becomes increasingly hard to justify a difference in treatment, if not on the basis of nationality then on sexual orientation.

20.6 Third-Country Nationals and Same-Sex Partners

Up to this point, the focus of this chapter has been on the free movement rights of EU citizens and their same-sex partners. Third-country nationals have a distinct and much less favourable position under EU law. In as far as they cannot claim rights as a family member of an EU citizen, only limited categories of third-country nationals are able to claim rights of entry and residence under EU law. These rights have been conferred in secondary legislation adopted under the EU competences in the field of migration and asylum, pertaining to the Area of Freedom, Security and Justice (AFJS).[158] The Treaty does not directly confer "free movement rights" on third-country nationals and their rights must be clearly distinguished from the internal market freedoms, which are enjoyed exclusively by EU citizens.

Nonetheless, just as the CJ may be called upon to interpret the Citizens Directive, the Court may be called upon to construe the rules contained in the EU's migration and asylum *acquis*. The question of how family members are defined in this legislation is important for two reasons. First, third-country nationals family members lack, unlike EU family members, the possibility to rely on independent rights of free movement as an EU citizen.[159] Second, the trend towards the formal

[158] Art. 79 TFEU.

[159] *Ferrer Laderer*, C-147/91, judgment of 25th June 1992 [1992] ECR I-4097, para. 7 and *Iida*, paras 51 and 66.

recognition of same-sex relationships is not limited to Europe, but can be seen almost worldwide.[160]

In order to assess to what extent same-sex partners of third-country nationals can join them when moving to or within EU territory, the definition of "family" in the Family Reunification Directive (2003/86) is of primordial importance, since it is referred to in most instruments regarding the status of legal third-country nationals.[161] The Family Reunification Directive determines the conditions under which third-country nationals lawfully residing on the territory of the Member States may exercise the right to family reunification.[162] If these conditions are fulfilled the Member State must authorize entry and residence.[163] The Family Reunification Directive contains a much more limited definition of family than the Citizens Directive. It includes spouses, but it is silent as regards registered partners or long-term stable partners. In respect of the interpretation of the term "spouse" *mutatis mutandis* similar arguments apply as in relation to the Citizens Directive.[164] However, if it were accepted that the term does not cover same-sex spouses, the consequences would be much graver than for the spouse of an EU citizen under the Citizens Directive, because of Member States' discretion in respect of unmarried partners under the Family Reunification Directive and the absence of a corresponding duty to facilitate the entry of long-term stable partners.

The initial Commission proposals for the Family Reunification Directive did include unmarried partners living in a durable relationship with the applicant, if the

[160] In addition to increased recognition in the form of registered partnerships, five countries have introduced same-sex marriage nationwide (Canada, South Africa, Argentina, New Zealand and Uruguay), some states recognize same-sex marriages (Israel), in some states same-sex marriage is legal only in some jurisdictions (Mexico, United States), other countries are in the process of discussing legislation aimed at introducing same-sex marriage, often as a result of Court rulings (Nepal, Colombia, Brazil).

[161] Council Directive 2004/114/EC of 13th December 2004 on the conditions of admission of third-country nationals for the purposes of studies, pupil exchange, unremunerated training or voluntary service (OJ 2004 L 375, p. 12) and the Proposal for a Directive on the conditions of entry and residence of third-country nationals for the purposes of seasonal employment (COM(2010) 379 final) are silent on family members. Council Directive 2005/71/EC of 12th October 2005 on a specific procedure for admitting third-country nationals for the purposes of scientific research (OJ 2005 L 289, p. 15) explicitly refers to the national law of the receiving Member State, although it emphasizes the importance of maintaining the unity of the researcher's family, Recital 19 and Art. 9.

[162] Council Directive 2003/86/EC of 22nd September 2003 on the right to family reunification, OJ 2003 L 251, p. 12. The Blue Card Directive (Directive 2009/50), which aims to attract highly qualified third-country workers, provides for more favourable conditions for family reunification and for access to work for spouses, by means of specific derogations to the Family reunification Directive. However, for the definition of the term 'family members' reference is made to Art. 4 (1) of the Family Reunification Directive. See recital 23 and Art. 2(f) and 15 of Council Directive 2009/50/EC of 25th May 2009 on the conditions of entry and residence of third-country nationals for the purposes of highly qualified employment, OJ 2009 L 155, p. 17.

[163] Art. 4(1)(a) Directive 2003/86.

[164] See Sect. 20.4.1.1.

legislation of the Member State concerned treated the situation of unmarried couples as corresponding to that of married couples.[165] The Directive as it was eventually adopted, however, merely enabled Member States to apply the Family Reunification Directive also to stable long-term partners and registered partners.[166] This is particularly problematic, if one realizes that also the Long Term Resident Directive refers back to the definition of family in the Family Reunification Directive.[167] The Long Term Resident Directive grants third-country nationals who have been legally present in EU territory a more permanent residence right, as well as a (limited) right to move to a second Member State. One can very well imagine a situation in which a long-term resident has entered into a (same-sex) registered partnership in one of the Member States.[168] If he then wishes to move to another Member State, it would be up to the discretion of the second Member State to allow him to bring his registered partner.

It must be stressed that also here the Court would be held to interpret the Directives in line with fundamental rights, and that Member States are bound to fundamental rights when implementing and applying the provisions of the Directive.[169] Moreover, it must be argued that as soon as Member States make use of their discretion as regards entry and residence for unmarried partners, they are bound by fundamental rights.[170] This means that the principle of non-discrimination would prevent them from distinguishing between same-sex couples and opposite-sex couples once they allow for the entry of registered partners and/or long-term stable partners. More generally, the weaker rights for third-country national partners appear difficult to reconcile with the EU's commitment to a "fair" policy towards third-country nationals who reside legally on the territory of its Member States, the aim of which should be to grant them rights and obligations comparable to those of EU citizens.[171] Just as within the internal market

---

[165] The Commission proposal had used the definition of 'family member' from the EU Asylum Qualification Directive (current Directive 2011/95/EC, OJ 2011 L 337, p. 9). Art. 2(j) of the Qualification Directive defines 'family member' as the spouse of the beneficiary of international protection or his or her unmarried partner in a stable relationship, 'where the law or practice of the Member State concerned treats unmarried couples in a way comparable to married couples under its law relating to third-country'. See also Art. 2(d) of Council Directive 2003/9/EC of 27th January 2003 laying down minimum standards for the reception of asylum seekers, OJ 2003 L 31, p. 25.

[166] Art. 4(3) Directive 2003/86.

[167] Art. 2(e) Directive 2003/109.

[168] Art. 16(1) Directive 2003/109.

[169] *Parliament v. Council*, C-540/0, judgment of 27th June 2006 [2006] I-5769, paras 62–64.

[170] Interestingly, when the previous Dutch government limited family reunification to spouses and registered partners, it provided for a special marriage visa for people who would not be able to marry in their home country because e.g. the spouse would be from a different religion or of the same-sex (Decree of 27th March 2012 amending the Aliens Act 2000 (Stb 2012, no 148). The limitation is now set to be repealed.

[171] Art. 67(2) TFEU and the Stockholm Programme (OJ 2009 C 115, p. 1), para. 6.1.4.

the presence of the EU's citizen's family in the host state is deemed to facilitate his integration, so should the presence of the third-country national's family members.

20.7 European Private International Law

Under the Area of Freedom, Security and Justice (further referred to as AFSJ) the EU does not only have the power to adopt legislation in the area of asylum and migration. Under Art. 81 TFEU it also has competence in judicial cooperation in civil matters having cross-border implications.[172] This includes a limited power to adopt harmonizing measures on family law with cross-border implications, including Member States conflict of law rules.[173] It is this provision that the EU legislator may turn to in order to address the issues that were identified in the preceding paragraphs.

The legal basis for judicial cooperation in cross-border civil matters was first introduced by the Treaty of Amsterdam. Art. 65 EC provided that measures could be adopted only "insofar as necessary for the proper functioning of the internal market". The Lisbon Treaty changed this into "particularly when necessary for the proper functioning of the internal market." Art. 81(1) TFEU now explicitly provides for the possibility of harmonization. Under Art. 81(3) TFEU a special legislative procedure applies, whereby unanimity in the Council is required, and whereby any national parliament can block the adoption of a proposal by the Council. The procedure forms a balancing act

> between the political desire to move forward in the area of family law and the politically sensitive nature of the area.[174]

The Commission has put forward two proposals for Council Regulations with regard to matrimonial property regimes as well as the property consequences of registered partnerships.[175] These evidence the Commission's awareness that obstacles to the free movement of EU citizens exceed questions of entry and residence only. Yet, for the present analysis the Commission's Green Paper of 2010 on the free movement of public documents and recognition of the effects of civil status records of 2010 is of greater relevance.[176] In the Green Paper, the Commission

---

[172] Art. 81(1) TFEU.

[173] Art. 81(2)(c) TFEU and Art. 81(3) TFEU.

[174] Storskrubb (2011), p. 307.

[175] COM(2011) 126 final and COM(2011) 127 final.

[176] COM(2010) 747 final, Green Paper "Less bureaucracy for citizens: promoting free movement of public documents and recognition of the effects of civil status records". The Green paper defines civil status records, i.e. "records executed by an authority in order to record the life events of each citizen such as birth, filiation, adoption, marriage, recognition of paternity, death and also a surname change following marriage, divorce, a registered partnership, recognition, change of sex or adoption."

argues that it should be possible to guarantee the continuity and permanence of a civil status situation to all European citizens exercising their right of freedom of movement:

> [. . .] the legal status acquired by the citizen in the first Member State [..] should not be questioned by the authorities of the second Member State since this would constitute a hindrance and source of objective problems hampering the exercise of citizens' rights.[177]

The Commission identified three policy options (1) administrative cooperation, (2) automatic recognition of civil status, or (3) the harmonization of conflict-of-law rules. The various national contributions in the Consultation Round indicate that the second option may be politically unfeasible.[178] Also the option to harmonize conflict-of-law rules met with considerable opposition. The European Parliament however, although deprived of legislative competence in this area, stressed "the need to ensure mutual recognition of official documents issued by national administrations" and "strongly" supported plans to enable the mutual recognition of the effects of civil status documents.[179] This would also be in line with the Art. 81 (1) TFEU and the Stockholm Programme, which both put mutual recognition at the heart of cooperation in civil law matters.[180]

Two principled objections plead against the adoption of legislation under the AFSJ to address the problems that same-sex couples encounter when exercising their free movement rights. Firstly, this issue is firmly rooted in the internal market and should be addressed as such, rather than under a related, yet clearly distinct policy area. Secondly, a number of Member States has opted-out under the AFSJ.[181] In practice this territorial limitation would be of limited importance since the Member States concerned do provide for same-sex marriage or registered partnership. However, problems could persist if legislation were to be adopted using enhanced cooperation on the basis of Art. 20 TFEU, since non-participating Member States would most likely include those opposing recognition of same-sex relationships.[182] At the same time, any initiative that may reduce obstacles to the free movement of same-sex couples must be welcomed. Hesitating Member States may still follow suit after the adoption of legislation under enhanced cooperation. Legislation adopted under the AFSJ is to be preferred over bilateral agreements between Member States, providing for some degree of legal certainty and uniformity for same-sex couples.

---

[177] COM(2010) 747 final, para. 4.1.

[178] See the various contributions by public authorities in the Member States on the official Commission website http://ec.europa.eu/justice/newsroom/civil/opinion/110510_en.htm (last visited 31st January 2012).

[179] European Parliament Resolution on civil law, commercial law, family law and private international law aspects of the Action plan implementing the Stockholm Programme, 23rd November 2010, P7_TA(2010)0426. See also the Opinions of the Economic and Social Committee (OJ 2011 C 248, p. 113) and the Committee of the Regions (OJ 2012 C 54, p. 23).

[180] Stockholm Programme (OJ 2009 C 115, p. 1), para. 3.1.2.

[181] Denmark, the United Kingdom and Ireland.

[182] See the application of enhanced cooperation with respect to the proposal on the law applicable to divorce and legal separation. Council Decision 2010/405/EU of 12th July 2010, OJ 2010 L 189, p. 12.

If the Commission's proposals from the Green Paper were to be adopted, this would not exclude the application of the rules of primary law on the free movement of persons to Member States that under opt-outs or enhanced cooperation are not bound by this legislation. The same holds true in general in the—not unlikely—scenario that the proposals are not adopted at all. In the absence of legislative action by the EU legislator, it would be left to the CJ to step in and ensure the full effectiveness of the free movement rights of same-sex couples. It would not be the first time for the Court to foster integration in the area of free movement of persons and by doing so to provide an impetus to the adoption of secondary legislation.[183]

20.8 Conclusion

It appears to be only a matter of time before a national court will make a preliminary reference to the CJ asking the Court to rule on the compatibility of a Member State's refusal to grant entry and residence rights to the same-sex partner of a migrating EU-citizen with EU law. The fact that this has not yet happened may be partly because same-sex partners simply decline to move or because they may prefer to use independent free movement rights where possible, instead of submitting themselves to the stress of legal proceedings.

Paradoxically, increased possibilities for same-sex couples to formalize their relationship in the EU, will on the one hand make it easier for same-sex couples to move freely. On the other hand, it will mean that a larger number of EU citizens may be negatively affected by the lack of recognition in some Member States. The restriction of the free movement rights of EU citizens in same-sex relationships is and remains real. In addition, same-sex couples who find themselves within the scope of EU law—whether EU citizens or not—must be able to rely on the protection of their fundamental rights, including the right to human dignity and the right to respect for family life.

This chapter has argued that the fundamental rights and freedoms as guaranteed by the EU plead in favour of an inclusive definition of family, which should however be based on the principle of mutual recognition so as to do justice to the existing divergences in Member States' national laws.

In having to rule in a controversial area such as the rights of same-sex couples, the CJ would once more confirm its role not only as Supreme Court, but also as constitutional adjudicator within the EU legal order.[184] The involvement of the

[183] For example, in *Antonissen*, C-292/89, judgment of 26th February 1991 [1991] ECR I-745 the Court attributed direct effect to the Treaty Articles on the free movement of workers in the absence of secondary legislation (presently Directive 2004/38). *Vlassopoulou*, C-340/89, judgment of 7th May 1991 [1991] ECR I-2357 formed the impetus for the adoption of secondary legislation on the recognition of higher-education diplomas (presently Directive 2005/36/EC of the European Parliament and of the Council of 7th September 2005 on the recognition of professional qualifications, OJ 2005 L 255, p. 22).

[184] Vesterdorf 2006, p. 609 and Rosenfeld 2006.

Court would seem to contradict conventional wisdom under which European gay rights activists lobby legislatures, whereas their American counterparts have recourse to the court system to achieve marriage equality.[185] It would join Supreme Courts and Constitutional Courts across the globe which have been asked to extend in full the rights granted in constitutional charters to citizens in same-sex relationships and to adjust to and support a rapidly changing societal reality. In a Union based on common values, the Court will be called to define these shared values. In doing so it will at the same time set the boundaries within which Member States can invoke their own national constitutional identity.

This all seems dangerous for a Court which sees its legitimacy questioned and is often accused of pursuing an integrationist agenda. The main role of the CJ may therefore be to bring the case back into proportions. In essence the Court is asked to deal with a fairly straightforward question of interpretation of secondary legislation (Directive 2004/38) and alternatively of the Treaty provisions on the free movement of persons. It may not even find it necessary to pronounce itself on the issue of fundamental rights. Even by simply applying the basic rules of free movement, the Court may do a great good to the emancipation and the equal treatment of gay men and women. As such it would contribute to the EU's duty to promote the rights laid down in the CFR, without having to take the praise nor the blame for it.

Acknowledgement Special thanks to prof. Kees Waaldijk for his valuable comments on an earlier draft. The usual disclaimer applies.

References

Barrington Wolff B (2005) Interest analysis in interjurisdictional marriage disputes. Univ Pa Law Rev 153:2215–2250

Bell M (2004) Holding back the tide? Cross-border recognition of same-sex partnerships within the European Union. Eur Rev Priv Law 12:613–632

Besselink L (2012a) General report. In: Laffranque J (ed) The protection of fundamental rights post-Lisbon: the interaction between the charter of fundamental rights of the European Union, the European convention on human rights and national constitutions. Tartu University Press, Tallinn, pp 1–139

Besselink L (2012b) Case C-208/09, Ilonka Sayn-Wittgenstein v. Landeshauptmann von Wien, judgment of the Court (second chamber) of 22 December 2010. Common Mark Law Rev 49:671–693

Clapham A, Weiler JHH (1993) Lesbians and gay men in the community legal order. In: Waaldijk C, Clapham A (eds) Homosexuality: a European community issue. Martinus Nijhoff Publishers, Dordrecht, pp 6–69

---

[185] Weiss (2007), p. 84. Note that recently US gay rights activists have become increasingly involved in the political process, especially since in a number of States the question of same-sex marriages has been put to a popular vote. European gay rights activists, on the other hand, become increasingly involved in strategic litigation. See also: 'To Have and to Hold', The Economist 17th November 2012.

Costello C (2009) Metock: free movement and "normal family life" in the Union. Common Mark Law Rev 46:587–622

De Witte B (2011) Direct effect, primacy and the nature of the legal order. In: De Burca G, Craig P (eds) The evolution of EU law. Oxford University Press, Oxford, pp 323–362

Van der Schyff G (2012) The constitutional relationship between the European Union and its member states: the role of national identity in article 4(2) TEU. Eur Law Rev 37:563–583

Ensig Sørensen K (2011) Reconciling secondary legislation and the treaty rights of free movement. Eur Law Rev 3:339–361

European Union Agency for Fundamental Rights (2010) Homophobia, transphobia and discrimination on grounds of sexual orientation and gender identity. Comparative legal analysis: Update, http://fra.europa.eu/sites/default/files/fra_uploads/1286-FRA-LGBT-report-update2010.pdf

Fallon M (2007) Constraints of internal market law on family law. In: Meeusen J, Pertegás M, Straetmans G, Swennen F (eds) International family law for the European Union. Intersentia, Antwerp, pp 149–181

Gallo D (2012) Développements récents en matière de citoyenneté européenne et regroupement familial. Revue du Droit de l'Union européenne 101:121

Groussot X, Pech L, Petursson GT (2011) The scope of application of EU fundamental rights on member states' action: In search of certainty in EU adjudication, Prague, Czech Society for European and Comparative Law, Eric Stein Working Paper No. 1/2011

Kochenov D (2009) On options of citizens and moral choices of states: gays and European federalism. Fordham Int Law J 33:156–205

Lenaerts K (2010) Federalism and the rule of law: perspectives from the European Court of Justice. Fordham Int Law J 33:1338–1387

Lenaerts K (2013) Exploring the limits of the EU charter on fundamental rights. Eur Const Law Rev 8:375–403

Lenaerts K, Gutierrez-Fons JA (2010) The constitutional allocation of powers and general principles of EU law. Common Mark Law Rev 47:1629–1669

McCrudden C (2008) Human dignity and judicial interpretation of human rights. Eur J Int Law 19:655–724

McInnes J (1999) Annotation to Case C-249/96, Lisa Jacqueline Grant v. South West Trains Ltd. Common Mark Law Rev 36:1043–1058

Melcher M (2012) Private international law and registered relationships: an EU perspective. Eur Rev Priv Law 20:1075–1096

Rosenfeld M (2006) Comparing constitutional review by the European Court of justice and the U.S. Supreme court. Int J Const Law 4:618–651

Singer JW (2005) Same sex marriage, full faith and credit, and the evasion of obligation. Stanford J Civ Rights Civ Liberties 1:1–50

Storskrubb E (2011) Civil justice – a newcomer and an unstoppable wave? In: Craig P, De Búrca G (eds) The evolution of EU law. Oxford University Press, Oxford, pp 299–321

Toner H (2012) Migration rights and same-sex couples in EU law: a case study. In: Boele-Woelki K, Fuchs A (eds) Legal recognition of partnerships in Europe. Intersentia, Antwerp, pp 285–308

Vesterdorf B (2006) A constitutional court for the EU? Int J Const Law 4:607–617

Von Bogdandy A, Schill A (2011) Overcoming absolute primacy: respect for national identity under the Lisbon Treaty. Common Mark Law Rev 48:1–38

Waaldijk C (2011) From A to B: first results of a comparative law survey in seven cases on the (non-) recognition of same-sex couples moving from one European country to another. Presentation at the conference 'The Lack of Mutual Recognition of Same-Sex Unions in Europe', Organised by l'Autre Cercle, Strasbourg, 18–19 November 2011

Waaldijk C (2012) The right to relate: on the importance of 'orientation' in sexual orientation law. Inaugural lecture delivered at Leiden University 2012

Weiss A (2007) Federalism and the gay family: free movement of same-sex couples in the United States and the European Union. Columbia J Law Soc Probl 41:81–124

Chapter 21
Employment Benefits for Same-Sex Couples: The Case-Law of the CJEU

Massimo F. Orzan

Abstract This chapter examines the case-law developed by the Court of Justice of the European Union (CJUE) with regard to employment benefits for same-sex couples (e.g., household allowance and survivor's pension), in the light of the principle of non-discrimination based on sexual orientation. The analysis focuses on two different categories of proceedings: EU staff cases and references for preliminary rulings. Despite a growing trend to extend employment benefits to same-sex couples, the case-law shows that a distinction must be made between those two categories. Since the adoption of Regulation 723/2004, which amended the Staff Regulations of Officials of the European Communities and the Conditions of employment of other servants of the European Communities, staff cases have seen the CJEU recognize a substantial equivalence between married couples and stable non-marital partnerships, including same-sex relationships. In preliminary rulings, the Court has had a more cautious approach, in accordance with EU law. Indeed, as EU law stands at present, a Member State is not obliged to recognize the equivalence between married couples and same-sex couples, since the marital *status* of a person falls within the competence of the Member States. This principle also applies to employment benefits: only if a Member State recognizes the equivalence of married couples and same-sex couples can employment benefits be granted to the latter pursuant to Directive 2000/78/EC.

The views of the author are entirely personal and in no way portray a position of the Court of Justice of the European Union.

M.F. Orzan (✉)
EU General Court, Luxembourg, Luxembourg
e-mail: massimo.orzan@curia.europa.eu

D. Gallo et al. (eds.), *Same-Sex Couples before National, Supranational and International Jurisdictions*, DOI 10.1007/978-3-642-35434-2_21,

21.1 Introduction

The recognition of same-sex couples is one of the most controversial topics in contemporary society, since it raises several legal problems to which different States provide different solutions. These problems include the difference between same-sex marriages and registered partnerships, as well as the access of same-sex couples to adoption, medically assisted reproduction, or employment benefits (e.g., household allowance, survivor's pension, etc.). Even though there is a growing trend to recognize the rights of same-sex couples, no consistent picture has yet emerged.

Because of the different ways in which sexuality is understood in the 28 Member States,[1] the situation is fragmented also within the European Union, and this prevents the harmonization of domestic laws with EU legislation. On the one hand, Art. 13 (TEC) of the Treaty of Amsterdam (now Art. 19 TFEU) establishes that the Union "may take appropriate action to combat discrimination based on [...] sexual orientation",[2] and Art. 21 of the Charter of Fundamental Rights (further referred to as CFR) provides that "[a]ny discrimination based on [...] sexual orientation shall be prohibited". On the other hand some directives aimed at implementing Art. 13 TEC do not require Member States to adopt EU rules on same-sex couples, but leave them the choice of whether to introduce laws on the subject.[3] In addition, the legislation currently being prepared also provides that Member States are free to decide whether or not to adopt rules on same-sex couples. The Proposal for a Council Directive on implementing the principle of equal treatment between persons irrespective of religion or belief, disability, age or sexual orientation,[4] for instance, states that the proposed directive is "without prejudice to national laws on marital or family status and reproductive rights."[5]

---

[1] Verschraegen (2012), p. 256.

[2] See Flynn (1999), p. 1127, Dubout (2006), p. 78 and Berthou (2012), p. 556.

[3] See, for instance, the Directive 2004/38/EC of 29th April 2004 on the right of citizens of the Union and their family members to move and reside freely within the territory of the Member States amending Regulation (EEC) No. 1612/68 and Repealing Directives 64/221/EEC, 68/360/EEC, 72/194/EEC, 73/148/EEC, 75/34/EEC, 75/35/EEC, 90/364/EEC, 90/365/EEC and 93/96/EEC, OJ 2004 L 158, p. 77 and the Directive 2003/86 on the right to family reunification, OJ 2003 L 251, p. 12.

[4] Formally the "Proposal for a Council directive on implementing the principle of equal treatment between persons irrespective of religion or belief, disability, age or sexual orientation", COM (2008) 426, 2 July 2008.

[5] See Art. 3(2) of the Proposal for a Council Directive on implementing the principle of equal treatment between persons irrespective of religion or belief, disability, age or sexual orientation [COM(2008) 426 final of 2nd July 2008]. See also the Proposal for a Council Regulation on jurisdiction, applicable law and the recognition and enforcement of decisions regarding the property consequences of registered partnerships [COM(2011) 126/2 of 16th March 2011] which applies only if a Member State has enacted provisions on registered partnerships. In particular, Art. 3(2), according to which "[t]he court [of another Member State] may decline jurisdiction if its law does not recognise the institution of registered partnership".

With regard to the development of EU law in this area, the Court of Justice of the EU (further referred as CJEU or the Court) has played a significant role in the application of the principle of free movement of persons[6] and the prohibition of sexual orientation discrimination. Moreover, it should be noted that, in so doing, the CJEU has been influenced by the jurisprudence of the European Court of Human Rights (further referred as ECtHR), to which it has often referred.[7]

This chapter aims to examine the CJEU's case-law relating to the employment benefits that, by virtue of the principle non-discrimination based on sexual orientation, are applicable to same-sex couples. It will discuss first the case-law developed in connection with disputes involving the EU civil service (also known as staff cases), and then the decisions rendered in the context of preliminary rulings. Finally, it will draw a brief conclusion summarising the current situation.

21.2 The Jurisprudence Concerning Same-Sex Couples in EU Staff Cases

The CJEU ruled on the issue of employment benefits for same-sex couples in *D v. Council*[8] and *W v. Parliament.*[9] The *status* of official of the EU was decisive, in both cases, as the relationship between an official and the EU is governed by the Staff Regulations of Officials of the European Communities and the Conditions of employment of other servants of the European Communities (further referred as Staff Regulations). Therefore, even though the general principles of EU law apply also to the European civil service, that relationship is seen in the context of labour law. As a consequence, discrimination based on sexual orientation must be examined in the light of the rules governing the EU civil service: that is, the relevant provisions of the Staff Regulations. In this perspective, it is not surprising that the CJUE came to different conclusions in the two cases, held differently the *D* and *W* cases, since the version of Annex VII to the Staff Regulations in force at the time of each decision was not the same.

Also relevant to our discussion is the judgment in *Roodhuijzen.*[10] Even though the case did not specifically concern a same-sex registered partnership, both the Civil Service Tribunal (further referred as CST) and the General Court (further

[6] See the chapter by Rijpma and Koffeman in this volume.

[7] See, in this volume, Crisafulli and Pustorino.

[8] *D v. Council*, T-264/97, judgment of 28th January 1999, [1999] ECR SC-I-A-1 and II-1and *D v. Council*, C-122/99 P and C-125/99 P, judgment of 31st May 2001, [2001] ECR I-4319.

[9] *W v. Parliament*, F-86/09, judgment of 14th May 2010, nyr.

[10] *Roodhuijzen v. Commission*, F-122/06, judgment of 27th November 2007, [2007] ECR SC I-A-1-00387 and II-A-1-02167 and *Commission v. Roodhuijzen*, T-58/08 P, judgment of 5th October 2009, [2009] II-3797.

referred as GC) clarified the meaning of the term 'non-marital partnership' used in the Staff Regulations.

21.2.1 D v. Council *and the Adoption of Regulation 723/2004*

D v. Council concerned the refusal of the Council of the European Union (further referred as Council) to award the applicant, Mr. D, the household allowance provided for in the Staff Regulations. Supported by Sweden at first instance and by Denmark and the Netherlands on appeal, Mr. D brought an action against the Council for its refusal to recognize the legal *status* of his registered partnership with another man. He submitted that the Council should have treated his registered partnership as equivalent to marriage for the purposes of granting the household allowance. On the contrary, the Council had rejected his application on the grounds that the provisions contained in the Staff Regulations could not be construed as allowing a registered partnership to be treated as the equivalent of marriage. Therefore, the applicant maintained that the decision of the Council violated the principle of equal treatment and constituted discrimination based on sexual orientation. In this respect, it should be noted that, at the time of the proceeding, Art. 1 (2) of Annex VII to the Staff Regulations provided that the household allowance would be granted to married, widowed, divorced, legally separated or unmarried officials with one or more dependent children.[11]

The applicant alleged that the refusal of the Council violated the principle of non-discrimination, Art. 8 of the ECHR, and Art. 119 TEC (subsequently Art. 141 TEC, now Art. 157 TFEU). The Court of First Instance (now GC) rejected all the pleas and established that (1) at the time, EU law did not consider same-sex unions as equivalent to marriage[12]; (2) despite the development of societal attitudes towards homosexuality, same-sex unions did not fall within the scope of Art. 8 of the ECHR[13]; and (3) the decision of the Council could not be considered discriminatory, since the conditions imposed by Art. 119 applied equally to female and male officials.[14] On appeal, the Court of Justice (further referred as CJ) confirmed the judgment of the GC. In particular, the CJ observed that the principle of equal treatment could only apply to comparable situations, and that the different approaches of the Member States to same-sex couple recognition made it

[11] It should also be noted that the Regulation 781/98/EC amending Staff regulations, which introduced the prohibition of discrimination based on sexual orientation, entered into force on 16 April 1998, that is, after the decision of the Council. The Court of First Instance was thus obliged to apply the law in force at the time of the decision, in accordance with the principle of *tempus regit actum*.

[12] *D v. Council*, T-264/97, paras 28–29. See Denys (1999), p. 419.

[13] *Ibidem*, para. 39.

[14] *Ibidem*, para. 43. For a critical view of the judgment see Scappucci (2000), p. 361.

impossible to consider same-sex unions as equivalent to marriage.[15] Nevertheless, the CJ left the door open to an alternative solution, noting that "the legislature can, where appropriate, adopt measures to alter that situation, for example by amending the provisions of the Staff Regulations."[16]

Some authors have criticized the *D* judgment, reproaching the CJ for a formalist approach, observing that it refused to examine the alleged violation of the principle of equal treatment on the grounds that the situation of an official in a registered partnership could not be compared to that of a married official.[17] However, as already noted, at the time neither ECtHR case-law nor the CJEU allowed a different interpretation. Moreover, the Staff Regulations did not recognize the equality of same-sex couples and married heterosexual couples.

Even though the rights of same-sex couples were not legally protected, the issue was debated at the institutional level and the judgment of the CJEU contributed to the debate, insofar as the CJ had established that only the legislature could adopt the necessary measures to alter the situation. This debate led to the insertion of a new point in Regulation 723/2004 amending the Staff Regulations of Officials of the European Communities and the Conditions of employment of other servants of the European Communities.[18] Contained in Art. 1(2) of Annex VII, this new point provides that, if certain conditions are met, the household allowance will be granted to an official registered as a stable non-marital partner.[19] The provision has thus filled the gap that existed in the Staff Regulations, and employment benefits are now granted also to officials registered as stable non-marital partners.

---

[15] *D v. Council*, C-122/99 P and C-125/99 P, paras 35–36. For a critical view see Caracciolo di Torella and Reid (2002), p. 86.

[16] *Ibidem*, para. 38.

[17] Berthou and Masselot (2002), p. 683.

[18] Council Regulation (EC/EURATOM) 723/2004 of 22th March 2004 amending the Staff Regulations of Officials of the European Communities and the Conditions of employment of other servants of the European Communities, OJ L 124, p. 1. See also Recitals 7 and 8 of this Regulation, according to which "[c]ompliance should be observed with the principle of non-discrimination as enshrined in the EC Treaty, which thus necessitates the further development of a staff policy ensuring equal opportunities for all, regardless of sex, physical capacity, age, racial or ethnic identity, sexual orientation and marital status" and "[o]fficials in a non-marital relationship recognized by a Member State as a stable partnership who do not have legal access to marriage should be granted the same range of benefits as married couples".

[19] According to Art. 1,(2)(c)(iv), the household allowance shall be granted to an official who is registered as a stable non-marital partner, provided that (1) the couple produces a legal document recognized as such by a Member State, or any competent authority of a Member State, acknowledging their status as non-marital partners; (2) neither partner is in a marital relationship or in another non-marital partnership; (3) the partners are not related in any of the following ways: parent, child, grandparent, grandchild, brother, sister, aunt, uncle, nephew, niece, son-in-law, daughter-in-law; (4) the couple has no access to legal marriage in a Member State; a couple shall be considered to have access to legal marriage for the purposes of this point only where the members of the couple meet all the conditions laid down by the legislation of a Member State permitting marriage of such a couple.

21.2.2 W v. Commission *and the Application of New Art. 1 (2)(c) of Annex VII to the Staff Regulations*

In the light of Regulation 723/2004, it seems appropriate to examine the judgment rendered by the CST in *W v. Commission*. The applicant, Mr. W, was a contractual staff member who held dual Belgian–Moroccan nationality, and whose same-sex relationship had been registered in Belgium. He brought an action against the Commission, challenging their refusal to grant him a household allowance on the grounds that he and his partner had access to marriage in Belgium and, therefore, did not satisfy one of the conditions laid down in Art. 1(2)(c)(iv) of Annex VII. As already noted, under the new provision officials registered as stable non-marital partners are granted a household allowance only if they satisfy four conditions, including that the couple have no access to legal marriage in a Member State. The applicant claimed that he could not contract legal marriage in Belgium because of his Moroccan nationality. More specifically, he pointed out that Moroccan legislation criminalises homosexual acts and, therefore, a marriage contracted in Belgium would have exposed him and his partner to danger.[20]

It is worth considering the *W* judgment from two separate points of view: first, the extension of entitlement to the household allowance to "officials registered as stable non-marital partners including those of the same-sex"; and second, the interpretation of Art. 1(2)(c)(iv) of Annex VII.

Concerning the first point, the CST noted that the extension of entitlement to the household allowance for stable same-sex couples "reflected the legislature's concern [...], that compliance should be observed to the principle of non-discrimination enshrined in article 13(1) EC."[21] That concern has been expressed in the seventh recital of Regulation 723/2004, which states that compliance with the principle of non-discrimination requires "the development of a staff policy ensuring equal opportunities for all regardless of sexual orientation and marital status." With regard to the household allowance, said policy is now enshrined in the new Art. 1(2)(c)(iv) of Annex VII.

Moreover, the CST observed that the extension of entitlement of the household allowance to same-sex couples found support in Art. 8 of the ECHR, since the exclusion of officials in same-sex partnerships would imply the administration's interference in the exercise to respect for their family and private life. From this, it is clear that Regulation 723/2004, according to which the EU cannot discriminate against its officials based on their sexual orientation, was regarded by the CST as filling the gap in the rules of the European Civil Service. We may thus conclude that the Staff Regulations, which govern the relationship between the EU and its

[20] According to Art. 489 of the Criminal Code of Morocco "[a]nyone committing an indecent or unnatural act with an individual of his or her own sex shall be sentenced to imprisonment of six months to three years and fined MAD 200-1000, unless the offending conduct constitutes a more serious offence."

[21] *W v. Parliament*, para. 42.

officials, recognize the substantial equivalence of stable non-marital partnerships with marriage.

As for the interpretation of Art. 1(2)(c)(iv) of Annex VII, the CST, referring to the well-known case-law of the ECtHR, emphasized that the provision must be interpreted in such a way as to make the rule as effective as possible, so that the right in question is not theoretical or illusory, but practical and effective.[22] This point is particularly important, especially because it was decisive in the Court's reasoning. The CST held, indeed, that the applicant's access to marriage in Belgium could not be considered practical and effective within the meaning of the ECtHR's case-law, since under the legislation in force in Morocco, a country with which he had close ties because of one of his dual nationalities, he did not have access to marriage.[23]

Even though this case had particular characteristics, it is significant that the CST, in order to ensure the equal treatment of EU officials, relied on the jurisprudence of the ECtHR and opted for a broad interpretation of Art. 1(2)(c)(iv).

21.2.3 *The* Roodhuijzen *Case and the Autonomous Notion of Non-Marital Partnership in the Staff Regulations*

In the *Roodhuijzen* case, the applicant challenged the Commission's refusal to grant his partner access to the Joint Sickness Insurance Scheme of the European Communities. The Commission maintained that the cohabitation agreement that the applicant and his partner had entered into in the Netherlands could not be considered a stable non-marital partnership within the meaning of Art. 1(2)(c) of Annex VII to the Staff Regulations.

Despite the case does not concern a same-sex partnership, it is interesting because both the CST at first instance and the GC on appeal were asked to rule on whether the term 'stable non-marital partnership', which includes same-sex partnership, had to be given an autonomous interpretation or whether it referred implicitly to national law.

Confirming the judgment of the CST, the GC ruled that the question whether two persons are non-marital partners within the meaning of the Staff Regulations cannot be solely a matter for the discretion of a Member State.[24] Thus, the GC established

22 *Scoppola v. Italy*, n. 10249/03, judgment of 17th September 2009.

23 Lagarde (2011), p. 371.

24 With regard to the first condition set out at art. 1(2)(c) (i.e., that a couple must produce a legal document recognized as such by a Member State, or any competent authority of a Member State, acknowledging their status as non-marital partners), the CST did not accept the certificate of the Embassy of the Netherlands in Luxembourg, which expressly granted the applicant and his partner the status of non-marital partners. The CST held, indeed, that said condition could not be solely a matter for the discretion of a Member State, since it had to be examined in the light of Staff Regulations. *Roodhuijzen v. Commission*, paras 35–40.

that the term 'non-marital partnership' had to be interpreted autonomously and not by reference to national law.[25] However, the GC also held that such an interpretation did not

> affect the exclusive competence of Member States [. . .] which are free to introduce statutory arrangements granting legal recognition to forms of union other than marriage.[26]

In other words, the provision of the Staff Regulations that establishes the substantial equivalence of marriage and stable non-marital partnerships as regards employment benefits cannot be directly transposed into national law, since the Member States have exclusive competence with regard to a person's civil *status*.[27]

21.3 Preliminary Rulings: A More Cautious Approach

The CJEU has examined the question of the extension of employment benefits to same-sex couples also in a number of preliminary rulings. Indeed, several national courts have made references for preliminary rulings in connection with whether EU law precludes national legislation which does not treat same-sex partnerships as equivalent to marriage for the purposes of benefits such as travel concessions or widower's pensions.

The CJ ruled on this issue in *Grant*, *Maruko* and *Römer*.[28] In order to clarify the distinction between discrimination based on sex and discrimination based on sexual orientation, we will also analyse the CJ's judgment in *K.B.*, which concerned discrimination against a transsexual, rather than against same-sex couples.

---

[25] The issue of the autonomous meaning of a term contained in the Staff Regulations is examined also in *Mandt v. Parlement*, F-45/07, judgment of 1st July 2010, nyr. In this case, the CST interpreted the term 'surviving spouse' used in Art. 18 of Annex VIII to the Staff Regulations. On this point, see Mosconi and Campiglio (2012), p. 309.

[26] *Commission v. Roodhuijzen*, para. 87.

[27] The conditions of the recognition of this equivalence are analyzed in the next paragraph.

[28] A new reference for preliminary ruling is currently pending before the CJ (*Frédéric Hay v. Crédit agricole mutuel de Charente-Maritime et des Deux-Sèvres*, C-267/12). In this case, the *French Court of Cassation* has asked whether Art. 2(2)(b) of Council Directive 2000/78/EC of 27th November 2000 must be interpreted as meaning that the choice of the national legislature to allow only persons of different sexes to marry can constitute a legitimate, appropriate and necessary aim such as to justify indirect discrimination resulting from the fact that a collective agreement which reserves an advantage in respect of pay and working conditions to employees who marry, thereby necessarily excluding from the benefit of that advantage same-sex partners who have entered into a civil solidarity pact.

21.3.1 The Grant *Case and the Adoption of Directive 2000/78*

In this case,[29] the Industrial Tribunal of Southampton referred for a preliminary ruling to the CJ. The question was whether Art. 119 TEC and Directive 75/117 on the approximation of the laws of the Member States relating to the application of the principle of equal pay for men and women precluded the application of a national law refusing travel concession for an unmarried same-sex couple living in cohabitation, while such concessions were available for spouses or unmarried opposite-sex couples.

It is worth noticing that the judgment in *Grant* is similar to that in *D v. Council,* insofar as they were both delivered before the entry into force of the Treaty of Amsterdam—and, thus, before the insertion of Art. 13 TEC, which prohibits discrimination based on sexual orientation.

Ms. Grant, who was in a lesbian relationship, brought an action before the Industrial Tribunal, challenging her employer's refusal to grant her partner travel concessions on the ground that such concessions applied only to spouses and unmarried cohabiting opposite-sex partners. The national court then made a reference for a preliminary ruling, asking whether the case at issue constituted discrimination based both on sex and sexual orientation.

Concerning the alleged discrimination on grounds of sex, the CJ compared the lesbian context of Ms. Grant with "a hypothetical gay context"[30] and observed that:

> travel concessions are refused to a male worker if he is living with a person of the same-sex, just as they are to a female worker if she is living with a person of the same-sex.

As a consequence, it concluded that:

> since the conditions imposed by the undertaking's regulations applies in the same way to female and male workers, it cannot be regarded as constituting discrimination directly based on sex.[31]

As for discrimination on the basis of sexual orientation, the CJ held that (1) at the time, EU law did not cover the issue; and (2) the ECtHR did not consider stable

[29] *Grant*, C-249/96, judgment of 17th February 1998, [1998] ECR I-621. See Bell (1999), p. 68 and Rofes i Pujol (1999), p. 211.

[30] Toggenburg (2008), p. 176.

[31] *Grant*, paras 27–28. It must be pointed out that the Advocate General Elmer on his Opinion delivered on 30th September 1997 proposed a different solution. Indeed, interpreting the *P v. S* judgment (*P v. S and Cornwall County Council*, C-13/94, judgment of 30th April 1996, [1996] ECR I-02143), he maintained that "the Court [. . .] took a decisive step away from an interpretation of the principle of equal treatment based on the traditional comparison between a female and a male employee [. . .] in a way that renders the principle appropriate for dealing with the cases of gender discrimination that come before the courts in present-day society. [. . .] Art. 119 of the Treaty must therefore be construed as covering all cases where gender is objectively the factor causing an employee to be paid less". Advocate General Elmer, Opinion of 30th September 1997, *Grant*, C-249/96, [1998] ECR I-621, paras 15–16.

homosexual relationships as falling within the scope of Art. 8 ECHR.[32] Therefore, the CJ concluded that there was no discrimination based on sexual orientation.[33] However, it also observed that, once entered into force, the Treaty of Amsterdam, would allow European institutions to eliminate various forms of discrimination, including discrimination based on sexual orientation. Indeed, just like after the judgment in *D v. Council* the Staff Regulations were amended to extend the rights of same-sex couples, after this judgment the EU legislator adopted Directive 2000/78 establishing a general framework for equal treatment in employment and occupation (further referred as Framework Directive) in order to combat direct and indirect discrimination in the Member States.[34] This clearly shows an effort of the EU to adapt its legal system to social transformations. However, as observed in Sect. 21.1, the Framework Directive does not require Member States to introduce legislation on registered partnerships or to recognize partners as equal to family members. Indeed, Art. 3 provides that the Directive applies within the limits of the areas of competence conferred on the EU.[35]

21.3.2 The K.B. *Case and the Different Approach of the CJEU to the Discrimination of Transsexuals*

In this case,[36] Ms. K.B., a member of the UK National Health Service (further referred as UK NHS), was in a relationship with Mr. R., a person born a woman who, following surgical gender reassignment, became a man. Ms. K.B. had requested to nominate her partner as the beneficiary of a widower's pension despite the fact that she and her partner were not married, on the grounds that they were excluded from marriage because UK law did not allow a change of sex on the birth certificate. The UK NHS, however, refused refused her permission to do so, maintaining that Mr. R. could not be granted the widower's pension because he was not entitled to marry. Before the national court, Ms. K.B. argued that this refusal constituted a discrimination based on sex, contrary to Art. 141 TEC and to Directive 75/117. The Court of Appeal (England and Wales, Civil Division) referred for a preliminary ruling to the CJ asking whether the exclusion of the female-to-male transsexual partner of a female member of the UK NHS Pension Scheme, which limited the material dependent's benefit to her widower, constituted sex discrimination.

[32] *X. and Y. v. the United Kingdom*, n. 9369/81, decision of 3rd May 1983.

[33] For a critical view see Armstrong (1998), p. 466.

[34] See Rivas Vãno (2001), p. 193, Schiek (2002), p. 290, Chacartegui Jàvega (2006), p. 53 and Bell (2008), p. 36. On the implementation of the Framework Directive see Waaldijk (2006), p. 17.

[35] See Sects. 21.3.3, 21.3.4 and 21.4.

[36] *K. B.*, C-117/01, judgment of 7th January 2004, [2004] ECR I-541. See Morozzo della Rocca (2004), p. 989 Quiñones Escàmez (2004), p. 507 and Bergamini (2012), p. 33.

Unlike the cases discussed in the preceding paragraphs, here the refusal to extend the benefit to Mr. R. was examined only from the point of view of sex discrimination. As noted by Advocate General Ruiz-Jarabo Colomer in his Opinion of 10 June 2003 "transsexualism is clearly different from the various conditions associated with sexual orientation" and "problems relating to transsexualism are not to be confused with those relating to sexual orientation."

The Advocate General also explained that:

> [i]f the discrimination to which transsexuals are subject were not regard as based on sex, the paradoxical situation would arise in which [they] would not have specific protection at Community level,[37]

since neither Art. 13 TEC nor the CFR make reference to transsexuals. For these reasons, transsexualism and sexual orientation do not raise, under EU law, the same legal issues with regard to the principle of non-discrimination. Therefore, they must be examined from different points of view.

Relying the *D v. Council* case, the CJ held that there was no discrimination on grounds of sex, since Community law did not prohibit the decision to restrict certain benefits to married couples for the purpose of awarding a survivor's pension.[38] However, following the Opinion delivered by the Advocate General, the CJ specified that the inequality of treatment did not relate to the award of a widower's pension, but to a necessary precondition for the grant of such a pension, namely the capacity to marry.[39] Referring to the *Goodwin* case (ECtHR),[40] the CJ thus concluded that UK law was in principle incompatible with Art. 141 EC. Nevertheless, based on the *Goodwin* judgment, the CJ added that (1) it is for the Member States to determine the conditions under which legal recognition is given to the gender of a person in R.'s situation[41]; and, (2) it is for national courts to establish whether a person in R's situation can rely on Art. 141 TEC.[42] Therefore, the groundbreaking nature of the decision in *K.B.* is ultimately tempered by the fact that the CJ regarded Member States as competent to determine the requirements for the recognition of a change of gender, and national courts as competent to assess whether a person can rely to Art. 141 EC.[43]

---

[37] Advocate General Ruiz-Jarabo Colomer, Opinion delivered on 10th June 2003 in *K. B.*, C-117/01, [2004] ECR I-541, paras 25 and 73.

[38] *K. B.*, para. 28.

[39] *Ibidem*, para. 30 and Opinion para. 74.

[40] *Goodwin v. United Kingdom*, n. 28957/95, judgment of 11th July 2002, paras 100–104. The ECtHR established that the impossibility for transsexuals to marry after gender reassignment surgery, due to the fact their newly acquired sex is not recognized in the civil registry, constituted a breach of their right to marry under Art. 12 ECHR. See Icard (2004), p. 979 and Canor (2004), p. 1113. For a critical view, see Wachsmann and Marienburg-Wachsmann (2003), p. 1157.

[41] *K. B.*, para. 35.

[42] *Ibidem*, para. 36.

[43] See Battaglia (2004), p. 617.

21.3.3 *The* Maruko *Case and the First (Apparently Revolutionary) Application of the Prohibition of Sexual Orientation Discrimination*

In order to understand the CJ's reasoning in *Maruko*,[44] two preliminary observations are necessary regarding the legal background of the case. First of all, by that time, and despite the *Grant* judgment, the EU had adopted the Framework Directive, whose Art. 1, as noted above,[45] established a general framework for combating discrimination in the Member States, including discrimination based on sexual orientation. Secondly, in 2001 Germany adopted the Law on Registered Partnerships, according to which same-sex partnership (further referred as life partnership) must be considered as somehow equivalent marriage, subject to certain conditions demonstrating the existence of a life-long partnership and the partners' mutual support and care for each other.[46] Moreover, in 2004, Germany amended its Social Security Code so as to recognize the equivalence of life partnership and marriages for the purpose of widow's or widower's pension. So, even if Germany does not allow persons of same-sex to contract marriage, it has created for them a separate regime that has been gradually made equivalent to that of marriage.[47]

Turning now to the case in question, Mr. Maruko entered into a life partnership with another man, who was a designer of theatrical costumes, in 2001. When the latter died in 2005, Mr. Maruko applied for a widower's pension but the German Theatre Pension Institution rejected his application noting that its regulation did not provide for the granting of this economic benefit to a surviving life partner. Mr. Maruko then brought an action against the decision before the Bavarian Administrative Court (further referred as BAC) which made a reference for a preliminary ruling to the CJ. Among the questions raised by the national court, the third is especially relevant to our discussion: the referring court asked whether the combined provisions of Arts. 1 and 2 of the Framework Directive precluded national legislation under which the surviving partner does not receive a survivor's benefit equivalent to that granted to a surviving spouse. The CJ ruled that, in principle, the Framework Directive precluded national legislation under which, after the death of his or her life partner, the surviving partner is not granted a benefit equivalent to that granted to a surviving spouse.

The CJ's judgment, however, is not as revolutionary as it might seem at first sight. First of all, the CJ established that it is for the national court to assess whether a surviving life-partner is in a situation comparable to that of a spouse.[48] So, despite

[44] *Maruko*, C-267/06, judgment of 1st April 2008, [2008] ECR I-1757. See Graupner (2012), p. 274.

[45] Section 21.3.1.

[46] Para. 2 of the Law on Registered Partnerships provides that: "[t]he life partner must support and care for one another and commit themselves mutually to a lifetime union. They shall each responsibility with regard to the other".

[47] See, in this volume, Repetto.

[48] *Maruko*, para. 73.

the fact that, referring to the argument of the BAC,[49] the CJ essentially ruled that the assessment must be based on a situation that is comparable rather than identical to that of a spouse, it is ultimately for the national court to determine whether the surviving partner satisfies the conditions for comparison. Secondly, the necessary precondition for the assessment of that comparability is the legal recognition of same-sex couples in the Member State concerned. Indeed, it is clear that if a Member State recognizes the equivalence of marriage and life partnership, as Germany did, that State must ensure this substantial equivalence is not contrary to the Framework Directive. As noted by Advocate General Ruiz-Jarabo Colomer in his Opinion of 6 September 2007:

> it is therefore necessary to establish whether those two types of union warrant equal treatment, for which purpose the national court must determine whether the legal situation of spouses is akin to that of persons in a registered civil partnership. In the event that it is not, the criteria for comparison would not be valid.[50]

Thirdly, it follows from the second point that if a Member State does not provide any legal protection for same-sex unions, the criteria for comparison will not be valid, because the national legislation in question does not recognize registered partnership as akin to marriage, thus making any comparison impossible.[51] In this respect, it should be noted that, at present, also the case-law of the ECtHR, to which the CJEU has constantly referred, does not require the Member States of the ECHR to recognize the equivalence of same-sex couples with married couples in terms of access to marriage.[52]

In essence, the *Maruko* judgment is less revolutionary than it may seem in that it does not recognize that, based on the Framework Directive, a surviving same-sex partner is entitled to pension benefits in every Member State. Indeed, each Member State remains free to decide whether to introduce the equivalence between same-sex couples and opposite-sex couples in its legal system. Of course, if that equivalence is introduced, the Member State concerned will be bound to ensure compliance with the Framework Directive. However, at present the EU cannot oblige Member States to introduce such equivalence.

---

[49] *Ibidem*, paras 68–71.

[50] Advocate General Ruiz-Jarabo Colomer, Opinion delivered on 6th September 2007 in *Maruko*, C-267/06, [2008] ECR I-1757, para. 100.

[51] Weisse-Marchal (2008), p. 1876.

[52] See, for instance, ECtHR, *Schalk and Kopf v. Austria*, n. 30141/04, judgment of 24th June 2010, para. 46: "[w]hile the Court had often underlined that the Convention was a living instrument which had to be interpreted in present-day conditions, it had only used that approach to develop its jurisprudence where it had perceived a convergence of standards among member States. [...] The issue of same-sex marriage concerned a sensitive area of social, political and religious controversy. In the absence of consensus, the State enjoyed a particularly wide margin of appreciation". The ECtHR also added that: "[i]n conclusion, the Court finds that Art. 12 of the Convention does not impose an obligation on the respondent Government to grant a same-sex couple like the applicants access to marriage".

21.3.4 The Römer *Case and the Confirmation of Member States' Freedom to Introduce the Equivalence Between Same-Sex Couples and Married Couples*

In the *Römer* case,[53] the benefit at issue in the domestic proceedings was, unlike that in *Maruko*, a supplementary retirement pension. Indeed, Mr. Römer, in life partnership with Mr. U., brought an action against the Administration for its refusal to amend the calculation of his pension on the basis of the more favorable deduction granted to married couples.[54] Mr. Römer essentially challenged the national law under which he would receive a lower pension than that granted to a retired married employee, alleging discrimination based on sexual orientation. The Labour Court of Hamburg (further referred as LCH) made a reference for a preliminary ruling asking whether the Framework Directive precluded the national legislation at issue.

Before answering to the question posed by the LCH, the CJ confirmed that, as EU law stood at the time, legislation on the marital status of persons fell "within the competence of the Member States."[55]

The Court then observed that, if a Member State decides to treat same-sex partnership as equivalent to marriage for the purposes of certain benefits, it cannot discriminate on the basis of sexual orientation. As a consequence, the CJ judged that the Framework Directive precluded a provision of national law under which the pension paid to a married employee is more favourable than that paid to an employee in a registered same-sex partnership. However, as in the *Maruko* case, the CJ ruled that national courts are competent to decide if a life partner is in a situation comparable to that of a married person.

21.4 Conclusion

Our analysis has shown that in the EU legal system there is a trend to recognize the substantial equivalence of same-sex couples with marriage as regards employment benefits.

---

[53] *Römer*, C-147/08, judgment of 10th May 2011, [2011] ECR I-03591. See Picarella (2011), p. 1325 and Winkler (2011), p. 1979 and Castellaneta (2011), p. 99.

[54] Paras 10 (8) and 12 (1) of the Law of the Land of Hamburg on Supplementary Retirement and Survivors provides that: "the notional net income to be taken into account for the purposes of calculating the pension shall be determined by deducting from the income included in the calculation of the pension [...] (1) the amount of income tax which would have to be paid [...] on the basis of tax category III/0 in the case of married pensioner not permanently separated at the date on which the retirement is first paid; (2) the amount of income tax which would have to be paid [...] on the basis of tax category I at the date on which the retirement pensions is first paid in the case of all other pensioners". It must be noted that the amount to be deducted under tax category III/0 is lower than the amount to be deducted under category I.

[55] *Römer*, para. 38.

This equivalence presupposes that the situations being weighed up are comparable, rather than identical. Despite certain differences, both EU staff cases and preliminary rulings have established that the condition for comparability is a stable, long-term life partnership. Nevertheless, a distinction must be drawn between EU staff cases and preliminary rulings.

Regarding EU staff cases, Regulation 723/2004 has introduced a substantial equivalence between all EU officials, prohibiting any discrimination based on sexual orientation with regard to employment benefits. Moreover, as established by the CST in the *Roodhuijzen* judgment, the term 'non-marital partnership' must be given an autonomous interpretation. However, this autonomous interpretation must be limited to the Staff Regulations, so that it applies only to EU officials in same-sex partnerships. Therefore, it is clear that, in the relationship between the EU and its officials, any discrimination based on sex or sexual orientation is prohibited.

On the other hand, the judgments rendered by the CJ in the context of preliminary rulings have different characteristics than those delivered in EU staff cases. Also in this case, there is a tendency to extend employment benefits arising from a long-term relationship to same-sex couples, provided that certain conditions are satisfied. However, there is neither an obligation to apply those benefits in all Member States nor a Community interpretation of the term 'non-marital relationship'. Indeed, as EU law stands at present, the Member States are not required to adopt legislative measures to recognize the equivalence of married couples and same-sex couples, since the marital status of persons falls within their competence. This principle obviously applies also to employment benefits.[56] As a consequence, employment benefits can be granted to same-sex couples, in accordance with the Framework Directive, only if a Member State treats same-sex unions as equivalent to marriages.

References

Armstrong KA (1998) Tales of the community: sexual orientation discrimination and EC law. J Soc Welfare Fam Law 20:455–479

Battaglia E (2004) "Sesso" e "orientamento sessuale" nell'interpretazione dell'art. 141 CE alla luce della sentenza K. B. c. Regno Unito. Il diritto dell'Unione Europea 3:599–618

[56] According to Vitucci (2011), p. 462, a possible development of the CJEU's case-law is the application to same-sex couples of the principle of the 'uniformity' of the status of EU citizens, a principle mentioned by Advocate General La Pergola in his Opinion of 3rd December 1996 in *Dafeki*, C-336/94, [1996] ECR p. I-6761, para. 6. The Advocate General noted that there are circumstances in which an individual's civil status is a condition for entitlement to a subjective legal position guaranteed by EU law, but held that it cannot be accepted in such circumstances that the status of the person concerned should be evaluated differently from one Member State to another. However, Vitucci (p. 463) recognizes that the Member States remain competent to adopt national rules on marital or family status. On this point, see also Marinai (2011), p. 181.

Bell M (1999) Shifting conceptions of sexual discrimination at the court of justice: from P v S to Grant v SWT. Eur Law J 5:63–81
Bell M (2008) The implementation of European anti-discrimination directives: converging towards a common model? Polit Q 79:36–44
Bergamini E (2012) La famiglia nel diritto dell'Unione europea. Giuffrè, Milano
Berthou K (2012) Articolo 19 TFUE. In: Curti Gialdino (a cura di) Codice dell'Unione europea. Simone, Napoli, pp 554–559
Berthou K, Masselot A (2002) Le mariage, les partenariats et la CJCE: ménage à trois. Cahiers de droit européen 5-6:679–694
Canor I (2004) Case C-117/01, K.B. v. National Health Service Pensions Agency, Secretary of State for health, judgment of the full court of 7 January 2004. Common Mark Law Rev 41:1113–1125
Caracciolo di Torella E, Reid E (2002) The changing shape of the "European Family" and fundamental rights. Eur Law Rev 27:80–90
Castellaneta M (2011) Pensioni: i partner di "unioni registrate" hanno gli stessi diritti delle coppie sposate. Guida al diritto 23:99–101, 24 giugno 2011
Chacartegui Jàvega C (2006) La direttiva 2000/78/CE e il principio di non discriminazione sulla base dell'orientamento sessuale nel diritto comunitario. In: Fabeni S, Toniollo MG (a cura di) La discriminazione fondata sull'orientamento sessuale. L'attuazione della direttiva 2000/78/CE e la nuova disciplina per la protezione dei diritti delle persone omosessuali sul posto di lavoro. Ediesse, Roma, pp 53–78
Denys C (1999) Homosexuality: a non-issue in community law? Eur Law Rev 24:419–425
Dubout E (2006) La clause communautaire de lutte contre les discriminations. Bruylant, Bruxelles
Flynn L (1999) The implications of article 13 EC – after Amsterdam, will some forms of discrimination be more equal than others? Common Mark Law Rev 36:1127–1152
Graupner H (2012) Sexual orientation discrimination and the court of justice of the European Union. In: Boele Woelki K, Fuchs A (eds) Legal recognition of same-sex relationships in Europe. National, cross-border and European perspective, Full revised 2nd edn. Intersentia, Cambridge/Antwerp/Portland, pp 271–282
Icard P (2004) Transsexualisme: un droit d'accès au mariage protégé par la CJCE. Recueil Le Dalloz 14:979–982
Lagarde P (2011) Jurisprudence. Conflits de lois. Revue critique de droit international privé 2:381–384
Marinai S (2011) Status familiari e libera circolazione. Gli Stranieri 1:181–188
Morozzo della Rocca P (2004) Recenti orientamenti di diritto europeo in materia di discriminazione dei transessuali. Europa e diritto privato 3:989–1000
Mosconi F, Campiglio F (2012) I matrimoni tra persone dello stesso sesso: livello «federale» e livello statale in Europa negli Stati Uniti. Rivista di diritto internazionale privato e processuale 48:299–316
Picarella G (2011) Le discriminazioni fondate sull'orientamento sessuale nella giurisprudenza della Corte di giustizia: dal caso P. alla sentenza Römer. Rivista italiana di diritto del lavoro 4:1325–1359
Quiñones Escámez A (2004) Derecho comunitario, derechos fundamentales y denegación del cambio de sexo y apellidos: ¿un orden público europeo armonizador? (a propósito de las SSTJCE, asuntos K.B. y García Avello). Revista de Derecho Comunitario Europeo 18:507–529
Rivas Vãno A (2001) La Prohibición de Discriminación por Orientación Sexual en la Directiva 2000/78. Temas Laborales. Revista Andaluza de Trabajo y Bienestar Social 59:193–220
Rofes i Pujol MI (1999) Crónica de la Jurisprudencia del Tribunal de Justicia de las Comunidades Europeas. La denegación de una reducción en el precio de los transportes en favor de la persona del mismo sexo con la que convive maritalmente el trabajador y el principio de igualidad de retribución entre hombres y mujeres en derecho comunitario. La sentencia del Tribunal de

Justicia de las Comunidades Europeas, de 17 de febrero de 1998 en el asunto C-249/96, Grant. Cuadernos Europeos de Deusto 20:211–223
Scappucci G (2000) Court of first instance refuses to recognize Swedish "Registered Partnership" rights and duties. Eur Public Law 6:355–366
Schiek D (2002) A new framework on equal treatment of persons in EC law? Directives 2000/43/EC, 2000/78/EC and 2002/73/EC changing directive 76/207/EEC in context. Eur Law J 8:290–314
Toggenburg GN (2008) "LGBT" go Luxembourg: on the stance of Lesbian gay bisexual and transgender rights before the European Court of Justice. Eur Law Rep 174–185
Verschraegen B (2012) The right to private and family life, the right to marry and to found a family, and the prohibition of discrimination. In: Boele-Woelki K, Fuchs A (eds) Legal recognition of same-sex relationships in Europe. National, cross-border and European perspective, Full revised 2nd edn. Intersentia, Cambridge/Antwerp/Portland, pp 255–270
Vitucci MC (2011) Lo status di coppia omosessuale fra Strasburgo e Lussemburgo (passando per Roma). In: Triggiani E (a cura di) Le nuove frontiere della cittadinanza europea. Cacucci, Bari, pp 447–468
Waaldijk K (2006) Legislation in fifteen EU member states against sexual orientation discrimination in employment: the implementation of directive 2000/78/EC. In: Weyembergh A, Castocea S (eds) The gays' and lesbians' rights in an enlarged European Union. Editions de l'Université de Bruxelles, Bruxelles, pp 17–47
Wachsmann P, Marienburg-Wachsmann A (2003) La folie dans la loi. Considérations critiques sur la nouvelle jurisprudence de la Cour européenne des droits de l'homme en matière de transsexualisme. Revue trimestrielle des droits de l'homme 56:1157–1185
Weisse-Marchal C (2008) Le droit à une pension de veuf du partenaire de vie du même sexe. Recueil Le Dalloz 27:1873–1876
Winkler MM (2011) I trattamenti pensionistici delle coppie dello stesso sesso nell'Unione europea: il caso Römer. Responsabilità civile e previdenza 11:1979–1996

Chapter 22
International Administrative Tribunals and Their *Non-Originalist* Jurisprudence on Same-Sex Couples: 'Spouse' and 'Marriage' in Context, Between Social Changes and the Doctrine of *Renvoi*

Daniele Gallo

Abstract The heterogeneous membership of international organizations—i.e. the existence of cultural, social and legal differences among member states—entails that, unlike what happens in the EU system, where the CJEU relies on an autonomous notion of 'family' in the interpretation of Staff Regulations and Staff Rules, international administrative tribunals generally base their decisions on the '*renvoi*' to the *lex patriae* of the staff member. As a result, a gay or lesbian staff member may be entitled to spousal rights for his/her partner only if his/her home country allows same-sex marriage or a certain kind of recognized same-sex civil partnership granting social benefits equivalent to those accorded by marriage. Moreover, in interpreting the term 'spouse', both the UN Administrative Tribunal and ILO Administrative Tribunal rely on a dynamic, systematic and teleological interpretation of the law, rather than a static, formal-constructivist and *originalist* approach.

22.1 Scope of Research: The Jurisprudence of the UNAT and ILOAT as a Privileged Tool of Analysis

This chapter focuses on the jurisprudence of international administrative tribunals[1] concerning employment benefits[2] for gay and lesbian people who are staff members of an international organization. By 'staff' I mean all agents/officials/officers/employees having an employed or self-employed work relationship, whether

[1] On international administrative tribunals, see Bastid (1957); Amerasinghe (2005), pp. 489–511; Sands and Klein (2009), pp. 421–434; Schermers and Blokker (2011), §§ 642–647; Elias and Thomas (2012).

[2] On the disputes involving the EU civil service, see the chapter by Orzan in this volume.

D. Gallo (✉)
Law Department, Luiss Guido Carli University, Rome, Italy
e-mail: dgallo@luiss.it

D. Gallo et al. (eds.), *Same-Sex Couples before National, Supranational and International Jurisdictions*, DOI 10.1007/978-3-642-35434-2_22,

indefinite or fixed term, with the organization.[3] The common feature is that, in carrying out their functions and activities, they all act on behalf and in the exclusive interest of the organization.

The analysis will be centered on two tribunals: the UN Administrative Tribunal (further referred to as UNAT)[4] and the ILO Administrative Tribunal (further referred to as ILOAT).[5] With regard to the UNAT, it must be recalled that the Tribunal was abolished on 31 December 2009,[6] following the decision of the UN General Assembly to establish a new two-tier internal justice system comprising a first-instance tribunal, the UN Dispute Tribunal (further referred to as UNDT), and an appellate body, the UN Appeals Tribunal (further referred to as UNAsT).[7] Moreover, to my knowledge, neither the UNDT nor the UNAsT have so far rendered rulings on same-sex couples' rights.

I have decided to focus on the UNAT and ILOAT as the most relevant international administrative tribunals[8]—choosing them as a privileged *sedes materiae* to illustrate the various issues concerning the *status* of gay and lesbian international officials—for three reasons. Firstly, both tribunals have generated abundant case-law in relation to a very high number of staff members, having ('having had' in the case of the now abolished UNAT) competence on the administrative decisions passed, as to the UNAT, by the great majority of the United Nations' (UN) entities and by a number of UN specialized agencies[9] and, as to the ILOAT, by 59 international organizations that have to date recognized its jurisdiction,[10] including, obviously, the ILO. Secondly, not only the UN's internal tribunals (before and after the reform) and the ILOAT influence each other, but their jurisprudence is apt to influence the case-law of other international administrative tribunals, thus strongly contributing to the development of general principles of administrative law as regards the international civil service.[11] Thirdly, unlike other systems of

---

[3] On these (partially overlapping) notions, see Pisillo Mazzeschi (1991), pp. 44–47; Aamir (2009); and Gallo (2012), pp. 273–278.

[4] On the UNAT see, among the others, Wood (2009).

[5] On the ILOAT see, among the others, Gutteridge (2009).

[6] See resolutions No. 61/261 of 4th April 2007 (A/RES/61/261), No. 62/228 of 22nd December 2007 (A/RES/62/228) and No. 63/253 of 24th December 2008 (A/RES/62/228).

[7] On the new internal justice system see, *inter alia*, Beigbeder (2009) and Hwang (2009).

[8] Among other important international administrative tribunals, the most active include those established within the World Bank (WB), the International Monetary Fund (IMF), the Organization of American States (OAS), and the Organization for Economic Cooperation and Development (OECD).

[9] In particular: all departments and offices of the UN Secretariat; peacekeeping and political missions; UN offices away from headquarters; UN regional commissions; international criminal tribunals; funds and programmes. See http://www.un.org/en/oaj/dispute/jurisdiction.shtml. As emphasized in note 8, some UN specialized agencies such as the WB and IMF have their own systems of internal justice.

[10] See http://www.ilo.org/public/english/tribunal/membership/index.htm.

[11] On the notion and relevance of this source of law see Sect. 22.2.

dispute resolution,[12] there is no doubt that both the UN's internal tribunals (before and after the reform) and the ILOAT are 'true' jurisdictions and their decisions are judgments *stricto iure*, being, as such, fully binding for the organization as well as its officials.

22.2 The Law Governing Employment Relations Between International Organizations and Their Staff: The Heterogeneous Notion of 'Family', 'Spouse', 'Marriage', and the *Renvoi* to the Official's *Lex Patriae*

As is well known, the internal legal order of international organizations[13] is constituted, in its essence, by the law governing the legal *status* and employment relationships of their personnel.[14] More precisely, the general rules regulating the rights and obligations of staff members are often contained in the statute/constitution of the organization—i.e. in its founding treaty—, in the headquarters agreement concluded with the host State, and in its administrative tribunal's statute. However, the main written sources of law providing a detailed number of provisions and regulations in this field are: the Staff Regulations, the Staff Rules, the recommendations or resolutions adopted by the deliberative organ (and the *plenum*) of the organization (such as the General Assembly of the UN), the circulars, guide (line)s or manuals (generally) implemented by its administrative body (such as the General Secretariat of the UN), as well as the contracts signed by and between the organization and its officials. Unwritten sources must also be mentioned: above all, the general principles of international administrative law or, more simply, the general principles on the international civil service (derived both from international organizations' and member states' contract, procedural, labour and administrative law), such as the principle of non-discrimination; the internal administrative practice of the organization; and equity.

Many of the rules provided for by international organizations on their staff's employment conditions concern the official's family members: spouse, dependent (children), relatives, widowers, survivors, and the like. Rights and obligations are attached to these statuses, both for the staff member and for his/her family.[15] Now,

[12] Examples are, for instance, the Appeals Boards of the North Atlantic Treaty Organization and of the European Space Agency. On this issue, see Sands and Klein (2009), p. 424.

[13] On its main characteristics see Jenks (1962); Amerasinghe (1988).

[14] On the legal character, *stricto sensu*, of the law regulating the employment conditions of international organizations' officials see Cahier (1963), p. 573; Akehurst (1967), p. 263; Amerasinghe (2005), p. 273; *contra*, Balladore Pallieri (1969), p. 13.

[15] On this topic see, in general, Gascon Y Marin (1932); Pellet and Ruzié (1993); Ruzié (2004); and Beigbeder (2012).

considering that family benefits—such as household, expatriate, or retirement allowances—depend precisely on the existence of family ties, the crucial problem is to give a precise meaning to the term ‘family’ and derive from this notion clear legal consequences. Well, when the issue of same-sex couples is at stake, what the member State of an international organization defines as ‘family’, ‘marriage’, ‘registered partnership’, ‘spouse’, or ‘couple’ could have a different meaning in another member State.

Moreover, since sexuality is understood in different ways even within national communities, as well as within (relatively) advanced systems of (economic, social, cultural and legal) integration such as the atypical *quasi*-constitutional regime represented by the European Union (further referred to as EU), it is evident that, within international organizations, establishing a single definition of ‘family’ that includes *per se* and always same-sex couples is very difficult, if not impossible. For this reason, international organizations’ regulations are, at present, extremely cautious in identifying the content and extent of the concept of family and, therefore, do not opt for a ‘horizontal’ and general recognition of same-sex couples’ rights. The heterogeneity of the membership—i.e. the existence of cultural, social and legal differences among member States—entails that, unlike what happens in the EU system, where the CJEU relies on an autonomous notion of ‘family’ in the interpretation of staff regulations and staff rules,[16] international administrative tribunals generally ground their decisions on the ‘*renvoi*’[17] to the *lex patriae* of the staff member concerned. As a result, it seems that, at present, a gay or lesbian staff member may be entitled to spousal rights for his/her spouse only if his/her home country allows same-sex marriage or a certain kind of recognized same-sex civil partnership granting social benefits equivalent to those accorded by marriage.[18]

22.3 The Jurisprudence of the UNAT on Same-Sex Marriage and Partnerships

To my knowledge, the UNAT has rendered only two judgments concerning the employment allowances of a gay or lesbian official: one in 2002 and the other in 2004.

---

[16] See the chapter by Orzan in this volume.

[17] On such notion see, from a private international law perspective, Davì (2012).

[18] On this topic, see the next sections.

22.3.1 *The* Berghuys *Case: The Legal Recognition of Same-Sex Marriages, But Not Partnerships*

In the *Berghuys*[19] case the applicant, Mr. Ronald Ernest Berghuys, was the partner of Mr. Nikolaas Roger Zegers de Bejil, a participant in the UN Joint Staff Pension Fund (further referred to as UNJSPF). Mr. De Bejil died on 29 July 1999, but on 30 June 1999 the partners, who were both nationals of the Netherlands, had formalized their relationship by entering into a registered domestic partnership agreement under Dutch law.

On 8 March 2000, Mr. Berghuys submitted to the UNJSPF a claim for survivor's allowance, in accordance with Arts. 34 and 35 of the UNJSPF Regulations and Rules.[20] By a letter dated 24 March 2000, the Chief Executive Officer (CEO) of the UNJSPF denied Mr. Berghuys' request on the grounds that the invoked provisions allowed the payment of the benefit only to a legally recognized surviving spouse, where 'spouse' meant that the deceased had to be married at the time of his death, which was not the case. The CEO was clear in stating that within the UN legal order only marriages, and not registered partnerships, are recognized. On 15 April 2000 the Applicant requested a review of the CEO's decision by the Standing Committee. On 8 August 2000, the Committee upheld the decision "on the grounds that the UNJSPF Regulations and Rules, as presently in force, did not provide for a survivor's benefit that might become payable to a 'domestic partner'".[21] On 10 December 2000, Mr. Berghuys filed the application with the ILOAT. Among various contentions, the applicant submitted that: firstly, the UNJSPF Regulations and Rules did not define the term "spouse"; secondly, the registered partnership agreement recognized by Dutch law should have been considered equivalent to marriage, as that equivalence had been ascertained by the UNJSPF with regard to other 'common law marriages'; thirdly, the denial of his request would be contrary to the organization's principles of non-discrimination.

Mr. Berghuys' application raises two main, interconnected, problems: the first concerns the notion of 'spouse'; while the second concerns the possibility to consider a registered partnership as equivalent to marriage under Arts. 34 and 35 of the UNJSPF Regulations and Rules.

[19] Case No. 1169, judgment No. 1063 of 26th July 2002, AT/DEC/1063.

[20] Art. 35 states that: "A widower's benefit, at the rates and under the conditions applicable in article 34 to a widow's benefit, shall be payable to the surviving male spouse of a participant." This article cross-references Art. 34, providing, *inter alia*, that: "A widow's benefit shall [...] be payable to the surviving female spouse of a participant who was entitled to a retirement, early retirement, deferred retirement or disability benefit at the date of his death, or who died in service, if she was married to him at the date of his death in service or, if he was separated prior to his death, she was married to him at the date of separation and remained married to him until his death."

[21] See *Berghuys*, p. 3.

The Tribunal begins its reasoning by rightly underlying that the meaning of the term "spouse" is "evolving and broadening in some nations".[22] Immediately after that, it clarifies that, in spite of "modern cultural notions of relationships and partners",[23] the applicant must not be seen as "the surviving spouse of the deceased participant, because they were not married" and, therefore, "his application for widower's benefit must be rejected".[24]

At paras II–IX of the judgment, the Tribunal makes a number of important observations. Firstly, it notes that the UNJSPF had determined the word 'spouse' on a case-by-case basis, since there is no definition of such term in the UNJSPF Regulations and Rules. As a consequence, the definition to be applied is the one used by the national law of the official, as stated in the opinion of the Office of Legal Affairs of 15 December 1981.[25] The *renvoi* to the law of a staff member's home country is thus the point of reference in the determination of an official's marital *status*. Secondly, the Tribunal, by observing that there is no common understanding of the term 'spouse' among the "peoples of the world", emphasizes that, up to that time, the UNJSPF had never been asked to consider "whether to pay benefits to the survivor of a same-sex partnership".[26] Most importantly, the Tribunal itself had never been resorted to decide on such an issue. Thirdly, the three UN judges refer to the UNAT's previous case-law, according to which interpretation of the law has to be carried out based on the "'ordinary meaning of the terms' in their context and in the light of [their] object and purpose"[27]—as provided for by Art. 31 (1)(4) of the Vienna Convention on the Law of the Treaties and specified in the advisory opinion of the International Court of Justice (ICJ) on the *Legal Consequences for States of the Continued Presence of South Africa in Namibia* (*South-West Africa*) of 21 June 1971[28]—and in accordance with the principle of equality enshrined, *inter alia*, in Art. 8 of the UN Charter and Art. 26 of the International Covenant on Civil and Political Rights (ICCPR).[29] Finally, and most importantly, the Tribunal concludes that: on the one hand, any definition of marriage which, like that provided by the Cambridge International Dictionary of English (1995), defines the term 'spouse' as "a person's husband or wife" is "outdated, since the traditional laws of several countries recognize that a pledge of marriage may be made by persons of the same sex"[30]; and, on the other hand, despite the evolution of the "pledges being made by couples and, especially, the changing nature of the parties

[22] *Ibidem*, para. I.

[23] *Ibidem*.

[24] *Ibidem*.

[25] *Ibidem*, para. II.

[26] *Ibidem*, para. III.

[27] *Ibidem*, para. IV.

[28] I.C.J. Reports 1971.

[29] See *Berghuys*, para. V.

[30] *Ibidem*, para. VI.

involved",[31] the word 'spouse' is "still linked to a pledge of marriage" and "law and custom still interpret a spouse as a partner in a legal marriage".

This last passage of the judgment is crucial in order to understand the approach, both 'progressive' and 'traditional', adopted by the Tribunal: while there is no doubt that a spouse can be either a heterosexual or a homosexual staff member, only those who are married to a straight or gay partner can apply for and enjoy social benefits. This is precisely the reason why Mr. Berghuys has been denied the right to receive the widow's benefit foreseen by Art. 35 of the UNJSPF Regulations and Rules.[32]

The reasoning of the Tribunal is welcome in that it goes beyond an *originalist* and static interpretation of the law. However, it may be argued that conditioning the application of social allowances for staff members provided for in the internal law of an international organization to the existence of a legal marriage under the national law of the staff member in question, as UNAT has done in *Berghuys* with regard to the UNJSPF, infringes the principle of non-discrimination based on sexual orientation. One could counter-argue that also unmarried straight couples may not be entitled to social benefits. This objection does not, in fact, seem decisive, in as much as many countries recognize registered partnerships but not same-sex marriage and, therefore, gay and lesbian officials coming from those States could not have access, *a priori*, to the enjoyment of the same rights conferred upon straight staff members who may decide to marry. The result seems to entail a *de facto* discrimination between straight and gay officials.

22.3.2 The **Adrian** *Case: An Atypical (and Indirect) Judicial* **Revirement** *and the UN Secretary General's* **Activism**

The approach adopted by UNAT in *Berghuys* has been abandoned in the judgment delivered by the same tribunal in the *Adrian* case of 30 September 2004.[33]

At stake was an application filed by Mr. Jean-Christophe Adrian, a French citizen and staff member of the UN Centre for Human Settlements (further referred to as UNCHS) based in Nairobi. Mr. Adrian filed an application with the UNAT after long proceedings begun on 21 August 2000, when he had requested the Human Resources Management Services of the UN Office in Nairobi (further referred to as HRMS/UNON) to review its decision of 10 July 2000. In the decision, the HRMS/UNON informed Mr. Adrian that his dependency status could be changed from 'single' to 'married'—and, thus, his gay partner could be granted spousal benefits—only if Mr. Adrian's national law recognized same-sex partnerships as equivalent to marriage. That, however, was not the case, since Mr. Adrian

[31] *Ibidem*, para. VIII.

[32] *Ibidem*, para. IX.

[33] Case No. 1276, judgment No. 1183, AT/DEC/1183.

and his partner had registered their domestic partnership under the French *Pacte Civil de Solidarité* (PACS) and, at the time, there was no French law allowing same-sex marriage.[34] The HRMS/UNON did not review its decision not to recognize Mr. Adrian's same-gender partner as a spouse for the purposes of UN entitlements. As a consequence, on 7 September 2000 the applicant requested the Secretary General to reform the administrative decision.[35]

On 5 December 2000, Mr. Adrian lodged an appeal with the Joint Appeals Board (further referred to as JAB) in Nairobi, which issued its report on 28 May 2002. The JAB stated, *inter alia*, that the decision on Mr. Adrian's application was not discriminatory because it was grounded on (1) the law of the home country of the staff member; and (2) the existence of a legal marriage recognized by such law, with the result that, having France made "a clear distinction between marriage and domestic partnership [PACS]", Mr. Adrian's request for the enjoyment of administrative privileges should be dismissed. The fact that there were several instances in which the UNON gave legal recognition to cohabitation contracts between unmarried straight partners was not considered as relevant practice, since that recognition was suspended once it came to the notice of the UN headquarters.[36] Thus, as noted by the JAB, this practice was neither uniformly applied nor was it carried by *opinion juris*.[37] On 24 October 2002 the Under Secretary General informed the applicant that the Secretary General had accepted the JAB's conclusion and, therefore, would not take further action on his appeal. For this reason, Mr. Adrian applied to the UNAT on 8 November 2002, requesting that the term 'spouse' be construed, for the purposes of all relevant UN entitlements, to include at least individuals in domestic partnerships which have been duly registered and recognized in the country of origin [...] "irrespective of the gender of the individuals".[38]

The applicant's principal argument was that the HRMS/UNON's refusal to grant spousal benefits to a gay staff member who could not enter into a marriage according to French law (which, *mutatis mutandis*, was in line with the UNAT's judgment in *Berghuys*), constituted discrimination. In addition, Mr. Adrian suggested that the UNAT opt for a substantive rather than a formalistic interpretation of the terms 'spouse' and 'marriage': in particular, he observed that "[t]he emphasis should be on substance rather than label".[39] The respondent's principal arguments, on the other hand, were as follows (1) the term 'spouse' must be construed as including only heterosexual relationships; (2) the reference/*renvoi* to the national law of the staff member in order to determine his or her marital *status* is the established practice and policy of the UN; (3) extending spousal benefits under

[34] On same-sex couples under French law see the chapter by Reyniers in this volume.

[35] See *Adrian*, p. 2.

[36] *Ibidem*, pp. 3–4.

[37] *Ibidem*, p. 3.

[38] *Ibidem*, p. 1.

[39] *Ibidem*, p. 4.

the Staff Regulations and Rules is a matter for the "appropriate organs of the UN to decide"[40] (i.e., for the 'legislator' and, thus, for the member States). The first argument is rather new and surprising, since in *Berghuys* the Tribunal had already recognized the possibility to define the term 'spouse' as including also married gay officials of international organizations. The second argument is in line with the UNAT's position in *Berghuys*. The third argument implies some crucial questions, not directly raised in *Berghuys*, concerning the dialogue between different organs of the UN (which, *mutatis mutandis*, exist in most international organizations): the administrative/executive body (Secretary General), the judicial body (UNAT), and the political/deliberative/legislative body (General Assembly).

First of all, the UNAT notes that the issue at the core of the *Adrian* case had already been raised in *Berghuys* and, before the ILOAT, in *Mr. R.A.-O.*[41] In this regard, it confirms that the reference to the law of nationality of the staff member is the only way to respect the cultural diversity among different countries.[42]

The Tribunal then turns to an important question connected with the legitimate distribution of competences between the UN Secretary General and UN member States. On 20 January 2004 the Secretary General adopted Bulletin ST/SGB/2004/4 ("Family *status* for purposes of UN entitlements"), which established that:

> [a] legally recognized domestic partnership contracted by a staff member under the law of the country of his or her nationality will also qualify that staff member to receive the entitlements provided for eligible family members. The Organization will request the Permanent Mission to the UN of the country of nationality of the staff member to confirm the existence and validity of the domestic partnership contracted by the staff member under the law of that country.

The UNAT observes that, in interpreting the concept of 'couple', the Bulletin, which the Tribunal denominates also 'circular', takes into account the recommendations published by the UN Consultative Committee on Administrative Questions in April 1998, and subsequently adopted by the UN Administrative Committee on Coordination in June 1998, which stated that "all agencies should strive to prevent discrimination with regard [not 'only' to marriage, but also] to same-sex partnerships".[43]

On 8 April 2004 the UN General Assembly adopted resolution No. 58/285 ("Human resources management"),[44] where the Assembly (i) invited

> the Secretary General to reissue Secretary-General's bulletin ST/SGB/2004/4 after reviewing its contents, taking into account the views and concerns expressed by Member States thereon;

---

[40] *Ibidem*, p. 5.

[41] On the (not so) relevant function of the referral to the official's *lex patriae* in that case and, more in general, on the ILOAT's jurisprudence see the next section.

[42] See *Adrian*, paras I–II.

[43] See *Adrian*, para. IV.

[44] A/RES/58/285.

(ii) noted

> the absence of the terms referred to in paragraph 4 of the bulletin in the context of the existing Staff Regulations and Rules

and (iii) decided that

> the inclusion of those terms shall require the consideration of and necessary action by the General Assembly.

As noted by the General Assembly and further emphasized by the UNAT in its judgment (paras V–XIII), the term 'spouse' must be interpreted in the light of a preliminary issue regarding the legal relevance and *status* of the Secretary General's circulars. The Tribunal refers to several decisions of the UNAT, including *Powell*,[45] according to which circulars

> have the same force and effect as the Staff Rules unless inconsistent with the Staff Regulations.[46]

As a consequence, the Tribunal had to answer two questions.

With regard to the first, the Tribunal wonders whether the circular should be regarded as an amendment to the Staff Regulations—in that case, the amendment would have been illegal, since it had not been approved by the General Assembly (i.e., the body that had issued the Staff Regulations)—or whether it simply offered an interpretation of their provisions.[47] In the first case, as countries such as Pakistan rightly maintained during the meetings of the Fifth Committee,[48] the Secretary General would have exceeded his mission. In this regard, the UNAT states that the Bulletin does not constitute "an amendment to the Staff Regulations", but, rather, "an interpretation of certain terms contained in them", since no definition of the terms "couple", "spouse" or "marriage" was given in the Staff Regulations and Rules and, therefore, there could be no amendments to previous definitions.[49]

The Tribunal then turns to the second question, that is whether said interpretation is consistent with the Staff Regulations. Divergent opinions also on this matter have been expressed by a number of States in the above mentioned Fifth Committee.[50] The UNAT clearly affirms that the Secretary General had acted within his authority and in accordance with the pivotal principle on which UN practice, including the case-law of the UNAT, is based: the family *status* of staff members must be determined by applying their national laws, as this principle is the best criterion

[45] Case No. 234, judgment No. 237 of 8th February 1979, AT/DEC/237, para. XIII.

[46] See *Adrian*, para. V.

[47] *Ibidem*, para. VII.

[48] A/C.5/58/SR.32, para. 36.

[49] See *Adrian*, para. VII.

[50] As reported *ibidem*, paras VIII–IX, Pakistan, Egypt and Iran considered the Bulletin in conflict with the Staff Regulations, whereas the EU, Canada and Australia expressed the opinion that it merely interpreted certain terms contained in those Regulations.

to respect social and cultural differences among UN member States. For this reason, the Tribunal maintains that

> [t]he position taken by the Secretary General is the only one that allows for such coexistence and such respect for diversity.[51]

According to the judges, this statement is confirmed by the fact that the term 'marriage' may not have the same meaning in different national legal systems: in some it refers also to polygamous unions (i.e., unions between one man and more than one woman), while in others it includes unions between same-sex partners.[52] In other words, the core public policy considerations of a given legislation must be excluded from other legislations' public policy notions.

As to the General Assembly's resolution No. 58/285, the UNAT explains that as long as the Secretary General's Bulletin has not modified—but only interpreted—the UN Staff Regulations and Rules, in principle, no prior approval of the Bulletin on the part of the Assembly was required. Furthermore, it must be noted that the Tribunal did not regard the General Assembly's invitation to reissue the Bulletin without reference to the term "domestic partnership" as an obligation for the General Secretary. Moreover, it did not give relevance to the fact that the Bulletin had been strongly criticized by a number of member States.[53]

In light of the above observations, the UNAT, considering the Bulletin as positive law, made it clear that UN judges were bound to apply it. As a consequence, it concludes that Mr. Adrian is entitled to all spousal benefits, with the important *caveat* that these benefits could be paid only from the date of the entry into force of the Bulletin (1 February 2004),[54] precisely because before that date the UN's internal law did not recognize registered partnerships such as the French PACS. Hence, it is reasonable to assume that, if the Bulletin had not been issued, the UNAT would have adopted the approach taken in *Berghuys* and applied the precedent.[55] For this reason, I do not think that the decision in *Adrian* represents a 'true' judicial *revirement* in the strict sense: the reversal in jurisprudence is in fact 'filtered' by another organ of the organization—which, quite interestingly, is neither a judicial nor a legislative body.

Regardless of the impact and influence of the Secretary-General's Bulletin ST/SGB/2004/4 on the Tribunal's decision to rule in favour of the applicant (at least partially, as previously noted with regard to the effect *ratione temporis* of the judgment), I strongly believe that the importance of the change vis-à-vis the *status* of same-sex couples within the 'UN family' entailed by the *Adrian* judgment cannot be underestimated. Following the Bulletin's spirit and letter, the UNAT subjected the granting of spousal rights to Mr. Adrian to the existence of a domestic

---

[51] See *Adrian*, para. X.

[52] *Ibidem*, para. IX.

[53] Moreover, the Tribunal notes that there is nothing in the resolution "to indicate what the contents of a new bulletin would be, much less if and when a new bulletin will be issued" (para. XII).

[54] See *Adrian*, para. XI.

[55] *Contra* Vitucci (2012), p. 133.

partnership, rather than a legal marriage, without requiring as a precondition that the partnership confer the same rights on the partners as those accorded by marriage under the legislation of the State of which Mr. Adrian is a citizen. Based on the UNAT's interpretation of the Secretary-General's Bulletin on "Family *status* for purposes of UN entitlements", the final conclusion seems to be that there is no need to verify the substantive equivalence between domestic partnerships and marriage in order to consider an official as a 'spouse' entitled to social benefits and allowances, since it is sufficient that one of these two forms of unions is recognized in the State of nationality.

Now, the Bulletin was eventually abolished and, then, replaced by the less explicit Bulletin ST/SGB/2004/13, which entered into force on 1 October 2004. This Bulletin simply states that

> [t]he practice of the Organization when determining the personal status of staff members for the purpose of entitlements under the Staff Regulations and Rules has been done, and will continue to be done, by reference to the law of nationality of the staff member concerned.

Only time will tell whether the change in jurisprudence brought about by the *Adrian* case on the basis of a Secretary-General's Bulletin will be capable of directing UNAT's future decisions on same-sex partnerships and related rights, allowances and benefits when the Tribunal will have to consider this issue without relying on Bulletin ST/SGB/2004/4 as applicable positive law.

22.4 The Jurisprudence of ILOAT on Same-Sex Marriage and Partnerships

ILOAT has ruled on same-sex couples in a number of cases, starting with its judgment of 3 February 2003 in *Mr. R. A.-O.*[56] Subsequent cases include: *Mrs. A. H.R.C.-J.*,[57] *Mr. D.B.*,[58] *Mr. E. J. P.*,[59] *Mr. A. J. H.*,[60] *Ms. J.L. H.*,[61] *Mr. A. J. H.* (further referred to as *Mr. A. J. H.nd*),[62] *Mr. E. H.*,[63] and, finally, *Mr. G. P.* (judgment of 8 February 2012).[64]

In two cases, the *Adrian* judgment examined in Sect. 22.3 above is expressly mentioned[65]; a reference is often made to the UN Secretary General's Bulletin

[56] Judgment No. 2193.

[57] Judgment No. 2549 of 12th July 2006.

[58] Judgment No. 2550 of 12th July 2006.

[59] Judgment No. 2590 of 7th February 2007.

[60] Judgment No. 2643 of 9th July 2008.

[61] Judgment No. 2760 of 9th July 2008.

[62] Judgment No. 2826 of 8th July 2009.

[63] Judgment No. 2860 of 8th July 2009.

[64] Judgment No. 3080.

[65] The *Adrian* case is cited in *Mrs. A.H.R.C.-J.*, para. 8 and *Mr. E. H.*, para. 2.

ST/SGB/2004/4 (cited above)[66]; and most decisions refer to the *Geyer* ruling delivered by the ILOAT on 29 January 1998.[67]

22.4.1 *The* Geyer *Case: Traditional (Heterosexual) Marriages and the* Renvoi *to the* Lex Celebrationis

The *Geyer* case concerns a complaint filed by Mr. Philip Gerhard Geyer against the United Nations Industrial Development Organization (further referred to as UNIDO). The UNIDO's official, who at the time was assigned to Colombo (Sri Lanka), requested the organization to pay him a dependency benefit for Miss Szabó, whom he defined as his "common-law wife", a term he asked the UNIDO to consider as equivalent to the notion of 'spouse'. Mr. Geyer thus claimed that he had the right to indicate his marital status as "Married" in the UNIDO's form entitled "Status report and request for payment of dependency benefits", since common-law marriages were valid in his country of residence (Austria), which was also the country of celebration of the marriage.[68]

The case is clearly relevant to the issue of the recognition of same-sex couples' rights by international administrative tribunals, for two reasons: first, the UNIDO Staff Regulations and Rules did not define the term 'spouse'; and, second, traditional marriages can be legally contracted in a limited number of countries—as is also the case for same-sex unions.[69]

On its part, the ILOAT clarifies that

> [a]s a general rule, and in the absence of a definition of the term, the status of spouse will flow from a marriage publicly performed and certified by an official of the State where the ceremony has taken place, such marriage being then proved by the production of an official certificate.

The Tribunal also states that:

> there may be *de facto* situations, of which 'traditional' marriages are examples, and which some States recognize as creating the status of 'spouse'.

Furthermore, in each case where there is no definition of 'spouse',

> it will be up to the staff member to prove not only the existence of the relevant fact but also the precise provisions of local law which give it consequences and the exact nature of those consequences, and he must show that such law is applicable in the context of the organization's staff regulations and rules.[70]

[66] See *Mrs. A.H.R.C.-J.*, para. 2, *Mr. D.B.*, para. 1, *Mr. A. J. H.*, para. E.

[67] With the exception of *Mr. A. J. H.*, *Mr. A. J. H.nd* and *Mr. G. P.*

[68] Judgment No. 1715.

[69] See http://legal-dictionary.thefreedictionary.com/Common-Law+Marriage and http://en.wikipedia.org/wiki/Common-law_marriage.

[70] *Geyer*, para. 10.

As a result, the Tribunal concludes that, in principle, a *de facto*/traditional marriage allows the official who has contracted it to claim the payment of benefits deriving from his/her new status. It is more a question of proving the existence of the marriage, rather than admitting a claim based on a domestic union. In this respect, the Tribunal asserts that the burden of proof is incumbent on the official who is unable to produce a marriage certificate. Now, the crucial point here is that the condition for obtaining benefits imposed by the ILOAT requires the applicant to rely on the law in force in the State of celebration rather than—as later established by the UNAT in the above examined *Berghuys* and *Adrian* cases with regard to same-sex couples—on the staff member's *lex patriae*.[71] In this connection, the main question is whether the ILOAT has recognized the legal principles arising from the *Geyer* case and applied them to gay and lesbian staff members. As we will see, the answer is both positive and negative, in the sense that same-sex unions are legally recognized, but there is no longer a referral to the *lex celebrations*.

22.4.2 *The Case-Law on Same-Sex Marriage and Partnerships, Between a Substantive Approach and the* Renvoi *to the Staff Members'* Lex Patriae

In this Sect. I will focus on the main legal issues raised by the judgments rendered by the ILOAT on same-sex couples' rights, trying to identify the common principles and the rationale that inform them.

22.4.2.1 The Applicants' Main Arguments

The first argument made by international organizations officials in their applications to the ILOAT concerns the reference to the *Geyer* case, which has been used to show that forms of opposite-sex marriage other than formally contracted marriages could, in principle, entitle also gay and lesbian staff members to be granted social benefits normally paid to other types of 'spouses', giving rise to a '*de facto* situation' in the case of same-sex domestic partnerships.[72]

The second argument lies in the changeover caused by the adoption of the UN Secretary General's Bulletin ST/SGB/2004/4, according to which all forms of (gay or straight) registered partnership should be considered equivalent to (gay or straight) marriages, with no need for the legislative/deliberative/governing body of the organization to amend the organization's Staff Regulations and Rules, having the Secretary General/Director General the power to interpret them.[73]

[71] On this issue—with reference also to the Hague Convention on Celebration and Recognition of Marriages of 1978—see Jessurun D'Oliveira (2009), pp. 512–514 and 526–530.

[72] See, for example, *Mrs. A.H.R.C.-J.*, para. 2.

[73] See, for example, *Mr. D.B.*, paras A and B.

The third argument is that prohibiting same-sex unions, whether in the form of marriage or legally recognized partnerships, infringes the principle of non-discrimination, which is both a general (and unwritten) justiciable principle of international (administrative) law and a justiciable rule enshrined in many international and European covenants concerning human rights, as well as in Art. 7 of the Universal Declaration of Human Rights.[74] Especially with regard to same-sex partnerships, reference is made also to the discrimination that may originate from the non-recognition of same-sex couples' rights as regards staff members whose State of nationality has legalized only domestic partnerships between homosexuals (and not same-sex marriage). On this point, in fact, the applicants generally stress that gays and lesbians would be discriminated not only in comparison to straight staff members who may opt for marriage rather than domestic partnership, but also, on one hand, to officials who work for the same organization and are nationals of a state where legislation is more 'progressive',[75] and, on the other, to international civil servants employed by UN entities and specialized agencies which, by contrast, recognize domestic partnerships.[76]

All the above arguments are based on two main, strongly interconnected, premises. First, unlike what was stated in *Geyer*, the applicants expressly rely on the legislation and jurisprudence of the state of nationality in order to show the similarities and, if possible, the equivalence between same-sex marriage and same-sex partnership. Second, by doing so, they urge the Tribunal to adopt a functional/substantive/non-nominalistic approach: in order for a domestic partnership to be treated like marriage and for a same-sex registered partner to be considered as a 'spouse', what is relevant is whether the law of the State of which the staff member is a national and that recognizes the partnership provides for the same social benefits as those provided for by the organization's internal law and claimed by the applicant before the Tribunal.[77]

22.4.2.2 The Defendant Organizations' Main Counter-Arguments

As a preliminary observation, defendant organizations maintain that the applicable law must be the law of the State of which the staff member in question is a national. Starting from this assumption, the first (and principal) counter-argument raised by the various organizations involved[78]—which obviously have different Staff

---

[74] See, for example, *Mr. R. A.-O.*, para. 5 and the concurring opinion of Justice Hugessen, paras 16–30.

[75] See, for example, *Mr. D.B.*, para. B.

[76] See, for example, *Mr. A. J. H.*, para. D.

[77] See, for example, *Mr. D.B.*, paras A, B, 1.

[78] The United Nations Educational, Scientific and Cultural Organization (UNESCO) (*Mr. R. A.-O.*), the International Labour Organization (ILO) (*Mrs. A.H.R.C.-J.* and *Mr. D.B.*), the International Telecommunication Union (ITU) (*Mr. A. J. H.* and *Mr. A. J. H.nd*), the International Atomic Agency (IAEA) (*Ms. J.L. H.*), the Food and Agriculture Organization of the United Nations (FAO) (*Mr. E. J. P.* and *Mr. E. H.*), and the World Health Organization (WHO) (*Mr. G. P.*).

Regulations and Rules, often (but not always)[79] lacking a definition of the term 'spouse' as including only 'husband' and 'wife', i.e. married heterosexual staff members—has been that the very existence of a national provision legalizing same-sex partnerships is sufficient proof that those unions must not be considered equivalent to marriage, since the national legislature has recognized the need to establish two different institutions. In this perspective, the term 'spouse' cannot be broadly interpreted as including also unmarried gay/lesbian officials.[80]

The reasoning of the defendant organizations is thus the opposite of that of applicant staff members (and understandably so), since what the Tribunal should consider are not the 'material' legal consequences attached to the domestic partnership in question. Hence, the ILOAT should not compare the partnership with same-sex marriage and consider whether the two forms of union may be treated similarly as regards dependency benefits for the organizations' staff. For this reason, in most cases the judgment in *Geyer* is not cited by the defendant or, when cited, it is used to show that the evidence provided by the staff member, rather than being understood in substantive terms, must be read in the sense of proving the existence of a marriage.[81] In other cases, the reference to *Geyer* is employed to stress the difference between the legal consequences of marriage and those of domestic partnerships.[82]

As a second counter-argument, the defendant organizations maintain that the only applicable internal law governing employment conditions are the Staff Regulations and Rules, thus excluding that the UN Secretary General's bulletins may be binding upon UN specialized agencies. For this reason, Bulletin ST/SGB/2004/4 may not be deemed as applicable[83]; in any case, the organizations clarify that, as already mentioned, the Bulletin "has been replaced with a less explicit test".[84] A closely connected point raised in a number of surrejoinders is that, having been created by an international treaty, an international organization is not bound by any European or national legislation.[85] As to international conventions and, more broadly, the UN legal order, the defendants submit that an interpretation of the term 'spouse' that excludes 'same-sex partner' does not infringe the principle of non-discrimination, as shown by the fact that "to date, none of the organizations has adopted any legal amendments concerning the status of domestic partnership".[86]

In one case, the defendant organization has clearly stated that the term 'spouse', as long as it is not defined by the Staff Regulations and the Staff Rules, "must be

[79] This will be clarified in Sect. 22.4.2.3.

[80] See, for instance, *Mr. E. H.*, paras C and E.

[81] See, for instance, *Mr. D.B.*, para. C.

[82] See, for instance, *Mr. A.H.R.C.-J.*, para. C.

[83] See, for instance, *Mr. D.B.*, para. A.

[84] See *Mrs. A.H.R.C.-J.*, para. A; on the new Bulletin see Sect. 22.3.2.

[85] See, for example, Mr. *R. A.-O.*, paras C and 8.

[86] *Ibidem*, para. C.

understood in the ordinary sense of 'husband' and 'wife'".[87] Moreover, for what concerns the two cases where the claimant wasn't a homosexual official who entered into a domestic partnership but a lesbian married official, it has been maintained that the term 'spouse' "refers only to persons of opposite sex".[88]

The third counter-argument is that the Director General/Secretary General of the organization is barred from amending the Staff Regulations in order to grant social benefits to the staff members, not only when those regulations clearly and repeatedly refer to "husband" and "wife",[89] but also when the organization's internal law contains passing references to those terms[90] or even when such references are absent.[91] A different approach would lead to modify both the spirit and scope implied in the notion of 'spouse'.

The fourth and conclusive counter-argument concerns the organization's practice not to recognize same-sex partnerships:

> [w]hilst it might be considered to have a discriminatory *effect* in certain cases involving countries where same-sex marriage is legally impossible, this would result from the laws of the country concerned, and the practice might nevertheless be justified by broader considerations, which warrant its continuing application "until such time as there is a change in underlying circumstantial differences, particularly in the direction of national laws which currently reflect the diversity of opinion on the subject among Member States of the UN.[92]

22.4.2.3 The Tribunal's Considerations

In all cases but three,[93] the Tribunal stated that the decision of the organization's Secretary General/Director General/Chairman must be set aside and consequently referred the case back to the competent body of the organization so that it may, in a few cases, re-examine the complainant's rights in accordance with the judgment's findings and, in most cases, grant the applicant the benefits he/she is entitled to.

As regards same-sex marriage, the Tribunal has held that the term 'spouse', if undefined, must be interpreted as including both straight and homosexual married couples. A passing reference to "husband and wife" contained in a few of the Staff Regulations (*Mr. E. J. P.*), Rules (*Mr. G. P.*) or other documents—such as guidelines—(*Ms. J.L. H.*) is not sufficient to defeat the claim. The only exception is when there is no ambiguity as to the definition of the term "spouse" as "husband" and "wife" (*Mr. A. J. H.*) according to the Staff Regulations, which are adopted—it

---

[87] *Ibidem*, para. C.

[88] See *Mr. E. J. P.*, para. C and *Ms. J.L. H.*, para. C.

[89] See *Mr. A. J. H.*, para. C.

[90] See, for example, *Mr. E. J. P.*, para. 6 and *Mr. G. P.*, para. 14.

[91] See, for example, *Mr. R. A.-O.*

[92] See *Mr. A.H.R.C.-J.*, para. C.

[93] See *Mr. R. A.-O.*, *Mr. A. J. H.* and *Mr. A. J. H.nd.*

must be recalled—by the legislative body of the organization, that is, by all member States.

As for same-sex partnerships, the Tribunal, when first resorted to rule on same-sex couples, referred to the *Geyer* judgment and stated that the status of 'spouse' can only arise in the context of marriage, "whatever form it may take".[94] This approach, however, is abandoned in later decisions, where the ILOAT combines the "long-established principle"[95] represented by the *renvoi* to the staff members' *lex patriae*[96] with a substantive interpretation of national law aimed at detecting an equivalence or even ('only') a (relevant) similarity between the rules governing (i.e. the rights and duties stemming from) same-sex partnerships and those governing (i.e. the rights and duties stemming from) marriages.[97] In this respect, the Tribunal notes that there may be situations in which the status of spouse can be recognized in the absence of a marriage, provided that the staff member concerned can show the precise provisions of local law on which he or she relies.[98]

The final outcome is that, unless otherwise clearly established in the organization's Staff Regulations, the applicant must always be granted the rights he/she claims if it can be inferred from national legislation and jurisprudence[99] that

> [r]egistered partners have the same rights and duties as married couples in relation to one another and to society.[100]

22.5 Concluding Remarks

The jurisprudence of ILOAT is most welcome insofar as it completes and develops that of the UNAT. It completes it in that it affirms the need for a substantive approach, which, by focusing on the legal consequences/effects, differs from the position adopted in the *Adrian* case, where all registered partnerships—regardless of the social benefits attached to them at the national level—were covered by the organization's internal law. It develops it in that, unlike the UN judges' implementation of the Secretary General's Bulletin on family statuses, it is the ILOAT itself that provides a broad interpretation of the term 'spouse'.

---

[94] See *Mr. R. A.-O.*, para. 10.

[95] See *Mr. G. P.*, para. 10.

[96] For an interpretation of the term 'spouse' only in the light of the organization's internal law, see the dissenting opinion by Gordillo in *Mr. E. H.*, further developed in Gordillo (2006).

[97] By developing a reasoning focused on the legal effects and consequences of domestic partnerships.

[98] See *Mr. D.B.*, para. 3.

[99] See the reference to the jurisprudence of the German Constitutional Court in *Mr. D.B.*, para. 4, and that to the reformed French PACS in *Mr. E. H.*, paras 19–21.

[100] See *Mr. G. P.*, para. 16.

The case-law of the two tribunals, however, converge on the following aspects: on the one hand, the referral to the law of the State of which the staff member is a national as a point of reference for determining his/her marital status; and, on the other, an evolutive interpretation of the law that, at first, accorded greater legal protection to same-sex married couples and, then, extended said protection to same-sex couples in a domestic partnership.

This approach raises a number of issues, including: on the one hand, the impact of a member State's law on the foreign partner of a gay international official who is a national of that State; on the other hand, the human rights implications and the role of the principle of non-discrimination based on sexual orientation. These concerns become extremely sensitive when the official's State of nationality does not provide any forms of legal recognition, i.e. neither same-sex marriages nor domestic partnerships between homosexuals are recognized.

However, despite these concerns, it must be strongly welcome that international administrative tribunals, unlike some national supreme/constitutional courts,[101] prefer to rely on a dynamic, systematic and teleological—even 'activist', according to others[102]—interpretation of the law rather than on a static, formal constructivist and *originalist* approach. Certain legal concepts naturally evolve and, as a consequence, must be interpreted taking into account changes in social and family behaviour, relations and perceptions: in different ways and various degrees, this notion informs the UNAT's and ILOAT's approach to the issue of same-sex couples' rights. The principal outcome of such an interpretation is that, even though only on condition that the home country recognizes same-sex partnership and/or marriage, the jurisprudence of both ILOAT and UNAT is clearly aimed at abandoning a 'traditional' conception of family and extending the scope of the provisions on family allowances, so as to include also gay and lesbian international officials.[103]

The (rationale behind the) choice to use the law of the staff member's home country as the point of reference for determining eligibility is indeed consistent with a flexible approach which, while leading to different results from country to country, allows international organizations to appreciate, tolerate and respect the world's many cultures as reflected in their membership, without imposing a single solution through a single conception of 'family'.

Considering the trend towards the recognition of same-sex couples' rights at both national and international levels,[104] it is not hard to imagine that, in the more

[101] It is the case, for instance, of the Italian Constitutional Court (see the chapter by Fidalgo de Freitas and Tega in this volume).

[102] On these terms and notions in the context of the relationship and dialogue between the legislature and the judiciary see, amongst others, Cappelletti (1984); Waldron (2006); Rubenfeld (2001). With specific regard to same-sex couples, see Gallo and Winkler (2013), pp. 23–26.

[103] We may assume that the jurisprudence of the UNDT and UNAsT will have the same purpose once they deal with the same issue.

[104] On the lack of a specific covenant aimed at protecting LGBT (lesbian, gay, bisexual, transsexual) people, see Hodson (2004).

or less near future, international administrative tribunals will apply the principle of non-discrimination (and, therefore, grant the social benefits provided for by an international organization in its internal law governing employment conditions) to situations where a staff member is prevented, in his or her country of nationality, from contracting a same-sex marriage and/or entering into a same-sex partnership. All the same, at present it seems that, by their nature, no general rules of international law are apt to prevail over the internal law of international organizations,[105] imposing a binding obligation on these organizations and their organs—including administrative tribunals—to treat married and unmarried (but registered) gay/lesbian partners as equivalent to married and unmarried (but registered) straight partners.[106] In this regard, international organizations and administrative tribunals have, in principle, an alternative option, which has been partly formulated in *Mr. R. A.-O.*, namely the application of the law in force in the State of celebration of the marriage or conclusion of the partnership.[107] It is, however, only a *de iure condendo* reasoning, not ready yet to combine it with the *lex patriae* principle, which remains the *Grundnorm* for recognition of family rights in the jurisprudence of international organizations' administrative tribunals.

References

Aamir AH (2009) The international civil service: the idea and the reality. In: De Cooker C (ed) International administration. Law and management practice in international organizations. Martinus Nijhoff Publishers, Leiden/Boston, pp 3–20

Akehurst MB (1967) The law governing employment in international organizations. Cambridge University Press, Cambridge

Amerasinghe CF (1988) The law of the international civil service (as applied by International Administrative Tribunals). Oxford University Press, Oxford

Amerasinghe CF (2005) Principles of the institutional law of international organizations, 2nd edn. Cambridge University Press, Cambridge

Balladore Pallieri G (1969) Le droit interne des organisations internationals. Recueil des cours 127 (II):1–37

Bastid S (1957) Les tribunaux administratifs internationaux et leur jurisprudence. Recueil des cours 92(II):343–517

Beigbeder Y (2009) Administrative and structural reform in the organisations of the UN family. In: De Cooker C (ed) International administration. Law and management practice in international organizations. Martinus Nijhoff Publishers, Leiden/Boston, pp 111–142

Beigbeder Y (2012) Civil service, international. In: Wolfrum R (ed) Max Planck Encyclopedia of Public International Law, vol II. pp 167–175

Cahier PH (1963) Le droit interne des organisations internationales. Revue générale de droit international public 3:563–602

[105] On general principles of law applied by international administrative tribunals see, amongst others, Germond (2009); on the primacy of general principles of international law over Staff Regulations and Rules see Gallo (2012), pp. 287–288.

[106] *Contra* see the dissenting opinions of Justices Hugessen and Rondón de Sansó in *Mr. R. A.-O.*

[107] See Jessurun d'Oliveira (2009), pp. 526–527.

Cappelletti M (1984) Giudici legislatori? Giuffrè, Milano
Davì A (2012) Le renvoi en droit international privé contemporain. Recueil des cours 352:3–521
Elias O, Thomas M (2012) Administrative tribunals of international organizations. In: Giorgetti C (ed) The rules, practice, and jurisprudence of international courts and tribunals. Martinus Nijhoff Publishers, Leiden/Boston, pp 159–188
Gallo D (2012) *Status*, privilegi, immunità e tutela giurisdizionale dei funzionari delle organizzazioni internazionali. In: Del Veecchio A (ed) Diritto delle organizzazioni internazionali. Edizioni Scientifiche Italiane, Napoli, pp 273–314
Gallo D, Winkler M (2013) The construction of same-sex families in Europe through vertical and horizontal dialogue: the role of Supranational Courts, National Judges and Legislators. http://www.jus.uio.no/english/research/projects/multirights/docs/paper-mrannual-2013/gallo-winkler-construction-same-sex-families-.pdf
Gascon y Marin J (1932) Les fonctionnaires internationaux. Recueil des cours 32(III):721–797
Germond L (2009) Les principes généraux selon le Tribunal administratif de l'O.I.T. Pedone, Paris
Gordillo A (2006) The administrative law of international organisations: checks and balances in law making – the case of discrimination. Eur Rev Pub Law 18:289–312
Gutteridge F (2009) The ILO administrative tribunal. In: De Cooker C (ed) International administration. Law and management practice in international organizations. Martinus Nijhoff Publishers, Leiden/Boston, pp 655–686
Hodson L (2004) Family values: the recognition of same-sex relationships in international law. Neth Q Hum Rights 22:33–57
Jessurun d'Oliveira HU (2009) How do international organisations cope with the personal *Status* of their staff members? Some observations on the recognition of (same-sex) marriages in international organisations. In: Bariatti S, Venturini G (eds) *Liber Amicorum* Fausto Pocar – Nuovi strumenti del diritto internazionale privato. Giuffrè, Milano, pp 505–531
Hwang PH (2009) Reform of the administration of justice system at the United Nations. Law Pract Int Courts Tribunals 8:191–224
Jenks CW (1962) The proper law of international organizations. Stevens, London
Pellet A, Ruzié D (1993) Les fonctionnaires internationaux. Pedone, Paris
Pisillo Mazzeschi R (1991) Funzionario internazionale. Digesto delle discipline pubblicistiche VII:44–55
Rubenfeld J (2001) Freedom and time – a theory of constitutional self-government. Yale University Press, New Haven
Ruzié D (2004) Les fonctionnaires internationaux. Pedone, Paris
Sands PH, Klein P (2009) Bowett's law of International Institutions, 6th edn. Martinus Nijhoff Publishers, Leiden/Boston
Schermers HG, Blokker N (2011) International institutional law. Unity within diversity, 5th edn. Martinus Nijhoff Publishers, Leiden/Boston
Vitucci MC (2012) La tutela internazionale dell'orientamento sessuale. Jovene, Napoli
Waldron J (2006) The core case against judicial review. Yale Law J 115:1346–1406
Wood M (2009) United Nations administrative tribunal, applications for review. In: Wolfrum R (ed) Max Planck Encyclopedia of Public International Law X:209–216

Chapter 23
Same-Sex Couples Before *Quasi*-Jurisdictional Bodies: The Case of the UN Human Rights Committee*

Luca Paladini

Abstract After giving an overview on the HRC and its competence to examine individual communications, the chapter analyses the case-law on LGBT and same-sex couples issues, in the latter case with regard to the right to marry and the right to the "widow pension", i.e. the aspects specifically considered in its case-law. Different interpretative methods in approaching same-sex couples issues arise; in the case of marriage the literal interpretation of the ICCPR (Art. 23) does not support the right to marry between same-sex partners, while a more teleological approach to the Covenant (Art. 26) allowed to recognize them some rights not expressly provided for in the same treaty. The future case-law will tell if the Covenant can constitute the basis for the recognition of new LGBT rights, also with regard to the recognition of the sentimental link between two same-sex partners independently of the marriage. The chapter ends with some brief considerations on the HRC as a "desirable forum" for the protection of LGBT rights for people living in countries both benefiting and not of a regional system of protection of human rights.

23.1 Preliminary Remarks

In addition to national and international courts, some international bodies, established and acting in the framework of the UN, can represent approachable *fora* for the protection of LGBT and same-sex couples' rights.

One first option is offered by the complaint procedure before the Human Rights Council, which can be initiated by individuals, groups of persons and NGOs in

*The Chapter is updated to the 107th session of the UN Human Rights Committee (11th–28th March 2013)

L. Paladini (✉)
University Institute SSML Carlo Bo, Rome, Italy
e-mail: l.paladini@ssmlcarlobo.it

D. Gallo et al. (eds.), *Same-Sex Couples before National, Supranational and International Jurisdictions*, DOI 10.1007/978-3-642-35434-2_23,

cases of violation of human rights and fundamental freedoms.[1] Nevertheless, that procedure seems more focused on getting States to respect human rights obligations than on affording individuals a remedy to guarantee their personal situations. In fact, the Council, which decides only on cases of gross and reliably demonstrable violations of human rights, adopts a non-binding act directed to involved States, providing, *inter alia*, for the monitoring of the situation, the request to give further information or the invitation to the UN High Commissioner of Human Rights to provide its technical cooperation.[2]

Another chance is represented by the expert bodies created by some human rights international treaties concluded in the framework of the UN. Those bodies (*rectius*, committees) are tasked with monitoring the respect of the rights protected by the relevant conventions and, under particular circumstances, they can receive and analyse communications coming from individuals and pronounce views on the merits of cases brought to their attention. Here the competence to ascertain a violation of human rights obligations implies the establishment of a remedy directly aimed to guarantee individual situations, thus the committees represent direct *fora* for the protection of individuals' rights.

This is the case of the CEDAW, i.e. the Committee established by the Convention on the Elimination of Discrimination against Women of 1979, or of the CAT, which is the Committee monitoring respect of the Convention against Torture and Other Cruel, Inhuman or Degrading Treatment or Punishment of 1984. Their practice on LGBT issues is quite limited: some (unsuccessful for the complainants) CAT views on cases of expulsion to another State entailing the risk of being tortured also because of sexual orientation[3] and a CEDAW General Comment on the interpretation of Art. 2 of the Convention of 1979, which underlines the States parties' legal duty to enact legislation against discrimination in all fields of women's lives and throughout their lifespan, also with regard to lesbians, considered as one of those women groups vulnerable to discrimination through laws and regulations.[4]

---

[1] Human Rights Council resolution 5/1 of 18th June 2007, para. 87.

[2] *Ibidem*, para. 109. As for the promotion of LGBT rights, see in general the Human Rights Council resolution 17/19 on human rights, sexual orientation and gender identity of 17th June 2011 and the subsequent High Commissioner's for Human Rights report on discriminatory laws and practices and acts of violence against individuals based on their sexual orientation and gender identity of 17th November 2011. The latter recommends to UN Member States, *inter alia*, to take measures to prevent torture and other forms of cruel treatment on grounds of sexual orientation and gender identity and to enact comprehensive anti-discrimination legislation that includes discrimination on grounds of sexual orientation and gender identity among prohibited grounds. In literature, see Maaldon (2009).

[3] Views in no. 31/1995 *Mr. X. and Mrs. Y v. The Netherlands* 20th November 1995 (unfounded), no. 190/2001 *K.S.Y. v. The Netherlands* 15th May 2003 (no violation) and no. 213/2002 *E.J.V.M. v. Sweden* 14th November 2003 (no violation).

[4] General Recommendation 28 on the Core Obligations of States Parties under Art. 2 of the Convention on the Elimination of All Forms of Discrimination against Women, para. 31.

The practice on LGBT and same-sex couples issues is more interesting when considering the Human Rights Committee (HRC or Committee), the treaty-based body composed by 18 experts of human rights also with legal experience,[5] established to monitor respect of the rights and principles proclaimed in the International Covenant on Civil and Political Rights of 1966 (ICCPR or Covenant).[6] Since it started its works, in 1977, the Committee has analysed a remarkable number of cases on the violation of ICCPR rights and, with regard to our field of investigation, it has considered cases both on LGBT individual rights and on same-sex couples—the latter with specific regard to the legal recognition of the sentimental link between two same-sex partners and to the survivor pension for the same-sex partner, i.e. one of the so-called material consequences. To date, the HRC has not adopted views on same-sex couples and parental consequences, but the privacy policy on pending cases, which remain confidential until the final decision,[7] does not allow reporting about the next pronunciation of the Committee on this sensitive issue.

It can be argued that the HRC represents for individuals the most relevant *forum* for the protection of LGBT and same-sex couples' rights in the constellation of the UN treaty monitoring bodies, and this chapter will address its decisions in this field of law. Before starting the analysis, a terminological clarification is due: even if the Committee does not pronounce judgments, the terms "jurisprudence" and "case-law" will be used in referring to its decisions because, as the following pages will highlight, there are meaningful similarities between the HRC and a court, and between the former body's decisions and courts' judgments.

23.2 The Human Rights Committee's Monitor Functions

According to the Covenant and its First Optional Protocol (the Protocol),[8] the HRC has four monitor functions. Under Art. 40 ICCPR it receives and examines reports from States parties on the measures they have adopted to give effect to the Covenant rights and, after a public dialog with the States involved, it publishes its concluding observation in response.[9] It also elaborates General Comments,

---

[5] On the Committee and the election of its members, see Arts. 28–39 ICCPR. In the literature, see the references at the end of this chapter, with specific regard to books and commentaries.

[6] This important human rights treaty was signed in New York on the 16th December 1966 and entered into force on the 23rd March 1976; currently there are 167 States parties.

[7] Rule 102 HRC Rules of Procedure (last version: 11th January 2012, available at: www.ohchr.org).

[8] The Covenant has also a Second Protocol on the abolition of the death penalty, signed in New York on the 15th December 1989. Currently there are 78 States parties.

[9] See Ando (2009), pp. 6ff. With regard to LGBT, recently the Committee invited, for instance, Japan to amend its legislation to include sexual orientation among the prohibited grounds of discrimination (HRC Annual Report A/64/40 (Vol. I), from 94th to 96th sessions, p. 34) and Jamaica to decriminalize sexual relations between consenting same-sex adults (HRC Annual Report A/67/40 (Vol. I), 103rd and 104th sessions, p. 23.

i.e. general statements of law interpreting articles or general issues of the Covenant.[10] Under Art. 41 ICCPR the Committee has jurisdiction on inter-State complaints on the alleged infringement of the Covenant,[11] while the Protocol confers on it the competence to receive and consider complaints lodged by individuals on the violation of their ICCPR rights and freedoms.

23.2.1 Focus on the Competence to Examine Individual Communications

The HRC competence to examine individual communications regards the States parties to the Protocol, thus only individuals subject to their jurisdiction can address a complaint to the Committee. At the end of 2012 there were 114 States parties to the Protocol (*versus* 167 ICCPR States parties), and this remarkable number is likely to increase in light of the growing attention for the respect of human rights at the international level.

23.2.1.1 Sending and Registration of Individual Communications

Individuals can send their communications to the HRC in Geneva, substantiating the violation of their ICCPR rights and including, in case of fear of irreparable damage or prejudice, a reasoned request for *interim* measures. The procedure before the Committee is informal and free and does not require legal representation. Anyway, the assistance of a lawyer could be useful, for instance in light of the several admissibility criteria provided for in the Protocol or considering that the procedure is entirely written.[12] Communications have to be registered prior to being brought before the HRC; communications that fail to be sufficiently substantiated cannot be registered, and in this case the UN offices open a provisional file and contact the complainant in order to obtain additional details and information.

---

[10] To date, the HRC has adopted 35 General Comments; the first one, on the reporting obligation under Art. 40 ICCPR, was adopted on the 27th July 1981, the last one, on Art. 9 ICCPR (Liberty and security of person) during the 107th session. General Comments can be found at: www.ohchr.org.

[11] To date this function has not been exercised.

[12] Potential complainants have to consider that there is no possibility to orally express their arguments during hearings. Guidance for potential complainants and their legal counsel can be found in the handbook by Joseph et al. (2006), also available on line, at http://www.omct.org/files/2006/11/3979/handbook4_full_eng.pdf.

Not always does a provisional file turn into a registered case. Pursuant to the principle of *audiatur et altera pars*, registered complaints are communicated to the State party concerned in order to obtain its comments.

23.2.1.2 The Admissibility Criteria Under the Protocol

The Protocol imposes several requirements in order to consider individual communications admissible. The practice shows that a considerable number of complaints are declared inadmissible and not brought to the attention of the HRC,[13] thus it is advisable to pay particular attention to the relevant criteria.

The Criteria Under Arts. 1, 2 and 3 of the Protocol

Arts. 1 and 2 provide that communications have to be submitted by individuals, who are allegedly victims of a violation of ICCPR rights, as a consequence of the conduct by a State party to the Covenant and the Protocol having jurisdiction on complainants.[14] The violation must have occurred after the entry into force of the Protocol for the State concerned. Before submitting a communication, all available judicial domestic remedies have to be exhausted by the victim.[15] Under Art. 3, communications which are anonymous, which consist in an abuse of the right of submission or which are incompatible with the ICCPR[16] are inadmissible.

Those criteria have been interpreted in the HRC case-law.[17] For instance, the Committee has clarified that only individuals (and not legal persons) can submit a communication and that an unexplained delay in submitting a complaint amounts to an abuse of right.[18] The Committee has also considered communications when domestic remedies had not been exhausted, if the application resulted unreasonably prolonged. Certainly those clarifications provide valuable guidance for future complainants.

---

[13] Forty-three percent, according to Hennebel (2007), p. 346.

[14] Being a resident is not a precondition for being under the jurisdiction of a State party, as the "passport cases" demonstrate (view in no. 57/1979 *S. Vidal v. Uruguay* 23rd March 1982 and view in no. 125/1982 *M.M.Q. v. Uruguay* 6th April 1984).

[15] Normally, it is not necessary to have exhausted also extraordinary remedies, e.g. administrative procedures or recourse to the Ombudsman (Hanski and Scheinin 2003, pp. 20–21).

[16] For instance, with regard to Art. 25 ICCPR and the non-elective nature of the Spanish monarchy, see view in no. 1745/2007 *Costa v. Spain* 1st April 2008.

[17] For an accurate analysis of the admissibility criteria under the Protocol, with references to the HRC case-law, see, *ex multis*, Bair (2005) and Möller and De Zayas (2009).

[18] For instance, see the view in no. 1591/2007 *Brown v. Namibia* 23rd July 2008.

The Coordination Clause Under Art. 5, Para. 2, of the Protocol

The admissibility of a communication also depends on compliance with the coordination clause *ex* Art. 5, para. 2: the HRC cannot examine communications if the same matter[19] is being handled via another procedure of international investigation or settlement.

The clause is aimed to avoid the simultaneous pendency of the same matter before the Committee and another *forum* for the protection of human rights, for instance another quasi-jurisdictional body or a regional court on human rights.[20] By staying the proceeding, Art. 5, para. 2 does not exclude that the HRC can examine the same matter after the other *forum* has decided the case, and this can happen when the latter decision is not favourable to the applicant.[21] *De facto*, the temporary suspension effect produced by Art. 5, para. 2 provides individuals with a further level of protection in case of unsuccessful complaint before a regional body.[22] Although this chain of complaints can give rise to conflicting decisions and enforcement problems, it should be also pointed out that the possibility to seek subsequent protection from different bodies also increases the chances to obtain justice, i.e. an outcome never to be taken for granted in judicial or quasi-judicial proceedings.

Declarations and Reservations on Art. 5, Para. 2

Individual communication regarding violations of ICCPR rights by some European Countries,[23] by El Salvador, by Sri Lanka and by Uganda cannot be considered by the Committee if another procedure of international investigation or settlement has already examined the same case, because those States entered a declaration of interpretation or a reservation on Art. 5, para. 2.[24] Also Austria made a reservation,

[19] More precisely, "... the concept of "the same matter" within the meaning of Art. 5 (2) (a) of the Optional Protocol had to be understood as including the same claim concerning the same individual, submitted by him or someone else who has the standing to act on his behalf before the other international body" (view in no. 75/1980 *Fanali v. Italy* 31st March 1983).

[20] Möller and De Zayas (2009).

[21] Which happened, for instance, with regard to previous ECHR bodies decision in the view in no. 201/1985 *Hendriks v. The Netherlands* 27th July 1988 and in the view in no. 1463/2006 *Gratzinger v. The Czech Republic* 25th October 2007. In the former case after the declaration of inadmissibility *ratione personae* adopted by the European Commission of Human Rights. In the latter one, a similar claim has been submitted to the European Court of Human Rights, which declared it inadmissible *ratione materiae*.

[22] Hennebel (2007), p. 390.

[23] Croatia, Denmark, France, Germany, Iceland, Ireland, Italy, Luxembourg, Malta, Norway, Poland, Moldova, Romania, Slovenia, Spain, Sweden, Turkey.

[24] The Russian Federation also made a declaration, reproducing the wording of Art. 5, para. 2, and thus leaving untouched the HRC competence on cases already decided by other international

but with regard to the competence of the Committee on cases already examined by the European Commission (now Court) of Human Rights.[25]

As to the European States, the spirit of declarations and reservations consists in the intention to avoid conflicts of decisions between the Strasbourg Court and the HRC, and can be traced back to the indication, adopted in 1970 by the ECHR Committee of Ministers, to normally utilize the ECHR procedures when both the Convention and the Covenant protect the invoked right.[26] Today, in light of the developments in the European Union and the entry into force of the Lisbon Treaty and of the Charter of Fundamental Rights, those declarations and reservations should produce their effects also with regard to the judgments by the EU Court of Justice, except for Austria. The same spirit underlies the reservations made by El Salvador with regard to the Inter-American Court of Human Rights and by Uganda in respect of the (newly operational) African Court on Human and Peoples' Rights.

The patchy picture emerging from the States parties' approach to the Protocol allows allocating the individuals under their jurisdictions to two separate groups: those who can benefit from an additional chance of obtaining justice, and those who have to decide in advance which *forum* to seize. For the latter the ultimate effect is a "forum closing" one along with the reduced chance to obtain justice following a violation of their ICCPR protected rights.

23.2.1.3 Pronunciation of Views and the Follow-Up Procedure

Normally the HRC decides on admissibility and on the merit in the same sitting, adopting a decision of inadmissibility or pronouncing a view. In case of violation of the Covenant, the view indicates which remedy or remedies the violator State has to implement in order to give satisfaction to the victim—for instance, a change of legislation, payment of compensation or the *restitutio in integrum.*

Since 1990 compliance of the States parties with the Committee's view has been monitored through the follow-up procedure.[27] A Special Rapporteur, appointed among the HRC members, keeps contacts with violator States in order to gather information on the enforcement of the measures taken to give effect to the views. Not always do States reply to the Rapporteur's requests. The procedure makes the level of compliance with the views visible and, since one of the Rapporteur's duties is to cooperate in preparing the Annual Report addressed to the UN General Assembly, it allows publicising all the cases of non-compliance. This "naming

settings bodies (accordingly, see view in no. 712/1996 *Smirnova v. Russian Federation* 5th July 2004, para. 9.2).

[25] For example, see the view in no. 998/2001 *Althammer v. Austria* 8th August 2003, para. 8.3.

[26] Some other ECHR parties (for instance, the UK) have not ratified the Protocol, removing *ex ante* the risk of conflict of decisions, but the majority of the ECHR States parties have not embraced that invitation and ratified the Protocol without reservations, in order to preserve the integrity of the universal system of human rights protection.

[27] On the follow-up of views procedure, see Ando (2002).

and shaming" policy should stimulate reluctant States parties to accomplish the Committee's decisions. The practice shows an encouraging level of compliance with views[28] and the progressive decrease of non-replying States parties.

Since *Kone v. Senegal* of 1994[29] the Committee has started coupling the indication of remedies with a formula aimed to underline the legal nature of obligations deriving from the Covenant and the Protocol—that is, in substance, the duty to comply with its views.[30]

23.2.1.4 Nature and Authoritativeness of the HRC and Its Views

The HRC is not a judicial institution and its members are not judges, and this is an unquestionable point, not only in the literature.[31] It is normally considered as a quasi-jurisdictional body, but this qualification is disputable as well since the Committee itself affirmed to be neither a court nor a body with a quasi-judicial mandate.[32] Certainly its views have no binding force in law and there is no enforcement mechanism aimed to guarantee compliance with them.

Nevertheless, it is fairly common to consider that the HRC behaves like a judicial body. In that regard, some indications come from the procedure on individual communications, which follows a judicial *iter*. For instance, communications have to respect precise admissibility requirements; the Committee acts as an arbitrator in an adversary proceeding; it decides on admissibility first and on the merits only afterwards for admitted cases; its views have a court-like design[33] and consist in conclusions of law; and finally, HRC members can submit individual opinions. Furthermore, the HRC function to elaborate interpretative General Comments on the ICCPR substantially mirrors the competence that some supra/international courts have to interpret authoritatively the relevant treaties—as it happens, for instance, with the Strasbourg Court in respect of the ECHR.

Certainly the strength of the HRC lies in its authoritativeness,[34] which results in turn from many factors such as its composition of independent experts, the judicial

---

[28] De Zayas (2009), p. 37.

[29] View in no. 386/1989 *Kone v. Senegal* 21st October 1994.

[30] The formula reads: "Bearing in mind that, by becoming a party to the Optional Protocol, the State party has recognized the competence of the Committee to determine whether there has been a violation of the Covenant or not and that, pursuant to Art. 2 of the Covenant, the State party has undertaken to ensure to all individuals within its territory or subject to its jurisdiction the rights recognized in the Covenant and to provide an effective and enforceable remedy when it has been determined that a violation has occurred, the Committee wishes to receive from the State party, within 90 days, information about the measures taken to give effect to the Committee's Views. The State party is also requested to publish the present Views and to have them widely disseminated in the official language of the State party".

[31] Case C-249/96 *Grant v South-West Trains Ltd.* [1998] ECR I-621, para. 46.

[32] Selected decisions of the HRC under the Optional Protocol, Vol. 3, 2002, para. 7.

[33] Nowak (2005), p. 892.

[34] Office of the United Nations High Commissioner for Human Rights 2005, p. 14.

spirit of its procedures, and the importance of its views[35] along with the independence and seriousness of its case-law.[36]

23.3 The HRC Case-Law on LGBT Rights

The case-law on LGBT rights does not directly regard same-sex couples issues, but a mention of the relevant views is due, in light of the delicate issues examined, i.e. the criminalization of homosexuality and freedom of expression.

In *Toonen v. Australia*,[37] "the first juridical recognition of gay rights on a universal level",[38] the Committee found that the provisions of the Tasmanian Criminal Code criminalizing homosexual intercourses were in contrast with Art. 17, which protects privacy and family, in connection with Art. 2, para. 1, ICCPR for the interferences they produced in the complainant's private life.[39] Australia's justifications on the need to maintain the contested provisions for moral reasons and to limit the spread of HIV/AIDS did not convince the Committee, since they did not appear reasonable in the circumstances of the case. In particular, the contested provisions had not been enforced for years, thus they were not so fundamental in protecting moral,[40] and there was no direct link with the effective control of HIV/AIDS spread. The Committee did not consider it necessary to verify the violation of the invoked Art. 26 ICCPR, disappointing those who expected an in-depth analysis of the discriminatory aspect of the contested provisions, e.g. the lack of prohibition of sexual intercourses between women.[41] It is worth underlining that here (and only in two more cases) the HRC found a violation of the prohibition of discrimination under Art. 2, para. 1, ICCPR, which affirms the general obligation of States parties to ensure the rights recognized in the Covenant, while normally those violations have been ascertained under Art. 26.[42]

---

[35] Tyagi (2011), p. 778, compares views to the teachings of the most highly qualified publicists of the various nations under Art. 38 of the International Court of Justice Statute.

[36] Independence has to be seen as lack of influence from other bodies' case-law (Conte and Burchill 2009, p. 16). Conversely, the HRC case-law has been applied and used in other contexts, both judicial—national and international—and not (Tyagi 2011, pp. 787ff).

[37] View in no. 488/1992 *Toonen v. Australia* 31st March 1994.

[38] Joseph (1994), p. 410. The case is important also for the notion of "victim" under Art. 1 of the Protocol, since the complainant had never been arrested or prosecuted because of his sexual orientation and the contested legislation had not been enforced for years. Nevertheless, the HRC found that future enforcement of the contested legislation could not be excluded and accepted the complainant's position on its impact on his and many people's life (paras 2.7 and 5.1), *de facto* extending the notion of victim to that of "potential victim".

[39] There are no details on the violation of Art. 2 ICCPR, but clearly the point is that all States parties have to guarantee the right recognized by the Covenant without discriminations.

[40] Thus public morality is a relative value, as Joseph et al. (2005), Art. 17, wittily observe.

[41] See individual opinion of HRC member Wennergren and, in the literature, *inter alia*, Joseph (1994).

[42] Nowak (2005), p. 47.

In two more cases that were decided with a 30-year interval between them, the Committee took into consideration the freedom of expression *ex* Art. 19 ICCPR with regard to sexual orientation, changing its position on public moral as a valid ground for the limitation of human rights.

Initially, in *Hertzberg v. Finland* of 1982[43] the HRC did not find a violation of Art. 19 in a case concerning both some decisions adopted by the Finnish Television to censure radio and TV programmes dealing with homosexuality and the criminal charges brought against the editor of a radio programme about job discrimination on the ground of sexual orientation. The Committee accepted the State's justification that freedom of expression could be limited for moral reasons, in particular the dis-encouragement of indecent behaviour between persons of the same sex (at that time punished by the Finnish Penal Code) and specifically minors. The HRC recognized a certain "margin of discretion" to States in protecting public moral, because it differs widely in ICCPR States parties and there is no universally applicable common standard.[44]

In *Fedotova v. Russian Federation* of 2012[45] the Committee reached opposite conclusions and established the violation of Art. 19 read in conjunction with Art. 26 ICCPR. The case regarded an openly lesbian woman activist in the field of LGBT rights, who was ordered to pay a heavy fine because in 2009 she had held a picket to promote tolerance towards gays and lesbians near a secondary school building in violation of a domestic provision. The State party argued that the picket constituted a public action aimed at involving minors in sexual activities or at encouraging any particular sexual orientation, i.e. substantially the same arguments adduced by the State party in *Hertzberg v. Finland.* The HRC did not share those arguments, observing that

> (w)hile noting that the State party invokes the aim to protect the morals, health, rights and legitimate interests of minors, the Committee considers that the State party has not shown that a restriction on the right to freedom of expression in relation to "propaganda of homosexuality" – as opposed to propaganda of heterosexuality or sexuality generally – among minors is based on reasonable and objective criteria. Moreover, no evidence which would point to the existence of factors justifying such a distinction has been advanced[46]

and, with specific regard to the freedom of expression, it affirmed that

> by displaying posters that declared "Homosexuality is normal" and "I am proud of my homosexuality" near a secondary school building, the author has not made any public actions aimed at involving minors in any particular sexual activity or at advocating any particular sexual orientation. Instead, she was giving expression to her sexual identity and seeking understanding for it.[47]

---

[43] View in no. 61/1979 *Hertzberg v. Finland* 2nd April 1982.

[44] This the only case in which the Committee adopted that "margin approach". As noted, *inter alia*, by Joseph et al. 2005, the recognized margin seems to mirror the ECHR margin of appreciation.

[45] View in no. 1932/2010 *Fedotova v. Russian Federation* 31st October 2012.

[46] *Ibidem*, para. 10.6.

[47] *Ibidem*, para. 10.7.

This is an important case for two reasons. It is the first one ascertaining infringement of a ban on discrimination on grounds of sexual orientation with regard to LGBT individual rights also under Art. 26 ICCPR,[48] thus it represents a milestone for activists, advocates and commentators. Secondly, it testifies to the decreasing importance of public moral in limiting human rights: while in *Hertzberg v. Finland* moral reasons represented a valid justification in limiting the freedom of expression, in *Fedotova v. Russian Federation* the Committee, along the trail of the General Comments 22 and 34[49] (and perhaps *Toonen v. Australia*),[50] stated that

> "the concept of morals derives from many social, philosophical and religious traditions; consequently, limitations... for the purpose of protecting morals must be based on principles not deriving exclusively from a single tradition". Any such limitations must be understood in the light of universality of human rights and the principle of non-discrimination.[51]

23.4 The HRC Case-Law on Same-Sex Couples Issues

Coming to same-sex couples issues, the relevant HRC case-law is confined to one case on same-sex marriages and two cases on the right to the deceased partner's pension. Even if reduced in number, those three views are interesting because of the conclusions reached by the HRC on the right to marry under Art. 23 and on the prohibition to discriminate under Art. 26 ICCPR.

[48] In the past, the Committee could not consider the merits of some cases brought to its attention but declared inadmissible (views in no. 480/1991 *Fuenzalida v. Ecuador* 12nd July 1996 and no. 1512/2006 *Dean v. New Zealand* 17th March 2009).

[49] See General Comment 22 on Art. 18 ICCPR (para. 8) and General Comment 34 on Art. 19 ICCPR (para. 32).

[50] *Supra*, note 37, para. 8.6: "The Committee cannot accept either that for the purposes of article 17 of the Covenant, moral issues are exclusively a matter of domestic concern, as this would open the door to withdrawing from the Committee's scrutiny a potentially large number of statutes interfering with privacy".

[51] *Supra*, note 45, para. 10.5. *Ante litteram*, Mr. Opsahl, Mr. Lallah and Mr. Tarnopolsky observed in their individual opinion in *Hertzberg v. Finland*: "... the conception and contents of public morals referred to in article 19 (3) are relative and changing. State-imposed restrictions on freedom of expression must allow for this fact and should not be applied so as to perpetuate prejudice or promote intolerance. It is of special importance to protect freedom of expression as regards minority views, including those that offend, shock or disturb the majority. Therefore, even if such laws as paragraph 9 (2) of chapter 20 of the Finnish Penal Code may reflect prevailing moral conceptions, this is in itself not sufficient to justify it under article 19 (3). It must also be shown that the application of the restriction is 'necessary'".

23.4.1 The Right to Marry

Joslin v. New Zealand of 2002[52] regarded two lesbian couples living in *de facto* relationships involving a sentimental link, sexual intercourse and shared responsibilities for their children out of previous marriages, finances and common home. Both couples applied for a marriage license, rejected under the New Zealand Marriage Act 1955 because it confines marriage to the union between a man and a woman. The internal courts, seized by the complainants, confirmed such an interpretation of the domestic law.[53]

The complainants alleged the violation of several provisions of the Covenant, i.e. Art. 16 on the right to be recognized as persons before the law, Art. 17 on the right to privacy and family life and Art. 26 ICCPR on equality before the law and prohibition of discrimination. Moreover, Arts. 17 and 23, paras 1 and 2, on the right to found a family and to marry, were invoked in conjunction with Art. 2, para. 1, ICCPR. Considering that their relationships exhibited all the criteria of a heterosexual family, the same-sex couples affirmed that since the New Zealand Marriage Act denied same-sex marriages, they suffered several harmful effects deriving from discrimination, impossibility to exercise civil rights, social exclusion, impossibility to assert their dignity, interference in private life and in having access to some important parental and material consequences, such as adoption, succession, matrimonial property, family protection.

The State party opposed to those arguments, *inter alia*, that the recognition of same-sex marriage does not meet the ordinary meaning of Art. 23, para. 2, ICCPR, which clearly refers to marriage between man and woman, and for this reason marriage as a legal institution cannot regard same-sex partners. Moreover, New Zealand argued that its law and policy protected and recognized gay couples in various ways, and that the Marriage Act did not interfere with the complainants' privacy or family life, as their personal relationships demonstrated.

The Committee adopted its view considering that the core of the communication was the denial of the right to marry under Art. 23, para. 2, ICCPR from which, like a cascade, the infringement of the other invoked provisions derived, and thus it decided the case focusing on the specific provision on marriage. Since the wording of Art. 23, para. 2, ICCPR, which protects the right of men and women of marriageable age to marry and to found a family, is specific—and not generic, like in other ICCPR provisions that refer to "every human being", "everyone" and "all persons"—the Committee concluded that the legal duty imposed on States

[52] View in no. 902/1999 *Joslin v. New Zealand* 17th July 2002.

[53] Complainants did not exhaust all available domestic remedies because they considered them futile, but New Zealand declined to draw a conclusion as to the admissibility of the communication on this or any other grounds, underlining, at the same time, that the Privy Council (unapplied to) could interpret the Marriage Act differently (*ibidem*, para. 4.1).

parties is to recognize as marriage only that between a man and a woman wishing to marry each other.[54] Consequently, the denial of same-sex marriages did not give rise to a violation of Art. 23, paras 1 and 2, and 16, 17 and 26 of the Covenant.

The decision in *Joslin v. New Zealand* is a matter of interpretation of the Covenant, and clearly the hermeneutic approach adopted by the Committee is textual, focused on the ordinary meaning of the wording of Art. 23 ICCPR in the context of the treaty as a reflection of what the parties intended[55]—i.e., it relies on the first (and prior) among the methods indicated in Art. 31, para. 1, of the Vienna Convention of the Law of Treaties (VCLT). The adoption of such a method is not surprising, firstly because the ICCPR is an international treaty and secondly because ever since *J.B. et al. v. Canada* of 1982 the Committee stated it would apply Art. 31 and, if necessary, 32 VCLT in interpreting the Covenant.[56] Thus, it can be said that there is a certain emphasis on its literal interpretation.[57] In that regard, it is interesting to quote what the International Court of Justice affirmed in 1950, i.e. that

> (...) the first duty of a tribunal which is called upon to interpret and apply the provisions of a treaty, is to endeavour to give effect to them in their natural and ordinary meaning in the context in which they occur. If the relevant words in their natural and ordinary meaning make sense in their context, that is an end of the matter.[58]

because it seems to mirror the brief reasoning of the Committee in *Joslin v. New Zealand*. In other words, Art. 23 ICCPR does not allow same-sex marriages because at the time of drafting the Covenant the States parties intended the marriage as an heterosexual institution—which is surely true, since the first ICCPR State party who legalized same-sex marriages was The Netherlands in 2000, and in 2002 the latter still was the only country in the world giving this right to same-sex partners.

One of the effects of the textual approach is to crystallize the meaning of the interpreted provisions and this could also have happened with Art. 23 ICCPR, but this does not mean that the Covenant is not a living instrument. On the contrary, the HRC stated that

> (w)hile recognizing that the Committee should ensure both consistency and coherence of its jurisprudence, it notes that there may be exceptional situations in which a review of the scope of application of the rights protected in the Covenant is required, such as where an alleged violation involves that most fundamental of rights - the right to life - and in particular if there have been notable factual and legal developments and changes

[54] The General Comment 19 on Art. 23 ICCPR, adopted by the HRC in 1990, did not provide any further interpretative elements to the complainants; in fact, it strengthened the State party's position on the possibility to accord different levels of protection to different kinds of families (*ibidem*, para. 4.8).

[55] Aust (2007), p. 235.

[56] See view in no. 118/1982 *J.B. et al. v. Canada* 18th July 1986, para. 6.3.

[57] Conte and Burchill (2009), pp. 14–15.

[58] ICJ, Advisory opinion on the competence of the General Assembly for the admission of a State to the United Nations, 3rd March 1950, p. 8.

> in international opinion in respect of the issue raised. . . . The Committee considers that the Covenant should be interpreted as a living instrument and the rights protected under it should be applied in context and in the light of present-day conditions[59]

and its jurisprudence confirms such a teleological approach, as some cases regarding death penalty demonstrate:

> (t)he provisions of the Covenant must be interpreted in the light of the Covenant's objects and purposes (article 31 of the Vienna Convention on the Law of Treaties). As one of these objects and purposes is to promote reduction in the use of the death penalty, an interpretation of a provision in the Covenant that may encourage a State party that retains the death penalty to make use of that penalty should, where possible, be avoided.[60]

This points to a variable interpretative method of the Committee in respect of the ICCPR,[61] unlike some regional human rights courts whose interpretative approach is, instead, mainly person-oriented. The effect of that variability is that the interpretation of the same legal instrument follows alternatively the textual and the teleological approach, and the choice probably depends on the kind and the importance of the issue at stake.[62]

Another effect produced by the textual approach is the de-contextualization of the Covenant from other human rights treaties of the UN system, to which it belongs.[63] The specific wording of Art. 23 allowed the Committee to deny the right to marry for same-sex couples, but the same outcome could not derive in cases similar to *Joslin v. New Zealand* brought before other treaty-based committees. For instance, the right to marry under Art. 5 of the Convention on the Elimination of All Forms of Racial Discrimination of 1965 or under Art. 16 of the Convention on the Elimination of Discrimination against Women of 1979 could not be denied when interpreting those provisions literally, since the former refers to the right of "everyone" to marry and the latter refers to the States Parties' duty to take all appropriate measures to eliminate discrimination against women in all matters related to marriage and family relations, the right to enter into marriage included.[64] In other words, the committees monitoring the respect of those treaties should adopt a more

---

[59] View in no. 829/1998 *Judge v. Canada* 5th August 2003, para. 10.3.

[60] View in no. 588/1994 *Johnson v. Jamaica* 22nd March 1996, para. 8.2, mirrored in no. 554/1993 *LaVende v. Trinidad and Tobago* 29th October 1997, para. 5.3, and no. 555/1993 *Bickaroo v. Trinidad and Tobago* 29th October 1997, para. 5.3.

[61] See Joseph et al. (2005), para. 1.62, and Conte and Burchill (2009), p. 16.

[62] Conte and Burchill (2009), p. 237, had the impression that in *Joslin v. New Zealand* the Committee considered the marriage only an inconsequential status, which clashes with the importance that the marriage received in other circumstances in the HRC jurisprudence.

[63] See the interesting considerations by Sudre (2011), pp. 46–47 and pp. 131–133, on the universality of human rights, their collectivization as an international phenomenon and the UN system for the protection of human rights, i.e. the UN Charter, the Universal Declaration of Human Rights of 1948, the Covenants of 1966 and, finally, the sectorial treaties.

[64] Moreover, also Art. 23 of Convention on the Rights of Persons with Disabilities of 2006 does not include specific wording, and the same is true with Art. 9 of the EU Charter of Fundamental Rights, solemnly proclaimed in 2000 and confirmed in 2007 as having the same legal value as the EU treaties (see Art. 6 TEU).

teleological approach in interpreting the said provisions, because the denial of marriage for same-sex partners could not be founded on the specific wording of the treaty provisions.

Concluding, reference should be made to the individual opinion of the HRC members Lallah and Scheinin in *Joslin v. New Zealand*, because they gave some important indications on prohibition of discrimination under Art. 26 ICCPR and differential treatment between married couples and same-sex couples. The Committee members recalled that, according to the previous case-law, reasonable and objective criteria can justify difference in the treatment under Art. 26, and this also regarded married couples and unmarried heterosexual couples, because heterosexual couples enjoy the right to marry and their living *more uxorio* amounts to a personal choice.[65] But the same is not true with same-sex couples:

> (n)o such possibility of choice exists for same-sex couples in countries where the law does not allow for same-sex marriage or other type of recognized same-sex partnership with consequences similar to or identical with those of marriage. Therefore, a denial of certain rights or benefits to same-sex couples that are available to married couples may amount to discrimination prohibited under article 26, unless otherwise justified on reasonable and objective criteria.
>
> However, in the current case we find that the authors failed, perhaps intentionally, to demonstrate that they were personally affected in relation to certain rights not necessarily related to the institution of marriage, by any such distinction between married and unmarried persons that would amount to discrimination under article 26. Their references to differences in treatment between married couples and same-sex unions were either repetitious of the refusal of the State party to recognize same-sex unions in the specific form of "marriage" (para. 3.1), an issue decided by the Committee under article 23, or remained unsubstantiated as to if and how the authors were so personally affected (para. 3.5). Taking into account the assertion by the State party that it does recognize the authors, with and without their children, as families (para. 4.8), we are confident in joining the Committee's consensus that there was no violation of article 26.[66]

It seems that the complainants applied to the HRC in order to affirm a principle, to "fight a battle" relying on the international duties of New Zealand under the ICCPR, i.e. the right to marry like heterosexuals. Indeed, their failure to refer to the right to be legally recognized as a couple before the law independently of marriage, which was not available at the time, seems to confirm it.[67]

That being said, the individual opinion of Mr. Lallah and Mr. Scheinin highlights the possibility to invoke Art. 26 ICCPR in cases of discrimination between same-sex couples and married couples in relation to certain rights, and this is what happened with the cases brought before the Committee with regard to a material consequence deriving from living in a same-sex couple.

---

[65] *Infra*, note 79.

[66] Individual opinion of Committee members Mr. Lallah and Mr. Scheinin (concurring), 3rd and 4th paras.

[67] New Zealand adopted the Civil Union Act in 2005, i.e. 3 years after *Joslin v. New Zealand*, affording same-sex and heterosexual couples the right to have a civil union. See the chapter by Rundle in this volume.

23.4.2 The Right to Benefit from the Deceased Partner's Pension

The HRC jurisprudence on material consequences consists in two cases on the same matter, i.e. the pension in favour of the same-sex survived partner, but nonetheless the adopted views are important because of the conclusions reached by the Committee with regard to the discriminations ascertained between same-sex couples and heterosexual couples.

Both cases are focused on Art. 26 ICCPR, which affirms equality before the law and the right of non-discrimination on any ground.[68] That provision enumerates some grounds of prohibited discrimination—e.g., race, colour, sex, language, religion, *et cetera*—but the list is merely indicative. Moreover, as the Committee affirmed in *Toonen v. Australia*,[69] the reference to "sex" includes the prohibition of discrimination on ground of sexual orientation. Prohibited forms of discrimination have to be intended as

> any distinction, exclusion, restriction or preference which is based on any ground . . ., and which has the purpose *or effect* (*italic* added) of nullifying or impairing the recognition, enjoyment or exercise by all persons, on an equal footing, of all rights and freedoms[70]

thus also indirect ("or effect", in *italic*) discriminations are prohibited under Art. 26.[71]

Differently from Arts. 2 and 3 ICCPR, which also regard the prohibition to discriminate, Art. 26 stands as an autonomous right.[72] While the former provisions have an accessory character and can be invoked in connection with a substantial right protected by the Covenant,[73] Art. 26 can be invoked autonomously and its field of application is not confined to discrimination in the matters covered by the Covenant, as it covers national legislations adopted in any field of law. In fact, as the Committee affirmed in the so-called Dutch Social Security cases:

---

[68] Hanski and Scheinin (2003), p. 329 define equality and non-discrimination as a "cross-cutting theme" in the Covenant, involving also Arts. 4 (derogation clause) 14, para. 1 (general clause of fair trial) and 20, para. 2 (advocacy of national, racial or religious), 23, para. 4 (equality of rights and responsibilities of spouses as to marriage), 24, para. 1 (discrimination of children on different grounds) and 25 (participation in public affairs) ICCPR.

[69] *Supra*, note 37, para. 8.7. This interpretation has been criticized in the literature as well as by some HRC members (Separate dissenting opinion by Mr. Amor and Mr. Khalil in the case *X v. Colombia*, examined at Sect. 23.4.2.2). Those criticisms have not prevented, for instance, the EU Advocate General Ruiz-Jarabo Colomer from taking up that approach as a point of reference in his opinion of 6th September 2007 on the Case C-267/06, *Maruko v. Versorgungsanstalt der deutschen Bühnen* [2008] ECR I-1757, para. 86.

[70] General Comment 18 on non-discrimination, para. 7, and, as to the HRC jurisprudence, view in no. 976/2001 *Derksen v. The Netherlands* 1st April 2004, para 9.3.

[71] For instance, see view in no. 516/1992 *Simunek v. The Czech Republic* 19th July 1995, para. 11.7.

[72] See Sect. 23.4.2.4.

[73] *Ex multis*, Nowak (2005), pp. 34 and 78.

> ... article 26 does not merely duplicate the guarantees already provided for in article 2. It derives from the principle of equal protection of the law without discrimination, as contained in article 7 of the Universal Declaration of Human Rights, which prohibits discrimination in law or in practice in any field regulated and protected by public authorities. Article 26 is thus concerned with the obligations imposed on States in regard to their legislation and the application thereof. Although article 26 requires that legislation should prohibit discrimination, it does not of itself contain any obligation with respect to the matters that may be provided for by legislation. Thus it does not, for example, require any State to enact legislation to provide for social security. However, when such legislation is adopted in the exercise of a State's sovereign power, then such legislation must comply with article 26 of the Covenant.[74]

In accordance with the HRC jurisprudence, the prohibition of discrimination is not absolute, since reasonable and objective criteria can justify differences in treatment.[75]

23.4.2.1 The Case of *Young v. Australia*

In *Young v. Australia* of 2003[76] a man who was in a long same-sex relationship with a war veteran was denied the pension after the death of his partner by the Repatriation Commission, because under the Veteran's Entitlement Act, which considers "couples" to be only married couples and *more uxorio* couples, he could not be considered as a member of a couple, thus a veteran dependant entitled to benefit from the bereavement payment. The internal authorities asked to review the Repatriation Commission's decision confirmed that interpretation, but Mr. Young did not exhaust all the available domestic remedies, because in his opinion a further appeal would have had no real prospect of success.

In his communication, Mr. Young argued the violation of his right to equal treatment before the law as an effect of the discrimination determined by VEA in relation with his sexual orientation; while widows and unmarried heterosexual survived partners could benefit from the pension, same-sex survived partners could not. In his opinion, that violation amounted to an infringement of Art. 26 ICCPR, because even if that provision does not oblige States parties to enact any particular legislation, social security included, according to the HRC jurisprudence on the invoked provision, when a legislation has been adopted, it has to comply with that provision. The State party, *inter alia*, opposed the lack of any form of discrimination: the former veteran did not meet the primary requirement under the VEA, in particular the serious disability or death caused as a result of war service, thus no survived partner, whether homosexual or heterosexual, would have been entitled to the pension under VEA.

[74] View in no. 182/1984 *Zwaan-de Vries v. The Netherlands* 9th April 1987, paras 12.3–12.4. Specularly, see views in no. 172/1984 *Broeks v. the Netherlands* 9th April 1987 and no. 180/1984 *Danning v. the Netherlands* 9th April 1987, same paras.

[75] *Infra*, note 79.

[76] View in no. 941/2000 *Young v. Australia* 6th August 2003.

The HRC considered the communication admissible[77] and ascertained that Australia, by denying Mr. Young a pension on the basis of his sex or sexual orientation, violated Art. 26 of the Covenant. It did not examine the State party's argument on the impossibility of Mr. Young's being entitled to the pension independently of his sexual orientation, as it was not in his competence, and concentrated on the domestic provisions applied by the internal authorities to deny the pension to the applicant, i.e. on the circumstance of being of the same sex as the deceased partner. The Committee considered that, independently of the other criteria provided for in the VEA, the applicant would never have been entitled to a pension because he was the same-sex survived partner of a former soldier, and added substantially the same considerations made by Mr. Lallah and Mr. Scheinin in their individual opinion in *Joslin v. New Zealand*, i.e. that

> . . . differences in the receipt of benefits between married couples and heterosexual unmarried couples were reasonable and objective, as the couples in question had the choice to marry with all the entailing consequences. It transpires from the contested sections of the VEA that individuals who are part of a married couple or of a heterosexual cohabiting couple (who can prove that they are in a "marriage-like" relationship) fulfill the definition of "member of a couple" and therefore of a "dependant", for the purpose of receiving pension benefits. In the instant case, it is clear that the author, as a same sex partner, did not have the possibility of entering into marriage.[78]

Certainly, distinctions can be admitted under Art. 26 if based on reasonable and objective criteria, for instance as in *Danning v. The Netherlands* with regard to differences in the insurance benefits for married beneficiaries and *more uxorio* beneficiaries:

> In the light of the explanations given by the State party with respect to the differences made by Netherlands legislation between married and unmarried couples (. . .), the Committee is persuaded that the differentiation complained of by Mr. Danning is based on objective and reasonable criteria. The Committee observes, in this connection, that the decision to enter into a legal status by marriage, which provides, in Netherlands law, both for certain benefits and for certain duties and responsibilities, lies entirely with the cohabiting persons. By choosing not to enter into marriage, Mr. Danning and his cohabitant have not, in law, assumed the full extent of the duties and responsibilities incumbent on married couples. Consequently, Mr. Danning does not receive the full benefits provided for in Netherlands law for married couples. The Committee concludes that the differentiation complained of by Mr. Danning does not constitute discrimination, in the sense of article 26 of the Covenant.[79]

[77] With regard to the exhaustion of internal remedies, the HRC observed that "domestic remedies need not be exhausted if they objectively have no prospect of success: where under applicable domestic laws the claim would inevitably be dismissed, or where established jurisprudence of the highest domestic tribunals would preclude a positive result. Taking into account the clear wording of the sections of the VEA in question, and noting that the State party itself admits that an appeal to the AAT would not have been successful, the Committee concludes that there were no effective remedies that the author might have pursued" (para. 9.4). On this point, see also the individual opinion of the Committee members Mrs. Wedgwood and Mr. De Pasquale.

[78] *Supra*, note 76, para. 10.4.

[79] *Supra*, note 74, para. 14.

But in *Young v. Australia* the same arguments cannot be relied upon, because same-sex couples cannot decide whether to enter into marriage or live in a *more uxorio* cohabitation. Moreover, Australia did not provide any arguments on reasonableness and objectiveness of the difference in treatment between same-sex partners and unmarried heterosexual partners under the VEA, like for any other justification, thus the Committee concluded that denial of the pension for Mr. Young was discriminative and in contrast with Art. 26 ICCPR.

Having ascertained a violation of the Covenant, the Committee indicated a remedy to give satisfaction to Mr. Young, i.e. the reconsideration of his pension application without discrimination based on sex or sexual orientation, if necessary through an amendment of the law, and invited Australia to ensure that similar violations of the Covenant would not occur in future.

23.4.2.2 The Case of *X v. Colombia*

Similarly, in *X v. Colombia*[80] (later, *Casadiego v. Colombia*)[81] the Committee examined the communication submitted by a Colombian citizen who was the survived partner of a same-sex couple and asked, in light of the neutral wording of the internal law, to benefit from the pension transfer after the death of his partner, who was dependant. The Social Welfare Fund of the Colombian Congress denied the benefit arguing that the law did not permit the transfer of a pension to a person of the same sex. The same interpretation had been confirmed in subsequent (and several) actions brought by the complainant in order to obtain the review the Fund's decision.[82]

In his communication, Mr. Casadiego recalled both the neutral wording of the internal regulation on pensions, which does not specify the sex of the partners, and that legislation had been amended in order to remove any form of discrimination between married couples and *more uxorio* couples with regard to the pension transfer benefit. The denial of the pension transfer in case of same-sex couples made him into a victim of the infringement of several ICCPR provisions, in particular: discrimination on the ground of sex and sexual orientation under Art. 2, paras 1, 3 and 26: failure to respect the principles of equality and non-discrimination under Art. 5,

[80] View in no. 1361/2005 *X v. Colombia* 30th March 2007.

[81] Initially, the complainant asked for his personal data and those of his partner to be kept confidential, but in the latest HRC Reports—follow-up section, the communication 1361/2005 regarding Colombia is quoted as *Casadiego v. Colombia*.

[82] It is worth mentioning that, in the appeal before the Bogotá Circuit Criminal Court No. 50, judges "ordered the modification of the earlier ruling [which did not specify that the two partners must be of different sexes] and called on the Procurator-General to conduct an investigation into errors committed by staff of the Fund" (para. 2.4).

paras 1 and 2[83]; failure to respect equality before the courts under Art. 14, para. 1; negative interference in his private life under Art. 17 of the Covenant. In its counterclaim, Colombia, *inter alia*, considered some of the invoked provisions irrelevant (e.g., Art. 3, on gender discrimination) and insufficiently substantiated (e.g., Arts. 5 and 17), thus it requested the communication to be declared inadmissible under Art. 2 of the Protocol.

In the wake of *Young v. Australia*, considering that Colombian same-sex partners are not allowed to marry along with the lack of arguments or justifications in support of the reasonableness and objectiveness of the distinction between same-sex partners, who are not entitled to pension benefits, and unmarried heterosexual partners, who are so entitled, the Committee declared that denying the complainant's right to his life partner's pension on the basis of his sexual orientation amounted to a violation of Art. 26 of the Covenant. The claims on Art. 2, paras 1, and 17 ICCPR were considered absorbed as it was not necessary to consider them, while the declaration of inadmissibility affected the other provisions invoked.

Just like in *Young v. Australia*, the Committee indicated, as a remedy for the victim, the reconsideration of his request for a pension without discrimination on grounds of sex or sexual orientation and the State party's obligation to take steps to prevent similar violations of the Covenant in future.

23.4.2.3 The Follow-Up of Cases on the Deceased Partner's Pension

In both cases the HCR ascertained a violation of Art. 26 ICCPR and indicated the reconsideration of the pension application as a remedy for the complainants, adding, as a further prescription, to avoid similar violations in future. The Committee also requested to be informed about the measures taken to comply with its view.

In 2008 Australia changed its legislation and from 1st July 2009 a same-sex partner can receive the war widower's pension,[84] thus it is likely that Mr. Young's pension application has been reconsidered without any discriminatory element. In 2010 the Colombian Constitutional Court stated that administrative, judicial and pension fund bodies could not deny the pension to same-sex partners opposing unjustified barriers and to this aim it adopted a group of orders with *intercomunis* effects, i.e. extended to all gay people.[85] Following this judgement, Mr. Casadiego

---

[83] According to the HRC jurisprudence, also Art. 5 has accessory character (see views in no. 1167/2003 *Rayos v. Philippines* 27th July 2004, para. 6.8, and in no. 1011/2001 *Madafferi and Madafferi v. Australia* 26th July 2004, para. 8.6).

[84] Information kindly provided by the Sexual Orientation, Sex and Gender Identity Team of the Australian Human Rights Commission, which the author thanks.

[85] Constitutional Court, T-051/10 of 2nd February 2010 (file No. T-2.292.035, T-2.299.859, T-2.386.935). On this judgement, see also the chapter by Cabrales Lucio in this volume.

received, from the Colombian Congress Pension Fund, some arrears and the monthly pension until he passed.[86]

Even if those States parties complied belatedly with the HRC view,[87] the outcome can be considered satisfying, since the discriminatory element in their legislations (or its effect) was removed as a consequence of its decisions. In fact, Australia changed its legislation after the Australia Human Right Commission's recommendation to the Australian Government to amend laws which discriminated against same-sex couples and their children also in light of the Committee's case-law.[88] Moreover, it is worth mentioning that in Australia a debate is in progress on the absence of a provision prohibiting discrimination on grounds of sexual orientation at the federal level.[89] As to Colombia, in its 2010 judgement the High Court affirmed that such judgment was also intended to implement the Human Rights Council's recommendations 112 and 113 on the protection and assertion of LGBT rights,[90] i.e. part of the outcome of the latest universal periodic review involving Colombia,[91] whose aim is to remind and to encourage States to respect their international human rights obligations, which include compliance with the treaty-based monitoring bodies decisions.

23.4.2.4 The Potential of Art. 26 ICCPR

The pension cases confirm the potential of Art. 26 as an autonomous right, which can be invoked independently of the other ICCPR provisions to sanction unreasonable, non-objective discrimination in the legislation adopted by States parties independently of the field of law.

It found expression initially in the aforementioned Dutch Social Security cases, originated from discrimination between heterosexual married and unmarried couples and decided by the HRC both by sanctioning unreasonable forms of discrimination and by admitting justified differences of treatment in the enjoyment of a

---

[86] Information kindly provided by the Colombian Fondo de Previsión Social del Congreso de la República, which the author thanks.

[87] *Young v. Australia* was decided in 2003, and *X v. Colombia* in 2007. Of note, the latest HRC Annual Report (A/67/40 (Vol. II), 103rd and 104th sessions) indicates that the follow-up dialogue on both cases is officially ongoing, but the situation may change on the basis of information received from one of the parties to the case (information kindly provided by the Petitions and Inquiries Section of the UN Office of the High Commissioner for Human Rights, which the author thanks).

[88] Final Report of 2007 "Same-Sex: Same Entitlements", available at http://www.humanrights.gov.au/human_rights/samesex/report/index.html.

[89] See the chapter by Rundle in this volume.

[90] *Supra*, note 85, para. 6.12.

[91] Human Rights Council Report on its 10th session, A/HRC/10/29, 9th November 2009, in particular decision n. 10/114 "Outcome of the universal periodic review: Colombia".

right not covered by the Covenant.[92] That jurisprudence played an important role in deciding the same-sex pension cases, which focused on the same field of law, i.e. social security legislation, and concerned allegedly differential treatment; in other words, it could be argued that the decisions in the Dutch Social Security cases solved the same-sex pension ones.

It is worth highlighting that the potential of Art. 26 ICCPR is the result of its liberal and forward-looking interpretation,[93] which is different from the method used in *Joslin v. New Zealand* regarding Art. 23 and which allowed the Committee to expand the field of application of the prohibition to discriminate to rights that are not directly protected by the Covenant. That progressive and expansive interpretation represents the core of the potential of Art. 26, which the Committee handled cautiously[94] and in order to bring the understanding of substantive equality to fruition into the field of social, economic and cultural rights.[95] Exactly this approach towards searching substantive equality in the enjoyment of rights could guarantee other rights in future to same-sex couples faced with national discriminatory legislation on other material consequences—such as tax issues, health insurance benefits or problems with tenancy in the deceased same-sex partner's name.

23.5 Final Remarks

The analysis of the relevant case-law has shown a patchy picture in the protections of same-sex couples issues. On the one hand, the literal interpretation of Art. 23 ICCPR in *Joslin v. New Zealand* did not support the right to marry; on the other hand, the forward-looking interpretation of Art. 26 in the pension cases sanctioned forms of discrimination against same-sex couples and could, in future, guarantee other material consequences. It seems that interpretation issues determine the extent of the protection of same-sex couples' rights under the Covenant, based on the problem at stake. That being said, some further (and concluding) considerations are due on two aspects.

[92] That potential is testified by some reservations on Art. 26, formulated after the "Dutch Social Security" cases by some States (for instance, Germany and Turkey) that had not yet become parties to the Covenant or the Protocol, in order to limit the competence of the HRC in applying Art. 26 over the Covenant, *de facto* denying its freestanding nature.

[93] *Ex multis*, Nowak (2005), p. 629 and Conte and Burchill (2009), pp. 14 and 17.

[94] Edelembos (2009), p. 79.

[95] Nowak (2005), p. 629.

23.5.1 Interpretation of the Covenant, Marriage and Same-Sex Partnership

An initial set of considerations have to do with the future interpretation of the Covenant in relation with the same-sex issues (mentioned or not) in *Joslin v. New Zealand*. In other words, can it be excluded that a less literal approach will be followed in future when interpreting Art. 23 of the Covenant in light of the social, cultural and legal changes that occurred over the last decade? And could one envisage that there will be an opening to same-sex marriages? Only practice will provide an answer to these questions; nonetheless some considerations can be made.

If in future the HRC adopts the textual approach in interpreting Art. 23 ICCPR, the outcome will be unquestionably (again) the denial of the right to marry for same-sex couples: indeed, only 13 out of the 114 States parties to ICCPR and its Protocol (and 14 out of 160 ICCPR States parties),[96] not covering all geographical areas and legal traditions, allow same-sex marriages as of today. But if the Committee adopts a different approach in cases dealing with same-sex marriage in light of social, cultural and legal changes,[97] some developments are possible, also in the direction of an extensive interpretation of Art. 23 ICCPR. For instance, this is what happened with the Strasbourg Court in *Schalk and Kopf v. Austria* of 2010[98]: the regional court denied the right to marry under Art. 12 ECHR for lack of consensus in the European area, but in light of social developments (and in spite of the reference contained in that provision to "men and women"), it offered a more extensive interpretation of marriage, affirming that

> the Court would no longer consider that the right to marry enshrined in Article 12 must in all circumstances be limited to marriage between two persons of the opposite sex. Consequently, it cannot be said that Article 12 is inapplicable to the applicants' complaint.[99]

Anyhow, if the HRC gave a (more or less) broader interpretation of Art. 23, the impact would be wide-ranging as the Covenant has an universal vocation and its legal obligations apply to a large number of States parties, belonging to different regional areas and legal traditions. Moreover, the latter observation would point to the unlikelihood of such a jurisprudential development in the next few years in respect of a sensitive issue like marriage, which is closely connected to family as an institution as well as being deeply rooted in States' societies and traditions.

---

[96] Some US States allow same-sex marriages, but USA is not party to the Protocol.

[97] Nowak (2005), pp. 526–527 and Conte and Burchill (2009). The latter consider the view in *Joslin v. New Zealand* outdated in light of recent developments and the dynamic nature of family law.

[98] *Schalk and Kopf v. Austria*, application n. 30141/04, judgment of 24th June 2010. See the chapter by Pustorino in this volume.

[99] *Ibidem*, para. 61.

Both factors make marriage proof against substantial changes (for instance, from being a heterosexual institution to becoming neutral gender-marriage), especially when not inspired by internal legislative processes.

A further consideration regards same-sex partnerships. The case of *Joslin v. New Zealand* was focused on the right to marry, so much so that, in their individual opinions, two HRC members underlined that the communication continuously referred to the recognition of same-sex unions in the specific form of marriage. But what could have happened if the New Zealand couples had simply applied for being legally recognized as a couple before the law? Does the ICCPR support such a right, for instance as a consequence of an individual right to the protection of privacy and family life? The answer belongs (again) to the future HRC case-law; however, unlike the marriage issue, some developments can be envisaged in the direction of affording legal protection to same-sex couples. Reference can be made in this regard to the (wide-ranging, in the HRC jurisprudence) notion of family,[100] the right to family life under Art. 17 ICCPR and the corresponding need for legal protection, as already happened, in cases involving same-sex couples, in the European and the American systems for the protection of human rights.[101]

23.5.2 *HRC as a* Forum *for Same-Sex Couples*

Secondly, in spite of its limits and deficiencies, the HRC represents an available and approachable *forum* for same-sex couples living in countries which have ratified the Protocol. Following the denial, at a national level, of LGBT and same-sex couples' rights, the Committee's competence to examine individual communications represents a further chance to obtain justice.

This is true for individuals living in countries not belonging to a regional system of protection of human rights, for instance Asian countries or Australia and New Zealand; but there is more to that. Also same-sex couples living in areas with a regional system of human rights can consider the Committee as a desirable *forum*. The HRC practice reports a certain number of communications coming from countries belonging to regional systems—for instance, Europe or Latin America—and often individuals' communications are sent after an unfavourable outcome before a regional body. Only individuals living in States parties which have entered a reservation and/or a declaration on Art. 5, para. 2, of the Protocol have to recall that *electa una via, non datur recursus ad alteram*: all the others can take advantage of the availability of a further *forum* for the protection of their rights.

[100] *Ex multis*, see Nowak (2005), pp. 393–394 and 515.

[101] See the chapters by Pustorino and Crisafulli on the Strasbourg Court and the one by Magi on the Inter-American Court of Human Rights. On the Strasbourg case-law, see also Johnson (2013), p. 113.

In particular, the Committee represents a desirable and available *forum* in cases of unreasonable and non-objective discrimination not only for individuals that are not covered by a regional system of human rights protection, but also for those who do not benefit from a general provision against discrimination in the framework of a regional system. For instance, this is the case of the ECHR. Following the entry into force of Protocol 12 attached to the European Convention, the prohibition of discrimination pursuant to Art. 14 ECHR stands as an autonomous right and it can be invoked also separately from another substantive right protected by the Convention.[102] This is a welcome development for the international protection of human rights, but it is worth mentioning that only 18 ECHR States parties out of 37[103] signatories have ratified Protocol 12, and the low number of ratifications, as Scheinin noted, is likely to slow down the emergence of a Strasbourg case-law on discrimination[104]—which *de facto* leaves it to the HRC jurisprudence to play a leading role in this highly controversial field of law.

References

Ando N (2002) The follow-up procedure of the human rights committee's views. In: Ando N, McWhinney E, Wolfrum R (eds) Liber Amicorum Judge Shigeru Oda, vol II. Kluwer Law International, The Hague/London/New York, pp 1437–1447

Ando N (2009) The development of the human rights committee's activities under the ICCPR and its optional protocol through my twenty-year experience as a committee member. In: Bariatti S, Venturini G (eds) Liber Fausto Pocar: Diritti individuali e Giustizia Internazionale. Giuffrè Editore, Milano, pp 3–17

Aust A (2007) Modern treaty law and practice. Cambridge University Press, Cambridge

Bair J (2005) The international covenant on civil and political rights and its (first) optional protocol. Peter Lang GmbH, Frankfurt an Main

Conte A, Burchill R (2009) Defining civil and political rights. Ashgate, Farnham/Burlington

De Zayas A (2009) Petitions before the United Nations treaty bodies: focus on the human rights committee's optional protocol procedure. In: Alfredsson G, Grimhemed J, Ramcharan BG, De Zayas A (eds) International human rights monitoring mechanisms: essays in honour of Jakob Th. Moller. Martinus Nijhoff Publishers, Leiden/Boston, pp 35–76

Edelembos C (2009) Jurisprudence under Article 26 of the ICCPR: the hidden revolution. In: Alfredsson G, Grimhemed J, Ramcharan BG, De Zayas A (eds) International human rights monitoring mechanisms: essays in honour of Jakob Th. Moller. Martinus Nijhoff Publishers, Leinden/Boston, pp 77–82

[102] On Protocol 12, see Harris et al. (2009) and Johnson (2013).

[103] http://conventions.coe.int, visited at February 2013. Of 47 ECHR States parties, 37 signed the Protocol and 10 did not (Bulgaria, Denmark, France, Lithuania, Malta, Monaco, Poland, Sweden, Switzerland and UK). Albania, Andorra, Armenia, BiH, Croatia, Cyprus, Finland, Georgia, Luxembourg, Montenegro, The Netherlands, Romania, San Marino, Serbia, Slovenia, Spain, FYROM and Ukraine have ratified the Protocol, while Austria, Azerbaijan, Belgium, Czech Republic, Estonia, Germany, Greece, Hungary, Iceland, Ireland, Italy, Latvia, Liechtenstein, Moldova, Norway, Portugal, Russia, Slovakia and Turkey have not.

[104] Scheinin (2008), p. 552.

Hanski R, Scheinin M (2003) Leading cases of the human rights committee. Institute for Human Rights, Åbo Akademi University

Harris DJ, O'Boyle M, Bates EP, Buckley CM (2009) The law of the European convention on human rights. Oxford University Press, New York

Hennebel L (2007) La jurisprudence du Comité des droits de l'homme des Nations Unies: Le Pacte international relatif aux droits civils et politiques et son mécanisme de protection individuelle. Bruylant, Bruxelles

Johnson P (2013) Homosexuality and the European court of human rights. Routledge, Abingdon, Oxon

Joseph S (1994) Gay rights under the ICCPR - commentary on Toonen v Australia. Tasman Law Rev 13:392–411

Joseph S, Schulz J, Castan M (2005) The international covenant on civil and political rights: cases, materials and commentary. Oxford University Press, New York

Joseph S, Mitchell K, Gyorki L, Benninger-Budel C (2006) Seeking remedies for torture victims: a handbook on the individual complaints, Procedures of the UN treaty bodies. OMCT Handbook Series, Geneva/Brussels

Maaldon T (2009) Sexual orientation discrimination: a necessary and emerging area of United Nations concern. In: Alfredsson G, Grimhemed J, Ramcharan BG, De Zayas A (eds) International human rights monitoring mechanisms: essays in honour of Jakob Th. Moller. Martinus Nijhoff Publishers, Leinden/Boston, pp 429–438

Möller JT, De Zayas A (2009) United Nations human rights committee case law 1977–2008: a handbook. NP Engel Publisher, Kehl am Rhein

Nowak M (2005) U.N. covenant on civil and political rights: CCPR commentary. N. P. Engel Publisher, Kehl am Rhein

Office of the United Nations High Commissioner for Human Rights (2005) Civil and political rights: The Human Rights Committee. Fact Sheet No. 15 (Rev. 1)

Scheinin M (2008) Human rights committee: not only a committee on civil and political rights. In: Langford M (ed) Social rights jurisprudence: emerging trends in international and comparative law. Cambridge University Press, Cambridge, pp 540–552

Sudre F (2011) Droit européen et international des droit de l'homme. Presses Universitaires de France, Paris

Tyagi Y (2011) The UN human right committee: practice and procedure. Cambridge University Press, Cambridge

Printed by Printforce, the Netherlands